Issues and Advocacy in Early Education

Issues and Advocacy in Early Education

MARY A. JENSEN

State University of New York—Geneseo

ZELDA W. CHEVALIER

State University of New York—Geneseo

Allyn and Bacon

BOSTON   LONDON   SYDNEY   TORONTO

Series Editor: Sean W. Wakely
Production Administrator: Annette Joseph
Production Coordinator: Susan Freese
Editorial-Production Service: TKM Productions
Text Designer: Denise Hoffman, Glenview Studios
Cover Administrator: Linda K. Dickinson
Cover Designer: Design Ad Cetera
Manufacturing Buyer: Tamara McCracken

Photo credits: SUNY—Geneseo Communications Office, page 3; Mary Jensen, page
54; Amy Miller/NAEYC, page 61; John Jensen, page 120; Mary Jensen, page 125;
John Jensen, page 163; Florence Sharp, page 184; Peter Scumaci, page 231; Mary
Jensen, page 275; Mary Jensen, page 307; Jacques Chevalier, page 341; David Gantt,
page 383

Library of Congress Cataloging-in-Publication Data

Issues and advocacy in early education / (edited by) Mary A. Jensen,
    Zelda W. Chevalier.
        p.   cm.
    Bibliography: p.
    Includes index.
    ISBN 0-205-12046-6
        1. Early childhood education.   2. Preschool teachers.
3. Professional socialization.   I. Jensen, Mary A.   II. Chevalier,
Zelda W.
LB1140.22.I87   1990   89-32041
372.21—dc20   CIP

Printed in the United States of America

10   9   8   7   6   5   4   3   2   1   94   93   92   91   90   89

BRIEF CONTENTS

CONTENTS

13 Advocacy: Influencing Policy and Regulations 355

PREFACE

Audience and Purpose

This book has been written for early childhood teachers and administrators at both preservice and inservice levels. Although written primarily to familiarize prospective teachers with critical issues in early education, this text is also suitable for teachers and administrators in the field who are interested in becoming more active in advocacy efforts.

Issues and Advocacy in Early Education is designed to involve readers in reflecting on issues with an eye to possible advocacy actions. Varied viewpoints, facts, cases, and research studies are presented to stimulate consideration of alternative positions and perspectives. The text includes topics now recognized to be important in the field of early education but generally not covered or only touched upon superficially in other textbooks. We closely examine the values underlying different views related to these topics, which include low wages and benefits for teachers of young children, the growing need for child care and early education services, the impact of television viewing on today's young children, and how to implement such goals as developmentally appropriate curriculum practices, culturally responsive programs for young children, and mainstreaming.

Overall, our goals are to expand the reader's knowledge about early education issues and to prepare him or her for advocacy work needed in the field. In addition, we seek to foster the professionalization of early childhood teachers and administrators through the examination of the core values that are the basis for professional decisions made in early childhood education.

Coverage and Features

During the past 10 years, grass-roots advocacy efforts among early childhood personnel have shown a dramatic increase. No longer are policy experts the only ones to testify at hearings or to address governmental representatives and the public concerning current issues in the field. At the same time, the knowledge base for issues in the field of early childhood education has mushroomed. Flourishing research related to young children has led to a need to review these contributions and select those that have meaning and value for the early childhood teacher and administrator. We have chosen articles based on their current and future-oriented viewpoints, their relevance to issues confronting people today in the field of early childhood education, their emphasis on values underlying particular actions or positions, and their clarity, liveliness, and brevity. In some sections of the book, we present articles that illustrate contrasting viewpoints in order to show that several views on a controversial issue can be well presented and to engage the critical thinking skills of the reader.

Chapter 1 of *Issues and Advocacy in Early Education* serves as an introduction and description of the approach to issues and advocacy used in the development of this book. Chapter 2 helps the reader understand the importance of advocacy for strengthening the professional status of early education. Chapters 3 through 13 range in content from issues most evident to the public through mass media coverage to issues given less media coverage but embedded in the policies and operation of early childhood programs and related organizations or institutions in our society. Each of these chapters provides intensive treatment of a particular topic and may be read independently of other sections. However, some chapters cover related topics and are grouped together. The order of subject matter is based on student reactions to the topics and their comprehension of the issues.

Chapter 3 launches an examination of critical issues regarding a topic receiving much media coverage in our culture: sex. Its relevance to early education is discussed in terms of sex-role development and sex education. Chapter 4 reviews ideas and evidence concerning the possible negative impact of television viewing on young children's development. Chapter 5 links the issue of child health with effective advocacy efforts and nutrition programs for young children. Also related to child health, the topic of child abuse and neglect is examined in Chapter 6. From a concern about child maltreatment, the issue of discipline or managing acting-out behaviors in a professional manner follows naturally in Chapter 7. Chapters 8 and 9 explore issues involved in the availability and quality of child care programs, such as funding, balancing the needs of children with those of working parents, and providing appropriate program settings, interactions, and curricula. Chapters 10 and 11 address the issues involved in education for children with special learning needs and in multicultural/bilingual education. Chapters 12 and 13 move beyond classroom policy issues. Chapter 12 considers topics related to the role of parents in early education. Finally, Chapter 13 deals with multiple perspectives on governmental child care policies and regulations in relation to legislative advocacy.

In addition to specific guidelines for organizing debates, this book provides an abundance of case examples, exercises, and discussion questions to involve the reader in developing his or her knowledge, skills, and dispositions for child advocacy. In order to facilitate this integration and make this text easy to use, we have included the following features:

Vignettes, presented at the beginning of each chapter, describe predicaments faced by early childhood teachers and child advocates. These vignettes may serve as a basis for initial discussion of key issues for the chapter topic.

Previews help the reader develop a framework for the readings and content of each chapter.

Ask Yourself sections, part of the material following readings at the end of each chapter, pose questions for self-reflection or group discussion. These questions will help the reader evaluate if he or she can identify various issues, values, and positions related to the chapter.

Application/Advocacy Exercises, also found at the chapter end, suggest activities that will help the reader: (1) relate viewpoints and reported evidence to personal experiences, (2) examine the values underlying various positions, and (3) further understand advocacy strategies.

References & Suggested Readings, the final section of each chapter, list some additional sources of information for the topic discussed.

Acknowledgments

Many people have helped us write this book. Our appreciation is extended to our students at the State University of New York—Geneseo, who made invaluable contributions to the development of the debating process and advocacy involvement activities. We are indebted as well to Allyn and Bacon's reviewers whose constructive comments and suggestions helped us improve the book: Professor Susan Ferrante, North Shore Community College, Lynn, Massachusetts; Professor Margie Kitano, New Mexico State University; Professor Susan Trostle, University of Rhode Island; and Professor Carol Vukelich, University of Delaware.

We gratefully acknowledge the efforts of the editorial and production staff at Allyn and Bacon, whose assistance greatly facilitated our work. We extend our special thanks to Sean Wakely, who coordinated and guided the project and readily provided advice and support.

Finally, we wish to acknowledge the outstanding contribution of Dawn Rowe, who typed the manuscript with amazing precision and speed.

Issues and Advocacy in Early Education

CHAPTER 1

Introduction

Advocacy: A Professional Challenge to Early Childhood Education

A commonly observed characteristic of early childhood teachers is their warm delight in young children. Practicing and prospective teachers work with children because they enjoy them and are concerned for their welfare. In assuming this role, teachers undertake to share with parents responsibility for helping children realize their full potential (Buchmann, 1986).

Recent social, political, and economic developments in our society, however, are challenging traditional images of the early childhood practitioner (Bronfenbrenner, 1986; Children's Defense Fund, 1987). Whereas conventional role definitions have been grounded in practices of early education and child care, today's practitioners are increasingly being faced with the need to become involved in public interest issues that impinge directly on their primary role obligations to the children in their care (Hostetler, 1981; Whitebook & Almy, 1986). For example, today's practitioner is required by law to report cases of suspected child abuse and may be involved with providing court-ordered services for abused children; therefore, social policies related to child abuse and neglect affect the practices of the early childhood teacher. Today's teachers also are acutely aware that, apart from parents, they are the most prominent agents who can act on behalf of children and protect children's rights. Thus, early childhood practitioners find themselves extending their concerns for children beyond immediate interactions within the classroom to seeking improvements in the responsiveness and relevance of social policies and services (Melton, 1983).

Other changes in our economy and society have impressed on early childhood practitioners the need to advocate for families as well as for children. Economic and social changes have brought about less stable communities and shifts in family makeup that have tended to isolate families and put additional strains on the family unit. Child advocacy is particularly important today in providing and bolstering support systems that help children cope with emotional needs. Supporting the family unit as well as helping children meet their full potential are primary goals of early childhood programs (Bredekamp, 1986; Melton, 1983).

The drive to become more involved in advocacy efforts on behalf of young children has been augmented in recent years by calls to advocate for improvement in the welfare of early childhood personnel. The occupation is plagued by low morale brought on by low wages, minimum employee benefits, and poor working conditions (Almy, 1985; Whitebook & Almy, 1986). Both for self-interest and for interest in the well-being of children, the role of the early childhood practitioner is being reconceptualized and restructured from one governed by parochial interests to one that acknowledges the direct and indirect linkages between quality child care, occupational welfare, and events in the public arena (Jorde-Bloom, 1986; Silin, 1985; Whitebook, Howes, Darrah, & Friedman, 1982).

To meet the advocacy challenge, some early childhood practitioners have taken a proactive stance. Their activities range from pursuing needed services for individuals and their families to seeking changes in procedures, laws, and resources that affect groups of families and children. In the process of effecting change, they have acquired the systematic knowledge and expertise needed to influence the decisions of legislators, agencies, and organizations whose mission it is to develop policies and legislation that protect the rights and needs of young children (Forgione, 1980; Kilmer, 1980).

Accompanying this quiet revolution in child advocacy (Jorde, 1986) have been efforts by early childhood personnel to professionalize the occupation (Almy, 1985; Feeney, 1985; Hostetler & Klugman, 1982; Katz, 1984; Raines, 1983). A critical step in this venture is clarifying and obtaining consensus on the beliefs and values of practitioners in order to establish a professional code of ethics. The construction of such a set of ethical principles provides an external framework for critical reflection and supports use of advanced professional knowledge in making judgments about positions and courses of action.

If the thrust toward advocacy and professionalization is to be expanded, preservice and inservice teachers not only will be asked to acquire the requisite knowledge and skills needed to deal with problem issues, but they must also be willing to expend the additional time and energy needed to effect change. Important to this enterprise is the task of overcoming feelings of powerlessness and anxiety about anticipated and unanticipated consequences (Jensen, 1986; Lombardi, 1986; Markus & Nurius, 1986). Put another way, if people perceive themselves as ineffective and conjure up possible calamities, they will be reluctant to attempt actions that exceed their ability to cope with unpredictable situations (Bandura, 1977).

In contrast, people who judge themselves adept in coping with potential threats are not deterred from entering into unknown territory (Bandura, 1977). The history of early education, in particular, documents how many practitioners and other interested parties have been instrumental in effecting the adoption of policies and programs that protect child and family welfare (Osborn, 1980). Whether their courage stemmed from motives of altruism or self-interest, these trailblazers of the past and those presently engaged in advocacy efforts provide a model for emulation.

Each of us has "possible selves"—what we would like to become and what we are afraid of becoming (Markus & Nurius, 1986). We can remain part of the advocacy problem, bogged down in helplessness and disillusionment, or we can become part of the solution by coming to grips with substantive issues in the field and obtaining, concurrently, the skills and dispositions needed to become effective advocates. Once again, early education has captured the public interest. Today, there is an unprecedented demand for child care by trained, qualified personnel. The time is right for action.

The time is right for action.

Characteristics of Effective Advocates

Learning how to become an effective advocate means obtaining information about advocacy issues, employing the skills needed to carry out the task, and developing and strengthening one's disposition to assume an advocacy role. For purposes of explication, these general goals can be redefined as specific attributes and skills (Dinham & Stritter, 1986), which represent outcomes that the reader will achieve as he or she engages in the strategies to be discussed in the next section. These intended outcomes include:

1. *Cognitive attributes*, which relate to the information base contained in this book and supplementary sources and become transformed for use in both analytical and intuitive reasoning
2. *Attitudinal attributes*, which reflect the values and ethics used to guide choice, argument, rationalization, and action and include the motivation and the disposition to engage in resolution of ethical problems and moral dilemmas
3. *Psychosocial attributes*, which underpin one's sensitivity to interpersonal relations when communicating with colleagues, clients, and members of the public
4. *Socialization attributes*, which reflect the gradual internalization of professional values and commitment to the role of advocate
5. *Learning skills*, which are needed to keep informed of events and changes in the field, to decide what needs to be learned and where to obtain information, and to know when learning has been accomplished.

These attributes and skills, in one combination or another, are brought into play through participation in activities incorporated in this book.

Strategies for Developing Advocacy Knowledge, Skills, and Dispositions

Suggestions for developing prospective advocates' knowledge of current child advocacy issues and strategies as well as strengthening their dispositions to assume advocacy roles come from several sources (Allen, 1983; Cahill, 1986; Deloria & Brookins, 1982; Fink & Sponseller, 1977; Jensen, 1986; Kilmer, 1980; New York State Child Care Coordinating Council, n.d.; Whitebook & Ginsburg, 1984; Zigler & Finn, 1981). These suggestions can be grouped in the following categories:

1. Issue debates
2. Issue interviews and advocacy speakers
3. Role-play simulation exercises
4. Advocacy journals, public information displays and me-

dia materials, advocacy letters, legislative visits, position papers, and testimony

5. Professional organization contacts, networking, lobbying coalitions, and task forces

Although most of these suggestions are incorporated as activities within this book, the remainder of this chapter will focus on the first strategy—issue debate. By engaging in the debate process, the five intended learning outcomes needed for effective advocacy can be made operational. More specifically, the debate strategy allows teachers to (1) acquire evidence to support their position; (2) actively test their arguments, evidence, and presentation skills against an opponent; and (3) better understand various perspectives on an issue. Beyond developing knowledge of current child care issues and debate/presentation skills, it also can strengthen students' dispositions to assume advocacy roles (Katz, 1982). Furthermore, the process has been refined and successfully implemented in teacher education classes over a four-year period. After each debate, students provided anonymous feedback about the value of the debate and the effectiveness of the strategies used. Although no substitute for action, the debate process has proven to be a solid foundation from which to take further steps in planning strategies and taking concrete actions to improve conditions for children, families, and child care practitioners in our society (Jensen, 1986).

A Framework for Analyzing Child Advocacy Knowledge, Skills, and Dispositions

To introduce teachers to the process of selecting a debate problem and formulating debate questions, this book provides a collection of selected readings on current issues. After reading relevant selections from the text, a framework for analyzing issues and developing arguments may be used (see Table 1–1). To facilitate understanding the nature of issue debate, subsequent pages chronicle a description of issues, debate questions, and debate arguments.

Identifying a Significant Issue for Debate

An issue is a point of genuine dispute that entails the desire for change on the part of some persons. When early education issues arise, underlying problems or questions are confronted in order to improve or protect the welfare of children, families, or staff involved in early education.

Selection of an issue for debate should rest on the belief that the issue is a *genuine* dilemma for the field of early educa-

TABLE 1–1 *Framework for Identifying and Analyzing Child Advocacy/Early Education Issues*

Step 1: Identification of a Significant Issue in Early Childhood Education Today	Step 2: Ways to Address This Issue	Step 3: Boundaries for Positions on This Issue	Step 4: Strategies to Justify or Clarify Your Position on This Issue
	1. Definition Questions: What is the meaning of a word, phrase, or problem? 2. Verification Questions: What is the true state of affairs, or how does the world operate? 3. Prescription (Value) Questions: What should or should not be done?	1. The significance of the issue for early education 2. The opposing positions and proposals 3. The views of the nature of childhood assumed by the opposing positions 4. The possible delimitations or constraints claimed by the opposing positions 5. The possible consequences of each position	1. Elaborating terms, making distinctions, or clarifying ecological contexts for the issue 2. Citing authoritative (expert) definitions or opinions, current legislation, or court rulings 3. Describing observational/clinical evidence: (a) personal experience, (b) others' anecdotes, or (c) case studies 4. Describing and evaluating empirical evidence: (a) research studies (reliable, valid, and representative), (b) evaluation studies, or (c) statistical surveys 5. Using an analogy or comparable situation 6. Calling for logical reasoning or common sense

tion. In other words, both sides of the issue to be debated can present plausible arguments and some sound evidence.

Examples of general issues selected by teacher education students for debate are:

1. Is television viewing at home or in a day care center detrimental to children?
2. Are family day care homes better places for young children than are day care centers?
3. Are laws and programs for bilingual/multicultural education effective?
4. Is infant education and stimulation provided in day care centers as beneficial to infants as home care by a parent?
5. Is formal parent education helpful in becoming an effective parent?

Addressing an Issue and Identifying Boundaries for Positions

In order to develop questions to investigate and pose for the debate, the main issue can be broken down into definition issues, verification issues, and prescription issues (Oliver & Newmann, 1969; Taylor, 1961). A definition issue poses a question about the meaning of a key concept, phrase, or problem. A verification issue poses a question about the true state of affairs or how the world operates. A prescription issue poses a question about actions that should or should not be taken based on certain core values or ethical principles.

Examples of definition, verification, and prescription issues for a debate are:

1. What is bilingual/multicultural education?   (definition)
2. What is child abuse?   (definition)
3. How does nutrition affect children's appearance and behavior?   (verification)
4. Is group care detrimental to infants and toddlers?   (verification)
5. Should preschool teachers encourage children's exploration of nontraditional sex roles in play?   (prescription)
6. Should an abused child generally be taken out of the home?   (prescription)

If we must limit the number of questions we address for the sake of clarity in our arguments, we should consider which questions are most pressing or most significant for the welfare of children, families, and staff involved in early education. (Some questions are necessary precursors to dealing with more significant ones.) When formulating questions to address, we should also consider: (1) the view of childhood our position and action proposals represent as well as the views of opposing positions, (2) the possible delimitations or disclaimers for our position as well as for opposing positions, and (3) the real and/or possible effects and side effects of our advocated actions as well as the effects and side effects of action alternatives.

Strategies for Justifying or Clarifying a Position

Specific strategies for justifying or clarifying a point of view or position on an issue include:

1. Elaborating terms or making distinctions
2. Citing authoritative (expert) definitions or opinions
3. Describing observational or clinical evidence such as personal experiences, anecdotes from others, or case study examples

7

4. Describing and evaluating empirical evidence such as research or evaluation results
5. Using an analogy or example of a comparable situation
6. Calling for logical reasoning
7. Appealing to common sense, common experience, or common emotions (Oliver & Newmann, 1969).

For example, an issue can be approached with logical reasoning. In this case, arguments based on relationships between propositions are prepared. Consider the following argument:

> *With an increase in the number of single, working mothers with preschool children, the demand for day care services is increasing. If these preschool mothers cannot find adequate and affordable day care services, they can be neither productive workers nor effective parents. Therefore, the government should provide tax credit for building day care facilities and purchasing equipment in areas that serve low-income families and should refund the current tax credit for child care to low-income families using day care who otherwise might not benefit from this income tax credit. (H.R. 5966, 1982)*

When both the propositions and the relationships have been verified, this type of argument can be very convincing.

When addressing an issue, use of an analogy can also be very persuasive. In the case of the issue "Should the state regulate day care homes in the same way it regulates day care centers?" the following analogy might be used:

> Let's consider Mrs. Conway who runs a day care home for neighborhood children. Now suppose Mrs. Conway instead sewed clothing for others in her home. You probably would not say that the same regulations should apply to her as apply to the local clothing manufacturing firm. Likewise, it can be said that the state should not regulate Mrs. Conway's day care home through licensing as it does day care centers.

Appealing to your audience's concerns, common experiences, and emotions can sometimes sway their opinion dramatically. Melton (1983) reports an incident about a conservative senator who became an adoption advocate when a lobbyist admired family pictures in his office and then shared pictures of her large family, including adopted children, and discussed the problems of supporting them without public subsidy.

Research and evaluation data and expert opinion are often used selectively by policy makers and advocates to advance their positions (Forgione, 1980). For example, initiation of legislation for the Head Start program relied on the work of Hunt and Bloom (Melton, 1983). Likewise, debate arguments can be bolstered by reference to research, evaluation, and expert opinion.

The framework presented here will not eliminate challenges, but it can help us to predict them. With practice in debating and increased knowledge of issues, we can clarify our values and make better decisions about the issues and policies that affect early education practice. (See Table 1–2 for an outline of how the framework can be applied to a sample issue.)

TABLE 1–2   *Application of Framework to Sample Issue*

Step 1: Identification of a Significant Issue in Early Childhood Education Today	Step 2: Ways to Address This Issue	Step 3: Boundaries for Positions on This Issue	Step 4: Strategies to Justify or Clarify Your Position on This Issue
Does removing abused children from their homes protect the well-being of children and improve family functioning?	1. Definition: What is child abuse? 2. Verification: Under what circumstances are abused children removed from the home? What percentage of abused children are removed? 3. Prescription: Should abused children generally be removed from their homes?	1. Teachers are required to report suspected cases of child abuse and are expected to support families in their task of nurturing children. 2. The child's vulnerability must be the foremost consideration in these situations. Only by considering the functioning of the family unit can long-term solutions be found. 3. Young children are vulnerable and exposure to abuse at this age has long-lasting effects. Children are part of an interactive family unit and only within that context can solutions to abusive relations be found. 4. In situations where extreme physical evidence is evident, the child must be removed from the home.	1. Describing types and indicators of child abuse 2. Citing definitions of child abuse found in state laws 3. Describing (a) own observations as a member of a foster-care family, (b) newspaper magazine articles about failure to remove an abused child, or (c) examples given by a child protective services worker during an interview 4. Describing an evaluation study that documents recurrence or severe abuse in families during different treatment programs Describing findings from the New York State Senate Report on Child Protective Services that shows 32% of indicated abuse and maltreatment cases receive foster care

TABLE 1–2 *Application of Framework to Sample Issue (cont.)*

Step 1: Identification of a Significant Issue in Early Childhood Education Today	Step 2: Ways to Address This Issue	Step 3: Boundaries for Positions on This Issue	Step 4: Strategies to Justify or Clarify Your Position on This Issue
		5. If removed, the child: (a) may be safer, (b) will become more trusting of others, (c) will develop self-esteem and more positive coping strategies, (d) will become lonesome and withdrawn, (e) will be placed in foster care, or (f) will or will not be reunited with his or her family.	5. Compare child abuse to actions taken to prevent cruelty to animals
			6. Call for need to consider how much responsibility governmental agencies can effectively assume for child rearing
		If not removed, the child: (a) will be subjected to further harm, (b) will participate in family assistance programs to improve family functioning, or (c) will maintain contact with family members.	

Guidelines for Orchestrating an Informal Debate

To prepare teachers for presenting an informal debate, the following guidelines are provided (Freeley, 1976; Guliano, 1985; Williamson-Ige, 1984; Windes & O'Neil, 1964; Ziegelmueller & Dause, 1975).

How Can Teams Prepare for an Informal Debate?

1. Research relevant journal and magazine articles, books, ERIC documents, government documents, and newspaper articles published within the last 10 years. Visit the library and learn how to find information by using various

resources such as the card catalog, Current Index to Journals in Education (CIJE), Resources in Education (ERIC), government document files, and newspaper machine index.

2. Select an issue and develop a debate question. Consult with your instructor if you need assistance in phrasing your debate question.

3. Set up two teams (two or three people on each team). One team will take the "pro" side of the debate question and the other team the "con" side.

4. Search for relevant, specific, and credible evidence (i.e., expert definitions, expert opinions, statistics, research findings, evaluation findings, testimony, and case descriptions) to support key arguments or propositions. Record evidence entries with complete reference citations (author(s) and copyright date) on separate note cards. Use a marker to highlight key terms or figures for easy retrieval during the debate.

5. Each team gathers or develops personal experience examples and analogies related to key arguments or propositions and records these entries on evidence cards.

6. Organize the evidence cards by evidence type and/or topic.

7. Each team organizes arguments and propositions in terms of:
    a. Significance of the issue for early education (need)
    b. Definitions of key concepts
    c. Child advocacy actions or early childhood programs/services that have been initiated
    d. Child advocacy actions or early childhood programs/services that could be initated
    e. Conclusions about the merit of various viewpoints, actions, programs, or services (advantages versus disadvantages or evidence of adequacy versus inadequacy)

8. Each team types a brief introductory statement, four or five challenge questions, a brief summary statement, and a reference list (10 to 20 selected references) with complete bibliographic information for all sources used.

What Is the Format of the Informal Debate?

1. The instructor serves as moderator and timekeeper.
2. Each team takes 3 minutes to present its introductory statements.
3. For the next 20 minutes, the teams take turns asking each other challenge questions.
4. During the next 25 minutes, the moderator solicits comments and questions from the audience.
5. Finally, each team is allowed 2 minutes to sum up and conclude its arguments.

6. Afterwards, each audience member responds to the debate practices questionnaire. (See Figure 1–1 for the debate questionnaire used during the debates.)
7. From process notes and submitted materials, the instructor later analyzes and evaluates the performance of individual team members and records audience contributions.

What Strategies Are Helpful During Delivery of a Debate?

1. Maintain eye contact. (Do not bury your head and read from note cards.) Try to convince the audience of your point of view. Be animated.
2. Use your three-minute introduction as a springboard.
3. Address the significance of the issue for early education in your introduction and/or summary.
4. While listening to the other team, take notes for possible followup or rebuttal statements.
5. Repetition of key points during the debate can be persuasive. Visual aids (containing a limited amount of print) can be effective for this purpose. Refer to your visuals during the course of the debate.

Following issue debates, teachers can make an easy transition to a variety of advocacy activities including letter writing, workshops, interviews, listening to speakers, displays at professional conferences, position papers, issue networking, and lobbying. Additional examples of advocacy training activities to extend teachers' learning can be found in other sources (Whitebook & Ginsburg, 1984; Fink & Sponseller, 1977).

Summary

The debate process presented here is not only an effort to incorporate advocacy training into teacher education but a way to encourage teachers to find their own answers to current issues. To advocate effectively for children and the teaching profession is one of the greatest challenges facing early childhood teachers and administrators today. We hope the material in *Issues and Advocacy in Early Education* will be a resource that teachers and administrators find stimulating and useful when seeking to meet this challenge.

References & Suggested Readings

Allen, K. E. (1983, January). Public policy report: Children, the Congress, and you. *Young Children, 38,* 71–75.
Almy, M. (1985, September). New challenges for teacher education: Facing political and economic realities. *Young Children, 40,* 10–11.

FIGURE 1–1 Debate Questionnaire

Please respond to this short followup questionnaire to let us know how you feel about our debate. Just mark an X on the line that best expresses your opinion regarding each statement.

Team 1 Members: _____

Issue (Viewpoint Argued): _____

	SUPERIOR	STRONG	AVERAGE	WEAK	UNSATISFACTORY
1. *Arguments:* Major arguments/propositions clearly stated. Relationships drawn between evidence, arguments, and propositions. Organized.					
2. *Supporting Material:* Variety of examples/testimony, statistics, expert opinion/definitions, comparisons/analogies, and visual aids. Appropriate, relevant, and credible evidence. Sufficient evidence.					
3. *Strategies to Persuade:* Adjustment/responsiveness to audience comments/questions. Balanced use of logical, emotional, and ethical appeals.					
4. *Delivery:* Effective voice quality, eye contact, gestures, and posture.					
5. *Tone of Argumentation:* Positive attitude toward self and other team. Orderly, courteous, and fair.					
6. *Overall Rating:*					

Comments:

Team 2 Members: _____

Issue (Viewpoint Argued): _____

	SUPERIOR	STRONG	AVERAGE	WEAK	UNSATISFACTORY
1. *Arguments:* Major arguments/propositions clearly stated. Relationships drawn between evidence, arguments, and propositions. Organized.					
2. *Supporting Material:* Variety of examples/testimony, statistics, expert opinion/definitions, comparisons/analogies, and visual aids. Appropriate, relevant, and credible evidence. Sufficient evidence.					
3. *Strategies to Persuade:* Adjustment/responsiveness to audience comments/questions. Balanced use of logical, emotional, and ethical appeals.					
4. *Delivery:* Effective voice quality, eye contact, gestures, and posture.					
5. *Tone of Argumentation:* Positive attitude toward self and other team. Orderly, courteous, and fair.					
6. *Overall Rating:*					

Comments:

	SA	A	D	SD	NA
1. This activity made me think about points that I had not considered before.					
2. My position on this issue most resembles that of Team 1.					

SA: Strongly Agree
A: Agree
D: Disagree
SD: Strongly Disagree
NA: No Answer or Can't Decide

13

Bandura, A. (1977). *Social learning theory*. Englewood Cliffs, NJ: Prentice-Hall.

Bredekamp, S. (Ed.). (1986). *Developmentally appropriate practice*. Washington, DC: National Association for the Education of Young Children.

Bronfenbrenner, U. (1986). Ecology of the family as a context for human development: Research perspectives. *Developmental Psychology, 22*, 723–742.

Buchmann, M. (1986). Role over person: Morality and authenticity in teaching. *Teachers College Record, 87*, 529–543.

Cahill, B. F. (1986). Training volunteers as child advocates. *Child Welfare, 65*, 545–553.

Children's Defense Fund. (1987). *A children's defense budget: FY 1988*. Washington, DC: Author.

Deloria, D., & Brookins, G. K. (1982). The evaluation report: A weak link to policy. In J. R. Travers and R. J. Light (Eds.), *Learning from experience: Evaluating early childhood demonstration programs* (pp. 254–271). Washington, DC: National Academy Press.

Dinham, S. M., & Stritter, F. T. (1986). Research on professional education. In M. C. Wittrock (Ed.), *Handbook of research on teaching* (3rd ed., pp. 952–970). New York: Macmillan.

Feeney, S. (1985, November). Professional ethics in early childhood education. Seminar presented at the Annual Conference of the National Association for the Education of Young Children, New Orleans.

Fink, J., & Sponseller, D. (1977, March). Practicing for child advocacy. *Young Children, 32*, 49–54.

Forgione, P. D. (1980). Early childhood policy-making. *Education and Urban Society, 12*, 227–239.

Freeley, A. J. (1976). *Argumentation and debate: Rational decision making* (4th ed.). Belmont, CA: Wadsworth Publishing Co.

Guliano, N. A. (1985, February). The identification of the most significant problems confronting high school novice debaters and recommended solutions. *Debate Issues, 18*, 9–13.

H. R. 5966. (1981, March). *Congressional Record, 128*(32), p. H 1145.

Hostetler, L. (1981, March). Child advocacy: Your professional responsibility? *Young Children, 36*, 3–8.

Hostetler, L., & Klugman, E. (1982, September). Early childhood job titles: One step toward professional status. *Young Children, 37*, 13–22.

Jensen, M. A. (1986, November). *Preparing early childhood teachers to become advocates: A new challenge for teacher education*. Paper presented at the Annual Conference of the National Association for the Education of Young Children, Washington, DC. (ERIC Document Reproduction Service No. ED 275 456)

Jorde, P. (1986). Early childhood education: Issues and trends. *The Educational Forum, 50*, 172–181.

Jorde-Bloom, P. (1986). Teacher job satisfaction: A framework for analysis. *Early Childhood Research Quarterly, 1*, 167–183.

Katz, L. G. (1980). Ethics and the quality of programs for young children. In S. Kilmer (Ed.), *Advances in early education and day care* (pp. 137–151). Greenwich, CT: JAI Press.

Katz, L. G. (1982). Helping others learn to teach: Some principles

Katz, L. G. (1982). Helping others learn to teach: Some principles and techniques. In N. Nir-Janiv, B. Spodek, and D. Steg (Eds.), *Early childhood education: An international perspective* (pp. 129–139). New York: Plenum Press.

Katz, L. G. (1984, July). The professional early childhood teacher. *Young Children, 39,* 3–10.

Kilmer, S. (1980). Early childhood specialists as policy makers. *Education and Urban Society, 12,* 241–251.

Lombardi, J. (1986, May). Public policy report. Training for public policy and advocacy: An emerging topic in teacher education. *Young Children, 41,* 65–69.

Markus, H., & Nurius, P. (1986). Possible selves. *American Psychologist, 41,* 954–969.

Melton, G. B. (1983). *Child advocacy: Psychological issues and interventions.* New York: Plenum Press.

New York State Child Care Council. (n.d.). *Lobbying techniques.* White Plains, NY: Day Care Council of Westchester.

Oliver, D. W., & Newmann, F. M. (1969). *Cases and controversies: Guide to teaching the Public Issues Series/Harvard Social Studies Project.* Middletown, CT: Xerox Corp.

Osborn, D. K. (1980). *Early childhood education in historical perspective.* Athens, GA: Educational Associates.

Raines, S. C. (1983). Developing professionalism: Shared responsibility. *Childhood Education, 59,* 151–153.

Silin, J. G. (1985, March). Authority as knowledge: A problem of professionalization. *Young Children, 40,* 41–46.

Taylor, P. W. (1961). *Normative discourse.* Englewood Cliffs, NJ: Prentice-Hall.

Whitebook, M., & Almy, M. (1986, September). NAEYC's commitment to good programs for young children: Then and now, a developmental crisis at 60? *Young Children, 41,* 37–40.

Whitebook, M., & Ginsburg, G. (Eds.). (1984). *Beyond "just working with kids": Preparing early childhood teachers to advocate for themselves and others.* Berkeley, CA: Child Care Employee Project. (ERIC Document Reproduction Service ED 255 299)

Whitebook, M., Howes, C., Darrah, R., & Friedman, J. (1982). Caring for the caregivers: Staff burnout in child care. In L. G. Katz (Ed.), *Current topics in early childhood education* (Vol. 4, pp. 211–235). Norwood, NJ: Ablex.

Williamson-Ige, D. K. (1984, May). Debate in the junior high school. *Debate Issues, 17,* 11–16.

Windes, R. R., & O'Neil, R. M. (1964). *A guide to debate.* Portland, ME: J. Weston Walch, Publisher.

Ziegelmueller, G. W., & Dause, C. A. (1975). *Argumentation: Inquiry and advocacy.* Englewood Cliffs, NJ: Prentice-Hall.

Zigler, E., & Finn, M. (1981, May). From problem to solution: Changing public policy as it affects children and families. *Young Children, 37,* 31–58.

CHAPTER 2

Advocacy for the Professional and the Profession

Professional Pursuits?

CECILY: No wonder we hear all this stuff about teacher burn-out! It's not enough that we're working for peanuts; I just found out that my request for leave pay so I can afford to attend the two-day state conference has been turned down by the board!

MONICA: Where did you hear that?

CECILY: Oh, Noah's mother, Mrs. Murdoch, stopped by the classroom after the board meeting and broke the news to me. She said that she was so sorry about my having to lose the pay, but she was sure that I would understand that, what with buying the new outdoor play equipment and fixing the leaking roof, the school was having real financial problems.

MONICA: Can't they get some more money somehow? Our enrollment is up from 70 children last year to 90 children this year. Did she say anything else?

CECILY: Nope. But she did say that everyone thought I was doing a great job! I sure wish they would forget those pats-on-the-back and begin to think about our problems. Not only do I feel like I'm treated as a babysitter, but I feel like I'm subsidizing this school!

MONICA: No arguments from me on that! I feel exploited too. When my daughter, Janie, got sick, I had no health insurance and my "ex" refused to help out.

CECILY: Look, a lot of us here are feeling exploited. Why don't we call around to other centers and find out about their salaries and benefits. Then we could make a real case.

MONICA: Gee, Cecily, I'd really like to help, but I'm in the doghouse now. Besides, I really don't think the board would listen to me. I'm rotten in those situations; I never can open my mouth without blowing my cool. Anyway, they've already made up their minds; they won't change.

CECILY: So much for sympathy—I'd think that if we worked together, it would help all of us in the long run.

MONICA: I suppose so. I really have my own problems hacking it as a single parent. Tell you what—why not ask the others first? If they will, then maybe I'll think about . . . You know, I just don't feel comfortable in those situations.

Questions

1. How do you account for differences in people's willingness to take a stand on personnel issues?

2. What would you say or do to persuade Monica to help in this situation?

3. How do you decide whether obligations to yourself, to the clientele, or to the organization are more important in your decision to act in this situation? When should a board decide whether obligations to personnel are more important than obligations to the center?

4. How may developing unity among staff members conflict with the welfare of the school organization?

5. What should early childhood teachers do to improve the professional status of their occupation?

PREVIEW

What do you believe to be the nature of a professional role in working with young children? How do your assumptions about the field of early childhood education affect your willingness to advocate for the profession? This chapter helps you begin making important decisions about advocating for professionalization in early childhood education. Lana Hostetler opens the readings with a persuasive argument for grass-roots involvement in advocacy. This is followed by a concise compilation of facts about the present status of child care in our country, which is provided by the National Commission on Working Women. Next, Caroline Zinsser questions the deplorable level of child care salaries and benefits. The Day Care and Human Services Local in Boston then argues for statewide unionization to improve wages, benefits, and working conditions. Finally, Jonathan G. Silin examines the progress of early childhood education toward professionalization.

Child Advocacy: Your Professional Responsibility?

Lana Hostetler

Child day care is at a crossroads. More parents of young children under five work outside the home so more young children need care for some or all of the day. Proportionately fewer dollars are being expended on family services. The world situation is tense and much of the federal budget is allocated for national defense. Inflation means that day care, along with many other services, is costing more. The federal day care regulations are in suspension, and there is internal fighting in the day care field between public and private sectors. The White House Conference on Families recommendations address the need for expanded day care services, but that report seems destined to gather dust on bureaucratic shelves. A strong conservative force in the country views day care as a threat to the family, as a move toward communal childrearing. Indeed, the future at times looks dismal.

If this were 1971 rather than 1981, I could be expressing the same views. In 1970, Congress was working to pass the Comprehensive Child Care Act which was then vetoed by former President Nixon on the grounds that it posed a threat to American families. In 1975, Senator Mondale's Child and Family Service Act was killed by a vast conservative outpouring of opposition. In 1979, Senator Cranston's attempt to develop child care legislation stagnated and died as the result of internal fighting in the child care field and external opposition from conservatives.

In short, in the past decade, little seems to have changed. We have had new crises: Iran and the fate of the hostages supplanted Vietnam; oil and energy and inflation became crucial concerns. Children, however, still remain a low priority and probably will as long as they cannot vote. People who advocate for children remain frustrated and angry; it sometimes seems we have made little progress. Perhaps it is true that the more things change, the more they remain the same.

However, one crucial element *has* changed—the children. Those children about whom we were concerned in the 1970s are no longer young children. Ten years ago I was looking for day care for my two-year-old son. Today he is twelve and in the "clean your pores but not your fingernails" stage. Instead of looking for day care, I spend a great deal of time looking for him at the skating rink or the junior high or wherever else he goes looking for girls. Some children who were in day care at the time he was are now parents—adolescent mothers looking for day care for their own babies. Yes, the children have changed. They have grown up.

As adults, we have a particular sense of time, an adult perspective. We view childhood as precious and fleeting, and we look to it with nostalgia, perceiving it as a time of joy. What we forget, from our adult perspective, is a child's outlook. When you are three, it is a long, long wait until Christmas or your birthday. It is also hard for a child in day care to wait every day until their parent comes for them. When the three-year-old child is in less than adequate care, the days do not dwindle down to a precious few—they do not need stretching out. Instead, they are like Macbeth's days, with " 'To-morrow, and to-morrow, and to-morrow, / Creep[ing] in this petty pace' (*Macbeth*, V.v. ll. 19–20)." Those petty-pace days may make up one-third or one-half or more of the young child's entire life span. We need to remember that for three-year-old children one year is one-third of their entire existence.

Source: Lana Hostetler (1981, March). Child Advocacy: Your professional responsibility? *Young Children, 36,* 3–8. Copyright © 1981 by the National Association for the Education of Young Children. Reprinted by permission of the publisher.

As adults, we often speak of time passing too quickly, especially if we have an overload of things to do. It seems it was only yesterday when I first carried that toddler into day care. But as adults we know that there are years ahead of us. That knowledge, perhaps, leads to our adult penchant to defer, to study, to plan, to await the results of a longitudinal study, to get our act together tomorrow. That penchant, however, should pale beside the three-year-old child's creeping todays and tomorrows, and should alert us that we must seek change now—indeed, we should have sought it yesterday.

Each of us wants more for children than petty tomorrows—we want precious and memorable days. We want to contribute to the quality of care for children because we have made a commitment to do so.

With that commitment comes the hard dilemmas—the questions of professional, ethical, and perhaps moral responsibilities. Once I was shopping with a young friend of mine who desperately wanted chewing gum. When all his persuasive techniques failed, and I continued to demur, he announced to me emphatically, "Now, Lana, this is my last truth. My Grandma June wants me to have gum." Like Kyle, I too have some last truths, the foremost of which is that commitment to caring for young children must also be a commitment to care about them in the fullest sense—not just on a day-by-day basis of wiping noses, kissing away hurts, and planning exciting and creative learning experiences; nor of seeking more funding, filling out forms, and completing a myriad of administrative tasks. Instead, we have to care about the children in our programs and the children without programs— and about their present status and what their future holds. Such commitment must necessarily carry some other last truths and some harsh realities.

I would assume that most of you, reading the title "Child Advocacy: Your Professional Responsibility?" probably focused on the word responsibility and may indeed have asked yourself if advocacy is a responsibility. Some of you may have thought of advocacy as a duty, an obligation, or perhaps a burden— something else you should be doing. Others may have centered on the word *advocacy* and questioned whether getting involved with politics was really professional, the right thing for human services professionals to do. I doubt that many of you focused on the word *professional* or even considered whether or not you are a professional in a professional field.

It is with this issue, however, that we must begin, if we are to answer the question of responsibility. Unfortunately, while we may consider ourselves professionals, the world at large probably does not. Certainly the wages that are paid to people who work with young children are not proportionate to other professions. Nor are we viewed as professionals by the Dictionary of Occupational Titles (U.S. Department of Labor 1977) which lists child care workers as domestics that need no more skills than offal workers, people who shovel chicken droppings. Most of us have encountered the attitude that day care is just babysitting, an easy job, a place for people who like to play with kids, a job that anyone who was once a child can do. Early childhood training programs often have students enrolled who have been advised to go into the field because they probably could not make it academically any place else. In the words of one high school counselor, they "should certainly be able to deal with three year olds, even if they cannot handle a real teaching job." That pervasive attitude on the part of other professionals is an extension of the educational pecking order—the notion that the more capable someone is, the higher level at which she or he should be teaching. It is this kind of notion that maintains abysmally low salaries, that reinforces public perceptions, and that once led an instructor at my college to leave his four-year-old child for me to care for while he taught his classes because "the babysitter is sick and you are in child care, after all."

Most assuredly, day care is not viewed as a profession. Indeed, it is hard sometimes for us to view ourselves as professionals. Have you caught yourself saying, "I'm in early childhood education" rather than, "I'm in day care?" Recently, I saw a questionnaire on job titles in the field. One of the questions was, "What do you call people who work with young children?" My first impulse was to answer "poor and crazy."

We must, however, view ourselves as professionals and work toward being recognized as such. Public perceptions of the field must change, and one part of advocacy efforts is to do just that. A last truth about our commitment (and our subsequent professionalism) is that we have to tell someone other than ourselves about it. One major component of values clarification is that for something to be a value, one must affirm it and act upon it; so too it is with our commitment and our professionalism.

Such commitment to a profession also carries with it responsibility. I do believe that child advocacy is a professional responsibility, although one that is not always easy to recognize nor fulfill. It is a responsibility that is made both easier and more difficult by the passion of commitment. Certainly we can see why we must advocate for children and the profession, but such a strong commitment often leads to some hard dilemmas.

If you are committed to young children, you cannot close your eyes and ignore what is happening to children and children's programs. While it might be easier to go into your classroom or office and close the door, you should not do so. If the city were closing down your street, few of you would go into your kitchen, shut the door, and scrub the floor or bake bread. Instead, you would meet with your neighbors, circulate a petition, and find someone to go down to city hall (or go yourself). You would probably even talk to the neighbor whose dog went through your flower bed last week or to the ones with whom you have been feuding because of their teenager's loud parties. Deciding how to spend your time, both with your family and on the problem, would pose a dilemma, but most likely you would find a way to solve that dilemma. If the city shut down your street, it would be harder to get home with the cleanser for the floor or the special rye flour for your bread. The fire department or paramedics would have trouble reaching your house. Your family might suffer. You would find a way to resolve the problem. So too might the children in your program and other programs suffer if you and your colleagues do not involve yourself with advocacy issues that affect them.

If we are truly committed to young children, it is probably easy to recognize this responsibility to become involved with advocacy issues. Acting on that responsibility, however, is not always so easy. There are many levels of advocacy in which one can become involved, but most require a very precious commodity—time. Advocacy efforts sometimes become burdens, another task to be completed. If we already feel underpaid and overworked, the thought of working even more is sometimes

overwhelming. I find that I am better able to deal with the time issue by thinking of a three-year-old child watching the clock and wanting to go home. I suddenly am able to find the necessary time, and you can too.

Acting on the responsibility to advocate also involves frustration (and the time to deal with frustration), especially when we think of how little we have accomplished in the last decade. Let me assure you, however, that despite the pessimistic outlook I shared with you earlier, there are some bright spots.

Certainly there is frustration and often anger. The political system, in Pennsylvania, California, Illinois, or in Washington is complex and moves slowly, if at all. The results are often not what we want to hear. The Navy still does not have to hold bake sales; day care does. We often feel that we are begging for half a loaf and settling for crumbs.

Even getting to know the system is frustrating. Just when you think you know the game, the players change and so does the strategy. You can get to know the basic rules; as in baseball, legislation has to go around the bases, through the teams, and it has to try to get home and score, at least most of the time. Presidential, gubernatorial, and legislative umpires may disagree on the rules or even change them.

Understanding the political system is a complex process not only because of its intricacies, but because of perceptions of that system which we have gradually developed. The political system does not operate in quite the way our eighth-grade civics textbook portrayed it. The view that the media has given us of the political process is incomplete. Often our understanding of the system is based on the same fragmentary impressions as those of a group of young children I know. When taken to the old State Capitol of Illinois, they looked around with apparent awe as their teacher explained that Abraham Lincoln had once worked there. As she talked to them about the importance of the Capitol, they were full of questions about the objects they were seeing, and she tried to explain the use of each one, including the brass spittoons by each desk. As they left the Capitol, she gathered the children together for a review. When she asked them what they had seen and learned, one girl remarked, "The people here weren't very nice. They wrote with feathers and spit a lot." Her perception, like ours sometimes is, was only fragmentary and based on what was real and immediate, rather than on more pertinent issues that were alien to her four years of experience.

Last fall former President Carter visited the campus where I teach. His motorcade slowed in front of the Lincoln Land Day Care Center so that he could wave to the children who were gathered on the front lawn waving flags and banners. After he had returned to the airport, the children were heard chanting, "We saw the policemen. We saw the policemen."

Like those children, and the four-year-old at the state capitol, we often perceive government and policy issues as remote from our daily lives. That remoteness, coupled with fragmentary impressions and with the complexity of the system, adds to our frustration and makes advocacy sometimes difficult.

Not only the system by which policy is made, but policies themselves are confusing and often frustrating. We can, however, learn about the system—with time and diligence and some sharing of resources. When I become terribly frustrated, I think of the young child who is constantly being frustrated because his care setting is less than adequate. I usually find that I can deal with the frustration; I hope you can too.

To act on the responsibility to advocate also involves guilt: guilt about for whom we are advocating—ourselves or young children. By advocating for more money for children's programs, are we being self-serving, seeking to feather our own nests? I would remind you that we are indeed a profession, and we must abandon some of the notions of guilt. Certainly, we advocate for ourselves when we advocate for children, but why shouldn't we? Aren't we more skilled than offal workers? Can't we do a better job with children if our own needs are met? Everyone does a better job if they feel good about themselves and that includes day care teachers and directors. As early childhood educators, we spend a great deal of time being concerned about children's affective development. We should also be concerned about our own self-concepts. Part of feeling good about oneself comes from doing a job that people value. Nurturing children should be valued. Ours is a capitalistic society, and valued work is work for which people are willing to pay appropriate wages. We need to give up our guilt, and the notion that because we are in the human services, we should be good, pure, noble, and underpaid. We do advocate for ourselves somewhat when we advocate for children, but if our commitment is to children and to building a profession, we should not feel guilty about this advocacy. Nor should we feel guilty about getting involved with the political system. It is time to take off our white gloves and recognize that it is the only system in town. What we should feel guilty about is not advocating at all.

Perhaps the last and hardest truth about advocacy as a professional responsibility lies in the dilemmas that are created by a passionate commitment to young children, and ultimately, our own personal integrity as it was involved in making that commitment. What do we do when our own causes come into conflict? What do we do when we know that the only program in a community is woefully inadequate, but that if it were closed, parents would have no other place to take their children? Do we say nothing, everything, or compromise? What do I as a trainer do if some of my students have special needs so severe that it seems likely they would be unable to provide for the safety and well-being of a group of young children? Where does my recognition and support for individual rights of access to education come into conflict with my basic commitment to young children? How do I determine whether a student is gaining skill at the expense of a group of young children? What do you do if your basic commitment to children leads to advocacy efforts that put you into direct conflict with your board? How do you reconcile voting for a candidate who has wonderful day care policies, but is the anathema of what you believe about foreign policy, the economy, or women's rights? If you had to rank the three most important issues facing Congress today, would you rank day care above energy, inflation, and the Middle East? Should you?

Perhaps resolving these dilemmas is not really the last truth; perhaps they cannot really be resolved. Recognizing that these and other dilemmas exist is, however, essential. As we make a commitment to a profession, to caring for and about children, we are committing ourselves to assuming not just a professional but also an ethical responsibility to grapple with these dilemmas and find our own answers. We will learn that it is easier to talk it than to walk it; that answers do not always come easily; that sometimes answers do not come at all unless we remember the three-year-old children waiting for their petty days to end and creeping tomorrows to begin. The ethics of our profession demand much of us. It is the children, the primary force behind our profession, who will reward us. Ultimately, I think we will view child advocacy not as a mere professional responsibility, but as an ethical responsibility and as a challenge we will be able to meet.

Lana L. Hostetler, M.S., is Instructor, Child Care Services, Lincoln Land Community College, Springfield, Illinois.

REFERENCES

Shakespeare, W. *Macbeth.* In *The Riverside Shakespeare,* ed. G. B. Evans. Boston: Houghton Mifflin, 1974.

U.S. Department of Labor. *Dictionary of Occupational Titles.* Washington, D.C.: U.S. Department of Labor (Employment and Training Administration) 1977.

Child Care Fact Sheet
Working Mothers and Children

In March, 1986, 62.8% of all women with children under 18 years old worked outside the home.

In all, nearly 20 million mothers were in the labor force. The highest increase in the rate of labor force participation was in women with children under 3 years old.

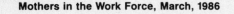

Mothers in the Work Force, March, 1986

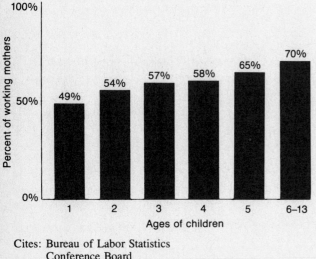

Cites: Bureau of Labor Statistics
Conference Board
Children's Defense Fund

In 1986, 1 in every 5 mothers in the work force was maintaining her own family.

Women work out of economic need. In March 1986, over 6.4 million women with children under 18 years old were single, divorced, separated, or widowed.

In 1986, 34.1 million or 58% of all children had mothers in the work force.

Numbers of children	Ages of children
9.97 million	0–5
15.08 million	6–13
9.01 million	14–17

The 25 million children age 13 and under were cared for in a variety of ways while their parents worked.

Types of care	Estimated numbers of children
family day care	5.5 million
child care centers	1.5 million
own homes; care by relatives or non-relatives or other arrangements	11 million
self care	7.0 million

Affordable, high quality child care is the combined responsibility of parents, providers, employers, and federal and state governments.

Parents, however, must determine what they consider important attributes of a care provider and of a nurturing environment for their child. The following factors are indicators of a high quality environment for children:*

• children are safe and well nourished
• children have adequate space
• ample materials and equipment for learning are provided
*NAEYC

• staff are trained in child development and teaching methods
• there is good planning and organization, and
• strong links to parents are maintained

About the Commission: The National Commission on Working Women was created to focus on the needs and concerns of the approximately 80% of women in the work force who are concentrated in low-paying, low-status jobs in service industries, clerical occupations, retail stores, factories, and plants.

Source: Used by permission of the National Commission on Working Women of Wider Opportunities for Women.

Child Care Fact Sheet
Kinds of Child Care

In 1982, over 55% of all working women chose care outside of their homes for their children under age 5. The rest chose care in their own homes or had other arrangements.

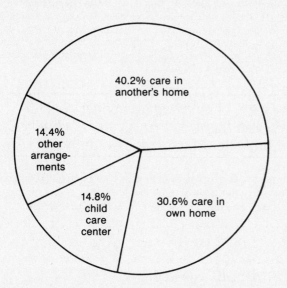

Care in another's home—family day care—40.2%

The largest percentage of children are cared for in family day care homes, especially infants and children under 3 years old. About 75% of care is given by non-relatives, while about 25% is provided by relatives.

Center care—14.8%

Child care centers include infant, preschool and mixed age centers accommodating groups of children. More and more women are choosing center care as the availability of centers increases. Most children in centers are 3–5 years old.

Care in own home—30.6%

Most care given in a working mother's own home is given by the father or another relative. Few parents can afford a full-time paid child care provider in their own home.

Other arrangements—14.4%

About 10% of working mothers care for their children themselves at their place of work. In addition, many mothers make part-time arrangements with more than one caregiver to cover their child's care throughout the day (i.e., nursery school in the morning, a neighbor's home in the afternoon).

Women leaving work for childbirth and care of infants

In 1984, 60% of all working women had no paid "parental (maternity) leave."

Paid time off from work to accommodate pregnancy and childbirth is called disability leave. Only 40% of women in 1984 were covered by some form of disability insurance or an employer's paid parental (maternity) leave policy. The Pregnancy Disability Act of 1978 prohibits discrimination because of pregnancy and requires insured wage compensation for the period (usually 6 to 8 weeks) a woman cannot work, if her employer provides other kinds of short term disability coverage. Some employers have a paid or unpaid "parental leave" policy (generally 4 to 16 weeks) which allows a woman time off from work to care for her newborn child. Women who are not covered by any policy often must use a combination of sick days, vacation days, and leave without pay during this period.

Children who care for themselves

By conservative estimates there are 7 million children aged 13 and under who care for themselves for at least part of every day while their parents work. Often brothers and sisters are responsible for younger siblings. There is an urgent need to make before and after school care for these "latchkey" children a national priority.

Cites: Census Bureau
       Association of Junior Leagues
       Children's Defense Fund
       Women's Legal Defense Fund

Child Care Fact Sheet
Affordability, Quality, and Wages: The Link

While costs vary according to the age of the child, most working families can expect to spend 10% of their income on child care.

Kind of care	Age of child	Yearly cost range
family day care	0–2	$1500–3250 +
	3–5	1500–3000
center care	0–2	1750–3800 +
	3–5	1750–3800
	6–13	900–1500

In 1984, the median annual income of female heads of household in the labor force with children under 18 years old was $13,213. Ten percent of $13,213 would not cover the cost of the least expensive preschool care.

In 1985, there were an estimated 2 to 3 million child care providers in the U.S. The majority earned minimum wage or less.

Center workers earn an average of $9200 per year, with the middle 50% of workers making between $6800 and $12,500. Family day care workers average about $1.00 per hour per child. The National Day Care Home Study (1981) estimated that 87% of family day care workers earn less than minimum wage. In 1985, 97% of all child care providers were women.

In 1980, the turnover rate of child care providers in centers was 41.7%; for family day care providers the rate was even higher.

Low pay, lack of benefits, and stressful working conditions are the major reasons child care providers leave their jobs in such high numbers. The rate for other occupations averages around 20%.

Only half (50.5%) of women entitled to child support received full payment in 1983. The other half received partial payment (25%) or no payment at all (24%).

The Child Support Enforcement Amendment of 1984 mandates the collection of support payments from non-custodial parents. If full payment of entitled child support had been paid in 1983, 80,000 fewer families would have lived in poverty, and many more would have been able to afford child care for their children.

Training of providers is essential to high quality child care.

Forty-two states do not require any special training in child care for staff, and only 24 states require any child development training for directors of centers. Federal and state governments support the Child Development Associate (CDA) credential, a competency-based program to train center workers and family day care and infant care providers. Lack of funds for in-service training and low wages act as barriers to increasing the number of well-trained child care professionals.

The ratio of child care providers to children and the size of the group of children are important factors in the quality of care.

Care providers can spend more time with each child if the provider/child ratio is small. Optimal ratios are:

Age of child	Ratio of providers to children
infants	1:3
1–2 years	1:4 or 5
3–5 years	1:7–9
6–13 years	1:25

Children under 3 years old should be in groups of 12 or less and 3–5 year olds in groups of 20 or less with the appropriate number of providers.

In 1984, of the 1 million child abuse cases reported to the American Humane Society, less than 1.5% were sexual abuse cases involving child care providers or babysitters.

Despite the recent publicity concerning sexual abuse in a small number of centers, the majority of child abuse occurs in the home by a parent, relative, or family friend. Child care programs have played an important role in the detection and treatment of abused children and their parents.

Cites: Conference Board
       Bureau of Labor Statistics
       Children's Foundation
       Department of Health and Human Services

Child Care Fact Sheet
National Outlook: Who Supports Child Care?

The United States has no comprehensive child care policy. Federal and state governments, employers, and unions offer some assistance to providers and parents.

In 1984, 7.6 million families used the Dependent Care Tax Credit, the largest source of government support for child care.

Under this tax law, parents may claim up to $2400 for the cost of care of one child and $4800 for two or more children. The deduction is based on a percent of that claim, according to the amount of income. Tax credits range between $720 and $480 for one child or $1440 and $960 for two or more children. The benefit totalled $2.7 billion in 1984.

Federal government programs for low-income families:

Social Services Block Grant/Title XX provides general funding to states for human services including child care. Parents with income below a state-established level can qualify for subsidized child care.

Child Care Food Program provides subsidies to centers and family day care homes for meals and snacks.

Head Start provides funds to local organizations which offer comprehensive preschool education to low-income children. It currently serves only 14% of eligible children.

Aid to Families with Dependent Children allows families to spend $160 of earned income per month per child for child care without reducing the family's AFDC grant.

About 20,000 out of an estimated 1 million center-based child care workers have been organized by unions.

In centers where workers are unionized, wages are higher, and child care workers have won such benefits as health insurance and paid vacations. Union involvement with child care has been primarily through informal negotiating with employers to improve the range of child care benefits and options offered to employees. Unions have also backed on-site centers, information and referral services, and community-based programs.

Cites: IRS
   Children's Defense Fund
   Census Bureau
   Child Care Employees Project (Berkeley)
   Service Employees International Union

In 1985, out of 6 million U.S. businesses of all sizes, only 2500 gave support to employee child care needs.

According to a January, 1986 Conference Board report, employers provided a variety of benefits for their employees:

- **On-site care.** Employer operates or provides care in or near the workplace.
- **Subsidies or vouchers.** Employers provide their staff subsidies or vouchers which they may redeem at a center or at the caregiver of their choice.
- **Discounts.** Employer arranges discounts for employees at selected child care programs.
- **Flexible benefits ("cafeteria plan").** Employee selects child care among other benefits.
- **Spending accounts (salary reduction).** Employee takes reduction in income and pays for child care out of a nontaxable account.
- **Information and referral service.** Employers devise an in-house information and referral system or contract with an outside company to provide one.
- **Establishing family day care homes.** Company recruits and pays for training and licensing of a caregiver who provides care for employees' children.
- **Sick child care.** Employer provides care for sick children through in-home nursing services or sick child care infirmaries.
- **Alternative work patterns.** Employer policies include: flex-time, job sharing, family leave, and parental sick leave.

More than 3 million American children are cared for in church-housed child care programs every day.

According to the National Council of Churches, up to 70% of all child care centers in the United States are in church buildings. Half of these programs receive free space, involving multi-million dollar subsidies by congregations.

The Disgrace of Child-Care Salaries

Caroline Zinsser

Policy makers and the press repeatedly call for more available and affordable child care through increased subsidies. But what is seldom publicly recognized is that day care is *already* heavily subsidized by the child-care workers themselves. Low wages and few benefits are the underpinnings of one of our most essential public services.

Although an underpaid and overworked staff keeps costs down—alleviating the need for other public or private subsidies—the quality of day-care programs suffer as a result. There's an exodus of experienced staff members from the field and finding qualified replacements is increasingly difficult. With more children moving into elementary school classrooms, public schools are siphoning off licensed day-care teachers at an alarming rate.

In an effort to document the extent of the problem in New York State, the Center for Public Advocacy Research conducted the first statewide survey of child-care-worker salaries and benefits. Although we were aware that day-care workers were underpaid, the actual figures were, in the words of one director, "shockingly low." In day-care centers outside of New York City, head teachers—those who are in charge of groups of children—earn an average of $4.98 per hour, or $10,358 annually. Assistant teachers earn an average of $4.14 per hour, or $8,611 a year. And classroom aides are paid only $3.69 an hour on the average, with many earning the minimum wage. The most recent Bureau of Census figures show that child-care wages are actually even lower than our survey indicates—$7,893 per employee.

It says something about our society's sense of values that even animal caretakers are paid more than those who care for our children. (In Orange County in 1984 nursery school attendants were offered $3.35 per hour, while animal caretakers were offered $4.00 per hour.) Teachers, who we entrust as experts in early childhood education, in child development, in nutrition and health—as well as in having a loving heart—are paid less than we pay bartenders, house cleaners and hotel clerks.

Even more disturbing, our survey shows that staff secretaries and bookkeepers at daycare facilities earn more than the teachers. Yet over 85 percent of head teachers and 52 percent of assistant teachers are college-educated. Aides, 26 percent of whom are college-educated, earn less than child-care-center custodians.

The benefits picture is equally disastrous. Only 54 percent of child-care employees outside of New York City receive any kind of individual health insurance. Although they devote their lives to other people's children, only 26 percent receive health insurance for their own families. Only 18 percent have a retirement plan, and an equally small percentage are covered by life insurance plans.

Turnover, always a problem, has reached a state of crisis. The average program statewide has a 40 percent turnover rate per year for teachers, 39 percent for assistant teachers and 37 percent for aides. Most day-care employees have been on staff for only three years or less—64 percent of all head teachers, 63 percent of assistant teachers and 76 percent of aides. The most often cited reason for leaving is to take a better-paying job.

National figures bear out the findings of our study. Center-based child-care workers rank among the lowest 10 percent of all wage earners in the United States. The Children's Defense Fund estimates that two out of three center-based caregivers earn below poverty-level wages, regardless of their experience,

Source: Caroline Zinsser (1987, February/March). The disgrace of child-care salaries. *Working Parents*, pp. 12–13. Reprinted by permission of Boyd & McGinnity Publishing.

training or education. Family child-care workers earn even less than center-based workers.

An unstable staff affects the quality of care. Children suffer when the bonds of trust in a caregiver are broken and a new person comes to take her place. Classroom routines are disrupted. When vacancies cannot be filled immediately, which is increasingly the case, other staff must cover the gaps by taking on extra responsibilities, resulting in fewer qualified adults caring for more children. When children are distressed, so are their parents, so much so that their own work may be affected.

Ironically, it is the economic facts of mothers entering the labor force that both cause the need for quality day care and at the same time undermine the compensation of those women we depend upon to provide that care. Taking care of children is a low-status job in our society, in part because it's work that has been traditionally performed by women in the home who received no wages. Unlike wage labor performed outside the home, which is recognized for its components of skill acquisition and specialized training, child care is generally viewed as an ability that comes "naturally" to all women.

Women are expected to be emotionally committed to the work of caring for children—to work for love rather than money. In fact, child-care workers who ask for wage increases are often viewed as lacking the proper attitude toward their job, as though the motivations for seeking a decent wage were at variance with commitments to children's care.

One might suppose that working mothers, realizing that skills and dedication are essential for quality child care, would champion child-care workers and would demand that they be paid a fair compensation for the value of their work. Unfortunately, many are themselves caught in a cruel bind that works against an alliance between mother and child caregiver.

It is not unusual for the cost of child care to be considered an expense of a woman's own earnings—instead of a joint family expense. These women measure what they can afford to pay in fees against salaries depressed by pay inequity. As a result, day-care workers are paid a lesser share of a lesser share. They bear the double weight of sex-based wage discrimination. Theirs is a sex-segregated occupation, undervalued by society and dependent upon the wages of other women workers.

Low pay for women's work, low status for work in women-dominated job categories, and the large number of single working mothers are all factors that unfairly not only depress the compensation of working mothers, but doubly depress the wages of those women who care for their children. When working women are so underpaid themselves that they cannot afford to pay adequate fees for child care, it is patently unfair to expect other women to subsidize these fees by low salaries and no benefits.

Child-care workers also are women who must work. And the work they have chosen is of great importance to our families and to our economy. But for too long they have been depended upon to support the public interest at their own expense. They are finally, in protest, beginning to leave the field and to choose other work. Child care must be given increased government and corporate support to subsidize fees, not only to empower working parents in obtaining quality care for their children but also to enable day-care workers to earn a decent wage with adequate benefits.

This problem has not yet received sufficient public recognition. It is time for us parents, employers, professionals, and policy makers to recognize and to correct this grossly unfair and harmful situation.

Caroline Zinsser is the director of the Center for Public Advocacy Research's Day Care Policy Study.

It Makes a Difference!

District 65, UAW
Daycare and Human Services Local, Boston, MA

Since the Daycare and Human Services Local in Massachusetts won its first election in 1979 in a daycare center with 12 employees, we have grown to represent over 1,500 workers across the country. Through unionizing, we have been able to improve wages and benefits, and have made gains in such things as child ratios, hiring policies, and equal treatment for all workers. It is apparent to unionized workers, however, that we will not get the decent wages and working conditions we all deserve until *all* childcare workers across the country speak up for themselves and demand decent wages for themselves, affordable child care for parents, and quality child care for children.

"I Have Never Heard of Anything Like This Before"

In Massachusetts, we have embarked on a history-making drive. We are the first daycare workers in the country to organize ourselves on a state-wide basis. Although the daycare employees in New York City funded centers are organized, that is the only city in the country where employees with the same funding source are organized into a Union with one contract covering the employees city-wide. Their contract is an outstanding example of what can be accomplished with a united workforce. As of this July, their contract includes *entry level* salaries ranging from $14,000 to $19,500; full health and dental benefits, paid prescriptions and eye glasses, free legal aid, etc. Our goal is to obtain comparable wage scales and other improvements in our working conditions and benefits on a state-wide basis.

On the National Level

The Union is also actively organizing in other states and we are available to assist other groups of workers throughout the country who are interested in organizing at their workplaces. We represent workers at non-profit centers and at proprietary chains in Illinois, Wisconsin, Massachusetts, New York, New Jersey and California.

The Union will continue to lobby for legislation that will expand the availability of quality, affordable day care as well as help daycare teachers. For instance, the Union will push for legislation to institute a loan forgiveness or deferred payment plan for daycare teachers who owe student loans.

As we all know, children are the future. We, as daycare employees, provide the crucial service necessary for parents to work. The Union believes that by organizing, by working *together*, we can provide higher quality child care and ensure that we receive wages, benefits and respect equal to the importance of our work.

Source: Childcare and Human Services Local, Boston, District 65, United Auto Workers. Reprinted with permission.

The following are just a few examples of changes in wages, benefits, and working conditions that can happen when people are united and organized.

Benefits

Before

Health Insurance: Most employers determine health plan available and employee/employer contributions.

Promotion/Transfer: Usually no preference for current employees; no standard criteria for selection; no emphasis on affirmative action.

Time Off: Most employers decide amount of time off available to employees.

Leave of Absence/Maternity Leave: No policy for arranging a personal leave from center, including maternity leave.

Layoff and Recall: No advance notice if center cuts staffing; no severance pay; no procedure for recall.

Full-Time, Part-Time Status: Most centers do not provide benefits to workers employed less than 35 hours/week.

After

Employees choose from a range of health plan options, including District 65 100% employer-paid health plan. Most centers negotiate 100% employer-paid health benefits.

Seniority determines the selection where applicants are relatively equally qualified; jobs filled in accordance with nondiscrimination clause/affirmative action language.

Centers negotiate increase in time off. Most centers have at least 11 guaranteed holidays; 12–15 sick days; sick days can be used as personal days; up to 24 vacation days.

Guaranteed leave of absence. Guaranteed maternity leave. No unreasonable denial of personal leave.

Employee notified as soon as practicable; seniority retained on recall list for 12 months; several centers negotiate severance pay.

Most centers negotiate prorated benefits for part-time workers.

Wages

Prior to 1979 when workers began to negotiate wages in their contracts, most centers were at or close to minimum wage, with no guaranteed wage increases; no additional money allotted to reward length of service.

Through lobbying efforts and contracts which demand guaranteed across the board increases, wages have risen substantially at many centers, setting increased wage standards for centers throughout Massachusetts (i.e., *Roxbury Tenants of Harvard:* 24% in 3 years; *Harvard Law School Childrens Center:* 17% in 2 years in addition to 5% annual step increases; *Hampshire Community Action:* 37% in 3 years with 5% step increases).

Working Conditions

Job Descriptions: Many job descriptions are vague; any additional duties can be added without consulting employee.

On first day of work, employee receives clear and accurate job description. Employees not required to do work not found in job description. Employer must consult with worker for any changes in job description.

31

Ratios: Limited only by OFC. Volunteers and trainees usually counted in ratios.

Ratios apply to number of permanent staff in each classroom (i.e., *Roxbury Tenants of Harvard:* Toddler—1 to 4, Pre-school—1 to 6; *Infants and Other People:* Infants—2 to 6, Afterschool—2 to 18).

Breaks: Understaffing often prevents workers from taking breaks.

Higher staff/child ratios. All employees are guaranteed breaks as specified by labor law (i.e., IOP—45 min. lunch, 15 min. break).

Consultation: Most employees have no say about planned changes in equipment, work procedures, work environment or location.

Union committees negotiate any changes in working conditions. Employees are given an accounting of supply money available to them. Some centers have paid setup days without children in center.

Hiring and Promotions: Most centers do not guarantee staff participation in hiring process. No consistent procedure for making internal promotions accessible.

Staff review resumés, participate in interviews, and have a voice in hiring new employees. Internal staff given preference for promotions/transfers based on seniority.

Job Security, Discipline, and Discharge: Totally arbitrary. Employees could be fired for little or no reasons, with no recourse.

Discipline limited to written warning procedures explicitly stating the charges; employees can only be discharged for just and good cause, subject to written grievance procedure and outside mediation; employees duly protected for reporting violations to OFC or DSS.

Authority as Knowledge
A Problem of Professionalization

Jonathan G. Silin

In recent years there has been a growing concern about the professional status of early childhood educators. This concern has led to a new awareness of the need to communicate to the public at large (Caldwell 1984) and a search for common nomenclature within the field (Hostetler and Klugman 1982; National Association for the Education of Young Children 1984). Underlying this interest in our professional status is the unspoken assumption that professionalization is a worthwhile goal. Indeed, it seems to be a struggle that we may not be able to avoid if we are to be successful advocates for young children and their families, and for the salaries that we so clearly deserve.

Is Professionalization the Answer?

As Caldwell points out (1984), the demand for professional recognition involves the development of increased conceptual clarity among child care workers themselves as to who they are and what they do. A look at the early childhood field and how individual teachers function within it confirms the saliency of Caldwell's remark.

For example, Lightfoot (1978) in her examination of the relationships between families and schools stresses the low status of teachers of young children. Joffe (1977) calls early childhood a weak or marginal profession lacking in the necessary mandate for the services it promises. She notes that early childhood educators are often uncertain as to the central acts which should characterize their professional lives. Dreeben (1970) decries the fact that teachers must rely on personal characteristics such as charisma for their authority. He advocates the development of a more highly defined technology of teaching as the key to increased professional standing.

Ade (1982) suggests that early childhood educators have only two alternatives when faced with the issue of professionalization: either to accede to the rigorous criteria set by sociologists for the determination of professional standing, or to create less stringent standards, thus allowing ourselves to be categorized with exterminators and dry cleaners.

But is professionalization the only legitimate answer to our problems? Is it even a realistic (Katz 1977) or desirable agenda for the 1980s? This article will explore some of the meanings that professionalization may have for us, especially in relation to pedagogic authority and the knowledge base which grounds our teaching practice.

Knowledge as Authority

As educators, our authority rests in part on our knowledge of teaching, children, and the world outside of the classroom. Our choices about how and what we teach reflect this knowledge and in turn affect the ways that others view our work, because we live in a society that values only certain kinds of knowledge (Habermas 1972).

As a novice teacher, I soon became aware of the relationship between knowledge and authority. At the first school open house I was greeted by parents asking how their children were faring in their initial school experience. These questions signaled that I had been cast in the role of the knowledgable one, the authority. But on what were these authoritative judgments to be based? We did not use the traditional markers of children's progress, and certainly personal opinions were an inappropriate basis for a professional dialogue with parents.

Authority, as a central aspect of teachers' professional practices (Arendt 1961; Peters

Source: Jonathan G. Silin (1985, March). Authority as knowledge: A problem of professionalization. *Young Children, 40,* 41–46. Reprinted by permission of the author.

33

1966; Vandenberg 1971), is integrally related to the knowledge we choose to present to our students or their parents. By the knowledge and teaching methods we use or exclude, we influence children's lives. Teachers are choice makers and the most important choices we make have to do with the nature of knowledge.

Knowledge and Curriculum

The nature of appropriate knowledge for young children, and the values implicit in the knowledge imparted, have often been poorly defined and remain a source of controversy among early childhood educators.

Programs for young low-income children (and the terminology used to describe them) in the 1960s reflected social values about low-income children. Early childhood programs still differ based on diverse conceptions of the child's developmental abilities, concerns, and needs (Kohlberg and Mayer 1972; Maccoby and Zellner 1970). Should knowledge, for example, focus on the expression and channelling of emotions, or should it focus on more social goals involving group interaction? Should it stimulate basic cognitive processes or should it train for specific academic objectives?

The question of appropriate knowledge also extends to the question of our professional expertise. Is our teaching expertise grounded in our knowledge of child development, understanding of materials, and ability to teach correct school behaviors, or in our personality?

Early childhood education has a unique history that needs to be taken into account when exploring these issues. Our tradition includes a concern for social reform, stress on the special qualities of the young child, and various attempts to change the nature of elementary education (Almy 1975).

The incorporation of kindergartens into the public schools has been influenced by educational trends stressing conformity, academic readiness, and behavioral objectives. However, much of the nursery and child care movements remained relatively free of such constraints well into the 1950s. In these small, less bureaucratically organized settings, a concern for the whole child could be practiced. It was not until the late 1950s and early 1960s, when the new interest in technical knowledge and social equity led to the popu-

larity of more cognitively oriented programs, that the traditional emphasis on socioemotional growth and the immediate interests of the child were questioned. Most recently, the use of computers with young children suggests the intensification of a technocratic approach to curriculum, one that may substantially affect the quality of children's experiences in schools (Cuffaro 1984).

Professional Expertise

The question of curriculum content in early childhood programs remains problematic not only because of different concepts of development but also because of the stress placed on technical forms of knowledge in the broader society. The kinds of knowledge possessed by young children and their ways of knowing have not been highly valued.

Traditionally, teaching was viewed as an extension of mothering. Through the Land Grant college system, child development evolved as one of several areas for the education of women, and until the last decade early childhood teachers were trained primarily within home economics departments (Spodek and Davis 1982).

Related to this female dominance of early childhood education (and the fact that women's fields were considered secondary to men's), is the problem of the knowledge base out of which we as teachers make our curriculum choices. Historically, the successful process of professionalization of any field has involved claims to a specialized body of knowledge and skills. This knowledge must be expressed in a highly technical language in order to be considered "professional knowledge." Joffe (1977) cuts to the heart of the issue.

> . . . the problem for childcare workers is that the care of normal preschoolers is very "familiar to everyone," and especially to their parent-clients. Thus for . . . early childhood education, the main struggle with clients is . . . to be acknowledged as "professional" . . . —to make the status leap from "babysitter" to "educator." (p. 22)

As a field of both study and action, early childhood education has been especially influenced by other disciplines (Williams 1978). In order to develop more relevant knowledge about both children *and* teaching, we need to support a knowledge base grounded in the work of practitioners. We need more qualitative research that relies on ethnographic standards, interpretive interviews, and participant observations.

> *Research on teaching . . . frequently views teachers in a fragmented way . . . and from a negative stance. This tends to reinforce the view of the teacher as an instrument; she is a cog in the educational machine, and one which often seems to fall below the quality-controlled standards of the whole. (Elbaz 1981, p. 45)*

We need to encourage research that not only focuses on and makes explicit the knowledge of practicing teachers, but allows participants to play a role in the creation and validation of theory itself. This would help ensure that research is meaningful to those who take part in it, and who are expected to apply it. Researchers should reorient themselves away from the collection of data and toward construction of meaningful theory that promotes positive social action (Fay 1975).

A few early childhood educators (Almy 1982; Katz 1977) have decried the distance between researcher and teacher. Others have traced the roots of this phenomenon to the desire of earlier child development researchers to establish their field as a more traditional science untainted by the practical considerations of educators in the classroom (Takanishi 1981). This may also contribute to inadequate descriptions of our teaching role. The majority of researchers in early childhood have their grounding in psychology. When Ade (1982) talks about the systematization of knowledge in early childhood, he mentions Sigmund Freud, Arnold Gesell, Erik Erikson, Jean Piaget, E. L. Thorndike, and B. F. Skinner. But, one must ask, what happened to Abigail Eliot, Patty Smith Hill, Susan Isaacs, Lucy Sprague Mitchell, and Caroline Pratt, among others? The division along gender lines of these two lists signals the complex ramifications of the professionalization issue.

Even if it were appropriate to base our authority on knowledge of child development alone, this research lacks the certainty demanded in the traditional professions (Katz 1977). The important decisions in education are not technical, but moral, and are based on differing notions of the good, the true, and the beautiful (Spodek 1977). But knowledge about teaching that is grounded in ethical and esthetic considerations is not highly prized in our society, which tends to celebrate empirical science, control, and predictability (Huebner 1975).

Exercising Protective Control

The current technical/scientific approach to education discounts value-related issues (Apple 1979; Bullough, Goldstein, and Holt 1984). Nevertheless, early childhood teachers have developed an implicit rationale for authority that is consistent with both this narrowly scientific view of education and with the traditional early childhood focus on the specialness of the young child and the promotion of nurturing care.

In interviews with a diverse group of teachers working in a variety of settings, I found that teachers understand their authority in terms of protective control (Silin 1982). They view children as open to the world, curious, and eager to learn; yet vulnerable to the threats posed by either internal emotional turmoil or external sources of influence. They see their task as one of protecting children by controlling the educational environment. The curricula designed by these teachers tend to focus on different aspects of children's development and to reflect specific knowledge interests— technical, interpretive, and critical (Habermas 1972).

Teachers view their students as choice makers. Authority for children is seen as an issue of self-development and identity formation. In contrast, teachers lack a real sense of choice about their work. They see themselves as being responsible for making decisions in reaction to children's needs. Authority is thus a question of acting for another in response to objective assessment of the children's needs. Authority, then, rests in *how* teachers teach, not in *what* they teach (their knowledge of the world).

This emphasis on developmentally appropriate curricula allows teachers to think of themselves as noncoercive, apolitical practitioners. These teachers do not seem to recognize the degree to which different approaches to development reflect alternative values. Neither do they acknowledge that there is a coercive aspect to their program, although children's attendance is mandated by their parents.

> [*The teacher's*] *intentions will inevitably be affected by the assumptions he makes regarding human nature and human possibilities. . . . If he is to achieve clarity and full consciousness, the teacher must attempt to make such assumptions explicit, for only then can they be examined, analyzed, and understood. (Greene 1973, p. 69)*

Teachers see their job as facilitative for children's learning and growth. Classroom structures, designed with the objective knowledge of child development in mind, are thought to insure freedom and choice for the child. Decisions in the classroom are made in the best interests of the child, without personal or social bias, and are not viewed as part of a larger sociopolitical process.

But many would argue that schooling does have implications outside the classroom and that teaching is indeed a very political process (Berlak and Berlak 1975; Grannis 1973; Peddiwel 1939). The psychological perspective has led us to view the child in isolation. If children are seen in context of family, peers, and community, then we realize the socioeconomic meanings that education may have for them. Attending to context involves moving beyond the *how* of teaching to the *what* and *why* of curriculum design.

How can we overcome the limited vision of our role as early childhood educators and strengthen the knowledge base of the field?

1. We can support qualitative research that looks directly to teachers to define questions for investigation, to corroborate findings, and to insure practical meaning (Porter 1982).
2. We can structure pre-service and in-service training to help teachers see themselves as choice makers. To do this, we need to give more attention to the history of our field, to alternative views of childhood (Greene 1978; Merleau-Ponty 1964), and to the values that underlie various forms of teaching practice.
3. We can begin to examine to what degree it is possible and/or advisable to remain a discrete field of action and study. We need to look more closely at the potential pitfalls and benefits of working toward greater

unity with teachers at other levels and with those who study education from diverse perspectives.

These three goals are worth pursuing because they will improve the lives of teachers and children, regardless of the professional status of the field.

Limits of Professionalization

Even if professionalization is feasible, is it desirable? This is not to deny the real need for improved salaries and working conditions, but rather to cause us to look at how these aims can be achieved most effectively. To do so, we must recall how the search for professional status has functioned in the past. Has it clarified or obscured the nature of teaching? What kinds of conflicts has it engendered within the school and between the school and community?

Three interlocking ideas are relevant to the critique of professionalization. First, professionalization might bring with it a devaluing of early childhood education's historic involvement in social reform and thus a withdrawal from community activism. Some critics of schooling are concerned that an emphasis on pedagogic reforms or technical knowledge can deflect attention from the need for socioeconomic changes in society at large (Lazerson 1971).

Second, borrowing from the history of English working-class education, we can infer that while professionalization can produce real gains in teacher autonomy, social honor, and economic rewards, it can function as a form of social control (Grace 1978). Teachers may find their enhanced status further narrows their perspective of students as people (Berlak and Berlak 1981). The real effects of economic and/or social class differences between students and teachers can be too easily overlooked.

Third, because the drive for professional status is consistent with the cultural demand for scientific neutrality, teachers may not ask themselves relevant questions about their professional practice. In contemporary usage, *professional* has multiple meanings (Grace 1978). For some, it may indicate a caring, but not emotionally involved, relationship between teacher and pupil. For others it may indicate that teachers are impartial, objective, and avoid controversy on political issues.

For many teachers, professionalism has meant the assumption of increased responsibilities and opportunities to make decisions (Apple 1983). But much of this new work engaged in by teachers is purely technical—implementing expertly designed tests rather than critically analyzing existing practice or designing new curricula. Ironically then, professionalism may actually entail a certain loss of control for teachers as the design and implementation of curriculum become two discrete functions.

Professionalism as a rallying cry can mask moral and political issues by transforming them into issues of control and management. The possibility of change and the subjective input of practicing teachers are lost sight of in the process of securing productive, efficient systems of education. Increasingly, teachers are seen as replaceable components in the curriculum machine, rather than as thinking people choosing to create meaningful lives for themselves and their students.

The process of professionalization is a complex one with both positive and negative, explicit and implicit meanings to be uncovered. It may also be inevitable.

Perhaps it would be most constructive to ask ourselves where we have been as a field and what we are currently about, rather than which strategies to use for attaining professional status. Just as we have been forced to rethink the nature of childhood in the contemporary world (Bronfenbrenner 1970; Skolnick 1976), perhaps it is time to rethink the field of early education if we are to improve the situations in which teachers work and children learn. Otherwise we may revert to a misplaced scientism that appears to be inherent in most claims to professionalization.

BIBLIOGRAPHY

Ade, W. "Professionalism and Its Implications for the Field of Early Childhood Education." *Young Children* 37, no. 3 (March 1982): 25–32.

Almy, M. *The Early Childhood Educator at Work.* New York: McGraw-Hill, 1975.

Almy, M. "An Early Childhood Education/Care Research Agenda." Paper presented at the Annual Conference of the National Association for the Education of Young Children. Washington, D.C.: November 1982.

Apple, M. *Ideology and Curriculum.* London: Routledge & Kegan Paul, 1979.

Apple, M. "Work, Gender, and Teaching." *Teachers College Record* 84, no. 3 (Spring 1983): 611–629.

Arendt, H. *Between Past and Future.* New York: Viking, 1961.

Berlak, A. and Berlak, H. *Dilemmas of Schooling.* New York: Methuen, 1981.

Berlak, H. and Berlak, A. "Toward a Political and Social-Psychological Theory of Schooling." *Interchange* 6, no. 3 (1975): 11–23.

Bronfenbrenner, U. *Two Worlds of Childhood.* New York: Russell Sage Foundation, 1970.

Bullough, R.; Goldstein, S.; and Holt, L. *Human Interests in the Curriculum.* New York: Teachers College Press, Columbia University, 1984.

Caldwell, B. "What Is Quality Child Care?" *Young Children* 39, no. 3 (March 1984): 3–13.

Cuffaro, H. "Microcomputers in Education: Why Is Earlier Better?" *Teachers College Record* 85, no. 4 (Summer 1984): 559–568.

Dreeban, R. *The Nature of Teaching.* Glenview, Ill.: Scott, Foresman, 1970.

Elbaz, F. "The Teacher's 'Practical Knowledge': Report of a Case Study." *Curriculum Inquiry* 11, no. 1 (Spring 1981): 43–73.

Fay, B. *Social Theory and Political Practice.* New York: Holmes & Meir, 1975.

Grace, G. *Teachers, Ideology and Control.* London: Routledge & Kegan Paul, 1978.

Grannis, J. "Informal Education and Its Social Context." *Teachers College Record* 74, no. 4 (May 1973): 547–552.

Greene, M. *Teacher as Stranger.* Belmont, Calif.: Wadsworth, 1973.

Greene, M. *Landscapes of Learning.* New York: Teachers College Press, Columbia University, 1978.

Habermas, J. *Knowledge and Human Interests.* Boston: Beacon, 1972.

Hostetler, L. and Klugman, E. "Early Childhood Job Titles: One Step Toward Professional Status." *Young Children* 37, no. 6 (September 1982): 13–22.

Huebner, D. "Curriculum Language and Classroom Meanings." In *Curriculum Theorizing: The Reconceptualists,* ed. W. Pinar. Berkeley, Calif.: McCutchan, 1975.

Joffe, C. *Friendly Intruders.* Berkeley, Calif.: University of California Press, 1977.

Katz, L. *Talks with Teachers.* Washington, D.C.: National Association for the Education of Young Children, 1977.

Kohlberg, L. and Mayer, R. "Development As the Aim of Education." *Harvard Educational Review* 42, no. 4 (November 1972): 449–496.

Lazerson, M. "Social Reform and Early Childhood Education: Some Historical Perspectives." In *As the Twig Is Bent,* eds. R. Anderson and H. Shane. Boston: Houghton Mifflin, 1971.

Lightfoot, S. *Worlds Apart.* New York: Basic Books, 1978.

Maccoby, E. and Zellner, M. *Experiments in Pri-*

37

mary Education: Aspects of Project Follow-Through. New York: Harcourt Brace Jovanovich, 1970.

Merleau-Ponty, M. *The Primacy of Perception.* Evanston, Ill.: Northwestern University Press, 1964.

National Association for the Education of Young Children. "NAEYC Position Statement on Nomenclature, Salaries, Benefits, and the Status of the Early Childhood Profession." *Young Children* 40, no. 1 (November 1984): 52–59.

Peddiwell, J. A. *The Saber-Tooth Curriculum.* New York: McGraw-Hill, 1939.

Peters, R. *Authority, Responsibility, and Education.* New York: Atherton Press, 1966.

Porter, C. "Qualitative Research in Child Care." *Child Care Quarterly* 11, no. 1 (Spring 1982): 44–54.

Shreve, A. "Careers and the Lure of Motherhood." *The New York Times Magazine* (November 21, 1982).

Silin, J. *Protection and Control: Early Childhood Teachers Talk About Authority.* Mimeo. Ph.D. dissertation, Teachers College, Columbia University, 1982.

Skolnick, A., ed. *Rethinking Childhood.* Boston: Little, Brown, 1976.

Spodek, B. "Curriculum Construction in Early Childhood Education." In *Early Childhood Education: Issues and Insights*, eds. B. Spodek and H. Walberg. Berkeley, Calif.: McCutchan, 1977.

Spodek, B. and Davis, M. "A Study to Prepare Early Childhood Personnel." *Journal of Teacher Education* 33, no. 2 (March–April 1982): 42–45.

Takanishi, R. "Early Childhood Education and Research: The Changing Relationship." *Theory into Practice* 20, no. 2 (Spring 1981): 86–93.

Tyler, R. *Basic Principles of Curriculum and Instruction.* Chicago: University of Chicago Press, 1949.

Vandenberg, D. *Being and Education.* Englewood Cliffs, N.J.: Prentice-Hall, 1971.

Williams, L. "Early Childhood Education in the 1970s." *Teachers College Record* 79, no. 3 (February 1978): 529–538.

Jonathan G. Silin, Ed.D., is Director of Education, Long Island Association for AIDS Care.

The author would like to express appreciation to Harriet K. Cuffaro for her comments on on earlier draft of this article.

ASK YOURSELF:
Identifying Issues for Debate and Advocacy

1. What is a profession?

2. In order for early childhood education to become a true profession, its practices must be grounded in a professional knowledge base. However, when discussing staff selection, some day care directors state that candidates with experience but little professional education are preferable to those with certification but little experience. What are some reasons that directors in early education often make this statement? What might cause directors to consider both education and experience as critical in staff selection?

3. What are the role obligations of a professional in early childhood education?

4. In what instances would an early childhood teacher's basic values conflict with his or her professional obligations? Are there priorities among professional core values?

5. Silin asserts that in the case of early education, professional development could mean loss of individual autonomy and control. What evidence is there that this claim does or does not hold true for professions such as medicine, dentistry, and law? Is there evidence that this claim holds true for labor unions?

6. What is the difference between professionalization and professionalism? (Consider individual attitudes or demeanor, the process by which a field or person becomes professional, unionism, unity among practitioners, how someone handles a difficult situation or dilemma, and cooperation with other professional groups.)

7. Jingle Jangle Day Care is a nonprofit corporation located in a small rural community. It serves 110 children with a budget of $120,000. Insurance for the program runs $6,500 and monthly rent runs $1,700. All employees start as substitutes and work their way up to part-time and full-time employees. After the first year of employment, an employee's salary is increased to $3.50/hour. After two years, it is increased to $3.62/hour. Two caregivers are certified (four-year degree) teachers. Relate this example to your readings and analyze the issues involved.

8. What effects does the work environment (climate) have on job satisfaction?

9. What factors contribute to overall job satisfaction? Why?

10. What is the most important challenge facing the profession today?

APPLICATION / ADVOCACY EXERCISES

1. Invite a local child advocate to speak about becoming an advocate and to share personal advocacy experiences. If possible, follow this presentation with further volunteer contact in relation to particular child advocacy issues.

2. Interview a local day care director about affordability, wages, and working conditions. Inquire about tuition fees, salaries, staff benefits, staff turnover, and adult–child ratios at the center. Compare your findings with those in the "Child Care Fact Sheet" and with those of peers. Discuss possible reasons for similarities and differences (e.g., profit/nonprofit status or additional funding sources).

3. In order to become familiar with the current advocacy efforts of various professional organizations and public interest groups, develop a networking file for two to four issues. This can be a team project. First, search for infor-

39

mation on the goals and current activities of these groups through publications and newsletters. Then contact these local, state, and national groups and ask them to send you information. (Be specific about what information you are seeking.) Organize the information received by issue and advocacy strategy. Identify ways collected resources could be used. The following list of addresses for national groups and governmental agencies may help you in getting started:

Group/Agency and Address	Area(s) of Focus
Action for Children's Television (ACT) 46 Austin St. Newtonville, MA 02160	Children's television: quality, diversity, violence, commercialism
Administration for Children, Youth and Families U.S. Dept. of Health and Human Services 330 Independence Ave., SW Washington, DC 20201	Programs: child nutrition; child abuse/neglect; child care/Head Start; bilingual/multicultural, high-risk/handicapped children; program regulations and evaluation
American Montessori Society 150 Fifth Avenue New York, NY 10111	Discipline, child care choices, developmentally appropriate curriculum, multicultural education
Association for Childhood Education International (ACEI) 3615 Wisconsin Ave., NW Washington, DC 20016 1(800) 423-3563	Professional status, child abuse/neglect, discipline, developmentally appropriate curriculum, high-risk/handicapped children, multicultural/bilingual education, parent involvement
Child Care Employee Project P.O. Box 5603 Berkeley, CA 94705	Wages, status, and working conditions of child care professionals
Child Welfare League of America 440 1st St., NW Washington, DC 20001	Child abuse/neglect, child care choices, regulations, program evaluation
Children's Defense Fund 122 C St., NW Washington, DC 20001	Federal programs: child health/nutrition, child abuse/neglect, child care choices, high-risk/handicapped children, minority children, bilingual education, parents
Center for the Study of Parent Involvement 303 Van Buren Ave. Oakland, CA 94610	Parent involvement
Children's Rights Group 693 Mission St. San Francisco, CA 94105	Child health, nutrition programs, child care choices
Committee for Children P.O. Box 11458 Washington, DC 20008	State/federal child care policies and regulations
National Association for Child Care Management	Child health and safety, child care choices, regulations

1255 23rd St., NW
Washington, DC 20037

National Black Child Development Institute 1463 Rhode Island Ave., NW Washington, DC 20005	Multicultural education, child care policies, regulations
Parents Anonymous 6733 S. Sepulveda, Suite 270 Los Angeles, CA 90045 1(800) 421-0353 (outside California) 1(800) 352-0386 (California)	Child abuse
Southern Association on Children Under Six P.O. Box 5403, Brody Station Little Rock, AR 72215	Developmentally appropriate practices, multicultural education, child care policy
The Children's Foundation 815 Fifteenth St., NW Suite 928 Washington, DC 20005	Rights, regulations, nutrition programs, child care choices, parent involvement, parent rights
Day Care and Human Service Local of District 65, UAW, AFL-CIO 636 Beacon St. Boston, MA 02215	Wages, status, and working conditions of child care workers
ERIC Clearinghouse on Elementary and Early Childhood Education University of Illinois 805 W. Pennsylvania Ave. Urbana, IL 61801	Research on all issues
High/Scope Research Foundation 600 North River Street Ypsilanti, MI 48198	Child care choices, developmentally appropriate curriculum, multicultural/ bilingual education, parent involvement, program evaluation
National Association for the Education of Young Children 1834 Connecticut Ave., NW Washington, DC 20009 1(800) 424-2460	All issues, governmental policies
National Center on Child Abuse and Neglect Department of Health and Human Services P.O. Box 1182 Washington, DC 20013	Child abuse/neglect
National Committee for Prevention of Child Abuse 332 S. Michigan Ave., Suite 950 Chicago, IL 60604	Child abuse/neglect
National Child Safety Council 4065 Page Ave. P.O. Box 280 Jackson, MI 49203	Child health/safety: toys, car seats, consumer awareness

National Council for Children's Rights, Inc. An Organization Helping Children of Divorce 2001 O Street, NW Washington, DC 20036	Child abuse/neglect, child care choices, parent involvement, parent rights
Organisation mondiale pour l'education prescolaire (OMEP) 1718 Connecticut Ave., NW Suite 500 Washington, DC 20009	Child care choices, cross-cultural child care policies
Parent Cooperative Preschools International P.O. Box 40123 Indianapolis, IN 46240	Child care choices, parent involvement
Woman's Action Alliance, Inc. Non-Sexist Child Development Project 370 Lexington Ave. New York, NY 10017	Nonsexist curriculum
U.S. Department of Education 400 Maryland Ave., SW Washington, DC 20202	Public school policies and programs

Also see: Koek, K. E., & Martin, S. B. (Eds.). (most recent volume). *Encyclopedia of Associations*. Detroit: Gale Research Company.

4. Develop an advocacy journal to become familiar with the political process of legislative and social change. Secure from the Board of Elections, the League of Women Voters, the Children's Defense Fund Annual Report, or other advocacy groups a list of local, state, and national legislators. Identify the representatives from your district. Find out from child advocacy groups or the representative's office what legislation these representatives are carrying that affects children. Start an advocacy journal organized around issues of professional concern or issues in the media. Include pertinent contacts (people and organizations), addresses and telephone numbers of government representatives, a glossary of key terms in the legislative process, as well as newspaper clippings and magazine or journal articles, letters, and so on that pertain to each issue. As an optional outcome of your research, draft a letter on an issue to an appropriate government representative or agency. Because such letters run the risk of being ignored or only casually read, the letter you compose should adhere to the following suggestions (Allen, 1983; Deloria & Brookins, 1982):

   a. Use clear language devoid of educational or developmental terminology unfamiliar to the reader.
   b. Keep the central issue clear throughout your letter.
   c. Organize paragraphs for the body of your letter around the questions you will address.

d. Whenever possible, clearly link the questions addressed to the real decisions the reader will be making or has made.

e. Use real-life examples to illustrate your point whenever possible.

f. Limit use of statistics to simple descriptive statistics (actual numbers or percentages).

g. Some attention should be given to the costs or cost tradeoffs of the proposed policy or action.

h. Open and close the letter with statements that will establish rapport.

REFERENCES & SUGGESTED READINGS

Ade, W. (1982, March). Professionalization and its implications for the field of early childhood education. *Young Children, 37,* 25–32.

Allen, K. E. (1983, January). Public policy report: Children, the Congress, and you. *Young Children, 38,* 71–75.

Deloria, D., & Brookins, G. K. (1982). The evaluation report: A weak link to policy. In J. R. Travers & R. J. Light (Eds.), *Learning from experience: Evaluating early childhood demonstration programs* (pp. 254–271). Washington, DC: National Academy Press.

Feeney, S. (1987, May). Ethical case studies for NAEYC reader response. *Young Children, 42,* 24–25.

Halpern, R. (1987, September). Major social and demographic trends affecting young families: Implications for early childhood care and education. *Young Children, 42,* 34–40.

Hendrick, J. (1987). What lies ahead? In *Why teach? A first look at working with young children* (pp. 25–32). Washington, DC: National Association for the Education of Young Children.

Houle, C. O. (1981). *Continuing learning in the professions.* San Francisco: Jossey-Bass.

Jorde, P. (1986). Early education: Issues and trends. *The Educational Forum, 50,* 172–181.

Kipnis, K. (1987, May). How to discuss professional ethics. *Young Children, 42,* 26–30.

Pettigrove, W., Whitebook, M., & Weir, M. (1984, May). Beyond babysitting: Changing the treatment and image of caregivers. *Young Children, 39,* 14–21.

Raines, S. C. (1983). Developing professionalism: Shared responsibility. *Childhood Education, 59,* 151–153.

CHAPTER 3

Sex Role Development and Sex Education

Having a Gay Time?

Mrs. Dodson was observing her son from the observation booth at Deb-N-Heir Preschool. As she was watching free play, she noticed her son, Seth, happily occupied with a group of girls in the housekeeping corner. All were busy decking themselves out in ruffly dresses and high heels. Once dressed, they pretended to apply makeup and nail polish. Then the children grabbed purses and pretended to go shopping with their babies. Doubts about this activity began to creep into Mrs. Dodson's mind: "Does Seth's enjoyment of this activity mean that he has homosexual tendencies? What will my husband say when I tell him what happened today? Should I ask the teacher to encourage Seth to spend more time with other boys playing boys' games?"

Questions

1. Should Seth's mother be concerned about her son's behavior? Why or why not?

2. From Seth's perspective, why do you think his behavior makes sense to him?

3. How would you, as a teacher, respond to this mother's concerns? (Option: Role-play a conference incorporating the mother's concerns and the teacher's attempt to convince the mother that the behavior is acceptable.)

4. Suppose a parent values maintenance of traditional male-female roles and insists that you redirect this type of play. What would you say and do?

5. What would you do if one of the other boys in the class called out to Seth, "Mr. Skirt, Mr. Skirt, better watch out or you'll get hurt!"?

PREVIEW

How do children learn to figure out appropriate behaviors for boys and girls in our society? How do they come to understand the birth of babies and their own beginnings? A quick flipping of the television dial is enough to reveal that messages related to sex and sex-role behaviors bombard most young children on a daily basis. What messages do parents and teachers convey about gender identity, gender role, and reproduction? What is the role of the teacher in relation to forming concepts of gender identity, gender role, and reproduction? Should young children be protected from exposure to some messages or experiences? At what point do parents' values and their rights to privacy become an issue? In this chapter, Carol Vukelich, Charlotte McCarty, and Claire Nanis provide evidence to indicate a need for more careful screening of young children's books for their sex prejudice. Eleanor Maccoby and Carol Nagy Jacklin, however, question the wisdom of trying to encourage greater choice of cross-sex playmates during free play. Similarly, Eleanor Roodenburg, a nursery school director, finds that sex-typed preferences and role perceptions as well as gender identity often influence the interview responses of three- and four-year-old children. Another disputed issue in our society is sex education. Sally Koblinsky, Jean Atkinson, and Shari Davis offer a comprehensive set of value statements and strategies for sex education with young children. Finally, a California hospital reports on a controversial class that prepares children to attend a sibling birth. Accompanying the report are two contrasting reactions to this new practice.

Sex Bias in Children's Books

Carol Vukelich, Charlotte McCarty, and Claire Nanis

Sex prejudice in books written for children is widely recognized. The collected evidence overwhelmingly indicates young women have few but sex-role stereotyped females to identify with in books. Research on sex bias in school textbooks, particularly reading textbooks, reports boy-centered stories outnumber girl-centered stories (McDonald, 1973; Chase, 1972; Beach, 1971; Frasher and Walker, 1972; Weitzman and Rizzo, 1974). Girls typically are depicted as passive, watching, weak, needing help, timid, dependent, incompetent and docile, while boys regularly are shown as active, brave, protective of women, powerful, possessing initiative, competitive, independent, intelligent, creative and industrious (Women on Words and Images, WOW, 1971; Frasher and Walker, 1972; Beach, 1971; Weitzman and Rizzo, 1974). Similarly, adult-role models reinforce the traditional patterns of female/male success; males are shown in the highly paid and prestigious occupations of politician, clergy, judge and athlete, while females are shown in the service occupations of secretary, stewardess, teacher, waitress and mostly homemaker (O'Donnell, 1973; Frasher and Walker, 1972). These findings have resulted in the effort by such companies as McGraw Hill to "eliminate sexist assumptions from (our) publications and to encourage greater freedom for all individuals to pursue their interests and realize their potential (McGraw Hill, 1975, p. 725)." Others (Feminists on Children's Literature, 1971; Weitzman et al., 1972) report similar findings in children's books, even in those books written for young children. These findings lead Mitchell (1973) to suggest that:

Nevertheless, parents and teachers of young children need to sharpen their awareness of the varied mechanisms of subtle tyranny restricting the healthy development of boys and girls. . . . The deliberate or careless selection of picture books may have an immeasurable and perhaps irreparable impact on the psychological growth of girls and boys (p. 230).

More recently, this same message has been echoed by Tibbetts (1975).

It therefore seems reasonable to investigate what sex biases, if any, are being presented to groups of young children through picture books.

Purpose and Procedures

The purpose of this study was to compare the activities, roles and relative importance assigned to males and females in selected picture books.

The picture books to be evaluated were selected from those identified as "favorite picture books that you use with your groups of children" by twenty-one teachers of young children. Only those books labeled a "favorite" by more than one teacher were included in the study. This procedure resulted in a total of thirty-two books for potential inclusion. Since the purpose of the study was to examine the depiction of sex roles, consideration was limited to those picture books dealing with human beings, or with animals who visually displayed human qualities; accordingly, eight picture books of the potential list were elimi-

Source: C. Vukelich, C. McCarty, & C. Nanis (1976). Sex bias in children's books. *Childhood Education, 52*(4), 220–222. Reprinted by permission of Carol J. Vukelich and the Association for Childhood Education International, 11141 Georgia Avenue, Suite 200, Wheaton, MD. Copyright © 1976 by the Association.

nated. Two additional books could not be located in the card catalogs of four searched libraries. Therefore, the writers and an independent examiner analyzed a total of twenty-two stories.

A method of illustration-analysis similar to that employed by the National Organization of Women (and reported by Jacobs and Eaton, 1972) to investigate sexism in children's readers was selected for the study.

Based on the findings of previous research, the following hypotheses were formulated:

1. The number of picture books with male main characters will outnumber the number of picture books with female main characters.
2. The number of illustrations of males will outnumber the number of illustrations of females.
3. Male children will be shown more often than female children in active play, using initiative, displaying independence, solving problems, receiving recognition, being inventive and giving help, while female children will be shown more often than male children as tearful or helpless, receiving help and in quiet play.
4. Female adults will be shown more often than male adults giving tenderness, scolding and being homemaker/shopper, while male adults will be shown more often than female adults taking children on outings, teaching, playing with children and being breadwinner/provider.
5. Male adults will be shown occupying the highly paid and prestigious occupational positions, while female adults will be shown occupying the service positions. In addition, males will hold more varied positions.

Analysis and Discussion of Data

Main characters. Table 1 clearly indicates the majority of favorite picture books analyzed had male main characters.

Males were main characters in three times as many picture books. This finding is consistent with all other research in the sexism in materials written for children area. The difference becomes even more accentuated when the list of favorite books with female main characters is examined. Two of the books, *Snow White* and *Cinderella,* are children's

TABLE 1 *Distribution of Main Characters*

	Frequency	Percentage
Male	15	68.2%
Female	5	22.7
None or Shared	2	9.1
Total Stories	22	100.0%

classics. Therefore, only three recently written books for young children with female main characters (of those in our study) have achieved acclaim as favorites of teachers of young children. In addition, one of these three books, *Madeline,* has been criticized because "the life of *Madeline* doesn't resemble our own (Bernstein, 1974)."

Number of illustrations of males and females. Contrary to the hypothesized finding, the number of illustrations of female children outnumbered the number of illustrations of male children, 484/331. However, a brief scrutiny of the data quickly suggests the reason for this unsuspected finding. A number of illustrations of "twelve little girls in two straight lines" in *Madeline* resulted in a total of 326 illustrations of females. Without the *Madeline* tally, the ratio of female children illustrations to male children illustrations was 158/331, or approximately $1/2$. Using the adjusted tally, each picture book contained an average of 7.2 female children illustrations and an average of 15 male children illustrations. Again, this finding is consistent with the finding of other researchers.

The ratio of adult female illustrations to adult male illustrations was 121/150. For each sex, one book accounted for $1/4$ to $1/3$ of the total number of illustrations. *Madeline* had 36 illustrations of female adults, while *Snow White* had 49 male adult illustrations.

Number of times children are shown. Table 2 presents the ratio of percentages of female to male children illustrations in the various categories.

As predicted, examination of these ratio percentages reveals the differential treatment of the sexes in the selected children's books. In particular, male children were more often shown as being active, as using initiative, as displaying independence, as receiving recogni-

TABLE 2 *Illustrations of Children*

Percentage ratio of times children were shown:

	Female	Male
in active play	15%	85%
using initiative	0	100
displaying independence	33	67
solving problems	50	50
receiving recognition	15	85
being inventive	10	90
tearful or helpless	50	50
giving help	40	60
receiving help	30	70
in quiet play	48	52

TABLE 3 *Illustrations of Adults*

Percentage ratio of times adults were shown:

	Female	Male
playing with children	100%	0%
taking children on outings	67	33
teaching	33	67
giving tenderness	75	25
scolding	100	0
being breadwinner/provider	12	88
being homemaker/shopper	100	0

tion, as being inventive, as giving help and as receiving help. With the exception of the last category, receiving help, the direction of the percentage ratios is similar to that reported in other studies (WOW, 1971, NOW, 1972; Beach, 1971) and that hypothesized. Contrary to other reported findings (WOW, 1971; NOW, 1972; Beach, 1971) and the hypothesis, male children were found to engage in quiet play, to be tearful or helpless and to solve problems equally as often as female children.

Another treatment of sex-role differences can been seen in the percentage ratios of number of times female and male children were shown in quiet and active play. This ratio of quiet to active play for female children was 46/54, while for male children the ratio was 14/86. For male children this ratio is consistent with the findings reported by such researchers as Frasher and Walker (1972), while female children were illustrated in more active play than has been previously reported (Frasher and Walker, 1972).

Number of times adults are shown. Table 3 presents the ratio of percentages of female to male adult illustrations in the various categories.

The hypothesized direction of the percentage ratios was found to be not always consistent with the observed direction. As predicted, and consistent with Frasher and Walker (1972), female adults were shown to give tenderness and to scold more often than male adults. They were also the only adults depicted in the role of homemaker/shopper. However, contrary to the predicted direction and Frasher and Walker's 1972 findings, they

also were shown to play with children more often and to take children on outings more often. As predicted, male adults were more often shown teaching and in the role of breadwinner/provider.

Adult occupations. Differential treatment of the sexes is much more evident in the assignment of occupations. As predicted, female adults were shown in the service occupations. Besides homemaker, the only occupations depicted were saleswoman and nun. Also as predicted, male adults held more varied and, in some instances, more prestigious positions. They were shown as a storekeeper, gentleman, policeman, soldier, doctor, judge, watchman, tailor and so on. In total, they held eighteen different occupation positions. The only occupational position held by both male and female adults was that of the circus worker.

Conclusions

Professional literature reflects a concern, dating back to 1971, about sex-stereotyping in books written for children. Yet, to date, teachers appear *not* to be evaluating picture books selected for use with their young children for sex bias. The most disconcerting findings are the total subservient image portrayed of female children and the suggestion to young females that males have a wide variety of prestigious occupational roles to choose among, while their choices are limited to the service occupational roles with homemaking being their number one available choice. With society's current concern for equal occupational opportunity for both sexes, this careless selection of picture books might also be restricting young males' consideration of service occupations, including the role of homemaker.

49

The evidence collected strongly indicates a need for more careful screening for this subtle sex-stereotyping tyranny in the picture books selected for use with young children.[1]

BIBLIOGRAPHY

Beach, Diana Lee. "Fun with Dick and Jane." *Spectrum* 47 (1971): 8–9.

Bemelmans, Ludwig. *Madeline.* New York: Viking, 1962.

Bernstein, Joanne. "Changing Roles of Females in Books for Young Children." *Reading Teacher* 27 (Mar. 1974): 545–49.

Chase, Dennis J. "Sexism in Textbooks?" *Nation's Schools* 90 (1972): 31–35.

Feminists on Children's Literature. "A Feminist Look at Children's Books." *School Library Journal* (1971): 19–24.

Frasher, Ramona, & Annabelle Walker. "Sex Roles in Early Reading Textbooks." *Reading Teacher* 25 (1972): 741–49.

Grimm, Jacob. *Snow White and the Seven Dwarfs.* New York: Coward McCann, 1938.

Jacobs, Carol, & Cynthia Eaton. "Sexism in the Elementary School." *Today's Education* 61 (1972): 20–22.

McDonald, Gilda. "Look, Jane, Look." *School and Community* 60 (Nov. 1973): 18.

McGraw Hill Book Company. "Guidelines for Equal Treatment of the Sexes." *Elementary English* 52 (May 1975): 725–33.

Mitchell, Edna. "Learning of Sex Roles Through Toys and Books." *Young Children* 28 (1973): 226–31. Reprinted by permission.

National Organization for Women. *Report on Sex Bias in the Public Schools.* New York: NOW, 28 E. 56th St., 1972.

O'Donnell, Richard W. "Sex Bias in Primary Social Studies Textbooks." *Educational Leadership* 31 (1973): 137–41.

Perrault, Charles. *Cinderella.* New York: Scribner's, 1954.

Tibbetts, Sylvia-Lee. "Children's Literature, A Feminist's Viewpoint." *California Journal of Educational Research* 26 (Jan. 1975): 1–5.

Weitzman, Lenore; Deborah Eifler; Elizabeth Hokada & Catherine Ross. "Sex-Role Socialization in Picture Books for Preschool Children." *American Journal of Sociology* 77 (May 1972): 1125–50.

Weitzman, Lenore, & Diane Rizzo. *Biased Textbooks: The Images of Males and Females in Elementary School Textbooks in Five Subject Areas.* Washington, DC: The Resource Center on Sex Roles in Education, 1974.

Women on Words and Images. *Dick and Jane as Victims. Sex Stereotyping in Children's Readers.* Princeton, NJ: WOW, 1971.

ENDNOTE

1. For assistance in book selection, write to Feminists on Children's Media, P.O. Box 4315, Grand Central Station, New York, NY 10017; request a copy of *Little Miss Muffet Fights Back.*

Carol Vukelich, Assistant Professor of Early Childhood Education, Department of Curriculum and Instruction, College of Education, University of Delaware, Newark

Charlotte McCarty, Teacher of Early Childhood Education, College of Education, Brisbane, Australia

Claire Nanis, Assistant Professor of Music Education, College of Arts and Sciences, University of Delaware, Newark

Gender Segregation in Nursery School: Predictors and Outcomes

Eleanor E. Maccoby and Carol Nagy Jacklin

There is now plentiful empirical confirmation for the widespread occurrence of gender segregation in childhood. Over a period of 50 years, from Parten's (Parten, 1933) report in the 30's to the present time, studies have reported that during free play periods, preschoolers and grade-school children interact with children of the same sex more often than they do with opposite-sex children. There is reason to believe that the degree of segregation becomes greater in the grade school years than it was in preschool. In our longitudinal study of approximately 100 children observed both in nursery school and the first grade, we found that the degree of sex segregation had doubled in the two-year period between our observations.

Lockheed and Klein (1985) report that in grade school classrooms, the rate of same-sex interaction is considerably higher than cross-sex interaction, but that the degree of segregation is not so great in teacher-supervised situations as it is in situations where children have more choice of activities and partners, as in most playground situations. In other words, in the presence of adults, or in situations where adults have structured the activities, children do not segregate themselves as greatly as they do when the choice of activities and partners is more unconstrained. We conclude from this that direct adult pressure is not the primary factor producing segregation by the time the children have reached school age. Children apply their own pressures, teasing one another for crossing gender lines, and monitoring one another's adherence to the gender norms. An interesting illustration of this fact comes from the recent work of John Gottman (Gottman, in press) who wanted to study same-sex and cross-sex friendships at

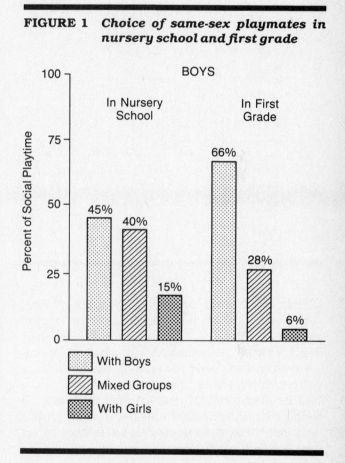

FIGURE 1 *Choice of same-sex playmates in nursery school and first grade*

two ages: preschool and the early grade-school ages. After the age of 6, he was able to locate almost no pairs of close cross-sex friends. A research assistant spent a month searching, including going door to door and asking parents, and finally located five pairs of cross-sex friends who were over six years of age. He learned, however, that all of these friendships were of long standing—the children had

Source: Reprinted by permission of Eleanor E. Maccoby. A longer version of this paper was presented at the Biennial Meeting of the Society for Research in Child Development, Toronto, April 1985.

51

FIGURE 2 *Choice of same-sex playmates in nursery school and first grade*

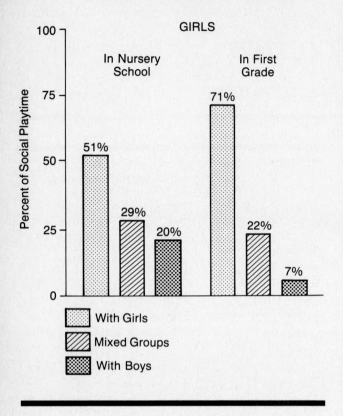

known each other since the age of three. Furthermore, the friendships had gone underground. That is, the children did not acknowledge their friendship when they encountered each other at school, but played together in secret in the privacy of their own homes after school. As we know from Damon's reports (Damon, 1977) children's segregation between the ages of 6 and 8 is backed up by an ideology which makes conformity to gender rules a kind of moral imperative.

How early does the tendency toward preference for same-sex playmates begin? In our 1978 study, we found a strong tendency for 33-month olders to play more actively with a same-sex partner than with an opposite-sex partner, when they were paired with an unfamiliar child of the same age as themselves. A recent report by La Freniere and colleagues (1984) involved observations of 200 children ranging in age from 1 to 6 years, enrolled in a day care center. They recorded affiliative behaviors of individual children, and noted the gender of the target toward whom these behaviors were directed. At the age of 18

months, there was no tendency for the children to discriminate by gender in choosing targets for their smiles, approaches, affectionate touches or social vocalizing. By 28 months, the girls were directing $^2/_3$ of their behaviors to other girls, while the boys were still showing no preference. The boys did increase steadily in their same-sex preference from that age on, however, so that by the age of $5^1/_2$, boys were directing $^3/_4$ of their overtures to other boys, and were more sex-typed than girls in this respect. There is some indication, then, that girls are the first to start the segregation, but that boys soon come to do their share of engineering the segregation.

How easy is it to change these sex-typed partner choices? Most of you are no doubt familiar with the study by Serbin and colleagues (Serbin, Tonick & Sternglanz, 1977), in which nursery school teachers mounted a behavior modification program, reinforcing children for cross-sex play over a period of two weeks. They got a nice Skinnerian acquisition curve, but found that when the reinforcement schedule was discontinued, the children returned immediately to their same-sex partner choices. Lockheed (personal communication) has worked with grade-school teachers to form mixed-sex work groups which met several times a week over a period of a year. There was some increase during the year in the rate of cross-sex interaction that occurred at other times than the work-group sessions. The attitudinal data, however, told a different story. At the beginning of the year, both boys and girls said that they would prefer to work with same-sex other children if they had a free choice of partners for a work group. By the end of the year's experience working in mixed-sex groups the boys had not changed: they still preferred other boys as partners. The girls *had* changed: they were now *less* willing to work with boys than they had been at the beginning of the year!

To summarize so far: sex segregation is a powerful phenomenon in childhood. To my knowledge, it occurs universally whenever children have a choice of playmates; parenthetically we would add that it is found in subhuman primates too. We would suggest, too, that sex differences on a variety of dimensions are more pronounced when children are functioning in groups than they are when children are acting individually. Sex-segregation is a robust phenomenon, in that it is resistant to change through adult efforts to engineer opportunities for cross-sex contact. It is our hypothesis that adults are not directly responsible for it.

However of course, they may be *indirectly* responsible for it. A popular view among many of us would be that children have acquired sex-typed play preferences and interaction styles through their socialization experiences within the family, before they move out into the peer group. If girls have been given dolls and tea sets and encouraged to help mother in the kitchen and to like pretty clothes, it would not be surprising if, when they entered nursery school, they would gravitate toward the doll corner or the play kitchen, or to the box of dress-up clothes; there they would encounter other girls with similar interests and their playmate choices would be shaped accordingly. In a similar vein, if boys have learned to like rough play because their fathers have tossed them in the air and played mock football with them from an early age, one would expect that they would seek out playmates who liked the same kind of play—primarily, other boys. In other words, early socialization would have created same-sex compatibilities in play styles and activity preferences, and this would bring same-sex children together when children are making spontaneous choices of playmates. One could expand on this hypothesis in the following way: the children who are already the most sex-typed by the time they enter a group setting should be the ones who will be the first to show same-sex playmate choice; that is, it will be the lady-like girls and the rough and active boys who will start the segregation process; these children will establish the pattern of interaction within the segregated groups, so that when the more androgynous children are recruited to these groups as the children grow older, the new recruits will have to adapt to the sex-typed group cultures already established by the most sex-typed children.

Our longitudinal study provides some limited opportunities to examine some of these hypotheses. For one of our cohorts, we sent observers to the children's homes when they were 45 months of age. A majority of the children were enrolled in some form of group care for at least a few hours a week at this age, but the children were seen only at home. During the following year, however, those who were enrolled in nursery school were observed at

their schools, at which time the degree of sex-typing of their playmate choices was scored. There were only 17 girls and 24 boys for whom data are available at both 45 months and the following year in nursery school, so the predictive correlations we will report should be regarded as exploratory.

At the 45-month home session, we observed the children in one play session with their mothers, and in another session with their fathers, and noted what kinds of toy choices and play themes were initiated by the children. We interviewed each parent about the child's play styles and activity preferences. We also gave the children a standard type of sex-typing measure, involving a choice of dolls (ranging from the Incredible Hulk to a bride doll) and a choice of headgear (ranging from football helmet to bridal veil). From these data sources we derived a number of measures of sex-typing. These measures did not always cluster together in expected ways—for example, we found that the girls who liked frilly dresses, were interested in how their hair looked, and were described by their parents as flirtatious, were more likely than other girls to be rough and noisy in their play. But the fact of greatest interest is that sex-typing at age 45 months does not predict significantly (not even marginally) to the choice of same-sex playmates in nursery school. That is, neither the toy-hat preference test, nor the masculinity or femininity of the child's toy and activity choices when playing with parents, is correlated with subsequent same-sex play. There is a tendency (of borderline significance) for the children who are rowdy at age 45 months also tended to select girl playmates a year later, so there is some cross-age consistency. At the same time, it was the girls who preferred masculine fantasy roles—who liked to play at being cowboys, spacemen, monsters or policemen—who were significantly more likely to choose girls rather than boys to play with in nursery school. This is consistent with the connection between rowdyism and same-sex play in girls, and runs counter to the hypothesis that it is the more ladylike girls who initiate same-sex play.

There were other measures taken at 45 months, other than those focused on sex-typing. Some of these reflected the quality of interaction between the child and the parents. We devised a score reflecting the degree of reciprocity in play; this score was based on the fre-

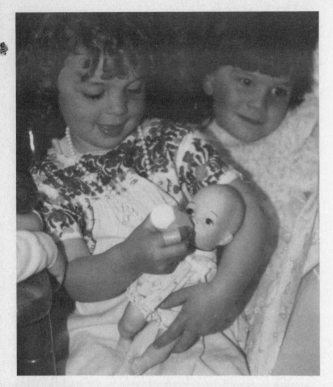

Are early play behaviors important for sex role development?

quency with which one partner—either parent or child—made an influence attempt (demand, suggest) to which the partner complied. For boys, it was the boys with the lowest reciprocity scores who were most likely to select other boys as playmates in nursery school. We have one other item of information that is consistent with this finding: at nursery school age, we observed our target children interacting in our mobile lab with two same-sex playmates. We scored the interactions for the level of mutual compliance, as well as for the amount of rough-and-tumble play. We found that boys who engaged in the roughest play showed the lowest levels of mutual compliance; and rough play, as you might expect, was associated with choosing same-sex playmates for boys. Thus, there are certain kinds of interactions that draw boys together and that appear not to depend on the skills that are involved in maintaining an interaction through mutual influence.

To summarize: the hypothesis that it is the most ladylike girls and the most boyish boys who first form the segregated play groups that emerge in nursery school receives no support from our data. On the contrary, there is some evidence that it is the more feisty girls who choose to play with other girls.

It is worth noting that for children of both sexes, it was the children who were already enrolled in group care of some sort at 45 months who were most likely to select same-sex playmates a year later. In other words sheer experience playing in group settings seems to foster segregation.

The next question we have asked is: given that a child does play in same-sex groups in nursery school, does this make any difference in the characteristics the child displays two years later, at the age of six? In our observation of first-grade groups, the girls who had previously played in all-girl groups were the most socially interactive, while the opposite was true for boys. For them, earlier experience in an all-boy playgroup did not appear to foster sociability, and indeed, may have dampened it.

To summarize: we have some modest evidence that the cultures developed by boys and girls in their segregated groups are distinctive, and serve different functions. It becomes increasingly important for us to understand why the segregation comes about in the first place, and why the two cultures develop the characteristics they do. We made an effort to develop an explanation of early segregation, based on widely accepted views about the origins of sex-typing. Our effort failed. We now want to suggest an alternative approach.

We want to suggest that the initial impetus for segregation stems from dominance relations between the sexes. We were initially alerted to this aspect of interaction in our study of 33-month old unacquainted pairs. We noted that when one child issued a vocal prohibition to the partner, in most cases the partner would desist and back away from the undesired activity. Thus when a boy was attempting to take a toy from a boy partner and the holder of the toy said "No!" or "Stop", the partner would generally desist. The same was true between girl partners. When a girl issued a vocal prohibition to a male partner, however, it did not appear to influence his behavior. Some recent work by Serbin and colleagues (Serbin, Prafkin, Elman & Doyle, 1982) illustrates the same point. They note that between the ages of 3½ and 5 there is an increase in the number of attempts children make to influence their play partners' behavior. Among girls, the increase takes the form of higher rates of polite suggestions; for boys, the increase is in direct demands. Furthermore, over this age range, boys are becoming less and less responsive to polite suggestions, and hence less responsive to the kind of influence attempts increasingly made by girls. These observations help us to understand the findings reported by Charlesworth and LaFreniere (1983). They brought mixed groups of preschool children—two boys and two girls in each group—into a playroom equipped with a movie viewer. In order to view the movie, one child had to stand in the viewing position while two other children cooperated—one by pressing a switch which lit up the screen, another by turning a crank that activated the video sequences. This was, then, an experiment in the ability of preschool-aged children to cooperate with one another. We should note that the overall level of cooperation was not very high. But for our present purposes, the interesting fact is that boys spent three times as much time in the viewing position, as did girls while the sexes were equal in the degree to which they played the helper roles. There is reason to believe, then, that when boys and girls find themselves in a position where they are competing for a scarce resource, the boys are likely to win out.

How early does this begin? We have little information about the interaction of mixed pairs of very young children. Some suggestive evidence comes from some observations by DeBoer (1984) of 10 pairs of mixed-sex twins and three sets of mixed-sex triplets. The children in this study were between the ages of 9 and 12 months, and the findings are that boy and girl infants were equally likely to start reaching for a sibling's toy, but the girls were more likely to inhibit the reach before actually grabbing the toy. Furthermore, when a boy saw that his sister was reaching for a toy he held, he would sit where he was and hang on to the toy; a girl in this situation, however, would quickly move away, trying to take the toy out of her brother's reach.

Some observations by David Goldfoot (1984) of the interactions of young rhesus monkeys may shed some light on the problem encountered by young females as a result of male dominance. He selected mixed pairs of young monkeys and put them into a fairly small cage with a single desirable tidbit of food or a single attractive toy. In pairs reared only with peers (without adults) the male would al-

most invariably get the object. In pairs reared with adults, however, the young female got a more equal share of the food and toys. This observation suggests to us a reason why preschool girls are more often found near the teachers: proximity to an adult may protect them to some degree from dominance by their male peers. The other solution available to girls is to play with other girls and avoid the boys. We suggest that we may have identified a reason why it is the girls who are the first to initiate segregation. Furthermore, it begins to make sense, if one thinks in terms of dominance, that it would be the most active, assertive girls who would least like to be dominated by boys and therefore most likely to select girl playmates. If there is any truth to these hypotheses, however, they constitute only a partial explanation of segregation. We have an explanation of girls' avoidance of playing with boys, but dominance relations do not help us to explain why boys should avoid playing with girls. Like all other aspects of behavioral development, gender segregation undoubtedly has multiple causes, and our hypothesis deals with only one of them.

In closing, let us say what we think some of the implications of these findings and ideas are. Gender segregation appears to be relatively intractable. We are not going to have much success if we try to prevent boys and girls from choosing same-sex playmates in unstructured play situations. In fact, we're not sure that we ought to try. Adults can play a very large role, however, in setting up structured situations where cross-sex interactions can occur without placing on children the burden of letting their peers see that they have chosen a cross-sex partner. Cultures differ enormously in the number of opportunities for non-sexual interaction that occur in the course of daily life, and here is where we think our choices lie. Our own preference is for maximizing the opportunities in childhood, so that when children reach the age for dating and mating, they have the background of experiences that will permit cross-sex pairs to become friends as well as lovers.

REFERENCES

Charlesworth, W., & La Freniere, P. (1983). Dominance, friendship utilization and resource utilization in preschool children's groups. *Ethology & Sociobiology, 4,* 175–186.

DeBoer, M. (1984). *Competition for toys in 9–12 month old twins and triplets.* Paper presented at the 4th International Conference on Infant Studies. New York, April.

Damon, W. (1977). *The social world of the child.* San Francisco: Jossey-Bass.

Goldfoot, D. (1984). *Behavioral sex differences in social contexts.* Paper presented at the Kinsey Symposium on Masculinity and Feminity: Concepts and definitions. Bloomington, Indiana, January.

Gottman, J. (in press). Conversations of friends: Speculations in affective development. New York: Cambridge University Press.

Jacklin, C. & Maccoby, E. E. (1978). Social behavior at thirty-three months in same-sex and mixed-sex dyads. *Child Development, 49,* 557–569.

LaFreniere, P., Strayer, F. F., & Gauthier, R. (1984). The emergence of same-sex preferences among preschool peers: A developmental ethological perspective. *Child Development, 55,* 1958–1965.

Lockheed, M. & Klein, S. (1985). Sex equity in classroom organization and climate. In S. Klein (Ed.), *Handbook for achieving sex equity through education.* Johns Hopkins University Press.

Parten, M. A. (1933). Social play among preschool children. *Journal of Abnormal and Social Psychology, 28,* 136–147.

Serbin, L. A., Tonick, I. J., & Sternglanz, S. H. (1977). *Child Development, 48,* 924–929.

Serbin, L., Sprafkin, C., Elman, M. & Doyle, A. B. (1982). The early development of sex differentiated patterns of social influence. *Canadian Journal of Behavioural Science, 14,* 350–363.

Interviews with Nursery School Children: Gender Identity and Gender Role

Eleanor Roodenburg

Interview Question: Who Am I?

Boy: I dig holes. I'm a boy. I got a sister. We play policeman. I'm the policeman, and she's the police girl.

Boy: I don't know anything about myself. I'm a boy. I'm $4^1/_2$.

Girl: I'm just a girl. I swing when I'm sitting up. I play "Dr. Set" and puzzles. I help Mommy set the table when it's supper time. Charlie chops the wood. He's got a big chopper. I don't.

Girl: I ride on a horse. I'm a girl, 'cause I wear ribbons.

Girl: My mom told me I'm a girl.

Boy: I play stuff. I play with Sean. I help Mom make cookies. I wrestle with Dad,—same thing I do with Uncle Robbie.

Girl: I laugh. I'm funny. My Grandma loves me. Even my Grandpa loves me,—and Amanda, too.

Boy: I have a brother Kyle. I have a mommy, and Daddy works at school. Me and Kyle and Daddy eat supper.

Girl: Sometimes I cook with Mommy. I help Daddy with my brother, if him being a bad boy, and he can't do it. I help him.

Interview Question: What Do Girls Like to Do?

Girl: Play with babies. Jump on bed.

Girl: Cheerleading. Help cook. Take horse-back riding lessons. Draw. Babysit.

Girl: Draw. Play with playdough. Play with a stuffed toy bear. Help Mommy do a few things,—not too many. Wash dishes.

Girl: They like to take naps.

Boy: Write.

Boy: Play with us (boys).

Boy: Record players.

Girl: Wash dishes.

Girl: Play on the swings.

Boy: Girls like to wear dresses, when they go to church.

Girl: Play by theyself,—like you are a super hero or you play house. Play in your room with your Barbies. Sometimes we go and play, and knock on the door of your friends, and see if they can play.

Girl: Like to write and play jumping jacks and maybe with a horsie. String beads.

Interview Question: What Do Boys Like to Do?

Girl: My brother likes to ride on the back of the horse with me. In the summertime, I told him he could wear my little dresses that I outgrowed; only in the summer, 'cause his legs would get colder than mine in the winter. He played in the sandbox and got them (the dresses) all messy, and I wasn't very happy.

Girl: Play with trucks in the sand. Play with smurfs.

Boy: They play with blocks and Legos.

Boy: They play with guns. They play cow-boys.

Boy: They play with their toys,—trucks and other things.

Girl: They work with their dad,—like if they had to go someplace and get steel or something.

Girl: Play in the sand.

Source: Reprinted by permission of the author.

Boy: Play guns.

Girl: Swing. Play with flashlights and blocks.

Boy: Like toys we get—like Mama buys—a policeman car and a police helicopter. I clean stuff up,—like toys.

Girl: Play with blocks. Boys like to play with babies sometimes, if they're girls.

Boy: Boys' toys, like fire trucks.

Boy: Play with puzzles and cars, and sometimes read books.

Interview Question: Who Would You Like to Play With? A Boy or a Girl?

Girl: A girl, 'cause you don't got any boy-friends.

Boy: A boy.

Girl: My brother, Charlie, and Matthew.

Girl: A girl.

Boy: A boy.

Girl: A girl.

Boy: A girl (Kathryn).

Boy: Tommy and Carrie (a boy and girl). I like to play with my brother, and he's a boy.

Girl: A boy,—my brother.

Girl: A girl, because they're nice. I like boys, too. Some boys I hate, and some I don't.

Girl: A girl.

Girl: Anybody.

Boy: A girl.

Boy: A boy.

Interview Question: What Are Your Favorite Toys?

Girl: Barbies, my blocks, my swingset.

Boy: The fire truck in my room.

Boy: My 2 cars,—my 8 & 6.

Boy: Guns.

Girl: Barbies are my best toys. I got one with long, long hair to the end of her back. She's got red hair like my mom do too.

Boy: Guns.

Boy: Pegboards (was playing with one).

Girl: I like to play with Mommy's makeup, 'cause she let me have a whole box. I like to play with my brother's trucks and cars. He gets mad at me, when I play with his hay baler and the big wagon that's behind it.

Girl: I like to color. I like to play with my doll-ies.

Boy: Guns.

Boy: Trucks.

Girl: Puzzles are my favorite. Jack-in-the-box that pops up and down.

Girl: A telephone.

Eleanor Roodenburg is Director of St. Michael's Nursery School, Geneseo, New York.

Sex Education with Young Children

Sally Koblinsky, Jean Atkinson, and Shari Davis

Michael (age 3) is watching Katherine (age 3) undress for swimming. As she begins to pull up her bathing suit, he stoops down to stare at her genital area. Student teacher Mary approaches the children with a frown on her face. Taking Michael by the hand, she states, "That's not nice. Go over and play with the boys."

The previous incident, recorded in Oregon State University's Child Development Laboratory, illustrates the anxiety and discomfort many teachers and parents experience in responding to children's sexual curiosity. Although early childhood is considered to be an important period in the formation of sexual attitudes (Gagnon 1965; Woody 1973), most adults have little background knowledge for dealing with children's sexual feelings and behaviors. A review of early childhood education texts reveals that the topic of sex education is generally omitted or limited to a discussion of plant reproduction.

Many teachers and parents want to learn more about children's emerging sexuality. Their daily experiences with children have increased their awareness of how much sexual learning occurs in the early years. Between the ages of two and six, children become aware of genital differences between the sexes; express curiosity about reproduction and birth; develop childhood romances; and engage in various types of sex play. Although many of us associate the topic of sex education with adolescence, young children ask more sex-related questions than do children in any other age group (Hattendorf 1932; Strain 1948).

Because young children are curious about human sexuality, more extensive teacher training is clearly needed in this area. Although parents remain the primary sex educators of their children, teachers may facilitate

the child's sexual learning and supply guidance for anxious mothers and fathers. We have been exploring ways in which teachers and parents may complement one another's efforts in providing responsible sex education. The Oregon State University Early Childhood Sex Education Project was initiated in the spring of 1978. We asked 150 parents of three- to five-year-old children in our Child Development Laboratory and community day care centers to complete questionnaires dealing with their attitudes toward sex education and responses to children's sexual behaviors. Meetings were held with parents to discuss early sex education and to explore parental expectations concerning the teacher's role in this process.

In response to the concerns of both parents and teachers, we have attempted to develop guidelines for sex education with young children. These guidelines are based upon our research (Koblinsky, Atkinson, and Davis 1979) and that of others, as well as the wisdom of fellow early childhood educators.

Guidelines for Teaching

Genital Differences

By the age of three, most children can distinguish between males and females (Gesell and Ilg 1949; Kreitler and Kreitler 1965). Although early distinctions are generally based on clothing and hairstyles, children soon become inquisitive about genital differences between the sexes. Such curiosity may be revealed in questions like "Why is Megan different?" or "Why don't I have a thing like Philip?" Adults who straightforwardly respond to those questions may provide a foundation for healthy and open communication about sexuality.

Use correct vocabulary. Children need correct terms for labeling their genitals, just as they need correct terms for other body parts (Calderone 1966; Gordon 1974). Such terms not only help them to learn about human anatomy, but also give them a vocabulary with which to ask questions.

Slang or nicknames such as pee pee or wiener are generally inappropriate for genitalia. Not only will children have to relearn new terms, but they may also suffer embarrassment when they use family words in the presence of their peers.

Adults frequently wonder about what terms to use in explaining genital differences. Our research indicates that adults are more likely to provide children with labels for the male genitals than the female (Koblinsky, Atkinson, and Davis 1979). This finding probably reflects the greater visibility of the male organs. Moreover, adults may have difficulty deciding which female organs (vulva, vagina, clitoris, labia, uterus) should be introduced to children. While young children may be confused by too many different labels, they need to know that both males and females possess unique and equally valuable genitalia. Therefore, one response to questions about body differences might be to say "Girls and boys are made differently. Girls have a vagina and boys have a penis."

Provide natural opportunities for children to observe each other. One natural place for children to learn about body differences is in the bathroom. Some early childhood programs have shared bathroom facilities so that girls and boys can use them together. This provides an especially good opportunity for a teacher in the bathroom area to clear up misinformation and model an accepting attitude about body differences. The following anecdote from our preschool illustrates this point:

> The teacher is helping David to use the toilet. Sara comments, "He gots a penis just like my brother." The teacher replies,

"That's right. David and your brother have penises because they are boys." Sara replies, "Yup! And I got a bagina." "That's right," responds the teacher, "you have a vagina."

Children's curiosity about genital differences may also lead them to question why boys and girls usually urinate differently. Here again, one might stress the differences in male and female anatomy. An adult could respond, "A boy stands up because he urinates through his penis. But a girl's urine comes out from an opening near her vagina. It doesn't stick out like a penis, so she sits down." Child-size toilets make it possible for boys to stand up, because some are not yet tall enough to reach adult facilities.

Regardless of how casual and open a teacher's attitude, there will always be children who have received strict modesty training at home. Teachers need to respect the needs of these children and their parents. Placing a portable screen or divider in the bathroom may help the modest child to feel more comfortable.

Use classroom resources when discussing body differences. Brenner's book, *Bodies* (1973, see Bibliography) provides an excellent introduction to the subject for preschool and elementary children. Black and white photographs depict clothed and unclothed children using their bodies to eat, sleep, defecate, bathe, and read. Another good book, *What Is A Girl? What Is A Boy?* (Waxman 1975, see Bibliography) uses both photographs and drawings to illustrate biological sex differences from infancy through adulthood. Magazine pictures and other photographs of nude children may also be posted on walls as conversation sparkers.

Another excellent stimulus for discussing body differences is anatomically correct dolls or puzzles (Constructive Playthings, Childcraft, Horsman). While such dolls may initially create a stir, children soon seem to enjoy differentiating between the girl and boy babies.

Reproduction and Birth
In addition to learning about body differences, children often display curiosity about reproduction. Children begin the questioning process at about the age of three with "Where do babies come from?" This question is typically followed by "How does it get there?" or "How

does it get out?" (Selzer 1974). Observations of pregnant women often stimulate curiosity about the origin of babies (Koblinsky, Atkinson, and Davis 1979). Children who are about to experience a birth in their own family are particularly likely to question teachers about reproduction.

Begin by finding out how much the child knows. Because young children will have encountered different information, it is important to determine how much they know. Therefore, a good rule to follow when answering questions is to ask a question. Throw the question back to the child by asking, "Well, where do *you* think babies come from?" or "How do *you* think it got there?"

Children often come up with remarkable and totally erroneous responses even though they have received accurate information. In our program, a child whose mother worked for Planned Parenthood gave the following explanation:

The baby grows and grows inside the mommy until she gets so big that the baby just about pops out! Then the mommy goes to the hospital to have the baby pop out. And if *you* go to the hospital, you'll have a baby too!

Although her mother had explained the birth process in great detail, Debbie's understanding was influenced by her level of cognitive development. Debbie, like other young children, is in Piaget's stage of preoperational thought and thus interprets information in terms of her own past experiences (Piaget 1929; Bernstein 1978). Just as balloons expand until they pop, babies will grow so big that they pop out of the mother. Debbie also uses transductive reasons to connect unrelated events. She reasons that anyone who goes to the hospital will return with a new baby.

Because children's ideas are influenced by their cognitive maturity, teachers should avoid laughing at fanciful explanations. Teachers should look for ways of correcting mistaken concepts, rather than telling children they are wrong. For example, a teacher overhearing Debbie's explanation might respond, "That's an interesting way of putting it, Debbie. You're right . . . The baby does come out of the mother. Do you know where the baby comes

out?" If the child is unable to answer, the teacher might describe the birth process or suggest that they look through a book on birth together. This approach enables the teacher to acknowledge the child's correct information as well as clear up any misinformation.

Give accurate information about reproduction. Our research indicates that adults explain the origin of babies in different ways, but the most common response is that they come from the mommy's tummy (Koblinsky, Atkinson, and Davis 1979). Some adults also explain that the baby began as a small seed. Few adults mention the uterus or union of sperm and ovum, and even fewer deal with the topic of sexual intercourse.

A major problem with these more common adult responses is that they are inaccurate. Babies do not grow in tummies, and they do not sprout from seeds! Children deserve a more accurate explanation of reproduction. Good responses are simple and contain correct terminology. These points are illustrated in the following suggested exchanges between a child and an adult:

Child: Where do babies come from?
Adult: Babies come from a place inside the mother called the uterus.

Children deserve an accurate explanation of reproduction.

61

That's where they grow until they're ready to be born.

Child: How does the baby get out?

Adult: There's an opening between the mother's legs called the vagina. When the baby's ready, the opening stretches enough to let the baby come out.

Child: How does the baby get in there?

Adult: The mother has a tiny ovum inside her uterus. The father has a tiny sperm. When the sperm and the ovum come together, the baby starts growing.

Child: How does the daddy get the sperm in the mommy?

Adult: The father and mother lie very close together and put the father's penis inside the mother's vagina. The sperm come out through the father's penis.

Child: Why can't a man have a baby?

Adult: They aren't meant to. A man's body doesn't have a uterus where babies grow. The man's part is to help make the baby and to help care for it after it's born.

As teachers discuss reproduction and birth, they should remember that these processes are not easily understood the first time around. They must be prepared to answer children's questions again and again and to present the information in a variety of contexts. With an open exchange of information, children will gradually bring their understanding of these events closer to reality.

Use books to explain reproduction and birth. Sex education books (see Bibliography) are especially helpful because they include pictures illustrating concepts that teachers cannot demonstrate. It is important to leave these books out on the shelf, right alongside children's other favorites, so that children may look at them again and again. Easy availability reinforces the notion that sexual curiosity is natural and healthy.

Avoid using plants and animals as substitutes for discussing human reproduction. Young children are greatly interested in reproduction and are intrigued by all new babies. Therefore, teachers are encouraged to plan experiences that familiarize children with the principles of reproduction in plants, fish,

rodents, and other animals (Holt 1977). However, there is some risk in attempting to use other species to convey an understanding of human reproduction and birth. Children may have considerable difficulty generalizing from plants and animals to human beings or vice versa. The following exchange illustrates the confusion that can be created by using analogies from the animal kingdom:

Adult: How would the lady get a baby to grow inside her?

Child: Um, get a duck. Cause one day I saw a book about them, and . . . they just get a duck or a goose and they get a little more growned . . . and then they turn into a baby. (Berstein and Cowan 1975, p. 87)

It is likely that this child had been read the popular book, *How Babies Are Made* (Andry and Schepp 1968). Although this book provides accurate information, it reviews reproduction in flowers, chickens, and dogs before it discusses humans. Because children are used to hearing stories in the once-upon-a-time to happily-everafter sequence, it is easy to understand why children might reason that humans were once ducks or flowers.

Individualize discussions about reproduction. It may be best to use a less formal instructional approach than might be used for concepts like colors or community helpers because young children vary widely in their knowledge of sexuality. When a teacher explains reproduction and birth, children will need an opportunity to ask questions. In one-to-one encounters or small groups, fewer of their questions are likely to go unanswered. Parents' concerns can also be responded to more easily when talking with individual children.

Masturbation

Masturbation is now widely accepted as natural and healthy for both children and adults (Arnstein 1976; Selzer 1974). Children will touch or rub their genitals because this behavior is pleasurable or soothing. Experienced teachers know that young children may absentmindedly fondle their genitals when they are tired, bored, or listening to a story. Children may also clutch their genitals when they are tense or nervous. Although some teachers may feel uncomfortable, adults will handle these situations most effectively if they adopt a relaxed approach to masturbation.

Ignore masturbation in most classroom situations. A teacher will probably notice that the child's behavior usually does not bother anyone else in the classroom.

Avoid negative responses. Adults should refrain from scolding or punishing children for engaging in masturbation. Responses like frowning or pulling the child's hands away from the genitals may communicate that these organs are bad or dirty. Criticisms or threats can lead children to develop unhealthy feelings of anxiety and guilt which can persist throughout life.

It is probably most difficult to refrain from scolding children when they are using masturbation as an attention-getting device. When a child masturbates to bring on laughter from others, you may say firmly and matter-of-factly, "Please put your penis back in your pants. That's where it belongs unless you're going to the bathroom."

Stress that there is a better time and place for masturbation. At times this behavior may interfere with other activities and may be bothersome to the entire class. A teacher might then take the child aside and explain, "I know that feels good, but other people don't like to see you play with your penis/vulva. You can do that when you're by yourself." This response acknowledges the pleasurable aspects of masturbation but also conveys the inappropriateness of its public display. However, teachers will need to be especially aware of any cultural prohibitions specific to their group of children.

Consult the child's parents if masturbation becomes compulsive. Compulsive masturbation, like compulsive scratching or nail biting, may be a symptom of deeper emotional problems. Should a teacher encounter a child who masturbates compulsively, we advise the teacher to discuss such behavior with the child's parents. The discussion may clarify factors contributing to the behavior and may inform teachers about the way masturbation is handled at home. Compulsive masturbation may be a reaction to family stress and may suggest that the child needs more time and attention from others. Parents and teachers can work together to help the child overcome anxiety and find other means of satisfaction.

Sex Play

Like masturbation, sex play is an extension of childhood curiosity about body differences and functions (Pomeroy 1976). Children engaged in sex play typically examine one another's bodies and may attempt to place objects into genital openings. Sex play often occurs within the context of children's games, such as doctor or house. Teachers may discover these games in a quiet corner of the classroom or outdoor play area.

Acknowledge children's curiosity. Teachers' responses to children engaged in sex play will vary according to assessments of each situation. It may be sufficient to acknowledge the children's behavior and redirect their interest. A teacher might respond, "Oh, you were just looking to see how boys and girls are different. That's the way we are made. Now, how about a game of hide and seek?" In some cases, sex play may appear to be motivated by unanswered questions about body differences. A teacher may then suggest that children join her in the story corner to review appropriate books on the human body.

Explain potential consequences. If children's play involves inserting objects into each other's genital openings, it is important to discuss the potentially dangerous consequences of this behavior. After acknowledging children's natural curiosity, a teacher may explain that this practice could hurt another child. Use a familiar example, like putting pencils in someone's ears, to suggest the harmful effects of placing objects in body openings.

Discuss consideration for others. If children repeatedly engage in sex play, despite efforts to distract them or satisfy their curiosity, teachers may wish to bring up the issue of consideration for others. A teacher might respond, "I know you're curious about each other's bodies, but it bothers people to see you playing like that. I'd prefer that you didn't do it here." In asking children to stop this behavior out of respect for others, avoid trying to instill a sense of guilt. Severe scolding or hysterical outbursts may have long-term negative effects on later sexual adjustment.

Obscene Words

Almost all adults have encountered children using such bathroom language as "This juice looks like pee" or "You're a poop face!" While such statements are generally accepted as

63

normal experimentation with language, teachers may experience real discomfort when children begin using the more offensive four-letter words. Adults often fear that use of obscene language will become rampant among children. Consequently, many teachers express concern about the proper method of handling obscenities in the classroom.

Ignore obscene language whenever possible. Because children are likely to experiment with any new words they hear, it is best to let a spate of obscene language run its course. Extreme teacher reaction will probably increase children's interest in using these words rather than reduce it. Some children may be scolded for using these words at home, and repeating them at school may help children get them out of their systems.

Explain the word's meaning when it is appropriate. Because children often parrot an offensive word without any idea of its meaning, teachers may question children about what a specific word really means to them. Should their responses indicate a lack of understanding, teachers may define the word and use it matter-of-factly. The following anecdote from our preschool illustrates how this strategy may diffuse the potency of a four-letter word for the child:

> *John screams that Billy is a "shithead." The teacher asks John, "Do you know what shit means?" John shakes his head. The teacher explains, "Shit is another word for bowel movement. Is that the word you wanted to use!" "No!" John exclaims, "I didn't want to say that!"*

Stress the offensive nature of obscene language if it persists. When children's repeated use of obscene language disturbs classroom activities, teachers may need to take firmer measures. Children should be told that obscene words offend many people, and that the times and places for their use are limited. The teacher might respond, "Most people don't like to hear words like that. I don't want you to use them here at school."

General Recommendations

Involve parents. It is extremely important to consider the specific backgrounds and concerns of parents because they remain the primary sex educators of their children. Early childhood educators must recognize that their own beliefs and values about sex education may not be shared by many parents. In some communities, sex education is a volatile issue. Consequently, efforts must be made to open discussions in which both parents and teachers can air views about the best ways of responding to children's sexual curiosity.

Teachers who represent their general philosophies of education at an initial get-acquainted parent meeting may allocate a portion of the program to discussing sex education. Parents should be encouraged to share their own ideas about handling sexual behaviors and should feel free to question the rationale behind any program policies. Placing an emphasis on an *exchange* of information will facilitate the development of mutual strategies for educating young children about sexuality.

Many parents seek extra help from teachers in communicating to their children about sexual issues. Therefore, we suggest planning at least one parent meeting to deal exclusively with the topic of sex education. Such meetings can be used to present information on normal psychosexual development and to address parental anxieties about specific behaviors. Meetings should be planned for a time when both mothers and fathers may conveniently attend. Teachers who feel uncomfortable directing a session on this topic may wish to solicit the services of speakers from a family planning agency or other community service organizations.

Parent involvement may play a crucial role in linking the young child's family experiences with those encountered in the school environment. Moreover, parents who establish family communication about human sexuality in the early years increase the likelihood that their children will approach them with sexual questions in the future. Finally, parents who develop an early concern for educating children about sexuality are likely to become active proponents of quality sex education programs in elementary and secondary schools.

Encourage staff members to participate. Lectures, group discussions, films, and other resources may be used to explore early childhood sexuality with all staff members. Time may be spent examining the ways in which teachers transmit sexual information and values to young children. Staff meetings provide an ideal opportunity to practice answers to children's questions about body differences and birth and to role play responses to specific sexual behaviors.

Examine personal sexual values. We believe that teachers must feel positively about their *own* sexuality before they attempt to discuss this sensitive subject with children. Therefore, discussion groups or values-clarification exercises may be used to explore sexual values and to increase comfort in responding to sexual issues. A relaxed and accepting attitude is just as important as the information provided.

Be a positive role model. Although we have focused on responding to children's overt sexual behaviors, sex education involves more than teaching facts about genital differences and birth. Indeed, sexuality is an integral part of the personality and involves the whole sense of what it is like to be a male or female. Teachers and parents are important role models for young children. Teachers who demonstrate warmth, affection, and support for others provide children with positive models for interpersonal behavior. The affective component of sexuality may also be stressed by reading children stories that describe the love, loyalty, and trust in human relationships.

Evaluate staff efforts. It is important to seek feedback from both teachers and parents about the effectiveness of sex education strategies. Efforts should be made to encourage a free exchange of feelings, attitudes, and personal experiences. Teachers may wish to evaluate their personal effectiveness as sex educators by answering such questions as "What have I learned?" "What have I relearned?" "How do I now feel about responding to various sexual behaviors?" It is wise to plan a specific time for dealing with sex education because the staff may be reluctant to bring up this subject in routine meetings.

Conclusion

Sex education is an important but often unrecognized component of early childhood programs. All children express curiosity about sexuality, and they deserve honest and thoughtful responses. The early childhood ed-

ucator with a background in sex education may play a vital role in helping children experience the joy and responsibility of their sexuality.

BIBLIOGRAPHY OF RECOMMENDED SEX EDUCATION BOOKS FOR PRESCHOOLERS

Suggested age levels are designated with overlapping age ranges as follows:

> N—nursery, up to age 5
> K—kindergarten, ages 4–6
> P—primary, ages 5–9

The Birth of Sunset's Kittens. Carla Stevens. New York: Young Scott, 1969. NKP
   Black and white photographs illustrate the birth of kittens. The text includes correct terminology for body parts and the birth process and subtly relates the birth of kittens to the child's own birth.

Bodies. Barbara Brenner. New York: Dutton, 1973. NK
   Beautiful photographs of males and females from all age groups and cultural backgrounds are used to explore the fascinating topic of bodies and what they can do. The text stresses the uniqueness of each child's body.

Did the Sun Shine Before You Were Born? Sol and Judith Gordon. Fayetteville, N.Y.: Ed-U Press, 1974. NKP
   With a focus on the family, the book explains male-female genital differences, intercourse, conception, and the birth process with multicultural illustrations and suggestions for parents and teachers.

Girls Are Girls and Boys Are Boys: So What's the Difference? Sol Gordon. Fayetteville, N.Y.: Ed-U Press, 1979. P
   The differences between boys and girls are explained in terms of body build and function, rather than play, clothing, or career preferences. Masturbation, menstruation, intercourse, birth, and breast-feeding are discussed. The illustrations are multicultural.

How Babies Are Made. Andrew C. Andry and Steven Schepp. New York: Time-Life, 1968. KP
   Simple, eye-catching illustrations enhance a long book that covers sexual differences, intercourse, and the birth process. Children may be confused by the sequential presentation of plant, animal, and human reproduction.

How Was I Born? Lennart Nilsson. New York: Delacorte, 1975. P
   A story of conception, prenatal development, and childbirth is told in a sequence of beautiful photographs by the author/photographer. The

text is clear and scientifically accurate and may be edited for younger children. The photos depict body differences in the sexes from early childhood to adulthood.

Making Babies. Sara Bonnett Stein. New York: Walker & Co., 1974. NKP

   One of the *Open Family* series, the book presents a simple description of pregnancy and birth with vivid photographs of the fetus. There is a separate text for children and adults on each page, with the adult text suggesting strategies for responding to children's sexual curiosity.

What Is a Girl? What Is a Boy? Stephanie Waxman. Culver City, Calif.: Peace Press, 1975. NKP

   Black and white photographs depict body differences between the sexes from infancy through adulthood. The book points out that, despite anatomical differences, both boys and girls can have the same names, enjoy the same activities, and feel the same emotions.

Where Did I Come From? Peter Mayle. Secaucus, N.J.: Lyle Stuart, 1973. P

   An amusing text with cartoon-like illustrations explains body differences, sexual arousal, intercourse, conception, fetal development, and the birth process. The text may be too long for some children.

Where Do Babies Come From? Margaret Sheffield. New York: Knopf, 1972. NKP

   A beautifully and sensitively illustrated book that discusses intercourse and fetal development and depicts natural childbirth and genital differences in infancy, childhood, and adulthood.

The books listed in this bibliography are available from the publisher or at your local bookstore.

Sources for anatomically correct dolls and dressing-undressing puzzles:

Constructive Playthings
P.O. Box 5445
Kansas City, MO 64131

Childcraft Education Corp.
20 Kilmer Road
Edison, NJ 08817

Horsman Dolls, Inc.
200 Fifth Avenue
New York, NY 10010

REFERENCES

Arnstein, H. "How Sex Attitudes Develop." *Day Care and Early Education* 3, no. 5 (May–June 1976): 11–14.

Bernstein, A. *The Flight of the Stork.* New York: Dell, 1978.

Bernstein, A., and Cowan, P. "Children's Concepts of How People Get Babies." *Child Development* 46 (1975): 77–91.

Calderone, M. S. "Sex Education and the Very Young Child." *The PTA Magazine* 61, no. 2 (October 1966): 16–18.

Gagnon, J. "Sexuality and Sexual Learning in the Child." *Psychiatry* 28 (1965): 212–228.

Gesell, A., and Ilg, F. L. *Child Development.* New York: Harper & Brothers, 1949.

Gordon, S. "Three Short Essays Toward a Sexual Revolution." *The Humanist* 34, no. 2 (March–April 1974): 20–22.

Hattendorf, K.W. "A Study of the Questions of Young Children." *Journal of Social Psychology* 3 (1932): 37–65.

Holt, B. G. *Science with Young Children.* Washington, D.C.: National Association for the Education of Young Children, 1977.

Koblinsky, S.; Atkinson, J.; and Davis, S. "Early Childhood Sex Education Project, 1979." Unpublished research report. Corvallis, Ore.: Oregon State University Family Life Department, 1979.

Kreitler, H., and Kreitler, S. "Children's Concepts of Sexuality and Birth." *Child Development* 37 (1965): 363–378.

Piaget, J. *The Child's Conception of the World.* New York: Harcourt, Brace, 1929.

Pomeroy, W. B. *Your Child and Sex: A Guide For Parents.* New York: Dell, 1976.

Selzer, J. G. *When Children Ask About Sex.* Boston: Beacon, 1974.

Strain, F. B. *The Normal Sex Interests of Children.* New York: Appleton-Century-Crofts, 1948.

Woody, J. D. "Contemporary Sex Education: Attitudes and Implications for Childrearing." *Journal of School Health* 43 (1973): 241–246.

Sally Koblinsky, Ph.D., is Assistant Professor, Family Studies and Consumer Sciences, San Diego State University, San Diego, California.

   Jean Atkinson, M.S., is a doctoral student in Human Development and Family Studies, The Pennsylvania State University, University Park, Pennsylvania.

   Shari Davis, M.S., is a doctoral student in the Department of Family Life, Oregon State University, Corvallis, Oregon.

Children in the Delivery Room

Seven-year-old Marisa wrinkles her face as the nurse says, "This is a real placenta. This is what surrounds a baby in your mom's uterus. It's OK to feel and touch it."

A few minutes later, Marisa is holding what another youngster calls "a purple blob."

She practices cutting the umbilical cord, something she expects to do after her mother has delivered a new baby to their family.

Meanwhile, five-year-old Neil struggles to pull a doll out of a knitted uterus. Neil is becoming so adept and repeats the process so often that someone jokes his mother won't need help from a doctor when her baby is ready for delivery.

Both Marisa and Neil are graduates of a new class that prepares youngsters to attend the birth of their new brother or sister.

Although children have been allowed into the Alternative Birth Center Room since 1977, they can now watch the delivery in any of the hospital's birthing rooms.

"This option isn't for everyone," explains Irene Terestman, RN, co-founder with Mary Beth Abarbanel, RN, of the sibling education program.

"We want to offer parents a range of involvement, so they can decide what is best for their family," says Terestman.

She explains that little research exists on what happens when children attend a birth and that the option is still controversial. Some pediatricians feel watching the birth is overwhelming and could have a negative effect on a child. Other experts feel this is the best and healthiest way to teach children about having babies and about sex.

Parents who choose the option are encouraged to attend a two-hour class with their child. The children tour labor and delivery rooms, climb up on the empty delivery beds, and see the nursery full of newborns.

Terestman tells them, "You will hear your mommy making sounds that you have never heard her make before. And you will see some blood. That is what is supposed to happen when she has a baby."

She tells them that the sounds only mean that their mother is working very hard. She also asks them all to make sounds like they might hear their mother make. She explains that the blood they will see doesn't mean that their mother is hurt.

The children also see a slide show of what happens during a birth. They play with dolls that represent newborns and look at books and charts that show the birth process. Even the most disinterested youngster is eager to don surgical gloves and handle the placenta.

Terestman stresses that once parents prepare children for a birth, they are getting into the realm of sex education. "We strongly feel that sex education belongs in the hands of the parents. That is why parents present most of the information and must attend the program with their children," she adds.

Children of any age can be present at the birth. Guidelines suggest that youngsters be at a verbal age so they will be able to tell someone that they want to leave if they are bothered by the birth. It also is required that each child have a support person, other than a parent, in the delivery room.

> Witnessing their mother giving birth threatens children's need to see mother as stable and in control of life. Adults often forget how critically important this need is for young children. Instead the child sees its mother relinquish her control to the powerful painful process of birth. Most adults who witness a woman giving birth are engulfed and overpowered by this experience. Matured psychological defense systems and intellectual understanding of the process of birth helps adults who see birth, cope with the experience. Yet days and even weeks later adults find themselves remembering

Source: Children in the delivery room (1986, January–February). *Alta Bates News, 16,* 5–7. Reprinted by permission of Alta Bates Corporation. Letters from Rose Weilerstein (1986, Spring). Early childhood research. *Cooperatively Speaking, 16,* 6–7. Reprinted by permission of Rose Weilerstein and Parent Cooperative Preschools International.

67

the experience, because of its powerful impact on them.

If the adult is someone with a close emotional tie to the mother giving birth, these reactions are even more intense.

Do we want to put young children through this experience, when, no matter how well they are prepared in advance, they are not capable emotionally and intellectually of understanding or coping with this powerful experience that is happening to their mother?

All recognized, reputable and knowledgeable child development specialists from around the world realize that during the first five or six years of life a child requires experiences through which he/she learns to trust in his environment and self and to have an increasing sense of control and influence over that environment. These stable nurturing experiences in the early years give the child the internal strength necessary for coping with the world later on.

Probably one of the most important dynamics for a child in his/her relationship with the mother is to be able to see the mother as someone who is strong and in control and thus reliable when it comes to meeting childhood needs and problems. This dynamic is the core of the bond between a child and its mother.

When a mother gives birth she gives up this control to an age-old process that is stronger than she is. Children who are present at birth can feel their mother losing control and strength. Their sense of security that comes from seeing their mother as strong and in control is violated. How can that be good for young children?

Witnessing a normal birth, can, therefore, damage the emotional core of a child—its sense of security and trust. If this happens, some children regress and thereafter become preoccupied with making demands upon the mother in an attempt to regain and reprove the security and trust in her that was damaged by witnessing the birth. Each demand is the

child's attempt to have the mother demonstrate to the child that she is strong and in control and can once again be trustworthy. Unfortunately young children do not know why they create a constant stream of demands on their mother and the mother does not understand the change in the child's behavior but only sees the increase in demands as bothersome—especially when she is busy with the care of her newborn baby.

For these reasons, which are only briefly developed here, it is unwise to have young children witness the birth process.

Peter Haiman, Ph.D.

Teacher of Child Psychology
and Child Development in the
San Francisco Bay Area

The sibling class at Alta Bates hospital was very worthwhile for the grown-ups as well as the children. The most impressive moment was when a real placenta was brought out for the children to examine. Each child was given a pair of gloves, a mask and a smock so they could actually touch and hold the placenta. The nurse explained to them that this was good blood. There were also cloth models of a baby attached to a placenta and a set of pelvic bones to demonstrate the birthing process. When the baby arrives the children were allowed to cut and clip the umbilical cord. A tasteful slide show of a mother giving birth accompanied by her family was shown. A tour of the birthing rooms and the nursery was also a big hit for children—especially playing with the buttons that move the bed up and down.

As adults, we are very glad that children now have the opportunity to see and participate in the birthing process.

Marilyn, Bill and Nicole Goward
Berkeley Hills Nursery School

Letters of Peter Haiman and Marilyn, Bill, and Nicole Goward are part of an article on the advisability of a young child being present at the delivery of his new baby brother or sister. The article dis-

cusses the new sibling education class at Alta Bates Hospital in Berkeley, California (Alta Bates News), which prepares children to watch the delivery in any of this hospital's birthing rooms. They have been allowed into the Alternative Birth Center Room since 1977. The new option isn't for everyone and parents are offered a range of involvement so that they can decide what is best for their family. (R.W.)

ASK YOURSELF:
Identifying Issues for Debate and Advocacy

1. In your experience, have you noticed any differences in how people respond to boy babies and girl babies?

2. What are behavioral and temperamental differences between boys and girls (Honig, 1983; Maccoby, 1980)? Are these differences significant? Should teachers adjust their ground rules to accommodate these sex differences (e.g., for a class of 15 boys and 5 girls)? Do teachers tend to reinforce aggressive behaviors in boys by giving boys who display aggressive behaviors a lot more attention? In contrast, do teachers tend to reinforce girls who display socially submissive behaviors?

3. Do attempts to reinforce a clear sense of gender identity in preschool children conflict with attempts to broaden their conceptions of responsibility and appropriate sex-role behavior? Note: Preschool children tend to associate gender identity with physical characteristics and they tend to view appropriate sex-role behavior as stereotypes associated with these physical characteristics (Carper, 1978; Kohlberg & Ullian, 1974; Maccoby & Jacklin reading).

4. Should books that depict females in a demeaning manner (i.e., in a manner similar to racist books) be removed from preschool library corners? In Iowa, a picture book, *The Pumpkin Patch*, was taken off the shelves because a character declared, "Boys can make jack-o'-lanterns better than girls" (Zepezauer, 1981). Do you consider this action to be censorship or careful screening of young children's picture books for sexist bias? Are young children able to critically listen to and view picture books for sexist bias?

5. In some preschool programs, boys will spend most of their free play time in the block and woodworking areas, and girls will tend to move into the housekeeping and cooking areas. During free play, should a preschool teacher attempt to draw both boys and girls into all activity areas of the classroom (e.g., housekeeping, blocks, manipulatives, art, music, sand/water play, library, cooking, and wood-

working)? Or is this forcing boys and girls to participate in an activity? Why or why not?

6. Why should parents be involved from the very start in program policies related to sex education? What is the importance of their role in sex education? Why is the early childhood period an important time to start sex education?

7. How should a preschool teacher handle questions about where babies come from (see Bernstein, 1976)? What is the value of simple responses and correct terminology? Why do adults often give inaccurate responses to young children, and what values or attitudes might this type of response represent?

8. Should preschool, kindergarten, or primary teachers discuss body differences with young children? Why or why not? Should dolls be anatomically correct? Why or why not? Should books depicting naked children be available in the classroom? (See, for example, Maurice Sendak's *In the Night Kitchen*.) Why or why not? If anatomically correct language is not included in the written program or school district health curriculum, should a teacher use these terms? Why or why not?

9. How should teachers respond to young children's use of obscene words or "bathroom language" in the preschool or kindergarten classroom?

10. You have been noticing that one boy in your preschool group tends to masturbate during nap and occasionally while listening to a story during circle time. You mention this behavior to his mother during a conference. She responds that she has noticed similar behavior at home during naps or while watching TV, and that she asked Tommy if anything was bothering him. He said, "No." When asked why he did this, he replied, "Because it feels good." His mother expresses concern to you about this response. What do you say?

11. Are healthy images of males and females portrayed in television programs aimed at young children?

APPLICATION/ADVOCACY EXERCISES

1. Refer to Table 3–1 of a brief chronology of the development of gender identity and gender role concepts. Also examine and analyze the responses of nursery school children to Roodenburg's interview questions in terms of the importance of gender identity in their self-definitions and in terms of their developing notions of gender role. To

TABLE 3-1 *Behaviors and Beliefs Associated with Gender Identity and Gender Role Development*

Age	Behaviors/Beliefs
	Gender Identity
Usually $1^1/_2$–2	Labels self correctly and labels the gender of others with partial accuracy.
4	Labels gender correctly and shows some awareness of gender stability (that gender is constant over the life cycle and that despite different physical changes (e.g., hairstyle or clothing) one's gender does not change).
6 or 7	Gender stability has a logical basis (the child provides reasons for his or her response) and is linked to genital differences.
	Gender Role
2–3	Both sexes show sex-typed toy and activity preferences.
$2^1/_2$–3	Boys are more aggressive and active than girls.
4–5	Girls are more compliant than boys.
5	Children often show strong preferences for same-sex people, objects, and activities.
6	Sex-role concepts are based on physical criteria, such as size, strength, depth of voice, skin characteristics, ornaments, and clothes.
10	Males and females are seen as occupying a particular role within a large social system. Conformity to existing sex roles (status quo) is preferred.
18	Sex-role characteristics are personally chosen from a conception of what one wants to be. The choice is based on a need for mutuality and equality of individuals in sexual relationships.

Based on Kohlberg, L., & Ullian, D. Z. (1974). Stages in the development of psychosexual concepts and attitudes. In R. C. Friedman, R. M. Richart, & R. L. Vande Wiele (Eds.), *Sex differences in behavior* (pp. 209–222). New York: John Wiley.

what extent do these children's responses conform or not conform to gender role behaviors described in Table 3–1? How do you account for similarities and differences?

2. After reading the Vukelich, McCarty, and Nanis article, examine five or six picture books in the children's collection of a local library. Include in your selection three books published since 1976. Using the criteria below, which incorporate the hypotheses of Vukelich, McCarty, and Nanis, look for evidence of sex bias in the books you screen. Compare and contrast your findings with those of Vukelich, McCarty, and Nanis. Also consider if differences exist among books with recent and older publication dates and if conditions have improved since the 1976 Vukelich, McCarty, and Nanis study.

*Criteria to Consider When Selecting
    Children's Books: Sexism*
These criteria may help you to decide if a children's book is sexist. But remember that a book's *overall* message

71

(the combination of plot, illustrations, words, and characterization) is most important, not simply the inclusion of characters representing sexist stereotypes. In other words, don't throw away *Goldilocks and the Three Bears*. Finally, use your own discretion in book selection by considering what is best for your group of children.

a. *Look for balance in characterization and illustrations.* Does the group of books you are examining include an equal number of male and female main characters? If not, could the balance of main characters be changed without altering the messages of the stories? Is the number of illustrations of males and females similar? If not, could the balance of illustrations be changed without altering the messages of the stories?

b. *Look for assumptions about social behavior.* Are girls depicted more often than boys as spotless, slim, pretty, demure, inactive, submissive, tearful, helpless or receiving help, and engaging in quiet play? Are boys shown more often than girls in physically active play, being competitive, showing independence, taking initiative, being inventive, solving problems, being brave, being strong, receiving recognition, and helping or protecting the opposite sex? Do women more often than men in the books show tenderness toward children and scold children? Do men more often than women in the books play with children, teach children, and take children on outings? Does the book downgrade or make fun of characters who display social behaviors traditionally associated with the opposite sex? Does acceptance depend on traditional boy/girl behavior? Are achievements of girls based on their good looks or on their own initiative and intelligence?

c. *Look for assumptions about occupations.* Are adult males shown more often than adult females as breadwinners or providers? Are adult males shown more often than adult females in prestigious, highly paid jobs? Are adult males shown in more varied job positions than adult females? Are adult females shown more often than adult males as homemakers and shoppers? Are adult females shown more often than adult males in service positions?

d. *Look carefully at the language.* Watch for "loaded" words and phrases (such as *sissy, tomboy, ladylike, manly, honey, boys will be boys,* etc.). Derogative adjectives and offhand remarks have subtle effects on a child's self-image and self-esteem.

e. *Look for antisexist messages.* Does the book let both boys and girls know they have many options open to them? Does the book encourage the listener to act against or to value action against injustices resulting from sexism?

Some Pre-1977 Books to Consider for Review

Beim, J. (1955). *Country school.* New York: William Morrow.

Darrow, W. (1970). *I'm glad I'm a boy! I'm glad I'm a girl!* New York: Simon & Schuster.

Eichler, M. (1971). *Martin's father.* Chapel Hill, NC: Lollipop Power Inc.

Hoban, L. (1976). *Arthur's pen pal.* New York: Harper & Row.

Kunhardt, D. (1961). *Billy the barber.* New York: Harper & Row.

Leaf, M. (1938). *The story of Ferdinand.* New York: Viking Press.

Seignobosc, F. (1957). *What do you want to be?* New York: Charles Scribner's Sons.

Van Woerkom, D. (1975). *The queen who couldn't bake gingerbread.* New York: Knopf.

Williams, B. (1975). *Kevin's grandma.* New York: E. P. Dutton.

Zolotow, C. (1972). *William's doll.* New York: Harper & Row.

3. View the film "The Sooner the Better" (Third Eye Films, 12 Arrow Street, Cambridge, MA 02138). Identify evidence of anti- or nonsexist classroom practices and discuss the value of these practices.

4. A recent, controversial practice is allowing young children to be present in the delivery room when their mother is giving birth to a new sibling. Review the description from Alta Bates Hospital of a sibling class preparing children for this experience and the two reaction letters. Next, contact three or four other people (e.g., parents, child development specialists, medical personnel, or child care personnel) and explain this practice to them. Elicit their reactions and the reasons for their feelings. Discuss their reactions in relation to those in the two reaction letters.

5. In a small group, review several of the following books about babies. Is information presented clearly, accurately, and sensitively? Explain. Which would be most appropriate for young children? Why? Which would be good additions to a parent library and which would be good additions to a classroom library? Why? Do you feel that any of the books would be inappropriate for parents or teachers to use with young children? Why or why not? As an outcome of your review, prepare a list of recommended books for a classroom library and one for a parent library. Be prepared to justify your choices.

73

Books about Babies

Ancona, G. (1979). *It's a baby.* New York: E. P. Dutton.

Andry, A. C., & Kratka, S. C. (1970). *Hi, new baby.* New York: Simon & Schuster.

Cole, J. (1984). *How you were born.* New York: William Morrow & Company.

Cole, J. (1985). *The new baby at your house.* New York: William Morrow & Company.

Girard, L. (1983). *You were born on your very first birthday.* Niles, IL: Albert Whitman & Company.

Herzig, A. C., & Mali, J. L. (1980). *Oh, boy! Babies!* Boston: Little, Brown & Company.

Holland, V. (1972). *We are having a baby.* New York: Charles Scribner's Sons.

Kitzinger, S. (1986). *Being born.* New York: Putnam.

Lasky, K. (1984). *A baby for Max.* New York: Charles Scribner's Sons.

Mayle, P. (1973). *Where did I come from?* Secaucus, NJ: Lyle Stuart, Inc.

Rogers, F. (1985). *The new baby.* New York: G. P. Putnam's Sons.

REFERENCES & SUGGESTED READINGS

Berg-Cross, G., & Berg-Cross, L. (1978). Listening to stories may change children's social attitudes. *Reading Teacher, 31,* 659–663.

Bernstein, A. C. (1976, September). How children learn about sex and birth. *Psychology Today,* 31–35.

Carper, L. (1978, April). Young minds at play: Sex roles in the nursery. *Harper's,* 51–53.

Collins, L. J., Ingoldsby, B. B., & Dellman, M. M. (1984). Sex-role stereotyping in children's literature: A change from the past. *Childhood Education, 60,* 278, 280–282, 284–285.

Gould, L. (1972, December). A fabulous child's story. *Ms.,* 74–76, 105–106.

Honig, A. S. (1983, September). Sex role socialization in early childhood. *Young Children, 38,* 57–70.

Kohlberg, L., & Ullian, D. Z. (1974). Stages in the development of psychosexual concepts and attitudes. In R. C. Friedman, R. M. Richart, & R. L. Vande Wiele (Eds.), *Sex differences in behavior* (pp. 209–222). New York: John Wiley.

Maccoby, E. E. (1980). *Social development: Psychological growth and the parent-child relationship.* New York: Harcourt Brace Jovanovich.

O'Brien, M., Huston, A. C., & Risley, T. R. (1983). Sex-typed play of toddlers in a day care center. *Journal of Applied Developmental Psychology, 4,* 1–9.

Project T.R.E.E. (1980). *Maximizing young children's potential: A non-sexist manual for early childhood trainers.* Newton, MA:

Educational Development Center, Inc., and Women's Educational Equity Act Dissemination Center. (ERIC Document Reproduction Service No. ED 194 198).

Ruble, D. N., Balaban, T., & Cooper, J. (1981). Gender constancy and the effects of sex-typed televised toy commercials. *Child Development, 52,* 667–673.

Zepezauer, F. S. (1981). Treading through the feminist minefield. *Phi Delta Kappan, 63,* 268–272.

CHAPTER 4

Television Viewing

Television as Curriculum?

Ever since your center's television set broke down, your staff seems to have done nothing but gripe about its loss. Particularly at issue are those transition times in the early morning and late afternoon.

When the day is just getting underway, the children straggle in, so only a few staff are needed. Yet, between setting up, doing health checks, greeting parents, and serving breakfast, it is difficult to monitor the children adequately. Inevitably, the first ones to arrive are the most lively. Unless closely supervised, these children tend to get out of hand, and the day begins on a negative note. You also have heard some parents complain about "wildness."

Things are not much better at the end of the day. Both staff and children have had it! They tend to be irritable and cranky. Fatigued parents faced with a tearful, grumpy child on their hands have been muttering, "Oh, no, not again!"

Clearly something needs to be done and done fast. Should you, against your better judgment, replace the set?

Questions

1. Should television be used in a day care center? Why or why not?

2. If television is used, should children watch only educational programs? State your reasons.

3. If television is not used, what activities could be substituted?

PREVIEW

Many parents have complained about excessive sex, violence, antisocial behaviors, and intellectual drivel in commercial television programs. Others say there is no need for concern and do not hesitate to rely on "Sesame Street" or "Mister Rogers' Neighborhood" to babysit their children. What impact does television viewing have on the socialization of young children? In the opening article, Neil Postman warns that the pervasive images and messages of television can deprive children of opportunities to experience the specialness and innocence of childhood. Patsy Skeen, Mac Brown, and D. Keith Osborn find age differences in preschool children's abilities to distinguish reality and fantasy in television programs. In the final selection, Peggy Charren, a leading advocate for quality in children's television, argues for the need to protect children from the TV marketplace.

The Day Our Children Disappear: Predictions of a Media Ecologist

Neil Postman

I am aware that in addressing the question of the future of education, one can write either a "good news" or a "bad news" essay. Typically, a good news essay presents readers with a problem, then proceeds to solve it (more or less). Readers usually find such essays agreeable, as well they should. A good news essay gives us a sense of potency and control, and a really *good* "good news" essay shows us how to employ our imaginations in confronting professional issues. Although I have not yet seen the other essays in this special *Kappan*, I feel sure that most of them are of the good news type, solid and constructive.

A bad news essay, on the other hand, presents readers with a problem—and ends (more or less). Naturally, readers find such essays disagreeable, since they engender a sense of confusion and sometimes hopelessness. Still, they have their uses. They may, for example, help us understand some things that need explaining. Let me tell you, then, that while I hope my remarks will be illuminating, you must prepare yourself for an orthodox—even classical—bad news essay. I wish it could be otherwise, because I know my temperament to be more suited to optimism than to gloom and doom. But I write as a person whose academic interests go by the name of media ecology. Media ecology is the study of the effects of communications technology on culture. We study how media affect people's cognitive habits, their social relations, their political biases, and their personal values. And in this capacity I have almost nothing optimistic to write about, for, if I am to respect the evidence as I understand it, I am bound to say that the effects of modern media—especially television—have been and will probably continue to be disastrous, especially for our youth. What I intend to do here is describe in some detail one important respect in which this is the case and explain how it occurred. As is the custom in bad news essays, I shall offer no solution to this problem—mainly because I know of none.

Before proceeding, I must express one bit of "good news" about what I shall be saying. It is to be understood that when I speak of some development as "disastrous," I mean that it is disastrous from my very limited point of view. Obviously, what appears disastrous to me may be regarded as marvelous by others. After all, I am a New Yorker, and most things appear to me disastrous. But even more to the point, what may appear disastrous at one historical moment may turn out to be marvelous in a later age. There are, in fact, many historical instances of someone's correctly predicting negative effects of a medium of communication but where, in the end, what appeared to be a disaster turned out to be a great advance.

The best example I know of concerns the great Athenian teacher, Socrates, who feared and mocked the written word, which in his time was beginning to be used for many purposes and with great frequency. But not by him. As you know, Socrates wrote no books, and had it not been for Plato and Xenophon, who did, we would know almost nothing about him. In one of his most enduring conversations, called the *Phaedrus,* Socrates gives three reasons why he does not like writing. Writing, he says, will deprive Athenians of their powerful memories, for if everything is written down there will be no need to memorize. Second, he says that writing will change the form of education. In particular, it will destroy the dialectic process, for writing forces students to follow an argument rather than participate in it. And third, Socrates warns that writing will change concepts of privacy and the meaning of public discourse, for once you write something down you never know

Source: Neil Postman (1981). The day our children disappear: Predictions of a media ecologist. *Phi Delta Kappan, 62,* 382–386. Reprinted by the permission of the author.

whose eyes will fall upon it—those for whom it is intended, perhaps, but just as likely those for whom it is not intended. Thus, for Socrates, the widespread use of writing was, and would be, a cultural disaster. In a sense it was. For all of Socrates' predictions were correct, and there is no doubt that writing undermined the oral tradition that Socrates believed to be the most suitable mode for expressing serious ideas, beautiful poetry, and authentic piety. But Socrates did not see what his student, Plato, did: that writing would create new modes of thought altogether and provide new and wonderful uses for the intellect—most especially what today we call *science.*

So without intending to suggest an unsupportable comparison, I write as a Socrates-like character, prophesying that the advent of the television age will have the direst outcome. I hope that among you there is a Plato-like character who will be able to see the television age as a blessing.

In order for me to get to the center of my argument as quickly as possible, I am going to resist the temptation to discuss some of the fairly obvious effects of television, such as its role in shortening our students' attention span, in eroding their capacity to handle linguistic and mathematical symbolism, and in causing them to become increasingly impatient with deferred gratification. The evidence for these effects exists in a variety of forms—from declining SAT scores to astronomical budgets for remedial writing classes to the everyday observations of teachers and parents. But I will not take the time to review any of the evidence for the intellectually incapacitating effects of television. Instead, I want to focus on what I regard as the most astonishing and serious effect of television. It is simply this: Television is causing the rapid decline of our concept of childhood. I choose to discuss this because I can think of nothing that is bound to have a more profound effect on our work as educators than that our children should disappear. I do not mean, of course, that they will physically disappear. I mean that the *idea* of children will disappear.

If this pronouncement, on first hearing, seems implausible, let me hasten to tell you that the idea of childhood is not very old. In fact, in the Western world the idea of childhood hardly existed prior to the 16th century. Up until that time children as young as 6 and 7 were not regarded as fundamentally different from adults. As far as historians can tell,

the language of children, their dress, their games, their labor, and their legal rights were the same as those of adults. It was recognized, of course, that children tended to be smaller than adults, but this fact did not confer upon them any special status; there were certainly no special institutions for the nurturing of children. Prior to the 16th century, for example, there were no books on child rearing or, indeed, any books about women in their role as mothers. Children, to take another example, were always included in funeral processions, there being no reason anyone could think of to shield them from knowledge of death. Neither did it occur to anyone to keep a picture of a child if that child lived to grow to adulthood or had died in infancy. Nor are there any references to children's speech or jargon prior to the 17th century, after which they are found in abundance. If you have ever seen 13th- or 14th-century paintings of children, you will have noticed that they are always depicted as small adults. Except for size, they are devoid of any of the physical characteristics we associate with childhood, and they are never shown on canvas alone—that is, isolated from adults. Such paintings are entirely accurate representations of the psychological and social perceptions of children prior to the 16th century. Here is how the historian J. H. Plumb puts it:

> There was no separate world of childhood. Children shared the same games with adults, the same toys, the same fairy stories. They lived their lives together, never apart. The coarse village festivals depicted by Breughel, showing men and women besotted with drink, groping for each other with unbridled lust, have children eating and drinking with the adults. Even in the soberer pictures of wedding feasts and dances, the children are enjoying themselves alongside their elders, doing the same things.

Barbara Tuchman, in her marvelous book about the 14th century titled *A Distant Mirror,* puts it more succinctly: "If children survived to age 7, their recognized life began, more or less as miniature adults. Childhood was already over."

Now the reasons for this are fairly complicated. For one thing, most children did *not* survive; their mortality rate was extraordinarily high, and it is not until the late 14th century that children are even mentioned in wills and testaments—an indication that adults did not expect them to be around very long. In fact, probably because of this, in some parts of Europe children were treated as neuter genders. In 14th-century Italy, for example, the sex of a child who had died was never recorded.

Certainly, adults did not have the emotional commitment to children that *we* accept as normal. Phillipe Aries, in his great book titled *Centuries of Childhood,* remarks that the prevailing view was to have several children in order to keep a few; people could not allow themselves to become too attached to something that was regarded as a probable loss. Aries quotes from a document that records a remark made by the neighbor of a distraught mother of five young children. In order to comfort the mother, the neighbor says, "Before they are old enough to bother you, you will have lost half of them, or perhaps all of them."

We must also not forget that in a feudal society children were often regarded as mere economic utilities, adults being less interested in the character and intelligence of children than in their capacity for work. But I think the most powerful reason for the absence of the idea of childhood is to be found in the communication environment of the Dark and Middle Ages. Since most people did not know how to read, or did not *need* to know how to read, a child became an adult—a fully participating adult—when he or she learned how to speak. Since all important social transactions involved face-to-face oral communication, full competence to speak and hear—which is usually achieved by age 7—was the dividing line between infancy and adulthood. There was no intervening stage, because none was needed—until the middle of the 15th century. At that point an extraordinary event occurred that not only changed the religious, economic, and political face of Europe but also created our modern idea of childhood. I am referring, of course, to the invention of the printing press. And because in a few minutes you will, perhaps, be thinking that I am claiming too much for the power of modern media, especially TV, it is worth saying now that no one had the slightest inkling in 1450 that the printing press would have such powerful effects on our society as it did. When Gutenberg announced that he could manufacture books, as he put it, "without the help of reed, stylus, or pen but by wondrous agreement, proportion, and har-

mony of punches and types," he did not imagine that his invention would undermine the authority of the Catholic Church. Yet less than 80 years later Martin Luther was in effect claiming that, with the Word of God on everyone's kitchen table, Christians did not require the Papacy to interpret it for them. Nor did Gutenberg have any inkling that his invention would create a new class of people: namely, children. Or more specifically, male children, for there is no doubt that boys were the first class of specialized children.

How was this accomplished? Simply by the fact that, less than a hundred years after Gutenberg's invention, European culture became a reading culture, i.e., adulthood was redefined. One could not become an adult unless he or she knew how to read. In order to experience God, one had to be able, obviously, to read the Bible, which is why Luther himself translated the Bible into German. In order to experience literature, one had to be able to read novels and personal essays, forms of literature that were wholly created by the printing press. Our earliest novelists—for example, Richardson and Defoe—were themselves printers. Montaigne, who invented the essay, worked hand in hand with a printer, as did Thomas More when he produced what may be called our first science fiction novel—his *Utopia.* Of course, in order to learn science one not only had to know how to read but, by the beginning of the 17th century, one could read science in the vernacular—that is, in one's own language. Sir Francis Bacon's *The Advancement of Learning,* published in 1605, was the first scientific tract an Englishman could read in English. And of course one must not forget the great Dutch humanist, Erasmus, who, understanding the meaning of the printing press as well as anyone, wrote one of the first books of etiquette for the instruction of young men. He said of his book, "As Socrates brought philosophy from heaven to earth, so I have led philosophy to games and banquets." (By the way, Erasmus dedicated the book to his publisher's son, and the book includes advice and guidance on how to convert prostitutes to a moral life.)

The importance of books on etiquette should not be overlooked. As Norman Elias shows in his book titled *The Civilizing Process,* the sudden emergence in the 16th century of etiquette books signifies that one could no longer assume that children knew everything adults knew—in other words, the separation of childhood from adulthood was under way.

Alongside all of this, Europeans rediscovered what Plato had known about learning to read: namely, that it is best done at an early age. Since reading is, among other things, an unconscious reflex as well as an act of recognition, the habit of reading must be formed in that period when the brain is still engaged in the task of acquiring oral language. The adult who learns to read after his or her oral vocabulary is completed rarely becomes a fluent reader.

What this came to mean in the 16th century is that the young had to be separated from the rest of the community to be taught how to read—that is, to be taught how to function as an adult. This meant that they had to go to school. And going to school was the essential event in creating childhood. The printing press, in other words, created the idea of school. In fact, school classes originated to separate students according to their capacities as readers, not to separate them according to age. That came later. In any event, once all of this occurred it was inevitable that the young would be viewed as a special class of people whose minds and character were qualitatively different from those of adults. As any semanticist can tell you, once you categorize people for a particular purpose, you will soon discover many other reasons why they should be regarded as different. We began, in short, to see human development as a series of stages, with childhood as a bridge between infancy and adulthood. For the past 350 years we have been developing and refining our concept of childhood, this with particular intensity in the 18th, 19th, and 20th centuries. We have been developing and refining institutions for the nurturing of children; and we have conferred upon children a preferred status, reflected in the special ways we expect them to think, talk, dress, play, and learn.

All of this, I believe, is now coming to an end. And it is coming to an end because our communication environment has been radically altered once again—this time by electronic media, especially television. Television has a transforming power at least equal to that of the printing press and possibly as great as that of the alphabet itself. It is my contention that, with the assistance of other media such as radio, film, and records, television has the power to lead us to childhood's end.

Here is how the transformation is happening. To begin with, television presents information mostly in visual images. Although human speech is heard on TV and sometimes assumes importance, people mostly *watch* television. What they watch are rapidly changing visual images—as many as 1,200 different shots every hour. This requires very little conceptual thinking or analytic decoding. TV watching is almost wholly a matter of pattern recognition. The *symbolic form* of television does not require any special instruction or learning. In America, TV viewing begins at about the age of 18 months; by 30 months, according to studies by Daniel Anderson of the University of Massachusetts, children begin to understand and respond to TV imagery. Thus there is no need for any preparation or prerequisite training for watching TV. Television needs no analogue to the McGuffey *Reader.* And, as you must know, there is no such thing, in reality, as children's programming on TV. Everything is for everybody. So far as symbolic form is concerned, "Charlie's Angels" is as sophisticated or as simple to grasp as "Sesame Street." Unlike books, which vary greatly in syntactical and lexical complexity and which may be scaled according to the ability of the reader, TV presents information in a form that is undifferentiated in its accessibility. And that is why adults and children tend to watch the same programs. I might add, in case you are thinking that children and adults at least watch at different times, that according to Frank Mankiewicz's *Remote Control,* approximately 600,000 children watch TV between midnight and two in the morning.

To summarize: TV erases the dividing line between childhood and adulthood for two reasons: first, because it requires no instruction to grasp its form; second, because it does not segregate its audience. It communicates the same information to everyone simultaneously, regardless of age, sex, race, or level of education.

But it erases the dividing line in other ways as well. One might say that the main difference between an adult and a child is that the adult knows about certain facets of life—its mysteries, its contradictions, its violence, its tragedies—that are not considered suitable for children to know. As children move toward adulthood we reveal these secrets to them in what we believe to be a psychologically assimilable way. But television makes this arrangement quite impossible. Because television operates virtually around the clock—it would not be economically feasible for it to do otherwise—it requires a constant supply of novel and interesting information. This means that all adult secrets—social, sexual, physical, and the like—must be revealed. Television forces the entire culture to come out of the closet. In its quest for new and sensational information to hold its audience, TV must tap every existing taboo in the culture: homosexuality, incest, divorce, promiscuity, corruption, adultery, sadism. Each is now merely a theme for one or another television show. In the process each loses its role as an exclusively adult secret.

Some time ago, while watching a TV program called "The Vidal Sassoon Show," I came across the quintessential example of what I am talking about. Vidal Sassoon is a famous hairdresser whose TV show is a mixture of beauty hints, diet information, health suggestions, and popular psychology. As he came to the end of one segment of the show in which an attractive woman had demonstrated how to cook vegetables, the theme music came up and Sassoon just had time enough to say, "Don't go away. We'll be back with a marvelous new diet and, then, a quick look at incest." Now, this is more—much more—than demystification. It is even more than the revelation of secrets. It is the ultimate trivialization of culture. Television is relentless in both revealing and trivializing all things private and shameful, and therefore it undermines the moral basis of culture. The subject matter of the confessional box and the psychiatrist's office is now in the public domain. I have it on good authority that, shortly, we and our children will have the opportunity to see commercial TV's first experiments with presenting nudity, which will probably not be shocking to anyone, since TV commercials have been offering a form of soft-core pornography for years. And on the subject of commercials—the 700,000 of them that American youths will see in the first 18 years of their lives—they too contribute toward opening to youth all the secrets that once were the province of adults—everything from vaginal sprays to life insurance to the causes of marital conflict. And we must not omit the contributions of news shows, those curious entertainments that daily provide the young with vivid images of adult failure and even madness.

As a consequence of all of this, childhood innocence and specialness are impossible to sustain, which is why children have disap-

peared from television. Have you noticed that all the children on television shows are depicted as merely small adults, in the manner of 13th- or 14th-century paintings? Watch "The Love Boat" or any of the soap operas or family shows or situation comedies. You will see children whose language, dress, sexuality, and interests are not different from those of the adults on the same shows. Like the paintings of Breughel, the children *do* everything the adults do and are shielded from nothing.

And yet, as TV begins to render invisible the traditional concept of childhood, it would not be quite accurate to say that it immerses us in an adult world. Rather, it uses the material of the adult world as the basis for projecting a new kind of person altogether. We might call this person the adult-child. For reasons that have partly to do with TV's capacity to reach everyone, partly to do with the accessibility of its symbolic form, and partly to do with its commercial base, TV promotes as desirable many of the attitudes that we associate with childishness: for example, an obsessive need for immediate gratification, a lack of concern for consequences, an almost promiscuous preoccupation with consumption. TV seems to favor a population that consists of three age groups: on the one end, infancy; on the other, senility; and in between, a group of indeterminate age where everyone is somewhere between 20 and 30 and remains that way until dotage descends. In *A Distant Mirror*, Tuchman asks the question, Why was childishness so noticeable in medieval behavior, with its marked inability to restrain any kind of impulse? Her answer is that so large a proportion of society was in fact very young in years. Half the population was under 21; a third under 14. If we ask the same question about our own society, we must give a different answer, for about 65% of our population is over 21. We are a nation of chronological grown-ups. But TV will have none of it. It is biased toward the behavior of the child-adult.

In this connection, I want to remind you of a TV commercial that sells hand lotion. In it we are shown a mother and daughter and challenged to tell which is which. I find this to be a revealing piece of sociological evidence, for it tells us that in our culture it is considered desirable that a mother should not look older than her daughter, or that a daughter should not look younger than her mother. Whether this means that childhood is gone or adulthood is gone amounts to the same thing, for if there is no clear concept of what it means to be an adult, there can be no concept of what it means to be a child.

In any case, however you wish to phrase the transformation that is taking place, it is clear that the behavior, attitudes, desires, and even physical appearance of adults and children are becoming increasingly indistinguishable. There is now virtually no difference, for example, between adult crimes and children's crimes; in many states the punishments are becoming the same. There is also very little difference in dress. The children's clothing industry has undergone a virtual revolution within the past 10 years, so that there no longer exists what we once unambiguously recognized as children's clothing. Eleven-year-olds wear three-piece suits to birthday parties; 61-year-old men wear jeans to birthday parties. Twelve-year-old girls wear high heels; 42-year-old men wear sneakers. On the streets of New York and Chicago you can see grown women wearing little white socks and imitation Mary Janes. Indeed, among the highest-paid models in America are 12- and 13-year-old girls who are presented as adults. To take another case: Children's games, once so imaginatively rich and varied and so emphatically inappropriate for adults, are rapidly disappearing. Little League baseball and Peewee football, for example, are not only supervised by adults but are modeled in their organization and emotional style on big league sports. The language of children and adults has also been transformed so that, for example, the idea that there may be words that adults ought not to use in the presence of children now seems faintly ridiculous. With TV's relentless revelation of all adult secrets, language secrets are difficult to guard, and it is not inconceivable to me that in the near future we shall return to the 13th- and 14th-century situation in which no words were unfit for a youthful ear. Of course, with the assistance of modern contraceptives, the sexual appetite of both adults and children can be satisfied without serious restraint and without mature understanding of its meaning. Here TV has played an enormous role, since it not only keeps the entire population in a condition of high sexual excitement but stresses a kind of egalitarianism of sexual fulfillment: Sex is transformed from a dark and profound mystery to a product that is available to everyone—like mouthwash or underarm deodorant.

In the 2 November 1980 *New York Times Magazine,* Tuchman offered still another example of the homogenization of childhood and adulthood. She spoke of the declining concept of quality—in literature, in art, in food, in work. Her point was that, with the emergence of egalitarianism as a political and social philosophy, there has followed a diminution of the idea of excellence in all human tasks and modes of expression. The point is that adults are *supposed* to have different tastes and standards from those of children, but through the agency of television and other modern media the differences have largely disappeared. Junk food, once suited only to the undiscriminating palates and iron stomachs of the young, is now common fare for adults. Junk literature, junk music, junk conversation are shared equally by children and adults, so that it is now difficult to find adults who can clarify and articulate for youth the differences between quality and schlock.

It remains for me to mention that there has been a growing movement to recast the legal rights of children so that they are more or less the same as those of adults. The heart of this movement—which, for example, is opposed to compulsory schooling—resides in the claim that what has been thought to be a preferred status for children is instead only an oppression that keeps them from fully participating in the society.

All of this means, I think, that our culture is providing fewer reasons and opportunities for childhood. I am not so single-minded to think that TV alone is responsible for this transformation. The decline of the family, the loss of a sense of roots (40 million Americans change residence every year), and the elimination, through technology, of any significance in adult work are other factors. But I believe that television creates a communication context which encourages the idea that childhood is neither desirable nor necessary—indeed, that we do not need children. I said earlier, in talking about childhood's end, that I did not mean the physical disappearance of children. But in fact that, too, is happening. The birthrate in America is declining and has been for a decade, which is why schools are being closed all over the country.

This brings me to the final characteristic of TV that needs mentioning. The *idea* of children implies a vision of the future. They are the living messages we send to a time we will not see. But television cannot communicate a sense of the future or, for that matter, a sense of the past. It is a present-centered medium, a speed-of-light medium. Everything we see on television is experienced as happening *now,* which is why we must be told, in language, that a videotape we are seeing was made months before. The grammar of television has no analogue to the past and future tenses in language. Thus it amplifies the present out of all proportion and transforms the childish need for immediate gratification into a way of life. And we end up with what Christopher Lasch calls "the culture of narcissism"—no future, no children, everyone fixed at an age somewhere between 20 and 30.

Of course I cannot know what all of this means to you, but my own position, I'm sure, is clear. I believe that what I have been describing is disastrous—partly because I value the charm, curiosity, malleability, and innocence of childhood, which is what first drew me to a career in education, and partly be-

cause I believe that adults need, first, to be children before they can be grown-ups. For otherwise they remain like TV's adult-child all their lives, with no sense of belonging, no capacity for lasting relationships, no respect for limits, and no grasp of the future. But mainly I think it is disastrous because it makes problematic the future of school, which is one of the few institutions still based on the assumption that there are significant differences between children and adults and that adults therefore have something of value to teach children.

So my bad news essay comes down to these questions: In a world in which children are adults and adults children, what need is there for people like ourselves? Are the issues we are devoting our careers to solving being rendered irrelevant by the transforming power of our television culture? I devoutly hope your answers to these questions are more satisfactory than mine.

Neil Postman is a professor of education, Department of Communication Arts and Science, New York University. His most recent book, Teaching as a Conserving Activity *(Delacorte Press, 1979), offers a sophisticated analysis of today's competing learning systems: the schools and TV.*

Young Children's Perception of "Real" and "Pretend" on Television

Patsy Skeen, Mac H. Brown, and D. Keith Osborn

Summary.—The Degree of Perceived Reality Scale was administered to 22 4- and 22 5-yr.-old children in a day-care center. The degree of reality perception of cartoon and human-fantasy televised episodes was measured. Five-yr.-olds had a more mature reality perception of both cartoon and human fantasy televised episodes than did 4-yr.-olds. Only 5-yr.-olds had a more mature reality perception of cartoon than of televised episodes of human fantasy.

By age 18, the average American child has watched 17,000 hours of television (Osborn & Osborn, 1977). In assessing the impact of television on the child, an important concern is when and how children develop their perception of what is real versus what is pretend on television. Piaget (1969) suggests that children's perception of reality passes through distinct stages as they gradually learn to separate themselves from the surrounding world and discriminate between what is real and what is not in the adult sense. Results from studies of children's perception of reality in various types of situations such as playing with a live animal (Kohlberg, 1968; DeVries, 1969), listening to stories (Lottan, 1967), looking at pictures (Taylor & Howell, 1973), and viewing television (Brown, Skeen, & Osborn, 1979; Noble, 1969) have generally indicated that a child's ability to distinguish between reality and fantasy increases with chronological age.

In addition to age, the content and type of the perceptual situation (story, picture, cartoon or live actors on television) appear to be important in determining how children perceive reality versus pretend. For example, children who realized that cartoon programs were pretend thought that fantasy programs which had live actors were real (Lyle & Hoffman, 1972).

Because preschool children are dependent upon immediate perception and lack the capacity for abstract reasoning, they are strongly influenced by appearance. When viewing television they find it difficult if not impossible to understand that actors play roles, cartoon characters are not alive, and scenes are artificial copies of real situations. Instead, they think that all events on television are real (Stevenson, 1972). Stein (1972) contends that children have a particularly hard time perceiving what is real versus pretend on television because it is such a realistic medium in which real and fictional events are presented in similar ways.

The purpose of this research was to study young children's perceived reality of cartoon and human fantasy in televised episodes.

Subjects

Subjects included 22 4- and 22 5-yr.-old Caucasian, middle-class children. They were equally divided by sex and randomly selected from children enrolled in a private day-care center located in an urban Northeast Georgia area.

Materials

Two 3-min. fantasy episodes of the television series "Star Trek" were video-taped from the

Source: Reprinted with permission of authors and publisher from: Skeen, P., Brown, M. H., & Osborn, D. K., Young children's perception of "real" and "pretend" on television. *Perceptual and Motor Skills*, 1982, 54, 883–887.

commercial series by the same name, one using live actors and the other an animated children's cartoon. Electronic splicing produced two equivalent episodes matched in storyline and amount of violence. The animated characters had identical voices, look-alike facial and body features, and dress and behavior patterns similar to the human actors.

The Degree of Perceived Reality Scale, an individually administered instrument designed by the authors to measure young children's reality perception of televised episodes of cartoons and human fantasy has three parts. In Part I rapport is established and demographic information elicited. Part II is designed to determine if a subject knows the meaning of "real" and "pretend" and is able to demonstrate behaviorally an ability to use both words appropriately. Part III consists of two Forms A and B. Form A is designed to measure the extent of a child's perception of reality of a particular event viewed in a cartoon episode of the television series "Star Trek." Form B measures the extent of perception of reality of a particular event viewed in a human-fantasy episode of "Star Trek."

Questions on both Form A and Form B are presented in nine pairs or a total of 18 questions on either form. The first question in each pair is designed to determine the child's perception of whether a particular event viewed in an episode is "real" or "pretend." The child receives one point if he gives a correct response indicating that the event is "pretend" and zero points for an incorrect response indicating that the event is "real." The second question in each pair is designed to determine the child's comprehension of why the event is "real" or "pretend." The child receives one point if he gives a correct response indicating he understands why the televised event is "pretend" and zero points for an incorrect response. An incorrect response is any response which does not indicate an understanding of why the event is "pretend." The values for all responses are summed. The highest possible score of 18 indicates a mature, adult-like perception of reality of the television episode, whereas a score of zero represents an immature perception of reality.

The Spearman rank-order correlation of "half" scores with application of the Spearman-Brown formula was used to compute internal consistency reliability. Correlations were .92 for 4-yr.-olds on Form A, .79 for 5-yr.-olds on Form A, .69 for 4-yr.-olds on Form B, and .79 for 5-yr.-olds on Form B.

Procedure
The children viewed the two "Star Trek" televised episodes and responded to the Degree of Perceived Reality Scale. Each child was administered both Forms A and B; however, the first form administered was randomly alternated. The complete testing procedure took about 20 minutes and was carried out during school hours in a quiet, distraction-free room with which the children were familiar.

Results and Discussion

Age and Degree of Perceived Reality
Five-yr.-olds had more mature perceptions of reality of televised episodes of both cartoons ($t = -3.05$, $p < .01$) and human fantasy ($t = -2.64$, $p < .01$) than did 4-yr.-olds. These results support other studies (Brown, Skeen, & Osborn, 1979; DeVries, 1969; Kohlberg, 1968; Lottan, 1967; Lyle & Hoffman, 1972; Noble, 1966; Taylor & Howell, 1973) which have showed a positive relation between age and degree of adult-like reality perception.

Several of the criteria underlying reality judgments were reminiscent of judgment categories delineated by Piaget (1966). Egocentric reasons irrelevant to the reality judgment were given by 27% of the 4- and 5% of the 5-yr.-olds. For example, "Captain Kirk" is "real" because "he is my Captain Kirk and I want to be a space Captain." Movement was used by 32% of the 4-, but only 5% of the 5-yr.-olds. "I know he's real because he moved and talked" or the space ship is "real because I saw it fly."

TABLE 1 *Mean Scores of Cartoon and Human Fantasy Reality by Age*

Factor	4-yr.-olds		5-yr.-olds		t
	M	SD	M	SD	
Cartoon Reality	4.86	2.18	8.00	4.16	−3.05*
Human Fantasy Reality	3.73	2.15	6.05	3.39	−2.64*

*$p < .01$.

This type of reasoning closely resembles Piaget's concept of animism (1966).

All children made incongruent judgments of reality. For example, a typical child answered all questions concerning the human-fantasy episode to indicate that it was "real" and then when asked if the show he had just seen was "real" indicated that it was not because "everything on TV is pretend."

Reality judgments also were influenced by sex-role perception or identification. In our society the traditional male-female sex-role pattern is that males are strong and must protect weak females. In the video episode women threw men on the ground, violating the traditional sex-role pattern. Thirty-two percent of the younger and 28% of the older males said this was "pretend" because "women can't throw men on the ground." Nine percent of the younger and 5% of the older females gave similar answers.

Type of Media

Five- but not 4-yr.-olds in this study made more mature reality judgments about the cartoon than they did about the human-fantasy episode ($r = .53$, p_1 .05). These results support the findings of Lyle and Hoffman (1972) and theories of Streicher (1972) and Stein (1972).

Further examination of judgment criteria categories is helpful in explaining the influence of type of media on reality judgments. Both 4- and 5-yr.-olds used appearance as a criterion. Cartoon and human fantasy women were not "real" because "their clothes don't look right" or were "real" because "their voice sounds real." The cartoon was "pretend" because it "was a cartoon" while the human fantasy was "real" because it "was not a cartoon."

While 32% of the younger children thought that everything on television was "real," all other children discriminated between "real" and "pretend" to some degree. No children made reality distinctions in the adult sense. The presence of live actors as opposed to animated cartoon figures was influential in reality judgments made by children who had begun to make such discriminations. For example, the opening scene of the space ship flying through space was identical in both episodes. The two episodes were judged to be equivalent in all respects except the presence of live actors versus cartoon animation. Yet 37% of all the children said the ship was "pretend" in the cartoon but "real" in the human-fantasy episode.

There may be several reasons why the presence of live actors is of paramount importance to children in making judgments of reality. Live actors look like the children themselves and those people in their immediate environment whom they know are "real." Cartoon characters do not look like "real" people. Piaget's (1966) contention that young children are able to focus on one, often isolated, attribute of a situation at a time suggests another explanation. It is difficult for children to understand that a human can be a "real" person and at the same time play a "pretend" role as an actor. The fact that television presents humans in both reality and fantasy situations further confuses the issue of humans who are "real persons," playing "pretend" roles, and appearing in "real"-life situations. Perhaps, one reason children perceive that cartoons are "pretend" before they make this decision about human fantasy is that cartoons are presented as "pretend" only, while confusion exists in presentation of live actors.

In an attempt to rule out as many variables as possible except type of media (cartoon versus human fantasy) and age, Star Trek episodes in the cartoon and human fantasy forms were used and subjects narrowly selected. Subjects were all white and from professional middle-class homes in the same geographic region. While the use of such subjects does rule out confounding factors of race, income level, and geographic region, their use also limits the generalizability of the findings to other populations. Further research needs to be carried out with more diverse populations and larger sample sizes.

REFERENCES

Brown, M. H., Skeen, P., & Osborn, D. K. Young children's perception of the reality of television. *Contemporary Education,* 1979, 50, 129–133.

DeVries, R. Constancy of generic identity in the years three to six. *Monographs of the Society for Research in Child Development,* 1969, 34, No. 4.

Kohlberg, L. Cognitive stages and preschool education. In J. L. Frost (Ed.), *Early childhood education rediscovered.* New York: Holt, Rinehart & Winston, 1968. Pp. 212–224.

Lottan, S. The ability of children to distinguish between the "make believe" and the "real" in children's literature. *Journal of Educational Thought*, 1967, 1, 25–33.

Lyle, J., & Hoffman, H. R. Children's use of television and other media. In E. A. Rubinstein, G. A. Comstock, & J. P. Murray (Eds.), *Television and social behavior*. Vol. 4. *Television in day-to-day life: patterns of use.* Washington: U.S. Government Printing Office, 1972. Pp. 1–32.

Noble, G. Reports on international evaluations of children's reactions to the Swedish television programme "Patrick and Putrik": the English report. In F. E. Briebel & A. E. Gurgar (Eds.), *Findings and cognition on the television perception of children and young people based on the prize winning programmes of Prix Jeunesse 1966.* München: Internationales Zentralinstitut für das Jugend und Bildungsfernsehen, 1969.

Osborn, D., & Osborn, J. Television violence revisited. *Childhood Education*, 1977, 54, 309–311.

Piaget, J. *The child's conception of physical cau-sality.* London: Routledge & Kegan Paul, 1966.

Stein, A. H. Mass media and young children's development. In N. I. Gordon (Ed.), *Early childhood education.* New York: National Society for the Study of Education, 1972. Pp. 181–202. (Yearbook No. 71)

Stevenson, H. W. Television and the behavior of preschool children. In J. P. Murray, E. A. Rubinstein, & G. A. Comstock (Eds.), *Television and social behavior*. Vol. 2. *Television and social learning.* Washington: U.S. Government Printing Office, 1972. Pp. 1–42.

Streicher, L. H. *Caricatural imagery in the mass media.* (Research Report, Vol. 9, No. 2) Chicago: Institute for Juvenile Research, 1972.

Taylor, B., & Howell, R. The ability of three-, and four-, and five-year-old children to distinguish fantasy from reality. *Journal of Genetic Psychology*, 1973, 122, 315–318.

Children's TV: Sugar and Vice and Nothing Nice

Peggy Charren

Television today is a four-billion-dollar industry. It is Beethoven and Batman, history and hysteria, creative entertainment and mindless mayhem. But above all, television in this country is big, big business. And children are a disproportionate part of that business. They are used, misused, manipulated, and misdirected by an industry that regards two-to-eleven-year-old children as a product to be sold to the highest bidder.

Few of our young people can remember life without television. The medium has grown up along with them. Over the last thirty years, television has grown from a novelty, a luxury for the wealthy, to become a staple in almost 98 percent of all American homes. Children today spend more time watching television than they spend in the classroom, or in any activity except sleep. By the time a child reaches age eighteen, he has spent two full years of his life staring at a small screen.

Although only 15 percent of a child's viewing time takes place during daytime hours on Saturdays and Sundays, the networks schedule hour after hour of what a recent Michigan State University study has called "the most violent and most deceitful time block of programming on television." In addition, a considerable portion of a child's TV viewing takes place during after-school hours, when independent and UHF stations recycle outdated situation comedies, westerns, and quiz shows to attract young viewers.

In the late 1960s, animated programs shifted from the standard Mickey Mouse and Donald Duck cartoons to series featuring monsters, superheroes, and science-fiction creatures. It is not uncommon for characters to resort to murder, bombings, car chases, and shootings to extricate themselves from sticky situations. And if all else fails, there's always the last resort: mysterious death rays!

These antisocial behavior patterns are often combined with racial and sexual stereotypes. The world children watch on television is peopled primarily by white American males, age eighteen to thirty-five. Women are more often witches than workers; blacks sing and dance; Orientals are villains; and the elderly are victims.

The commercial broadcaster has no incentive to develop innovative, age-specific programming for children as long as ratings is the name of the game. In the early days of television, programs were the bait used to sell TV sets. Now that more people in this country have a television set than have indoor plumbing or refrigerators, programs are the bait used to attract audiences to the advertising messages.

Television advertising to children has evolved into a complex, highly sophisticated industry. In 1939, $300,000 was spent on radio advertising to children. Today, the two-to-eleven-year-old market is the object of a $400,000,000-a-year advertising assault, with ads for toys, candy, cereal, record offers, amusements, and fast-food chains. Advertisers obviously have not made this kind of investment to attract nickels and dimes from a child's allowance. They recognize the persuasive powers of children as surrogate salesmen. If a child doesn't have the resources to buy a product himself, advertisers know that he has ways of getting Mom and Dad to buy it for him. As an Oscar Mayer executive puts it:

Source: Peggy Charren (1977, Summer). Children's TV: Sugar and vice and nothing nice. *Business and Society Review, 22,* 65–70. Reprinted by permission of the author.

When you sell a woman on a product and she goes into the store and finds your brand isn't in stock, she'll probably forget about it. But when you sell a kid on your product, if he can't get it, he will throw himself on the floor, stamp his feet and cry. You can't get a reaction like that out of an adult.

During a single week, the average child will see almost three thousand commercial messages; that's five hours of advertising every week for the nation's 35 million children. There are more commercials on children's TV than on adult prime time.

No wonder the issue of selling to children has become a matter of intense concern to all those who care about the health and well-being of children. Many people believe that because children are neither able to distinguish fact from fantasy, nor understand the functions of the marketplace, advertising to children is inherently misleading and unfair. Dr. Richard Feinbloom, Medical Director of the Family Health Care Program of Harvard Medical School, expressed this opinion in a statement to the Federal Trade Commission:

An advertisement to a child has the quality of an order, not a suggestion. The child lacks the ability to set priorities, to determine relative importance, and to reject some directions as inappropriate.

Sugar in the Morning

Almost half of the advertisements directed to children are for heavily sugared foods. Less than 2 percent of the food ads are for milk, fruit, or vegetables. Candy, junk food, and supersweet cereals are marketed to children as nutritious, delicious, and fun to eat. Some cereals advertised as appropriate breakfast choices contain so much sugar, more than 50 percent, that nutritionist Jean Meyer has suggested they be relabeled as "imitation cereal" and placed on the candy counter. Pediatricians, dentists, and even the FDA state that sticky sugar between meals causes cavities, yet Mars, Inc. markets Milky Way to children, with the oft-repeated slogan, "At work, rest, or play—all day, Milky Way." Do the executives of Mars, Inc. encourage their own children to nibble these sticky snacks at any hour of the day,

or do they carefully teach the facts of dental life to their vulnerable offspring?

When they are not sweet-talking the young, TV's admen are busy turning the living room into a toy store. The TV commercial is the answer to a toy maker's dream. It affords the opportunity for visual demonstration, loud music, slow motion, fast action, engines whining, and babies crying. Armed with market research, pretested packaging, and program tie-ins, the toy salesman appears early and often during the pre-Christmas season. There was a time when toys were inexpensive, simply made, and related to the developmental needs of the child. Now the pressure to create an effective TV commercial affects the design of toys. A rag doll looks dead on television, but the doll that walks, talks, blows bubbles, and burps is a star attraction in a thirty-second drama. Despite the disclaimers "batteries not included" or "each item sold separately," a child is often disappointed to find that Barbie doesn't come with a fur coat and four friends, or that the Hot Wheels race-car set doesn't really look that much like Indianapolis after all.

Toy commercials accounted for 84 percent of all children's advertising during the after-school hours on a New York City station in November, 1975. *Broadcast Advertisers Report* calculates that manufacturers of toys, games, and hobbycrafts spent about $32,866,000 on network advertising in 1975, nearly half of it directed to young viewers on Saturday and Sunday morning programs. The proliferation of licensed toys with TV tie-ins creates a boomerang effect. A program like "S.W.A.T." spurs a demand for S.W.A.T action figures, which in turn serve as an ever-present reminder to watch the heroes on the tube.

Until recently, the broadcasters' Code of Good Practice permitted pills to be pushed to youngsters, pills that said on the back of the bottle, "Keep out of reach of children," because in overdose, they would put children into coma or shock. It was not until Action for Children's Television (ACT) petitioned the Federal Trade Commission to prohibit the selling of vitamins directly to children that the industry took action.

Hudson Pharmaceuticals ignored the Code ban in an attempt to market Spiderman vitamins, using the comic book hero Spiderman to endorse the special qualities of the pills. (Hudson is owned by Cadence Industries, which also owns Marvel Comics.) In response to a

91

complaint from ACT, the FTC issued a consent order prohibiting the company from selling vitamins to child audiences.

In another illustration of corporate disregard for the vulnerability of childhood concerns, WDCA, an independent TV station in Washington, D.C. In 1975, during the two weeks before the Fourth of July, that station scheduled fifty-four commercials promoting the sale of fireworks. The manufacturer of the fireworks had arranged for all these sales pitches to be broadcast on popular children's programs, including "Bugs Bunny," "Bozo's Circus," "Gilligan's Island," and "Superman." Complaints from the American Academy of Pediatrics convinced the broadcaster to cancel the potentially dangerous campaign.

Children for Market

In defense of self-regulation, the television industry argues that outside regulation is an unnecessary imposition and would result in extraordinary expenditures. Industry and government talk a lot about the costs of regulation—in time, money, energy, and paperwork. But the real issue is the cost of no regulation. The state of the art of commercial children's television proves that self-regulation does not work; that left to its own devices, business does not make the right decision; that the nation's children are not as important as the bottom line.

The costs to society will be enormous if we continue to treat two-to-eleven-year-old children as a market to be captured. Some of the costs are obvious: poor dental health and nutritionally disastrous food habits. The toll in dental bills has reached a staggering $5 billion annually. Dentists recognize that the single biggest threat to dental health is sugar. And yet television continues its super-sweet sales pitches hundreds of times a week.

Some of the costs of inaction are more subtle. What are the effects on a child's perceptions of society when he is constantly exposed to racial and sexual stereotypes? In the world of television, capable, self-assured, ruggedly handsome males predominate in the leadership roles. Women, in contrast, are often shown as weak, insecure, scatter-brained, and submissive. In a typical Saturday morning of cartoon shows, an animal is more apt to have a speaking part than a black.

What are the effects of incessant exposure to violent interaction on television? Are children learning that violence and aggression are acceptable solutions to problems? If it works for their heroes, why not for them? What is the effect of violence on people's perceptions of real-life violence and danger? Drs. George Gerbner and Larry Gross of the Annenberg School of Communications have found:

heavy viewers significantly overestimated the extent of violence and danger in the world. Their heightened sense of fear and mistrust is manifested in their typically more apprehensive responses to questions about their own personal safety, about crime and law enforcement, and about trust in other people.

What are the results to society of an atmosphere that encourages materialism and consumption in children at a very early age? With all the sophistication that Madison Avenue can muster, television advertisements are beamed to children who lack even the basic ability to tell where a program ends and an ad begins. Through commercials, children are led to believe that unless they own a certain toy they won't be happy; that there is something intrinsically "better" about a cereal which comes with a prize in the box; that they can actually buy a device which will make them bionic. We're raising a new generation of children who know Peter Pan only as peanut butter, and think Mother Nature is a middle-aged lady who sells margarine. Although it is no longer permissible to exhort a child to be "the first kid on your block" to own a certain product, advertisers still aim at a child's sense of security and worth in ads like the one for a footwear company that promised, "Wear our sneakers and you'll never be lonely again."

Advertisers don't market moderation. They don't suggest that a particular toy may be too expensive for the family budget. They don't warn that too much candy can lead to cavities or weight problems. They don't volunteer the information that sweet cereals do not contribute to a balanced, nutritious diet. Advertising to children has little educational value. It is there to encourage them to acquire, not inquire.

American society historically has provided special protection for its children: child labor laws, restrictions on the legal drinking age, and laws governing the ability of minors to enter into contracts. Until the regulatory agencies act to protect children from the TV marketplace, broadcasters must exercise restraint and responsibility in program practices directed to children. At present, the industry, by both its actions and inactions, is not responsive to the social and human needs of developing children.

Who Is "ACT"?

Action for Children's Television (ACT) is a nonprofit, national consumer organization, based in Newtonville, Massachusetts, working to improve broadcast practices related to children. Through legal action, education, and research, the group is trying to reduce violence and commercialism and to encourage quality and diversity on children's television.

ACT's activities include petitions and complaints to regulatory agencies, maintenance of a reference library and speaker's bureau, annual conferences on various aspects of children's television, and distribution of materials to parents, physicians, teachers, and industry. ACT publishes a quarterly newsletter, sponsors research studies, and currently is preparing a series of handbooks on specialized areas of children's programming.

ACT's accomplishments include successful lobbying to reduce weekend children's advertising time by 40 percent, eliminate vitamin pill advertising on children's programs, and eliminate "host" commercials. (No longer can the children's favorite performers act as salesmen for a sponsor's product.)

ACT has a paid staff of ten, over a hundred volunteer representatives, and fifteen affiliated groups across the country. ACT is funded by members and by foundations, including the Ford Foundation, the Carnegie Corporation of New York, and the National Endowment for the Arts. For more information, contact ACT at 46 Austin Street, Newtonville, Mass., 02160.

Peggy Charren is president of Action for Children's Television (ACT).

ASK YOURSELF:
Identifying Issues for Debate and Advocacy

1. Does television viewing rob children of their childhood? Why or why not?

2. Is the child who does not view television deprived of information about the larger world? Why or why not?

3. What are the positive or negative effects of television viewing on young children? (Also see Anderson, 1985; Forge & Phemister, 1982; Lesser, 1979; Singer & Singer, 1979, 1983.)

4. What kinds of television shows are worthwhile and appropriate for young children? Inappropriate?

5. Positive correlations have been found between viewing violent or aggressive episodes on television and increased aggressive behavior in young children (Rubenstein,

93

1983). How can you explain the abundance of violence that still exists in children's commercial television programming?

6. To what extent does television portray stereotypes (race, age, gender, culture), self-importance, and escapism versus an accurate view of life in the real world?

7. Do children's television programs and commercials portray poor nutritional habits? Explain.

8. Professional values indicate that children have the right to be protected from commercial exploitation. In what ways may the teacher help protect this right given the current state of children's television programming? Do the TV commercials that young children watch affect what their parents buy?

9. Do children who watch more television engage in more pretend play (Kostelnik & Whiren, 1986; Singer & Singer, 1976)? Does pretend play stimulated by TV watching tend to have a positive or negative influence on socioemotional development?

10. What is the average number of hours per day that preschool children watch television?

11. Does the amount of TV viewing in the preschool years affect later school achievement? Sociability? Choice of playmates? Level of anxiety? Explain.

APPLICATION/ADVOCACY EXERCISES

1. Interview a program developer at a local public television station. Compose a set of interview questions concerning the availability and quality of children's programming in your local area. Base some of your questions on issues raised by Action for Children's Television (ACT). Also inquire about local efforts of public stations to fund and develop television programs geared to young children. In your report, relate your findings to readings found in this chapter or elsewhere.

2. After reading about the possible negative impact commercial television can have on your children, complete the television program evaluation form in Figure 4–1. Share and discuss your results in terms of the readings with four or five other students.

FIGURE 4–1 *Television Program Evaluation Form*

Program _____ Evaluator _____

I.* Rate a commercial children's TV program viewed against the following positive and negative characteristics to help you decide whether or not you would recommend the program be viewed by preschool children. Add comments to clarify rating. Enter a check in the last column if the characteristic is not applicable.

Characteristic	Positive		Negative	N.A.
A. Content fits the interests of the intended audience.	Content relates to children's interests and experiences.	← 4 3 2 1 0 → Comments:	Not relevant; children lose interest in content quickly.	
B. If an entertainment show, the tone is appropriate.	Wholesome, exciting, and/or humorous.	← 4 3 2 1 0 → Comments:	Gruesome, violent, and/or antisocial behavior.	
C. It aids the child in self-understanding and/or understanding of others.	Deals with problems relevant to young children. Supports positive relationships with others.	← 4 3 2 1 0 → Comments:	Problems are not relevant to young children. Promotes incorrect ideas about people and their characteristics.	
D. It promotes positive social values.	Fair play, kindness, honesty, empathy.	← 4 3 2 1 0 → Comments:	Crime, cheating, lying, hurting.	
E. It promotes and encourages constructive play and activities.	Promotes and encourages behavior such as constructive fantasy play, working with others, an interest in appropriate play materials (such as books or paint) or further inquiry and problem solving.	← 4 3 2 1 0 → Comments:	Shows details of criminal activities; inappropriate materials being used; or extremely competitive or very aggressive behavior.	
F. The program production is high quality.	Production has high-quality script, music, artwork, sets, sound effects, photography, and acting.	← 4 3 2 1 0 → Comments:	Production is sloppy; artwork or sets are poorly done; cartoons are oversimplified and unattractive; acting and/or voice dubbing is poor; action is hard to follow, too fast, or too slow.	
G. Program is free of prejudice and fair in treatment of different groups of people.	Nonsexist and nonracist. Equality and understanding are promoted. All ages, races, cultures, handicapping conditions, and sexes are presented fairly and honestly.	← 4 3 2 1 0 → Comments:	Unfair to any age, race, sex, culture, or handicapping condition. Presents unrealistic stereotypes, or omits different ages, races, cultures, handicapping conditions, and sexes.	

(cont.)

95

FIGURE 4–1 *Television Program Evaluation Form* (cont.)

Characteristic	Positive		Negative	N.A.
H. If program presents them, emergent reading, math, and writing skills/concepts are age appropriate and well presented.	Concepts presented clearly, repeated in a variety of formats, and illustrated concretely.	← 4 3 2 1 0 → Comments:	Concepts/skills beyond the preschool child's level; presentation misleading and confusing.	

II. Check the program against the following criteria by circling a yes or no response.

    A. Crime is never suitable as a major theme of a program for children.   Yes   No

    B. There should be immediate resolution of suspense, and the program should avoid undue stress or fear.   Yes   No

    C. A clear differentiation should be made between fantasy and fact.   Yes   No.

Commercials:†

III. Respond to the following questions with yes or no responses and descriptive statements.

    A. Is the size of the product made clear?

    B. Is a child or adult shown doing something unsafe?

    C. Does the ad promote poor eating habits?

    D. Does the ad promote sexist or racist attitudes or behaviors?

    E. Are children shown using a product not intended for children?

    F. Are children shown using a product in a way that the average child could not?

    G. Does the ad suggest that a child will be superior to friends or more popular if he or she owns a given product?

    H. Does the ad suggest that an adult who buys a product for a child is better or more caring than one who does not?

    I. Do program hosts or characters appear in commercials within their own programs?

    J. In ads featuring premiums, is the premium offer clearly secondary?

IV. Write a summary reaction for your analysis of the program and the commercials.

*Adapted from Charlesworth, R. (1987). *Understanding child development,* 2nd ed. Albany, NY: Delmar.

†Adapted from Children's Advertising Review Unit, National Advertising Division Council of Better Business Bureaus, Inc., 845 Third Avenue, New York, New York, 212/754-1353.

REFERENCES & SUGGESTED READINGS

Anderson, D. R. (1985). *The influence of television on children's attentional abilities.* Amherst, MA: University of Massachusetts and Children's Television Workshop. (ERIC Document Reproduction Service No. ED 265 933)

Burton, S. G., Calonico, J. M., & McSeveney, D. R. (1979). Effects of preschool television watching on first-grade children. *Journal of Communication, 29,* 164–170.

Eron, L. D. (1982). Parent-child interaction, television violence, and aggression of children. *American Psychologist, 37,* 197–211.

Forge, K. L. S., & Phemister, S. (1982). *Effect of prosocial cartoons on preschool children.* San Diego, CA: San Diego State University. (ERIC Document Reproduction Service No. ED 262 905)

Kostelnik, M. J., & Whiren, A. P. (1986). Living with he-man: Managing superhero fantasy play. *Young Children, 41,* 3–9.

Lesser, G. S. (1979, March). Stop picking on Big Bird. *Psychology Today,* 57–60.

Rubenstein, E. (1983). Television and behavior: Research conclusions of the 1982 NIMH Report and their policy implications. *American Psychologist, 38,* 820–825.

Singer, D. G., & Singer, J. L. (1976). Family television viewing habits and the spontaneous play of preschool children. *Journal of Orthopsychiatry, 46,* 496–502.

Singer, J. L., & Singer, D. G. (1979, March). Come back, Mr. Rogers, come back. *Psychology Today,* 56–60.

Singer, J. L., & Singer, D. G. (1983). Psychologists look at television: Cognitive, developmental, personality, and social policy implications. *American Psychologist, 38,* 826–834.

CHAPTER 5

Child Health and Nutrition

No Freebie Food?

Dear Editor:

I would like to comment on your editorial concerning the need for government food programs such as Women, Infants, and Children (WIC). To me, it's just another giveaway welfare program. So what if the food supplement is restricted to foods rich in protein and vitamins! What guarantee is there that the babies will get the nourishment they need? From what I have seen of these people, the mothers and their boyfriends will eat the food.

My husband and I have worked hard for everything we own. We scrimped and saved to buy our own home, to clothe and feed our children, and to send them to college. Why should we pay taxes to support people who were not even born here? Answer me that!

Signed,
Not a Bleeding Heart

Questions

1. In your opinion, what is the value of spending tax dollars on supplemental food programs such as WIC, the Child Care Food Program, Food Stamps, or the School Lunch Program?

2. Based on your observations and experiences, what are the pros and cons of the programs mentioned in question 1?

PREVIEW

In recent years, there has been a marked increase in emphasis on the interrelatedness of good nutrition and child health and development. Joseph H. Stevens, Jr., and Delia H. Baxter provide a comprehensive survey of what is known about the effects of nutrient intake on optimal child development and argue for more careful screening of children for nutritional problems, for nutrition education programs for both parents and children, and for family food assistance as well as child nutrition programs. The second reading in this chapter, written by Mary A. Jensen, traces the history of a federal child nutrition program that has successfully used diverse advocacy efforts to secure funding. This is the WIC program (Special Supplemental Food Program for Women, Infants and Children). In addition to policies that seek to support good nutrition through supplemental food programs, this chapter addresses the issue of educating young children about good nutrition. Should young children be educated about nutrition, and if so, how? Margaret G. Phillips points to nutrition education experiences used in the Head Start program. And in the final reading, Ligaya P. Paguio and Anna V. A. Resurreccion describe children's developmental food preferences as a basis for planning appropriate nutrition education experiences.

Malnutrition and Children's Development

Joseph H. Stevens, Jr., and Delia H. Baxter

The past 15 years have been active ones for research about the effects of malnutrition on children's development. Some of this work has been conducted in the United States but much of it has come from developing countries. Chronic undernutrition, rather than severe malnutrition, is more prevalent in the United States; in this condition the frank signs are not yet present, but can be detected by anthropometric and biochemical measures. Such children simply do not get enough food, and consequently do not get enough nutrients. The undernourished child typically grows less well, and is generally small for age.

In contrast, moderate and severe malnutrition is more common in developing countries. Severe malnutrition has been defined as infantile marasmus or kwashiorkor (Winick 1976). They occur where there is a low intake of both calories and protein (marasmus) or a reduced protein intake accompanied by adequate calorie consumption (kwashiorkor); clinical features differ in the two conditions. We cannot generalize with assurance from research conducted in developing countries to our own because of significant cultural, social, and economic differences, as well as differences in the levels and extent of malnutrition encountered. However, evidence about malnutrition in other countries provides further support that the nourishment of children plays an important role in development and particularly in their mental development.

The impact of malnutrition is related to its severity, age of onset, and length of the deprivation period (Read 1973). Both severe and moderate malnutrition have been associated with poor sensorimotor development, intellectual functioning, intersensory organization, visual discrimination ability, and language development in children (Cravioto and De Licardie 1979), although performance appears to be more depressed when the malnutrition occurs earlier, for a longer time period, and when nutrient intake is much more limited.

In addition to such effects on children's performance, very severe malnutrition has been linked to structural changes in the brain. For example, there appear to be at least two critical periods in brain development. One is during the second and third trimester of pregnancy when there is a rapid increase in the number of fetal neuronal cells. The second is during the first two years of life when glial cell development and synaptic formation is rapid (National Academy of Sciences, Food and Nutrition Board 1974; Read 1973). According to one theory, glial changes facilitate synaptic functioning and the efficient transmission of impulses, and these changes may be important in explaining the development of long-term memory. However, there are other theories (Guyton 1976). Chase (1976) reported that about 25 percent of the adult number of brain cells are present at birth, 66 percent by age six months, and 90–95 percent by age one year. During these periods of rapid expansion, the brain is probably particularly vulnerable to insult like limited nutrient intake. Very severe malnutrition occurring early in development appears to decrease brain weight, cell number, and cell size, as well as inhibit myelin formation. There is no evidence that chronic undernutrition also results in structural changes in the brain.

In virtually all of the investigations about malnutrition done with humans, it is difficult to separate the effects of limited nutrient intake from the effects of other environmental factors (Brozek 1978). Humans are fed and nourished in a rich social context. Some of the social relationships connected with feeding and the securing of food may well represent a unique adaptation of *Homo sapiens,* distinguishing them from other primates (Lancaster 1980). Further speculation about the interdependence of malnutrition and other environmental influences on development leads to the suggestion that limited nourishment may result in diminished vigor, energy, attentiveness in children which is associated with decreased exploratory behavior, lowered responsivity, and fewer environmental encounters. This diminished responsiveness may elicit less stimulation from others in the environment. An environment with less food may have similar effects on all members of the social group, resulting in lowered interaction and social interchange for all family members.

Research in Other Countries

Several studies document that malnourished children perform less well on cognitive and developmental measures (Herrera, Mora, Christiansen, Ortiz, Clement, Vuori, Waber, De Paredes, and Wagner 1980; Engle, Irwin, Klein, Yarbrough, and Townsend 1979; Hertzig, Birch, Richardson, and Tizard 1972; Graham 1972; Stoch and Smythe 1976; Cravioto, Birch, De Licardie, Rosales, and Vega 1969). Two large-scale and long-term nutritional supplementation studies have provided particularly interesting data.

Engle, Irwin, Klein, Yarbrough, and Townsend (1979) selected four rural Guatemalan villages in which mild to moderate malnutrition was widely evident. The yearly income of families was below $300; most adults did not read nor write; drinking water was contaminated; and there were no indoor sanitary facilities in the villages. Pregnant and nursing women and their children from birth to seven years received nutritional supplementation twice daily, at a central facility, on demand. Residents in two of the villages received a highly nutritious, protein-calorie drink. The other two villages received a drink containing fewer calories but no protein. Three categories of 3-, 4-, and 5-year-olds were identified, based on their caloric supplementation for three-

month periods since conception. Children were tested on batteries appropriate for each age group. Learning, memory, perceptual analysis, reasoning, response style, and cognitive style were among the abilities assessed. At each age-level children who were more adequately nourished obtained significantly higher composite scores. Significant differences due to supplementation were found for all three age levels on the Vocabulary Naming and the Draw-a-Line Slowly tests. Level of supplementation was related to performance differences on the Embedded Figures, Sentence Memory, Vocabulary Recognition, and Reversal Discrimination Learning tasks for at least two age groups.

Both prenatal and postnatal supplementation was associated significantly and independently with the cognitive measures at ages three and four, suggesting that adequate nourishment during these periods may contribute separately to later mental development. Differences in children's performance were unrelated to degree of parental cooperation, or village differences. Measures of family economic level, and opportunities for learning and stimulation, as well as nutritional supplementation were related to children's mental development. Adequate nutrition alone did not account for the differences observed in performance but it did appear to make a unique contribution. Even when children of the same mother were compared, the better nourished outperformed the less well-nourished. However, children who both received less supplement and whose family socioeconomic status was lower were more likely to perform poorly.

The individual and combined effects of early nutritional supplementation and a home-based educational program on development were assessed in a second major study (Herrera, et al. 1980). Four hundred fifty Colombian families with young children at nutritional risk were selected; mothers began the program during their second trimester of pregnancy. The average family size was 5.1 persons; most lived in no more than two rooms. Fewer than 10 percent of the mothers and 20 percent of the fathers had obtained more than a primary-grade education. At entry, maternal food intake was at least one standard deviation below the recommended calorie/protein allowance for pregnant Colombian women. Intakes were very low in protein, calories, and other nutrients. All program and control families received free obstetrical and pediatric care.

Participants were randomly assigned to one of six service programs: nutritional supplementation beginning when target infants were six months and continuing to age three; nutritional supplementation from the second trimester of pregnancy to the infants' six-month birthday; nutritional supplementation from the second trimester to the infants' third birthday; a home-based education program from birth to age three; nutritional supplementation beginning during the second trimester, with home visitation beginning at birth and both continuing to age three; and a control group receiving only medical services.

The nutritional supplement was provided to all family members and consisted of dry milk, bread, vegetable oil, and vitamins. Duryea (a food made of rice, soybeans, corn, and milk) was provided for weaned infants. The supplement accounted for a portion of the daily recommended dietary allowance. A nutritionist demonstrated the use of the supplement, visited regularly to consult with parents, and monitored the amount of unused supplement. The researchers estimated that during pregnancy mothers consumed 490 of the 850 calories and 26 grams of the 39 grams of protein provided daily. This was a gain of 133 calories per day and 20 grams of protein.

The home-based education program used was the Ypsilanti Carnegie Infant Education model (Lambie, Bond, and Weikart 1974). Families were visited by paraprofessionals twice weekly for about one hour and shown how to use developmentally appropriate activities with their infants.

Nutritional supplementation was associated with significantly fewer stillbirths and lower mortality for newborns. The birth weights of supplemented and unsupplemented girls were no different, although the supplemented male group weighed 95 grams more than unsupplemented males. Those pregnant women whose initial diet approached the Recommended Dietary Allowance (RDA) had heavier newborns. For these women, the supplement increased the amount and quality of protein they ate. However among pregnant women whose initial intake of calories and protein was substantially below the RDA, supplementation had no effect on birth weight.

Differences in newborns' behavior due to supplementation were also reported. When a checkerboard was repeatedly shown to newborns, those supplemented were more likely to habituate, or to look at the figure for increasingly shorter periods, evidencing greater efficiency in processing visual information. Unsupplemented females appeared less efficient at habituating than supplemented females or either of the male groups. Lasley and Klein (1980) also found that malnourished six-month-old Guatemalan infants were less efficient in processing visual stimuli.

Herrera, et al. (1980) reported that supplementation was associated with significant differences in Griffith locomotor, personal-social, eye-hand coordination, and performance scores as well as total scores at 4, 6, 12, and 18 months. Infants in the home visitation program scored significantly higher on personal-social, speech-language, and eye-hand coordination subscales and the full scale. (In this study infant stimulation but not supplementation enhanced language development, while supplementation but not stimulation improved locomotor development.)

The influence of malnutrition interacts with aspects of the home environment to affect the child's mental development. Richardson (1976) studied the intellectual development of 74 Jamaican boys six to ten years old who had been hospitalized for severe malnutrition during their first two years of life. The children were inpatients for an average of eight weeks and follow-up visits by nurses were made up to two years afterwards. Parents were interviewed to assess socioeconomic factors including caretaker capability, home furnishings and appliances, and degree of intellectual stimulation. Children who were chronically malnourished were from homes rated lower in these factors.

Richardson compared malnourished children with a group of classmates or neighbors matched on sex, race, and age. An episode of severe malnutrition was especially detrimental for the intellectual performance of children from less favorable social backgrounds and who were chronically undernourished (short-for-age). However when a child from a more favorable social background with a history of being well-nourished (tall-for-age) did experi-

103

ence an episode of severe malnutrition the effect on intelligence was much smaller. Richardson concluded that the effects of severe malnutrition were most severe when this occurred in the context of lower levels of stimulation, greater poverty, and chronic undernutrition. This is comparable to Sameroff and Chandler's (1975) findings that the possible negative developmental consequences of prematurity are moderated by the quality of the infants' home environment.

Richardson (1976) also found that the entire group of severely malnourished children performed more poorly than those children never hospitalized for malnutrition. In an earlier report, Hertzig, Birch, Richardson, and Tizard (1972) found that the severely malnourished children obtained intelligence scores lower than those of a never-hospitalized comparison group, whose scores were lower in turn than the classmate/yardmate comparison group. Hertzig, et al. (1980) suggested that the siblings of a child hospitalized for malnutrition are more likely to experience chronic undernourishment.

The Nutritional Status of U.S. Children

Malnutrition and chronic undernutrition are not unknown in this country. While they may be less common, when they do occur the consequences may be no less severe. Just how well nourished are children here? Are some children at nutritional risk?

The Ten-State Nutrition Survey (U.S. Department of Health, Education and Welfare 1972) in 1968–1970, sampled approximately 40,000 people from five high-income and five low-income states. Demographic, clinical, anthropometric, biochemical, and dietary data were collected. For the preschool and early elementary children surveyed, poor nutrition increased as income decreased, especially for Blacks and Hispanics. Yet irrespective of ethnicity, more undersized children were found among the low-income children than among other income groups. There were also more low-income children with low levels of hemoglobin (an index of iron anemia). For all age groups and both sexes, hemoglobin values were significantly lower for Blacks and Hispanics. Deficient levels were found in 1.8 percent of the Whites, 7.6 percent of the Blacks,

and 8.3 percent of the Hispanics studied. When those having low iron levels were considered, the percentages increased: 13.8 percent of Whites, 29.8 percent of Blacks, and 12.3 percent of Hispanics. Of the pregnant and nursing women surveyed three times more Blacks than Whites or Hispanics had hemoglobin levels of less than 11 gm/100 ml, evidencing iron anemia. Kotz (1979) reported that many Native American children, especially in the South and Southwest also experience serious nutritional problems. Owen, Dram, Garry, Lowe, and Lubin (1974) collected data on over 5000 children ages one to six. Their national probability sample included 80 percent White, 14 percent Black, and 5 percent Hispanic children. Teams of investigators collected community relations, demographic, dietary, clinical, laboratory, and anthropometric data. The evidence of overt nutritional deficiencies were minimal. However, many more low-income children had low hemoglobin values, low dietary intake, and were small for their age. The diets of many, while not poor in quality, were low in quantity. These data were comparable to those from the Ten-State survey; in both low-income children were more likely to be at nutritional risk.

The first Health and Nutrition Examination Survey (HANES) was conducted in the U.S. from 1971–1974 (U.S. Department of Health, Education and Welfare 1974, 1979). Additional data are still to be analyzed and reported. The sample included people from 1 to 74 years old with approximately 1600 children under age 6. Dietary, clinical, dental, anthropometric, and biochemical data were collected, and findings have generally been in agreement with the other surveys. Low-income preschool children were slightly smaller and had lower caloric consumption than their counterparts from higher-income levels. Consistently low caloric intakes result in poor growth. There were no classic signs of protein deficiency found among the children. However it is likely that some of the protein consumed was used to meet energy needs not met by calories, rather than for growth. The low mean iron intake observed for low-income Black preschoolers was due to insufficient total food intake rather than to low intake of iron-rich foods.

In rural southwest Mississippi, Koh and Caples (1979) found the caloric intake of all groups was well below recommended allow-

104

ances. These data were collected in 1974 from 250 Black households with annual incomes below $1,000. The findings for low energy consumption were consistent with the Ten-State and HANE surveys.

Valentine and Valentine (1972) conducted a participant observation study of low-income Blacks in a northeastern city. All but two of the families studied received Aid to Families with Dependent Children (AFDC), with an average income for a family of four approximating $3,000 yearly. The investigators recorded what the infant or child ate during at least one day from waking to sleeping; dietary histories were also collected through interviews. No data about height, weight, or biochemical measures of iron anemia were collected, so it is not possible to say whether children would be at nutritional risk on these measures. The Valentines concluded that the children did have adequate diets; however, they did not seem to consider the children's utilization of nutrients. Several children whose parents were surveyed received cow's milk as early as three months of age, a few as early as one month. Plain cow's milk without added modifiers such as syrup is not utilized well by most infants less than six months of age because of its high protein and mineral content. Therefore while the infants in this study may have had an adequate intake of nutrients, complete utilization of these nutrients is questionable.

Research in the United States

The pattern of the findings from U.S. research on malnutrition parallels that conducted in developing countries. Chase and Martin (1970) compared 19 Denver preschoolers who had been hospitalized for malnutrition when under one year of age with a control group matched for birth date, birth weight, sex, and socioeconomic status. Fifteen of the children in each group were Hispanic. The malnourished infants were all free of organic disease and had no neonatal problems, although 17 of the 19 were low birth weight (less than 2,000 grams). No significant group differences were found for family variables: number of children, use of community resources, housekeeping standards and practices, community relations, family relations, and economic functioning. However, more malnourished children had family members who were in poor health than did control children. The homes of the malnourished children also were rated as less stimulating and less supportive of development. When the children were tested three-and-one-half years after hospitalization, the malnourished children were less well-grown than were controls. Their scores on the Yale Revised Developmental Examination were significantly lower than controls. And their subscale scores in gross motor, fine motor, adaptive, language, and personal-social areas were also lower.

A second study confirms that even in this country some children are at nutritional risk. Vietze, Falsey, O'Connor, Sandler, Sherrod, and Altemeier (1980) conducted a prospective study of child maltreatment. Seven percent of the group of 500 had infants who were subsequently identified as failing to gain sufficient weight. These 35 infants did not evidence either severe growth retardation or have other organic problems, but were designated as non-organic failure-to-thrive. For one-third of these children, the failure to gain weight was problematic enough to warrant hospitalization. No differences in demographic variables, attitudinal variables, and very few differences in mother-infant interaction during the neonatal period were found to distinguish the subsequently malnourished children's families from the comparison families. However, the former infants were more likely to be younger in gestational age and lighter in birth weight. During feeding, mothers also looked less at their newborn infants than did mothers whose infants later grew well.

Winick, Meyer, and Harris (1975) reported some of the most dramatic evidence about the ability of children to recover from early nutritional insult, given a supportive environment. They identified well-nourished and malnourished Korean female infants who had been adopted by middle-class U.S. parents. All children were full term, had no organic problems or chronic illnesses at birth, were admitted to the adoption service before age two and placed by age three, had adoptive parents who agreed to participate, and were current U.S. residents. Using both weight-for-age and height-for-age when admitted to the adoption agency, three groups were constituted: malnourished infants, moderately nourished infants, and well-nourished infants. Diverse estimates of intelligence, school achievement, as well as height and weight were obtained from school records. At follow-up all children surpassed

105

the fiftieth percentile for height and for weight for Korean children. No group differences in weight for the three groups were significant although the well-nourished group was significantly taller than the malnourished group. A comparable difference was found for both IQ and for achievement scores, although mean scores were in the average range for all three groups on both types of measures. The moderately nourished group also had significantly higher achievement test scores than the malnourished group. No data about the quality of the children's home learning environment were gathered, nor were data about differential placement practices.

An experimental study provided further evidence that specific nutritional supplementation improves performance on developmental measures. Honig and Oski (1978) identified iron-deficient Black and White infants (9 to 26 months of age) and randomly assigned them to an experimental or control group. Groups were equivalent in parental education, and in infant weight, age, and measures of iron levels (i.e., hemoglobin, serum iron, and transferrin saturation). The Bayley Scales of Infant Development (mental, motor, and behavior record) were administered by an examiner not informed of group assignment. After testing, experimental infants received an injection of supplemental iron and the controls were given an injection of a saline solution. Infants were retested five to eight days later; this time the control group received the iron supplement after testing. Supplemented infants had gained scores that were significantly higher than controls on the mental scale but not on the motor scale. The scores for both groups were higher at the second testing; whether these differences were significant was not reported. A significant correlation for supplemented infants between initial iron levels and mental score gains ($r = - .72$) was found, with infants having the lowest initial levels of iron evidencing the largest gains. Honig and Oski also reported that after iron supplementation infants were more likely to be rated as normally reactive, rather than either over- or underreactive. Pollitt, Greenfield, and Leibel (1979) appropriately cautioned in the interpretation of these findings; one can most validly conclude that infants' test performance rather than their mental development was enhanced by one supplementation.

Iron deficiency also may be implicated in the poorer intelligence test performance of preschool children (Sulzer, Hansche, and Koenig 1973). Over 300 4- and 5-year-old Black Head Start children were administered the Kahn Intelligence test, a picture vocabulary test, and tasks assessing reaction time, recall, and endurance. Iron deficiency was associated with significantly lower scores on the intelligence and vocabulary tests, and slower reaction time on one task. No significant differences between anemic and normal children were found on most SES variables used (i.e., parents' education and occupation, household size, housing characteristics, health, aspirations for child, and mothers' child-rearing practices). However, anemic children had fathers with significantly lower levels of education. This difference may reflect the greater economic well-being of the non-anemic children. Recent data suggest that as years of schooling completed increased, median earnings for Blacks also increased (U.S. Commission on Civil Rights 1978).

A report about the effects of participation in the Women, Infants and Children (WIC) nutrition programs in 13 states indicated that many children entered the program with iron deficiency anemia, significant growth retardation, and some evidence of overweight (Center for Disease Control 1977). Those children who remained in the program for 12 months ($N = 5,692$) manifested considerable improvement in iron levels. Some evidenced no change; however the percentage of those whose iron levels increased was three times the percentage of those whose levels decreased. The greatest changes in iron were observed for those having the lowest initial levels.

Cook, Hulburt, and Radke (1976) compared the nutritional status of Maine Head Start children with private nursery school children. Three day food records, anthropometric, and biochemical measures were obtained in the fall and the spring of the school year. No differences were found in the anthropometric measures. The Head Start program did have a positive effect on nutrient and energy intakes of the children in regular attendance and their levels of intake improved from fall to spring. Home dietary patterns did not seem to change, despite a nutrition education program.

Summary

1. Significant numbers of children in this country have diets which are low in quantity although they appear to be adequate in general quality. These mildly undernourished children tend to be small-for-age and are more likely to be from low-income families. The consequences of such mild undernutrition in intellectual development and performance on developmental measures is far from clear-cut, and appears to be only weakly associated with differences in such measures.

Some children in this country also appear to manifest iron anemia. Two of the studies reviewed here examined the impact of this specific deficiency on development and raise the possibility that iron deficiency may be related to performance on infant developmental tests and on preschool picture vocabulary measures. However, in an extensive review of the effects of iron deficiency, Leibel, Greenfield, and Pollit (1979) suggested that the entire body of evidence available to date does not provide firm evidence that iron deficiency is associated with significantly lower intelligence, learning, attention, or motivation. Much more evidence, however, is needed about the role of mild undernutrition and specific nutritional deficiencies with respect to U.S. children's development and functioning.

2. Severe and moderate malnutrition, particularly that found in developing countries, is associated with poorer performance on developmental, intelligence, and vocabulary tests, as well as on some learning and memory tasks.

3. In the research conducted to date we have been unable to separate the effects of malnutrition from those of other important environmental factors: parental behavior, the family's general economic well-being, and even characteristics of the malnourished child. Perhaps due to greater poverty, malnourished children are more likely to grow up in less stimulating home environments. (This alone we know influences development and intelligence.) Yet the consequences of an episode of severe malnutrition may be particularly detrimental for children when their home environment is less stimulating.

4. Does nutritional supplementation make a difference in children's development? In developing countries supplementation for moderate malnutrition in children results in improved performance on developmental and intellectual measures, especially when both supplementation and educational experiences are provided. We have little comparable evidence of supplementation programs on the development and nutritional status of U.S. children. This is an area where carefully designed and executed research is very much needed.

Implications

When examined cumulatively, using evidence from developing countries and our own, the research indicates that nutrition plays an important role in children's development, including their mental development. While to date we have been unable to adequately separate out the unique contribution of nutrient intake to intelligence, learning, and other areas of functioning, adequate nutrition is one of the factors which supports more optimal child development. From this perspective the continuing importance of comprehensive child development programs with effective nutrition components should be clear. We will need to ensure that our nutrition education programs and feeding practices assure that all the children we serve are well-nourished and they and their parents are knowledgeable about optimal food consumption practices.

This will require us to establish and maintain close, ongoing working relationships with nutritionists in community health centers, hospitals, home economics extension programs—wherever the expertise is available in our communities. Our classroom programs are likely more effective in feeding children well during the hours they are in attendance. However, we will probably be much less successful in helping parents to effectively utilize and exploit the food resources they have available. A wide range of materials are available for use in nutrition education programs (The Nutrition Foundation 1977). Involving children and parents in food preparation is one of several very effective ways to accomplish this (Wanamaker, Hearn, and Richarz 1979; Endres and Rockwell 1980).

We will need to become more systematic about screening children for nutritional prob-

107

lems. This may involve routine biochemical tests for iron anemia for all children enrolled, dietary records (including systematic observation during meals and snacks) on selected children, and accurate measures of height and weight. While inadequate intake will be a problem for some, obesity may be problematic for others. If this information is gathered across several years we can begin to document the effectiveness of our supplemental feeding and nutrition education programs.

Gutherie (1976) found that a relatively few measures accurately identified those U.S. preschoolers at nutritional risk. Data from biochemical measures of transferrin saturation (for iron anemia) and dietary iron values from a two-day food record would identify the majority of all children considered at nutritional risk. Then if dietary intake data for calories, calcium, vitamin C, thiamine, and vitamin A were also included, all children at risk would be selected. Gutherie emphasized that this would be an appropriate screening procedure even though it does not include all the measures necessary for a complete nutrition assessment.

We need much more evidence about effective strategies of nutrition education for both parents and children as well as research about the effects of comprehensive child development programs on children's nutritional status. Those programs with ready resources to undertake this research may well be the university child development centers based in colleges of home economics, consumer science, or human ecology. Research activity in early childhood education seems to have entered a more quiescent period; this is an area crying out for additional data.

Other important implications are related to social and governmental policy. Continued advocacy for comprehensive programs is essential; but we also need to insure that families can adequately feed their children. Important federal services include child nutrition programs for day care and residential facilities; school food programs such as school breakfast, lunch, and the supplemental milk program; Head Start; special supplemental food programs for women, infants, and children (WIC); family food assistance programs including food stamps; and food distribution (Egan 1979). Severely diminished funding for many of these programs may well be a threat to low-income children's development. Those programs which enable all parents to provide an adequate diet for their children are as essential to children's well-being and their bright futures as are quality day care and effective parent education programs.

REFERENCES

Brozek, J. "Nutrition, Malnutrition, and Behavior." In *Annual Review of Psychology,* Vol. 29, eds. M. R. Rosenzweig and L. W. Porter. Palo Alto, Calif.: Annual Reviews, 1978.

Center for Disease Control. *Analysis of Nutritional Indices for Selected WIC Participants.* Atlanta: U.S. Department of Health, Education and Welfare, Public Health Service, 1977.

Chase, H. P. "Undernutrition and Growth and Development of the Human Brain." In *Malnutrition and Intellectual Development,* ed. J. D. Lloyd-Still. Littleton, Mass.: Publishing Sciences Group, 1976.

Chase, H. P., and Martin, H. P. "Undernutrition and Child Development." *New England Journal of Medicine* 282 (1970): 933–939.

Cravioto, J.; Birch, H. G.; De Licardie, E.; Rosales, L.; and Vega, L. "The Ecology of Growth and Development in a Mexican Pre-industrial Community Report 1: Method and Findings From Birth to One Month of Age." *Monographs of the Society for Research in Child Development* 129 (1969).

Cravioto, J., and De Licardie, E. R. "Nutrition, Mental Development and Learning." In *Human Growth, Vol. III: Neurobiology and Nutrition,* eds. F. Falkner and J. M. Tanner. New York: Plenum, 1979.

Cook, R. A.; Hulburt, R. A.; and Radke, F. H. "Nutritional Status of Head Start and Nursery School Children." *Journal of the American Dietetic Association* 68 (1976): 120–132.

Egan, M. C. "Federal Nutrition Support Programs for Children." In *Pediatric Nutrition Handbook,* ed. Committee on Nutrition, AAP. Evanston, Ill.: American Academy of Pediatrics, 1979.

Endres, J. B., and Rockwell, R. C. *Food, Nutrition, and the Young Child.* St. Louis: Mosby, 1980.

Engle, P. L.; Irwin, M.; Klein, R. E.; Yarbrough, C.; and Townsend, J. W. "Nutrition and Mental Development in Children." In *Nutrition: Pre- and Post-Natal Development,* ed. M. Winick. New York: Plenum, 1979.

Graham, G. G. "Environmental Factors Affecting the Growth of Children." *American Journal of Clinical Nutrition* 25 (1972): 1184–1188.

Gutherie, H. A. "Nutritional Status Measures as

Predictors of Nutritional Risk in Preschool Children." *American Journal of Clinical Nutrition* 29 (1976): 1048–1050.

Guyton, A. C. *Textbook of Medical Physiology.* Philadelphia: W. B. Saunders, 1976.

Herrera, M. G.; Mora, J. O.; Christiansen, N.; Ortiz, N.; Clement, J.; Vuori, L.; Waber, D.; De Paredes, B.; and Wagner, M. "Effects of Nutritional Supplementation and Early Education on Physical and Cognitive Development." In *Life-Span Developmental Psychology: Intervention,* eds. R. R. Turner and H. W. Reese. New York: Academic, 1980.

Hertzig, M.; Birch, H. G.; Richardson, S. A.; and Tizard, J. "Intellectual Levels of School-Age Children Severely Malnourished During the First Two Years of Life." *Pediatrics* 49 (1972): 814–824.

Honig, A. S., and Oski, F. A. "Developmental Scores of Iron Deficient Infants and the Effects of Therapy." *Infant Behavior and Development* 1 (1978): 168–176.

Koh, E. T., and Caples, V. "Nutrient Intake of Low-Income, Black Families in Southwestern Mississippi." *Journal of the American Dietetic Association* 75 (1979): 665–670.

Kotz, N. "Hunger in America: The Federal Response." In *Hunger in America: Ten Years Later,* U.S. Congress Senate, Committee on Agriculture, Nutrition and Forestry, Subcommittee on Nutrition. Washington, D.C.: U.S. Government Printing Office, 1979.

Lambie, D. Z.; Bond, J. T.; and Weikart, D. P. *Home Teaching with Mothers and Infants.* Ypsilanti, Mich.: High/Scope, 1974.

Lancaster, J. B. "The Evolution of the Human Family." *Dimensions* 9 (1980): 8–11.

Lasley, R. F., and Klein, R. E. "Fixation of the Standard and Novelty Preference in Six-Month Old Well and Malnourished Infants." *Merrill-Palmer Quarterly* 26 (1980): 171–178.

Leibel, R. L.; Greenfield, D. B.; and Pollitt, E. "Iron Deficiency: Behavior and Brain Biochemistry." In *Nutrition: Pre- and Post-natal Development,* ed. M. Winick. New York: Plenum, 1979.

National Academy of Sciences, Food and Nutrition Board. "The Relationship of Nutrition to Brain Development and Behavior." *Nutrition Today* 9, no. 4 (1974): 12–13, 16–17.

The Nutrition Foundation. *Index of Nutrition Education Materials.* Washington, D.C.: The Nutrition Foundation, 1977.

Owen, G. M.; Dram, K. M.; Garry, P. J.; Lowe, J. E.; and Lubin, A. H. "A Study of Nutritional Status of Preschool Children in the United States, 1968–1970." *Pediatrics* 53 (1974): 597–646 (Supplement).

Pollitt, E.; Greenfield, D.; and Leibel, R. "Significance of Bayley Scale Score Changes Following Iron Therapy: II." *Infant Behavior and Development* 2 (1979): 235–237.

Read, M. S. "Malnutrition, Hunger and Behavior. I.: Malnutrition and Learning." *Journal of the American Dietetic Association* 63 (1973): 379–385.

Richardson, S. A. "The Relation of Severe Malnutrition in Infancy to the Intelligence of School Children with Differing Life Histories." *Pediatric Research* 10 (1976): 57–61.

Sameroff, A. J., and Chandler, M. J. "Reproductive Risk and the Continuum of Caretaking Casualty." In *Review of Child Development Research,* Vol. 4, ed. F. D. Horowitz. Chicago: University of Chicago Press, 1975.

Stoch, M. B., and Smythe, P. M. "Fifteen Year Developmental Study on Effects of Severe Undernutrition During Infancy on Subsequent Physical Growth and Intellectual Functioning." *Archives of Disease in Childhood* 51 (1976): 327–336.

Sulzer, J. L.; Hansche, W. J.; and Koenig, F. "Nutrition and Behavior In Head Start Children: Results from the Tulane Study." In *Nutrition, Development and Social Behavior,* ed. D. J. Kallen. Washington, D.C.: U.S. Government Printing Office, DHEW Publication No. (NIH) 73-242, 1973.

U.S. Commission on Civil Rights. *Social Indicators of Equality for Minorities and Women.* Washington, D.C.: U.S. Commission on Civil Rights, 1978.

U.S. Department of Health, Education and Welfare, Health Services and Mental Health Administration. *Ten-State Nutrition Survey 1968–1970.* Washington, D.C.: U.S. Government Printing Office, DHEW Publication No. (HSM) 72-8134, 1972.

U.S. Department of Health, Education and Welfare, Public Health Service, Health Resources Administration. *Preliminary Findings of the First Health and Nutrition Examination Survey, United States, 1971–72: Dietary Intake and Biochemical Findings.* Rockville, Md.: National Center for Health Statistics, DHEW Publication No. (HRA) 74-1219-1, 1974.

U.S. Department of Health, Education and Welfare, Public Health Service, Office of Health Research, Statistics and Technology. *Dietary Intake Source Data, United States 1971–1974.* Hyattsville, Md.: National Center for Health Statistics, DHEW Publication No. (PHS) 79-1221, 1979.

Valentine, B. L., and Valentine, C. A. "Poor People, Good Food, and Fat Babies: Observations on Dietary Behavior and Nutrition Among Low-Income, Urban Afro-American Infants and Children." In *Practices of Low-Income Families in Feeding Infants and Small Children with Par-*

ticular Interest to Cultural Groups, eds. S. J. Fomon and T. A. Anderson. Rockville, Md.: U.S. Department of Health, Education and Welfare, 1972.

Vietze, P. M.; Falsey, S.; O'Connor, S.; Sandler, H.; Sherrod, K.; and Altemeier, W. A. "Newborn Behavioral and Interactional Characteristics of Nonorganic Failure-To-Thrive Infants." In High Risk Infants and Children, eds. T. Field, S. Goldberg, D. Stern, and A. M. Sostek. New York: Academic Press, 1980.

Wanamaker, N.; Hearn, K.; and Richarz. S. More Than Graham Crackers: Nutrition Education and Food Preparation with Young Children. Washington, D.C.: National Association for the Education of Young Children, 1979.

Winick, M. Malnutrition and Brain Development. New York: Oxford University Press, 1976.

Winick, M.; Meyer, K.; and Harris, R. "Malnutrition and Environmental Enrichment by Early Adoption." Science 190 (1975): 1173–1175.

Delia H. Baxter, Ph.D., is Assistant Professor, Department of Community Health Nutrition, Georgia State University, Atlanta. She is on the Nutrition Advisory Committee for the Atlanta Parent-Child Center. She coordinates laboratory experiences in maternal-infant and child nutrition for junior students in five day care centers in Atlanta and teaches a child development course for community nutrition and medical assistants students.

Joseph H. Stevens, Jr., Ph.D., is Professor, Department of Early Childhood Education, Georgia State University.

We are most appreciative of the critical comments provided by Sara Hunt and Ronald Weinstein on an earlier version of this review.

Multiple Voices for Advocacy: The Story of WIC

(Special Supplemental Food Program for Women, Infants, and Children)

Mary A. Jensen

Views differ on the extent to which governmental agencies should provide nutritional assistance to people in the United States. In a land of plenty, competitive food prices, and numerous charitable groups, some people contend that adequate nutrition is readily available to all. Others point to the rise in number of children living in poverty in our country and the nutritional risks associated with poverty.

A key governmental response to concern about adequate child nutrition has been the WIC (Special Supplemental Food Program for Women, Infants and Children) Program. WIC is a federally funded program that provides nutritional foods and nutrition education to women who are pregnant, breastfeeding, or have recently delivered a baby, and to infants and children up to the age of five. To be eligible, participants must establish nutritional need through a medical exam and must meet income guidelines.

The WIC program is a classic example of how advocacy can dramatically affect policy making and program expansion, even in times of fiscal restraint. WIC began in 1972 as a $20 million pilot program aimed at a few thousand participants. By 1985, it was serving approximately 3.1 million participants and had a budget of more than $1.5 billion (Scheffler, 1987). This dramatic expansion cannot be attributed to any single cause or to the isolated efforts of a few. Many forces coalesced and contributed to the establishment and growth of WIC: prevalent social values and beliefs, political climate, economic conditions, media attention, constituency letter writing, opportune research findings, court decisions, and "umbrella" legislative packages. Also, diverse voices at many levels shaped the present WIC program: farm interests, antipoverty groups, antihunger groups, social service providers, lawmakers, judges, administrators in the Department of Agriculture, evaluators, health clinics, child advocacy groups, public interest law firms, and so on. The interactive dynamics of this process involved numerous decisions by a broad array of people who had various agendas and value systems. To understand the establishment and expansion of WIC, we must consider the political, social, and economic contexts of participants' decisions, the complex interactions among various forces, and shifting influences and alliances (Hayes, 1982). This article traces and examines the changing issues and various forms of advocacy in the history of the WIC program.

Setting the Stage for the WIC Program

Several federal initiatives that began in the mid-1930s set precedents for today's child nutrition programs. During the Roosevelt administration, the U.S. Department of Agriculture (USDA) offered grants to a number of school lunch programs reaching up to 400,000 children by 1941. The USDA also piloted a food stamp program in Rochester, New York that eventually spread to other parts of the country reaching about 4 million people (Nelson, 1982). Congress did not continue support for the food stamp program in the 1940s, but did pass the National School Lunch Act (P.L. 79-396) in 1946, making the program a permanent piece of legislation. Under this act, the lunch programs that received monies and commodities were required to (1) meet USDA nutritional standards, (2) be nonprofit, (3) be available to all children offering free or reduced rate lunches to the needy, and (4) provide some matching funds (Committee on Education and Labor, 1987).

Another nutritional assistance program

that affects today's children is the Food Stamp Program. Roughly half of the program's participants are children (Nelson, 1982). The Kennedy administration revived the program as a series of pilot projects in 1961. In 1964, Congress passed the Food Stamp Act (amended in 1977, P.L. 95-113), giving legitimacy to guidelines established by the Kennedy administration for the pilot programs. During the late 1960s, concerns grew about the lack of participation among the poorest of the poor. After some eligibility reforms and a downward swing in the economy, participation rates leaped upward. (The number of participants was 2.9 million in 1969 and 18.9 million in 1975.) But, by the mid-1970s, the public began to voice the opinion that food stamps were too easy to obtain and that lax eligibility review led to cheating and fraud. Although food stamps can be used to purchase almost any food item, some thought that participants should not be using tax dollars to buy steaks. These voices began to dominate in the 1980s, leading to a series of changes in eligibility and benefit regulations as well as to spending cuts in fiscal year 1982 (Berry, 1984).

A third federal nutrition program that has set precedents for WIC and that reaches many young children is the Child Care Food Program (CCFP). This program began in 1968 as a pilot program under the National School Lunch Act. It expanded and in 1978 became a permanent piece of legislation (P.L. 95-627). CCFP provides federal reimbursement for two meals and one snack to nonprofit child care centers (or to child care centers where at least 25 percent of the child care is subsidized by Title XX Social Services monies) and to day care homes. To be eligible, centers or homes must be licensed or approved by federal, state, or local standards. For centers, reimbursement rates are based on individual family income and are similar to those for school lunches and breakfasts. Also like the school lunch program, food served in day care centers or homes has to meet USDA nutritional requirements (Committee on Agriculture, Nutrition, and Forestry, 1983). Like WIC, this program has grown dramatically in recent years, perhaps as a result of the growing numbers of mothers in the work force and the growing need for child care. (For a comparison of funding and participation levels in these four major child nutrition programs, see Table 1.)

The Supplemental Food Program: A Precursor of WIC

Reminiscent of values espoused during the Roosevelt administration, the Johnson administration promised to build a Great Society through domestic legislation. Spending for the Vietnam War, however, curtailed Johnson's plans. By the mid-1960s, nutritional aid to poor families was being provided by the revival of the Food Stamp Program. Also, the comprehensive Child Nutrition Act of 1966 provided food for children in school or institutional settings. Neither of these efforts proved to be sufficient, however. In 1967 and 1968, the astonishing extent of hunger in the United States was discovered by the media, researchers, government officials, and the public. CBS televised its much acclaimed documentary, "Hunger in America." Researchers published *Hunger, U.S.A.* and *Your Daily Bread.* Both charged the government with ineptitude in meeting the needs of the poor. Senate hearings were held on malnutrition in Mississippi. Among those who testified was Robert Coles of Harvard University, well known for his work in Mississippi with poor children. At the hearings, he raised the question of possible permanent physical damage in infants and young children caused by malnutrition. The public also generated political pressure through the 1968 Poor People's Campaign and their march on Washington (Nelson, 1982).

In response, the Johnson administration initiated regulations for a $15 million Supplemental Food Program (SFP) that supplied commodity food packages to pregnant and postpartum women, infants, and young children. The legal authority for creation of this program came from an act in 1935 for commodity distribution to low-income groups. Now known as the Commodity Supplemental Food Program, this program continues to operate under the Food and Nutrition Service, but participation has dropped since the start of the WIC program (Committee on Agriculture, Nutrition, and Forestry, 1983).

At the beginning of his administration in 1969, Nixon showed interest in the congressional hearings on hunger, particularly testimony regarding relationships between malnutrition and prenatal brain damage or infant retardation. Plans were made to expand the Supplemental Food Pro-

TABLE 1 *Federal Appropriations and Selected Participation Figures (in Millions) in Four Major Nutrition Programs Serving Children, Fiscal Years 1981–1986*

Program	$ in FY 1981 (enrollment)	$ in FY 1982 (enrollment)	$ in FY 1983 (enrollment)	$ in FY 1984 (enrollment)	$ in FY 1985 (enrollment)	$ in FY 1986* (enrollment)
WIC (less than 50% eligible)	900.0 (2.1)	904.3 (2.2)	1,160.0 (2.3)	1,360.0 (3.0)	1,500.0 (3.1)	1,560.0
Child Care Food Program	290.5 (.78)	276.9 (.87)	332.5	356.9	434.9 (1.03)	483.5
National School Lunch Program (56% of eligible)	2,372.5	2,045.3	2,353.9	2,556.3	2,656.0	2,734.3 (23.7)
Food Stamp Program ($^2/_3$ of eligible)	11,308.0	11,117.0	12,734.0	12,470.0 (21.0)	12,599.0	12,600.0

Sources: Committee on Agriculture, Nutrition, and Forestry, 1983; Committee on Education and Labor, 1987.

* Estimated funding level

gram (SFP), but SFP suffered two major setbacks. The first was a study of the local program in Washington, DC. Results indicated that distribution of commodity parcels accounted for 35 percent of program costs, transportation problems of participants reduced parcel pickup to 60 percent, and all family members ate the foods. These findings led to a decision by the Food and Nutrition Service to either consolidate the Supplemental Food Program with the Food Stamp Program or to transform SFP into a voucher program. In 1970, the Food and Nutrition Service started a pilot voucher program for low-income, pregnant women and infants in five areas of the country. The women received booklets of $.25 coupons for milk, infant formula, and baby cereal. While pregnant, women received $5 coupon booklets each month. After giving birth, they received $10 coupon booklets each month for one year. Those referred by local health clinics as well as welfare recipients were eligible for the program.

A second major setback for SFP came when evaluator David Call found that the pilot voucher program failed to significantly increase the quantity of formula or milk intakes or the nutrient intakes in infants and that it did not increase the milk intakes of women. With the results of this second study in hand, the Food and Nutrition Service was convinced that the Supplemental Food Program was ineffective and was prepared to abandon the program. Politics, however, slowed the process down. Constituents and congressional representatives were still expressing concerns about hunger among pregnant women and infants. Moreover, research was accumulating that confirmed a relationship between nutrition and mental development. It was this growing body of research as well as the political climate that spawned the WIC Program (Nelson, 1982). (See Table 2 for an overview of key events and advocacy strategies in the initiation of WIC.)

TABLE 2 *Time Line of Key Events and Advocacy Strategies in the Creation and Expansion of WIC*

1966	1967	1968	1970	1971	1972
Child Nutrition Act passed	Senate expert testimony on malnutrition and physical development; TV documentary: "Hunger in America"; research reports on U.S. hunger	Poor People's Campaign and March; Supplemental Food Program (SFP) created	1st negative evaluation: distribution system; pilot voucher program for SFP created	2nd negative evaluation: pilot voucher program; public outcry about hunger persists; research on malnutrition and mental development accumulates	Photos, x-rays, and research testimony on mental development support creation of $20 million WIC program with provision for medical evaluation in Child Nutrition Act

1973	1976	1977	1978	1979
Article in *Redbook* and letter writing; class action suit against USDA for spending slowdown	Class action suit against USDA for spending slowdown (1974–1975); lobbying coalitions formed; 1st medical evaluation = positive	2nd medical evaluation = positive, but calls for more stress on nutrition education	P.L. 95-627 requires states to spend $ on nutrition education	Funding reaches $712.3 million

Establishment and Early Expansion of the WIC Program

In 1972 during Senate hearings on the child nutrition bill, Humphrey introduced an amended bill with a $20 million annual provision for a Special Supplemental Food Program for Women, Infants, and Children (WIC). This proposal was distinct in that it more closely linked food assistance with health care. Unlike previous programs, WIC included: (1) a medical examination and referral rather than income as the chief criterion for eligibility, (2) children up to the age of four, and (3) vouchers for specific foods medically known to be essential for proper nutrition (i.e., protein and vitamins in iron-fortified formula or cereal, fruit juice, milk, cheese, eggs, or vegetable juices). In hearings and a subsequent Senate floor fight, Humphrey dramatized his case with photographs and x-rays of malnourished infants and their underdeveloped brains and with research testimony on the effects of infant malnutrition. When challenged by the conclusions of the Call evaluation, he refuted the methodology of Call's study and pointed out that Call's study did not include medical data. In the end, the child nutrition bill was amended to include a two-year experimental program subject to a medical evaluation prior to reconsideration of any extension. The bill passed both houses of Congress with a veto-proof majority (Nelson, 1982).

In 1973, several advocacy efforts focused attention on the new WIC program. Having been convinced that the Supplemental Food Program was ineffective, the USDA and the Food and Nutrition Service reluctantly began to execute the WIC program (Nelson, 1982). By March, efforts to design the program were under way (Committee on Agriculture, Nutrition, and Forestry, 1983). But during the spring, *Redbook* magazine published a provocative article by Virginia Hardman called "How to Save Babies for Two Dimes a Day." Her article chronicled personal observations of and conversations about efforts at St. Judes Hospital in Memphis to help large numbers of malnourished children. Descriptive accounts supported by photographs of children over time, statistics, medical testimony, and a personal appeal from actor Danny Thomas created a powerful message. The author urged readers to write to Butz, Secretary of Agriculture, to persuade him to end delays in feeding hungry children and to write to their congressional representatives for a copy of the bill containing provisions for WIC. The public responded. About the same time, the Food Research and Action Center, a public interest law firm, learned that the USDA planned to implement WIC in 1973 with only a limited amount of the $40 million allocated for 1973–74 (i.e., $5–6 million). Seeing the potential of WIC as a major feeding program, the firm filed a class action suit on behalf of the beneficiaries to speed up implementation of WIC, charging that funds had been unused or misspent in terms of congressional intent. The suit called for all authorized funds ($40 million) to be spent by the end of June 1974. The effect of this strategy was to double the program's size. In June, the court ordered USDA to publish regulations by July 1973, and in August, ordered USDA to spend all allocated funds by July 1974 (Nelson, 1982).

By the end of 1974, WIC was operating at around $100 million. And in 1975, carryover from 1974 was added to the $100 million allocated. Despite a veto by President Ford, Congress then allocated $250 million annually for WIC over the three-year period of 1976–79 and extended eligibility to include children up to age five. But another USDA slowdown in spending during 1974–75 and USDA's attempt to spread annual spending for 1976 over five quarters rather than four—after changes in federal fiscal year dates—led to another class action being filed. In June 1976, the judge ordered the USDA to spend $687.5 million on the WIC program by September 1978 and to submit quarterly reports on WIC spending and development (Committee on Agriculture, Nutrition, and Forestry, 1983; Nelson, 1982).

Delayed for over a year, the first medical evaluation of WIC (Endozien, Switzer, & Bryan, 1976) was completed and released by the USDA in July 1976. Although the U.S. General Accounting Office had raised questions about the value of results from human nutrition evaluations, these long awaited results were critical for WIC funding deliberations. And unexpectedly, the results of the Endozien study indicated that except for eggs, food intake of all participants increased, and for infants, physical growth and hemoglobin levels increased while anemia decreased. The researchers concluded that the WIC program was a clear-cut success. The methodology and conclusions of the study, however, received much criticism. About the same time, the USDA released another WIC study that noted an increase in health clinic visits for WIC participants, but questioned the value of the nutritional counseling component (Nelson, 1982).

In 1977, the Centers for Disease Control (CDC) in Atlanta completed a third evaluation of WIC for USDA's Food and Nutrition Service. Sensitive to criticism of the Endozien study, CDC carefully noted the delimitations of their study and findings. Children who entered the program were found to have a high prevalence of anemia, delay in linear growth, or excessive weight gain. After a year in the WIC program, these children evidenced improved hematocrit/hemoglobin levels (anemia), gains in weight-to-length ratios and linear growth, and decreases in overweight. Also, the proportion of infants entering the program with low birth weight decreased. Other findings led CDC to recommend that more stress be placed on nutrition education as an adjunct to food assistance (Nelson, 1982). A governmental response to this suggestion came in November 1978 with the passage of P.L. 95-627, which requires states to spend at least one-sixth of their administrative funds on nutrition education activities (Stansfield, 1984).

Although originally proposed as a way to prevent expansion of WIC, the USDA evaluations basically confirmed the convictions of WIC supporters. By 1978 and 1979, funding for the WIC program had become a mother-and-apple-pie issue. Congressional representatives were reluctant to vote against additional funding for an apparently effective program aimed at feeding low-income, pregnant women and babies (Nelson, 1982). In 1978, WIC funding reached $527.3 million, and for 1979, funding rose to $712.3 million (Commit-

Chapter 5

tee on Agriculture, Nutrition, and Forestry, 1983).

The successes and cost-benefits of WIC have been documented many times. For example, a 1979 study by the Harvard School of Public Health concluded that as much as $3 was saved on neonatal/infant medical care for every $1 spent on prenatal care in the WIC program. Nevertheless, WIC evaluation studies continue to encounter skepticism and resistance from some policy makers. For example, a five-year, $5 million study by David Rush found numerous positive outcomes for WIC, but disputes arose when USDA delayed its release, omitted Rush's favorable summaries, and substituted their own compendium of results ("U.S. Accused of Altering Study," 1986). In his study of WIC, Rush found improvements in length of gestation, iron intake for infants, and women's use of prenatal care and their weight gain during pregnancy. He also found that WIC participants spent less on foods away from home and more on WIC-type foods than did the control group. However, WIC participation had no effect on the mother's intent to breast-feed, rate of breastfeeding, or use of tobacco or alcohol. He recommended improvements be made in the health education component of WIC (Committee on Agriculture, Nutrition, and Forestry, 1985).

A number of other studies in recent years have focused on the effects of WIC on anemic children. Perhaps the most comprehensive of these studies was one reported in the *Journal of the American Medical Association* (Centers for Disease Control, 1986). In 1974, CDC established the Pediatric Nutrition Surveillance System to monitor growth and anemia prevalence in low-income children enrolled in programs such as WIC in six selected states. Between 1975 and 1985, CDC found a 60 percent decline in prevalence of anemia which, given the magnitude and consistency of the difference, they primarily attributed to WIC. This conclusion is impressive because anemia can adversely affect intellectual development.

Recent Concerns: Adequacy of Regulations and Effectiveness of State and Local Management

By 1984, WIC was able to serve 3.1 million participants. Census data show, however, that more than 10 million women, infants, and children are income-eligible, and it is estimated that most of these potential participants could meet WIC nutritional risk guidelines (Committee on Agriculture, Nutrition, and Forestry, 1984, 1985). Moreover, of the more than 10 million eligible individuals, an estimated 2.7 million are high-priority cases (pregnant women and infants)—almost the total number now being served (General Accounting Office, 1985).

Current discussions of the merits of WIC tend to focus on regulatory or management needs more than on funding needs. Given the estimated numbers of high-priority cases in our population, concerns have been raised about local systems for determining eligibility, targeting benefits to the most needy, and monitoring vendors (Committee on Agriculture, Nutrition, and Forestry, 1985). According to an investigation of the WIC operations in five states by the General Accounting Office (1985), income documentation is nonexistent in many local files and procedures for verifying income documentation are not always adequate. Problems, however, can arise with income determination. When a teenage parent lives with her parents because she can't afford or can't manage to live alone, should her parents' income be used in determining eligibility (English, 1987)?

Another concern in recent years has been the lack of uniformity and imprecise application of nutritional risk criteria in various states. Variations occur in specific conditions included on state referral forms. A participant who smokes may be eligible in one state for benefits, but not in a neighboring state. Questions also arise when new infectious diseases, not on referral forms, begin to affect children (e.g., AIDS). Another question has been the more frequent use of inadequate dietary pattern than of medical factors as a nutritional risk criterion. Some contend that many Americans have poor diets and that assessments of dietary patterns using 24-hour recall interviews are unreliable. Others point out that inadequate diet is authorized in WIC legislation as a risk criterion. This dispute, in part, reflects different views of the purposes of WIC. Although WIC was established as a preventive program, much emphasis has been placed on cases of children whose health has improved as a result of WIC participation rather than on helping at-risk children before health deteriorates. To address concerns about greater uniformity and rigor in the application of nutritional risk criteria, the USDA is making efforts to establish greater professional consensus on appropriate nutritional risk criteria for WIC referrals and to improve methods of assessing inadequate dietary patterns (General Accounting Office, 1985).

A third concern has been lack of local targeting given the limited WIC funds available. By 1985, seven service priority categories had been established in WIC regulations. Participants classified as high-risk included pregnant and breast-feeding women, and infants referred for medical conditions rather than for inadequate dietary patterns. WIC legislation, however, does not mandate targeting. And program policies have not encouraged targeting benefits to those at highest risk except at year's end when the maximum caseload has been reached and additional funding has become uncertain (Committee on Agriculture, Nutrition and Forestry, 1984, 1985; General Accounting Office, 1985). To monitor state and local targeting performance more carefully, recent USDA regulatory changes require WIC programs to report semiannually caseloads and numbers of participants served in each of the seven priority categories (General Accounting Office, 1985). This information may allow USDA in the future to reward states that do a better job of targeting and to allocate to them the unspent funds of less productive states. Some states are presently rewarding local programs for targeting. For example, New York offers local programs a "bounty" for cases in the top-risk category (English, 1987).

A fourth management issue has been adequacy of vendor monitoring. A number of states have adopted strategies to assure proper use of WIC vouchers. California has instituted a training program for vendors or grocers to improve understanding of which foods can be purchased with WIC checks (Serrano, 1986). Other states such as Texas and New York maintain aggressive monitoring schemes to assure that vendors do not overcharge WIC customers, exchange WIC vouchers for unauthorized foods, or trade vouchers for cash. Surprise visits are made to stores to check on prices, stock, and receipts, and sometimes investigators will pose as WIC recipients and attempt to make illegal purchases. If violations are found, vendors will be dropped from both WIC and Food Stamp Programs (English, 1987; Rhodes, 1983). Computerized vouchers

also are being used in some states to monitor vendors and WIC purchases (Stansfield, 1984).

Finally, lack of end-of-year funding flexibility has also become a management problem for WIC programs. Now with annualized budgets, WIC programs are less likely to experience USDA slowdowns in spending. However, at the end of each fiscal year, unspent program funds cannot be carried over to the next year. Moreover, programs are never certain if they suddenly will be allocated additional unspent funds from other programs. This budget management policy causes disruption of sound program planning. Congress has been urged by the National Association of State WIC Directors and by the General Accounting Office to allow carryovers of funds not to exceed 3 percent at the end of the year, but Congress has not adopted this recommendation (Committee on Agriculture, Nutrition, and Forestry, 1984, 1985).

In the course of its development, WIC has garnered broad support from many quarters. Although not permanently authorized in legislation, WIC seems to be here to stay as a program. It is now considered to be one of the federal government's most cost-effective programs (Committee on Education and Labor, 1987). Advocacy strategies that have fostered development of this program have taken many forms: congressional testimony, television documentaries, letter writing campaigns, displays of photos and x-rays, magazine articles, class action suits, newspaper articles, developmental research, evaluation studies, and formation of lobbying coalitions. Perhaps WIC can serve as a model of advocacy orchestration for other child advocacy efforts. In any case, WIC supporters hopefully will enjoy continued success in their advocacy efforts as they face new challenges and issues.

REFERENCES

Berry, J. M. (1984). *Feeding hungry people: Rulemaking in the Food Stamp Program.* New Brunswick, NJ: Rutgers University Press.
Centers for Disease Control. (1977, December). *Analysis of nutrition indices for selected WIC participants.* Atlanta: Author.
Centers for Disease Control. (1986, October 24–31). Declining anemia prevalence among children enrolled in public nutrition and health program, Selected states, 1975–1985. *Journal of the American Medical Association, 256,* 2165.

Committee on Agriculture, Nutrition, and Forestry. (1983). *Child nutrition programs: Description, history, issues, and options* (S. Prt. 98-15). Washington, DC: U.S. Government Printing Office.

Committee on Agriculture, Nutrition, and Forestry. (1984, March 15/April 9). *Evaluation and reauthorization of the Special Supplemental Food Program for Women, Infants, and Children (WIC)* (S. Hrg. 98-985). Washington, DC: U.S. Government Printing Office.

Committee on Agriculture, Nutrition, and Forestry. (1985, June 17). *Reauthorization of WIC, the Commodity Supplemental Food Program and the Temporary Emergency Food Assistance Program* (S. Hrg. 99-401). Washington, DC: U.S. Government Printing Office.

Committee on Education and Labor. (1987, October 7). *The Chairman's report on children in America: A strategy for the 100th Congress, A guide to federal programs that affect children* (Vol. II). (H. R. Serial No. 100-0). Washington, DC: U.S. Government Printing Office.

Endozien, J. C., Switzer, B. R., & Bryan, R. B. (1976, July). *Medical evaluation of the Special Supplemental Food Program for Women, Infants, and Children (WIC)* (6 vols.). Chapel Hill, NC: University of North Carolina, School of Public health.

English, C. (1987, October). Personal communication.

General Accounting Office. (1985). *Need to foster optimal use of resources in the Special Supplemental Food Program for Women, Infants, and Children (WIC)*. Report to the Secretary of Agriculture. Washington, DC: Author.

Hardman, V. M. (1973, April). How to save babies for two dimes a day. *Redbook, 68, 70, 72–75.*

Hayes, C. D. (1982). *Making policies for children: A study of the federal process.* Washington, DC: National Academy Press.

Nelson, J. R. (1982). The Special Supplemental Food Program for Women, Infants, and Children. In C. D. Hayes (Ed.), *Making policies for children: A study of the federal process* (pp. 85–150). Washington, DC: National Academy Press.

Rhodes, R. J. (1983, April). How Texas works with WIC vendors. *Food and Nutrition, 6–7.*

Scheffler, W. (1987, January). Food programs are stronger than ever. *Food and Nutrition, 2–7.*

Serrano, T. (1986, July). Special effort in California helps grocers understand WIC. *Food and Nutrition, 14–15.*

Stansfield, C. M. (1984, January). WIC celebrates its tenth anniversary. *Food and Nutrition, 2–8.*

U.S. accused of altering study of food program. (1986, January 30). *New York Times, 9.*

Nutrition Education for Preschoolers:
The Head Start Experience

Margaret G. Phillips

The Head Start program has always had a nutrition component, one that includes nutrition education. Some major aims of the program are to help Head Start staff, families and children understand the relationship of nutrition to health, and the variety of foods that can be utilized to meet nutritional needs, so that children and families develop sound food habits.

The program is focused primarily upon children from low-income families who have not reached the age of compulsory school attendance. Data from the Census Bureau shows that there are 9,530,000 children aged three to five in the United States. Twenty percent of this age group—1,943,000 children—are in families below the poverty line. Head Start serves approximately 395,800 or one out of five of the eligible low-income preschool children.

The nutrition program is also planned to respond to the multiracial and multicultural composition of the children served in Head Start nationwide: 42 percent of the children are black, 33 percent are white, 20 percent are Hispanic, 4 percent are American Indian and 1 percent, Asian. As the number of families from different cultures immigrating to the United States increases, the need for nutrition education is even more crucial to help families maintain optimal nutrition while adjusting to the different foods confronting them in food markets, restaurants and schools.

Local Head Start programs may vary considerably from this national average in terms of the racial and cultural backgrounds of the children served. The enrollment in one Head Start program, for example, in Manhattanville Preschool Program in New York City, recently represented at least seven different countries. There were children whose parents had come from El Salvador, Peru, the Dominican Republic, Haiti, Puerto Rico and Jamaica. Other Head Start programs provide equally rich opportunities for learning about various cultures.

Approximately 12 percent of the children enrolled in Head Start are handicapped and some of these children and their families may need special nutrition education and services. Children with handicaps, for instance, may need to be trained to use specially modified dishes and utensils to promote self-feeding. Teachers and parents may need instructions on how to position handicapped children for feeding and on ways to modify equipment to facilitate eating—modifying the design of a chair or table for the child with cerebral palsy, for example, in order to stabilize and lessen the movement so that the child can hold utensils more easily. The consistency or composition of children's usual diets may also need to be changed to meet the special requirements of a child's diet.

Low-income families need information and help in applying for such food assistance programs as the U.S. Department of Agriculture's Food Stamp Program and the Supplemental Food Program for Women, Infants and Preschool Children (WIC). In a national nutrition survey of preschool-aged children from low-income families, the major problem identified among children who were rated low in nutritional status was simply the insufficient amount of food available to them.[1]

Families also need information related to child nutrition and food selection and food preparation and storage.

Source: Margaret G. Phillips (1983, July–August). Nutrition education for preschoolers: The Head Start experience. *Children Today,* 20–24. Reprinted by permission of the author.

Young children have a growing desire to be independent and to perform independently.

Beginning Nutrition Education

Early childhood is the ideal time to begin nutrition education. The food habits and attitudes of adults are shaped and molded during infancy and the preschool years; they influence nutrition attitudes and health throughout the entire life span.

In selecting and developing nutrition education activities for the preschool child, Head Start teachers keep in mind the basic principles of how children learn. They recognize that young children have a growing desire to be independent and to perform independently, and that they want to be actively involved in the process of learning. They know that young children want to reach out to feel things and to explore and that children are stimulated by sounds, color and smells. And the Head Start programs focus on the child as a learner in real life situations.

The nutrition education programs for parents are integrated with those for the children so that both will have mutually harmonious objectives. Parents participate in the classroom as volunteers; they assist at the table at mealtimes and often demonstrate a recipe for a snack food.

Learning Activities

Meals and snack times can be a source of a variety of learning situations that will help to promote positive food habits and attitudes. Using family style food service in Head Start helps to promote socialization among children and adults. It also provides an opportunity for teaching children about safe and hygienic food practices, and it encourages children to try new foods. The children are also involved in such tasks as setting the table, folding napkins, serving food and clearing the table. They also help to prepare some snacks.

In addition to the classroom activities relating to nutrition, field trips are planned to help children learn about the community and food sources. Visits to local fruit and vegetable markets also help children learn about a wide variety of foods and encourage them to try unfamiliar ones.

The diversity of cultures represented in Head Start classrooms offers a valuable opportunity to teach children about the food habits and practices of families in many countries. Such activities as participating in the planning of an international luncheon or food fair and exhibits illustrating typical foods and dress of a country or region can be an enriching experience.

Patsy Thomas, director of a Head Start program in Gainesville, Florida, developed a nutrition component with an international flair. The one-month curriculum unit was designed to help children understand and accept the cultural differences reflected in eating styles and food habits of families from other countries. The Head Start director and the nutritionist planned the project on the basis of the countries represented by the children in the Head Start center: India, Brazil, China, Laos and Vietnam were highlighted. Typical foods of each country were served, and eaten in the style of that country. For the Chinese meal of rice, sauteed fresh vegetables and diced meat, for example, the children ate with chopsticks and sat on cushions at low tables. For the Brazilian meal, rice, black beans and fruit were served.

The teachers discussed the food customs and geographic area of each country included in the international project and parents, dressed in colorful native dress, brought artwork, linens and pictures showing typical homes and customs. Some parents performed folk dances for the children.

At Project Head Start in Montgomery County, Maryland, the teachers developed a nutrition education activity based on "hot and cold" foods. The class observed the preparation of hot apple juice, for example, tasted it and then discussed the effect of heating a food.

The Newark Preschool Council, Inc. in New Jersey reports that interns in dietetics from the College of Medicine and Dentistry participated in nutrition education sessions for preschoolers in more than 23 New Jersey Head Start centers. The children were introduced to such concepts as the importance of a good breakfast, how fruits and vegetables grow and the fundamentals of a nutritious diet.

Many Head Start programs are utilizing "Food—Early Choices: A Nutrition Learning System for Early Childhood" developed by the National Dairy Council.[2] The system includes a teacher's guide, learning activity cards, materials for parents, food picture cards and a puppet, Chef Combo. The puppet, an instant success with preschoolers, also helps convey ideas on food and nutrition to teachers and parents.

A booklet originally prepared by General Mills, Inc. and the U.S. Department of Agriculture, *The Thing the Professor Forgot,* discusses basic foods in a simple manner suitable for young children and also offers pages to color.[3]

Program Linkages

Linkages with other nutrition programs are developed by Head Start projects in order to strengthen their nutrition services. Close coordination is maintained at the national level between Head Start and programs of the U.S. Department of Agriculture, particularly WIC, the Child Care Food Program, the Food Stamp Program, the National School Lunch Program, the Extension Service and the Nutrition Education and Training Program (NET).

The Extension Service and the Nutrition Education and Training Program (NET) have contributed significantly to the success of various nutrition education and training programs in Head Start. For example, the Head Start programs in Wayne County and the Wayne County Intermediate School District's Nutrition Education and Training Resource Center have been working cooperatively since the beginning of the NET program. Each year, a Nutrition Fair has been held, sponsored by NET and Out-Wayne County Head Start. Nutrition education sessions for parents and staff are offered on such subjects as diet and exercise, nutrition and preschoolers and "Nutrition and You." A display and a lunch, composed of a variety of nutritious snacks for children, are part of the fair.[4]

Sharing the Head Start Experience

What have Head Start programs learned about nutrition education that can help others involved in nutrition programs for children? The following suggestions and examples, grouped under five major headings, should be useful.

Relate nutrition learning activities to real life situations.

• Help children learn to identify foods by color, feel, smell, shape, taste and temperature.

• Plan field trips to include one or more visits to local markets to help children learn more about familiar foods and discover unfamiliar ones.

• Develop learning activities based on cultural food patterns represented by children in the program, as discussed earlier.

• Offer children opportunities to observe the growth of plants and animals—in the classroom, during daily outdoor play periods, in walks to nearby parks and through field trips to zoos, greenhouses and other sites.

Children can also initiate and maintain such special projects as planting an herb garden.

• Have children assist in the preparation of simple snacks.

121

Share nutrition education objectives with parents and encourage them to participate as partners in the learning process.

• Offer a series of nutrition seminars for parents based on their expressed needs. The sessions can focus on these needs and on current findings related to health and nutrition.

• Explain the program's nutrition goals to parents and demonstrate the related classroom learning activities for their children so that continuity in approach to nutrition, food and health will be maintained at school and home.

• Invite parents to participate in classroom activities. Parents can demonstrate preparation of their favorite, healthful snack foods and they can help serve during mealtimes.

Develop ongoing nutrition education programs for staff members.

• A series of nutrition education seminars can be held for staff members based on current nutrition information and on national nutrition goals, as expressed in *Dietary Guidelines for Americans.*[5]

• Teachers and other classroom personnel should be provided with easy-to-use examples of food and nutrition learning activities.

Involve the community in nutrition activities.

• Work with local radio and T.V. stations to present programs on nutrition for preschool children and their parents.

• Invite members of the community—representatives from such local food-producing companies as a milk plant or bakery, and from the consumer department of a supermarket chain, for example—to talk with the children and/or parents.

• Similarly, children's field trips can include visits to a local farm, bakery or dairy, for instance.

• Coordinate nutrition activities with such federal, state and local programs as the WIC Program (Supplemental Food Program for Pregnant Women, Infants and Children), USDA; NET (Nutrition Education and Training Program), USDA; the County Extension Program, USDA; county and city health departments; and community colleges.

Consider the child's stage of growth and development.

• Learning activities for preschoolers should be matched to their developmental levels. For example, nutrition education for 3-year-olds is best accomplished on a one-to-one basis. Older preschoolers can work in groups of five to six children.

Four-year-olds like to work on activities with immediate results or rewards, such as the preparation (and consumption) of such foods as mixed dried fruit and cereal snacks or stuffed dates and prunes. For 5-year-olds, independent activities are favored, such as setting the table.

• All materials and objects used in classroom projects should be ones that children can grasp and handle easily.

In summary, the preschool years provide rewarding opportunities to help children develop sound food habits and positive attitudes toward mealtimes. A well-planned nutrition education program involving the preschool child, parents and staff will contribute enormously to a healthier childhood and future adult life.

ENDNOTES

1. G. M. Owen, et al., "A Study of Nutritional Status of Preschool Children in the United States, 1968–1970, *Pediatrics* (Supplement), Vol. 53, No. 4, Part II, April 1974.

2. Information on the learning system is available from the National Dairy Council, 6300 N. River Road, Rosemont, Ill. 60018.

3. Single copies of *The Thing the Professor Forgot* are available from Nutrition Department, General Mills, Inc., Department 45, P.O. Box 1112, Minneapolis, Minn. 55440.

4. More information on the fair is available from the Director, NET Resource Center, and the Head Start Health Specialist, Wayne County Intermediate School District, 33500 Van Born Road, Wayne, Mich. 48184.

5. *Nutrition and Your Health: Dietary Guidelines for Americans,* U.S. Department of Agriculture and U.S. Department of Health and Human Services, February, 1980. (Single copies are available free from the National Health Information Clearinghouse, Department CT, P.O. Box 1133, Washington, D.C. 20013. (Please include self-addressed mailing label.)

Margaret G. Phillips, Ed.D., R.D., is nutrition specialist, Administration for Children, Youth and Families, OHDS.

Children's Food Preferences: Development and Influences

Ligaya P. Paguio and Anna V. A. Resurreccion

Adequate nutrition during the early years is an important issue because of the impact on development, learning and emotions. Early malnutrition interferes with the development of the central nervous system and has negative effects on learning performance (Raman, 1975). Optimum learning cannot be achieved, even in an enriched environment, if children's capacity to learn is impaired through poor nutrition (Lee, Schvaneveldt & Sorenson, 1984). Nutrition also affects the growth rate of young children (Tanner, 1970) and iron deficiency affects the emotional behavior of infants (Honig, 1984). Iron deficient infants are harder to involve with play materials and are less likely to smile than iron sufficient infants. Children's food preference is a critical factor in children's nutrition.

The purpose of this paper is to review studies concerning the development and influence of children's food preferences and discuss implications of these findings for parents and educators.

Based upon a review of relevant studies, Birch (1980a) concluded that there may be sensitive periods early in life that are important in the formation of food preferences and aversions. Reports of individuals interviewed at different points in their life span indicated that most food dislikes originated in early childhood. Additionally, food preferences established early in life continued throughout the life span, affecting preferences and consumption patterns during adulthood. Several factors appeared to have an impact on children's food preferences:

1. Cultural beliefs, attitudes and knowledge about food
2. Characteristics of food
3. Social environment in which incidents with food occur.

Cultural Beliefs, Attitudes and Knowledge About Food

Children's food habits and taste for food are influenced by culture and family (Church, 1979). The beliefs and attitudes about food vary from culture to culture, and children develop food preferences regarded as acceptable and palatable in their culture. For example, school children in North Dakota and Georgia react differently to rice used as a vegetable (Lowenberg, 1977). Preference for bitter and sour foods greatly varies from culture to culture. Whereas Westerners find the taste of sour and bitter to be unpleasant, Kartanaka laborers in India report increased concentration of bitter and sour solutions to be pleasant (Moskowitz, Kumaraiah, Sharma, Jacobs & Sharma, 1975).

Ethnic groups in the United States vary not only in food patterns (Lowenberg, 1977) but also in their consumption of dairy products, vegetables and meat (Price & Price, 1982). Price and Price studied the school lunch program in the state of Washington and found that black, white and Mexican-American children significantly differed in their consumption of the various food groups. They reported that children whose parents were raised in the Northeast or Central United States had significantly higher consumption of meat and fresh

Source: L. P. Paguio & A. V. A. Resurreccion (1987). Children's food preferences: Development and influence. *Childhood Education, 63*(4), 296–298, 300. Reprinted by permission of Ligaya P. Paguio and the Association for Childhood Education International, 11141 Georgia Avenue, Suite 200, Wheaton, MD. Copyright © 1987 by the Association.

vegetables than did children whose parents were raised in the West.

Characteristics of Food

Children tend to prefer sweet foods. This preference for sweet is present at birth (Birch, 1980a). Newborns were able to discriminate between sweet and nonsweet, and they consumed increasing amounts and concentrations of sweet solutions when given a choice between sweet and nonsweet solutions. Also, when given a choice of sweet and nonsweet open-faced sandwiches and sweet and sour, tart fruits, 3- and 4-year-olds preferred sweets (Birch, 1979a; 1979b).

Texture, flavor, color and temperature of food also influence children's choices of food (Hui, 1985; Lowenberg, 1977). Lowenberg reported that children liked soft, fluffy food, such as pudding and mashed potatoes, and crisp, firm vegetables, such as carrots and rutabagas. She stated that pieces of meat were difficult for a young child to eat because the teeth of 2- and 3-year-old children do not grind meat as easily as adult teeth do. In addition, she found that finger foods were popular with young children because of their developing fine motor skills.

Plain and unmixed foods were preferred by children (Ireton & Guthrie, 1972). Children, however, also preferred *au gratin* preparations of green vegetables more than creamed vegetables (Dudley, Moore & Sunderlin, 1960). Foods with strong flavors were disliked (Ashbrook & Doyle, 1985; Hui, 1985). Taste and odor of foods such as cabbage, broccoli and onions seem to overwhelm children. Colorful foods were preferred (Hertzler, 1983). Green, orange, yellow and pink were popular colors in food (Lowenberg, 1977). Children usually preferred their food to be lukewarm. Hui (1985) asserted that temperature is an important criteria in the acceptability of food among young children.

Social Environment

The social-affective climate in which food is presented influences food preferences (Birch, 1980a). Children's preferences have been associated with the eating behaviors of peers (Birch, 1980b), parents (Birch, 1980c; Bryan & Lowenberg, 1958; Burt & Hertzler, 1978;

Harper & Sanders, 1975) and siblings (Eppright et al., 1972). Birch (1980b) investigated the influence of peers' food selections on 3- and 4-year-olds' food preferences during lunch. He found that when target children were exposed to peers who selected and ate the target children's nonpreferred foods, target children changed preference and consumption patterns. Modeling appeared to have both immediate and more lasting effects on food preferences. It is interesting to note that younger children as opposed to older children showed more positive preference shifts, supporting the contention that there is a sensitive period during the early years for the formation of food preferences (Birch, 1980a).

Parental influence on children's food preferences has been investigated. Harper and Sanders (1975) studied young children's willingness to eat novel food when mothers and strangers modeled the eating of food and found that mothers were more influential than strangers. Interestingly, children were more likely to eat novel food if the adult actually modeled eating the food rather than if the adult merely offered the food. Other researchers have found significant correlations between mother-child and father-child preferences. Bryan and Lowenberg (1958) found a significant correlation between fathers' and children's preferences for vegetables, and Burt and Hertzler (1978) reported that father and mother influenced the child's food preferences equally. Birch (1980c) not only found significant relationships between mother-child and father-child preferences but also with child-unrelated adults' preferences. Eppright et al. (1972) found that "Fathers, through their likes and dislikes, played a role both in foods selected by the mother for family use and in the attitudes toward food formed by the adult" (p. 329).

Older siblings influence younger children's dislikes of vegetables (Eppright et al., 1972). Younger siblings' dislikes of vegetables were more closely associated with dislikes of older siblings than with parents' dislikes.

Verbal praise, recognition or tokens have been cited as techniques to affect food preferences. Ireton and Guthrie (1972), in an effort to increase vegetable consumption, gave children tokens and verbal reinforcement when they consumed premeasured servings of vegetables. Results indicated that this technique resulted in significant increases in consumption. Birch (1981) and Birch, Zimmerman and Hind (1980) found that presenting foods as rewards and presenting them noncontingently paired with adult attention produced significant increases in preference of snack food among 3- and 4-year-olds.

Familiarity due to constant exposure of food to children is a salient dimension in children's preferences. Birch (1979a) found that after constant exposure to an unfamiliar food, preschoolers significantly shifted their food preferences. Frequent exposure to food through television and advertising was reported to affect children's requests for food (Stoneman & Brody, 1982).

Implications

Even young children are able to learn basic concepts of good nutrition (Davis, Bassler, Anderson & Fryer, 1983). Studies have shown increased nutrition knowledge, food acceptance and selection after teaching children about nutrition. Lee et al. (1984) used food profile cards to enable preschool children to demonstrate understanding and competence about concepts in nutrition. Results indicated that those taught at school by the teachers and at home by the parents showed significantly higher scores than those children who did not receive instruction.

Church (1979) used concrete experiences in the classroom to teach children nutrition concepts similar to those included in Lee et al. Concrete experiences included involving the children in food preparation; reinforcing activities with stories, games and discussions; and conducting nutrition field trips. Also, parents of the children were given mini-lessons about nutrition. The parents accompanied the children during field trips and prepared a variety of ethnic dishes. After six weeks, there was an increase in children's food knowledge; changes in children's behaviors were also noted. The teachers observed children's interest in new foods and participation in food preparation. Parents reported that some children asked for vegetables they disliked before the study was conducted. Church recommended that concrete experiences should be planned in the classroom to increase children's knowledge about food and that parents and teachers

Participation in food preparation develops positive attitudes and knowledge about foods.

who work with children must be knowledgeable about foods and food groups as well as be good role-models.

Guiding principles in serving meals. In serving meals to young children at school, it is helpful if we:

• Consider the food and cultural patterns of children, serving foods that are acceptable to the cultural beliefs of the group.
• Serve food with a variety of colors and textures. Serve both raw and cooked food. Food should be arranged in an attractive manner and served in small, bite-size pieces that may be eaten with the fingers.
• Introduce new foods slowly, giving children time to be familiar with the new food. Serve small portions of the new food and encourage children to try at least one bite, giving attention to those who try but not discouraging those who reject the food.
• Serve strong-flavored foods with mild-flavored cream sauce, grated cheese or cheese sauce to cover the strong flavor.
• Seat picky eaters with good eaters. Also, there should be an adult with 5–6 children at each table to act as facilitator and role-model.

125

• Use eating utensils that can be comfortably managed by small hands.

• Make the eating arrangement pleasant with a bright, clean eating area and calm, interesting conversations. When table accidents happen, accept them calmly. Simply help the child in cleaning-up and remind everyone that we all have accidents.

Involve the family to influence food habits. Studies have shown the important role parents and siblings play in changing children's food preferences. Mothers, fathers and other adults responsible for planning and preparing meals in the home must know the basic concepts in nutrition and be willing to share and use this information in the home. As Hertzler (1983) suggests, "If family members share information and decide to use it, then food problems will be solved. However, if the family is a passive audience or does not agree on the use of the information, behavior change is unlikely" (p. 558).

Parents can be involved in nutrition programs in the school through discussion groups, newsletters and parent participation in the classroom. During discussion groups, nutritionists and other resource persons with a knowledge of foods and nutrition can be invited. Topics of discussion should be based on the interests and needs of the parents. School newsletters may include: tips on how to prepare balanced meals and how to cook food without losing food nutrients, recipes and a question-and-answer section from parents about food and nutrition. Tips on how to deal with eating problems can also be included during discussion groups and in newsletters. For example, many mothers use sweet foods as rewards and deprivation of sweet foods as a punishment, yet they are concerned that children eat too many sweets (Eppright et al., 1972). Parent participation in the classroom may include helping children prepare snacks and special recipes, accompanying children on field trips and helping children compile a recipe book of favorite snacks and dishes.

Adequate nutrition during the early years is of great concern to educators, since good nutrition promotes the biological growth of children and enhances their capacity for learning and social-emotional development. Educators can help influence young children's preferences for nutritious food by teaching them about nutrition, observing some guiding principles in serving meals at school and involving the family in the nutrition program.

REFERENCES

Ashbrook, S., & Doyle, M. (1985). Infant's acceptance of strong and mild-flavored vegetables. *Journal of Nutrition Education, 17,* 5–6.

Birch, L. L. (1979a). Dimensions of preschool children's food preferences. *Journal of Nutrition Education, 11,* 77–80.

Birch, L. L. (1979b). Preschool children's food preferences and consumption patterns. *Journal of Nutrition Education, 11,* 189–192.

Birch, L. L. (1980a). Experimental determinants of children's food preferences. In L. Katz (Ed.), *Current topics in early childhood education* (pp. 29–47). Norwood, NJ: Ablex.

Birch, L. L. (1980b). Effects of peer models' food choices and eating behaviors on preschoolers food preferences. *Child Development, 51,* 489–496.

Birch, L. L. (1980c). The relationship between children's food preferences and those of their parents. *Journal of Nutrition Education, 12,* 14–18.

Birch, L. L. (1981). Generalization of a modified food preference. *Child Development, 52,* 755–758.

Birch, L. L., Zimmerman, S. I., & Hind, H. (1980). The influence of social-affective context on the formation of children's food preferences. *Child Development, 51,* 856–861.

Burt, J. V., & Hertzler, A. A. (1978). Parental influences on the child's food preference. *Journal of Nutrition Education, 10,* 127–128.

Bryan, M. S., & Lowenberg, M. E. (1958). The father's influence on young children's food preferences. *Journal of the American Dietetic Association, 34,* 30–35.

Church, M. (1979). Nutrition: A vital part of the curriculum. *Young Children, 35,* 61–65.

Davis, S. S., Bassler, A. M., Anderson, J. V., & Fryer, H. (1983). A nutrition education program for preschool children. *Journal of Nutrition Education, 15,* 4–5.

Dudley, D. T., Moore, M. E., & Sunderlin, E. M. (1960). Children's attitudes toward food. *Journal of Home Economics, 52,* 678–680.

Eppright, E. S., Fox, H. M., Fryer, B. A., Lampkin, G. H., Vivian, V. M., & Fuller, E. S. (1972). Nutrition of infants and preschool children in the north central region of the United States of America. *World Review of Nutrition and Dietetics, 14,* 269–332.

Harper, L. V., & Sanders, K. (1975). The effects of adults' eating on young children's acceptance of unfamiliar food. *Journal of Experimental Child Psychology, 20,* 206–214.

Hertzler, A. A. (1983). Children's food patterns—a review: Food preferences and feeding problems. *Journal of the American Dietetic Association, 83,* 551–560.

Honig, A. S. (1984). Risk factors in infants and young children. *Young Children, 39,* 60–73.

Hui, Y. H. (1985). *Principles and issues in nutrition.* Monterey, CA: Wadsworth.

Ireton, C. L., & Guthrie, H. A. (1972). Modification of vegetable-eating behavior in preschool children. *Journal of Nutrition Education, 4,* 100–103.

Lee, T. R., Schvaneveldt, J. D., & Sorenson, A. W. (1984). Nutritional understanding of preschool children taught in the home or a child development laboratory. *Home Economics Research Journal, 13,* 52–60.

Lowenberg, M. E. (1977). The development of food patterns in young children. In P. L. Pipes (Ed.), *Nutrition in infancy and childhood* (pp. 85–100). St. Louis, MO: Mosby.

Moskowitz, H. W., Kumaraiah, V., Sharma, K. N., Jacobs, H. L., & Sharma, S. D. (1975). Cross-cultural differences in simple taste preference. *Science, 190,* 1217–1218.

Price, E. W., & Price, D. Z. (1982). *The effects of school lunch participation, socioeconomic, and psychological variables on food consumption of school children.* Pullman, WA: College of Agriculture Research Center, Washington State University, XB 0912.

Raman, S. P. (1975). Role of nutrition in the actualization of the potentialities of the child: An anisa prospective. *Young Children, 31,* 24–32.

Tanner, J. M. (1970). Physical growth. In P. H. Mussen (Ed.), *Carmichael's manual of child psychology,* (3rd ed.), pp. 77–155. New York: Wiley.

Stoneman, Z., & Brody, G. H. (1982). The indirect impact of child-oriented advertisement. *Journal of Applied Developmental Psychology, 2,* 369–375.

Ligaya P. Paguio, Assistant Professor, Department of Child and Family Development, College of Home Economics, University of Georgia, Athens, and Anna V. A. Resurreccion, Assistant Professor, Department of Food Science, Georgia Experiment Station, University of Georgia, Experiment

ASK YOURSELF:
Identifying Issues for Debate and Advocacy

1. What is the difference between undernourishment and malnutrition?

2. Which is the more common child nutrition problem in this country: diets lacking in quality or diets low in quantity?

3. How and to what extent does the government provide nutritional assistance to children in our society?

4. Are supplemental nutrition programs accountable and effective?

5. The Children's Defense Fund (1987) documents the large percentage (23 percent) of young children who live in poverty in this country. How may the advocacy efforts used to support development of the WIC program serve as a model for others who wish to improve the quality of life for children and their families?

6. In a preschool program, why is it more important to provide concrete preparation experiences with food and to hold conversations about necessary ingredients and the

127

preparation process than to show food pictures and to ask questions like "Are peas vegetables?"

7. At Tiny Tikes Child Care Center, a small group of three-year-olds sat at the art table as their preschool teacher ladled from a big bowl a glob of chocolate pudding for each child and placed it on the art table. Then the teacher told the children that today they were going to fingerpaint with pudding! The three-year-olds began cautiously to stick their fingers in the glob of pudding. One child giggled and squeezed the pudding through his fingers. Another child spread the pudding around and then slapped her hands on the table several times. Next, a child stuck a pudding-covered hand in her mouth and grinned. The other children began to lick pudding from their hands and to giggle at each other's chocolate-covered hands and faces. What attitudes and values about food are being conveyed by this activity? Discuss the choice of food as a medium for art.

8. At a parent-teacher conference in your nursery school, Mrs. Goodman shares her concern about three-year-old Amy's picky eating habits. Amy will seldom eat anything but spaghetti and fruit-flavored yogurt. What is your response?

9. What can schools do to help parents become informed consumers who get good nutritional value for their dollar at the grocery store?

10. Freedberg (1983) asserts that next to farm and chemical workers, children face the greatest health risks from pollution and hazardous wastes. Do current policies prohibit construction of playgrounds or child care settings on abandoned industrial sites or landfills? Are children exposed to high levels of lead poisoning when child care settings or playgrounds are located near freeways? Are children exposed to dangerous pesticides or wood preservatives on playgrounds or child care sites?

APPLICATION / ADVOCACY EXERCISES

1. Invite a WIC representative to speak to your group about WIC eligibility requirements, screening forms, and the application process. Also discuss efforts to reach possible participants, and the nature of their nutrition consultation program.

2. After reading and listening to presentations about the WIC program, make arrangements to visit one of your county legislators or supervisors. (See Chapter 13 for ad-

ditional tips on visiting public officials). Be prepared to discuss the purposes and accomplishments of WIC. Point out that WIC checks bring money into the county and that the WIC program provides employment for people in the county. Make plans to discuss the feasibility of more county support for the WIC program (e.g., greater coordination of social service programs or assistance in contacting eligible WIC participants).

3. Request an interview with a grocery store employee. Explain that you want to learn more about how the WIC program works and to discuss the employee's impressions of the program. (Be sure that the grocery store employee has had sufficient experience with WIC customers.) Based on the readings in this chapter as well as information received from a WIC representative (if available), compose four to six interview questions that you wish to ask this person. (Avoid questions that can be answered with a yes-no only response.) In framing your questions, consider issues such as:

   a. Do grocery store employees or vendors understand the purposes of WIC, WIC eligibility requirements, and what foods are acceptable for WIC purchases?

   b. Do they encounter pressure to allow substitute purchases?

   c. Do they believe that the program is necessary and effective in supplementing the nutrition of the women and children enrolled in the program?

Take notes during the interview in order to obtain a record of the interviewee's responses. After the interview, write a synopsis of the interview, including the interview questions asked, the interviewee's responses, and your interpretation and comparison of these responses in relation to chapter readings and information you received, if any, from a WIC representative.

4. Suppose that you are composing a parent newsletter for your preschool program. What parent-child activities might you suggest to strengthen positive attitudes toward good nutrition? (Relate your activities to ideas found in articles by Phillips and by Paguio and Resurreccion.)

REFERENCES & SUGGESTED READINGS

Children's Defense Fund. (1987). *A Children's defense budget: FY 1988*. Washington, DC: Author.

Evans, R. (1986). *The violation of childhood: A review of possible effects on development of toxic chemical and nuclear waste*. Paper presented at the 18th Conference of the World Organization for Early Childhood Education, Jerusalem. London, Eng.:

Roehampton Institute, Southlands College. (ERIC Document Reproduction Service No. 280 562)

Freedberg, L. (1983). *America's poisoned playgrounds: Children and toxic chemicals.* Paper presented at the Conference on Alternative State and Local Policies, Washington, DC. Oakland, CA: Youth News. (ERIC Document Reproduction Service No. 231 519)

Martin, E. A., & Beal, V. (1978). *Robert's nutrition work with children* (4th ed.). Chicago, IL: University of Chicago Press.

Sleator, E. K. (1986). *Infectious diseases in day care.* Champaign, IL: University of Illinois. (ERIC Document Reproduction Service No. ED 269 157)

Van Heerden, J. R. (1984). Early undernutrition and mental performance. *International Journal of Early Childhood, 16,* 10–16.

Winick, M. (1976). *Malnutrition and brain development.* London: Oxford University Press.

CHAPTER 6

Children: Abuse, Neglect, and Privacy

Fast Talk with Fast Foods

Observation Notes:

6:25 p.m.   A mother, about 21 years old, walks toward a restaurant table followed by 6-year-old Jason and 4-year-old John. Straggling at the rear is 2-year-old Johanna. The mother sets the tray and her purse on the table and takes off her jacket. She doesn't help the kids with their jackets. John tugs on the strap of her purse; she swats his hand and caustically remarks, "Why don't you break that like you break everything else?"

Jason and John sit down on one side of the booth, the mother and Johanna on the other. The mother shoves a Cheery Meal in front of each child, and they open the boxes. Jason wails, "I didn't want a burger!"

"I didn't *give* you a burger," his mother snaps.

"I wanted fries, too," Jason peevishly mumbles.

"I don't care. Don't ask for anything else for the rest of the day," yells the mother.

Johanna takes a bite of her hamburger and then spits it out, exclaiming, "No like pickles! No like pickles!"

The mother grabs the hamburger away and says, "So don't eat them."

They all sit in silence for a few seconds.

John pulls out his package of Legos from the Cheery Meal box and asks, "Can I open the Legos?"

The mother responds, "No! Will you be quiet and just eat? We're *not* staying." John sighs and eats a couple of fries.

6:30 p.m.   Jason demands, "Gimme one," and grabs at his brother's fries. John quickly pulls away his fries.

The mother intervenes: "John, give him one. You always hog everything. How many times have I told you to share stuff with your brother?"

John stands up on the bench. The mother growls, "Sit! We're gonna go, so *eat.*" Jason starts to kick his feet against the bench so hard that the booth shakes. His mother glares, raises her hand, glances around, and then withdraws it. She warns, "Jason, we're going now; you better be ready." She leaves the table to throw out the garbage.

When she returns, Jason whines, "Johanna messed her pants, Johanna messed her pants." Johanna starts to whimper and shrinks back into the corner of the booth.

The mother grabs Johanna by the arms, shakes her, and shrieks, "You're gonna get it! You dirty, dirty girl! Don't I have enough to do!" The mother drags sobbing Johanna off to the bathroom.

Questions

1. Are there clues to suggest that the dynamics displayed are typical patterns for this family? Or do they represent "just one of those days when nobody should have gotten out of bed"?

2. Consider the interaction in this episode. In what ways did the actions of the mother influence the actions of the children? In what ways did the actions of the children precipitate the actions of the mother?

PREVIEW

The past decade has witnessed an upsurge in reports of suspected child abuse and neglect. This upsurge reflects, in part, dramatic changes in laws and in public concern about the problems of abuse and neglect. In Sweden, public concern about child abuse led to passage of an antispanking law. To assess the impact of this law, Richard J. Gelles and Ake W. Edfeldt, in the first reading, compare the use of violence in Swedish and American families. In 1986, the state of New York found that the upsurge in reporting of child abuse and neglect resulted in a higher level of overreporting (unfounded cases) than in the past. What signs of child abuse and neglect should be reported? The readings in this chapter include a summary of indicators of child abuse and neglect as well as two case studies with accompanying questions for case analysis. What is the difference between neglecting a child and respecting a child's need to be alone? Barbara Lonnborg ends the readings with a discussion of children's needs for privacy.

Violence towards Children in the United States and Sweden

Richard J. Gelles and Ake W. Edfeldt

Abstract—This paper reports the results of a cross-cultural comparison of violence towards children in the United States and Sweden. Data from the United States are based on interviews with a nationally representative sample of 1,146 households with at least one child between the ages of 3 and 17 years living at home. Data from Sweden are based on interviews with a nationally representative sample of 1,168 households with a child 3 to 17 years of age at home. Violence and abuse were measured using the Conflict Tactics Scales. In general, Swedish parents reported using less violence than did parents in the United States. There was no significant difference between the two countries in the rate of reported severe or abusive violence. The paper compares factors found associated with violence towards children in the two countries, including age, marital status, education, and parents' background. The results are analyzed by considering methodological and cultural factors that explain the similarities and differences in the use of violence towards children in the two countries.

Much of the research carried out on child abuse and violence towards children has focused on the problem in the United States. Yet, students of child maltreatment have long been aware that American children are not the only, or even the most likely, victims [1–3].

While there has been a tremendous growth of an international perspective on abuse and neglect, there have been few actual cross-cultural studies conducted or published [4]. Problems with definitions, costs, and access have limited the ability of researchers to field cross-cultural investigations. This paper reports the results of a cross-cultural study of violence towards children in the United States and Sweden. A comparison of the incidence and patterns of violence towards children in the United States and Sweden is presented.

Background

Sweden and the United States offer important contrasts when it comes to cultural and social factors which may be related to violence and abuse. Child abuse has not generally appeared to be an overwhelming problem in Scandinavian countries, including Sweden. Vesterdal lists four reasons [5]. First, social conditions are generally good. Second, there is widespread use of contraceptives and free abortions, reducing the number of unwanted babies. Third, many mothers work and leave their children in day-care institutions. Last, premature babies are kept in a neonatal ward until they are a certain weight. The babies are released only when their parents are taught to handle a newborn.

There are stark contrasts between the United States and Sweden in terms of social attitudes towards violence. While in the United States the majority of states permit the corporal punishment of school children, corporal punishment has been outlawed in Sweden since 1952. Legislation prohibiting the spanking of children was passed in 1979, and has since been adopted in all other Scandinavian countries. Firearm ownership is rigorously controlled in Sweden. While nearly half of all American households contain guns, mostly handguns, gun ownership in Sweden is mostly limited to weapons used for hunting. Television violence offers another important contrast. American children witness as many as 15,000 killings each year on television; violent programming in Sweden is severely restricted. (Actually, Swedish television is barely on the air as many hours as the average American child watches television in a week.) The level of concern for children's programming in Sweden can be seen in the decision to limit the popular American movie, *ET*, to audiences over 11 years of age. A final contrast is in public violence. Capital punishment is banned in Sweden, but it is allowed and growing in use and popular support in the United States.

There is considerable difference in one area of social complexity. While the United States is a heterogeneous nation which is made up of numerous ethnic, religious, and cultural groups and communities. Sweden is more homogeneous in terms of such cultural and social attributes. There are, of course, innumerable similarities in the lives of children and families in the United States and in Sweden. However, the contrasts, especially in the area of attitudes towards violence, make a compelling case for comparing the level of violence towards children in the two countries.

Measures of Extent of Abuse and Violence

Research in the United States. Various techniques have been used to measure the extent of child abuse and violence towards children in the United States [6, 7]. Two of the most widely cited studies are the National Center on Child Abuse and Neglect report titled "Recognition and Reporting of Child Maltreatment" [8] and the "National Analysis of Official Child Neglect and Abuse Reporting," published yearly by the American Humane Association. Both studies provide interesting

data on officially recognized cases of abuse and neglect that come to public attention. However, the studies do not provide a direct measure of the true incidence of the occurrence of abusive events. As Burgdorf admits, a study of reported cases of maltreatment only identifies the "tip of the iceberg of child maltreatment" [8]. Measures of reported child abuse tend to focus on the more injurious forms of violence towards children. Such research cannot be used to examine the total range of violent acts experienced by children.

Not only do official report data fail to inform us about the true extent of violence towards children, such data also do not offer an accurate representation of the factors related to violence and abuse of children. Official reports of child abuse include a number of biases. Certain individuals and families are more likely to be reported due to the nature of the injury, social status of the alleged abuser, and social characteristics of the victim. Minority, poor, and single parents are more likely to be correctly and incorrectly reported as abusers than are wealthy, white and intact families [9–11]. Infants are more likely to be identified as victims than are teenagers [9].

Research in Sweden. The State Board of Social Welfare in Sweden undertook two national investigations in which they tried to establish the extent and character of child abuse in Sweden. The first study, which was reported in 1969, examined the period from 1957 to 1966. Data were collected from all general hospitals and all surgical, children's surgical, neurological, pediatric, and children's and youth psychiatric clinics. In addition, data were collected from all medico-legal centers in Sweden. In all, 178 places were contacted as part of the survey. Two cases were reported in 1957; by 1966 there were 66, with an average of 11.9 cases annually for the 10-year period.

A second report was published in 1975 and described the conditions during the period 1969 to 1970. For this period, there was an average of 147 cases of bodily abuse each year and 7 cases titled "sexual outrage."

Sweden, like all countries with the exception of the United States and Canada, does not have laws mandating the reporting of child abuse and neglect [12]. Thus, most of the iceberg of child maltreatment remains below the surface of official recognition in Sweden.

Methods

The United States Survey

One source of data which is not biased by official reports or awareness and which examines a range of violent acts experienced by children is the National Family Violence Survey carried out in 1976 by Murray Straus, Richard J. Gelles, and Suzanne Steinmetz [13]. This survey served as the comparison data for a national survey of violence toward Swedish children conducted by Ake Edfeldt.

A full description of the National Violence Survey in the United States, and specifically the portion of the survey which focused on violence towards children, has been published elsewhere [13]. This section briefly reviews the definitions, measurement, and sample used in the survey.

Defining violence and abuse. Violence was nominally defined as "an act carried out with the intention, or perceived intention, of physically injuring another person." The injury could range from slight pain, as in a slap, to murder. The motivation might range from concern for a child's safety (as when a child is spanked for going into the street) to hostility so intense that the death of the child is desired [14]. Abusive acts were those acts which had a high probability of causing an injury to the child (an injury did not have to actually occur).

Operationalizing violence and abuse. Violence was operationalized through the use of the Conflict Tactics Scales (CTS). First developed at the University of New Hampshire in 1971, this technique has been modified extensively and used in numerous studies of family violence [15–20]. The Conflict Tactics Scales contain items to measure three variables: (1) use of rational discussion and argument (discussed the issue calmly; got information to back up one's side; brought in/tried to bring in someone to help settle things); (2) use of verbal and nonverbal expressions of hostility (insulted or swore at the other; sulked or refused to talk about it; stomped out of the room or house; did or said something to spite the other; threatened to hit or throw something at the other; or threw, smashed, hit or kicked something); and (3) use of physical force or violence as a means of managing the conflict (threw something at the other; pushed, grabbed, shoved the other; slapped or spanked; kicked, bit or hit with a fist; hit or tried to hit with something; beat up the other; threatened with a knife or gun; or used knife or gun). The abuse items were those acts that had a high probability of causing an injury: kicked, bit or hit with a fist; beat up; threatened with a knife or gun; or used a knife or gun.

The Conflict Tactics Scales were presented to subjects in the order enumerated, and the subjects were asked to say how often they used each technique when they had a disagreement or were angry with a child, both in the previous year and in the course of the relationship with the child.

The Conflict Tactics Scales' definition of violence and abuse is different from traditional definitions of child abuse. First, in one sense, the definition is broader than most definitions since it is not limited to acts of violence that only result in injury (operational definitions of child abuse that rely on official reports almost invariably are limited to instances of violence that result in a diagnosable injury). In another sense, the Conflict Tactics Scales are narrower than many definitions of abuse because the Scales are limited to a specific list of violent acts. Omitted, for example, are burnings or scaldings of children. Another limitation of the Scales is that they rely on the parents' recollection and willingness to report specific acts of violence.

Reliability and validity. The reliability and validity of the Conflict Tactics Scales has been assessed over the 15-year period of its development and modification. A full discussion of reliability and validity can be found elsewhere [13, 21]. There is evidence of adequate internal consistency reliability, concurrent validity, and construct validity.

Sample. A national probability sample of 2,143 households comprised the National Family Violence Survey [13]. In each family where there were two caretakers present and there was at least one child at home between the ages of 3 and 17, a referent child was selected using a random procedure. An important limitation of the sample was the omission of referent children under the age of 3 years and single parents. Many experts believe that children under 3 years of age and children of single parents are at the greatest risk of physical abuse [22–24]. Because of the examination of violence towards children was imbedded in a larger survey designed to measure all forms

135

of family violence, including violence between couples and violence between siblings, single parents and children less than 3 years of age were excluded from the sample (acts perpetrated by children younger than 3 years of age could not be considered violence in the same way as acts committed by older children).

Of the 2,143 families interviewed, 1,146 had two caretakers and children between the ages of 3 and 17 living at home. The data on parent-to-child violence in the United States are based on the analysis of these 1,146 parent-child relationships.

The Survey in Sweden

Sample. A basic sample of 1,618 individuals representative of Swedish children aged 3 to 17 was purchased by the research team in Sweden. The list contained the name, address, and national registration number of the children as well as an identifier which indicated who was officially responsible for the household. The head of the household's name, address, and national registration number were obtained also. (In Sweden, the male partner in a two-parent household is automatically identified as the head of the household; thus, a female name automatically indicated a single parent household.) As the Swedish survey was not concerned with violence between partners, the Swedish sample included two-parent and single-parent households.

There was an initial loss of 3.3% of the sample due to incorrect or insufficient identification data. Forty-one households (2.5%) refused to participate in the survey, although telephone interviews were completed with 11 of these individuals. Additional cases were lost due to language barriers. Interviews were completed with 78.9% of the sample—a higher completion rate than the United States survey. However, a random subsample of 171 completed interviews were lost in transit between two offices of the Swedish State Data Processing Unit. Due to the complete anonymity of the survey, researchers were unable to identify and recontact these individuals.

A final completion rate of 68% was obtained for 1,105 usable interviews. There were 255 single-parent households (only 3 of which were headed by men) and 850 two-parent households. The age and regional distribution of the sample approximated the distribution in Sweden.

Differences between the Two Surveys

Although the Swedish survey was designed as a replication of the study in the United States, there were some important differences. First, the United States survey was conducted in 1976 while the Swedish survey was completed four years later in 1980. Second, while both studies collected data by using in-person interviews in the homes of the respondents, the United States investigators employed a professional survey research company and professional interviewers. The Swedish interviews were conducted by trained psychologists.

The Conflict Tactics Scales were translated into Swedish. In the process, there were two changes from the original scales. Whereas the American research group asked how often did you threaten/use a gun or knife, the Swedish project asked how often did you threaten/use a weapon. The American version of the Scales asked about slapping or spanking, while the Swedish version asked about hitting. In America, respondents were asked how often they hit or tried to hit their children with objects. These items could include attempted and/or completed hits. In Sweden the interviewers qualified this item by measuring only completed hits.

Results

Because of the contrasts between the United States and Sweden, especially with regard to social and cultural attitudes about violence and because the Swedish survey was conducted a year after the passage of the anti-spanking law, we expected that the reported rates of violence towards children would be lower in Sweden than in the United States. The results, however, do not generally support this hypothesis.

Physical Punishment

In addition to the administration of the Conflict Tactics Scales, respondents in the United States and Sweden were asked whether they had used any form of physical punishment towards their children in the previous year. Slightly more than half (51.3%) of the Swedish parents reported using physical punishment compared to more than three-quarters (79.2%) of the Americans.

Violence towards Children

The responses to the Conflict Tactics items offer a more precise comparison as shown in

Table 1. In general, Swedish parents reported less use of violence towards their children during 1980 than the American respondents reported in 1975 (29.8% vs. 63%). Swedish parents reported less violent conflict tactics during the course of raising their children than the Americans, but the difference here is smaller than for the one-year recall period.

There is no significant difference between Swedish and American parents in the reported use of severe or abusive violence (kicking, biting, hitting with a fist, beating up, threatening or using a weapon—gun or knife). If one includes hitting (or trying to hit) with an object, there are differences; but these differences are not reliable since the Swedish item only examined completed hits while the item in the United States asked about trying to hit as well.

A rate of abusive violence of 4% in Sweden means that each year 62,000 of the more than 1.5 million Swedish children 3 to 17 years of age are at risk of physical abuse (considering sampling error, the range is from 39,000 to 84,000). In the United States, between 1.4 and 1.9 million children 3 to 17 years of age living with two caretakers were at risk for physical abuse during the survey year.

An item by item examination of the two surveys reveals that Swedish parents report more pushing, grabbing or shoving than American parents (which accounts for the difference between the Swedish previous year figures) and double the rate of beating children both in the last year and over the course of raising their children. American parents report more spanking (about double the rate of Swedish parents in the previous year, a bit less than 50% more over the course of the child's life). In general, there were far more similarities in the two countries than there were differences.

Factors Associated with Violence towards Children

A complete profile of the factors associated with violence towards children in the United States has been previously published [13, 25]. This section briefly compares the factors found related to violence and abusive violence which are comparable in the two countries.

Age. In both the United States and Sweden, younger parents are more likely to use violence towards their children than older parents.

Marital status. Only intact families were surveyed in the United States. However, much of the child abuse literature claims that single parents are at a greater risk for abusing and striking their children due to higher stress and low income [25–27]. There were no significant differences in the rates of violence towards children between Swedish parents who were married and those who were single parents at the time of the interview.

TABLE 1 *Violence Towards Children in the United States and Sweden*

Type of Violence	United States 1975	United States Ever	Sweden 1980	Sweden Ever
1. Threw things at	5.4%	9.0%	3.6%	13.2%
2. Pushed, grabbed, or shoved	40.5	46.0	49.4	63.3
3. Hit (spanked or slapped)	58.2	71.0	27.5	51.2
4. Kicked, bit, or hit with a fist	3.2	8.0	2.2	8.4
5. Hit with an object*	13.4	20.0	2.4	7.7
6. Beat up	1.3	4.0	3.0	8.0
7. Threatened with a weapon	0.1	2.8	0.4	1.5
8. Used a weapon	0.1	2.9	0.4	1.3
All forms of Violence (3–8)	63.0	73.0	29.8	66.0
Severe Violence (Index A: 4 thru 8)	14.2	—	4.6	—
Severe Violence (Index B: 4, 6 thru 8)	3.6	—	4.1	—

*In the United States this item referred to attempted or completed hits. In Sweden, the item referred only to completed hits.

Education. A curvilinear relation was found between violence towards children and education in the United States—those parents with the highest (at least some college) and lowest (no high school) levels of education were the least likely to use violence. In Sweden, education was unrelated to the rate of abusive violence towards children. Those who had the highest levels of education actually were more likely to report using some form of violence towards their children.

Parents' backgrounds. Violence begets violence, we are told. And, to a certain degree this is borne out in both surveys. Being spanked as a teenager and observing one's parents hit one another raises the chances that a person will be a violent parent both in the United States and in Sweden.

Discussion

The results of the comparison of violence towards children in the United States and Sweden are complex and do not generally support the hypothesis that Swedish parents are less likely to use violence than American parents. However, Swedish parents tend to be less likely to use the least harmful forms of violence. There is less spanking and slapping in Sweden than there is in the United States. There were no appreciable differences in the rates of abusive violent acts between the two countries.

What accounts for the differences and similarities? First, there are methodological artifacts that may have entered into the comparison study.

Methodological Factors

There were important differences in the qualifications of the interviewers employed in the United States and Sweden. The Swedish interviewers were trained psychologists. We know that they were able to obtain a higher response rate than the American survey research firm. They may have been more successful in eliciting more truthful answers from the respondents. Thus, the rate of violence towards children may be larger in Sweden because the Swedes were more inclined to provide accurate reports of their use of violence, while American respondents systematically under-reported violence.

If one continues to assume that Swedish parents are indeed less violent, then this too could have produced more accurate reporting.

If violence is indeed unusual in Sweden, then Swedish parents may have been more likely to remember these unusual behaviors. If violence is "as American as apple pie," then American parents may have been more likely to under-report the routine use of all forms of violence. Thus, Swedish parents may be less violent towards their children than American parents even though a combination of methodological biases produced similar rates for the abusive forms of violent behavior.

Cultural Factors

In the absence of certain known biases, researchers are trained to believe their data. Thus, even though methodological explanations are a plausible explanation for the findings, we still must accept another plausible explanation that the similarities and differences are real. This being the case, why are Swedish parents more moderate in their use of spanking, slapping, general hitting and throwing things than American parents, but as likely to beat, kick, bite, punch and even use weapons?

A close examination of the yearly rates of violence compared to the "ever" reports, provides some evidence that the anti-spanking law has had some impact on the lives and behavior of Swedish parents. While the differences between the yearly rates of spanking, slapping, pushing, grabbing and throwing things are small in the United States, the differences are much greater in Sweden. Since 1980 was the first year that the anti-spanking law was in force (the year of the Swedish survey), parental use of the less harmful forms of violence may have begun to decline.

Spanking, slapping, pushing, and grabbing tend to be the more instrumental forms of violence used by parents. Thus, when hitting children became illegitimate in Sweden, parents may have found it easier to moderate their use of violence as an instrumental technique. Kicking, biting, punching, beating, and using weapons could be considered either more expressive forms of violence (i.e., expressed out of anger or rage) or forms of violence consciously designed to inflict serious injury on a child. These behaviors may be less amenable to control by imposing a cultural standard that spanking is wrong (note the anti-spanking law carries with it no punishment for violation).

At the risk of over-generalizing from a

cross-sectional survey, Swedish parents may be responding to the anti-spanking law and lowering their use of the less harmful forms of physical punishment. The more abusive forms of violence appear to be less sensitive to change, at least in the short run.

The fact that there are essentially no differences in the use of abusive violence is still surprising given the differences in cultural attitudes, cultural complexity and social support in the two countries. One simple explanation is that the attitude changes and levels of social support (e.g., day care, health care) have not gone far enough in Sweden to curtail the use of abusive violence. A more complex formulation is that the differences between the two countries are not nearly as major as one would think. The similarities are those factors which are related to the use of abusive violence towards children. Both societies are western, industrial nations—Sweden tending more towards a socialist economy than the United States. Family life in both countries conforms to the norm of western, industrial nations. Nuclear residence and a premium on family privacy and family rights are the cultural norm for both nations. An exchange/social control explanation of family violence [28] explains that privacy and primacy of the family limits the amount of external social control (formal and informal) that is exerted on family members. With limited social control, the costs of using abusive violence are frequently quite minimal—even if there is a public anti-spanking law. In the extensive report from the Swedish study another more sophisticated explanation is given to the obvious similarities in the two national samples [29].

Injurious Physical Violence
One of the important limitations of the Conflict Tactics Scales used to measure violence towards children in the United States and Sweden is that it does not measure whether a child was actually ever injured or harmed by the physical violence. While we can measure violent behavior in the two countries, we have little insight into the actual harm inflicted on children. Official reporting records on child maltreatment in the United States are useful means of measuring the harm inflicted on children (at least the harm that comes to public attention). Unfortunately, there is no official reporting of child maltreatment in Sweden and, therefore, there is no opportunity to compare levels of harm experienced by children.

We do have at least some anecdotal data that would seem to imply that, although Swedish and American children are about equally likely to experience violence that could cause harm, there is less of what one would call classic child abuse in Sweden.

At the U.S. and Swedish Symposium on Physical and Sexual Abuse of Children, held in Satra Bruk, Sweden, in June 1985, the American pediatrician, Eli Newberger, presented a report on hospital management of physical abuse. He described a number of cases, including slides of various physically abused children. All Swedish participants agreed that, while they had occasionally seen similar abuse cases in the past, they were no longer seeing these types of cases in 1985.

Thus, although we cannot empirically verify this claim, the changes in social attitudes and social support in Sweden may have been successful in reducing the outrageous, grievous injuries experienced by children. Although Swedish parents are still violent, the violence is not allowed to escalate to the point of injury. However, it is just as possible that, since data on physical abuse are not routinely reported and tabulated in Sweden, the rates of injurious violence are the same in both countries (as our data suggest) but abusive violence in Sweden is simply not recognized or reported as such.

Conclusion

Research often tends to raise as many questions as are answered. Such was the case with this first cross-cultural comparison of the rate of violence towards children. We thought that the rates of violence would be lower in Sweden than in the United States, but we found a more complex pattern. Clearly, the relationship between social and cultural attitudes, social support, and societal complexity and the use of physical violence towards children is not simple or unitary. Only with continued and expanded cross-cultural research will we be able to refine our understanding of the socio-cultural factors that relate to the physical abuse of children.

REFERENCES
1. Gelles, R. J. and Cornell, C. *International Perspectives on Family Violence.* Lexington Books, Lexington, MA (1983).
2. Kempe, C. H. Recent developments in the field

of child abuse. *Child Abuse & Neglect* 2:261–267 (1978).

3. Korbin, J. (Ed.). *Child Abuse and Neglect: Cross Cultural Perspectives.* University of California Press, Berkeley (1981).

4. Straus, M. A. Methodology of collaborative cross-national research on child abuse. Unpublished paper presented at the Swedish/American Symposium on Physical and Sexual Abuse of Children, Satra Bruk, Sweden (1985).

5. Vesterdal, J. Handling of child abuse in Denmark. *Child Abuse & Neglect* 1:193–198 (1977).

6. Gelles, R. J. Violence towards children in the United States. *American Journal of Orthopsychiatry* 48:580–592 (1978).

7. Gelles, R. J. and Cornell, C. *Intimate Violence in Families.* Sage, Beverly Hills, CA (1985).

8. Burgdorf, K. *Recognition and Reporting of Child Maltreatment.* Westat, Rockville, MD (1980).

9. Gelles, R. J. The social construction of child abuse. *American Journal of Orthopsychiatry* 45:363–371 (1975).

10. Newberger, E., Reed, R. B., Daniel, J. H., Hyde, J. N. and Kotelchuck, M. Pediatric social illness: Toward an etiologic classification. *Pediatrics* 60:178–185 (1977).

11. Turbett, J. P. and O'Toole, R. Physician's recognition of child abuse. Unpublished paper presented at the annual meetings of the American Sociological Association, New York (1980).

12. Kamerman, S. Eight countries: Cross national perspectives on child abuse and neglect. *Children Today* 4:34–37 (1975).

13. Straus, M. A., Gelles, R. J. and Steinmetz, S. K. *Behind Closed Doors: Violence in the American Family.* Anchor/Doubleday, Garden City, NY (1980).

14. Gelles, R. J. and Straus, M. Determinants of violence in the family: Toward a theoretical integration. In: *Contemporary Theories about the Family,* (Vol. 1), W. R. Burr, R. Hill, F. I. Nye, and I. Reiss (Eds.), pp. 549–581. The Free Press, New York (1979).

15. Allen, C. and Strauss, M. Resources, power and husband-wife violence. Unpublished paper presented to the National Council on Family Relations in Salt Lake City (1975).

16. Cate, R. M., Henton, J. M., Christopher, F. S. and Lloyd, S. Premarital abuse: A social psychological perspective. *Journal of Family Issues* 3:79–90 (1982).

17. Henton, J., Cate, R., Koval, J., Lloyd, S. and Christopher, S. Romance and violence in dating relationships, *Journal of Family Issues* 4:467–482 (1983).

18. Hornung, C., McCullough, B. and Sugimoto, T. Status relationships in marriage: Risk factors in spouse abuse. *Journal of Marriage and the Family* 43:679–692 (1981).

19. Jorgensen, S. Societal class heterogamy, status striving, and perception of marital conflict: A partial replication and revision of Perlin's contingency hypothesis. *Journal of Marriage and the Family* 43:679–692 (1977).

20. Straus, M. A. Leveling, civility, and violence in the family. *Journal of Marriage and the Family* 36:13–30 (1974).

21. Straus, M. A. Measuring intrafamily conflict and violence: The Conflict Tactics (CT) scales. *Journal of Marriage and the Family* 41:75–88 (1979).

22. Fergusson, D. M., Fleming, J. and O'Neil, D. *Child Abuse in New Zealand* Research Division, Department of Social Work, Wellington NZ (1972).

23. Gil, D. *Violence Against Children: Physical Child Abuse in the United States.* Harvard University Press, Cambridge, MA (1970).

24. Johnson, C. *Child Abuse in the Southeast: An Analysis of 1172 Reported Cases.* Welfare Research, Athens, GA (1974).

25. Gelles, R. J. Violence in the family: A review of research in the seventies. *Journal of Marriage and the Family* 42:873–885 (1980).

26. Parke, R. D. and Collmer, C. Child abuse: An interdisciplinary analysis. In: *Review of Child Development Research,* (Vol. 5), M. Hetherington (Ed.), pp. 1–102. University of Chicago Press, Chicago (1975).

27. Maden, M. F. and Wrench, D. F. Significant findings in child abuse research. *Victimology* 2:196–224 (1977).

28. Gelles, R. J. An exchange/social control theory. In: *The Dark Side of Families: Current Family Violence Research,* D. Finkelhor, R. Gelles, M. Straus, and G. Hotaling (Eds.). pp. 151–165. Sage, Beverly Hills, CA (1983).

29. Edfeldt, A. Research and theory on violence towards children in Sweden. Unpublished paper presented at the Sweden/American Symposium on Physical and Sexual Abuse of Children, Satra Bruk, Sweden (1985).

Are There Signs of Child Abuse and Neglect?

(Are There Signs That a Family May Be in Trouble?)

There are many indications that a family may be in trouble. Any one of them may not mean abuse or neglect and may have other explanations. If there are a number of them or if they occur frequently, child abuse or neglect may be suspected.

Type of Child Abuse/Neglect	Physical Indications/ Child Appearance	Child Behavior	Parent/Caretaker Behavior
Physical Abuse 1. Assault with an implement 2. Assault without implement	Unexplained bruises and welts Unexplained burns Unexplained head or skeletal injuries Unexplained lacerations or abrasions	Wary of physical contact with adults Seeks affection from any adult Apprehensive when others cry Behavioral extremes (e.g., aggressiveness or withdrawal) Frightened of parents or little distress at separation Afraid to go home; hangs around school Reports injury by parents Exhibits anxiety about normal activities (e.g., napping)	Harsh discipline, inappropriate for age and condition No explanation or offers explanation that doesn't make sense for child's injury Lack of concern about child Views child as "bad" Misuses alcohol or drugs Attempts to conceal child's injury History of abuse as a child
Physical Neglect 1. Abandonment 2. Refusal of custody 3. Failure to provide needed care for health condition 4. Inadequate physical supervision	Consistent hunger, poor hygiene, inappropriate dress Consistent lack of supervision, especially in dangerous activities or for long periods Unattended physical problems or medical needs	Begging, stealing food Constant fatigue, listlessness, or falling asleep States there is no caretaker at home Frequent absence from school	Misuses alcohol or drugs Disorganized, unstable home life Apathetic Isolated socially Long-term chronic illness History of neglect as a child

(cont.)

Source: Based on Broadhurst, D. D. (1979). *The educator's role in the prevention and treatment of child abuse and neglect* (DHEW Publication No. OHDS 79-30172). Washington, DC: National Center on Child Abuse and Neglect; and Broadhurst, D. D., Edmunds, M., & MacDicken, R. A. (1979). *Early childhood programs and the prevention and treatment of child abuse and neglect* (DHEW Publication No. OHDS 79-30198). Washington, DC: National Center on Child Abuse and Neglect.

Type of Child Abuse/Neglect	Physical Indications/ Child Appearance	Child Behavior	Parent/Caretaker Behavior
5. Disregard of home hazards 6. Inadequate nutrition, clothing, or hygiene 7. Other (e.g., disregard for child's safety)			
Sexual Abuse 1. Intrusion 2. Molestation with genital contact 3. Other	Difficulty in walking or sitting Torn, stained, or bloody underclothing Pain or itching in genital area Bruises or bleeding in genital area Venereal disease	Unwilling to participate in some physical activities Withdrawal; fantasy or unusual infantile behavior Bizarre, sophisticated, or unusual sexual behavior or knowledge Poor peer relations Reports sexual assault by caretaker	Very protective or jealous of child Encourages child to engage in prostitution or sexual acts Misuses alcohol or drugs Frequently absent from home
Emotional Maltreatment 1. Verbal or emotional assault 2. Close confinement 3. Inadequate nurturance/affection 4. Knowingly "permitted" drug or alcohol abuse or delinquency 5. Other	Speech disorders Lags in physical development Failure-to-thrive	Habit disorders (sucking, biting, rocking, etc.) Conduct disorders (antisocial, self-destructive, defiant, etc.) Neurotic traits (sleep disorders, inhibition of play) Psychoneurotic reactions (hysteria, obsession, compulsion, phobias, hypochondria) Behavior extremes (e.g., compliant, passive, apathetic, aggressive, demanding) Overly adaptive behavior (e.g., inappropriately adult or inappropriately infant) Developmental lags (mental, emotional)	Blames or belittles child Cold and rejecting; withholds love Treats children in the family unequally Indifferent about child's problems

Case Studies:
The Carrs and the Thomases

The Carr Family

The Present Problem

On November 25, 1974, Mrs. Thelma Carr brought her three daughters (Dolores, 7; Laura, 4; and Mindy, almost 2) to the police station. She told the officer on duty that neither she nor the children's father, Mr. Henry Carr, was capable of taking adequate care of their children, nor did they have any friends or relatives who were. That same day, the police assisted Mrs. Carr in placing the three children in the county Department of Social Services youth shelter. Shortly thereafter, Mr. Carr appeared with a babysitter he had just hired and asked to take the children home.

Family History

Married in 1967, the Carrs have a history of separations, unemployment, and financial difficulties. When they separated in 1972 (before their youngest child was born), Mrs. Carr placed the two girls in the care of a babysitter during the hours she worked in an amusement park. One day Mr. Carr appeared at the babysitter's and took Laura away without his wife's knowledge. The uproar that ensued was resolved by placing the children in foster care, where they stayed for six months until the Carrs reconciled. The family later moved to their present address, the third city they have lived in since their marriage.

In February of 1974, when Mr. Carr lost his job as a taxi driver, the family applied for assistance from the Department of Public Welfare. During this period the children stayed with Mrs. Carr's parents in a nearby city. Before the assistance could be granted, however, Mr. Carr obtained another job, and the case was closed.

Two weeks before Mrs. Carr appeared with her children at the police station, she and her husband separated again; Mrs. Carr left the girls with her husband in the hope that he would find an adequate caretaker for them. Neighbors report that he did not make adequate provision for them, they were poorly fed and supervised, and were sometimes seen outside late at night, poorly clothed and in the rain. The neighbors were apparently convinced that the children were not developing normally (especially Laura and Mindy, the younger two), and a group of them told Mr. Carr that they would call the police unless he had his children checked by a doctor. This warning prompted Mr. Carr to take the girls to the hospital clinic, where the attending pediatrician noted that all three children were filthy. He also diagnosed Mindy, the two-year-old, as a failure-to-thrive child due to poor nutritional and hygienic care. He sent a referral form for Mindy to the probation department, which arrived after Mrs. Carr had already placed the children in the department's youth house.

The following information has been collected regarding family members:

Mr. Henry Carr. The eligibility worker on the Carr's assistance case noted that Mr. Carr is an apparently good worker and union member, who occasionally loses a job because of two- to three-day binges. He is also apparently able to get another job as a taxi driver fairly quickly. From other sources it was determined that he did not follow up on the hospital pediatrician's instructions given two weeks before the children were placed in the youth house.

Mrs. Thelma Carr. Herself an only adopted child, she seems to be the dominant member of the family, according to the eligibility worker, but leaves responsibility for child care to her husband when he is home. The Carr's landlord complained to the eligibility worker that while the two older girls seemed ade-

Source: National Center on Child Abuse and Neglect (1979). Case history and discussion questions: The Carr family; The Thomas case with discussion questions. *Resource materials: A curriculum on child abuse and neglect* (DHEW Publication No. OHDS 79-30221). Washington, DC: U.S. Government Printing Office, pp. 31–32, 38–39.

143

quately cared for, Mindy was seldom changed or dressed properly. Both parents admit that their children had not received medical care for a period of two years prior to Mr. Carr's "enforced" visit to the hospital clinic.

Dolores Carr. Now seven years old, Dolores is developmentally normal. Her first grade teacher reports that she comes to school regularly, but is always very unkempt. Although her work habits are sloppy, she is one of the brightest children in the class. She has been largely responsible for the care of her two younger sisters.

Laura Carr. Laura is four. When she was born she had so much difficulty retaining food that she had to spend ten days in the newborn intensive care section of the hospital. During her first year she cried most of the time, and according to her parents did not walk until she was two and one-half years old. Mrs. Carr reports that she began to catch up in her development during the six months she spent in foster care in 1972. When she was returned to her parents she continued this growth, but not at such a rapid rate. Youth house officials saw her developmental difficulties primarily in her speech and motor coordination: she is enuretic (consistent bed-wetter), does not speak intelligibly, will not walk without assistance, and tends to drag her right leg. A psychologist who examined her found her likeable and co-operative, but fearful of new tasks and of guessing, and while she found her speech intelligible, she reported a definite need for speech therapy. She also stated that Laura's emotional attachment remains with her natural family, particularly with her mother.

Mindy Carr. Now almost two, Mindy is an extremely thin child with a large head. She weighed seven pounds at birth, would not cry and had to be given oxygen. The attending physician noted a distended stomach and felt a spinal tap was necessary. Mindy was kept in intensive care for 11 days before she was allowed to go home. Mrs. Carr states that Mindy did not receive follow-up medical care, but gained weight and ate well after coming home. At the youth house, Mindy is unable to sit up or to engage in play. A psychologist who tested her found that her responses are on a level of a 10- or 11-month-old child.

Discussion Questions:
1. What are the indicators of neglect in this case?
2. How does this case fit (or not fit) your State's definition of child neglect?
3. What seems to be the Carr family's underlying problem?
4. Are there any contra-indicators in this case (factors which suggest an explanation other than neglect that would account for the conditions and behaviors of the family)?
5. What additional information, if any, do you need to decide what you would recommend be done to insure adequate care for the Carr children?

The Thomas Case

The Report
On August 17, 1976, at 12:10 p.m., the Child Protective Service office in Port City was contacted by Lorraine Shotwell of 3742 55th Street, Apt. 5, concerning possible child beating. Miss Shotwell said she had seen a man in Apartment 2 beating his four-year-old daugher with a wide belt and that the child had numerous bruises resulting from the beating. Miss Shotwell also stated that she had seen the man in Apartment 2 pick his three-year-old son up by the hair and lift him roughly over a fence.

The Investigation
Ms. Louise Allen was assigned to make the Child Protective Service's investigation on this report. She arrived at the home of Mr. and Mrs. Peter Thomas, in Apartment 2 of 3748 55th Street, at 4:15 p.m. the same day. Mr. Thomas was informed that Ms. Allen was there to investigate possible child abuse. Mr. Thomas was concerned and cooperative. Ms. Allen asked if she could examine and talk to Mari, his four-year-old daughter.

Ms. Allen found fresh bruises from the middle of Mari's shoulder blades to the middle of her buttocks. The bruises were elongated, as if caused by a belt. Mari also had a horse shoe shaped bruise on her stomach which appeared to Ms. Allen as though it could have been caused by the buckle of the belt flicking around her waist and hitting her on the stomach. Though clearly in pain, Mari did not cry while Ms. Allen examined her back. The

Thomases' three-year-old son, Peter, Jr., was also examined and there was a scratch and redness on his right cheek. There were no other visible signs of possible abuse on the boy. Peter was quite frightened as Ms. Allen examined his torso and went immediately to his mother for comfort when she had completed her examination. When Mr. Thomas was questioned about the bruises, he said Mari had gone to the corner where she knew she was not allowed to go. Mr. Thomas said his father had strapped him until it hurt to sit for days and it had not left any scars on him. Mr. Thomas stated that it was his business how he disciplined his children and not his nosey neighbors'.

Mrs. Thomas stated that her husband was even-tempered normally and that Mari deserved the strapping that she got.

Discussion Questions:

1. What are the physical indicators of child abuse?
   • Mari
   • Peter, Jr.
2. What are the behavioral indicators of child abuse?
   • Mari
   • Peter, Jr.
3. What are parental characteristics that suggest a possible child abuse problem?
4. What other kinds of information would you like to know about the Thomases?
5. If Mari's bruises had first been discovered by you, either in your professional role or as a neighbor, would you have called Child Protective Services? Why? Why not?

The Background

Mari is Peter and Noreen Thomas' first child. Mrs. Thomas states that Mari's birth and development have been normal. The mother further indicates that Mari has always been a happy, well-behaved child. She further said that Mari is not now and never has been in preschool because she is not completely toilet-trained.

Mr. Thomas readily admits that he strapped his daugher. He believes he should have.

There is no prior history with the Port City Child Protective Services unit or the Police Department indicating abusive behavior on the part of the Thomases.

At the time of the Child Protective Service investigation in this report, the Thomases became somewhat hostile and apparently felt that they were being singled out by the agency.

Interviews with the parents disclosed several facts about the parents, including a belief that unacceptable behavior should result in "strict" corporal punishment, a lack of familiarity with appropriate child-rearing techniques and anxiety about chronic financial difficulties.

The Thomases' youngest child, Peter, is an epileptic. His condition is controlled with medication. Peter is also somewhat hyperkinetic. Mr. and Mrs. Thomas sometimes find it difficult to keep Peter under control.

Parents' History

Noreen Thomas was born in Ogdensburg, New York. She was raised in a small community north of Albany. Her parents divorced when she was an infant and she has had little contact with her father throughout her life. Mrs. Thomas is a high school graduate. She worked for an insurance company for four years.

Mr. Thomas was born in San Francisco, California. He is one of four brothers. While Mr. Thomas was growing up, his father pursued a career in both the Navy and the Coast Guard, necessitating the family's continual movement. His parents remained married until his father's death several years ago.

Mr. Thomas is a high school graduate. He is a career man in the Navy, enlisted for approximately ten years. He is an electrical specialist and his rank is E-6.

The Thomases have resided in Port City for eighteen months. They have a two-bedroom apartment in an apartment complex. The apartment is somewhat cluttered although adequate housekeeping standards are met. It appears that the Thomases have more possessions than their apartment can accommodate.

The Thomases are expecting a child in October. The baby was planned. Since the birth of their two children, Mr. and Mrs. Thomas have taken out insurance policies for the children's college educations. Mr. Thomas also stated that when he was in Vietnam, he earned a silver star. This award entitles his children to a free education at a military school and at certain nursing schools.

Discussion Questions:

1. What factors in Noreen's and Peter's individual histories are significant in determining whether they need help as parents?
2. What additional factors in the Thomases' present life circumstances are significant in determining whether they need help?
3. What kinds of help might be offered?
4. Should a child abuse petition (or case) be filed with juvenile court in order to have supervision over this family to attempt to insure the protection of the children or to remove the children temporarily for their own protection? Why? Why not?

Children and Privacy

Barbara Lonnborg

Do you remember what private world you sometimes escaped into as a child?

Did you captain a pirate ship from the deck of a rock beside a stream? Did you build your own castle from cattails in a field? Or perhaps you traveled to outer space by pulling the bedcovers up over your head.

You may recall with delight the private places and moments of your childhood. Beyond that, you may hope your own children discover the joyous side of time spent alone. But you probably have other expectations of children too—that they be friendly with others, accessible to your family, and willing to share their thoughts with you.

There is plenty of evidence that children need social contact with others, but it is only recently that researchers have begun looking at the other side—whether also being able to choose privacy is important for children.

Some of their studies indicate that children allowed to choose when they want to be alone have higher self-esteem. Others show that a lack of privacy can be related to aggression or psychological withdrawal. In one study, children from crowded households were more aggressive in school than children who had more space and therefore more opportunity for privacy at home.

Youngsters themselves seem to know they need some time alone. For example, when children helped design a playground in California, they wanted it to include rocks, caves, and trees for seclusion, as well as open space for games and swing sets. In New York, child-development specialist Marilyn Rothenberg, Ph.D., asked children to arrange classrooms and found they repeatedly featured a quiet reading corner, screened off by bookshelves and with comfortable furniture or pillows to sit on.

All Children Need Time Alone

From infancy on, children need and benefit from some form of privacy. A series of studies has indicated that noisy, crowded homes have negative effects on infants. Those babies who could occasionally escape to another room away from excessive noise and stimulation showed enhanced mental development during their second year.

Slightly older children may also at times need privacy to withdraw from others and their demands or to rehearse new behavior and enjoy fantasy play.

When Ellen Jacobs of Montreal's Concordia University observed children between the ages of three and five in a day-care center, one-third of them regularly sought some kind of privacy, often late in the day after having spent long hours in the company of others.

Some took a favorite toy or book and climbed into a big cardboard box they called "the house." Others moved furniture around to create private spaces or crawled under tables, pulling the chairs in after them.

Dr. Maxine Wolfe of the Environmental Psychology Program at The Graduate School of the City University of New York and her colleagues interviewed more than 900 children in Wisconsin and New York and discovered that even the youngest children interviewed, at age five, understood what privacy meant. If the children could not remember when *they* had been alone, they could describe times when their parents had privacy.

The seven- to ten-year-olds in the study described for Wolfe the first time they went home alone—for many of them, the most significant opportunity for privacy. "At first they were nervous, but soon they felt terrific," she says. "They realized the positive side of not having

Source: Barbara Lonnborg (1982, May). Children and privacy. *Parents Magazine,* 57, 68–71. Reprinted by permission of Barbara Lonnborg, Director of Public Service, Boys Town, Nebraska.

147

anybody around. It wasn't that they wanted to do things their parents wouldn't approve of—it was just feeling free to be themselves."

The Quest for Independence

Privacy experiences for children can be exhilarating steps in their struggle for independence from parents. Young children believe all of their movements are known by adults even when they are out of sight. When they catch on that this is not true, children learn to enjoy the greater freedom and power of operating alone. This realization—that they can control others' information about them—is important in helping children discover themselves as unique individuals.

On their own, children can be resourceful and inventive. Ten-year-old Sara plays chess with her cat.

Billy, also ten, says, "I put together puzzles, read books, and sometimes I make up movies in my head using the *Star Wars* people."

"I like to talk to my dog and pretend she can talk to me," says nine-year-old Adam. "I want to be alone then, so I don't have to answer any questions."

Children seek privacy in different ways. Suburban or rural children will be more likely than urban children to have outdoor places where they go to be alone. Privacy for children living in cities may mean keeping a secret or being unbothered by others or undisturbed by noise even if other people are within sight.

Children can feel private in many situations, but what counts most to them, says Wolfe, is whether the choice to be alone is theirs. And that doesn't happen often. In her study, nearly all of the children who could recall personal moments of privacy also said their parents could and did invade their private space at any time. "That power seemed to be given to parents by definition," she says.

For example, one youngster pointed out to Wolfe, "It's not *really* my bedroom; it's my parents' house."

Respecting a Child's Privacy

Parents often give mixed signals to children about privacy.

Parents, Wolfe says, often demand and attach status to their own privacy but believe they need to know everything their children are doing and thinking—and feel hurt, angry, or rejected when a child seeks time alone or refuses to share information with them.

Twelve-year-old Julie struggles with this contradiction: "Sometimes I'm reading a book or playing solitaire and I don't want to be disturbed. But I don't know how to tell my parents; I'm too afraid to hurt their feelings."

As a result, children reaching the teenage years may decide that wanting to be alone at times or to keep some feelings private is wrong. Unlike the younger children in Wolfe's study, who saw privacy as a privilege and enjoyed it, adolescents in another study reported being in low spirits when they were alone, even when it was *their* choice to be private.

Dr. Mihaly Csikszentmihalyi, who conducted the study with Dr. Reed Larson at the University of Chicago, thinks that when younger children, up to about age twelve, are alone and daydream, "they spin out stories and visualize themselves doing positive things. It broadens their imagination, gets them in touch with their feelings, and helps them learn about themselves."

On the other hand, when adolescents are alone and unoccupied, many of their thoughts tend to be disconnected and self-critical. Csikszentmihalyi had the teenagers in his study record what they were thinking when a pocket beeper they carried for a week went off at random times. What they reported when alone was often negative; "I'm getting fat." "Jerry doesn't like me." "I'm just wasting time; I should be doing my homework."

But despite these negative feelings, most of the teenagers were spending about one-quarter of their waking hours alone and were apparently benefiting from it, the researchers discovered. For example, even when the teenagers did not enjoy their time alone they still had improved concentration for hobbies and homework and rejoined their families and friends feeling stronger and more alert after periods of solitude.

"Those kids who don't have any time alone are worse off in the long run than those who spend at least some time alone," says Csikszentmihalyi. For many adolescents, he says, solitude is like "bitter medicine"—they don't always enjoy it, but they often feel better because of it.

Is My Child Hiding Something?

Despite the positive effects of privacy, you may be afraid the reason your child wants to be alone is to do or hide something you disapprove of. This suspicion can become a real battleground between parents and teenage children.

"I caught my mother going through my pockets looking for cigarettes," says Brian. "I just blew up."

In other cases, parents listen in on phone calls, go through closets and drawers, read diaries, and literally interrogate children about their whereabouts, actions, even thoughts and feelings.

Wolfe found that privacy invasion by parents only caused adolescents to feel guilty, become defensive, and withdraw further. "There will be times when children need extra support in being with people or instances when they may be doing something destructive to themselves," she says. "But the evidence will not be hidden in the child's dresser drawers. It will be in their eyes, their behavior."

She suggests there are ways that parents can begin showing trust in their children's use of privacy when they are young.

First, try to recognize the times when your children may need to be alone. For example, how often have you asked your youngster what happened during his or her day and gotten the answer "Nothing"? Occasionally this frustrating reply is simply the child's way of saying, "Give me some time, I can't talk about it yet." When you can, grant that time to your child—you may be swamped with conversation later.

"I Want to Be Alone"

Sometimes when children want some privacy, they won't say so directly but will offer an excuse. They may tell you they are tired or not feeling well. Fidgeting or restlessness when playing with others also may be a signal that children need some time alone.

"When my daughters start squabbling," says one mother, "I suggest that they read a book, listen to music, or take a walk by themselves."

Children sometimes stomp away in the middle of an argument. A typical response, according to Wolfe, "is, 'Don't you slam that door on me; come out here and discuss this right now.' But by leaving, the child is saying that the argument is only going to escalate. They sense that they must have time to cool off, think things over, and get some perspective."

You can also provide a time and place for your child to be alone. The home is crucial because in the neighborhood, at school, or on the playground, children have little control over their privacy. Most of the time spent alone by adolescents in the Chicago study, for example, was at home.

If you have taught your child to knock at the door and wait for an answer before entering your room, you can do the same in return so the child knows his or her privacy is equally respected.

Wolfe also suggests that for a week you keep a list of the times you are tempted to invade your child's privacy—insisting he or she play with another child, demanding information on thoughts and feelings, listening at a door—and then try to cut in half those occasions when you do intrude.

When Siblings Share a Room

Providing space to be alone is not difficult when children have their own bedrooms.

"My oldest son would love a room of his own, but that isn't possible," says a mother of two sons, ages three and nine. "So I try to give him time in the bedroom by himself or with his friends and keep his younger brother with me."

Children who share a room may need to feel that part of it is theirs alone. You might let them arrange the furniture and decorate their own portions as they like. You can also provide some individual drawers or shelves for their possessions. The purpose is not to duplicate everything, so your children never have to cooperate or work together, but to give them a few opportunities where *they* can decide whether to share their time or belongings with others.

You may think of picnics and camping trips as *family* activities. But for children who live in apartments or urban areas, these trips may offer a rare chance to explore nature quietly. A walk by himself through the park or a silent vigil on a riverbank can be a special time for a child.

When your child reaches adolescence, try to be aware of the times he or she is most sensitive to preserving privacy. Young people, for example, feel very protective of their telephone conversations, diaries, and personal belongings. There are ways to accommodate these needs.

Judy's family of seven shares one telephone in the busiest room of the house. "We just got a long cord. We're always tripping over it, but now we can take the phone into the bedroom, even down the basement stairs, for privacy," she says.

Too Much Solitude?

What if you become worried that your child is spending too much time alone? Csikszentmihalyi thinks 15 to 30 hours spent alone per week is normal for adolescents.

"If they spend a lot more time alone, then I think you would want to know what they are doing," he says. "If a teenager is only watching television, listening to the same song over and over, or just staring into space, you might be concerned and try interesting him or her in other activities."

However, you probably don't have to worry, Csikszentmihalyi says, if the youth is deeply involved during that time in a hobby or special interest.

Wolfe declines to set boundaries on how much time younger children should spend alone. That will depend, she says, on where they live, the size of their family, and the availability of playmates. But she does suggest that the problem for some young children lies in having almost no chance for private moments.

"But once they have a choice in being alone," says Wolfe, "they do what adults do—they make choices. Sometimes they choose to be with others and sometimes to be alone, sometimes to share and sometimes not."

Allowing young children to reasonably control their own privacy won't be mistaken for lack of concern, according to Wolfe, if you respond warmly when they do seek you out for contact. By letting your child sometimes choose to be private, you are demonstrating your trust in him or her. And that is when the sharing between you truly begins.

Barbara Lonnborg, a former newspaper reporter and editor, is director of public service at the Boys Town Center, Boys Town, Nebraska.

ASK YOURSELF:
Identifying Issues for Debate and Advocacy

1. Does society have the right to interfere in a family's private life? Why or why not?

2. How might certain cultural values in American society (e.g., beliefs in self-reliance, individual control, and the rights of those in authority positions to use force, if necessary, to maintain authority) contribute to potential situations of child abuse?

3. Are current child abuse/neglect laws effective and sufficient? Why or why not?

4. What happens to someone in your state when he or she reports a suspected case of child abuse or child neglect? Can a reporter be held liable for an unfounded report? Should a reporter be able to remain anonymous? Why or why not?

5. Should an abused child generally be taken out of the

home? What general standards are to be used when deciding to remove the child from his or her home?

6. What alternatives can you suggest other than taking an abused child from his or her home? (Also see Rosenberg & Reppucci, 1985.)

7. A number of states (New York, Kentucky, South Carolina, Georgia, Indiana, Missouri, California, and Washington) have been advocating screening day care workers as a means to combat the child sexual abuse problem. Among the policies being instituted are:
   a. Checking state child abuse registers for substantiated reports of child abuse or neglect
   b. Fingerprinting of all day care workers to check for a record of violent or sexual crime
   c. Checking federal and state records for felony convictions

   What are the pros and cons of each of these screening procedures?

8. What staff behaviors in a preschool setting would you consider to be forms of physical, sexual, or emotional maltreatment? Would you include overemphasis on academic skills, overreliance on packaged materials, dislike of particular children, or physical coercion (Paulson, 1983)? Why or why not?

APPLICATION / ADVOCACY EXERCISES

1. Suppose the interaction reported in the vignette at the beginning of this chapter occurred at a school-sponsored family picnic. In small groups, discuss the following issues:
   a. Is there enough evidence here to file a report of suspected child abuse? Why or why not?
   b. Should the school get involved? Why or why not?

   In reaching a decision, use the indicators of child abuse included in this chapter as well as your state's legal definition of child abuse and your state's reporting guidelines.

2. Using the indicators of child abuse and neglect included in this chapter as well as your state's legal definitions of child abuse and neglect and your state's reporting guidelines, analyze the two case reports included in this chapter and respond to the case report questions.

3. Request an interview with a child protective services caseworker. Explain to the individual that you wish to learn more about the prevention, identification, and treatment of child abuse and neglect. Based on information gathered

151

from readings, class presentations, and your own personal experiences, compose at least six interview questions to ask this person. (Consider issues such as who is reporting, confidentiality of reporting, the investigation process, the percentage of unfounded cases, removal of the child from the home, delivery and time frame of services, and case load.) Take notes during the interview in order to obtain a record of the interviewee's responses. After the interview, write a synopsis of the interview, including the interview questions asked, the interviewee's responses, and your interpretation based on chapter readings and other information gathered from class presentations. Cite references used. Share and discuss your report with your classmates.

4. Interview a school nurse about the incidence of child abuse and neglect cases among school children. In framing your interview questions, consider readings, class presentations, and your own experiences related to issues such as identification, reporting procedures, school-home relations, linkages with social and public health agencies, and pupil classroom adjustments. (Also remember to respect the nurse's need to maintain confidentiality.) Take notes during the interview. After the interview, write a synopsis of the interview, including the interview questions asked, the interviewee's responses, and your interpretation based on chapter readings and other information gathered from class presentations. Cite references used. Share and discuss your report with classmates.

REFERENCES & SUGGESTED READINGS

Gelles, R. J., & Cornell, C. P. (1982, September). *International perspectives on family violence.* Paper presented at the annual meeting of the American Sociological Association, San Francisco. (ERIC Document Reproduction Service No. ED 230 830)

George, C., & Main, M. (1979). Interactions of young abused children: Approach, avoidance, and aggression. *Child Development, 50,* 306–318.

Kadushin, A., & Martin, J. A. (1981). *Child abuse: An interactional event.* New York: Columbia University.

Meddin, B. J., & Rosen, A. L. (1986, May). Child abuse and neglect: Prevention and reporting. *Young Children,* 26–30.

Paulson, J. S. (1983). Covert and overt forms of maltreatment in the preschools. *Child Abuse and Neglect: The International Journal, 7,* 45–54.

Rosenberg, M. S., & Reppucci, N. D. (1985). Primary prevention of child abuse. *Psychological Bulletin, 98,* 576–585.

Stuart, D. (1985, November/December). I did what I had to do. *Kiddie Kare,* 33–34.

White, S., Strom, G. A., Santilli, G., & Halpin, B. M. (1986). Interviewing young sexual abuse victims with anatomically correct dolls. *Child Abuse and Neglect: The International Journal, 10,* 519–529.

Wilson, C., & Steppe, S. C. (1986). *Investigating sexual abuse in day care.* Washington, DC: Child Welfare League of America.

CHAPTER 7

Discipline/Group Management

What's the Matter with Melissa?

Melissa Conover, a four-year-old, has just enrolled in your day care center. After observing her for a week, you no longer chuckle about her mother's response to your question, "Does Melissa tire easily?" Her response, "No, just the parents," is all too accurate.

In spite of all your efforts to engage Melissa in a sustained activity, the child seems to be everywhere. One minute she's grabbing a doll away from another child. The next minute she's dashing over to the puzzle table busily tucking pieces into her pocket. You've tried all the reasonable interventions, but nothing you say or do seems to make much difference. In fact, whenever you approach her, she runs in the opposite direction. Melissa, however, will listen to stories and thoroughly enjoys participating in movement activities. Nevertheless, the constant monitoring of her behavior is beginning to wear you down. You wonder how you should proceed.

Questions

1. Often we tend to look at what is wrong with the child instead of looking for what is positive. Are there ways this teacher could build on Melissa's strengths?

2. Melissa's mother indirectly implies that Melissa is a very active child. What kinds of questions could you have asked her to help you better understand Melissa?

3. What effects might an unfamiliar situation have on children's behavior?

PREVIEW

What child behaviors do you consider to be disruptive in a program for young children? What happened the last time you were faced with a child displaying such behavior? What did you do? What values guided your actions or behaviors? The first article, by Irwin A. Hyman and Dolores Lally, describes five approaches to children's acting-out behaviors that do not rely on physical punishment or public humiliation. Lilian G. Katz advocates for use of advanced professional knowledge, professional judgment, and professional standards in making decisions about how to respond to instances of acting-out behavior as opposed to reliance on common sense, personal predilection, or one's feelings. Following Katz's article is a letter to the editor rebutting Katz's view of time out and Katz's response.

Discipline:
Some Alternatives to Corporal Punish

Irwin A. Hyman and Dolores Lally

Most Americans believe that hitting is a perfectly appropriate and often necessary disciplinary method in order to change children's behavior. In the schools, suspension is frequently used as a disciplinary procedure. These approaches to discipline are even more pervasive in the growing private school movement. Public school children have rudimentary constitutional protection in suspension cases, although they have none regarding corporal punishment. However, in private schools, children have little or no protection, an especially crucial factor since the number of private schools is increasing.

We at the National Center for the Study of Corporal Punishment and Alternatives in the Schools, Temple University, are attempting to convince the public that hitting is an unnecessary and ineffective form of discipline—one that may lead to unintended consequences for children. The elimination of physical punishment of children, we believe, could lead to the elimination of most child abuse cases.

We are currently working to inform the public about what is happening in the schools and to help educators, parents and institutional personnel develop repertoires of alternative, positive approaches to discipline. One of the ways in which we do this is through information gathering—by documenting examples of corporal punishment and gathering statistical data on it. For example, our files, based on newspaper clippings, articles and letters from the public, show that students in American schools have been subjected to the use of the paddle, strap, hand, arrow, stick, rope, belt and fist. In addition, students have been subjected to having hair cut off; they have been placed in storerooms, boxes, cloakrooms, closets and school vaults; they have been thrown against walls, desks and concrete pillars; and they have been forced to run the "gauntlet" or "belt line." Other forc[...] ments include making a child perfor[...] tary style push-ups; sticking a pin in a c[...] taping a child's mouth, hands or body; u[...] dressing a child in private or before peers; making a child stand on toes for long periods of time; punching, choking or dragging a child by the arm or hair; withholding meals; forcing a child to stand in pajamas in 20-degree weather, to lay on a wet shower floor in clothing, or to eat cigarettes; tying a child to a chair—all documented examples of child abuse perpetrated by school staff members under color of school law.

The cases mentioned here represent the tip of the iceberg since they were culled mainly from newspaper clippings. Other statistical data, especially that obtained from the Office of Civil Rights Surveys of Education, indicate massive use of corporal punishment and suspensions on children of minority groups.

Center Workshops

Of practical significance are the variety of workshops the Center provides, all tailored to individual and institutional needs. One major workshop, "Seven Approaches to Discipline," is based on research performed by the Center under contract to the National Institute of Education and is designed to help participants gain a broad perspective on theory and practice in the area of discipline.

During the first segment of the all-day workshop, the major theories of human behavior—psychodynamic-interpersonal, behavioral, human potential, ecological, sociological and biophysical—are outlined and discussed. An eclectic process approach is used to align and integrate complementary components of the six major theoretical orientations.[1]

After these theoretical explanations for be-

Source: Irwin A. Hyman & Dolores Lally (1982, January–February). Discipline in the 1980's: Some alternatives to corporal punishment. *Children Today, 11,* 10–13. Reprinted by permission of Irwin A. Hyman.

ed punish-
m mili-
hild;
n-

strategies is develop... reconvene to report, contrast and evaluate the conclusions of each theoretical analysis.

For instance, in a situation in which a child is too noisy, behaviorists would suggest ignoring the noisy behavior and reinforcing positive behavior; those employing the ecological approach would seek to stop the behavior immediately; and advocates of the human potential view would specify that the child be allowed to discuss what being noisy means to him or her and the other children.

After viewing a segment that portrays a senior high school girl becoming agitated and verbally aggressive with her teacher, the group examining the psychodynamic-interpersonal approach might recommend family counseling to help the student resolve her problems in dealing with authority figures. Behaviorists might suggest a specific behavioral contract between the student and teacher listing expectations and contingent consequences. The ecological group may conclude that the curriculum is not meeting the student's academic needs. The biophysical group might raise the issue of a possible drug dependence problem. The human potential group might suggest a class meeting to discuss classroom rules and the roles of students and teachers in an educational system. The sociological group could discuss community norms for teenage behavior and the value of education.

The following example illustrates how some of these approaches might be applied to a very severe discipline problem.

Mrs. Jones, a kindergarten teacher, had been having great difficulty with Johnny, a 5-year-old who was extremely active in class, always grabbing other children's things. Johnny, who seemed in general to be immature for his age, was also prone to hit other children and he had had several temper tantrums. When Mrs. Jones tried to control him, he struck her.

Using a psychodynamic-interpersonal approach to handling the problem of disciplining Johnny, a teacher might hypothesize that some problem related to Johnny's home life was the cause of his difficulties. Consistent with this approach, the teacher would spend time interviewing the parents in an attempt to discover what developmental stages were being disrupted—and why. In this kind of situation the teacher might discover, for instance, that Johnny's mother had recently remarried and so his developing relationship with his biological father had been interrupted, at a time when male role identification was important to his development. The stepfather may have been seen by the child both as a competitor for his mother's attention and as one who was displacing his real father, with whom he wished to be. If so, Johnny might be acting out his aggression and frustration as a result of his inability to complete a normal developmental stage of identification with his father.

Using a behavioral approach, the teacher might assume that Johnny's negative aggressive behavior was also being reinforced in some way. She might observe the instances and tally the number of times he exhibited such a specific behavior as hitting, and then begin to analyze why and how it was being reinforced. Concurrently, she might begin to reinforce his positive behaviors and to offer rewards for short periods of time when he didn't hit other children. She might also set up a similar schedule for the parents at home, so that he would begin to get more and more reinforcement for his non-aggressive behavior.

From an ecological point of view, the teacher might analyze which classroom situations seemed to promote Johnny's aggressive behavior. She might then discover that she let the situation get out of hand when the children had free play time. As a result, she might rearrange his schedule and have an aide spend more time with him during the free play period. She would also learn to anticipate Johnny's outbursts and to move him out of a situation as soon as it looked like a confrontation was about to occur. She might begin remediative processes by teaching the whole class how to negotiate the use of toys on a shared time basis.

With the biophysical approach, the teacher would want to investigate what physical causes might be associated with Johnny's hyperactive behavior. A thorough medical and psychological evaluation could be undertaken to help determine whether his acting out had a medical basis. It might be found that certain medications were necessary to help him gain control of his behavior. Or, it might be found that his sleeping or eating habits were responsible for his irritability.

From a human potential approach, the teacher might try to understand what was frustrating Johnny and keeping him from meeting some of his needs for love, affection, safety and accomplishment. She might find that the routine of the class was too structured for him. He might be a very bright child who was extremely frustrated in his inability to do the kinds of things which he might want to do. She might find that his activities were preventing him from achieving certain accomplishments and that a vicious cycle, in which Johnny would function as if he truly were a bad child, was occurring.

As a result, the teacher would attempt to provide an atmosphere in which Johnny could learn to appropriately act out his frustration and aggressions. When he became angry, an opportunity could be provided for him to vent his feelings on an inflatable punching bag instead of hitting other children. The teacher might also provide him with artistic means for expressing his frustration and anger, play therapy might be utilized and parents might be recruited to help Johnny develop a more positive self-image by decreasing the kinds of negative statements made to him about his behavior.

As indicated by Johnny's example, application of a variety of theoretical orientations can result in a number of practical solutions to a single behavioral problem. The purpose of the Center's training activities is to help educators generate a vast repertoire of theoretical and practical solutions to discipline problems. Most teachers do not appear to have a consistent approach to discipline based on theoretical assumptions; this workshop helps teachers to identify their own orientation and to contrast it with others. And, to help reinforce the training received in the workshop, the center makes tapes and other materials available for use by schools.

Another workshop is on physical restraint. Most teachers have had to deal with students' uncontrollable behavior and it is important for them to understand the legal, pedagogical, psychological and physical parameters involved in physical restraint.

The workshop emphasizes that in utilizing physical restraint teachers should analyze the situation vis-a-vis the child's background and his or her current state of mind. Environmental restrictions and dangers must be considered, and vocal control should always be tried first. If physical restraint is necessary, after all prevention measures have been eliminated, the teacher should move himself or herself behind the child and out of the way of possible attack. A procedure for placing the child in a "basket hold" or "wrap up" is demonstrated in the workshop.

This method of physical restraint may be necessary and can be effective when the teacher is physically able to control the child. But if a teacher is smaller than the student or not as strong, it is inadvisable for him or her to physically engage the child. Other practices, however, can be employed to help reduce the possibility of violence occurring—and the Center urges that schools, especially ones in which there are older, potentially more aggressive children, develop procedures which anticipate this possibility. (In a recent research study conducted by the Center in the Philadelphia schools, junior high school teachers indicated a high priority for establishing set procedures for dealing with aggression against teachers in the classroom.) For example, we point out the importance of making certain that the school intercom system always works properly so that a teacher can get help quickly. We also suggest that teachers who are physically small or unable to handle larger, aggressive children always be assigned classrooms that are near other teachers who could be helpful in such a situation. In our workshop, teachers learn methods of identifying and verbally handling children when they appear to be moving toward an outburst and they receive appropriate training to help them avoid needlessly antagonizing students and precipitating violent episodes.

Other Center workshops include approaches to stress management for teachers and the measurement and adjustment of classroom climate in preventing severe disciplinary problems.

Center Research

One Center study of processes common to various inservice teacher training programs has been of great importance in developing workshops and generating further research. The first stage of the study was a comprehensive review of research on the effectiveness of such popular teacher training programs as Teacher Effectiveness Training, Behavior Modification and Classroom Ecology. Twenty-seven programs were examined and common practices identified and sorted into seven teaching process categories.

The study showed that teachers used verbal methods most frequently to show students that their ideas and feelings were recognized and accepted as valid forms of self-expression. Here, a teacher might say: "John, I realize that you are angry with the group for not letting you play in the kickball game at recess. You must feel as though you have no friends here." Also included in this category are statements of objective verbal feedback in regard to students' positive behavior: "Jean, I noticed that you tried very hard to control your temper when Jill stepped in front of you in line. That is a real improvement."

The second most common classification of the teacher processes considered relates to their gathering of objective diagnostic information about students' feelings and behaviors. Also included in this category is the influence of a teacher's beliefs and characteristic behaviors on classroom interaction. For example, when Ms. Scott was discussing with her students their responses to a questionnaire about their math lessons, she discovered that her apparent dislike of the subject had influenced the entire period. In other words, many of the in-service programs urged teachers to gather information on classroom behavior so that they might obtain objective feedback about what was happening.

Classroom ecology, including the physical arrangement of the room, the structure of class activities and decision-making policy,

was found to be a common concern. For example, a teacher could decide that Tim and Martha should not work at the same learning center after lunch, because sitting together made it hard for them to concentrate and return to work, a factor the teacher might not have recognized before she, Tim and Martha had discussed what situations might be causing behavior problems.

Because occasional student misbehavior is inevitable, many of the training programs examined included methods of dealing with inappropriate behaviors. However, it was interesting to note that the majority of these programs strongly emphasized the use of reward and encouragement to prompt cooperative behavior, rather than punitive techniques to decrease disruptive behavior. (A teacher would attempt to "catch" a student engaged in an appropriate task and then verbally praise him for his cooperation.)

Several training programs encouraged specific instruction and practice in devising and using problem-solving strategies in attempts to insure student cooperation and participation. Some of these programs suggested direct involvement of students in classroom policy negotiations—for example, Mr. Johnson would hold a class meeting in which the students would determine the work requirements that had to be met each morning to earn extra privileges.

Recognition of teachers' feelings in the classroom was considered an important factor in cooperative student-teacher relationships. Several programs encouraged teachers to share their relevant feelings with their students: "Tom and Bob, I get angry when you talk to your friends while I'm trying to teach a new lesson."

The expression of student feelings is equally important. Peers and teachers often fail to realize the impact a careless comment can have. Structured group activities may help students express their own feelings and to understand how others may feel. The use of a "magic circle," which is classified within the human potential approach, is one popular affective technique.

Other Center research activities focus on the causes of teachers' use of corporal punishment, the relationships between corporal punishment, suspension and vandalism and school disciplinary codes.

We believe that together the Center workshops, advocacy, research and information programs represent a unique effort on the part of parents and professionals to stem and turn back the current tide of punitiveness towards children.

ENDNOTE

1. I. Hyman and D. Lally, "Effectiveness of Staff Development Programs to Improve School Discipline," paper presented at the annual convention of the American Psychological Association, Montreal, Canada, September 1980.

Irwin A. Hyman, Ed.D., is Director, National Center for the Study of Corporal Punishment and Alternatives in the Schools, Temple University, Philadelphia, Pa. Dolores Lally is a doctoral candidate in school psychology at Temple University.

The Professional Early Childhood Teacher

Lilian G. Katz

How would you handle a situation in which two children are fighting over a tricycle? Lilian Katz holds up a mirror to our teaching in early childhood programs and urges us to reflect on the uses of professional judgment and how our teaching techniques can become more professional.

The term *professional* means many things (Ade 1982; Hoyle 1982). This article discusses two aspects of professionalism in particular: the use of *advanced knowledge* in the formulation of *judgment* (Zumeta and Solomon 1982), and the adoption of *standards of performance* for the early childhood profession.

Advanced knowledge in early childhood education is derived from developmental psychology as well as from many other fields. Professional judgment involves diagnosing and analyzing events, weighing alternatives, and estimating the potential long-term consequences of decisions and actions based on that knowledge.

One of the major functions of a professional organization is to set standards of performance based on the best available advanced knowledge and practices. Practicing professionals are committed to performing at the same high standards consistently, without allowing personal matters or moods to affect their work or their relations with those with and for whom they work. Nonprofessionals may be very skillful, may enjoy their work, and often work very effectively as volunteers. A major difference between professionals and nonprofessionals lies in the commitment to maintain professional standards.

Professional standards are set for typical or standard situations all members of the profession can be expected to encounter, and are based on the best available knowledge and practices. In order to illustrate how a professional early childhood teacher might use advanced knowledge and judgment and apply standards of performance, let us look at a common predicament faced by early childhood teachers.

Imagine a teacher of about 20 four-year-olds whose outdoor equipment includes only two tricycles! Squabbles will inevitably arise over whose turn it is to use them. A child named Robin goes to the teacher and protests, "Leslie won't let me have a turn!"

Professional Responses to a Common Predicament

There are probably scores of ways to respond. What does a professional teacher know that has implications for handling such an incident?

What Can I Be Teaching in This Situation?

Ideally a trained teacher would ask: *What can I be teaching the children in this situation?* A professional considers the most reliable knowledge about how children learn plus the goals of the parents, the school, and the

Source: Lilian G. Katz (1984, July). The professional early childhood teacher. *Young Children*, 39, 3–10. Copyright © 1984 by the National Association for the Education of Young Children. Reprinted by permission of the publisher.

An inadequate amount of outdoor equipment inevitably leads to squabbles.

community at large. The following responses depict the kind of judgment that might be expected of a well-trained, experienced teacher at the stage of "maturity" (Katz 1972).

Social Skills

Turn-taking skills. The teacher can help children learn to read another's behavior for signs of when a request for a turn is most likely to work, when to give up, when to come back for another try, and similar behavioral cues that help determine the next best move. These processes are similar to learning the turn-taking skills required for participation in conversation (Shields 1979; Wells 1981; Frederiksen 1981). The teacher might suggest that Robin do something else and then ask Leslie for a turn again, or that Robin observe Leslie for signs of weariness or boredom with the tricycle.

Negotiating skills. Children during the preschool years can begin to refine their bargaining skills by learning to predict what will appeal to another child (Rubin and Everett 1982).

To help the child learn these skills, the teacher could encourage Robin to consider what might appeal to Leslie. Thus she might say: "Why don't you go to Leslie and say, 'I'll push you on the swing if you give me a turn on the tricycle'?" The teacher provides verbal model of how the negotiation might go.

Coping skills. Teachers can help children learn to cope with having their requests rejected and to accept defeat gracefully.

For example, the teacher can help Robin learn to deal with rejection by responding matter-of-factly: "Alright. Maybe Leslie will have a change of heart later. What would you like to do in the meantime?"

Verbal Skills

The tricycle situation is a good one in which to help children learn how to express their feelings and assert their wishes more clearly and effectively.

Assertive phrases. Perhaps Robin simply tugged at the tricycle, or even whined a bit, hardly a clear statement of desire for a turn with the tricycle. The teacher could respond to Robin by saying "It might help to say to Leslie, (modeling a mildly assertive tone) 'I've been waiting a long time . . . I really want a turn'." The teacher introduces a simple phrase that the child can use when an adult is not there, and models a tone of moderate but firm assertiveness.

Conversational phrases. It may be that these children have few appropriate phrases and are only just learning to engage in heated conversations. Teaching the needed verbal skills can be done through what is called "Speaking-*for*-Children" (Schachter and Strage 1982) in which the adult speaks to each child on behalf of the other.

The teacher might say to Leslie, "Robin really wants a turn." If Leslie refuses, the teacher can say to Robin, "Leslie isn't ready to give up the tricycle yet." Robin might protest, in which case the teacher can paraphrase what Robin is feeling to Leslie: "Robin really would like a turn now."

Social Knowledge

Nucci and Turiel (1978) have shown that preschool children understand the distinction between social conventions and moral transgressions and thus can be helped with moral and social insights. This typical incident provides a good opportunity for children to gain social knowledge.

Social perspective. A trained teacher can help children to learn what is a tragedy and what is not. Not getting a turn to ride a tricycle is not a tragedy. The teacher helps the child put desires into perspective by responding to the complaint with gentle good-humored empathy, rather than with tragic tones or by rushing to rescue the child from distress.

The teacher might assert, "I know you're disappointed not to get a turn on the tricycle, but there are other things you like to do." Again, the tone is matter-of-fact and pleasant, without hint of reprimand.

Rudiments of justice. Preschoolers probably are ready to absorb some of the rudiments of justice (Johnson 1982), particularly in the form of *ground rules* that everyone is asked to observe. A professional teacher's response would be "Leslie, you have been riding the tricycle for five minutes and it is time for you to give Robin a turn now," followed by, "And when you need help getting a turn with something I will be glad to help you to."

Similarly, if the situation were to lead to combat the teacher might say to the instigator, "I won't let you hit him, *and I won't let anyone hit you either.*" This reassures aggressors that they are in a just environment in which everyone's rights are protected and everyone's needs are considered. One of the important elements of professionalism is the teacher's acceptance of responsibility for the learning and development of both the victim and the aggressor (Grusec and Arnason 1982).

If Leslie monopolizes the tricycle and refuses to give Robin a turn, when other techniques have failed, the teacher might say to Leslie, "Five more minutes, Leslie. Then I want you to let Robin have a turn. When you need help with something just let me know." And the teacher insists that Leslie yield after five minutes, removing her physically if necessary.

Observers' understandings and skills. Professional judgment includes taking into account what the children observing the incident might be learning. All the teacher's responses outlined so far can provide indirect instruction for the uninvolved children. They might learn techniques of negotiation and verbal strategies for use in confrontation, and are likely to feel reassured that they are in a just environment.

Dispositional Learning

In addition to teaching social skills and knowledge, the professional teacher would also consider which personal dispositions could be strengthened or weakened in this situation.

Empathy and altruism. Young children are capable of strengthening empathy and altruism in various ways (Grusec and Arnason 1982). For example, if Leslie resists giving up the tricycle, the teacher might say, "Leslie, Robin has been waiting for a long time . . . and you know how it feels to wait a long time . . . ," thereby stimulating empathy and nurturing sharing capabilities as well. This should not be said in a tone that implies guilt, of course.

Sometimes children refuse to accede to the requests of others because *they do know what it feels like to be in the other's position. In such cases empathy exists, but charity does not.* It is not very useful for adults to say things like, "How would you like someone to do that to you?" If charitable attitudes are lacking, the teacher must judge how to respond in the long-term interests of the children. At times, confrontations like these are inevitable and benign; their significance should not be exaggerated or overinterpreted.

Disposition to experiment. Many situations arise in which the teacher can strengthen children's dispositions to approach social situations experimentally as problem-solving situations in which alternative solutions can be invented and tried out, and in which a few failures will not be debilitating.

When Robin complains that Leslie won't take turns, the teacher can respond by saying something like, "Go back and say to Leslie, 'I really want a turn. I've been waiting a long time' (in a mildly assertive tone). *If that doesn't work, come back and we'll think of something else to try.*" This tag teaches a disposition to be experimental.

Complaining and tattling. Professional judgment may be that Robin complains too often. The trained teacher tries to assess the legitimacy of complaints and to determine which of them require action. If, in the teacher's best judgment, the complaint requires no intervention, the teacher sends Robin back to the situation with some suggested strategies for coping. If complainers do succeed often, complaining can become persistent.

Similarly, with tattling the teacher may send the child back to cope with the conflict. When children are older, perhaps after age six or seven years, the teacher can explain the conditions under which telling on another child to an adult is warranted, for example, when the consequence of some activity unknown to the teacher may be dangerous.

Clinical Judgments

Clinical describes the processes of taking into account the *meaning* of the children's behaviors. Professional teachers attempt to put behavior into the context of everything they know about the children. A teacher might ask questions such as the following:

- Is this a typical day for Robin? If so, is Robin a chronic attention seeker? Are Robin's expectations for receiving attention too high to be satisfied by the teacher?
- How much experimentation can Robin tolerate? Robin's disposition to be self-assertive may not be strong enough to risk failure yet.
- Does Leslie's behavior reflect progress? Perhaps this is the first time Leslie has been assertive.
- Will the children develop healthy ways of interacting if they resolve the situation themselves? For children's long-term interests, the professional teacher will try to minimize the success of the bully or bossy child.
- Will the pattern of behavior of the children cause them trouble later on if it is left unattended now?
- Have these children's characters been defined (Leslie as selfish and a bully or Robin as weak and a complainer) so that they are matching their behavior to the traits attributed to them (Grusec and Arnason 1982)?

Curriculum and Management Considerations

The professional teacher might ask these questions regarding the program.

- Is the behavior to be expected for this age group? In the children's culture? Preaching and moralizing are ineffective methods for changing the behaviors of preschool children. However, the teacher may tell a story with a relevant moral at an appropriate level of complexity for the children.
- Have I provided the right kind and/or quantity of equipment for children of this age, background, and culture? Are there enough suitable alternative activities? Is the curriculum sufficiently appropriate and challenging for children?

Nonprofessional Responses to Common Incidents

Many people without professional education work with children in groups. In many settings parents and volunteers contribute greatly to the quality of the program. The term *nonprofessional* does not imply inferiority, but is used to contrast the application of knowledge and professional experience and practices with common sense responses, and to focus attention on how training and judgment come into play in daily work with *other people's children*.

How would people without professional education and experience respond when confronted with the same hypothetical situation? Typically nonprofessionals focus on what is happening rather than on what is being learned. They may wish simply to stop the incident rather than consider which of many possible interventions is most likely to stimulate long-term development and learning. If teachers saw teaching as fire-extinguishing, they would be smoke detectors rather than teachers!

Distraction. Many people without professional education and experience might respond by distracting Robin. Distraction seems to make sense, very often works, and is therefore a probable technique. However, for three-or four-year-olds it is not a preferred technique. It does not *help children learn* alternative approaches to the situation. On the contrary, it may teach children that complaining gets adult attention.

Exhortions. Other nonprofessional responses in situations like the tricycle squabble

165

include saying things to children such as *Cut it out!*, *Don't be so selfish!*, *Be nice!*, *We take turns in this school!*, and *Don't be nasty!* Such exclamations are also unlikely to help the participants develop alternative approaches.

Removal. A nonprofessional might respond to squabbling over equipment by putting it away or locking it up. This eliminates the situation, of course, but *it does not teach*. A professional's commitment is to teaching.

Empty threats. A nonprofessional may issue a threat as a means of control. For example: "If you don't let Robin have a turn you can't go to the zoo with us on Friday . . ." Will the threatener really keep Leslie away from the zoo? How does one make the sanction match the seriousness of the behavior? Sometimes threats are out of proportion to the transgression. Then when a truly serious transgression comes along, what is left to threaten?

Perhaps four-year-olds cannot yet sense that threats indicate that the adult has lost or given up control. But some four-year-olds do. Then their testing behavior is apt to increase and the relationships in the class focus on the rules, on what happens when they are broken, and on who is really in charge.

Bribery. Some adults resort to bribery: "If you give Robin a turn with the tricycle, I'll let you give out the raisins." The danger in using a bribe is that it tends to devalue the behavior you want. The values of generosity and concern for others are discounted as not worth engaging in for their own sake. While bribery often works, the professional question is *what does it teach?*

Time out. Some adults use time out in cases of persistent refusal to cooperate with other children. Time out often seems to work and, indeed, many teachers are trained to use it. The main problem is that time out does not teach new skills or desirable dispositions, although it does change behavior. If the child's mental ability is reasonably normal, it is not necessary to circumvent the mind by insisting on a time out chair. The cognitive connection between sitting on a particular chair and granting another child's request for a turn must be fairly obscure if not confusing to a four-year-old (Katz 1977).

Preaching. Many adults moralize or preach about the virtues of sharing, kindness, generosity, and the evils of selfishness. None of these approaches are likely to help children learn strategies to use when adults are not present.

Sympathy. Another common response of adults without training is to become preoccupied with the feelings and needs of the victim and to neglect the feelings, needs, and the development of the aggressor. The professional is committed to responding to the feelings, needs, and development of *all* children.

Guilt. Some untrained adults, when confronting situations like the tricycle squabble, would say to Leslie "What you did makes me sad" or "That makes me feel bad." Such statements draw attention to the adults' own internal states and can cause the child to feel guilty for not pleasing the adult. Again, the basic problem with guilt is that it fails to teach the participants ways of coping with and resolving the predicament.

Other manipulative techniques. An untrained person is apt to combine common sense with impulse, customs, folk tales, and shaming comparisons with other children in order to intimidate children so they will give in to the adult's demand.

Unprofessional Responses to Common Incidents

One of the characteristics of a fully developed profession is that its members subscribe to a code of ethics which serves as a guide to professional conduct (Katz 1977). Conduct which violates any part of the code is unethical and therefore unprofessional. *Nonprofessional* behavior is determined by personal predeliction, common sense, or folk wisdom rather than by professional knowledge and practices. *Unprofessional* behavior is that which contravenes agreed-upon standards of performance of the society of professional practitioners and their code of ethical conduct.

In general, unprofessional behavior is the result of giving in to the temptations of the situation at hand. It could be, for instance, that Leslie and/or Robin's behavior frequently puts the teacher into this kind of predicament. The adult might be a bit weary of it, and silently hope that aggressive children will "get what they deserve." Not only is it unethical to let one's feelings dictate the response to a situation, but the school of hard knocks, although powerful, is likely to provide the wrong lessons to children.

The trained teacher is not without feelings of the kind alluded to here. What is professional is to temper one's feelings with the knowledge and insight that constitutes professional judgment rather than the feelings or temptations of the moment.

Occasionally we are tempted to blame the children for creating the predicament or to blame their parents for not raising them properly. However, what is relevant is not whom to blame, but what to teach in this situation.

Conclusion

The professional responses presented here use judgment based on the most reliable knowledge and insight available. They reflect only a sample of the potential uses of contemporary knowledge about children's development and learning. They are intended to add weight to the proposition that the effective training and education of early childhood teachers can make a significant contribution to children's development and learning.

REFERENCES

Ade, W. "Professionalization and Its Implications for the Field of Early Childhood Education." *Young Children* 37, no. 3 (March 1982): 25–32.

Frederiksen, C. H. "Inference in Preschool Children's Conversations: A Cognitive Perspective." In *Ethnography and Language in Educational Settings*, ed. J. Green and C. Wallat. Norwood, N.J.: Ablex, 1981.

Grusec, J. E., and Arnason, L. "Consideration for Others: Approaches to Enhancing Altruism." In *The Young Child: Reviews of Research.* Vol. 3, ed. S. G. Moore and C. R. Cooper. Washington, D.C.: National Association for the Education of Young Children, 1982.

Hoyle, E. "The Professionalization of Teachers: A Paradox." *British Journal of Educational Studies* 30, no. 2 (June 1982): 161–171.

Johnson, D. B. "Altruistic Behavior and the Development of Self in Infants." *Merrill-Palmer Quarterly* 28, no. 3 (1982): 379–387.

Katz, L. G. "Developmental Stages of Preschool Teachers." *Elementary School Journal* 23, no. 1 (1972): 50–54.

Katz, L. G. *Ethical Issues in Working with Children.* Urbana, Ill.: ERIC Clearinghouse on Elementary and Early Childhood Education, University of Illinois, 1977.

Nucci, L. P., and Turiel, E. "Social Interactions and the Development of Social Concepts in Preschool Children." *Child Development* 49 (1978): 400–407.

Rubin, K. H., and Everett, B. "Social Perspective-Taking in Young Children." In *The Young Child: Reviews of Research.* Vol. 3, ed. S. G. Moore and C. R. Cooper. Washington, D.C.: National Association for the Education of Young Children, 1982.

Schachter, F. F., and Strage, A. A. "Adults' Talk and Children's Language Development." In *The Young Child: Reviews of Research.* Vol. 3, ed. S. G. Moore and C. R. Cooper. Washington, D.C.: National Association for the Education of Young Children, 1982.

Shields, M. M. "Dialogue, Monologue and Egocentric Speech by Children in Nursery Schools." In *Language, Children and Society*, ed. O. I. Garnica and M. L. King. London: Pergamon, 1979.

Wells, G. *Learning Through Interaction: The Study of Language Development.* London: Cambridge University Press, 1981.

Zumeta, W., and Solomon, L. C., "Professions Education." *Encyclopedia of Educational Research.* Vol. 3, 5th ed. New York: Macmillan and Free Press, 1982.

Lilian G. Katz, Ph.D., is Professor of Early Childhood Education and Director of ERIC Clearinghouse on Elementary and Early Childhood Education at the University of Illinois, Urbana, Illinois.

Time Outs and Professionalism

After reading Lilian Katz's article "The Professional Early Childhood Teacher" (July 1984 *Young Children*), I am concerned with her listing of time out as a nonprofessional response. If Katz means that time out is a nonprofessional response in the cited hypothetical situation, then I agree that other responses would be more appropriate. In the particular child-child situation presented in the article, it is up to the teacher to set guidelines before play begins. With only two tricycles, a teacher knows that problems could erupt, so the teacher sets time limits before the children go to the play yard. After these guidelines are set, children tend to monitor themselves.

Time out seems to be a good professional response in other situations. When one child is disrupting the whole group, I think time out is a good professional response. Is it more important to stop the whole class and negotiate with one child, or to continue class with those paying attention and ask one to leave? Time out teaches that being part of a group means responsibility. It means following certain guidelines of behavior. If this responsibility is not met, a child is asked to leave until she or he is ready to handle that responsibility. Time out teaches respect for others in a group. If children can't respect the rights of others in that group, then they can't be part of that group.

I don't believe that time out is a nonprofessional response in all learning situations. I think the proper use of time out stimulates a child's long term development in a group.

Joyce A. Daniels
Pueblo, Colo.

Katz Responds to Daniels

Before commenting on Joyce Daniel's letter regarding my article "The Professional Early Childhood Teacher" (July 1984 *Young Children*), I would like to assure readers that the point of view and practices suggested in my article reflect my own view of appropriate methods for teaching normal young children. Other methods are indeed advocated and taught as professional competences and readers must select the methods that make the most sense to them. I cannot prove the approach I have advocated is right or that others are wrong. The suggestions are based on *my* best understanding of what we know about children today.

Daniels agrees that time out would not be appropriate in the situation I used to illustrate the contrasts between professional and nonprofessional responses (children squabbling over a tricycle). Yet I am not sure that setting up time limits in advance, as she suggests, is the preferred response either—even if it would work. It seems more appropriate and practical to teach children turn-taking and other skills for *coping* with such situations.

Ms. Daniel's letter reminds us that *time out* is ambiguous (Gifford 1984). If, in the case of disrupting the activities of the whole group, *time out* means encouraging a child to find an alternative activity, I would agree to that as preferable to disrupting other's pleasure. There is no evidence that I know of that participation in a whole group activity should be required at the preschool level.

If *time out* means to remove the child from all action and interaction then it still seems to me to be a flawed procedure. It may represent a case of what Bandura calls "cognitive bypass" (1978, p. 348), or failure to appeal directly to the child's mind. Bandura points out that impulse control and self-regulation become increasingly possible to growing children because they adopt standards of behavior—which are cognitions, of course. Thus it would be far more desirable to teach children what they could do as an alternative activity, or to address the child's mind by discussing expected standards of behavior. If the behavior persists, it may be useful to look at the total curriculum and examine the extent to which this child's interest, skills, and dispositions are given sufficient opportunities to flourish.

When disruptive behavior persists in spite of the use of time out procedures, it may be that the child is enjoying all the stir and fuss. It seems to me that the preferred response is to offer the child alternative activities without any hint of punishment so that the others are not disturbed.

The other major concern with time out procedures in such cases is the assumption that it can teach respect for other's rights. How can we be sure of that? We really do not know what meaning children give to being removed from the group. Do we really believe that young children go off into isolation saying to themselves ". . . from now on I will respect other's rights . . ." and otherwise engage in self-chastisement? It is highly unlikely.

We need some retrospective interviews with individuals who can recall having been punished by ostracism early in life. The chances are that even very young children nurse feelings of anger and shame, and perhaps even hopes of revenge on such occasions.

Furthermore, the idea that time out teaches respect for others could lead to the absurd and ridiculous implication that every child should have regular time outs in order to be taught respect for others!

Time out may teach that one has behaved badly or in ways that are unacceptable to the group. But by itself it cannot give a child new standards of behavior, insight into how one's actions affect others, or strategies for coping with an uncomfortable or painful situation. It is unlikely that the time out procedure "stimulates a child's long-term development in a group," but it would be most helpful to have some good longitudinal empirical data on the subject.

Lilian G. Katz
Urbana, Ill.

REFERENCES

Bandura, A. "The Self System in Reciprocal Determinism." *American Psychologist* 33, no. 4 (April 1978): 344–358.
Gifford, L. "Do They Really Deserve the Time-Out Chair?" *Texas Child Care Quarterly* 8, no. 2 (Fall 1984): 18–21.

ASK YOURSELF:
Identifying Issues for Debate and Advocacy

1. What are the intended and unintended consequences of different approaches to discipline?

2. Can you reason with a child about acting-out behavior when according to Piaget a preschool child is still in the preoperational period and not able to reason logically yet? Explain.

3. In some day care licensing regulations (e.g., New York), corporal punishment (spanking) and humiliating or frightening methods of control and discipline are prohibited. Moreover, punishment may not be associated with food, rest, toilet training, or isolation. Discuss the implications and reasons for these policies.

4. Refer to the vignette at the beginning of this chapter. If Melissa's parents indicate that they respond to Melissa's misbehavior with a good spanking and give the teacher

permission to spank Melissa, how should the teacher respond?

5. How can the teacher in the vignette determine the cause(s) or reinforcers of Melissa's behavior?

6. In using behavior modification procedures, who decides what is normal and acceptable behavior? In behavior modification, for whose benefit is the behavior changed—the teacher's or the child's? Explain.

7. Should a child be punished if she or he hits a teacher? Why or why not?

8. How should a teacher respond when children display signs of overstimulation (e.g., become silly, overly excited, or carried away in repetitive motions or chasing behaviors)?

9. Do the ways children reinforce peers reflect the reinforcement patterns of the teacher? Discuss.

APPLICATION/ADVOCACY EXERCISES

1. Using each of the five approaches described by Hyman and Lally, interpret the possible origins of Melissa's acting-out behavior as documented in the opening vignette. For each approach, describe in specific terms how to respond to the situation. Finally, determine which approach might best explain Melissa's behavior, ranking the approaches 1–5 and indicating your reasons for ranks given.

2. Analyze the following episodes in terms of Katz's view of a professional response, a nonprofessional response, and an unprofessional response:

   At Punkin' Patch Preschool, the children enjoy finding, collecting, and hoarding the "jewels" (beaded necklaces) during free play. One child said to the teacher assistant, "Stacy took almost all of my jewels when I wasn't looking!" The teacher assistant responded in a matter-of-fact tone, "Well, maybe you will be able to get them back later."

   At St. Mark's Preschool, when a child acts out or is in a bad mood, he or she is told to sit in the "Grumpy Bear Chair." While sitting there, the child can talk to Grumpy Bear about what he or she has done wrong, and what he or she can do to behave in a more acceptable manner. The children are told that it is okay to feel bad, upset, and mad at times—everybody does.

   At Kiddie Korner Day Care, two-year-old Teddy was being active and aggressive at an inappropriate time and was disrupting the whole group. Teddy received a few warnings but did not change his behavior. Teddy was being reinforced by laugh-

ter from other children. He was then placed in the time-out chair for several minutes and invited to return "if he felt he could behave."

At Mother Goose Day Care, children are placed in time out for spitting, choking another child, hitting, saying bad words, and so on. They are placed in time out for 10 minutes. They are given two chances. After the third incident, the child is sent to the director. If this still does not work, a child is told that his or her parents will be called. This usually stops the undesirable behavior.

3. Bushell (1982), a well-known behaviorist, says, "Time-out from positive reinforcement (although sometimes misunderstood) is a direct and humane procedure for eliminating inappropriate behavior. As the name indicates, time-out is a brief period during which no reinforcement is provided. In a setting rich in reinforcement for appropriate behavior, it is an effective consequence for inappropriate behavior" (p. 164). Bijou (1976), another well-known behaviorist, defines time-out as "the removal of opportunities for positive reinforcement . . . (taking the child out of an exciting play situation)" (p. 118). After reading the letters to the editor of *Young Children* and considering these expert definitions of time out, form a discussion group with three or four other students. Appoint a person to take notes. Analyze how each letter writer addresses the issues and how each writer's notion of time out compares or contrasts with the two expert definitions above. Try to reach a group consensus as to whether or not you agree with Katz or Daniels and why.

4. View Seymour Feshbach's film "Children's Aggression: Its Origins and Control" (Davidson Films). Discuss the difference between assertion and aggression and how adults should respond in different ways to various types of aggressive behavior.

5. View High/Scope's film "Contrasting Teaching Styles: Circle Time" (High/Scope Press). Analyze and discuss the contrasting management strategies used in the two large-group lessons.

REFERENCES & SUGGESTED READINGS

Bijou, S. W. (1976). *Child development: The basic stage of early childhood.* Englewood Cliffs, NJ: Prentice-Hall.

Bushell, D. (1982). The behavioral analysis model for early education. In B. Spodek (Ed.), *Handbook of research in early childhood education* (pp. 156–184). New York: The Free Press, Macmillan.

Canter, L. (1988, January). Assertive discipline and the search for the perfect classroom. *Young Children, 43,* 24.

Cryan, J. R. (1987). The banning of corporal punishment: In child care, school and other educative settings. *Childhood Education, 63,* 146–153.

Hitz, R. (1988, January). Assertive discipline: A response to Lee Canter. *Young Children, 43,* 25.

Kounin, J. S. (1970). *Discipline and group management in classrooms.* New York: Holt, Rinehart and Winston.

Suransky, V. P. (1983, March). The preschooling of childhood. *Educational Leadership, 40,* 27–29.

CHAPTER 8

Child Care Choices and Selection

Making a Choice or Taking a Chance?

MRS. CASEY: Hello, is this Wee Ones Day Care? I need day care for my two kids. My neighbors didn't know of any nearby places for day care. But I looked in the yellow pages, and I found out you're right on my way to work. How much do you charge?

MRS. QUINN: How old are your children, ma'am?

MRS. CASEY: Well, Dina is three, and my little Davy is six months. You do have room, don't you? I need to go to work immediately because my husband has been seriously injured and will be laid up for six months. I sure hope you have room.

MRS. QUINN: It just so happens that one family suddenly moved last week to another state. So there now are vacancies for children of the ages you mentioned. The cost for a three-year-old is $65 per week and for the baby, $75. I think you'll find this is the "going rate," Mrs. . . . ?

MRS. CASEY: Oh, my name is Sara Anne Casey. When can they start?

MRS. QUINN: Anytime, Mrs. Casey. Would you like to come and visit first?

MRS. CASEY: Gosh, I'd really love to. But what with everything that's going on in my life, I'm going to have to take your word for it. Maybe I can look around a little when I drop the kids off.

MRS. QUINN: Well, Mrs. Casey, we are a state-licensed center, so we meet state health and safety standards. Also, we serve hot meals, have a lovely yard for outdoor play, and have lots of interesting activities for children. Do you want to know anything else about our program?

MRS. CASEY: Oh, that sounds good! I'm also hoping Dina will learn her ABCs soon. She's a good colorer and we want her well-prepared for kindergarten.

MRS. QUINN: Mrs. Casey, our program does not emphasize those kinds of preacademic skills.

MRS. CASEY: Really!? Why not? I thought preschools were supposed to prepare children for school! Do you just babysit the children?

MRS. QUINN: Not exactly. We do try to provide experiences that children will enjoy for their ages.

MRS. CASEY: Look, I guess I'll just have to take your word for it. I'll bring in the kids at 8 A.M. tomorrow.

Questions

1. In what ways are differences between the goals of Wee Ones and the expectations of Mrs. Casey, the parent, likely to cause problems in home/school relationships? If a center's goals differ from those of parents, should the center refuse admission to the children? Why or why not?

2. The parent's responses in this vignette are based on a telephone survey of 85 parents in a medium-sized city in a Middle Atlantic state. What seems to be the most common considerations of parents in selecting child care?

3. On what past experiences does Mrs. Casey seem to be basing her perceptions of what preschool programs should be like? Why?

4. Should a visit be required by a quality center? Why or why not? Should a child care program screen families and children as part of admissions procedures before admitting the children? Why or why not?

PREVIEW

Many Americans feel ambivalent toward child care. In fact, the United States, unlike other industrialized nations, does not have a national child care policy. Nevertheless, the demand for child care, especially infant care, is rising rapidly. Are concerns about the effects of child care justified? Is high-quality, reliable child care generally available and affordable? How do parents choose child care? How should parents be educated about choosing child care? Will child care advocacy efforts receive more attention in the upcoming years? Should the government subsidize child care programs or provide economic support for parental leaves?

174

Deborah Lowe Vandell and Carol P. Powers provide evidence that children experience more positive interactions with adults in high-quality centers than in moderate or low-quality centers. Jay Belsky, however, argues that nonmaternal care in the first year of life may have undesirable emotional and social side effects on infants. Deborah Phillips, Kathleen McCartney, Sandra Scarr, and Carollee Howes counter that Belsky's review of infant day care studies is too narrow, and then propose that quality of care, not age of entry, is the critical issue. To this, Stella Chess adds a note of caution about assessment strategies used in infant day care research. Next, Deborah Burnett Strother examines the pros and cons of placing preschool programs in the public schools. Addressing the needs of working parents and latchkey children, Ellen Gray and Peter Coolsen report research findings on the feelings of school-age children who care for themselves at home. Finally, Anne C. Lewis addresses the need for policy makers at all levels to pay more attention to child care problems.

Day Care Quality and Children's Free Play Activities

Deborah Lowe Vandell and Carol P. Powers

A critical issue explored during the 1970s was the effect of day care attendance on children. A number of researchers examined the effects of day care on children's relationships with their mothers, [1, 6, 17, 19] children's ability to get along with their peers and their teachers, [10, 15, 16, 25] and children's intellectual and academic functioning. [7, 9, 11, 14, 20] Because a central question underlying many of these studies was whether day care must necessarily have a negative effect on children, a common research strategy was adopted. Children who attended excellent, typically university-affiliated, centers were contrasted with home-reared children. From these studies, a general statement was derived that middle-class day care and home-reared children did not differ significantly on most variables and that lower-class day care children may surpass their home-reared counterparts in intellectual functioning. [4, 5]

There is, however, an important qualifier to this statement: Children who attend less than optimal day care centers have not been studied in detail. In fact, even most studies of community-based day care have focused on high quality programs. Rubenstein and Howes, [22] for example, contrasted the behavior of mothers and their home-reared infants with the behavior of caregivers and their day care infants who attended community-based programs in which adult-child ratios were often 1:3 and the facilities were "bright, well-equipped" playrooms. The National Day Care Study [24] examined the activities and performances of preschoolers who attended federally funded day care in three cities. Most of these centers had adult-child ratios between 1:5 and 1:9, class sizes between 12 and 24 children, and teachers with slightly less than 14 years of education.

Day care standards in many states are considerably less stringent than those adopted in the programs studied by Rubenstein and Howes [22] or Ruopp et al. [24] According to a survey conducted as part of the National Day Care Study, the average adult-child ratio for four-year-olds in programs across the U.S. is 1:14.7; and 18 states have ratios of 1:15 or greater. The survey also indicated that staff members' levels of educational attainment varied widely across programs, from fewer than 12 years of education to greater than 16 years. Some states have no requirements for the quantity or quality of toys or equipment.

A limited number of studies have examined the effects of variations in program quality on children's activities in day care. Rohe and Patterson, [21] for example, found that as the number of children per square foot increases, children's aggressiveness, destructiveness, and unoccupied behavior also increase. Prescott, Jones and Kritchevsky [18] observed that programs enrolling more than 60 children placed a greater emphasis on following rules and controlling children than did programs with 30 to 60 children. These larger centers also appeared to have less flexible scheduling and offered children fewer opportunities to initiate and control activities. [13] These studies, then, argue that variations in program quality can have substantial effects on children's activities in the centers.

It was the purpose of the current study

to examine further the relationship between variations in program quality and children's functioning. Comparable groups of white, middle-class children were observed in day care programs which varied widely in adult-child ratio, teacher training, toy availability, and square footage per child. The specific question addressed was whether there were differences associated with center quality in children's positive and negative behavior with adults, children's positive and negative behavior with peers, and children's solitary and unoccupied activities. These areas of activity were selected because they were seen as indicative of the range of activities in which preschoolers could engage and because prior research related these activities to subsequent important developmental outcomes. Carew[7] and others[3, 8] have found positive adult-child interactions to be important for children's intellectual and emotional development while unoccupied behavior (*i.e.*, aimless wandering) has been negatively associated with cognitive development.[23] Experience in peer interactions has been associated with enhanced social skills and emotional well being.[12] In the current study, it was hypothesized that the relatively large number of well-trained adults in high quality programs would result in children having more positive interactions with adults and less time in aimless wandering. Peer interactions were expected to be more positive in the high quality programs.

Method

Subjects

Fifty-five three- and four-year-old children from six different day care centers were observed. All of the children were from two-parent, white, middle-class families and had attended day care an average of two years. Table 1 summarizes the children's characteristics distributed across the six centers.

Selection of Centers

Initially information was collected on 16 area day care centers. Questionnaire and on-the-spot observations were used to determine *1)* the number of children at each age present at the center, *2)* the number of teachers, *3)* the adult-child ratio, *4)* the staff educational level, *5)* square footage per child, and *6)* the number, condition, and availability of toys. From these observations, six centers representing three types of day care were selected for further study. (See Table 1 for the summary characteristics of these programs.)

Two centers were designated as high quality programs. These centers were university laboratory programs with low adult-child ratios ($M = 1:5$), abundant toys readily accessible to the children, teachers with bachelor's degrees in child development, and high allotments of space per child ($M = 60$ *sq ft* per child). Two centers designated as moderate quality programs were characterized by mod-

TABLE 1 *Summary Description of Children and Day Care Centers of High, Moderate, and Low Quality Programs*

Factor	High		Moderate		Low	
	Ctr 1	*Ctr 2*	*Ctr 3*	*Ctr 4*	*Ctr 5*	*Ctr 6*
Boys observed (N)	3	3	3	5	4	5
Girls observed (N)	7	3	7	4	6	5
Mean age (months)	52	53	44	51	50	56
Children in class	13	24	26	32	38	90
Children in center	42	50	58	132	160	215
Sq. ft. per child	60	60	48.8	30.5	54	23
Adult-child ratio	1:6	1:4	1:13	1:15	1:23	1:25
Toy availability[1]	E	E	E	G	P	G
Staff training[2]	H	H	H	M	L	L
Monthly tuition per child	$140	$170	$185	$178	$175	$185

[1]E = excellent amount, condition, and availability of toys; G = good, P = poor.

[2]H = college degree; M = some college; L = no college.

erate adult-child ratios ($M = 1:14$), good to excellent toy condition and availability, and less square footage per child ($M = 39.6$ *sq ft*). Staff education varied in the two programs. Center 3's teachers had college degrees in child development. Center 4's teachers had some college, but no degrees. The two low quality centers were lacking the facilities and features of the other two types of programs. They had high adult-child ratios ($M = 1:24$), poor to good toy availability, and less well-trained teachers. Teachers were only required to be 18 years old and none had attended college. The square footage varied in the two programs, with Center 5 having ample square footage (54 *sq ft* per child) and Center 6 being very crowded (23 *sq ft* per child).

Procedure

Each child was observed in a randomly determined order for 16 minutes in his or her regular classroom during unstructured indoor free play. The teachers were asked to continue with their normal routine during the observations and the observer was instructed not to initiate conversations or direct any activities of the children or teachers during this time. A time sample was used in which behavior was observed for 20-second intervals and recorded during 15-second intervals. Coders were asked to record any and all of the following activity that occurred within a time interval, with the restriction that only one tally per variable could be made within a time frame:

Solitary behavior. The child *a)* was engaged alone in a nonverbal activity with an object and showed little regard for other people for at least 15 consecutive seconds or *b)* was engaged in solitary, make-believe play. Each of these acts was coded separately and combined to create this category.

Unoccupied behavior. The child was not engaged in any activity beyond sitting alone or wandering around the room for at least 15 consecutive seconds.

Positive behavior with adults. The child *a)* touched an adult, *b)* gave an object to an adult, *c)* joined in an activity with an adult, or *d)* accepted an object from an adult. Each of these acts was coded separately and combined to create this category.

Positive vocalization with adults. The child talked to an adult, and could ask a question, tell of an event that happened, or request the adult's participation in a play activity. A positive vocalization was not coded as a positive behavior.

Negative interactions with adults. The child hit, kicked, pushed, or acted otherwise negatively toward an adult, or directed negative vocalizations to the adult. Negative behavior and vocalizations were coded separately and combined for an overall frequency of negative interactions with adults.

Total adult-directed behavior. The sum of incidents of positive behavior, positive vocalization, and negative interaction with adults.

Positive behavior with peers. The child positively *a)* touched, *b)* comforted, *c)* gave toys to, *d)* shared toys with, *e)* accepted toys from, *f)* joined in play with, or *g)* participated in fantasy with a peer. Each of these acts was coded separately and combined to give the overall frequency of positive behavior with peers.

Positive vocalizations with peers. The child talked to a peer, and could ask a question, tell of an event that happened, or request the peer's participation in play.

Negative interactions with peers. This category was coded as were negative interactions with adults, the only difference being the child's partner.

Total peer-directed behavior. The sum of incidents of positive behavior, positive vocalization, and negative interaction with peers.

Interobserver Reliability

Prior to the actual data collection, interobserver agreement was assessed on six preschoolers (3 boys, 3 girls, M age $= 3.11$ years) who attended a nursery school program, not one of the programs observed in this study. Each child was observed during free play by two observers working independently for 16 minutes in a way analogous to the regular data collection. One of these observers then collected all of the data for the main study. Interobserver agreement was determined frame-by-frame using the formula (agreement)/(agreement +

disagreement). The range of agreement varied from 96.2% to 99.6%.

Results

During free play, the preschoolers in all three types of day care centers were very likely to engage in solitary behavior ($M = 16.43$). The children also frequently engaged in social behavior with their peers ($M = 15.60$), in particular, positive vocalizations ($M = 9.88$). Negative behavior with adults ($M = .11$) or peers ($M = 1.24$) was rare in all three types of centers. Unoccupied behavior ($M = 5.55$) and behavior with adults ($M = 4.53$) occurred with intermediate frequency and varied widely according to center type.

To determine whether the observations from Centers 1 and 2, 3 and 4, and 5 and 6 could be combined to represent high, moderate, and low quality programs respectively, independent sample t tests were conducted for each of the variables listed in Table 2. No significant differences were found for any variable in the children's performance in Centers 3 and 4 or in children's performance in Centers 5 and 6. Only one difference was found in children's performance in Centers 1 and 2: Children were more likely to vocalize positively to a peer in Center 2 ($Ms = 6.1$ and 12.3), $t(14) = 2.60$, $p < .02$. Given the number of comparisons, however, this difference may have been spurious. Consequently, for all subsequent analyses, performance in Centers 1 and

2, 3 and 4, and 5 and 6 were combined to create three quality levels.

To determine whether there were significant differences in the preschoolers' behavior associated with day care quality, a 3 (type of center) × 2 (sex) multivariate analysis of variance, which included all variables listed in Table 2, was calculated. A significant effect was found for center quality, $F(20, 78) = 1.91$, $p < .03$, but not for sex or for the interaction between sex and center quality. Univariate 3 × 2 ANOVAs were then computed to determine what the specific differences associated with center quality were. As shown in Table 2, significant differences were found in the three types of center in the frequencies of the children's solitary behavior, $F(2, 49) = 4.54$, $p < .05$; unoccupied behavior, $F(2, 49) = 3.61$, $p < .05$; total behavior directed to adults, $F(2, 49) = 6.86$, $p < .01$; positive behavior with adults, $F(2, 49) = 2.98$, $p = .06$; and positive vocalization with adults, $F(2, 49) = 6.51$, $p < .01$. Newman-Keuls post hoc analyses indicated that children in high quality centers were more likely than children in moderate or low quality centers to interact with adults with respect to positive behavior ($p < .05$), positive vocalization ($p < .05$), and total behavior ($p < .05$). No significant differences in the children's activities with adults were found between moderate and low quality centers. Children in low and moderate quality centers were significantly more likely ($p < .05$) to engage in solitary and unoccupied behavior than were

TABLE 2 *Mean Frequency of Preschoolers' Social and Nonsocial Behavior in Three Types of Day Care Programs*

Variable	High	Moderate	Low	F(2,49) Values
Solitary behavior	12.19	17.42	19.90	4.54*
Unoccupied behavior	2.00	4.70	9.10	3.38*
Total adult-directed behavior	8.19	4.32	1.80	6.86**
Positive behavior	.56	.21	.10	2.98***
Positive vocalizations	7.38	4.15	1.70	6.51**
Negative interactions	0	.16	.15	
Total peer-directed behavior	16.19	17.79	13.05	
Positive behavior	1.50	2.42	1.65	
Positive vocalizations	8.43	11.47	8.60	
Negative interactions	1.13	1.16	1.40	

*$p < .05$; **$p < .01$; ***$p < .10$.

179

children in high quality programs. No significant differences were found in the children's peer-directed behavior in the three types of centers. Paralleling the multivariate analysis, no significant univariate sex or sex-by-center-quality interaction effects were found.

Discussion

Day care quality defined in terms of adult-child ratio, educational level of the teacher, and toy availability was found to be clearly associated with the children's free play activities. While there were no significant differences in the children's peer interactions in the three types of programs, children in the high quality programs had significantly more positive interactions with adults. In contrast, children in the low and moderate quality programs spent more time in aimless wandering and in solitary behavior. It was especially notable that, while the variables appeared to be consistently ranked, with frequencies for low and high quality programs being at opposite ends of the continuum and the moderate quality programs in between, significant differences were found only between comparisons of the high quality versus the moderate and low quality programs. No differences were found in the post hoc analyses between the children's activities in the moderate and low quality programs.

These results may be important for several reasons. First, they support the argument that quality issues must be considered in the evaluation of day care research. Although previous researchers were justified in stating that no negative effects were associated with excellent day care, they may be less justified in this statement with poor, or even moderate, quality programs. The results of the current study suggest that the interactions observed in high quality programs (characterized by low adult-child ratios, well-trained teachers, and ample, well-equipped space) do not generalize to programs without these assets.

Second, these results may be important because they caution us against premature statements about the effects of particular quality variations. One conclusion drawn by the National Day Care Study was that variations in staff-child ratios had only minimal effects on program processes and products. This conclusion may not be justified, however, because

the range of ratios they observed (typically 1:5 to 1:9) was so restricted. The ratios in even the moderate programs observed in the present study were greater than 1:13, and the low quality programs had ratios greater than 1:23. Before the issue of the effects of quality variations can be addressed more definitively, much wider variations must be explored.

Unfortunately, our results do not indicate which (or what combination of) quality variables observed in the current study resulted in the differential pattern of behavior. In our study, three distinct types of day care were described, and adult-child ratio covaried with other quality dimensions such as number of children in the class, level of teacher education, and toy availability. Future research is needed to isolate the relative effects of various quality dimensions on children's functioning in day care. Future research is also needed to determine how these quality indices affect the teachers' behavior. One might expect that teachers in programs with lower adult-child ratios and more training would be more responsive and positive in their interactions than those teachers who have less training and more children in their class.

Finally, a critical question that must be addressed is the long-term effect of attending moderate or poor quality programs. Based on our observations that peer interactions did not differ significantly in the three types of programs, one might expect that peer relations would not be particularly vulnerable to wide quality variations. At the same time, however, children's intellectual performance and emotional security may be more affected by center quality. Anderson et al,[2] for example, found that preschoolers were more likely to use their caregivers as a source of emotional security and for object exploration if they were from programs in which the teachers were highly involved with the children. In contrast, those preschoolers with low-involved caregivers were more likely to interact with an unfamiliar adult. Those children with both highly involved teachers and rich day care environments were more likely to explore an unfamiliar playroom than children from centers with poor physical quality and low caregiver involvement. Based on Anderson et al's results, one might expect that the differences in unoccupied behavior and adult-child interactions found in the current study would also affect the children. What we do not know, however, is whether these effects are generalizable and lasting.

REFERENCES

1. Anderson, C. 1980. Attachment in daily separations: reconceptualizing day care and maternal employment issues. Child Devlpm. 51:242–245.
2. Anderson, C. et al. 1981. Attachment to substitute caregivers as a function of center quality and caregiver involvement. Child Devlpm. 52:53–61.
3. Belsky, J., Goode, M. and Most, R. 1980. Maternal stimulation and infant exploratory competence: cross-sectional, correlational, and experimental analyses. Child Devlpm. 51:1163–1178.
4. Belsky, J. and Steinberg, L. 1978. The effects of day care: a critical review. Child Devlpm. 49:929–949.
5. Belsky, J., Steinberg, L. and Walker, A. 1982. The ecology of day care. In Childrearing in Nontraditional Families, M. Lamb, ed. Lawrence Erlbaum Associates, Hillsdale, N.J.
6. Blehar, M. 1974. Anxious attachment and defensive reactions associated with day care. Child Devlpm. 45:683–692.
7. Carew, J. 1980. Experience and the development of intelligence in young children at home and in day care. Monogr. Soc. Res. Child Devlpm. 45(6–7, Serial No. 187).
8. Clarke-Stewart, K. 1973. Interactions between mothers and their young children: characteristics and consequences. Monogr. Soc. Res. Child Devlpm. 38(6–7, Serial No. 153).
9. Cochran, M. 1977. A comparison of group day and family child-rearing patterns in Sweden. Child Devlpm. 48:702–707.
10. Farran, D. and Ramey, C. 1977. Infant day care and attachment behaviors towards mothers and teachers. Child Devlpm. 48:1112–1239.
11. Golden, M. et al. 1978. The New York City Infant Day Care Study. Medical and Health Research Association of New York City, New York.
12. Hartup, W. The peer system. In Carmichael's Manual of Child Psychology: Social Development, E. Hetherington, ed. Wiley-Interscience, New York (in press).
13. Heinicke, C, et al. 1973. The organization of day care: considerations relating to the mental health of child and family. Amer. J. Orthopsychiat. 43:8–22.
14. Kagan, J., Kearsley, R. and Zelazo, P. 1978. Infancy: Its Place in Human Development. Harvard University Press, Cambridge, Mass.
15. Macrae, J. and Herbert-Jackson, E. 1975. Are behavioral effects of infant day care programs specific? Devlpm. Psychol. 12:260–270.
16. McCutcheon, B. and Calhoun, K. 1976. Social and emotional adjustment of infants and toddlers in a day care setting. Amer. J. Orthopsychiat. 46:104–108.
17. Moskowitz, D., Schwarz, J. and Corsini, D. 1977. Initiating day care at three years of age: effects on attachment. Child Devlpm. 48:1271–1276.
18. Prescott, E., Jones, E. and Kritchevsky, S. 1967. Group day care as a childrearing environment. Final report to Children's Bureau. Pacific Oaks College, Pasadena, Calif.
19. Rogozin, A. 1980. Attachment behavior of day care children: naturalistic and laboratory observations. Child Devlpm. 51:409–415.
20. Ramey, C. and Campbell, F. 1977. The prevention of developmental retardation in high risk children. In Research to Practice in Mental Retardation, Vol. 1: Care and Intervention, P. Mittler, ed. University Park Press, Baltimore.
21. Rohe, W. and Patterson, A. 1974. The effects of varied levels of resources and density on behavior in a day care center. In Man-Environment Interactions, D. Carson, ed. EDRA.
22. Rubenstein, J. and Howes, C. 1978. Caregiver and infant behavior in day care and in homes. Devlpm. Psychol. 15:1–24.
23. Rubin, K., Fein, G. and Vandenberg, B. Play. In Carmichael's Manual of Child Psychology: Social Development, E. Hetherington, ed. Wiley-Interscience, New York. (in press)
24. Ruopp, R. et al. 1979. Children at the Center: Summary Findings and Their Implications. Final report of the National Day Care Study, Vol. 5. Abt Associates, Cambridge, Mass.
25. Schwarz, J., Strickland, R. and Krolick, G. 1974. Infant care: behavioral effects at preschool age. Devlpm. Psychol. 10:502–506.

Infant Day Care:
A Cause for Concern?

Jay Belsky

Every essay on day care invariably begins with an opening comment regarding the social changes we have all witnessed during the past two decades. These changes—and their consequences vis-a-vis child care—are not news to readers of *Zero to Three*. One point worth noting, though, involves the rapid growth of employment not simply for women in general, or for those with young children in particular, but specifically for those with infants under one year of age (Klein, 1985). Not only is this the fastest growing sector of the employed-mother labor market, but the most recent statistics reveal that virtually one of every two women with a child under one year of age is now employed (Kamerman, 1986).

When it comes to considering the care which the infants of these mothers receive, it is imperative that we understand what we are talking about—and we are not, for the most part, talking about day-care centers. The overwhelming majority of infant care is provided in private homes—in 1982, a full 77%; not even 10% of infants whose mothers are working are to be found in centers (Klein, 1985). Moreover, tremendous diversity characterizes infant care in private homes. The most recent statistics describing the care of children under three years of age reveal that (as of June, 1985) 45% of these infants and toddlers were cared for by a relative (27% in own home, 18% in relative's) and 24% were cared for in family day care (Kamerman, 1986).

The diversity of arrangements that constitutes the reality of infant care in America today poses serious challenges to scientists who seek to discern the "effects" of day care on young children (to say nothing of its effects on their families). After all, families that use day care and those that do not may differ from each other in a myriad of ways, as families that use one type of care may differ from families using another type. Thus, the very concept of "effects of day care" appears misplaced, as between-group comparisons are plagued with a host of confounds that cannot be teased apart by most statistical or design controls. How are we to know whether so-called "day-care effects" are effects of day care or of being in families that have others share in the rearing of their infants? We must recognize that comparisons between day-care-reared and home-reared infants represent comparisons of early development in contrasting ecologies rather than "effects" of day care in the pure, causal, or experimental sense of the word.

Having cautioned the reader regarding the nature of conclusions that can be drawn from research regarding any "effects" of day care, I feel compelled to make a final introductory comment before proceeding to consider the developmental correlates of nonmaternal care initiated in the first year of life. This has to do with the political and personal contexts in which research on day care is conducted, reported, and discussed. Day care is a very emotionally-charged topic, especially when we are talking about babies. The moment a poor scientist stumbles on evidence suggesting a potentially negative effect of day care and reports it, a host of ideologues are raising questions, criticizing methodology, mounting ad hominem attacks, or simply disregarding the data entirely in their pronouncements. As I went to testify before Congress in the fall of 1984, people warned me not to raise concerns about infant day care because of their political implications. I decided, however, to behave as a scientist and present the evidence as I regarded

Source: Jay Belsky (1986, September). Infant day care: A cause for concern? *Zero to Three*, 7, 1–7. Reprinted by permission of the National Center for Clinical Infant Programs, 733 15th St., NW, Suite 912, Washington, DC 20005.

it. My own personal sense is that few individuals are truly open-minded about infant day care. Politicians, like many others, are either for day care or against it; they sift through the research looking for ammunition for their arguments while finding fault with, and thus dismissing, any evidence that reads the other way.

Scientists, of course, are susceptible to similar biases, however much we try not to be. This fact was brought home to me recently in a most vivid way as part of a correspondence with a colleague whose work on and opinions about day care I admire and respect immensely. In sharing with me her plans to carry out a meta-analysis of research bearing on the influence of day care on infant-mother attachment, this mother of a young infant in sitter care wrote to me that "I think historical and cross-cultural data can be used *to support the position* that shared caregiving, which is what day care is, is not detrimental to child development" (emphasis added).

Since holding a point of view, either consciously or unconsciously, and for whatever reasons, prior to the analysis of the evidence may involve a considerable risk of bias entering into the reading of such evidence, I feel it is important to make several facts clear about my circumstances: I am the father of two darling and demanding young sons who spent their entire infancies in the primary care of their mother and who did not start preschool (on a three half-day a week schedule) until they were $2\frac{1}{2}$ and 3 years of age. Because I am not sure that this family reality of mine does not influence my reading of the scientific evidence, I share it here.

Concern with the Development of Infants in Day Care: A 15-Year Perspective

In the early 1970s, prevailing cultural attitudes led to the belief that exclusive maternal rearing, particularly during the early years, was essential for healthy psychological development. The principal organizing question of day care research thus became "Does rearing outside of the confines of the family in a group program adversely affect intellectual, social and, especially, emotional development?" This specific interest in the developmental consequences of day care, and particularly a concern for negative effects, derived from poli-

cymakers' and scientists' feeling of obligation to protect the public from harm. If day care proved detrimental to child development, they would not want to be in the position of advocating policies to promote, or even support, the group-rearing of young children beyond the confines of the family. If such early rearing experience was found to disrupt the normative course of early childhood, the best interests of the public would be served if mothers or fathers did not work unless it was absolutely essential.

When I reviewed the literature on the effects of day care in 1977 (Belsky & Steinberg, 1978) and again in 1980 (Belsky, Steinberg, & Walker, 1982), I found little if any evidence of detrimental effects of nonmaternal child care on infant development. This was especially the case for model, university-based, research-oriented programs. Only one conclusion could be reached: infant day care *need not* disrupt the child's emotional development.

In terms of most day care research, emotional development has been conceptualized in terms of the quality of the affective tie linking child to mother. This focus upon the attachment relationship was based upon a great deal of theory suggesting that the emotional security which this bond promoted in the child would affect his/her future well-being, particularly his/her feelings about self, others, and capacity to form relationships. In order to study the effect of day care on the security of the infant-mother attachment relationship, researchers employed the Strange Situation, a laboratory procedure in which the baby is subjected to a series of brief separations and reunions with mother and stranger and his/her behavior is observed.

Early studies of infant day care which employed this procedure or some variant of it revealed not only that day care infants were as likely to get distressed as home-reared children when confronting a stranger or being separated from mother, but also that they clearly preferred their mothers as objects of attachment. Caregivers, then, were not replacing mothers as the source of infants' primary emotional bonds, and this was, and still is, regarded as a good thing—especially since the evidence also indicates that day-care infants can and do form healthy affectional ties to individuals who respond to their needs in their day care environment.

It is of special significance that in all the

183

initial work done on infant day care, and on which the preceding conclusions were based, attention was paid to whether or not the infant became distressed upon separation and whether or not s/he approached and interacted with a strange adult. In the years which *followed* the first wave of studies of infant day care, it became abundantly clear that the most revealing and developmentally meaningful aspect of the infant's behavior in the Strange Situation was his/her orientation to mother upon reunion following separation, something which simply had not been considered in the early studies. Indeed, attachment researchers now distinguish between three types. Infants who positively greet their mothers (with a smile or by showing a toy) and/or who approach mother to seek comfort if distressed are characterized as having secure attachments. Those who fail to greet mother (by averting gaze) or who start to approach mother but then turn away are considered to be anxious-avoidant in their attachment; and those who seek contact yet cannot be comforted by mother and who cry in an angry, petulant manner or hit away toys offered by mother are considered anxious-resistant in their attachment relationship.

In numerous studies these patterns of secure and insecure attachment relationships have been found to be predictive of individual differences in later development, such that those infants who are characterized as having secure attachments look, as a group, more competent than their agemates whose attachments to mother are characterized as insecure (Bretherton, 1985; Lamb et al., 1985). All of this is not meant to imply that the child's future development is solely or unalterably determined by the nature of the infant-mother attachment bond, but merely to indicate why a focus upon reunion seems so important to understanding the developmental correlates of infant day care.

Another Look at the Evidence

In the time since my initial reviews of the day care literature, a number of additional investigations have been reported which not only have raised concerns in my mind about the developmental correlates of nonmaternal care initiated in the first year of life, but have also led me to re-examine earlier research. It is not my intention to provide an exhaustive summary of my current reading of the evidence (see Belsky, 1986), but rather to outline my thinking.

In my 1980 review, only a single investigation raised any real concern in my mind regarding infant care. Vaughn and his colleagues (1980), studying a sample of low-income Caucasian women and their firstborn in the Minneapolis-St. Paul area, found that infants who were reared in what appeared to be low quality, if not frequently changing, child care arrangements were especially likely to show a particular pattern of attachment to mother if they had been enrolled in care in the first year of life. Specifically, they were disproportionately likely to display a pattern of avoidance in which they refused to look at or approach mother when reunited with her after brief separations in the Strange Situation paradigm.

In addition to the Minnesota study which first raised some concerns in my mind, several other findings in the literature in 1980 *could* also have been regarded as *potential* evidence of negative effects. For example, Ricciuti (1974) found that at one year of age day-care-reared infants cried more in response to separation than did a home-reared group. In another study of a very small sample, Rubenstein, Howes, and Boyle (1981) observed that

Does infant day care disrupt the formation of mother-child attachment?

children who were in day care during the first year of life had more temper tantrums than those cared for at home by mothers on a full-time basis. In my writings I have consistently, and I believe wisely, cautioned against overinterpreting such group differences, particularly because they emerged in a context in which virtually all other measures revealed no differences. We should look for trends and patterns, I counseled, and not be swept away by a single variable, especially when other studies fail to discern a similar day care-home care difference that could be interpreted as an effect of day care.

When it came time for me to review the literature again in 1982, I found that a few more studies revealed what could conceivably be viewed as evidence of negative effects of day care on the development of infants (see Belsky, 1984). In fact, each time I have gone back to my files of day care reports, first to prepare my congressional testimony in 1984 and then to prepare a talk to the American Academy of Pediatrics in 1985, I have found that disturbing evidence keeps accumulating. I am not talking about a flood of evidence, but at the very least a slow, steady trickle.

Consider first the fact that, at the same time that Vaughn and his colleagues (1980) were following their Minneapolis sample at two years of age and Farber and Egeland (1982) were discerning no significant differences between day-care and home-reared infants, another study provided further evidence of a pattern of avoidance associated with early substitute child care. This study of middle-class infants in Michigan revealed that those babies who began day care (in a variety of arrangements) in the first year of life displayed greater avoidance of their mothers in the Strange Situation separation procedure (Schwartz, 1983) at 12 months of age than did home-reared infants. This heightened avoidance was also chronicled by Willie and Jacobson's (1984) investigation of 45 18-month-olds from the Detroit area; when studied with their mothers in the Strange Situation, those children displaying insecure-avoidant attachment patterns were found to have experienced more than three times as much extra-familial child care as their securely attached (to mothers) counterparts (15.9 hours/week versus 4.5 hours). And, in still another study, this one of affluent families in the Chicago area, Barglow (1985) found higher rates of avoidance as well

as decreased rates of proximity-seeking and contact maintenance for those infants experiencing good quality, stable "other-than-mother" care in the home than for a comparison group whose mothers did not work outside the home during the baby's first year.

These newly emerging data, it is of interest to note, turn out to be quite consistent with trends in the more general day care literature concerning preschoolers. As Clarke-Stewart and Fein (1983) observed in their comprehensive review of the evidence appearing in the most recent edition of the authoritative *Handbook of Child Psychology*,

> *children in day care are more likely than children at home to position themselves further away from mother, and to ignore or avoid mother after a brief separation. The difference is not observed in every child or every study, but the consistent direction of the differences is observed.* (p. 948)

There is, then, an *emerging* pattern here in which we see supplemntary child care, *especially that initiated in the first year*, whether in home or in centers, sometimes associated with the tendency of the infant to avoid or maintain a distance from the mother following a series of brief separations. Some, as I have already indicated, contend that such behavior reflects an underlying doubt or mistrust about the availability of the mother to meet the baby's needs and, thus, an insecure attachment. Moreover, since it is known that heightened avoidance of the mother is related to a set of developmental outcomes such as noncompliance and low frustration tolerance which most developmentalists would regard as less than desirable, some are inclined to conclude that the quality of the mother-child bond and thereby, the child's future development may be jeopardized by nonmaternal care in the first year of life.

Other scientists read *the very same evidence* in a *very different way.* Even though they observe the same pattern of avoidance among infants in day care, they interpret this not as a deficit or disturbance but rather as positively adaptive and possibly even precocious behavior. Since day care infants experience many separations, they reason, it is sensible for them not to orient toward mother. In addition, because the tendency for children as they get older is to remain more distant from their parents, the avoidance of mother among day-care-reared 12–18 month olds is seen as evidence of early maturity:

> *In children receiving care exclusively from mother, avoidance may be a pathological response reflecting an interactive history with a rejecting mother, while for children in day care greater distance from, or ignoring of, mother at reunion may be an adaptive response reflecting a habitual reaction to repeated daily separations and reunions. In these latter children, greater physical distance from mother and apparent avoidance may, in fact, signal a precocious independence. (Clarke-Stewart & Fein, 1986, p. 949)*

Which interpretation is correct? I concur with Clarke-Stewart and Fein (1983) that "there is no way to determine at this point if the apparent avoidance of mother observed in day care children in *some* studies is a disturbed or adaptive pattern" (p. 949; emphasis in original). But this very uncertainty leads me to wonder about the meaning of other data regarding the subsequent social development of those children who experienced nommaternal care in the first year.

The Long Term Development of Day-Care-Reared Infants

The very first investigation of the social development of preschoolers with infant day-care histories involved the developmental follow-up at three and four years of age of children who began nonmaternal, group care toward the end of their first year at the Syracuse University Infant Care Center (Schwarz et al., 1974). When compared to a group of children reared exclusively at home until entering a preschool day-care program, those with infant care histories were found, four months after entering the preschool, to be more physically and verbally aggressive with adults and peers, less cooperative with grown-ups and less tolerant of frustration. When the children from the Minnesota studies, which first linked infant care with insecure-avoidant attachment, were studied at two years of age, somewhat similar results emerged. Although Farber and Ege-

land (1982, p. 120) were led to conclude on the basis of their analysis of the problem-solving behavior of the Minnesota toddlers that "at two years of age the effects of out-of-home care were no longer striking" and "that the cumulative adverse effects of out-of-home care were minimal," careful scrutiny of the data leads a more cautious reader to a different conclusion. Not only was it the case that toddlers whose mothers began working prior to their infant's first birthday displayed significantly less enthusiasm in confronting a challenging task than did children who had no day care experience, but it was also the case that these day-care-reared infants tended to be less compliant in following their mothers' instructions, less persistent in dealing with a difficult problem, and more negative in their affect. A more thorough analysis of these same data by Vaughn, Deane, and Waters (1985) further revealed that although 18-month attachment security was a significant advantage to the children who were home-reared as infants when studied at 24 months, the securely attached infants who had entered day care in their first year looked more like toddlers with insecure attachment histories (from home- and day-care groups) than like home-reared children with secure infant-mother relationships. That is, early entry to day care in the first year appeared to mitigate the developmentally beneficial effects of a secure attachment that is so often noted in studies of home-reared middle- and lower-class children.

What is most notable about these findings from the Syracuse and Minneapolis studies, and even from other investigations (see below), is that the very child development outcomes associated with early entry into supplementary child care are the same as, or at least similar to, those that have been implicated in the attachment literature as the (undesirable) child development outcomes correlated with early insecure attachment to mother. Indeed, the tendency of the early day care infants in the Minneapolis and Syracuse studies to be less compliant at two years of age leads me to wonder whether I was too ready in early reviews to explain away Rubenstein, Howes, and Boyle's (1981) similar findings regarding the significantly more frequent temper tantrums and decreased compliance of $3\frac{1}{2}$ year olds who had been in supplementary care in their first years.

Other studies in the literature which do not focus specifically on attachment also raise concerns about infant day care. These studies report results that are not inconsistent with the notion that infant care *may* promote anxious-avoidant attachments. For example, a study conducted in Bermuda involving virtually all two year olds on the island found that "children who began group care in infancy were rated as more maladjusted (when studied between three and five years of age) than those who were cared for by sitters or in family day care homes for the early years and who began group care at later ages" (McCartney et al., 1982, p. 148). These conclusions, it is important to note, were based upon analyses which controlled for a variety of important background variables, including child's age at time of assessment and mother's IQ, age, and ethnicity. In a retrospective investigation of eight to 10 year olds who varied in their preschool experiences, Barton and Schwarz (1981) also found that day care entry prior to 12 months was associated with higher levels of misbehavior and greater social withdrawal, even after controlling for the educational level of both parents.

Finally, and perhaps most noteworthy, are results emanating from a longitudinal investigation of kindergarten and first graders reared since they were three months old in an extremely high-quality day care center at the University of North Carolina. Comparison of these children with others reared for varying amounts of time in nonmaternal child care arrangements initiated sometime after the first year of life revealed that children who received center-based care in the first year of life, in contrast to those receiving care any time thereafter, were rated:

> . . . as more likely to use the aggressive acts hit, kick, and push than children in the control group. Second, they were more likely to threaten, swear, and argue. Third, they demonstrated those propensities in several school settings—the playground, the hallway, the lunchroom, and the classroom. Fourth, teachers were more likely to rate these children as having aggressiveness as a serious deficit in social behavior. Fifth, teachers viewed these children as less likely to use such strategies as walking away or discussion

> to avoid or extract themselves from situations that could lead to aggression (Haskins, 1985, p. 700).

Conclusion

What are we to make of the evidence just summarized? The first point which must be made before drawing any conclusions is that not every study of infant day care reveals a heightened risk of insecure-avoidant attachment or of aggression, noncompliance, and disobedience. Nevertheless, it is clear that if one does not feel compelled to draw only irrefutable conclusions, a relatively persuasive *circumstantial* case can be made that early infant care *may* be associated with increased avoidance of mother, *possibly* to the point of greater insecurity in the attachment relationship, and that such care *may* also be associated with diminished compliance and cooperation with adults, increased aggressiveness, and possibly even greater social maladjustment in the preschool and early school-age years.

What is most noteworthy about these very *possiblities* is that they are *strikingly* consistent with basic theoretical contentions of attachment theory. It is certainly not inconsistent with attachment theory that repeated separations in the first year of life, as routinely associated with day care usage, might affect the emerging attachment relationship, and even disturb it from the standpoint of security (or at least avoidance). Further, the theory clearly assumes that avoidance reflects some doubt on the part of the infant with respect to the availability and responsiveness of the mother and may well serve as a coping strategy to mask anger. Finally, the theory clearly assumes that an avoidant attachment places the child at risk (probabilistically) for subsequent social difficulties, with diminished compliance and cooperation, increased aggressiveness and even maladjustment being, to some extent, expectable outcomes (or at least subsequent correlates).

The point of this essay, and my reason for writing it, is not to argue that infant day care invariably or necessarily results in an anxious-avoidant attachment and, thereby, increased risk for patterns of social development that most would regard as undesirable, but rather to raise this seemingly real possibility by organizing the available data in such terms. I cannot state strongly enough that there is sufficient evidence to lead a judicious scientist to doubt this line of reasoning; by the same token, however, there is *more than enough* evidence to lead the same judicious individual to seriously entertain it and refrain from explaining away and thus dismissing findings that may be ideologically disconcerting. Any one who has kept abreast of the evolution of my own thinking can attest to the fact that I have not been a consistent, ideologically-driven critic of nonmaternal care, whether experienced in the first year of life or thereafter. Having struggled to maintain an open mind with respect to the data base, so that the evidence could speak for itself, I know how difficult a task this is. I am well aware, too, that my gender and the more or less traditional nature of my family structure could bias my reading of the evidence.

It is certainly true that the very same evidence that I have presented for purposes of raising concern (not alarm) and encouraging others to reconsider the developmental correlates of infant day care could be organized in a different manner. This not only should be, but has been done, and very well indeed (Clarke-Stewart & Fein, 1983; Hoffmann, 1983; Rubenstein, 1985). It is also the case that virtually any one of the studies cited above could be dismissed for a variety of scientific reasons. But in the ecology of day care, perfect field research seems almost impossible; moreover, it would seem that the more perfect it is, the less generalizable it might be.

This complexity inherent to infant day care research underscores a most important point that also cannot be sufficiently emphasized. When we find infants in care we are not only likely to find them in a variety of arrangements usually resulting from their mothers working outside of the home, but also for a variety of reasons and with a variety of feelings and family practices associated with these care arrangements. Thus, infant day care refers to complex ecological niches. This means, then, that any effects associated with care are also associated with a host of other factors. Thus, it would be misguided to attribute any effects associated with nonmaternal care to the care per se, or even to the mother's employment.

Not to be lost in this discussion, however, is the fact that the correlates of day care which

have been chronicled (i.e., avoidance, aggression, noncompliance, withdrawal) have been found across a host of ecological niches and caregiving milieus. Thus, these "effects" or correlates of early supplementary care have been found in samples of impoverished (Haskins, 1985; Vaughn et al., 1980), middle-class (Rubenstein, Howes, & Boyle, 1981), and upper-class families (Barglow, 1985), and with children cared for in unstable family day care (Vaughn et al., 1980), high quality centers (Haskins, 1985; Schwarz, Strickland, & Krolick, 1974), poor quality (McCartney et al., 1982), and even in-home, babysitter care (Barglow, 1985). Such variation in the samples studied, yet similarity in the developmental outcomes associated with nonmaternal care in the first year, lead me to conclude that entry into care in the first year of life is a "risk factor" for the development of insecure-avoidant attachments in infancy and heightened aggressiveness, noncompliance, and withdrawal in the preschool and early school years. Under a variety of imaginable conditions, particularly pertaining to the quality and stability of the care arrangement, the temperamental vulnerability of the child, and the economic-social stresses to which the family is subjected, it seems likely that risk associated with early care would increase.

REFERENCES

Barglow, P. (1985). *Other-than-mother, in-home care, and the quality of the mother-child relationship.* Paper presented at the biennial meetings of the Society for Research in Child Development, Toronto.

Barton, M., & Schwarz, J. (1981, August). *Day care in the middle class: Effects in elementary school.* Paper presented at the American Psychological Association's Annual Convention, Los Angeles.

Belsky, J. (1984). Two waves of day care research: Developmental effects and conditions of quality. In R. Ainslie (Ed.), *The child and the day care setting* (pp. 1–34). New York: Praegner.

Belsky, J. (1986). *The effects of infant day care reconsidered.* Paper presented to National Academy of Sciences Ad Hoc Committee on Policy Issues in Child Care for Infants and Toddlers, Washington, D.C.

Belsky, J., & Steinberg, L. D. (1978). The effects of day care: A critical review. *Child Development, 49,* 929–949.

Belsky, J., Steinberg, L. D. & Walker, A. (1982). The

ecology of day care. In M. Lamb (Ed.), *Child-rearing in nontraditional families* (pp. 71–116). Hillsdale, NJ: Erlbaum.

Bretherton, I. (1985). Attachment theory: Retrospect and prospect. In I. Bretherton & E. Waters (Eds.), Growing points in attachment theory and research. *Monographs of the Society for Research in Child Development*, No. 209, Vol. 50, Nos. 1–2, pp. 3–36.

Clarke-Stewart, K. A., & Fein, G. (1983). Early childhood programs. In M. M. Maith & J. J. Campos (Eds.), P. H. Mussen (Series Ed.), *Handbook of child psychology: Vol. 2. Infancy and developmental psychobiology.* New York: Wiley.

Farber, E. A., & Egeland, B. (1982). Developmental consequences of out-of-home care for infants in a low income population. In E. Zigler & E. Gordon (Eds.), *Day Care* (pp. 102–125). Boston: Auburn.

Haskins, R. (1985). Public school aggression among children with varying day-care experience. *Child Development*, *56*, 689–703.

Hoffman, L. (1983). Maternal employment and the young child. In M. Perlmutter (Ed.), *Minnesota symposium on child psychiatry* (pp. 101–127). Hillsdale, NJ: Erlbaum.

Kamerman, S. (1986, February). *Infant care usage in the United States.* Report presented to National Academy of Sciences Ad Hoc Committee on Policy Issues in Child Care for Infants and Toddlers, Washington, D.C.

Klein, R. (1985). Caregiving arrangements by employed women with children under one year of age. *Developmental Psychology*, *21*, 403–406.

McCartney, K., Scarr, S., Phillips, D., Grajek, S., & Schwarz, J. C. (1982). Environmental differences among day care centers and their effects on children's development. In E. Zigler & E. Gordon (Eds.), *Day care: Scientific and social policy issues* (pp. 126–151). Boston: Auburn House Pub. Co.

Ricciuti, H. N. (1974). Fear and the development of social attachments in the first year of life. In M. Lewis & L. A. Rosenblum (Eds.), *The origins of fear* (pp. 73–106). New York: Wiley.

Rubenstein, J. (1985). The effects of maternal employment on young children. *Applied Developmental Psychology*, *2*, 99–128.

Rubenstein, J., Howes, C., & Boyle, P. (1981). A two year follow-up of infants in community-based day care. *Journal of Child Psychology and Psychiatry*, *22*, 209–218.

Schwartz, P. (1983). Length of day-care attendance and attachment behavior in eighteen-month-old infants. *Child Development*, *54*, 1073–1078.

Schwarz, J. C., Strickland, R. G., & Krolick, G. (1974). Infant day care: Behavioral effects at preschool age. *Developmental Psychology*, *10*, 502–506.

Vaughn, B., Deane, K., & Waters, E. (1985). The impact of out-of-home care on child-mother attachment quality: Another look at some enduring questions. In I. Bretherton & E. Waters (Eds.), *Growing points in attachment theory and research.* Monographs for the Society for Research in Child Development.

Vaughn, B., Gove, F. L., & Egeland, B. (1980). The relationship between out-of-home care and the quality of infant-mother attachment in an economically disadvantaged population. *Child Development*, *51*, 971–975.

Wille, D., & Jacobson, J. (1984, April). *The influence of maternal employment, attachment pattern, extrafamilial child care, and previous experience with peers on early peer interaction.* Paper presented at the meetings of the International Conference on Infant Studies, New York.

Work on this paper was supported by a grant from the National Institute of Child Health and Human Development (RO1HD15496) and by an NIMH Research Scientists Development Award (K02MH 00486).

189

Selective Review of Infant Day Care Research: A Cause for Concern!

Deborah Phillips, Kathleen McCartney, Sandra Scarr, and Carollee Howes

In the September, 1986 issue of *Zero to Three*, Jay Belsky states that "entry into care in the first year of life is a 'risk factor' for the develoment of insecure-avoidant attachments in infancy and heightened aggressiveness, noncompliance, and withdrawal in the preschool and early school years" (p. 7). This is a startling conclusion with far reaching implications for both political and personal decisions about reliance on infant day care. And despite the caveats and qualifiers sprinkled through the article, it is this grave pronouncement that will become the heritage and most quoted of Belsky's remarks.

This is unfortunate. Belsky's admonition that infant care—apparently *any* nonmaternal infant care—exposes infants to risk constitutes one individual's interpretation of research on infant care that is at best, selective, and at worst, misinterprets the available data. Under any condition, a selective review is cause for concern. But when the stakes are as high as they are in the area of infant day care—anxious parents and precariously funded programs—the review requires careful scrutiny, and, we believe, substantial revising.

With respect to the issue of insecure attachment, Belsky refers to, but does not report, the results of a meta-analysis of research examining the influence of child care on infant-mother attachment. This meta-analysis was conducted by two of the current authors (McCartney & Phillips, in press). The complete findings will soon appear in an edited volume of research on motherhood (Birns & Hay, in press).

Belsky implies that the meta-analysis was biased by the family status and ideology of the authors. A meta-analysis is a statistical method for analyzing the combined results of multiple studies that, by definition, holds less potential for bias than a personal literature review. Several precautions were also taken in this instance: a search of *Child Development Abstracts and Bibliography* was conducted, excluding only those studies that did not use the Strange Situation to assess attachment or that did not report data for proximity to mother and avoidance of mother. Fourteen studies were identified. A research assistant who was unaware of the purpose of the analysis coded each of the articles. Finally, given the frequent criticism of meta-analysis on the grounds that less valid studies are given equal weight with carefully controlled studies, the moderating influence of methodological strengths and weaknesses of each study was explicitly examined.

What did we discover? Two results are important. First, the effect-size estimates for the four measures of attachment (explore, cry, proximity, avoidance) showed negligible day care-home differences. This suggests that children attending day care are no different from children reared at home on mother attachment as assessed through the Strange Situation. Second, the examination of methodological moderators revealed that ratings of

Source: Deborah Phillips, Kathleen McCartney, Sandra Scarr, & Carollee Howes (1987, February). Selective review of infant day care research: A cause for concern! *Zero to Three*, 7, 18–21. Reprinted by permission of the National Center for Clinical Infant Programs, 733 15th St., NW, Suite 912, Washington, DC 20005.

avoidance were affected by whether judges were "blind" to the children's substitute care experience. Judges who were *not* blind were more likely to find differences between day care and home-reared children, such that day care children were rated as more avoidant. This documents an unfortunate experimenter expectancy effect.

Belsky draws heavily upon one longitudinal study—the Minneapolis sample studied by Farber and Egeland (1982) and by Vaughn and his colleagues (Vaughn, Deane, & Waters, 1985; Vaughn, Gove, & Egeland, 1980)—in his analysis of this attachment literature. It is critical for your readership to know that this research was designed to study early *maladaptation* in parent-infant interactions. As described by Farber and Egeland, "The sample was drawn from a local maternal and child care clinic which serves families of lower socioeconomic backgrounds. The majority of the mothers were single and receiving some form of public assistance at the time their babies were born. Most of the pregnancies were not planned" (pp. 107–8). Infant day care, in this study, was most frequently provided by an adult female, often a relative or friend of the infant's mother. At least 80% of the infants experienced a change in the substitute caregiver during the period they were receiving out-of-home care. The authors conclude, "In sum, out-of-home care arrangements were quite varied and changes in these arrangements were a routine" (Farber & Egeland, p. 111).

We do not have any quarrel with Belsky's reporting of these data. They have been reported in reputable journals and edited volumes. Given the meta-analyses results and other available evidence, we do, however, question his subsequent conclusion that "the very child development outcomes associated with early entry into supplementary child care are the same as or at least similar to, those that have been implicated in the attachment literature as the (undesirable) child development outcomes correlated with early insecure attachment to mother" (p. 5). Nowhere is it ascertained, for example, to what degree the results of the Minneapolis project are due to the multiple family stresses associated with poverty or the unstable care arrangements of the children in conjunction with, or instead of, the age at which the children entered child care. And regardless of causality, we question

the validity of premising a generalized argument about infant care largely on a sample of very low-income, single mothers with unplanned pregnancies and inconsistent child care.

One of us (Howes & Stewart, 1986) has recently completed a study that compares directly the influence of age of entry into child care and the stability of child care in 55 toddler-age children who were enrolled in family day care when they were between 2 and 23 months old. Only 36% of this middle-class sample stayed in the same family day care home from the time they entered day care until they were observed in the study. Children who changed child care arrangements more often were less competent in their play with peers. Boys who entered child care as younger babies and had few child care changes were most likely to engage in high level play with objects. This suggests that the stability of the child care arrangement is more important than the age the child begins child care.

It should also be noted that the results of the Schwartz study (1983), as discussed by Belsky, are overgeneralized. Belsky states that this study shows that "babies who began day care in the first year of life displayed greater avoidance of their mothers . . ." (p. 4). In fact, only those babies who began *full-time* care as infants showed greater avoidance of their mothers. Those in part-time care were not different in attachment from infants not in child care.

The only other available review of the research on attachment and infant care (Gamble & Zigler, 1986) is more circumspect in its conclusions, and we believe far more in line with the evidence. Gamble and Zigler state as a "tentative" conclusion, "*In families facing significant life stresses*, substitute care during the first year increases the likelihood of insecure parent-child attachments" (p. 35, emphasis added). And in an accompanying article (Young & Zigler, 1986), policy recommendations that include efforts to improve the quality of infant care and make parental leaves more widely available are outlined.

The second argument put forth by Belsky concerns the effects of infant day care on children's social development, specifically maladjustment and aggression. Belsky concludes on the basis of the Bermuda child care study (Mc-

191

Cartney, Scarr, Phillips, Grajek, & Schwarz, 1982), data from the Abecedarian Project (Haskins, 1985), and data reported by Rubenstein, Howes, and Boyle (1981) that early infant care, "may be associated with diminished compliance and cooperation with adults, increased aggressiveness, and possibly even greater social maladjustment in the preschool and early school-age years" (p. 6). In our opinion, a far more cautious and restricted conclusion is, in fact, warranted.

Specifically, the Bermuda study (also reported in McCartney, 1984; McCartney, Scarr, Phillips, & Grajek, 1985; and Phillips, McCartney, & Scarr, in press) did not examine "poor quality" centers, as Belsky claims (p. 7), but centers that ranged widely in quality from excellent to poor. The central purpose of this research was to examine whether variation in the quality of center-based care affects children's cognitive, language, and social development. Family background and age of entry into child care were controlled statistically prior to examining the effects of day care quality.

The most significant finding of this research is that child outcomes are affected by the quality of their child care programs. Age of entry into care showed only one significant effect out of a total of 20 outcome measures, while quality showed consistent effects. Child care is not a uniform intervention and should not be discussed as such—a point that has been emphasized by many reviewers of child care research (Clarke-Stewart & Fein, 1983; Etaugh, 1980; Rutter, 1981; Scarr, 1984; Zigler & Gordon, 1982), including Belsky, (Belsky, Steinberg, & Walker, 1982). Just as home environments are not all the same, day care environments are not all the same and some are better for children than others.

Belsky sidesteps this major finding, and states, instead, that the Bermuda study demonstrates that maladjustment is a consequence of early entry into child care. The "maladjustment" measure used in this study actually consists of three scales, each of which was rated by a parent and a caregiver. Only *one* of the six ratings showed a significant effect for age of entry—caregiver ratings of children's anxiety. Moreover, quality of care was just as important a predictor of the caregiver anxiety ratings as age of entry. Perhaps most important, we must ask if any of the children in the study were, in fact, overly anxious. The

answer is no. The actual range of caregiver anxiety ratings was 1.00 to 2.67 on a scale on which the highest possible score is 10.00. Thus, the highest score actually obtained for a child in this study was 2.67—a score of 6.73 is considered "anxious" by the authors of the scale (Behar & Stringfield, 1974). So to portray any of the children in this study as over-anxious, let alone maladjusted, is inappropriate.

Belsky also bases his conclusions about the social development of children who enter child care as infants on a study conducted by Haskins (1985). Belsky characterizes these data as showing greater aggressiveness for "children who received center-based care in the first year of life, in contrast to those receiving care at any time thereafter . . ." (p. 6). In fact, Haskins states that "my results will not support these conclusions" (personal communication, October 1986).

What Haskins' data *do* show is that "children with extensive experience in a cognitively-oriented day-care program were rated by their public school teachers as more aggressive" (p. 700). In direct comparisons with children who had extensive experience in licensed child care centers that did not place a great emphasis on a cognitive curriculum, significant differences emerged, such that only the children in the cognitively-oriented programs showed higher aggressiveness upon school entry. Thus, we must again circumscribe Belsky's conclusions—they apply only to children who attended a single intervention program with a particular type of curriculum. In fact, the children with extensive experience in licensed child care centers showed *lower* amounts of hitting, kicking, and pushing than did children with less day care experience.

The results of the Haskins study relate directly to questions about the type of day care curriculum to which young children are exposed. They have little to say about age of entry into child care and, to the extent that conclusions can be drawn about *amount* of day care experience, it appears that this factor alone does not predict aggressiveness in kindergarten and first grade. These are quite different—almost opposite—conclusions from those that Belsky draws from this research.

A third published study that Belsky cites to draw conclusions about the social development of children who enter child care as infants was conducted by Rubenstein, Howes, and Boyle (1981). In this study, preschool-age children who had been in child care as infants were found to be less compliant when asked by their mothers to complete a boring task than children who had been at home. Furthermore, mothers of child care children reported more temper tantrums than mothers of children reared exclusively at home.

Belsky does not, however, report a follow-up study of these children (Rubenstein & Howes, 1983) which revised several of the conclusions reached in the initial study. Thus, the authors later conclude that "For later emotional development, individual differences in the actual experiences and behaviors of the toddlers in day care are more important than is attendance in day care per se. We found that later behavior problems, test anxiety, and aspects of the mother-child affective relationship were predicted by individual differences in the toddlers' experiences and behaviors in day care and they were not predicted by whether the toddler had been in day care or at home" (pp. 41–42).

Similarly, Howes & Olenick (1986) report that toddlers in high quality child care centers demonstrated accelerated self-regulation while toddlers in low quality centers lagged behind both children who were in high quality centers and at home with their mothers. Therefore, when critical studies are not eliminated from the review, they converge to suggest that early entry into day care may be less important than the kind and quality of care children receive while in day care.

An additional problem must be noted with respect to Belsky's review of research on the social effects of infant day care. On page 5, he refers to the Farber and Egeland (1982) study and concludes, "Not only was it the case that toddlers whose mothers began working prior to their infant's first birthday displayed significantly less *enthusiasm* in confronting a challenging task than did children who had no day care experience, but it was also the case that these day-care-reared infants tended to be less *compliant* in following their mothers' instructions, less *persistent* in dealing with a difficult problem, and more negative in their *affect*."

In fact, only one of these results showed *significant* effects for the mother's work status—enthusiasm—and then *only for boys*. The other results failed to reach significance, e.g., $p = .09$ for compliance, $p = .13$ for persistence, $p = .10$ for negative affect. Nonsignificant group differences are also included

among significant effects in Belsky's reporting of Schwarz, Strickland, & Krolick (1974) (Schwarz, personal communication, October, 1986). It is highly unconventional to report nonsignficant effects as reliable group differences.

Finally, it is instructive to examine other evidence which should also be weighed in a comprehensive review of the effects of infant day care. Benn (1985), in a study of 41 upper-class children from intact families using family day care homes with fewer than 3 children or a sitter for child care, found that male infants who started child care during the latter half of the first year of life were more likely to be insecurely attached to their mothers than were male infants who began child care earlier. Howes & Rubenstein (1985) report that children who entered center or family day care earlier (children entered between 2 and 15 months of age) had higher frequencies of touching and laughing with their caregiver than children who entered care later. Schwarz and his colleagues (Schwarz, Krolick, & Strickland, 1973) studied peer interactions among children who entered center-based care earlier (5–22 months, average = 9.5 months) versus later (24–47 months, average = 36 months). The results showed that the early entry group exhibited more positive affect upon entering the peer group, showed less tension upon entering the group and five weeks later, and also had higher (more positive) social interaction scores than the late group on day one and five weeks later.

Scientists who study controversial and emotion-laden issues sometimes find it difficult to suspend judgment in the face of complex and contradictory research evidence. Infant day care is among the most controversial and emotion-laden issues that developmentalists study. It is precisely under these circumstances, however, that it is incumbent on the scientific community to use the utmost caution. Sometimes "good science" means saying "I don't know—the evidence is inconclusive." At a minimum, when we venture to draw conclusions from a relatively small and contradictory collection of research evidence, we must qualify our conclusions to explain to whom they apply, under what circumstances, and with what remaining questions.

The evidence on infant day care is not all in. In fact, carefully controlled studies of infant day care are rare. Yet, we do know that quality makes a difference and that treating infant child care as a homogeneous environment fails to reflect the real diversity of infant care. We also know that the existing data confound family stress, the child's age of entry into care, the length of time in care, and the stability and quality of care, thus leading us to be very cautious about attributing the consquences of care to any single one of these variables. Many other equally important issues have received scant empirical attention, such as the role of child care as a support system for working families and the role of fathers in children's (and mothers') adjustment to child care.

Of course, any *consistent* findings of detrimental effects would be cause for concern, as noted by Belsky. And any clues in the research literature about how to define high quality infant care should be studied carefully. This latter issue is particularly compelling. Because, while we continue to debate the merits of infant care, the realities of economic and demographic life in America tell us that infant day care is here to stay.

REFERENCES

Behar, L., & Stringfield, S. A. (1974). A behavior rating scale for the preschool child. *Developmental Psychology, 10*, 601–610.

Belsky, J. (1986). Infant day care: A cause for concern? *Zero to Three*, Vol. VI, No. 5, pp. 1–9.

Belsky, J., Steinberg, L. S., & Walker, A. (1982). The ecology of day care. In M. Lamb (Ed.), *Childrearing in nontraditional families*. Hillsdale, NJ: Erlbaum.

Benn, R. (1985). *Factors associated with security of attachment in dual career families*. Paper presented at the biennial meeting of the Society for Research in Child Development, Toronto, Canada.

Birns, B., & Hay, D. (Eds.), (in press). *Different faces of motherhood*. New York: Plenum Press.

Clarke-Stewart, K. A., & Fein, G. (1983). Early childhood programs. In M. M. Haith & J. J. Campos (Eds.), P. H. Mussen (Series Ed.) *Handbook of child psychology: Vol. 2. Infancy and developmental psychobiology*. New York: Wiley.

Etaugh, C. (1980). Effects of nonmaternal care on children: Research evidence and popular views. *American Psychologist, 35*, 309–319.

Farber, E. A., & Egeland, B. (1982). Developmental consequences of out-of-home care for infants in a low income population. In E. Zigler & E. Gordon (Eds.), *Day Care: Scientific and Social Policy Issues*. Boston: Auburn.

Gamble, T., & Zigler, E. (1986). Effects of infant day care: Another look at the evidence. *American Journal of Orthopsychiatry, 56*, 26–42.

Haskins, R. (1985). Public school aggression among children with varying day-care experience. *Child Development, 56*, 689–703.

Howes, C., & Stewart, P. (1986). *Child's play with adults, peers and toys*. Unpublished manuscript, University of California at Los Angeles.

Howes, C., & Olenick, M. (1986). Family and child care influences on toddler compliance. *Child Development, 57*, 206–216.

Howes, C., & Rubenstein, J. (1985). Determinants of toddlers' experience in day care: Age of entry and quality of setting. *Child Care Quarterly, 14*, 140–151.

McCartney, K. (1984). The effect of quality of day care environment upon children's language development. *Developmental Psychology, 20*, 244–260.

McCartney, K., & Phillips, D. (in press). Motherhood and child care. In B. Birns, & D. Hay (Eds.), *Different faces of motherhood*. New York: Plenum Press.

McCartney, K., Scarr, S., Phillips, D., & Grajek, S., (1985). Day care as intervention: Comparisons of varying quality programs. *Journal of Applied Developmental Psychology, 6*, 247–260.

McCartney, K., Scarr, S., Phillips, D., Grajek, S., & Schwarz, J. C. (1982). Environmental differences among day care centers and their effects on children's development. In E. Zigler and E. Gordon (Eds.), *Day care: Scientific and social policy issues*. Boston: Auburn House.

Phillips, C., McCartney, K., & Scarr, S. (in press). Child care quality and children's social development. *Developmental Psychology*.

Rubenstein, J., & Howes, C. (1983). Adaptation to infant day care in S. Kilmer (Ed.) *Advances in early education and day care*. Greenwich, CT: JAI Press.

Rubenstein, J., Howes, C., & Boyle, P. (1981). A two year follow-up of infants in community-based day care. *Journal of Child Psychology and Psychiatry, 22*, 209–218.

Rutter, M. (1981). Social-emotional consequences of day care for preschool children. *American Journal of Orthopsychiatry, 51*, 4–28.

Scarr, S. (1984). *Mother care, other care*. New York: Basic Books.

Schwartz, P. (1983). Length of day-care attendance and attachment behavior in eighteen-month-old infants. *Child Development, 54*, 1073–1078.

Schwarz, J. C., Krolick, G., & Strickland, R. G. (1973). Effects of early day care experience on adjustment to a new environment. *American Journal of Orthopsychiatry, 43*, 340–348.

Schwarz, J. C., Strickland, R. G., & Krolick, G. (1974). Infant day care: Behavioral effects at preschool age. *Developmental Psychology, 10,* 502–506.

Vaughn, B., Deane, K., & Waters, E. (1985). The impact of out-of-home care on child-mother attachment quality: Another look at some enduring questions. In I. Bretherton & E. Waters (Eds.), *Growing points in attachment theory and research.* Monographs for the Society for Research in Child Development.

Vaughn, B., Gove, F. L., & Egeland, B. (1980), The relationship between out-of-home care and the quality of infant-mother attachment in an economically disadvantaged population. *Child Development, 51,* 971–975.

Young, K. T., & Zigler, E. (1986). Infant and toddler day care: Regulations and policy implications. *American Journal of Orthopsychiatry, 56,* 43–55.

Zigler, E., & Gordon, E. (Eds.). (1982). *Day Care: Scientific and Social Policy Issues.* Boston: Auburn.

Comments: "Infant Day Care: A Cause for Concern"

Stella Chess

I wish to express my reaction to Dr. Jay Belsky's article, "Infant Day Care: A Cause for Concern." It is a curious article, in that it disclaims personal bias as a scientist, views with alarm those scientists who have personal bias that day care is not detrimental to child development, explains the great variability in quality and type of day care utilized by working parents, gives a nod to the hetereogeneity of family environments of children in day care, yet concludes that entry into day care in the first year of life is a risk factor for undesirable developmental outcomes. I also wonder why Belsky places so much emphasis on the personal bias among the proponents of day care, and fails to give equal weight to the biases of opponents of day care.

I have read the excellent paper by Phillips, McCartney, Scarr & Howes taking issue with Belsky's article in terms of the selectivity of the day care research findings that he reports. I am grateful for their scholarship and careful statistical critique. My remarks will be clinical in nature.

Dr. Belsky's paper brings echoes of an earlier judgment spearheaded by the reports of Bowlby and Goldfarb that institutional rearing of children was always to be condemned. However, later careful studies by B. Tizard and Rees and J. Tizard and colleagues in the 1970s provided evidence that the issue was really a good versus a bad institution rather than a blanket attack on all institutions for children. We could now identify the factors that would make institutional care a positive experience. And we are finally brought up to date in the 1980s by the long term studies by Quinten, Rutter & Liddle showing that "Institution

reared women showed a worse psychosocial outcome in adult life compared with controls, but there was great hetereogeneity, with some women functioning very well." Surely this outcome cries for an examination of the factors involved in the positive outcomes so that, when institutional upbringing is needed, it can strive toward increasing the proportion of those who have good outcomes. A cry of alarm over the poor outcomes ending in elimination of all institutional care is of no help unless it were true that all institutional care is in fact disastrous.

Surely we should not duplicate, with day care, this first overall condemnation, based primarily on the results of poorly functioning units.

A second point that strikes one in reading Belsky's article is his statement, highlighted on page 5 by repetition in large type, that "the child development outcomes associated with early entry into supplementary child care are similar to those undesirable developmental outcomes correlated with early insecure attachments to mother." As a clinician I am made quite uneasy by oversimplified one-to-one judgments. Throughout the article, the Ainsworth Strange Situation is assumed to be the valid mode of determining the child's actual attachment to the mother. Substantial clinical doubts have been voiced about the ability of a short, simple laboratory procedure to judge a complicated child-mother relationship. To quote Rutter (1981), who cautioned about drawing conclusions from ". . . curious procedures involving mother, caretakers and strangers not only going in and out of rooms every minute for reasons quite obscure to the

Source: Stella Chess (1987, February). Comments: "Infant day care: A cause for concern." *Zero to Three,* 7, 24–25. Reprinted by permission of the National Center for Clinical Infant Programs, 733 15th St., NW, Suite 912, Washington, DC 20005.

child but also not initiating interactions in the way they might usually do" (p. 160). Also in the Strange Situation rating, the infants who ignore the mother when she returns are called "avoidant," indeed a pejorative term, and classified as insecure. But is it not possible that in a child who is confident that his or her mother will return after a brief absence, the mother's return does not call for any special recognition of this event?

Surely, in view of the fact that one of every two women with a child under one year of age is employed and hence needs child care arrangements, our aim should be to supply good substitute care to all these working women of all economic levels. An unsupported dictum that such day care is a "risk factor" can only cause unnecessary guilt among working mothers and provide ammunition for the many elements in our society who are hostile to the idea of spending public funds suffi-

ciently to provide good day care facilities for all young children.

REFERENCES

Quinten, D., Rutter, M., & Liddle, C. (1984) Institutional Rearing, Parenting Difficulties, and Marital Support. *Psychological Medicine* 16: 151–169.

Rutter, M. (1981) *Maternal Deprivation Reassessed.* Second edition. Middlesex, England. Penguin Books.

Tizard, B., & Rees, J. (1974) A Comparison of Adoption, Restoration to the Natural Mother, and Continued Institutionalization on the Cognitive Development of Four-Year-Old Children. *Child Development* 45: 92–99.

Tizard, J. (1974) The Upbringing of Other People's Children: Implications of Research and For Research. *Journal of Child Psychology and Psychiatry* 15: 161–173.

Preschool Children in the Public Schools: Good Investment? Or Bad?

Deborah Burnett Strother

Early childhood education has become a hot topic, with several forces working together to push the issue onto the national agenda. For example, the excellence movement has brought more stringent coursework requirements—and greater pressures on children who were already at risk of school failure. Meanwhile, as the world market grows increasingly competitive, the public recognizes that American young people must be better educated and more adaptable. Some parents, hoping to rear academic superstars, are pushing their youngsters to read and write at a very early age. Many observers are concerned about the increasing number of children who suffer the harmful effects of poverty.

But the growing number of working mothers is perhaps the strongest force pushing early childhood education onto the national agenda. In 1984–85 approximately 55% of women with children under the age of 15 were in the labor force, according to the U.S. Census Bureau. Nearly 25% of these working mothers enrolled their children in organized child-care facilities, such as nursery schools and day-care centers.[1]

Inspired by these forces and by the highly publicized positive effects of some preschool programs, business leaders and legislators (including several Presidential candidates) have begun to maintain that high-quality early education for all children is not an expense, but a necessary investment. As commission and task force reports, congressional bills, and the mass media have begun to deal with the growing need for child care, the term *child care* itself has expanded to cover a spectrum of meanings from preschool programs to custodial care.

Though the words they use may vary, legislators, business leaders, and parents agree that a need exists for more daylong programs for preschoolers. There is little consensus, however, on such issues as curriculum, funding, location of the programs, criteria for admission, teacher preparation, and teacher certification.

The Committee for Economic Development (CED) has recommended that the federal government fund broad-scale "prevention programs" for all at-risk children from birth through age 5.[2] Members of the House Select Committee on Children, Youth, and Families have maintained that "better use of the public school would expand the number of safe, affordable, child-care options available to parents."[3] And the National Governors' Association recommended that states work with 4- and 5-year-old children from poor families "to help them get ready for school and to decrease the chances that they will drop out later."[4]

Policy

Policy making in the field of early childhood education is in its infancy, and most states have little experience in setting up programs, according to Norton Grubb.[5] If the current push for early childhood education programs comes to shove, most states will have the opportunity to create an early childhood education policy from scratch. To develop an effective policy, however, policy makers must first agree on what constitutes effective programming. In order to do this, according to Grubb, they must reconcile such issues as the conflict between the goals and methodology of elementary educators and those of early childhood educators.

Grubb points out that most child-care cen-

Source: Deborah Burnett Strother (1987). Preschool children in the public schools: Good investment? Or bad? *Phi Delta Kappan, 69,* 304–308. Reprinted by permission of Phi Delta Kappan, Inc.

ters and preschool programs rely on a Piagetian model, whereby children learn through their own experimentation and initiative. Most elementary teachers, by contrast, implicitly follow a behaviorist model, whereby children learn through structured interaction with the teacher and are graded on their performance. If preschool programs are placed in the public schools, some educators and parents are concerned that these programs will emphasize formal academic instruction for children as young as age 3. David Elkind has warned that formal learning programs for the very young are "risks to the child's motivation, intellectual growth, and self-esteem and could well do serious damage to the child's emerging personality."[6]

Funding

The federal government currently provides nearly $2 billion in relief for families that have incurred child-care expenses.[7] But two-thirds of that sum goes to families with incomes above the median, and none goes to the large number of families who lack sufficient disposable income to take advantage of the tax credits that provide the relief.

To reach such families, a variety of bills related to preschool and child-care programs have been—or are about to be—submitted to Congress. There are bills to provide tax incentives for employers who develop child-care centers in the workplace, a bill to cap the tax credit for child care (so that dollars now going to middle-income families can be diverted to low-income families to help them pay for child care), and bills to provide adult education for parents with limited parenting skills and to provide school-readiness training for their young children. Last fall the Alliance for Better Childcare, a coalition of more than 80 national organizations, proposed a bill calling for $2.5 billion, 85% of which would go to help low-income families pay for child care. The remaining 15% would pay for such services as training, the dissemination of information, and referral services. Meanwhile, the Welfare Reform Bill has new child-care provisions designed to serve women enrolled in job-training programs.

Legislators and business leaders who are pushing the child-care initiatives cite research findings on early childhood programs to support their position. However, some educators are raising important questions about this

practice. Last May, at a symposium inaugurating a new early childhood education research center in Memphis, several speakers expressed concern about the speed with which legislation is being enacted, policy is being set, and programs are being created using inadequate or inappropriate research data.

Jane Stallings, head of the Department of Curriculum and Instruction at the University of Houston, talked about the growing number of state-mandated programs created without supporting research. "We are being told what should be taught with very little evidence (to back up these assertions)," she said. "So much of the legislation is aimed at raising achievement test scores. Are we evaluating what we value?"[8] Stallings urged educators to take a more active role in helping to shape those laws.

Evelyn Moore, executive director of the National Black Child Development Institute, questioned whether public school programs for 4-year-olds will adopt the methods and procedures of elementary education, which she feels have often operated to segregate black children and to label them as nonachievers. The institute she directs has published criteria designed to insure that preschool programs based in the public schools will meet the needs of black children.

Herbert Zimiles, senior research fellow with the Institute for Social Research at the University of Michigan, has warned against viewing preschool programs as a panacea for immensely complicated social problems that cannot be solved by education. Further, he believes that much of the value of preschool education depends on how expertly it is implemented, and he wonders whether the quality and value of preschool education can be maintained if it is implemented on a broad scale. He notes:

Once regarded as a vitamin supplement painstakingly designed to serve as an enhancer of psychic growth, whose dosage was carefully prescribed by experts for different clients in a restricted age range, early education has begun to serve other purposes and has become, so to speak, an over-the-counter medication, available without prescription. And now, in order to make it universally available, we are about to put it in the drinking water.[9]

Other educators are worried that researchers may be overpromising what early child-

199

hood programs can do. In a recent policy report, Carolyn Morado said that some reformers "look to early childhood programs as a solution for complex educational and social problems that have not been solved by other means."[10] Morado warned that such an approach may lead to unrealistic expectations for some programs.

In its own recent report, the Committee for Economic Development cited researcher David Weikart's claim, made in testimony to the Select Committee on Children, Youth, and Families,[11] that every $1 spent on early prevention and intervention can save $4.75 in the costs of remedial education, welfare, and crime further down the road.[12] Yet these figures were derived from Weikart's most recent follow-up study of 98 of the original 123 children with I.Q. test scores between 60 and 90 who had been enrolled in a preschool program with a per-pupil expenditure of $6,187, a figure nearly double the cost of Head Start programs.[13]

Exemplary programs cost money. Many educators warn that it makes no sense to cite evidence regarding the educational benefits of such programs and then to enact legislation that provides inadequate funding for new programs, which must limp along with low expenditures, high pupil/teacher ratios, low teacher salaries, and inadequate teacher preparation.

The Research

Several studies conducted during the last 20 years suggest that high-quality early childhood programs have a positive effect on children. Such programs as Head Start, the Institute for Developmental Studies at New York University, the Perry Preschool Program in Ypsilanti, Michigan, the prekindergarten program in New York State, and the Brookline Early Education Program in Massachusetts have succeeded in spurring the developmental and cognitive growth of 3- and 4-year-olds.[14] Researchers found that during the early elementary school years children who participated in the experimental preschool programs had better grades, had fewer failing grades, had fewer absences, and were less often retained than nonparticipants. The participants had greater self-confidence and self-esteem— and so did many of their parents. The participants had better-developed literacy skills, greater curiosity, and less need for special edu-

cation services. They were more likely than nonparticipants to finish high school. They were more employable, less dependent on public assistance, and less likely to engage in criminal activity.

One study comparing preschool curricula found evidence that, over time, child-initiated learning can have a positive effect on social development. Lawrence Schweinhart, David Weikart, and Mary Larner compared three curricula, one of them relying on teacher-initiated learning (direct instruction) and two of them designed to foster child-initiated learning. They found that participants in the three programs did not differ significantly in I.Q. or in their achievement test scores over time. However, when the researchers interviewed 79% of those same children at age 15, they found fewer incidents of delinquent acts among the children who had taken part in the two programs using methods designed to foster child-initiated learning.[15]

At the Memphis symposium, David Weikart called that study "a red flag on the play—it doesn't say direct instruction should not be used on young children. It does say that, if you do prefer to use direct instruction, you'd better have a research design in place in order to assess the outcome."[16] Weikart theorizes that child-initiated learning gives children a greater sense of responsibility because it encourages them to act on their own initiative, both physically and mentally.

Despite the encouraging long-term benefits of preschool reported by Weikart and others, some researchers maintain that generalizing from studies such as these is inappropriate because the researchers followed small numbers of children (and some children dropped out of the studies along the way), because most of the children were economically disadvantaged, and because the programs in which they participated had very high per-pupil expenditures.[17] Those programs provided health and social services, in addition to a preschool curriculum—and they often provided such services to entire families, not just to program participants. The programs used curricula that adhered to principles of child development, and they employed appropriate assessment procedures. The teachers were trained in early childhood development, and they enjoyed strong administrative support. Moreover, parents played an active role in the education of their children.

Indeed, Zimiles has suggested that some of

the long-term effects found by Weikart and others may reflect the degree of parental involvement in children's education, not the quality of the program per se. If some children in the group originally selected for preschool later dropped out because their families were unwilling to bring them to school, self-selection may have operated to eliminate those children whose families were least supportive. Zimiles points out that when samples are self-selected (even in part), it is difficult to interpret the meaning of research findings.

Public School Early Childhood Study

How involved are the public schools in preschool education, and what are the characteristics of existing programs? Researchers with the Center for Children's Policy at the Bank Street College of Education and researchers with the Center for Research on Women at Wellesley College recently investigated the involvement of public schools in the development of early childhood programs that are educationally and developmentally sound and responsive to the child-care needs of the families that use them.

The researchers surveyed and analyzed state-level policy and legislation related to preschool education and child care in all the states and the District of Columbia. They surveyed 2,800 U.S. school districts with prekindergarten programs, and they examined a small sample of early childhood programs in depth to see how these programs relate to the communities they serve. (They received information on 1,700 programs, and they explored 12 programs in detail.)

The researchers found that 28 states and the District of Columbia support early childhood education through one of three funding arrangements: 1) pilot or statewide prekindergarten programs, 2) parent education programs (in lieu of direct service to prekindergarten-aged children), or 3) introduction or expansion of the Head Start program. According to Fern Marx, research director of the study at Wellesley, two-thirds of the state programs are intended to serve children at risk of school failure because they come from low-income families or suffer such problems as limited proficiency in English or lack of school readiness.[18]

Of those states offering programs, half contract directly with private agencies and half permit only public schools to provide programs, either directly or through subcontracts with other agencies (primarily private non-profit schools or Head Start). Marx finds the acceptance of multiple systems of delivering child care exciting, because it increases the likelihood that the needs of working parents and their children will be met. However, the absence in some states of coordination of planning, services, and funding at the local level has caused Head Start programs and state prekindergarten programs to compete increasingly for students, for staff, and for space.

According to Anne Mitchell, director of the study at Bank Street College, the public school programs serve a wide variety of purposes.[19] Thirty-three percent serve special education students, 11% are Head Start programs, 16% are prekindergarten programs funded by the state, 8% are locally funded prekindergarten programs, 9% are Chapter 1 prekindergarten programs, 6.5% are child-care programs, 2% are child-care programs for teenage parents, 3% are preschool programs operated by high school students, 3% are parent education programs, and 8% are magnet school or summer programs.

Eighty percent of the public school programs operate only during the school year, and 60% of them operate three hours or less per day. (Child-care programs for the general public and some Chapter 1 programs have longer hours.) The mean class size and the mean teacher/pupil ratio are well within the limits established by high-quality programs; no public school program had classes larger than 18 or a teacher/pupil ratio greater than 1:10. Teachers in some of the early childhood programs in the public schools receive lower salaries than their counterparts in grades K–12; teachers in Head Start, child-care, and locally funded programs receive the lowest salaries.

Half of all the responding school districts in the Wellesley/Bank Street study reported that preschool teachers must be certified in early childhood education. Almost 75% of the districts require that preschool teachers hold bachelor's degrees; two-thirds of the districts indicated, however, that previous teaching experience is not a criterion for hiring. Nonetheless, when they were hired, slightly more than half of the preschool teachers in these districts were certified in early childhood education and had already spent at least one year teaching children younger than 5. About 20% of the paraprofessionals who were hired by those districts had both one year of training in early childhood education and at least one year of working with young children. Case studies from the Wellesley/Bank Street project showed that strong leadership and active parent participation are key ingredients of high-quality programs. Ninety percent of the districts reported that their early childhood programs offer parent/teacher conferences; about half said that they have parent advisory councils or boards, and a similar number reported that their programs use parent volunteers.

The researchers found great variety in teaching methods and curricula among the early childhood programs they studied. In some programs, the children received breakfast and then spent the entire school day with a given teacher. They chose their own activities, receiving help and companionship from the teacher when necessary. In other programs, the children ate breakfast with aides and had one teacher for "school," another teacher for "day care"—with little communication or coordination among the different caretakers. Some programs were divided into 15-minute periods (marked by bells), during which the teachers directed all activities. The children in these programs were rarely (if ever) allowed to engage in open-ended, creative activities. In some programs, the teachers even determined which child would jump rope, work a puzzle, or climb on the climbing frame. Where skills-based curricula were in use, the children were often given written tests to assess their mastery of the skills being taught. Most of the programs studied had adequate materials and supplies, but some of the more structured programs apparently did not make daily use of these items.

Between Promise and Practice (a book to be published in the spring of 1988 by the Bank Street College Center for Children's Policy) will describe in detail the schools that Mitchell and her colleagues visited. Three technical reports, describing the district survey, the state survey, and the case studies, will be available this winter.

A Dual System

Edward Zigler, the first director of the Office of Child Development and an early defender of the Head Start program, now a professor of psychology at Yale University, suggests a new way to use school buildings to deal with the child-care issue.[20] We should "think of two major systems within the school building," he says.

"One system is the formal educational system that we have today, and it won't change. This system will remain in the hands of educators, and they will continue to try to improve it as best they know how," Zigler explains. The second system, according to Zigler, is the child-care system, composed of a child-care center, outreach services, and a referral system.

In other words, each elementary school will contain a center equipped to provide high-quality all-day child care to 3- and 4-year-olds whose parents work outside the home. Five-year-olds will attend kindergarten for half of each school day; they will spend the remainder of the day at home (if a parent is there to oversee them) or at the child-care center (if both parents work outside the home). The child-care center will be available before and after school to serve children between the ages of 6 and 12.

Three kinds of outreach programs will also be available, Zigler predicts, because "not all families' needs are going to be met in the school building." One kind of outreach programs will offer support services for new parents. A second kind of outreach program will coordinate and monitor all the local facilities that provide day care for children from birth to age 3 and will provide training and support for workers in these facilities. A third kind of outreach program will provide information and make referrals for parents who have problems related to health, education, or social services.

Zigler believes that child care, like education, should be a state-level responsibility. He recommends that parents pay for child care (with fees adjusted to their incomes) and that the federal government continue to subsidize the program (much as it does now).

Zigler would like to see the federal government support at least one pilot day-care center within the public school system in each state. He maintains that we must work child care into the very structure of the system, rather than expect the private sector and the churches to take care of the problem. The public schools are ideal places for child-care centers, in Zigler's view, because they are social institutions that are permanent, reliable, and close to home.

Zigler and Mitchell both note that close coordination between the day-care center and the host elementary school is important. When there is continuity between the two programs, the young participants will benefit. "You can run a terrific early childhood program," according to Mitchell, "but if you send the children from that program into a rigid, highly structured elementary program that differs considerably in philosophy and approach, it's bound to be a hard transition for them."

Zigler maintains that we have the knowledge to put this vision into effect immediately—if only we could gain access to school buildings. "The people we are serving with day-care centers are not teachers and principals; they are American families," he points out. "We can't allow turf battles to stand in the way of putting together a logical system that combines two of the basic needs of children—education and child care."

REFERENCES

1. U.S. Bureau of the Census, *Who's Minding the Kids?* (Washington, D.C.: Current Population Reports, Household Economic Studies, Series P-70, No. 9, 1987). The figures cited were calculated from this and other sources by Amaru Bachu, a statistician with the U.S. Bureau of the Census.
2. *Children in Need: Investment Strategies for the Educationally Disadvantaged* (New York: Committee for Economic Development, 1987).
3. Select Committee on Children, Youth, and Families, U.S. House of Representatives, 98th Congress, Second Session, *Families and Child Care: Improving the Options* (Washington, D.C.: U. S. Government Printing Office, 1984), p. xviii.
4. *Time for Results: The Governors' 1991 Report on Education* (Washington, D.C.: National Governors' Association, 1986), p. 3.
5. W. Norton Grubb, "Young Children Face the States: Issues and Options for Early Childhood Programs," Center for Policy Research in Education (CPRE) Note Series, sponsored by the U.S. Department of Education in conjunction with the Eagleton Institute of Politics at Rutgers University, the Rand Corporation, and the University of Wisconsin-Madison, May 1987.
6. David Elkind, "Formal Education and Early Childhood Education: An Essential Difference," *Phi Delta Kappan*, May 1986, pp. 631–36.
7. Select Committee, p. viii.
8. Remarks by Jane Stallings at a symposium hosted by the College of Education of Memphis State University and the Barbara K. Lipman Early Childhood Research Institute, 22–23 May 1987.
9. Herbert Zimiles, "Rethinking the Role of Research: New Issues and Lingering Doubts in an Era of Expanding Preschool Education," *Early Childhood Research Quarterly*, vol. 1, 1986, pp. 189–206.
10. Carolyn Morado, "Prekindergarten Programs for 4-Year-Olds: Some Key Issues," *Young Children*, July 1986, p. 62.
11. "Prevention Strategies for Healthy Babies and Healthy Children," 30 June 1983.
12. *Children in Need . . .*, p. 6.
13. Grubb, p. 47.
14. See, for example, Lawrence J. Schweinhart and David P. Weikart, "Evidence That Good Early Childhood Programs Work," *Phi Delta Kappan*, April 1985, pp. 545–53; Consortium for Longitudinal Studies, *As the Twig Is Bent . . . Lasting Effects of Preschool Programs* (Hillsdale, N.J.: Erlbaum, 1983); and Donald E. Pierson, Deborah Klein Walker, and Terrence Tivnan, "A School-Based Program from Infancy to Kindergarten for Children and Their Parents," *Personnel and Guidance Journal*, April 1984, pp. 448–55.
15. Lawrence J. Schweinhart, David P. Weikart, and Mary B. Larner, "Consequences of Three Preschool Curriculum Models Through Age 15," *Early Childhood Research Quarterly*, vol. 1, 1986, pp. 15–45.
16. Remarks by David Weikart at a symposium hosted by the College of Education of Memphis State University and the Barbara K. Lipman Early Childhood Research Institute, 22–23 May 1987.
17. See, for example, Edward F. Zigler, "Formal Schooling for Four-Year-Olds? No," *American Psychologist*, March 1987, pp. 254–60.
18. Telephone conversation with Fern Marx, 10 September 1987.
19. Telephone conversation with Anne Mitchell, 10 September 1987.
20. Telephone conversation with Edward Zigler, 15 September 1987.

Deborah Burnett Strother is editor in the Phi Delta Kappa Center on Evaluation, Development, and Research, Bloomington, Ind.

How Do Kids Really Feel about Being Home Alone?

Ellen Gray and Peter Coolsen

When the First National Conference on Latchkey Children convened in Boston in May 1984, it immediately became clear that the subject of children in self care polarizes people. In a session dealing with research on the topic, one panelist stressed the fear and safety risks school-age children face when they are taking care of themselves during the out-of-school hours. A second researcher, whose survey had just been published in a popular parents' magazine, argued that we simply do not know whether being a latchkey child has negative consequences. Incensed with his viewpoint, the audience hardly gave him a chance to present his case.

When we ask, "How do kids really feel about being home alone?," we get different answers depending to a great extent on who gives the answer and where it is reported. Many child care professionals believe that self care brings with it a number of risks and should not be taken for granted as an adequate child care solution for school-age children. However, popular magazines and newspapers that target a working mother audience favor the view that self care is safe and quite manageable if children are prepared with the necessary skills to protect, discipline and entertain themselves.

What is it about this subject that generates such controversy? Perhaps it is the realization that there is so much at stake for parents. Working parents are being forced to choose between perhaps their two highest priorities: working (in many cases for financial survival, not for professional fulfillment) and adequate child care. Many of these parents would not have chosen self care if given an option. Since it was the only available solution, emotions about the situation run high.

The practice of leaving children in self care is widespread in every community. Currently, well over half of all mothers with children under 18 years of age and 54 percent of mothers with children under six are in the work force.[1] This is in marked contrast to 1940, when under nine percent of mothers with minor children were employed, and even after World War II, when just twice that many mothers of minor children were working. As a result of this shift, the majority of America's children are growing up in situations where either both parents or the sole parent is employed outside the home.

It has become increasingly difficult to provide supervision for school-age children when community institutions established for this purpose have not kept pace with the changing structure of the family. While recent census data suggest that only 7.2 percent of children between the ages of five and 13—about two million children—spend time in self care,[2] a number of other sources estimate that over a quarter of the children between six and 14 years old spend time in self care, most of them regularly. (There are several plausible explanations why census figures would be artificially low. Among them are guilt on the part of the responding parent for leaving the child alone, and a hesitancy, stemming from safety concerns, to reveal that the child is sometimes left unsupervised.)

Research on the impact of self care is mixed. Some studies support the practice. Hyman Rodman and his associates at the University of North Carolina compared 4th graders in adult care with 4th graders in self care on measures of self-esteem, sense of control over their own lives and social skills.[3] They found no difference in feelings between children in self care and those supervised by parents. In their study of 1,200 children in kindergarten through 8th grade, Diane Hedin and her colleagues at the University of Minnesota had

Source: Ellen Gray & Peter Coolsen (1987, July–August). How do kids really feel about being home alone? *Children Today, 16,* 30–32. Reprinted by permission of Ellen Gray.

tended in their own homes, the incidence of experimentation with alcohol and sex increases.[7]

In a demonstration and research project conducted for the National Committee for Prevention of Child Abuse (NCPCA) and funded by the Head Start Bureau, ACYF, we gained some new insights about how kids feel when they are home alone, in addition to testing a self-care preparation curriculum. The project, "Balancing Work and Family Life," tested an educational curriculum called "I'm in Charge," developed by the Kansas Committee for Prevention of Child Abuse for children in self care and their parents. The course—which was taught by trained volunteers from local NCPCA chapters in over 40 sites in eight states—teaches children and parents the skills necessary for safety and survival in self care settings.[8] It does not promote or encourage self care, but rather assists families in deciding if self care is an appropriate option for them within their own unique environment.

The course consists of five sessions. Children attend all five sessions, while parents attend the first and last. In the first session, parents learn to evaluate their child's ability to stay successfully in a self-care situation with a minimum of risk. They also discuss the benefits and risks of self care and explore alternative strategies and placements. Appropriate rule making and the importance of consistency are emphasized, and parent and child are given tasks to complete together.

In session two, children describe the current rules in their homes, and they receive instruction in effective communication techniques that they can use with their parents when discussing their feelings about these rules. Personal safety skills regarding telephone calls, responding to strangers and protection from sexual assault are reviewed and clarified. Reviews of existing educational prevention programs are also provided.

Session three focuses on discrimination between emergency and nonemergency situations. Children practice using the 911 emergency number and review procedures that they can use in non-emergency situations. They also learn a problem-solving strategy that they use later in the course and complete a homework assignment to identify fire escape routes and potential home safety hazards.

The fourth session examines the serious re-

similar findings.[4] When asked how they felt about being in self care, 80 percent of the children in self care said that they loved it or liked it. It is interesting to note that both of these studies were cited in popular magazines that write for a working mother audience. While Deborah Vandell of the University of Texas automatically assumed that going home to a latchkey situation would prove to be bad for children, her study showed that there were no differences in parents', peers' or the children's own ratings of social and study skills between those who went home to their mothers and those in latchkey situations.[5]

Other studies are not so optimistic about the impact of self care on school-age children. Laurence Steinberg of the University of Wisconsin questions Rodman's results on common sense grounds and in light of his own research on latchkey children. He states that the effects of self care are considerably more subtle than measurable loss of self-esteem or other sophisticated psychological constructs.[6] He points out that the public's concern about latchkey children revolves mainly around the fears and worries of these children, the dangers unsupervised children may be exposed to and their susceptibility to peer pressure, particularly when they reach adolescence. His own studies indicate that the more removed from adult supervision adolescents are, the more susceptible they are to peer pressure to commit antisocial acts. This view is echoed by another researcher, Thomas Long, who found that as more children spend more time unat-

sponsibility assumed by children caring for brothers and sisters and other children. Participants apply the problem-solving strategy that was introduced in the third session to devise realistic solutions for a variety of common problem situations. Three different models of division of power are discussed and the children identify the model used in their homes. The children also receive instruction in basic child care techniques, again emphasizing the importance of clear and continuing communication.

Parents and children attend the last session together and raise any concerns or questions they may have about material covered in previous meetings. Each family develops its own contract for self (or supervised) child care and the house rules are committed to paper for future use.

From this project—conducted with more than 1,000 children and 600 parents—we learned that it is possible to communicate self care techniques to children between eight and 12 years old through methods suggested in the curriculum. As the course progressed, parents and their children talked more about what could happen when the child was home alone, and the children understood more clearly what their parents wanted them to do in these situations. Tangible preparation gradually replaced the guilt or fear that had prevented acknowledging real, if unlikely, disasters when children are unsupervised by adults.

After the course ended, there was greater awareness and acknowledgement of the parents' actions when the child was home alone—such as how frequently the parents came home when expected and how often they left telephone numbers for the children—suggesting that more honest communication about these sensitive issues was taking place.

Some people, however, were not relieved by open discussion of these issues. The comments of one Nevada woman reflect the reservations many have about all prevention programs that offer anticipatory guidance for children. The woman removed her child from the course, explaining:

"I felt the program left my daughter feeling paranoid. It didn't apply to our family at all. If you are describing community families and rules, then we live in a sick society. We live in a rural community. Our doors are never locked. My daughter has to answer the phone every time it rings because of her father's business . . . I did not see any sense in continuing the program since it just didn't apply."

Notwithstanding the legitimate fears of some about scaring children and damaging their trust, there were positive results for children participating in this course that went beyond improved communication. These children—who initially reported being frightened of noises, worried that they would have to deal with someone at the door or on the telephone, and wanting their parents to come home when they were alone—felt much more confident about handling emergencies and everyday events after completing this course.

In spite of these gains in confidence, however, the children still strongly wished their parents were home with them. This fact was brought home poignantly in a sentence completion exercise used in the course. One question designed to determine the specific types of information or preparation the children would like their parents to provide when they had to be home alone ("When I am home alone, I wish Mom and Dad . . .") instead highlighted the fact that the children wanted their parents' physical or telephone presence. Over 80 percent of the children said they wished their parents "would come home" or "would call me." Another statement, included to pinpoint skills and knowledge the children felt they lacked ("When I'm home alone, I wish I knew . . ."), elicited sentence completions having to do with companionship 35 percent of the time, and most of these specifically mentioned parents.

One fact that came through loud and clear from our research on children who participated in this course was the ambivalence of latchkey children about their situation. On the one hand, they experience some sense of independence and accomplishment because they are taking care of themselves. On the other hand, being all alone at age nine or 10 can be a frightening experience. Although the children experienced an increased sense of competence as a result of staying alone and knowing how to handle various emergencies as the course went on, they also reported more loneliness, which we interpret as increased acknowledgement of the loneliness they have been feeling all along.

It would appear from these children's responses that while fear and boredom are significant problems for children in self care, they can be decreased significantly by a course like this. Loneliness, however—particularly missing the parents when they aren't there—is a problem more difficult to deal with. Parents can leave numbers where they can be reached, call the children frequently and go home when promised; these measures seem to help somewhat. But there is only so much that can be done to combat the loneliness of the child in self care.

When children and parents were asked what changes had come about as a result of their experience in the Balancing Work and Family Life project, by far the most frequently cited change was added rules for the child in the self care situation. Next most often mentioned was the revision of some self care rules. Interestingly, some families increased the number of self care hours for a child or children, some initiated self care for the first time, some stopped self care and some decreased the number of self care hours. However, more families reduced or stopped self care than increased or initiated this arrangement. This is significant, given the concern in some communities that providing a course such as this is condoning or encouraging parents to leave their children in self care.

What are we to make of the differing study findings regarding the impact of self care on children? If we are realistic, we will acknowledge that some kids probably do quite well in self care, while others—especially the younger ones—will have problems with it. In either case, self care is an arrangement set up to meet the needs of working parents and not necessarily the needs of the child. The findings of this project accentuate the fact that for most children, self care is no substitute for adult-supervised child care.

ENDNOTES

1. Children's Defense Fund, *Employed Parents and Their Children: A Data Book,* Washington, D.C., 1982.
2. U.S. Bureau of the Census, "After School Care of the School-Age Child," *Current Population Reports,* Series P-23, No. 149, Jan 1987.
3. H. Rodman, D. J. Pratto and R. Smith Nelson, "Child Care Arrangements and Children's Functioning: A Comparison of Self-Care and Adult Care Children," *Development Psychology,* 21, 1985.
4. D. Hedin, K. Hannes, R. Saito, A. Goldman and D. Knich, "Summary of the Family's View of After School Time," St. Paul, University of Minnesota, Center for Youth Development and Research, July 1986.
5. D. Vandell and M. Corasaniti, "Forms of After School Care: Choices and Outcomes," submitted for publication.
6. L. Steinberg, "Latchkey Children and Susceptibility to Peer Pressure: An Ecological Analysis," *Development Psychology,* 22, 1986.
7. T. Long and L. Long, manuscript in press, New York, Time, Inc., 1987.
8. The "I'm in Charge" curriculum and the accompanying *Lord of the Locks* film can be ordered from the Kansas Committee for Prevention of Child Abuse, 35 S. Kansas Ave., 2nd Floor, Topeka, Kans. 66603.

   The full report of the "Balancing Work and Family Life" project is entitled *The Modern Dilemma of Latchkey Children: A Report of the Balancing Work and Family Project* and can be ordered from the National Committee for Prevention of Child Abuse, 332 S. Michigan Ave., Suite 950, Chicago, Ill., 60604.

Ellen Gray, formerly Research Director, National Committee for Prevention of Child Abuse, is currently Senior Research Associate, National Council of Jewish Women, Center for the Child, New York City. Peter Coolsen, formerly NCPCA Associate Director, is a consultant with The Phoenix Group, Chicago.

Will Uncle Sam Help Mind the Children?

Anne C. Lewis

Day care rarely sparks much interest among education lobbyists in Washington or among public educators in general. Except in a few urban districts, where education programs and day care have been combined (primarily for using federal funds for low-income families), day care is not viewed as a responsibility of the public schools. This is especially true today, when the public schools are being asked to narrow their focus.

That view may need to change in the next few months. The one area in which Congress is likely to go beyond its already-set agenda for education (renewal of the Higher Education Act and protection of existing programs from drastic cuts) is that of day care and early childhood education in general. Some of the first bills introduced in this session of Congress deal with the specific problem of preventing child abuse in day-care facilities and with the larger issues of expanding access to and setting standards for day care.

More than 12 years ago, some of the education leaders in Congress recognized a need for attention to the area of child care and developed proposals to establish a "prime sponsor" system to expand child-care options in local communities. But the effort failed, primarily because the Nixon Administration branded the proposals "anti-family." One reason that the Nixon Administration took this tack was a campaign against the proposals by fundamentalist churches that felt threatened by government regulations and by the competition from new providers of child care.

Since then, the issue of a federal interest in child care has remained dormant, save for the persistent mention of its importance by Albert Shanker, president of the American Federation of Teachers (AFT). At first, extending services to younger children was seen as a way to make use of a teacher surplus. Now, the need for public school involvement in day care dovetails with changes in the population that could only have been guessed at by early supporters of federal involvement in day care.

In 1983 and 1984 the House Select Committee on Children, Youth, and Families laid the groundwork for congressional interest in child care. Alarmed by the social and economic trends facing American families, the committee heard testimony in Washington, D.C., and four other cities, with witnesses coming from 22 states. The committee's activities were endorsed by 65 national organizations concerned with young children. In the fall of 1984 the committee released a report, *Families and Child Care: Improving the Options,* which proposed some new approaches to federal involvement that rely heavily on changes in the tax code and on incentives rather than mandates.

At one of the final hearings before the committee prepared its report, George Miller (D-Calif.), the committee chairman, commented that the committee wanted "to move public policy on child care from the 1950s to the 1980s. The simple truth is that the need for affordable child care is now a very real, everyday problem for the majority of American families. Unlike a decade ago, the need today cuts across the entire spectrum of economic and social lines, and, as a result, child care is a less partisan issue."

The population statistics assembled by the committee illustrate why child care deserves the immediate attention of policy makers at all levels. Statistics from the U.S. Census Bureau for 1983, along with the testimony of researchers and child-care experts, confirm the following demographic changes:

- For the first time, slightly more than half of all mothers of preschool-age children are in the workforce. Fifty-eight percent of mothers with children between the ages of 3 and 5 are in the workforce.
- Nearly 45% of mothers with children under the age of 1 are working—an increase of nearly 30% in less than five years.
- More than 70% of children between the ages of 3 and 5 whose mothers work outside the home attend some kind of preschool program, but these are largely part-day services, a fact that forces families to put together "packages" of school and day-care programs.
- A U.S. Census Bureau survey found that more than one-third of mothers in families with incomes under $15,000 would seek employment if they could obtain decent, affordable child care. In addition, most married women are working out of necessity; for more than 70%, the incomes of their husbands are less than $20,000.
- The cost of child care is creating a two-tiered system. In 1982, 53% of 3- and 4-year-olds from families with incomes above the national median attended preschool programs; only 29% of those from families with lower incomes did so.
- According to the Children's Defense Fund, the average costs of child care range from a low of $1,200 for family-provided day care to more than $5,000 a year for enrollment in some day-care centers. A single woman with children, who is most in need of child care, earns an average of $9,495 a year.
- Since 1981, cuts ranging from 21% to 30% in child nutrition and Title XX of the Social Security Act—the two major federal programs aiding very young children—have triggered cuts at the state level, creating even greater difficulties for low-income families. Despite an increase in the number of poor children, 32 states are now providing Title XX child care to fewer children than they did in 1981.

The Bureau of the Census projects another demographic change fraught with all sorts of problems for child care and the schools. By the year 2000, if current trends continue, 30% of U.S. women will delay childbearing until after age 30. These women are likely to be career oriented, to reenter the labor force as soon as possible after they give birth, and to demand (and be able to pay for) more and better child care.

These parents are already being siphoned off into private schools. A recent survey by the National Association of Independent Schools showed that more than half of the independent day schools are now offering extended day care to their patrons.

Witnesses consistently pointed out at the committee hearings that the U.S. is the only industrialized nation without a child-care policy. The professional expertise to deliver good child care exists across the U.S., but it is primarily available only to those who can afford it.

To create a system that is more equitable and to be prepared for a growing demand for child-care options, the House Select Committee laid the foundation for a federal initiative. First, witnesses frequently criticized the Dependent Care Tax Credit—now the largest child-care program, costing about $1.5 billion annually. It benefits primarily families with disposable income. The committee recommended that the tax policy be revised immediately to direct federal resources toward allowing full participation by families with little or no tax liability.

Tackling the problem of child abuse in child-care settings, the committee recommended that Congress discontinue federal funds to states that "have failed to provide adequate health, safety, and law enforcement standards for the protection of children in out-of-home care." Furthermore, the Department of Health and Human Services should continue current national training and credentialing programs for family day-care providers and infant care-givers, and Congress should establish a modest matching-funds program to expand local information and referral services for parents and information and referral networks for those who provide day-care services.

Recognizing that research findings on out-of-home care for infants are mixed, the committee urged caution but recommended that options be explored with employers on revising current leave and related personnel policies. Employees should not be penalized for having children, the committee report said. (Testimony at the hearings revealed that, despite the media attention focused on employer-sponsored day care, only 600 employers provide their employees with some help with child care—and about half of those 600 are hospitals.)

209

The committee recommended that Congress fully fund the maximum level authorized for Title XX of the Social Security Act, with an emphasis on child-care services; require states to adjust payments made through Aid to Families with Dependent Children to reflect reasonable child-care costs; and increase child nutrition programs for eligible children. The committee report also said that Congress should review "the legislative authorities for child care under vocational, post-secondary, and training programs to determine if they are adequate to meet the child-care needs of participating parents."

To enlarge the role of the private sector, the committee report recommended that Congress develop incentives for private employers to expand the child-care options that they make available to their employees and that Congress review current barriers and incentives to the formation of proprietary and other child-care facilities.

As to the public schools and child care, the committee found that "parents and communities are struggling to provide safe, supervised, and developmentally appropriate before- and after-school activities for their 'latchkey children.'" The committee included its recommendation to expand school-based programs in a catch-all Head Start reauthorization bill, which passed the last Congress at the end of its term.

The committee had another recommendation regarding schools. Noting the large number of working mothers of children between the ages of 3 and 5, it recommended that Congress provide incentive grants to public and private nonprofit agencies to help local school districts and private schools that voluntarily develop programs for 4-year-olds. One approach, the committee said, would be to provide enrichment programs for disadvantaged children that charged fees on a sliding scale.

Some committee members, all Democrats, would have gone further than the committee report, which was signed unanimously by all 25 committee members. Noting the proven success of Head Start, these Democrats called for an annual incremental increase in the number of children who can participate in Head Start, which now serves fewer than one in five eligible children. Because of the scandals in child-care services, they recommended that the federal government call a national conference of policy makers, professionals, and day-care consumers to discuss ways to provide high-quality care; that a Federal Commission on Child Care be established to review and evaluate the status of child-care licensing and regulation; and that the federal government operate a clearinghouse on standards, regulatory definitions, and actions that affect the quality of day care.

But there were other dissenters, as well—from the other side of the aisle. Three Republican members objected to the expansion of funding, unless other options were considered first. They suggested that "economic and social incentives for mothers who want to be at home" be explored more fully. Rep. Dan Burton (R-Ind.) questioned the ultimate price tag of the committee's recommendations. He estimated that the cost of the recommendations would be around $727 million.

The question of which level of government is best able to pay for extended day-care services was a central concern of a meeting of policy makers, early childhood educators, and day-care professionals held this winter at the Spring Hill Center in Minnesota. It was the first time in the memory of those present that day-care and public school officials had met to discuss issues of mutual concern and the possibility of joining forces. Some policy makers argued that integrating child-care services into the schools is a state issue and that states are more likely to be able to finance expanded services than the federal government. However, staff members of various congressional committees and members of Congress interested in the issue optimistically pushed for united support of a modest approach, such as that recommended in the select committee's report.

The attention being paid to education inevitably will turn to what happens to children from the very beginning of their learning, Shanker said at the Spring Hill meeting. "We lost several years ago, but the time is ripe now," he said. Michael Kirst of Stanford University pointed out one barrier to a partnership between child-care and public school interests. "Child care is federally oriented in its politics," he said, "while public schools are state oriented." Public schools, under attack for not doing well with the responsibilities they already have, probably cannot be expected to take the lead on this issue, he added.

But they can be "lured" into placing child care on their agenda.

The important point, said Helen Blank, director of child care for the Children's Defense Fund, is that the federal and state levels must stop bickering and get together. "There is no doubt that, if we are honest about it, we need billions of dollars," she said, "but we can't get it unless we form a coalition."

Anne C. Lewis is executive editor of Education USA.

ASK YOURSELF:
Identifying Issues for Debate and Advocacy

1. Should the cost of day care be funded by the federal and/or state government(s) in the same manner as are kindergarten and elementary education?

2. In San Francisco, the Office Affordable Childcare Program requires office and hotel developers to provide at least 2,000 square feet of floor space for an on-site child care center or to contribute $1 for every square foot of floor space to a city fund that supports child care facilities for low- and moderate-income families. Is this a "social cost" businesses should bear, or is this the work of political pickpockets (Will, 1985)? Why or why not?

3. What are the possible benefits and adverse effects of day care?

4. According to Burton White (1981), eight hours is an eternity for a one- to two-year-old child. Should a baby spend this much time each day away from his or her mother or father? Explain.

5. In 1984, the Maryland Committee for Children reviewed research showing that children in large day care centers have runny noses 40 percent of the time, and that day care center infants under one year old have 9.6 respiratory illnesses per year. Clarke-Stewart (1982), reviewing day care research, found numerous studies that indicate children who attend day care do not suffer negative consequences in terms of physical growth and development. However, day care children usually do have more bouts with flu, colds, coughs, rashes, and runny noses than do children not enrolled in day care. Stevens (1982), on the other hand, reported that health care, health surveillance, and nutritional programs in day care centers are better than those in family day care programs. What is your reaction to these figures and findings?

6. Are the advantages for child care in homes offset by the problems these settings have in obtaining a license? Explain in terms of quality child care.

7. Are day care centers better for enhancing the young child's development than are family day care homes?

8. How should a parent choose a day care program for a preschool child?

9. Should day care programs accommodate their purposes to those of public schools?

10. Public libraries have recently voiced concerns about parents regularly dropping off their children for hours as a substitute for day care (Noble, 1988). Should libraries adopt rules prohibiting parents from leaving unattended children at a library? Should libraries post signs warning parents that they can be prosecuted for child neglect if they leave their children unattended? Or do such actions create a punitive or unreceptive impression and discourage children from using the library?

APPLICATION/ADVOCACY EXERCISES

1. As a small group exercise, prepare a public information display for parents on child care selection. Printed information (e.g., brochures such as "How to Choose a Good Early Childhood Program" available from the National Association for the Education of Young Children) and nonprint visuals should be included. Consider the following characteristics.
   a. Display is attractive and eye-catching.
   b. Amount of print is limited.
   c. Lettering is large.
   d. Program features are described in observable terms; professional jargon is avoided.
   e. Facts about sources of information for local child-care alternatives are included.
   f. Suggestions for visiting and observing child-care programs as well as interviewing a staff person in relation to child and family needs are included.

   Make arrangements with a local business, library, or social service agency for a showing of your display. Include free information flyers or brochures with the display. Write a brief paragraph describing the display and any observed or reported responses.

2. Figure 8–1 shows a cartoon that appeared in local newspapers across the nation. Incorporating information from the readings in this chapter, write a model letter to the ed-

FIGURE 8-1

"CHEER UP, HANSEL. YOU AND GRETEL COULD BE IN A DAY CARE CENTER."

Reprinted by permission: Tribune Media Services.

itor, responding to this editorial cartoon. As you compose your letter, consider the following guidelines (Allen, 1983; Deloria & Brookins, 1982):

a. Use clear, vivid language devoid of educational or developmental terminology unfamiliar to the public.

b. Keep the central issue clear throughout your letter.

c. Organize paragraphs for the body of the letter around the questions you will address.

d. Whenever possible, clearly link the questions addressed to the real decisions the public (parents as consumers, taxpayers, etc.) is or has been making.

e. Use real-life examples to illustrate your point whenever possible.

f. Limit use of statistics to simple, descriptive statistics (actual numbers or percentages).

g. Open and close the letter with statements that will establish rapport with public readers.

3. Interview a member of the policy committee of one of your local early childhood professional organizations. Inquire about local and state child care needs as well as current advocacy efforts to secure more support for quality child care. In your report, include your interview questions, responses from the interviewee, and your interpretation of responses in terms of chapter readings.

4. Imagine that you are a young parent (male or female) and are contemplating either returning to work and placing your infant in day care or not returning to work and keeping your infant at home. Using information from the readings in this chapter, prepare an argument for each position.

REFERENCES & SUGGESTED READINGS

Allen K. E. (1983, January). Public policy report: Children, the Congress, and you. *Young Children, 38,* 71–75.

Clarke-Stewart, A. (1982, September). The day-care child. *Parents,* 72–74, 142, 144.

Deloria, D., & Brookins, G. K. (1982). The evaluation report: A weak link to policy. In J. R. Travers & R. J. Light (Eds.), *Learning from experience: Evaluating early childhood demonstration programs* (pp. 254–271). Washington, DC: National Academy Press.

Flamholz, M. L., Aukamp, A., Edlund, M. J., & Leslie, L. (1984). *Care of infants in groups: A resource paper.* Baltimore: Maryland Committee for Children. (ERIC Document Reproduction Service No. ED 247 006)

Hill, C. R. (1978). Private demand for child care: Implications for public policy. *Evaluation Quarterly, 2,* 523–546.

Noble, K. B. (1988, February 15). Libraries as day care: New curbs and concerns. *The New York Times,* Section A, pp. 1, 17.

Prescott, E. (1978, January). Is day care as good as a good home? *Young Children, 33,* 13–19.

Rubenstein, J. L., & Howes, C. (1979). Caregiving and infant behavior in day care centers and homes. *Developmental Psychology, 15,* 1–24.

Stevens, J. H. Jr. (1982, January). The New York Infant Day Care Study. *Young Children, 37,* 47–53.

White, B. (1981, November). Viewpoint: Should you stay home with your baby? *Young Children, 36,* 11–17.

Will, G. F. (1985, July 28). Political pickpockets at work in San Francisco. *Los Angeles Times,* Section 4, p. 5.

CHAPTER 9

Developmentally Appropriate Curriculum Practices

The Delight of Learning to Read?

Grandma Kramer, Cindy's mother-in-law, breezes in the front door with a package under her arm and exclaims, "How's my darling grandson? Come here, sweetie. Look at the nice present Grandma brought you!" With a gleeful twinkle in her eye, Grandma Kramer shakes the box. Jimmy toddles toward her as she starts to open it. Grandma Kramer gushes, "Oh, Cindy, I found the most marvelous kit for teaching a two-year-old to read. It's just what our genius, Jimmy, needs." Grandma Kramer produces an assortment of word cards, phrase cards, and picture books (cost = $29.95).

"Cindy, the kit is as easy as pie to use. It'll take you only a few minutes a day to teach Jimmy to read. Oh, what a thrill it will be to hear little Jimmy read his first words!" exudes Grandma Kramer. Grandma continues, "Besides, you know we can't depend on today's schools to teach children—especially young boys—to read. If we use this kit with Jimmy now, we can be sure our little darling will never have a reading problem in school. Don't you think that would be worth the few minutes a day this kit takes, Cindy?"

Questions

1. If a child spends time learning to read in the preschool years, might other critical areas of development be slighted? Explain.
2. Why is there a trend in today's society to expose children to school-related activities at earlier ages? Can this instruction be harmful for children? Explain.
3. Suppose Jimmy does learn to recognize some sight words through exposure to this kit. Is this really reading? Is there value in teaching Jimmy to recognize some sight words (e.g., names of body parts) at this young age? Explain.
4. If Jimmy learns to read before he starts school, will he be bored in kindergarten? Why or why not?

PREVIEW

The prevailing point of view about teaching young children has shifted from nurturant waiting for certain indicators of readiness to appear to active efforts to provide appropriate early experiences that promote learning at the child's present level of development. Today, the early childhood teacher needs not only to identify appropriate early experiences to broaden children's understanding, but must build on children's existing knowledge and experiences. With the explosion of child development research as well as the expanding diversity of early childhood programs in the last 25 years, the National Association for the Education of Young Children recently developed and published a position statement and set of guidelines for developmentally appropriate practice for children, ages zero to eight (Bredekamp, 1987). Questions and debate about what is developmentally appropriate practice, however, will continue as times and our knowledge about children change.

The first reading, a position statement developed by a committee of leading educators in Nebraska, addresses concerns about the role of academic learning in the kindergarten. In contrast, Russell Gersten and Thomas Keating argue that academic skills instruction that starts in kindergarten is more effective in terms of students' later achievement than is academic skills instruction that begins in first grade. Lawrence J. Schweinhart, however, recognizes several developmental issues, including child-initiated activity, as important features of early childhood curricula. Charles H. Wolfgang and Tobie S. Sanders defend the value of play as an appropriate approach to the development of literacy and representational abilities. The next selection, by Mary A. Jensen and Zelda W. Chevalier, addresses the question: Is the calendar routine a meaningful activity for young children? The article discusses what is known about children's developing understanding of time. Finally, Laura D. Goodwin, William L. Goodwin, and Mary Beth Garel critique the present body of research on microcomputer use by preschoolers, noting the gap between claims for usefulness and research results.

What's Best for Five-Year-Olds?

Position Statement on Kindergarten

Nebraska State Board of Education

Introduction

Nebraska has a long history of providing kindergarten programs for the young children of the state. Both the Constitution and state laws affirm the entitlement of all five-year-old children to receive free public education. The State Board of Education supports this legal entitlement and urges public schools to offer kindergarten programs without qualification to all eligible resident children and further to assure that kindergarten programs meet the developmental learning needs of the children they are designed to serve.

Changes in Kindergarten Programs

During the first two-thirds of this century, kindergarten programs were designed expressly for five-year-olds, curriculum decisions were based upon increasing knowledge about child development, and kindergarten teachers used content and methods appropriate for five-year-old children. In recent years a number of conflicting societal pressures and attitudes have caused changes in the focus of kindergarten programs. This shift in emphasis has caused many schools to begin to use content and methods unsuited to the learning needs of most five-year-old children, for whom kindergartens were originally designed. Commonly stated examples of these conflicting pressures include the following:

Five-year-old children are often perceived to be more advanced than they used to be. This perception causes many teachers and ad-ministrators to think that the kindergarten program should require mastery of content that was formerly expected in later primary grades. Many people also believe that today's children should be taught more at an earlier age so that they can keep up with expanding knowledge. BUT AT THE SAME TIME . . .

. . . many five-year-old children are judged to be unready for today's kindergarten program. A growing arm of the testing industry now provides a variety of instruments designed to ascertain whether children are likely to be successful in kindergarten. Ironically, at the same time that such tests are being used to discourage enrolling many "typical" five-year-olds in kindergarten, recent legislation assures that handicapped youngsters receive appropriate educational services, whether they are "ready" or not.

Many preschoolers and child care centers are now presenting inappropriate concepts and skills that were formerly taught in kindergarten or even first grade. This causes many people to believe that children who have been to preschool will be bored by kindergarten. BUT AT THE SAME TIME . . .

. . . many of the preschools, as well as the educational components of many child care centers, erroneously believe the center must "get children ready" for the more demanding kindergarten programs. Unfortunately, children who have not attended a private preschool are increasingly, and often mistakenly, viewed as disadvantaged upon reaching kinder-

Source: Nebraska State Board of Education, "Position statement on kindergarten." Lincoln, NE: Nebraska Department of Education, 1984. Reprinted by permission of the Nebraska State Board of Education. And "Follow-up: The Nebraska position statement." High/Scope *Resource*, Vol. 5, No. 2, Spring 1986, p. 8. Reprinted with permission.

garten age. (The number of these programs is rapidly expanding in all sizes of communities across the state. They are often staffed by people who have no professional preparation to work with young children. In many instances these programs use content and methods entirely inappropriate for the three- and four-year-old children they serve.)

Parental pressure to teach reading earlier has contributed to changes in the kindergarten program in many communities. Parents often view the traditional activities of kindergarten as trivial and expect the school to "teach" children content formerly reserved for later in the school program. BUT AT THE SAME TIME . . .

> . . . many parents decide against entering their five-year-olds in kindergarten because they are afraid their children won't be able to adjust to increased academic demands or to score well on standardized tests. Such parents are especially susceptible to suggestions by school personnel that children should wait a year or attend a preschool.

These conflicts cause confusion and create uncertainly among many parents, teachers, and administrators . . .

• Among parents because, with rare exceptions, they want what is best for their children. They put trust in educators to advise them.
• Among kindergarten teachers, who feel pressured by parents, by administrators, but especially by first grade teachers. Most kindergarten teachers know that the increased expectations are unsuitable for most five-year-old children.
• Among administrators, who must try to juggle everyone's expectations, but who often have a limited background in early childhood education, either through training or through teaching experience.

Desirable Characteristics of Kindergarten Programs

Hundreds of studies on the development of young children have been completed during the past two decades. This research has largely supported what, until recently, constituted the practice and content of kindergarten programs. The research also confirms that the course of the social, physical, emotional, and cognitive development of young children has not changed, in spite of major sociological and technological changes in our society. Developmental rates have not accelerated, nor are children more intelligent than they used to be—only the variety and intensity of early experiences have changed.

We know more now about how young children learn and can express that knowledge more professionally. This does not mean that the children are different because of it. Young children of today still need supportive environments geared to their needs rather than driven by inflexible curricula. If schools are to adequately serve the unique educational needs of five-year-old children, a kindergarten should provide a place where:

• Children are enrolled based upon their legal right to enter . . .
> . . . not counseled to attend preschool or to wait a year because pre-screening suggests that many who are five are "not ready" for the program.
• Parents and school personnel work cooperatively to build a partnership between home and school that will support the child throughout the school experience . . .
> . . . not a place where the expectations of the parents and the school are in conflict or where parents feel isolated from their child's experience.
• Children experience a planned, child-centered environment that encourages learning through exploration and discovery . . .
> . . . not a sit-down-be-quiet classroom dominated by desks, paper, and workbooks.
• Children have access to multilevel experiences and activities of varying degrees of complexity. They should be able to use concrete materials which allow for individual differences and natural variations in each one's ability to perform . . .
> . . . not a place where all children are expected to perform the same task, reach the same level of performance, and accomplish the same objectives.
• Children can make choices and decisions within the limits of the materials provided . . .
> . . . not a largely teacher-directed room where children seldom choose.

219

- Children learn there is often more than one right answer. Divergent thinking is developed and encouraged through use of open-ended materials and many informal conversations among the children and with adults . . .

    . . . not a place where the day's activities are largely dominated by worksheets and discussions with predetermined answers.

- The children's own language, experiences, and stages of development form the basis of reading and writing activities . . .

    . . . not the almost universal use of commercial, formal pre-reading and early-reading programs.

- Children learn to enjoy books and to appreciate literary language through a daily story time, creative dramatics, and repeated opportunities to hear and learn simple rhymes and other poems . . .

    . . . not a place where the day is too short for story time and the opportunity to appreciate literature comes *only* by way of educational television.

- Children participate in daily, planned activities fostering both gross and fine motor development, including such activities as running, jumping, bouncing balls, lacing cards, hammering nails, playing with clay, etc. . . .

    . . . not a place where children are expected to sit quietly for long periods of time and perform fine motor skills beyond the current ability of many of them. For example, it is inappropriate to expect many five-year-old children to be able to form letters correctly on lined paper.

- Children develop mathematical understanding through use of familiar manipulatives such as sand, water, unit blocks, counters, and other concrete materials . . .

    . . . not a place where children mark an X on the right answer in a workbook.

- Children's curiosity about natural, familiar elements forms the basis of scientific observations, experimentation, and conclusions. Both planned and spontaneous interaction with real objects such as plants, animals, rocks, soil, water, etc., is considered to be essential . . .

    . . . not a place where science is included only when time permits or where the books tell outcomes and the teachers do the experiments.

- Experimentation, enjoyment, and appreciation of varied forms of music are encouraged *on a daily basis* . . .

    . . . not a place where music is included only when time permits or the music teacher works with the class.

- Many forms of art expression are encouraged through the use of a wide assortment of media integrated *within the daily curriculum.* The final product is never as important as the process of creating . . .

    . . . not a place where art usually consists of copying a model, coloring a ditto, or cutting and pasting a pattern, and/or where art is delegated to the specialist.

- The mental and physical well-being of each child is of paramount importance . . .

    . . . not a place where external pressures for group achievement, especially as measured by group achievement tests, are more important than the individual needs of children.

- All the activities are planned to promote a positive self-image and attitude toward school and peers . . .

    . . . not a place where the child's worth is measured only by his or her ability to conform to expectations.

- Play is respected for its value as an appropriate learning medium for children of this age . . .

    . . . not a place where play is deemphasized because the child "played enough" in preschool and should now be ready for "real" learning.

- Different levels of ability and development are expected, valued, and accepted . . .

    . . . not a place where attempts to narrow differences within a class or group through prescreening, entrance procedures, and transition classes result in *de facto* tracking.

Important Outcomes of Kindergarten

In order to encourage the development of kindergarten programs which meet the needs of both children and the larger community in which they live and grow, the State Board of Education encourages local boards of education to implement kindergarten programs which will help:

• Children learn to work both alone and in cooperation with other children in both informal and more formal settings.
• Children learn that the things of a classroom—toys, books, paints, blocks, easels, record player and records, computer, etc.—have both purposes and places. They learn how to use them and where to put them when the time comes to stop using them.
• Children learn about rules—why we have them, how people (including children) make them, and how to follow the rules for the classroom and the school.
• Children learn about time, taking turns, sharing, respecting the rights of others, responsibility, and about the role of the teacher as instructor, mediator, sustainer, counselor, and interpreter of rules.
• Children increase their knowledge of language, especially the relationship between words and the things and processes they represent. As appropriate, individual children should begin to learn how speaking relates to writing and the two relate to what they say and do.
• Children increase their knowledge of the number system and how it is related to quantities of real things in their environment—books, children, blocks, beans.
• Children increase their knowledge of space and the things within that space—space and things in the classroom, space and things in the school, and space and things in the neighborhood.
• Children increase their awareness of colors and shapes in nature and how these colors and shapes relate to the properties of real things in their environment.
• Children learn about their bodies and how to keep them healthy and fit. They learn to develop strength, coordination, balance, dexterity, and motor control through active vigorous physical activity.
• Children acquire and maintain excitement about learning. They look forward to continuing the learning process with a sense of wonder and anticipation.

Recommendations

An earlier section of this document elaborated on interwoven trends and practices which have produced unsuitable changes in kindergarten programs in recent years. Because the reasons for the changes are so complex, recommendations for improvement must be directed at the various entities which can be helpful in bringing about the positive redirection of kindergarten programs.

A. The State Department of Education should:
   1. Provide for wide distribution of this position statement and urge its endorsement by interested organizations and groups.
   2. Develop and seek support for legislation which will guarantee equal access to kindergarten programs in public schools for all five-year-old children in Nebraska.
   3. Develop and distribute a curriculum guide for kindergarten which suggests suitable activities for five-year-old children and addresses concerns about articulation with later schooling.
   4. Develop voluntary standards for early childhood programs (both preschool and kindergarten) to encourage quality in both public and private programs and to attempt to positively influence articulation between public kindergarten programs and the growing number of often nonprofessionally staffed private preschool programs.
   5. Develop and distribute materials for administrators which provide current basic information about early childhood development and education.
   6. Provide for regular department contact with kindergarten teachers and elementary administrators through workshops, consultation, newsletters, and information about exemplary materials and practices consistent with this position statement.
B. The Nebraska Council on Teacher Education should:
   1. Expand the elementary education teacher training program criteria to include specific coursework in kindergarten/early childhood methods and materials as related to child growth and development. (Many of the practicing kindergarten teachers do not feel that general elementary

methods courses were adequate to prepare them for teaching in kindergarten.)

2. Include practica and coursework in early childhood education as a part of the elementary and general administration program criteria.

3. Reconsider the current criteria for the early childhood endorsement in light of the new National Council for the Accreditation of Teacher Education (NCATE) standards.

C. Approved teacher training institutions should:

1. Regularly offer kindergarten/early childhood courses and practica required by the program approval criteria of the Nebraska Council on Teacher Education. Practica should closely link experience with course content.

2. Regularly provide kindergarten/early childhood courses in summer and evening sessions to accommodate practicing elementary teachers and administrators.

3. Provide personnel to teach such courses who are optimally prepared in early childhood development and education.

4. Encourage elementary education students interested primarily in working with young children to pursue an additional endorsement in early childhood education. (Nine of the fifteen Nebraska teacher training institutions offer this endorsement program.)

D. The central administration and building level administrators in local school districts should:

1. Become informed about the growth and development of young children and about kindergarten/early childhood education.

2. Recommend policies to local boards which acknowledge children's constitutional right to free public education at age five and which encourage parents to enroll eligible children.

3. With the participation of elementary administrators and kindergarten teachers, recommend kindergarten curriculum goals to local boards which are consistent with the characteristics of five-year-old children's growth and development.

4. Limit prescreening of kindergarten children to the identification of handicapping conditions and/or gaining information about the learning needs of incoming students. (If such testing is deemed necessary, it is most valid when conducted just prior to or just after the opening of school.)

5. Avoid the trend to group children perceived to be "less ready" in special classes. (These are often called transition rooms, developmental, or readiness kindergartens. Educational research continues to support heterogeneous grouping over homogeneous grouping as most beneficial for children.)

6. Attempt to hire and/or assign to the kindergarten teachers who hold an early childhood endorsement or who have significant specific preparation to teach kindergarten.

7. Work to create a climate which diminishes the pressure teachers feel from those teaching at higher grade levels. (Although this is often cited as a problem by teachers at all levels, kindergarten teachers bear the weight of the entire system.)

8. Assist and support the kindergarten teacher in interpreting the goals and program of the kindergarten to parents.

9. Discourage the purchase and use of kindergarten instructional materials that consist primarily of worksheets, workbooks, and similar non-concrete materials. Provide support for the selection of varied age-appropriate materials for the kindergarten classroom.

10. Consider holding periodic meetings for parents of preschool-age children. Such meetings would provide a forum for parents to learn about appropriate expectations for their young children. Contact with parents of preschool children would also assist in the early identification of handicapped children.

11. Provide incentives for currently assigned kindergarten teachers to expand their knowledge of kindergarten/early childhood education through professional growth activities.

E. Kindergarten teachers should:
    1. Participate in professional growth activities which expand knowledge of child growth and development and kindergarten/early childhood education.
    2. Explore the suitability of adding the early childhood endorsement. (Seventeen percent of current kindergarten teachers hold an early childhood endorsement.)
    3. Recommend the purchase of varied, age-appropriate materials for the kindergarten classroom. (Many kindergarten teachers cite the need to reduce the use of workbooks, worksheets, and other non-concrete materials.)
    4. Participate in early childhood professional organizations in order to gain the support of peers in advocating for quality kindergarten/early childhood programs.
F. Parents of preschool and kindergarten-age children should:
    1. Become informed about the programs and services available to children in public school districts.
    2. Expect that the public school will provide a kindergarten program suited to the learning needs of five-year-olds and will welcome all children who reach age five by October 15.
    3. Develop reasonable expectations for their children which are suitable for each child's age and stage of development.
    4. Take advantage of developmental evaluation services available to all children through local public school districts, if the growth and development of a child of any age appears to be impaired in any way.

REFERENCES

Cohen, Dorothy H. and Marguerite Rudolph. *Kindergarten and Early Schooling.* 2nd Edition. Englewood Cliffs, NJ: Prentice Hall, Inc., 1984.

Katz, Lilian G. and others. "Assessing the Development of Preschoolers." Maharaja Sayajiro University of Baroda, India, March 1983, ERIC Document Number ED 226 857.

National Association for the Education of Young Children. *Early Childhood Teacher Education Guidelines.* Washington, D.C.: National Association for the Education of Young Children, 1982.

Nebraska. *Revised Statutes of Nebraska.* (79-444).

Nebraska. *The Constitution of the State of Nebraska.* (Article VII, Section 1).

Ramsey, Marjorie and Kathleen Bayless. *Kindergarten Program and Practices.* St. Louis, MO: The C. V. Mosby Co., 1980.

Spodek, Bernard. "The Kindergarten: A Retrospective and Contemporary View." In *Current Topics in Early Childhood Education*, Vol. 4., Lilian Katz (ed.). Norwood, NJ: Ablex, 1982.

Weber, Evelyn. *The Kindergarten: Its Encounter With American Thought in Education*, New York, NY: Teachers College Press, 1969.

Follow Up:
The Nebraska Position Statement

The Position Statement on Kindergarten reprinted here has had a widespread impact throughout Nebraska. Harriet A. Egertson, an early childhood consultant with the Nebraska Department of Education and one of the authors of the statement, has compiled a list of some of the things that have happened since the statement was released. Some of her findings:

1. Many kindergarten teachers have reported that the paper has helped them in their efforts to institute more age-appropriate practices in their schools.

2. Kindergarten teachers have "discovered" each other. Many teachers have reported more communication with other teachers and more visits to classrooms in other communities. About a dozen teachers have organized a "round robin" group to share slides, ideas, parent materials, evaluation methods, etc.

3. A number of teachers and principals have reported that, for the first time in many years, more 5-year-olds are coming to school.

4. There has been a noticeable increase of memberships in early childhood profes-

sional organizations and attendance at conferences dealing with early childhood education.

5. The Nebraska Council of School Administrators has convened a Task Force on Early Childhood Education to address specific issues in preschool, kindergarten, and primary education. The Council is also providing day-long inservice sessions on early childhood education for administrators.

6. Due primarily to the recommendations addressed to the Nebraska Council on Teacher Education, the Council appointed ad hoc committees in elementary and early childhood education. The committees have been meeting to make recommendations to the Council. If the Council accepts the recommendations, new standards for the preparation of teachers endorsed in early childhood education could be in effect by this summer.

7. A new kindergarten curriculum guide is being developed and reviewed; it should be ready for distribution to all schools by Fall 1986.

8. Many schools that hired kindergarten teachers for the 1985–86 school year looked for persons with Early Childhood endorsements, i.e., those who are specifically prepared to teach kindergarten.

9. The September 1985 state conference of the Nebraska PTA focused on kindergarten issues.

10. Authors of the Position Statement have carried their message to groups of principals, parents, and teachers through numerous speaking engagements and inservices.

Long-Term Benefits from Direct Instruction

Russell Gersten and Thomas Keating

A growing consensus about effective teaching practices for at-risk students in the elementary grades has been developing during the past ten years. This research (Brophy and Good 1986, Stebbins et al. 1977) shows that teachers using direct instruction can enhance academic growth. Direct instruction is a highly interactive approach to teaching. The lesson is structured so that teachers can assess immediately whether students understand the concepts being taught. If there are problems, the teacher guides the students toward comprehension by providing immediate feedback and modeling a pertinent problem-solving strategy (Gersten and Carnine 1986).

Direct instruction, however, has its critics. They assert that students may be stifled by the structure and that the effects dissipate when students are left on their own. In fact, some say direct instruction can cause students future harm.

These criticisms intensified with the release of a study of the later effects of preschool programs for at-risk children (Schweinhart et al. 1986). According to these authors, although 18-year-olds taught with direct instruction in preschool accelerated academic achievement during elementary years, the early academic focus harmed these students in later life, especially in the sphere of social behavior.

On the other hand, eminent educators such as Benjamin Bloom (1981) have asserted that structured instructional programs for at-risk students in the primary grades have enduring effects on students' lives. These eductors argue that students who develop academic competence in reading, language, and mathematics in the primary grades are more likely to benefit from any type of instruction in higher grades. Children who can read, for example, will always be able to learn new material, regardless of the quality of teaching in later years. In addition, if young students feel competent, they are more likely to approach learning positively, even when they encounter difficult academic and social situations in inner-city schools.

Because of this debate, the findings of a recent longitudinal follow-up study of over 1,000 low-income minority students in compensatory education are illuminating. In both rural and urban areas, we found positive long-term effects, with students achieving higher reading, language, and mathematics scores on standardized tests than students who either had not participated in direct instruction or who had participated in other programs. Participating in direct instruction also lowered dropout rates and raised the proportion of students applying to college.

Project Follow Through

At the time of its inception in 1968, Project Follow Through was the largest educational experiment in history. The U.S. Office of Education implemented Project Follow Through by applying innovative programs from 20 universities and research centers to the real world of inner-city and rural schools to determine their effectiveness for educationally at-risk students. Twelve of these interventions were evaluated, including the direct instruction program developed by Englemann and Becker (Becker et al. 1981) and the cognitive curriculum developed by Weikart and his colleagues.

Among the inner-city schools chosen for the experiment were those in Flint, Michigan; New York City; East St. Louis, Illinois; and Washington, D.C. The rural schools included were in Uvalde, Texas; and Williamsburg

County, South Carolina. At that time, the U.S. Census ranked Williamsburg County as the poorest county in the 48 mainland states, with one of the highest illiteracy rates in South Carolina.

Abt Associates, who conducted an independent evaluation, concluded that direct instruction was the most effective in teaching academic skills in mathematics, reading comprehension, and language (Stebbins et al. 1977). Low-income students in the four-year kindergarten-to-third-grade direct instruction programs performed at or near the national norm on standardized achievement tests in reading (median of 41st percentile), mathematics (median of 48th percentile), and language (median of 50th percentile), often significantly above their peers in traditional programs in local schools. In contrast, at-risk students using David Weikart's Cognitive Curriculum performed at the 21st percentile in reading and at the 11th percentile in mathematics (Stebbins et al. 1977). Direct instruction students also produced the highest scores in self-concept, self-confidence, and sense of personal responsibility for success or failure.

Two features that distinguished direct instruction from the other Follow Through models were the curriculum and assistance to teachers. The curriculum taught skills in a detailed, step-by-step process, and teachers were provided with specific remedies to their problems.

Longitudinal Study

In June 1981 and June 1982, the first two groups of Follow Through students were slated to complete high school. We decided to investigate whether direct instruction in the primary grades had an effect on their high school careers.

A major problem plaguing our study was finding students in each neighborhood comparable to those in the Follow Through program. By using information from welfare agencies, we found a comparison school for each Follow Through school with equivalent ethnicity and percent of families on welfare in four communities.

These served as the basis of our study (Gersten et al. 1984). Three inner-city schools were in New York City; Flint, Michigan; and one city that chose to remain anonymous, which we labeled Finley. The fourth community was in rural Williamsburg County, South Carolina.

Computerized student files were unknown to school districts in 1969; therefore we retrieved data by searching manila folders in the principal's office, school basements, and other storage areas. Student mobility was also a huge problem. The most extreme case was New York City. From the one experimental and one comparison elementary school in the New York study, students had dispersed to 67 different high schools in all five boroughs. We visited each of these to retrieve the files.

Underlying Hypotheses

First, we hypothesized that the more successful their learning experiences in the primary grades, the more likely children were to stay in school and graduate. Although we knew that the quality of instruction in higher grades would also affect high school performance, we hypothesized, nonetheless, that some effects would endure. If students could read and write and had relatively positive attitudes about learning, they could learn new material, regardless of the quality of instruction.

A secondary issue was the effect of academic kindergarten. Some students had direct instruction only from first through third grades; others, from kindergarten. We thought that students in a four-year program might display more enduring effects than those in a three-year program, and Finley provided a perfect opportunity to examine this possibility. In 1969, their direct instruction program was limited to three years, then was expanded to include kindergarten in 1970, allowing a comparison.

Results

In Finley, the median family income is among the lowest in urban areas. Over 70 percent of the students are in families receiving welfare. In the six participating schools, 98 percent of the students are black. We found that direct instruction produced consistent positive effects in all areas of academic achievement (Table 1). The most dramatic effects are found in the 1970 group of students who received the program starting in kindergarten.

For Follow Through students whose direct instruction began in kindergarten, the average reading score in the ninth grade on the California Achievement Test was at the 40th percentile, or almost grade level, while comparison

TABLE 1 *Finley 9th Grade Achievement (California Achievement Test)*

Group	N	Reading		Language		Mathematics	
		Percentile	*G.E.*	*Percentile*	*G.E.*	*Percentile*	*G.E.*
1968 (Began in First Grade)							
Follow Through	118	22nd*	7.2	25th	7.3	18th*	7.3
Comparison	158	17th	6.7	24th	7.2	14th	6.8
1970 (Began in Kindergarten)							
Follow Through	54	40th**	8.8	59th	10.2	30th**	8.3
Comparison	121	26th	7.6	39th	8.6	20th	7.5

* $p < .05$, one tail
** $p < .01$, one tail

students were at the 26th percentile. In language, they were above grade level: 59th percentile vs. 39th for the comparison group. In mathematics, they were significantly higher than comparison students, but still below middle income students.

For students who received direct instruction starting in first grade, the effects are more modest but still significant in reading and mathematics. Without kindergarten, both direct instruction students and students in the district's traditional program perform at a lower achievement level. The direct instruction academic kindergarten seems to accelerate the effect with demonstrable benefit to the students six years later.

In Flint, Michigan, both groups of direct instruction students began school in kindergarten. Through high school, direct instruction students demonstrated significantly fewer attendance problems: 20 percent versus 42 percent for the comparison group. An attendance problem was defined as 10 or more absences per year. Significantly fewer direct instruction students had to repeat grades after Follow Through: 23 percent versus 39 percent. More direct instruction students were accepted at college than comparison students, although the effect was not significant.

In the ninth grade SRA achievement tests, direct instruction students outperformed comparison students in reading at a level that bordered on significance. In mathematics, the comparison for the second group of students significantly favored direct instruction students. They performed at grade level in the ninth grade SRA Achievement Test.

We conducted the New York City study in the Ocean-Hill Brownsville section of Brooklyn, one of the lowest achieving districts

throughout the 1970s. This four-year program is one of the most effective direct instruction programs (Meyer et al. 1983), and the results of this follow-up study were the most positive. They are reported in Table 2, adapted from Meyer (1984).

In the rural community of Williamsburg, South Carolina, direct instruction students repeated grades less often, and more students successfully completed high school. For example, 34 percent of direct instruction students repeated grades while 55 percent of the comparison students did so. No differences were found in academic achievement here. The Williamsburg program did not include direction instruction in kindergarten. Three years of intervention may not be sufficient, especially in a community with extreme educational problems.

Findings: Positive and Disturbing

In each of the four communities we studied, we found positive long-term effects for students in the direct instruction programs. These effects were consistent at all places and among all groups of students. In some places, such as Finley, the effects were in achievement but not dropout rate; while in others, such as Williamsburg County, they were in graduation rates but not achievement.

Fewer students who participated in direct instruction Follow Through programs dropped out, and more applied to college. In three of the four communities, ninth-grade reading achievement was within ten percentile points of the national median and appreciably above the levels typical of low-income students (NAEP 1979), and students who went through the direct instruction program from

TABLE 2 *New York City Aggregated Cohorts from 1968, 1969, 1970: Graduation, Drop-out and College Acceptance Data (Adapted from Meyer, 1984)*

Group	N	Percent Graduated	Percent Dropped Out	Percent Accepted to College
1968, 1969 1970				
Follow Through	65	60***	28***	34***
Comparison	100	38	46	17

***p < .001

kindergarten through third grade benefited the most. These findings lead us to wonder what effects comprehensive, direct instruction K–6 to K–8 programs could have on educationally at-risk students.

Some findings were at once positive and disturbing. We found it gratifying to see adolescents from one of the poorest sections in New York City perform at grade level in reading in junior high, six years after the program ended. These students consistently outperformed the local comparison students and demonstrated a significantly lower dropout rate and a higher college acceptance rate. Despite these important gains, however, 40 percent still dropped out of high school. This is significantly less than the comparison group dropout rate of 58 percent, but it is far from ideal.

But there is more to the study than numbers. I spent six months of 1982 in the communities to work out details of the study, riding the subway lines to every vocational high school in Brooklyn and driving through swampy country roads in South Carolina to isolated high schools. It was impossible not to see how segregated education is or to ignore consistently low teacher expectations, as well as the apathy, sarcasm, and latent hostility present in some of the high schools.

We know that, without effective instruction in grades 4–12, these students lose ground against their middle-income peers and fail to realize their potential. Limited English-speaking students and students in rural communities appear to lose the most (Gersten and Woodward 1985). The same concern for providing an intense, successful experience for students that typified the direct instruction model in Follow Through needs to be extended to continuing grade levels. For at-risk

children to succeed as adults, they need high-quality instructional programs not only in kindergarten and the primary grades, but also in the intermediate grades and beyond.

REFERENCES

Becker, W. C., S. Englemann, D. Carnine, and R. Rhyne. "In The Direct Instruction Model," edited by R. Rhyne. *Encouraging Change in America's Schools: A Decade of Experimentation.* New York: Academic Press, 1981.

Becker, W. C., and R. Gersten. "A Follow Up of Follow Through: Meta-analysis of the Later Effects of the Direct Instruction Model." *American Educational Research Journal* 19, 1 (1982): 75–93.

Bloom, B. *All Our Children Learning.* New York: McGraw-Hill, 1981.

Brophy, J., and T. Good. "Teacher Behavior and Student Achievement." In *Third Handbook of Research on Teaching*, edited by M. C. Wittrock. New York: MacMillan, 1986.

Gersten, R., D. Carnine, and T. Keating. "Lasting Impact of the Direct Instruction Follow Through Program: Preliminary Findings of a Longitudinal Study of 1500 Students." Paper presented as part of a symposium at the American Educational Research Association, New Orleans, April 1984.

Gersten, R., D. Carnine, T. Keating, and M. Tomsic. "Long-Term Benefits of Effective Academic Programs in the Primary Grades: A Longitudinal Study." Technical Report 87.1. Eugene, Oreg.: Project Follow Through, 1987.

Gersten, R., and J. Woodward. "A Case for Structured Immersion." *Educational Leadership* 43, 1 (1985): 75–78.

Meyer, L., R. Gersten, and J. Gutkin. "Direct Instruction: A Project Follow Through Success Story in an Inner-city School." *Elementary School Journal* 84 (1983): 241–252.

Meyer, L. "Long-Term Academic Effects of the Direct Instruction Project Follow Through." *Ele-*

mentary School Journal 84 (March 1984): 380–394.

National Assessment of Education Progress (NAEP). "Mathematical Knowledge and Skills." ERIC #ED 176964, August 1979.

Rosenshine, B. V. "Synthesis of Research on Explicit Teaching." *Educational Leadership* 43, 7 (1986): 60–69.

Schweinhart, L. J., D. P. Weikart, and W. B. Larner. "Consequences of Three Preschool Curriculum Models Through Age 15." *Early Childhood Research Quarterly* 1, 1 (1986): 15–45.

Stebbins, L. B., ed. *Education as Experimentation: A Planned Variation Model*, vol. IIIA. Cambridge, Mass.: Abt Associates, Inc., 1976.

Stebbins, L. B., R. G. St. Pierre, E. C. Proper, R. B. Anderson, and T. R. Cerva. *Education as Experimentation: A Planned Variation Model*, vols. IVA-D. *An Evaluation of Follow Through*. Cambridge, Mass.: Abt Associates, 1977.

Russell Gersten is Associate Professor, Division of Teacher Education, College of Education, University of Oregon, Eugene 97403-1215.

Thomas Keating is Research Associate, Division of Special Education and Rehabilitation, at the same institution.

How Important Is Child-Initiated Activity?

Lawrence J. Schweinhart

If you believe young children can—and should—learn at their own pace, the answer is very important—that is, if we are to believe child development experts, early childhood education leaders, and longitudinal studies of program effects. All the same, some early childhood curricula do not take full advantage of this practice.

By child-initiated activity, we at High/Scope mean that children carry out an activity as they see fit, but within a framework provided by a teacher. As an example, think of children painting pictures. The teacher arranges the paint, paper, space, time, and other conditions of use, but the children design the pictures. They are unconstrained by the teacher's definition of the "right" composition or "correct" use of materials.

The purposefulness of child-initiated activity distinguishes it from random activity. Allotting the child some control over what happens also makes child-initiated activity distinct from its chief alternative, teacher-directed activity. This partial ceding of control often requires a departure from tradition, since many people think of teacher-directed activity—lectures, teacher-centered discussions, and paperwork—as being virtually equivalent to formal schooling.

Some people would like to see such teacher-directed practices adopted in early childhood education as well. In recent studies, we have found, however, that though either child- or teacher-directed activity can stimulate cognitive development, the child-initiated approach outstrips teacher-directed activity in fostering at least some aspects of social development. To better understand how we arrived at this finding, we should take a quick look back at curriculum developments over the past few decades.

What Works in Preschool?

The debate over curriculum for young children stems from the 1960s, when psychologists became involved in early childhood education (a span that includes learning from birth to age eight, but concentrates particularly on age three to five). From different and sometimes conflicting psychological theories came different and sometimes conflicting curriculum models. Some favored teacher-directed instruction. Others emphasized child-directed activity, an approach grounded in the work of venerable early childhood education figures like Friedrich Froebel, Susan Blow, Maria Montessori, and John Dewey.

Another change in the 60s was an addition. Early childhood education had previously emphasized only social-emotional and physical development. As some curriculum developers (including David Weikart and his colleagues at the High/Scope Educational Research Foundation) began to acknowledge the value of developmental theory, especially that of Swiss psychologist Jean Piaget, they concluded that cognition could also be enhanced. According to developmental theory, though, the right curriculum to develop the young child's mind would have to be different from that suitable for older students. The cognitive development of preschoolers, Piaget had cautioned, is *not centered on the symbolic world* of reading, writing, and arithmetic, *but on thinking about the physical world* of toys and objects.

The federal government stepped into these curriculum development efforts when it financed the brief Planned Variation Head Start Project (1969–1972) and the National Follow Through Project, which began in elementary schools in 1968 and continues today. In both projects, various curricula were implemented,

Cognitive development of preschoolers is not centered on the symbolic world of reading, writing, and arithmetic, but on thinking about the physical world of toys and objects.

though some more completely than others. Subsequent evaluations did find evidence that any of the curricula could contribute to children's success and produce enduring effects.[1] What the evaluations could not determine was whether one approach works better than another if all curricula are fully implemented.

High/Scope's Preschool Curriculum Comparison Study[2] corrected this methodological problem. Though our foundation's continuing, longitudinal study is smaller in scope than the Follow Through evaluations, it has examined only well-implemented instances of three distinctly different preschool curriculum models.

A *Direct Instruction* model emphasized academic objectives and teacher-directed instruction. *High/Scope* and traditional *Nursery School* models differed from each other in the extent of teacher involvement; High/Scope's teachers and children planned activities jointly, while Nursery School teachers only responded to the child's expressed needs and interests. Both models, however, included social as well as academic objectives and called for child-initiated activity.

The mean IQ of children in all three kinds of programs, we found, rose a remarkable 27 points (from 78 to 105) during the first year. A lot of the gains seemed to endure over time, too—IQs remained in the normal range, averaging 94 at age ten. We hypothesized that, regardless of the curriculum used, all three well-implemented preschool programs had virtually identical and positive effects. We

thought so right up until we analyzed the age-15 data.

We were quite surprised to discover that adolescents from the High/Scope and Nursery School groups each reported engaging in only about *half* as many delinquent acts as the Direct Instruction group. The child-initiated activity groups had far fewer high-frequency offenders, too: adolescents reporting over 15 delinquent acts made up only 8 percent of the High/Scope and Nursery School groups, but constituted 44 percent of the Direct Instruction group. Hence, though Direct Instruction strategy appears to be as good as (though not superior to) the two other models in stimulating the intellect, it seems to be less successful at developing young children's social problem-solving skills.

Developmental psychologist Constance Kamii interprets the differential effects on social adjustment in terms of Piaget's theory of moral development. The authoritarian teachers and the rewards and punishments inherent in Direct Instruction, Kamii believes, prevent children from developing autonomy. The two other curricula encourage children's autonomy by allowing teachers and children to discuss their points of view.[3]

Child-Initiated Activity: Who Cares?

Researchers are hardly the only sources of support for child-initiated activity. In recent decades, more *parents* have also become strong advocates. According to Duane Alwin of the University of Michigan's Institute for Social Research, there has been a change in what parents value in children. Alwin's comparison of 1950s and 1980s surveys shows that contemporary parents prefer children to be independent and self-reliant, in stark contrast to parents of three decades ago, who cited obedience and good manners as the most desirable characteristics.[4] The values shift, Alwin believes, is attributable to various changes in society: more working mothers, more single-parent families, more highly-educated parents, smaller families, increasingly complex technology, urbanization, and changed childrearing ideas, especially among Roman Catholics.

Business and education leaders also tacitly recognize the importance of child-initiated activity through their calls for education that produces self-directed and goal-oriented adults. The Committee for Economic Development, a group that speaks for the business community, defines the employable future worker, for example, as responsible, self-disciplined, able to learn, and equipped with problem-solving skills.[5] The influential Carnegie Forum on Education and the Economy expresses the same idea in different words: tomorrow's adults must be able "to figure out what they need to know, where to get it, and how to make meaning out of it."[6]

The *early childhood field* values child-initiated activity as a way to help young children achieve their full potential. Position statements[7] issued by the 54,000-member National Association for the Education of Young Children (NAEYC), for example, assert that in exemplary and developmentally appropriate practice:

• Adults provide opportunities for children to choose from among a variety of activities, materials, and equipment; adults provide time so that children can actively explore.
• Children select many of their own activities from among a variety of learning areas that the teacher prepares.
• Much of young children's learning takes place when they direct their own play activities.
• Learning takes place as children touch, manipulate, and experiment with things and interact with people.

The Principles of Child-Initiated Activity

From early childhood development theory, research, and practice, we at High/Scope have drawn together three principles of child-initiated activity:

Child-initiated activity acknowledges both the developmental limits of young children and their potential for learning. Educational thinkers undervalue early childhood education when they claim that the developmental limits of young children preclude meaningful learning outside the home. Just as faulty is the polar opposite view, which virtually denies any developmental limits in young children, insisting that children can learn anything (including reading, writing and arithmetic) as long as it is organized in small steps.

Early childhood learning activities should be child-initiated, developmentally appropriate, and open-ended. Child-initiated activities promote curiosity and motivation to learn from experiences. Activities must be developmentally appropriate, meaning neither too easy nor difficult for the child's interests and abilities. In permitting more than one response or way of acting, open-ended activities closely parallel real-life learning situations, which are usually not highly structured.

If a child learns to share ideas with teachers and peers, instead of having them imposed by an authority, the reciprocal communication will broaden the child's perspective. A body of research on teaching and childrearing affirms the superiority of a democratic style over both authoritarian and permissive styles in helping children appreciate the viewpoints of others.[8] Growing children, Piaget explained, will learn to see situations from other people's perspectives, provided they are given the opportunity to interact. If instead, most communication is with highly authoritarian adults, children do not have occasions to learn the give-and-take that is often essential in human interaction.[9]

Child-Initiated Activity in Practice

Child-initiated activity is now embraced by many formal and informal curricula. Some prominent early childhood education schools and training institutions—Bank Street College in New York, the Erikson Institute in Chicago, Pacific Oaks College near Los Angeles, and the High/Scope Educational Research Foundation in Ypsilanti, Michigan—make child-initiated activity central in the curricula they espouse. Similarly, the practice is endorsed in NAEYC's Child Development Associate training and in the early childhood departments of most American universities.

Despite such widespread endorsement, three well-known early childhood curricula do not emphasize all aspects of child-initiated activity. A fourth major force in early childhood education promotes rigorous readiness screening largely because of the *absence* of child-directed activity in elementary instruction. Let's look at the part that child-initiated activity plays in these four philosophical stances:

Direct Instruction. As a specialized version of teacher-directed instruction, Direct Instruction programs try to make the teaching process more efficient by scripting the teacher's spoken words and the student's expected responses. The teacher's job is to identify the entering child's skills and then to place the student in a predetermined course of instruction according to the assessed skill level. As with any teacher-directed format, the teacher transmits spoken and written information to children, who demonstrate that they have received it by answering questions, doing paperwork, and taking tests.

In Direct Instruction programs, teachers initiate all the activities (which may be developmentally appropriate, but sometimes are not—as when flash cards are used to teach reading or arithmetic to very young children). Since questions have single correct answers, they are not open-ended. Interaction among children is not part of the model.

Direct Instruction advocates believe that anyone can learn virtually anything if the task is organized into understandable steps. Thus, Direct Instruction at its best encourages teachers to believe in children's potential. Like all teacher-directed forms of instruction, though, it tends to undervalue the importance of maturation as a major determinant of developmental status. Indeed, Carl Bereiter, a designer of the Direct Instruction program studied in the High/Scope Curriculum Comparison, believes that the program's objectives for preschool children can and ought to be *academic,* and not *preacademic.*[10]

It may be true that young children *can* learn academic skills. Marva Collins, who is widely known for educating Chicago ghetto children with teacher-directed instruction, high expectations, and "tough love," claims that her students read two grade levels above national norms. She implies that others can apply her philosophy and duplicate her success.

Perhaps Collins is right, but demonstrating that children *can* does not establish that they *should.* As the High/Scope Curriculum Comparison study showed, the concentration on

FIGURE 1 *Developmental Issues and Selected Early Childhood Curricula*

	Diagnostic-Prescriptive	Direct Instruction	High/Scope	Montessori
Emphasis:	learning	learning	maturation & learning	maturation & learning
Child-initiated activities	some	no	yes	yes
Developmentally appropriate activities:	usually	usually	yes	yes
Open-ended activities:	some	no	yes	no
Teacher role:	authoritarian	authoritarian	democratic	democratic
Interaction among children:	some	no	yes	some

academic skills may attain achievement by sacrificing social skill development. A second danger is that, though some children may succeed beyond expected norms, others may be pushed beyond their developmental limits and begin a downward spiral that leads to failure and frustration.

Diagnostic-Prescriptive special education. In this testing and teaching combination, which is the prevalent approach to early childhood education for the handicapped, the child is first tested to establish eligibility for the program.[11] Next, a diagnostic test identifies deficient skill areas. The teacher then directs the child in activities intended to correct the weaknesses. Often, improvement results, at least to some extent. Finally, the child is re-tested, and the sequence is repeated.

The elimination of ambiguity that is possible through concentration on discrete, achievable steps may account for the popularity of Diagnostic-Prescriptive special education. Because the teacher remains in full control of the testing-teaching process, though, the curriculum leaves only occasional opportunities for child-directed activities. Consequently, the cost of the greater clarity may well be less social development.

Furthermore, exclusive attention to fixing what is wrong may bypass chances to strengthen what is right. Each of us has strengths and weaknesses. Encouraging handicapped children to initiate their own activities enables them to develop strengths *and* correct weaknesses. As children are permitted to develop their strengths, they also develop attitudes that are important to learning. As they find out that they can do things that they want to do, they acquire a sense of competence and self-confidence.

Diagnostic tests categorize children, sometimes unfairly, and teaching to such tests seldom completely liberates children from their designated "handicapping conditions," even if the labels were incorrect to begin with or cease to be relevant. We at High/Scope believe that the number of diagnostic categories in early childhood education should be held to a minimum and perhaps even limited to a single designation of eligibility for service. Michigan, for example, has such a category, called "preprimary impaired."

The Montessori method. The educational method formulated by Maria Montessori in the early 1900s is one of the oldest formal curriculum models in early childhood education. It is a child-centered approach that accepts developmental characteristics and still places great faith in children's potential. Mutual respect of teacher for child and of children for each other is considered important, so strong emphasis is placed on understanding the perspectives of others. Montessori children are encouraged to undertake independent activity and expected to become good workers.

Though the Montessori curriculum has a solid tradition of child-initiated activities, and sensitivity to child development, the self-teaching and self-correcting materials do exercise a great deal of control over the child's learning. Montessori cylinder blocks, for example, fit together in only one way. Teachers encourage discovery and understanding within the limits of somewhat restrictive materials.

The effectiveness of the Montessori approach has been more asserted by testimonial than confirmed by research. Generalizations are difficult because, though the approach is a worldwide movement, both teacher backgrounds and the interpretation of curriculum principles vary widely. Another problem is the lack of demonstrated efficacy with the various kinds of student populations. During the past three decades in the U.S., the Montessori curriculum has been used mainly in private schools serving prosperous families; only recently have programs focused on children in less fortunate circumstances (which was actually Maria Montessori's original intent). The Montessori curriculum, ideally implemented, deserves to be subjected to rigorous scientific evaluation and longitudinal research involving all kinds of students.

Gesell Institute approach. From the Gesell Institute of Human Development, comes not a formal curriculum model, but a set of ideas about child development, child observation, and school readiness. The institute's active training program for public school personnel and promotion of the Gesell School Readiness Screening Instrument are consistent with a curricular emphasis on child-initiated activity. Indeed, the institute views readiness as crucial because of *the absence* of child-initiated activity in our preponderently teacher-directed elementary curriculum. If child-initiated activity were more commonplace in early childhood education, the institute would consider precise placemement as far less critical.

The work of Arnold Gesell is associated with a maturationist viewpoint, that is, that ability level is primarily a function of growth. Gesell's namesake institute, though, now accepts the proposition that both maturation and experience affect the young child's developmental status.

Determination of this status is very important to the institute, since it recommends grade placement based not on age, but on stage of development. Failure in school, according to the institute, results either from placing less mature children in grades for which they are chronologically, but not developmentally, ready[12] or *from a lack of developmentally appropriate learning experiences in the preschool years.*

A school district using the Gesell approach would consequently be inclined to offer prekindergarten programs as well as transition programs before or after kindergarten. Districts may also be using the Gesell School Readiness Screening Assessment to help direct students into appropriate programs.

A full-scale effort has been mounted to demonstrate the assessment's predictive validity (meaning success in correctly placing a very high percentage of students). Until the instrument's validity and reliability are confirmed, however, the institute recommends that it not be used as the sole basis for routine placement decisions, but as a clinical indicator, that is, one source of information in a problem-solving procedure that also considers data from parents, teachers, and other forms of assessment. It should be noted, however, that researchers have recently questioned the validity of both the Gesell Assessment[13] and the extra-year-of-kindergarten programs.[14]

Pressurizing the Children's Garden

Screening children for kindergarten readiness has become more of an issue because of the emphasis that educational reform has placed on performance. Since government leaders, administrators, and parents have declared that it's "time for results," the pressure to expect academic achievement in kindergarten has increased.

Child psychologist David Elkind, who is also NAEYC's 1987–88 president, has argued emphatically that children are harmed by such pressure, both in education and in American society as a whole.[15] Though technological advancements have given children more access to information, making them appear sophisticated, Elkind firmly believes that the way young children relate to the world has not changed.

Froebel's vision of kindergarten as a "children's garden" in which preschoolers play is just as valid as it was in the early 1800s. The Gesell Institute expresses the general opinions of the early childhood education field when it declares that most five-year-olds are not ready for *academic* kindergartens and the developmental kindergartens should serve *all* children, not just those ill-prepared for academic competition.

Variety among early childhood curricula enriches the early childhood field, but within the variety lie fundamental disputes that ought to be resolved. Some choices are not a matter of preferring one valid practice over another, but of distinguishing the beneficial from the detrimental. We trust that researchers will continue to clarify these issues.

Meanwhile, we ought to keep in mind that early childhood education is not merely the transmission of numbers, letters, shapes, and colors. It is our first public statement on the values we wish our children to have. If we say that we value personal initiative, collaborative problem solving, and respect for others, then these are the values that should be evident wherever young children spend their time and create their future.

ENDNOTES

1. L. B. Stebbins and others, *Education as Experimentation: A Planned Variation Model* Vol. IV-A (Cambridge, Mass.: Abt Associates, 1977). For long-term effects, see P. P. Olmstead and M. J. Szegda, *Long-Term Effects of Follow Through Participation* (Ypsilanti: High/Scope Foundation. 1987).

2. Lawrence J. Schweinhart; David P. Weikart; and Mary B. Larner, "Consequences of Three Preschool Curriculum Models Through Age 15," *Early Childhood Research Quarterly* 1 (1986): 15–35.

3. Constance Kamii, "Autonomy vs. Heteronomy," *Principal* 66 (September 1986): 68–70.

4. Duane F. Alwin, "Trends in Parental Socialization Values: Detroit, 1958–1983," *American Journal of Sociology* 90 (1984): 359–382.

5. Research and Policy Committee, Committee for Economic Development, *Investing in Our*

Children (Washington, D.C.: Committee for Economic Development, 1985): 17, 18.

6. Task Force on Teaching as a Profession, Carnegie Forum on Education and the Economy, *A Nation Prepared: Teachers for the 21st Century* (Washington, D.C.: Carnegie Forum on Education and the Economy, 1986): 20.

7. "NAEYC Position Statement on Developmentally Appropriate Practice in Early Childhood Programs Serving Children from Birth to Age 8," *Young Children* 41 (September 1986): 4–19; and "NAEYC Position Statement on Developmentally Appropriate Practice in Programs for 4- and 5-Year-Olds," *Young Children* 41 (September 1986): 20–29.

8. For example, Diana Baumrind, "Current Patterns of Parental Authority," *Developmental Psychology Monograph* 4, Part 2 of 4 (1971).

9. Jean Piaget, *The Moral Judgment of the Child* (London, Routledge and Kegan Paul, 1932).

10. Carl Bereiter, "Does Direct Instruction Cause Delinquency?" *Early Childhood Research Quarterly* 1 (1986): 290.

11. Samuel J. Meisels, *Developmental Screening in Early Childhood: A Guide* (Washington, D.C.: National Association for the Education of Young Children, 1985).

12. Louise B. Ames, Clyde Gillespie, and John W. Streff, *Stop School Failure* (Flemington, N.J.: Programs for Education, 1985): 44.

13. Samuel J. Meisels, "Uses and Abuses of Developmental Screening and School Readiness Testing," *Young Children* 42 (January 1987): 4–9, 68–73, and related articles.

14. Lorrie A. Shepard and Mary Lee Smith, "Synthesis of Research on School Readiness and Kindergarten Retention," *Educational Leadership* 44, 3 (November 1986): 78–86.

15. David Elkind, *The Hurried Child* (Reading, Mass.: Addison-Wesley, 1981). Also, David Elkind, "Formal Education and Early Childhood Education: An Essential Difference," *Phi Delta Kappan* 67 (1986): 631–636. For elaboration, see David Elkind, *Miseducation: Preschoolers at Risk* (New York: Knopf Publishing Company, 1987).

Lawrence J. Schweinhart directs the Voices for Children Project at the High/Scope Educational Research Foundation, Ypsilanti, Michigan. This article is adapted from one that appeared in High/Scope ReSource, *Spring 1987.*

Defending Young Children's Play as the Ladder to Literacy

Charles H. Wolfgang and Tobie S. Sanders

"When is my child going to learn something—all he does is play all day!" This is a common criticism directed toward many early education programs which use play as the central curriculum vehicle. When we investigate further to determine what this "learn something" really means, we discover parents are talking about "basic skills," such as those involved in reading, writing, and arithmetic, or "readiness" for public school and first grade. The attack against play curriculum has come not only from parents, but also from the educational community where, because of demands for "back to basics," the traditional first grade reading or math programs have been moved down into the kindergarten and even early childhood education programs for three- and four-year-old children.

Historically, those educators who have committed themselves to play programs and curricula have attempted to defend their position by saying that play is a child's natural or developmental form of learning. Such educators have claimed play programs provide a holistic approach to educating the young child. Providing for play experiences that enable the child to grow physically, socially, cognitively, and especially emotionally, has been underscored. However, critics of early childhood education, who erupted out of the latter '60s from compensatory programs such as Head Start, dismissed this defense of play as having lacked solid theoretical or empirical research support and as being reflective of a sentimental bias. Concerned about helping children catch up to their peers, childhood educators accepted a narrow viewpoint which held that since time is limited, the available time should be used to drill basic skills. Now those educators who wish to continue to defend play as a valid curriculum vehicle must enter the arena and demonstrate clearly the relationship between play and such basic skills as reading. In this paper, we will examine the defense of play with respect to beginning literacy, based on current research and development of new theory.

A Developmental Defense

We find our first line of defense in the works of Piaget and Vygotsky, who saw in both play and reading the process of using symbols or indicators—one thing in reality stands for another in thought. In play, a child picks up a toy block and by her actions and language she has a "CB," an airplane, or whatever meaning she wishes to project. The child, through this imaginative play, is using and manipulating representation or symbols to express meaning.

Reading, in its most fundamental definition, is a process of deriving meaning from the printed page or written words. Understanding of meaning is related to cognitive development and the ability to understand representation; i.e., one thing (such as a written word) stands for another (such as an idea or concept) (Vygotsky, 1962, 1978).

Piaget has delineated a number of cognitive stages from birth to adolescence. The stages that relate to our question are those of preoperational thinking, which gradually ends near the age of seven, and concrete operational thinking, which generally comprises the elementary school years. In preschool chil-

Source: Charles H. Wolfgang & Tobie S. Sanders (1981). Defending young children's play as the ladder to literacy. *Theory into Practice*, 20, 116–120. Reprinted by permission of Charles H. Wolfgang and *Theory into Practice*, College of Education, The Ohio State University.

dren, the preoperational stage is characteristically associated with the lack of full development of conceptual forms of thinking. This is evidenced by an inability to make fine discriminations between ideas and objects and to classify or establish a meaningful relationship with ideas and objects. During this stage, for example, the preschooler "fans" a paper before his face and feels the wind blow. He reasons that moving paper causes wind to blow. Later, when outdoors on a windy day, he feels the wind and sees the trees swaying (similar to the action of the fanning paper) and preoperationally reasons "moving trees cause the wind to blow." Such transductive reasoning does not enable preschoolers to understand concepts, ideas, and reality as adults do. Their thinking is egocentric in the sense that they cannot project themselves to truly comprehend other points of view and perceptions.

It is during this preoperational period from ages two through seven that representational make-believe play tends to dominate the young child's activities. Such play is the central curriculum vehicle used in many preschool programs. During the beginning of the concrete operational period, around the age of seven, we see the make-believe play generally dissipate, and the child enters the world of symbols as representation. Vygotsky, in fact, theorized that the vehicle of make-believe play is essential in enabling a child to build up stores of represented meanings necessary for success in learning to read. It is important to note that many children who are not yet reading successfully at the end of first grade are still at a preoperational stage of thinking (Wolfgang, 1974).

Both Piaget and Vygotsky draw a direct relationship between representation in make believe and in reading, using the term *symbols* for the representation in play and *signs* for the representation in reading. A symbol is defined as a projection, with toys or gesture, of the child's egocentric and personal ideas expressed externally in play. A sign, as in the written and spoken word, is a form of representation that is socially agreed upon and arbitrary in nature. Generally, there is no visual relationship to the real concept or object being represented.

If we ask several people to make a symbol for *cat*, each person's enactment or drawing of cat would be different because it would express his/her personal concepts and ideas of what a cat is. In contrast, if we ask them to write the sign for cat, everyone (unless they had a different language) would write *c-a-t*. We can read and write with the representative form of signs, and we understand the arbitrary, socially agreed-upon system.

Piaget and Vygotsky, therefore, theoretically demonstrate that the use of symbols in play by young children (preoperational period) provides the foundational ability used in representation that will be needed later when using the higher abstract form that we know as signs or the written word. There has been research to demonstrate that those children who have not developed the first level of representation as symbolic play during the preschool years are the very ones who generally have difficulty when entering public school, with its demands for use and manipulation of socially agreed-upon, arbitrary sign systems in reading and similar academic subjects (Wolfgang, 1974).

Preschool curriculum may be viewed from a play-oriented or work/skill-oriented, dichotomous position. Play-oriented curriculum emphasizes child-directed representations of symbols through activities in which constructive materials, imaginative sequences, and/or elements of language are freely used. At the work/skill end of the dichotomy, we find teacher-directed instruction in the decoding of arbitary signs.

Developmental Stages of Representational Ability

Fein (1979) presented a framework for viewing the sequential development of representational play discussed by Piaget and Vygotsky. She noted several developmental strands which combine within play to help create a child's representational ability. These strands include: 1) separation of the play activity from real-life settings; 2) reduction of dependence on concrete, real-life objects; 3) addition and manipulation of actors and roles; and 4) group participation facilitated through negotiations and role standardization. Within this developmental framework, the child progresses from use of symbols to use of signs, and from egocentric behavior and thinking to social behavior requiring conceptual manipulation of social rules. Characteristic examples of play from each of Fein's stages follow.

Stage 1   Separation of activity and object from real-life setting.

Example: The child attempts to drink from a cup when it is empty for pure play purposes. (Symbol used in simplistic form).

Stage 2 Reduction of dependence on concrete objects.

Example: Child uses orange rind as pretend cup. (Higher, more abstract use of symbol).

Stage 3 Addition and manipulation of actors and roles.

Example: Child uses pretend cup and pitcher to serve tea to his dolls. (Still higher and more abstract use of symbol, combined with beginning aspects of social behavior toward others).

Stage 4 Group participation facilitated through negotiation and role standardization.

Example: Child says to playmate, "Let's pretend you come to my house for a tea party. You sit there and I'll serve you." Imaginary guests are also included and the children act out an elaborate drama while pretending to have cookies with tea. They use no props. (Highest level of symbolic behavior; symbols approach use of signs, as roles are standardized and socially agreed upon.)

Reading implies that communication can occur in the absence of another person. In reading, meaning is indicated by interpreting abstract symbols, the precursors of which have been traced above. The child must be able to act upon those symbols as if another person, or in Vygotsky's terms, interlocater, was communicating with him or her. The ability to take such an internalized approach in order to gain meaning from symbols seems to be present in Fein's fourth stage, in which the child attains the most abstract level of symbol development from which signs are approached as an abstract set of indicators. When this stage is attained, there has been transition from the egocentric thinking of a child to the social ability of a child to act as though there are others present who are filling standardized roles. When we discover children who have been unable to learn to read within a traditional work/skill instructional program, we suggest that those children may not have arrived at the highest level of representational ability through play. Also, if we look closely at children who have learned to read through the work/skill approach, we may find that some of them are merely decoding; that is, they may not be reading in the sense of gaining meaning from print (Foss and Hakes, 1979). Therefore, if we wish to meet the needs of children to acquire reading in its fullest sense, we are theoretically and empirically justified in suggesting that reading should be viewed as only the top rung on the ladder of representational growth. Early developmental stages of symbolic play then may be seen as means of moving up the rungs of the ladder.

A Psycholinguistic Defense

Our defense of play as a preparation for literacy has thus far come from developmental theorists. What support for preschool play curriculum, as opposed to work/skill curriculum, can be gained from investigations of the reading and writing process?

Traditional notions of reading readiness dictated the use of work/skill activities based upon inventories of isolated skills, such as verbal knowledge of sound/symbol relationships, and the ability to trace right to left progression across a page. Such skills were believed to be the prerequisites or building blocks of reading. Emphasis on the acquisition of these traditional skills reflected the demands of an instructional program, rather than the nature of the reading process. Advances in the field of psycholinguistics point toward a revised concept of reading readiness. From a psycholinguistic perspective, learning to read is viewed as a "continual process of making more and more sense of written language, advancing with every reading experience and beginning with the first insight that print is meaningful" (Smith, 1979, p. 155). In this sense, readiness to read implies competence in symbolic representation of meaning, more than it implies facility in any given set of specific skills as seen in the programs of work/skill instruction mentioned earlier.

The psycholinguistic reconceptualization of reading readiness may be demonstrated with samples drawn from Clay's (1975) investigations of early stages in writing development. Parallels between Fein's (1979) stages in representational ability described earlier and Clay's stages of developmental principles of early writing ability are evident (See Figure 1).

Clay presented a strong case for examining beginning writing as a component of beginning reading from a "total language" or psycholinguistic perspective. She noted that a young child who engages in writing is manipulating the units of written language and is likely to be gaining some awareness of how those symbols may be combined to convey unspoken messages. When such manipulation is spontaneous and unbidden, it is symbol play.

First, a child realizes there is a written system. Clay calls this the *sign* stage. Next, an awareness of the function of the system develops, as the young writer develops the *message* concept in relation to print. She realizes what she says can be written down. A child at this stage may make "writing-like" marks on paper, which appear to be scribbling, and optimistically pretend to read what he or she has written. Or the child may ask an attending adult, "What did I write?" As the child moves into the next stage, she becomes aware of the elements of the system. Letters and word forms are copied and/or invented. Practice with the elements occurs as the child makes inventions of elements, replicates patterns, and combines elements in generative patterns. Finally, the young writer strives for mastery of the adult rule-governed forms. Directional principles are adhered to as are spacial conventions, and eventually page and book arrangement patterns. As with Fein's

FIGURE 1 *Comparison of Clay and Fein Stages*

CLAY'S DEVELOPMENTAL CONCEPTS OF EARLY WRITING ABILITY (Condensed)		FEIN'S STAGES OF REPRESENTATIONAL ABILITY IN PLAY
Adherence to convention in writing, including directionality and spatial arrangement.	Mastery of standardized forms of representational system	Stage IV: Role standardization and negotiations used to facilitate group participation.
	↑	
Copy principle, inventories, and invention of letter and word forms.	Awareness of standardized representational system and practice with elements of that system	Stage III: Addition and manipulation of actors and roles.
	↑	
Message Concept: Child asks "What did I write?" or pretends to read marks on paper.	Awareness of the function of representational systems	Stage II: Reduced dependence on concrete objects.
	↑	
Sign Concept: Child attempts writing-like scribbles on paper.	Awareness that there are representational systems	Stage I: Separation of play activity from real-life setting.
	↑	
	PARALLELS IN DEVELOPMENT OF REPRESENTATIONAL ABILITY: MOVEMENT TOWARD HIGHER LEVELS OF SYMBOLIC BEHAVIOR	

model of representational ability, elements appearing in early stages are internalized in the later stages. Through development of a representational system, the child moves toward attainment of this important aspect of literacy.

The psycholinguistic perspective relates reading to total language use. Play, which involves elements of language, serves both as a facilitator and an indicator of representational ability. Play presents the child with a situation removed from real life demands. Thus, play within the school setting is removed from intrusive teacher intervention and arbitrary evaluations. This allows for freedom to explore a wide range of representational possibilities. In play, a child's attention is most typically focused on the function or meaning of his/her representational system. In this sense, language, which is part of the representational system, facilitates the functions of play sequences. When functions break down, play must be facilitated by negotiations and attention may shift to the form of the representational system. Thus, language, as a representational system patterning with play, goes through sequences of being roughed out and polished, further extended in a functional fashion, and then again polished in terms of form or adherence to arbitrary, socially agreed-upon conventions.

Summary

Educators need to demonstrate more clearly to parents the relationship between play with symbols and the ability to use signs in reading. This defense of play, based upon the work of developmental and psycholinguistic theorists, suggests movement away from reliance upon scope and sequence charts, which yield normative comparisons of children in work/skill programs, to an individualized, diagnostic profile. The latter would reflect stages in sequential growth of symbol representation as found both in Fein's (1979) and Clay's (1975) frameworks.

Such a profile would enable a teacher to pinpoint each child's location in a sequence as s/he moves toward arbitrary use of signs and toward literacy. The teacher could use this profile to diagnose and as the basis of a plan to
support a child's growth with appropriate teaching techniques and learning experiences. Such techniques and experiences would then be based on a developmental unfolding rather than on an arbitrary inventory of curriculum-bound activities.

If representational ability is necessary in becoming literate, as both developmental and psycholinguistic theorists suggest, then play provides a vehicle for enhancing such ability both in a general sense and more specifically with respect to language as a representational system. Play also provides the means for a child to progress through the stages of representational development which conclude with a drive toward mastery of rule governed, socially approved forms. This end product reflects the desired outcome of both the play-oriented and work/skill-oriented preschool curricula described earlier. The arbitrariness and threat of failure inherent in the work/skill-oriented format, however, suggests that, although the goal may be reached by either road, the play-oriented curriculum marks a path that is not only defensible but far more fruitful for exploration than the narrow and restrictive one paved by the work/skill extreme on the dichotomy.

REFERENCES

Clay, M. *What did I write?* Auckland, New Zealand: Heinemann Educational Books, 1975.

Fein, Greta. Play and acquisition of symbols. In *Current topics in early childhood education*, Vol. 2, Lilian G. Katz, (Ed.), New York: Ablex Publishing, 1979.

Foss, D. J., and Hakes, D. T. *Psycholinguistics: An introduction to the psychology of language.* Englewood Cliffs, N.J.: Prentice Hall, 1979.

Piaget, J. and Inhelder, B. *The psychology of the child.* New York: Basic Books, 1969.

Smith, F. *Reading without nonsense.* New York: Teachers College Press, 1979.

Vygotsky, L. S. *Thought and language.* Cambridge, Mass.: MIT Press, 1962.

Vygotsky, L. S. *Mind and society.* Cambridge, Mass.: Harvard University Press, 1978.

Wolfgang, C. H. An exploration of the relationship between the cognitive area of reading and selected developmental aspects of children's play. *Psychology in the Schools, 11,* July, 1974, 338–343.

Charles H. Wolfgang is associate professor of education and Tobie S. Sanders is senior research associate, both at The Ohio State University.

The Calendar and the Clock: When Is the Right Time?

Mary A. Jensen and Zelda W. Chevalier

Because the concept of time permeates every aspect of modern life, it is understandable why preschool and kindergarten teachers feel some urgency in helping young children come to grips with this concept. Toward this end many early educators routinely focus instruction on external timekeepers as they display models of the clock or the calendar, the two most common symbol systems for keeping time in our society.

Scenario I

Fifteen three-year-olds have been gathered in a circle, and the teacher begins to discuss the concept of time. "What day of the week is it?" she asks. "That was good remembering," she tells Shawn, who gives the correct answer. "What season is it?" she prods. "How can we tell?" Gently, she leads the group into a discussion. "There's something shining in my eyes and on your back," she tells them, pointing to the sun. Carefully, she shows them that the sun has moved, and so have the hands of the clock. "That means time has gone by," she says. (Excerpt from *Rochester Times Union,* January 21, 1984).

Scenario II

Every day as the kindergartners eagerly enter the classroom, they take off their coats, put their belongings in their cubbies, and take out their individual calendar sheets. The task is to write in the square the correct date for that day. Some children look up on the chalkboard or at their peers to find out which number is "today's number." (On Mondays, they can fill in three days, but on every other day they are to fill in only one day. At the end of the month, the children take their calendars home to show their parents.) After attendance and the flag salute, the children look at the big calendar at the front of the room and cho-

rally respond to the teacher's prompting of the day, the month, the date, and the year as the teacher writes this information on the chalkboard. One child is then chosen to pick a figure (e.g., a snowman for January) with the number that corresponds to the date on the chalkboard and to place that figure on the big calendar. (E. Merkel, personal correspondence, July 29, 1987).

Scenarios akin to these are being enacted daily in many preschool and kindergarten classrooms. Apart from questionable practices that foster an erroneous notion of the solar system, instruction that tries to assign meaning to highly complex abstract systems such as the clock and calendar may cause genuine confusion, distaste, boredom, and frustration (Baroody, 1987; Harner, 1975; Piaget, 1981; Springer, 1952).

To understand abstract systems like the clock and calendar, a number of understandings and experiences must be coordinated. A critical feature of these systems is their cyclic recurrent structure based on astronomical and social regularities. For example, the intervals of time on the clock and calendar are cyclically ordered. Any two elements can occur either before or after one another, and any two elements can recur (Friedman, 1982). Whereas adults have come to understand that the cyclic units of time are quantifiable but arbitrary inventions, young children experience considerable difficulty comprehending these concepts. Reconstructing a temporal order is not an intuitive process but requires the consideration of multiple points in time. The coordination of multiple cycles and the conceptualization of recurrent cycles does not occur until about the age of eight or nine (Friedman, 1978).

Time is not a simple perception, but a complex invention of humanity requiring comprehension of not only cognitive and linguistic concepts, but social concepts as well (Lewis & Weigart, 1981; Zerubavel, 1981). Time is experienced in many ways and imbued with various levels of meanings: (1) as a physical passage (the earth's orbit around the sun, the seasons) and as a geological change; (2) as references to social and historical events ("For the last five years, we have played bridge on a weekly basis with the Sandlins"); (3) as mechanical, mathematical demarcations ("Let's meet at a quarter to 8:00"); and (4) as biological time (birth to old age).

Faced with explaining these multiple meanings, many practitioners put their trust in highly visible sources of information readily at hand—the calendar and the clock, which, though concrete, represent abstract symbols. In many preschools and kindergartens, instruction on the calendar emphasizes rote memorization of the days, weeks, and months. Often, these verbal association lists are divorced from children's practical concerns and experiences. Young children may be able to learn to recite the days of the week as a rote verbal list, but this kind of teacher-directed learning is likely to be superfluous or ineffectual in terms of children's understanding and use of time. These routines make little sense to young children because their grasp of temporality is subjective, based on their feelings at the moment, and action-bound (Baroody, 1987; Friedman, 1982; Nash, 1979; Schultz & Theophano, 1987).

Relationships between days, weeks, and months are complex and difficult to detect. Days of week can indeed be named in a predictable linear sequence of Sunday through Saturday. Such recitation produces a useful verbal list that serves similar functions as recitation of the alphabet. But this regularity is not coordinated with relational information about the cyclic nature of the week. Moreover, schools and the workplace often make a distinction between work (or school) days and the weekend and treat the days of the week as Monday through Sunday. To further complicate matters, at the onset of each month, listings of days have multiple, seemingly arbitrary starting points. (Any day of the week can be labeled the first and/or last day of the month.) And the number of weeks in a month varies as does the number of days in a month ("Thirty days hath September. . ."). Small wonder that children are muddled! Recall that not until the age of eight or nine do they grasp cyclic time systems such as the calendar (Friedman, 1982).

In his research on the development of time concepts in children, Friedman (1977, 1982) examined children's ability to understand elements of cyclic time systems. He started with temporal, social regularities such as daily routines and moved on to conventional time systems. Using pictorial representations, his findings revealed that when four-year-olds were asked to place in order four cards depicting activities in their daily cycle (waking in morning, working at school, eating dinner, and sleeping at night), nearly half could arrange the cards correctly. For similar instructions and cards representing holidays, seasonal activities, or natural phenomena associated with seasons, most six- to seven-year-olds could correctly order four cards. By age seven, the children began to show the first signs of coordinating time systems, matching holiday cards with season cards. By the age of eight, children could order cards with month names and could match season cards with month cards. Evidence for understanding the recurrent, cyclic nature of months did not occur until the age of nine. In other words, the cyclic recurrent nature of conventional time orders emerged about two years after mastering the particular time order.

In an early normative study, Springer (1952) focused on clock time and used children's verbal and motor responses to questions to determine the ages at which they developed various understandings of clock time. As found in other studies (Ames, 1946; Friedman, 1982), Springer found that some four-year-olds can tell the time of activities in their daily cycle by using descriptive comments or by listing a sequence of activities. But most of her four-year-old subjects gave unreasonable numerical responses to questions about time (e.g., "69 o'clock"). In contrast, six-year-olds were more likely to respond with correct numerical responses. By age five, many could recognize hours on the clock, but few could identify half or quarter hours. Setting a clock for certain times proved to be a much more difficult task, even for six-year-olds. The most difficult concept assessed was the purpose and functioning of the hands of the clock. This entails the ability to coordinate unequal speeds of the clock hands. Since the clock's circumference is fixed, the minute hand completes the cycle in a shorter time than the hour hand. Also there is a fixed relationship between the movement of the faster moving hand and the movement of the slower moving hour hand which is not readily discerned but must be understood (Friedman, 1978). Only 23 to 36 percent of the six-year-olds could answer these questions correctly. These studies illustrate that young children are just beginning to realize that time can be measured systematically, and that a number system can be used to represent that process.

There are a number of other task-related reasons why the comprehension of cyclic time is so troublesome. Full comprehension of conventional time markers involves the gradual construction of a temporal cognitive map where a number of intangible abstract ideas need to be associated. As we have seen, a first step in this process appears to be the ability to order and sequence events (Brown, 1976; Fivush & Mandler, 1985; French & Nelson, 1985; Kayra-Stuart, 1977). Once the ordering principle is grasped, the related temporal concept of duration—how long events last—needs to be conceptualized. Friedman (1978) found that four- and five-year-olds use conventional time words spontaneously, but their estimates of time in minutes or hours are unreasonable and unstable because they have difficulty relating duration (how long) or when events start and stop to time labels. Even when trained to estimate duration, a four-second waiting period was described as "a couple of minutes" or "10 minutes." These two important temporal concepts, ordering and duration, must be coordinated, synthesized, and translated into the language of a conventional time system. For young children this is a formidable problem (Piaget, 1969).

Furthermore, when the clock and calendar are used to denote duration, the intervals between events (hours, minutes, days, weeks, months) must be discriminated and quantified. Studies have shown that young children focus on perceptually salient cues that interfere with their ability to quantify and integrate duration of time. In judging amount of time, they focus entirely on spatial end points, ignoring the amount of time actually passed (Levin, 1982; Levin, Wilkening, & Dembo, 1984).

Other intangible aspects of temporality need to be discerned as well: the notion of location, which specifies where events or situations take place, and the rate of recurrence, which registers how often they take place (Zerubavel, 1981). For young children, these

ideas are impalpable. For example, play time is not understood as a distinct event located in time. The child must have had sufficient experiences with play time in a particular place to recognize that this event occurs in a daily routine. Similarly, snack time is not understood as a recurrent event until the child has had sufficient experience with the regular, repeated occurrence of the activity. When words used by adults are disembedded from the immediate situation, children have trouble linking time vocabulary and action.

The idea that time can be quantified in a systematic fashion is counterintuitive. For adults as well as children, the passage of time is not uniformly experienced. It is a personalized happening. The tempo is sometimes patterned, slow, fast, haphazard, or amorphous depending how one feels about what is going on at that moment. These illusory perceptions are anchored in the social context. In the natural environment, there are no clues about days of week, minutes, or hours. Time-anchored inventions such as the calendar and the clock represent tools designed to enhance predictability and to reduce the uncertainty of events with respect to our environment. They help to tell people what is going on around them (Zerubavel, 1981). As we have seen, conventional time has little meaning for children under five or six years old. The subtle intricacies of timekeeping devices (e.g., associating time units with counting numbers) and facets of cyclic time are mastered at the concrete operational level (Friedman, 1978). The evidence suggests that we move away from ineffectual practices that drill children on the perplexities of the clock and the calendar, and that we substitute experiences and devise tasks that make sense to children in terms of what they can do rather than what they cannot.

We are all born with a partially developed set of biological, temporal rhythms. As babies, we are able to synchronize these rhythmic actions with external rhythms. Condon (1977) noted this interactional synchrony in mother speech and infant movements. Social schedules and culturally derived temporal norms soon impinge on the life of the infant. Socializing the baby's rhythms in terms of a culture's temporal expectations and norms occurs through early interactions between parents and the infant. Gradually, the infant is trained to adapt internal rhythms to external demands and learns to use actions to regulate social interactions (Rifkin, 1987). Fogel (1977), for example, noted cycles of attention and mutual accommodation of movements in mother-infant interactions. Also, we see how young children, ages 13 and 15 months, will seek to establish social communication cycles by accommodating and repeating their actions and accompanying utterances:

> *Larry sits on the floor, and Bernie turns and looks toward him. Bernie waves his hand and say "da," still looking at Larry. He repeats the vocalization three more times before Larry laughs. Bernie vocalizes again and Larry laughs again. Then the same sequence of one child saying "da" and the other laughing is repeated twelve more times before Bernie turns away from Larry and walks off (Mueller & Lucas, 1975, p. 241).*

In the context of familiar everyday activities, even young children are surprisingly competent in their social uses of temporality. A naturalistic study of a preschool classroom by Shultz and Theophano (1987) revealed that three-year-olds are able to use temporal concepts to negotiate taking turns ("Can I be after you?" "Can I have your place when you are done?" pp. 40, 43), to create social boundaries (Joel asks each of four boys at the table for a place. Each says that he will take a long time. Joel goes away crying. All four laugh at him loudly. p. 43), and to socially demarcate desirable activities (David to Kenny at the play dough table where four are allowed to sit: "Now is it my turn? Are you going to take a long time?" Eventually he squeezes in beside Kenny on the bench and tells him he will wait there, but then picks up a small piece of the play dough and starts rolling it. p. 40). Note that these understandings of temporality are embedded in and shaped by the social environment, are action-bound, and express territoriality more than duration of events.

Young children are able to draw proper inferences about the marking of time imposed by scheduling of events in familiar institutions such as their home or school and in familiar community settings. Within these contexts, they learn the meanings of quantifiers such as *always, never,* and *sometimes* (Kucjaz, 1975), and they gradually discern the meanings of temporal terms such as *now, not now, today, tomorrow, yesterday, then, daytime, nighttime, morning, afternoon, winter,* and *summer* (Ames, 1946; French & Nelson, 1985; Harner, 1975; Nelson, 1978; Zerubavel, 1981). Preschoolers also acquire scripts for temporal events in familiar contexts. Nelson, for example, compared preschoolers' ability to recapitulate the sequence of events of an important daily routine: eating lunch at home, at a day-care center, or at McDonald's. Comparisons among the three locations showed that children had similar understandings of the sequence of habitual actions. Although differences occurred in elaborations and specific types of action associated with each place, the basic constructions of temporal sequence were orderly and organized. Nelson posits that such scripts, when anchored to personal action, assist the development of memory for temporal events and their recurrence.

Exposure to different institutional scheduling patterns has been found to generate variations in children's conceptualization of duration of time and consequent patterns of behavior. In a five-year observational study, Nash (1979) evaluated time scheduling and time management by kindergarten teachers as well as children's time management, their understanding of task duration, and their view of themselves with respect to locus of control and autonomous behavior. The effects of experimental classroom schedules, consisting of large, flexible blocks of time with ample opportunity for play, were compared with regular schedules where time allocations were arranged into shorter, discrete activity periods (e.g., exercise, gym, snack time, and story time). Free play in regular classrooms was limited. The results showed that when time arrangements were more consonant with children's natural proclivities, they were better able to set criteria for task completion, and were able to make more realistic judgments about duration with respect to task completion. Unlike children in the experimental program, children in the regular program decreased the amount of time they spent on tasks over the course of the school year. In terms of locus of control, differences in children's feelings of self-directedness during free play were strongest in the experimental programs. Children's feelings of other-directedness were strongest in the regular programs. Apparently, the time dimension of programs is a powerful one, influencing classroom climate and interpersonal relationships as well as the child's view of himself or herself as a learner.

245

These studies indicate that young children are deeply involved in the process of learning to reproduce and distinguish important characteristics of time. Although there are numerous gaps in our understanding of the development of time concepts, there is mounting evidence for delaying formal instruction of cyclical time. Research has shown that before the age of eight, concepts associated with the clock and the calendar are inaccurate and poorly understood. Even systematic exposure to these devices is apt to be ineffective until changes occur in basic memory capacities, in the use of appropriate strategies, in the formation of networks of related associations and distinctions, and in knowledge of content (Baroody, 1987; Friedman, 1978).

The research findings also suggest that other approaches and activities can enable children to use or comprehend time. A program environment rich in materials with ample opportunities for social interaction is an important basis for young children's learning about time. Through action-oriented activities that respect the child's sense of temporality, children can be helped to begin to cope with the complexities of cyclic time, its sequence, duration, and the recurrence of events. Discussion of events in the child's daily cycle as well as building associations for special events such as birthdays appears to be an appropriate instructional focus for preschool and kindergarten children. Listening to and reenacting favorite stories would also help the young child to understand event sequencing and event relationships in terms of a cohesive, meaningful whole. The reader also is urged to consult Hohmann, Banet, and Weikart (1979) for activities that will make sense to children. Questionable, premature instruction of one of the most basic and complex concepts in our culture is an issue deserving attention from persons committed to advocating for developmentally appropriate practices (Bredekamp, 1987).

REFERENCES

Ames, L. B. (1946). The development of the sense of time in the young child. *The Journal of Genetic Psychology, 68,* 97–125.

Baroody, A. J. (1987). *Children's mathematical thinking.* New York: Teachers College Press.

Bredekamp, S. (Ed.). (1987). *Developmentally appropriate practice in early childhood programs serving children from birth through age 8.* Washington, DC: National Association for the Education of Young Children.

Brown, A. L. (1976). The construction of temporal succession by preoperational children. In A. D. Pick (Ed.), *Minnesota symposia on child psychology: Vol. 10* (pp. 28–83). Minneapolis, MN: The University of Minnesota Press.

Condon, W. S. (1977). A primary phase in the organization of infant responding behavior. In H. R. Schaffer (Ed.), *Studies in mother-infant interaction* (pp. 153–176). New York: Academic Press.

Fivush, R., & Mandler, J. M. (1985). Developmental changes in the understanding of temporal sequence. *Child Development, 56,* 1437–1466.

Fogel, A. (1977). Temporal organization in mother-infant face-to-face interaction. In H. R. Schaffer (Ed.), *Studies in mother-infant interaction* (pp. 119–151). New York: Academic Press.

French, L. A., & Nelson, K. (1985). *Young children's knowledge of relational terms.* New York: Springer-Verlag.

Friedman, W. J. (1977). The development of children's understanding of cyclic aspects of time. *Child Development, 48,* 1593–1599.

Friedman, W. J. (1978). Development of time concepts in children. In H. W. Reese & L. P. Lipsitt (Eds.), *Advances in child development and behavior: Vol. 12* (pp. 267–298). New York: Academic Press.

Friedman, W. J. (1982). Conventional time concepts and children's structuring of time. In W. J. Friedman (Ed.), *The developmental psychology of time* (pp. 171–208). New York: Academic Press.

Harner, L. (1975). Yesterday and tomorrow: Development of early understanding of terms. *Developmental Psychology, 11,* 864–865.

Hohmann, M., Banet, B., & Weikart, D. P. (1979). *Young children in action: A manual for preschool educators.* Ypsilanti, MI: High Scope Press.

Kayra-Stuart, F. (1977). *The development of the concept of time.* Paper presented at the Biennial Meeting of the Society for Research in Child Development, New Orleans, LA. (ERIC Document Reproduction Service No. ED 136 915)

Kucjaz, S. A. (1975). On the acquisition of a semantic system. *Journal of Verbal Learning and Verbal Behavior, 14,* 340–358.

Levin, I. (1982). The nature and development of time concepts in children: The effect of interfering cues. In W. J. Friedman (Ed.), *The developmental psychology of time* (pp. 47–85). New York: Academic Press.

Levin, I., Wilkening, F., & Dembo, Y. (1984). Development of time quantification: Integration and nonintegration of beginnings and endings in comparing durations. *Child Development, 55,* 2160–2172.

Lewis, J. D., & Weigert, A. J. (1981). The structures and meanings of social time. *Social Forces, 60,* 432–462.

Mueller, E., & Lucas, T. (1975). A developmental analysis of peer interaction among toddlers. In M. Lewis & L. A. Rosenblum (Eds.), *Friendship and peer relations* (pp. 223–257). New York; Wiley.

Nash, B. C. (1979). Kindergarten programmes and the young child's task orientation and understanding about time scheduling. *British Journal of Educational Psychology, 49,* 27–38.

Nelson, K. (1978). How children represent knowledge of their world in and out of language: A preliminary report. In R. W. Siegler (Ed.), *Children's thinking: What develops?* (pp. 255–274). Hillsdale, NJ: Erlbaum.

Piaget, J. (1969). *The child's conception of time.* London: Routledge & Kegan Paul.

Piaget, J. (1981). Time perception in children. In J. T. Fraser (Ed.), *The voices of time* (2nd ed.) (pp. 202–216). Amherst, MA: The University of Massachusetts Press.

Rifkin, J. (1987). *Time wars.* New York: Henry Holt and Company.

Shultz, J., & Theophano, J. S. (1987). Saving place and marking time: Some aspects of the social lives of three-year-old children. In H. T. Trueba (Ed.), *Success or failure? Learning and the language minority student* (pp. 33–48). New York: Harper & Row.

Springer, D. (1952). Development in young children of an understanding of time and the clock. *The Journal of Genetic Psychology, 80,* 83–96.

Zerubavel, E. (1981). *Hidden rhythms.* Chicago: University of Chicago Press.

Use of Microcomputers with Preschoolers: A Review of the Literature

Laura D. Goodwin, William L. Goodwin, and Mary Beth Garel

Research related to microcomputer use by preschool-age children is a timely topic given the rapid increase in interest in, and acquisition of, microcomputers by preschool personnel. This review summarizes and critiques the research in this area. Also synthesized is the relatively large body of literature that consists of unsupported claims and speculations about microcomputer effects. Conclusions drawn from this review suggest that (a) there is a general lack of congruence between the actual research findings and the numerous "pronouncements and speculations" about microcomputer effects; (b) many methodological weaknesses limit the utility of research findings; and (c) little is known, empirically, about important process and outcome variables associated with preschoolers' use of microcomputers. Some recommendations for research are presented, based on the findings from the research and other literature reviewed.

The acquisition of microcomputers by elementary and secondary schools in the 1980s has been dramatic (Bork, 1984; Magarrell, 1982; *School Uses of Microcomputers*, 1983; Snyder, 1985). Preschools, day care centers, and other settings for very young children likewise have become entranced with this new technology. Chin (1984a) has noted that approximately 25% of the 20,000 licensed preschools in the country (not including nursery schools operated by churches, universities, and the federal government) have microcomputers and has predicted that all preschools will have access to them by 1989. Exposure of preschoolers to microcomputers at home is also markedly increasing.

Much has been written about the actual and potential uses of microcomputers with young children. However, there have been relatively few reports published on the findings from research studies on the effects of micro-

computer use, particularly with preschoolers (Brady & Hill, 1984; Chin, 1984b; Hoot, 1984; Ziajka, 1983). Brady and Hill (1984) have described several research studies in progress to illustrate the kinds of questions that early childhood researchers are asking about microcomputer use by preschoolers; they have concluded that much research still needs to be conducted, especially in terms of what constitutes appropriate microcomputer experiences for young children. Exacerbating this problem is the fact that much of the existing research information is published in varied and difficult-to-obtain sources, such as trade magazines and technical journals (Dickerson & Pritchard, 1981).

The major purpose of this article is to describe, summarize, and critique the empirical research that has been conducted on microcomputer use by preschoolers. The discussion is organized into three sections. In the first,

Source: Laura D. Goodwin, William L. Goodwin, & Mary Beth Garel (1986). Use of microcomputers with preschoolers: A review of the literature. *Early Childhood Research Quarterly, 1,* 269–286. Reprinted by permission of Laura D. Goodwin, William L. Goodwin, and Ablex Publishing Corporation.

the large number of unsupported claims and speculations that have been published about the effects of microcomputer use by preschoolers are briefly summarized. These "pronouncements and speculations" are included because they provide some direction for future needed research. The second section—which is most directly related to the major purpose of the article—contains a review and analysis of the actual research that has been conducted in this area. As will become evident in this second section, there is a dearth of sound, empirically based evidence available to date on the impact of microcomputer use by preschoolers. In the third and final section, some research suggestions and recommendations are offered. These are based on both the unsupported pronouncements and speculations and on the results of the actual research studies mentioned in this review.

Pronouncements and Speculations

The literature on presumed effects of microcomputer use by young children can be sorted, generally, into two categories. The first includes the work of authors with very positive opinions about the likely effects of microcomputer use on young users. In the second category are commentaries expressing negative, or at least cautious, views about the appropriateness of exposing preschoolers to microcomputers.

Positive Views

The positive claims or speculations involving preschoolers and microcomputers are many and diverse. One way to classify them is according to the type of presumed outcome: cognitive, affective, or psychomotor. The majority of these speculative effects belong in the cognitive domain and range from simple to quite complex.

Some of the cognitive outcomes that have been claimed or proposed include (a) the acquisition of computer or keyboard familiarity (Lucas, 1980; Monahan & Monahan, 1982); (b) the acquisition of programming skills, especially using Papert's (1980) LOGO, or KINDER (Bitter, 1982; Campbell, 1985; Chin, 1984b; Hirshberg, 1981; Martin, 1981; Tursman, 1982; Vaidya, 1984); (c) alphabet recognition (Lucas, 1980; Mandell, 1983) and improvement of language skills in general (Burg, 1984; Damarin, 1982; Monahan & Monahan, 1982); (d) learning to write stories via word process-

ing programs (Chin, 1984b; Monahan & Monahan, 1982); (e) acquisition of basic mathematics concepts and skills (Burg, 1984; Damarin, 1982); and (f) learning spatial and relational concepts (Chin, 1984b; Lucas, 1980). The relatively more abstract or complex proposed cognitive outcomes include increases in creative thinking, problem-solving skills, decision-making abilities, the understanding of cause-and-effect relationships, and the ability to engage in Piaget's (Piaget & Inhelder, 1969) "symbolic representation" (Burg, 1984; Chin, 1984b; Damarin, 1982; Gallini, 1983; Jones, 1980; McCrory, 1984; Olds, 1982; O'Malley, 1985; Silvern, 1983; Tan, 1985; Ziajka, 1983).

Claims concerning affective outcomes for preschoolers from microcomputer use have been quite varied. Included in this category are such expectations as the development of autonomy and a sense of power through being "in control" of the microcomputer (Bitter, 1982; Burg, 1984; Chin, 1984b; Spencer & Baskin, 1983; Weir, Russell, & Valente, 1982; Ziajka, 1983). Other claimed affective outcomes are increased sociability, social interaction skills, and cooperation and collaboration abilities, as well as improved self-esteem and self-confidence (Burg, 1984; McCrory, 1984; Muller, 1983; Silvern, 1983; Spencer & Baskin, 1983; Weir et al., 1982; Ziajka, 1983). Two claims that have been made about psychomotor effects are that microcomputer use fosters fine motor skills and eye-hand coordination (Ziajka, 1983). An additional positive speculation—not easily categorizable as either cognitive, affective, or psychomotor—has been made by Ross and Campbell (1983). They argue that microcomputers are compatible with Montessori instruction in that their use can enhance such traditional Montessori objectives as freedom, structure and order, control and acceptance of error, meaningfulness of materials, and multisensory stimulation.

Negative or Cautious Views

The views of those authors who have been critical or cautious about young children's use of microcomputers can be categorized into four general areas of concern. The first relates to the adequacy of the available software packages. Some of the specific concerns that have been discussed include the appropriateness of the suggested age ranges for the software, the alleged ability of children to use them without adult assistance, and the inadequacies of the accompanying texts and workbooks (Barnes & Hill, 1983; Hoot, 1984; McCrory, 1984; Staples, 1984; Swigger, 1983b; Tan, 1985).

The second area of concern relates to the preparation of teachers. The lack of adequate preservice and inservice education for teachers in computer technology, generally, and in using microcomputers with young children, specifically, has been lamented (Bork, 1984; Dickerson & Pritchard, 1981; Lee, 1984; Walker, 1983). Relatedly, Steffin (1982) and Ohanian (1983) have emphasized the importance of the teacher's role in providing successful microcomputer experience and have been critical of teacherless uses of microcomputers by young children.

The third area deals with requisite skills and abilities that preschoolers need in order to use microcomputers beneficially. According to some authors (Getman, 1983; Kimmel, 1981; Swigger, 1983a), preschoolers' lack of reading ability, problem-solving skills, and eye-hand coordination place limits on what they can realistically be expected to do with microcomputers. Other authors (Barnes & Hill, 1983; Cuffaro, 1984; Favaro, 1983) have discussed this area of concern in terms of Piagetian stages and indicated that children need to be at the concrete operations stage (about age 7) before they are ready to use microcomputers, except perhaps to draw pictures with joysticks and paddles. Some of the specific skills that are considered necessary for effective microcomputer use (not usually demonstrated by preoperational children) are basic arithmetic skills, sequencing ability, and memory and mnemonic skills.

Finally, a few authors have raised concerns about possible adverse effects of microcomputer use by preschoolers. Bowman and Rotter (1983) have expressed worry about competition rather than cooperation and "computer catatonia" resulting from the use of microcomputers. It also has been suggested that microcomputer use may actually stifle cognitive development, language acquisition, social-emotional development, play behaviors, and ability to create images (Barnes & Hill, 1983; Partridge, 1984; Simon, 1985; Streibel, 1984).

Summary
The literature discussed in this section illustrates how numerous and diverse the unsupported claims about both positive and negative effects of microcomputer use on pre-

schoolers have been. Further, such related issues as the adequacy of available software, the readiness of young children to use microcomputers, and the preparation of teachers have been addressed and debated by numerous authors. This literature is valuable because it suggests several areas of needed research and can aid researchers in delineating specific questions and identifying independent and dependent variables. Following the review of actual research conducted in this area, some of these suggested research questions and variables will be discussed.

Results of Completed Research

The search for reports of completed research dealing with microcomputer use by preschoolers (3 to 5 years of age) resulted in disappointingly few studies, especially ones that were methodologically strong and/or included adequate information about the research design, measurement, and data analysis procedures. Because of these limitations, the search was extended beyond preschool age to include studies involving slightly older children (i.e., 6- and 7-year-olds). The focus of the search (and of this review) remained, however, on studies involving children ages 3 to 5. The discussion that follows is organized according to the principal type of design used in each study: true-experimental; quasi-experimental; pre-experimental and correlational; and descriptive.

True-experimental Studies
Eight studies were located that utilized true-experimental designs (random assignment of subjects to groups), but only five of them involved preschool-age children. These studies represent a myriad of different purposes, independent variables, and dependent variables.

Chatman, Love-Clark, and Ash (1984) investigated the effects of "touch-tone feedback" on task learning. Twenty 4-year-old Head Start children worked individually with a software program designed to teach the emergency number 911. A random half of the group received touch-tone feedback on correct and incorrect responses; the other group received no feedback. The results were reported sketchily but seemed to show no significant differences between the groups in the ability to perform the task successfully. In a study of the relative effectiveness of different computer-assisted instruction (CAI) programs, Watkins and Abram (1985) randomly divided 103 first graders into two groups. The experimental group used a reading software program for 12 weeks; the other group (called a "placebo control group") used a math software program instead. There were no significant differences between the two groups' average scores on the Iowa Test of Basic Skills reading subtest.

Three of the true-experimental studies involved comparisons of LOGO (or LOGO-like) programs with CAI-type programs. Clements and Gullo (1984) studied 18 6-year-olds over a 12-week period to determine the relative effects of learning to program with LOGO versus CAI microcomputer programs. On the post-tests, the LOGO group performed significantly better than the CAI group on measures of cognitive style (reflectivity and divergent thinking), metacognitive ability, and ability to describe directions; there were no significant differences between the groups on measures of cognitive development (operational competence and general cognitive measures). In a somewhat similar study (Emihovich, Miller, & Clare, 1985), cognitive processing, comprehension, and "self-monitoring" skills were compared for two randomly assigned groups of seven children ages 4 to 6: one that had used LOGO for 3 weeks and another that had instead spent the time in play activities and in using CAI-type software. Apparently, there were no significant differences between the two groups on any of the dependent variables except one—the ability to detect errors—on which the LOGO group did significantly better. Shade and Watson (1985) randomly assigned 41 2- and 3-year-olds, and their mothers, to either a "microworld computer experience" (a LOGO-type activity that taught the concept of inside/outside) or an "alphabet computer experience" (a CAI-type program that taught ABC's). There was no significant main effect for the group differences on the post-test (a sorting task).

The other three studies in this category dealt with differential effects of various types of interactions that children can have while using microcomputers. Strein and Kachman (1984) randomly assigned 26 children (ages 4 and 5) to either a "cooperative," a "competitive," or an "individualistic" condition of microcomputer use. The children used a microcomputer software game for six 10- to 15-min. sessions. No significant differences were found among the three groups on either of two measures of cooperative behaviors. Pettito and Newman (1984) conducted a study with 19 second-grade students to compare a "turn-taking" with a "collaborative" approach to using microcomputers. Working in small groups, the children used a software program that taught numerical concepts and graphing; all sessions were audiotaped and videotaped. Although the findings were not presented in detail, they seemed to indicate that less talking occurred in the turn-taking groups and that the collaborative groups used a more systematic approach to solving the problem presented by the software. Finally, Goodwin, Goodwin, Nansel, and Helm (in press) investigated the relative effectiveness of "adult-assisted," "adult-unassisted," and no microcomputer use in terms of 3- and 4-year-olds' knowledge of reading readiness concepts and their attitudes toward the microcomputer. Children in each of the two microcomputer groups worked with CAI programs designed to teach prereading skills. There were no significant differences in the three groups' average scores on the cognitive posttest. On the attitudinal posttest, however, the control group demonstrated significantly higher interest in the microcomputer than did either of the experimental groups.

Quasi-experimental Studies

Six studies were located that appeared to have used quasi-experimental designs, but only four were pertinent to this review. Keller and Shanahan (1983) taught a group of 19 kindergarten children to program and control a robot ("Big Trak") over a 28-week period. The control group consisted of children matched with the experimental group on gross and fine motor skills, age, and concepts and communication skills. The findings were not presented in detail, but the authors implied that the Big Trak group scored higher than the control group on listening and mathematics subtests of a standardized achievement test.

Three studies employed repeated measures or time series types of design. Worden, Kee, and Ingle (1985) compared parent-child interaction in two contexts for a group of 20 children (all 3 years old): a book-reading and a CAI-type microcomputer activity. Each parent-child dyad was videotaped in two 12-min. sessions of each activity. There were significantly more verbalizations, and more content was covered, in the book-reading activity than in the computer activity; parents were more directive and the children asked more questions during the computer sessions. Another study that used this type of design was reported by Warash (1984). The 10 children in this study were asked to talk about pictures they drew under two conditions: first with markers (i.e., hand drawn) and then with a computer program. On average, they verbalized significantly more about their computer pictures than about their hand-drawn ones. This suggested to the author that use of the microcomputer may enhance the development of young children's language and motor skills. In a project conducted at North Carolina University, 31 4-year-olds' free play choices were observed and recorded before, during, and following the introduction of a microcomputer into the center (Lipinski, Nida, Shade, & Watson, 1984). Although the presence of the microcomputer initially changed the children's free play choices, the pattern of choices returned to baseline levels after just a few weeks. Also studied with this same sample were the social interactions of the children at the microcomputer as compared with other free play areas in the center (Nida, Lipinski, Shade, & Watson, 1984). Generally, no significant or consistent differences in social interaction patterns were found among the play areas or across the weeks of the study period.

The final two quasi-experimental studies were conducted in the early 1970s (thus preceeding the age of microcomputers) and involved first graders; hence, they are only indirectly related to this review. In both, the academic achievement of a group of children who had used CAI programs was compared with that of a control group (no CAI). Feldman and Sears (1970) found no significant differences between the two groups. Other researchers (Atkinson & Fletcher, 1972; Fletcher & Atkinson, 1972) reported larger pre-post gains for the CAI group as compared with the control group.

Pre-experimental and Correlational Studies

Studies in this category are of two general types: (a) ones that used either a one-group, pre-post design or a two-group, posttest-only design and attempted to answer cause-and-effect research questions; or (b) ones that used correlational methods and attempted to answer correlational questions. Because the pre-experimental type tend to have so many threats to internal and external validity (Campbell & Stanley, 1971), they are discussed here along with the correlational studies. It should be noted, too, that a few of the studies discussed in this section may actually have used quasi-experimental designs; however, the information provided in the reports or articles was insufficient to make that kind of assumption easily.

Five studies used a one-group, pre-post design and all reported positive pre-post changes for young children exposed to microcomputers. Hines (1983) studied five kindergarten children who spent 10 weeks learning LOGO. She reported increases in their number and letter recognition skills; their understanding of spatial concepts and number quantity; their abilities to perform Piagetian tasks; and their understanding of, and attitudes toward, the microcomputer. Casey (1984) described what happened when five 5-year-olds used a microcomputer with a speech synthesizer and special software to develop a group story; she reported that the microcomputer experience increased the children's participation and involvement in the activity as well as their language and print production. Smithy-Willis, Riley, and Smith (1982) claimed that six children (ages 3 and 4) significantly improved their ability to discriminate letters after using a visual discrimination software program for 3 weeks. Prinz, Nelson, and Stedt (1982) found significant gains on word recognition and identification among 10 deaf preschoolers who used specially designed microcomputers and individually designed programs that taught beginning reading concepts and skills. Piestrup (1981, 1982; "Preschoolers Learn," 1982) conducted a study at Stanford University's Bing Nursery School with 55 3- and 4-year-olds. For 3 weeks, the children used a microcomputer software program that dealt with the concepts of "right," "left," "above," and "below." Significant pre-post increases in their knowledge of these concepts were reported.

Three studies used a two-group, posttest-only design. Hungate (1982) compared the performance of four microcomputer-experienced and six microcomputer-inexperienced kindergartners on six tasks like those taught by the software. The experimental group had spent 9 months working with software programs that covered basic math concepts, visual discrimination skills, and name and telephone number practice. The average difference in proportion of correct responses for the two groups was .095, favoring the experimental group. Using 75 3- to 6-year-old Head Start children, Hungate and Heller (1984) investigated differences in "on-task performance" (the number of software programs mastered and the average number mastered per unit of time) according to whether, and what type of, feedback was provided by the software. No significant differences were found for the feedback versus no-feedback comparison. Among those children receiving software feedback, however, the group who had received global feedback (i.e., information on long-range progress toward a goal) demonstrated greater on-task performance than the group who had received local feedback (i.e., feedback on the last keypress only). Muller and Perlmutter (1984) observed 27 4-year-old children using microcomputer learning games for 9 weeks and 18 children engaged in jigsaw puzzle problem-solving for 5 weeks. They found that the microcomputer group displayed more peer interaction than did the jigsaw puzzle group.

Six studies belonging in this category were correlational in purpose, and all of them used a "criterion-group" design (Vockell, 1983). Further, four of these studies investigated relationships between sex (male vs. female) and variables related to microcomputer use. Vartuli, Hill, Loncar, and Caccamo (1984a) compared the "computer success" (ability to use the microcomputer hardware and CAI-type software, program interest, and robot use and simple LOGO programming skills) of boys and girls ages 3 to 5. They reported that, although the girls had higher levels of computer competency and interest than the boys, the boys outperformed the girls on the robot tasks. In two of these studies, the preferred type of software (LOGO or "problem-solving" type versus CAI or "drill and practice" type) was compared for boys and girls. Swigger, Campbell, and Swigger (1983) found that girls chose the CAI-type programs more often than the LOGO-type programs, whereas boys displayed the reverse pattern. Sherman, Divine, and Johnson (1985) found no sex differences in preferences for the two types of programs but did report that both boys and girls consistently preferred the problem-solving software programs to the drill and practice ones. In a study with 4- and 5-year-

olds, Klinzing (1985) observed children's and teachers' behaviors at computer stations as well as at other activity stations within a preschool and concluded that there were no significant sex (or age) differences in the children's activity choices or their types of play behaviors.

The fifth criterion-group study, reported by Cuneo (1985), examined the relationship between age (4- and 5-year-olds vs. 6- and 7-year-olds) and the number and type of misunderstandings demonstrated by the children as they tried to program the LOGO turtle. She found that the younger children more often systematically misunderstood the turtle commands and that their types of misunderstanding were predictable by Piaget's theory. Finally, Johnson (1985) described the results of a study that investigated the relationships between interest in the microcomputer (high, moderate, or low) and various cognitive and social variables. There were no significant relationships between microcomputer interest and the variables of social maturity, potential creativity, social-cognitive ability, or social knowledge; however, the highly interested group had high levels of "representational competence" and displayed more organized and less concrete forms of free play behaviors than did the other groups.

Descriptive Studies

This last category of completed research studies represents a "mixed bag" of variables studied and research approaches used. The unifying characteristic of the studies cited here is their use of some type of descriptive research method.

Several investigators have used a case study approach. Weir et al. (1982) reported on the reactions of two preschool-age children with cerebral palsy to microcomputer experiences. After being taught LOGO on specially modified microcomputers for several weeks, both were able to use the program to draw steps, houses, and the like, and were reportedly more communicative than before. Lawler (1980) discussed how one 6-year-old girl learned to write a short story with the aid of a microcomputer. Staples (1981) described the experiences of two children (ages 3 and 9) in the Computer Gallery at Sesame Place in Pennsylvania. The older one used and enjoyed most of the microcomputer learning programs

253

and games, but, due to his inability to read, the younger did not.

In a number of studies, observations of young children in the process of using microcomputers constituted the principal research and measurement methodology. Hungate and Heller (1984) observed 75 preschoolers and concluded that most of them could find and press particular keys but that they often engaged in random, playful key pressing. Others who have reported similar findings—that preschoolers are able to use the keyboard—include Paris and Morris (1985); Shade, Daniel, Nida, Lipinski, and Watson (1983); and Vartuli, Hill, Loncar, and Caccamo (1984b). In addition, these groups of researchers indicated that the children were able to help or teach each other effectively; that they preferred programs that allowed them to press any key to get a response and were animated, colorful, and accompanied by music; and that plenty of social interaction occurred among them while using the microcomputer. By observing 44 preschoolers for 3 weeks, Swigger and Swigger (1984) also discovered that the microcomputer did not disrupt pre-existing social patterns in the classroom.

Two descriptive studies involved programming. Ross and Campbell (1983) described a class of 28 first graders in a Montessori school who learned to use microcomputers as calculators and for writing simple BASIC programs. The Lamplighter School LOGO Project in Dallas, in which 50 microcomputers were made available for use by children ages 3 to 9, was discussed by Watt (1982). He observed that 4-year-olds constructed geometric figures with LOGO but also noted that the microcomputers had not been integrated into the curriculum nor been used in research studies as originally planned.

In a study of the kinds of questions children ask while using microcomputers, 7- and 8-year-old children were taperecorded while they used CAI-type programs in math, language arts, and social sciences. Their questions were classified into eight categories, and the majority fell in the categories of "keyboard," "program instruction," and "data entry" (Shaw, Swigger, & Herndon, 1984). Finally, Rotenberg (1984) reported descriptive program evaluation results for "Writing to Read," a program that uses specially designed software to teach kindergartners and first graders how to write stories. Teachers and parents perceived that the children had improved their creativity and attitudes toward reading and writing; however, "outsiders" (e.g., university professors) were critical of the program's emphasis on monotonous drill and practice.

Summary

Certainly, the combination of young children and microcomputers has generated much enthusiasm and many interesting ideas about fruitful use of this new technology. At the same time, our review of published and unpublished research results highlights the paucity of methodologically strong research studies on the effects of microcomputer use by preschoolers. Six major limitations—methodological and substantive—can be noted. First, only five studies (Chatman et al., 1984; Emihovich et al., 1985; Goodwin et al., in press; Shade & Watson, 1985; Strein & Kachman, 1984) directly involved preschoolers *and* used true-experimental designs. Because the majority of the investigations were aimed at detecting *effects* of microcomputer use on young children, or the *relative effectiveness* of such characteristics as type of software or type of feedback provided by the software programs, the lack of well-controlled designs is unfortunate and weakens the overall credibility of this body of research. Second, the samples used in most of the studies tended to be drawn by convenience sampling methods, and thus their representativeness of larger populations of chidren was unknown. Relatedly, the size of most of the samples was fairly small. Of the 37 studies cited that reported sample sizes, the mean and median number of subjects were 32.82 and 28, respectively. Third, the psychometric properties (validity and reliability) of the instruments used in these studies were largely unknown (or at least were not discussed in the written reports.) Exceptions occurred, of course, in that a few researchers used well-known standardized tests and/or discussed the instrumentation and psychometric properties in some detail (e.g., Clements & Gullo, 1984; Keller & Shanahan, 1983; Shaw et al., 1984). A fourth and related weakness of many of the studies was that too few details were provided about the design, sampling, instrumentation, data analysis, and results—rendering it difficult indeed to comprehend, synthesize, and summarize the research. Fifth, relatively few studies (only 22, or 55%, of all 40 studies mentioned here) were focused on the use of microcomputers by *preschoolers*—children ages 3 to 5—although those that included kindergartners or first graders certainly are relevant to the general research area.

A final weakness or limitation in the literature concerns the incongruity between the pronounced or speculated effects of microcomputer use on preschoolers and the actual effects documented via completed research. Of the long "laundry list" of presumed effects described earlier—ranging from the acquisition of programming skills to the development of thinking skills and self-confidence—very few have been studied empirically, and even fewer have been studied with appropriate designs and procedures. In addition, the reservations and cautions—such as those pertaining to requisite skills needed for beneficial use of microcomputers by preschoolers—have not been empirically tested. Because so much of the literature on this topic is in publications easily accessible to parents and teachers, the critical need for more careful empirical research is obvious.

From this body of research, what do we know about microcomputer use by preschoolers? Very little, actually, although a few possible trends emerge from viewing the findings as a whole. One is that most preschoolers probably can learn to operate the keyboard, although the most appropriate or effective role for teachers is unclear. Second, it does not appear that children's social interaction patterns or free play/activity choices are markedly disrupted by the introduction of microcomputers in preschools. Third, there is a very weak suggestion that some learning, specific to the content of the software programs, may occur as a result of using CAI-type programs; it must be noted, however, that most of the studies that have yielded this kind of finding have used a one-group, pretest-posttest design. The results of the stronger true- and quasi-experimental designs tend to demonstrate no consistently significant effects. Fourth, the presence or absence of specific or local feedback in the software programs seems to make little difference in terms of learning outcomes. Fifth, differential learning effects of LOGO or other problem-solving programs versus CAI-type, "drill and practice" programs generally have not been found. And, sixth, there appear to be no consistent sex differences in microcomputer competency, interest, or choice of various types of software.

Research Recommendations

The research recommendations presented below are based on our critical review and analysis of pronouncements and speculations concerning microcomputer use with young children and the research results currently available in this area. This is not an exhaustive list of recommendations, but it does represent some major ideas that emerged after reviewing how previous research studies were conducted and what research questions were (and were not) investigated.

1. Before researchers attempt to answer cause-and-effect research questions (which have been largely uppermost thus far), they might first consider conducting descriptive and correlational research studies on some basic, unanswered questions about preschoolers and microcomputers. Included here would be the following general question areas: (a) Are preschoolers interested in using microcomputers and, if so, at what age does this interest develop? (b) What verbal and nonverbal behaviors do preschoolers exhibit when sitting in front of a microcomputer? (c) Do preschoolers react differently to microcomputers when confronted with them alone versus in pairs or small groups? Do such reactions differ if an adult is present? (d) How long will preschoolers remain at the microcomputer before becoming bored, inattentive, or disruptive? Do they remain interested for longer periods of time with certain types of software? (e) What are the characteristics of the software programs that preschoolers prefer? (f) What changes occur in interest level, type of use, etc. after preschoolers have been exposed to microcomputers for several weeks or months? (g) What are the concerns and questions that teachers and parents have about preschoolers' use of microcomputers? (h) How do such personological variables as sex, age, ethnicity, outside-school experiences with microcomputers, aptitude, and so on, correlate with microcomputer-related interest and behavioral variables?

2. Optimally, the results of this descriptive and correlational research would help in planning relevant and well-controlled experimental research studies. The list of possible experimental (cause-and-effect) research ques-

tions is practically endless. Finding out whether microcomputers are responsible for all of the cognitive, affective, and psychomotor outcomes that have been presumed by others would constitute numerous research studies. Besides using tightly controlled true- or quasi-experimental designs, the samples should be representative and fairly large, and subjects should be stratified on relevant attribute-independent variables. Further, the exact nature of the active independent variable (loosely conceived of as "microcomputer use or no use") needs to be made clear. What software programs were used and for how long? What role did the teachers or other adults assume during the study? Did the subjects use the microcomputers individually or in small groups? In what kind of setting did the study take place? What activities did the children in the control or comparison groups engage in during the study? Answers to these questions are important in interpreting and generalizing the findings.

The active independent variables in experimental studies might also involve systematic variation of software- and use-related conditions. Among these variables are (a) type of software; (b) content area of software; (c) type of use (e.g., group vs. individual); (d) type of teacher role (e.g., active instructor vs. observer); (e) type of sequencing of presentation of different kinds of information; (f) presence versus absence of humor, animation, color, music, and the like; (g) time of day when microcomputers are used; and (h) length of sessions at the microcomputer as well as length of total exposure time. Determining the relative effectiveness of microcomputer use for a wide variety of instructional purposes and software contents is certainly important to persons wanting to use research findings to make wise decisions about introducing or using microcomputers in preschools.

3. The instruments used to measure the dependent variables should be carefully developed, pilot tested for validity and reliability estimation, and thoroughly described in the research reports. As indicated earlier, one weakness of the existing research literature is the dearth of information about measurement procedures.

4. A final recommendation is that short-time *and* long-term effects of microcomputer use by preschoolers be studied. As Clark (1984) noted in his discussion of previous computer research (primarily on the effects of computer-based instruction, or CBI), the novelty effect was apparent when shorter and longer term studies were compared. Immediate effects, favoring CBI, frequently disappeared when dependent variables were remeasured at a later point in time. Such a situation could easily occur when preschoolers are the subjects. Longitudinal studies, with repeated measurements of the dependent variables (and with measurements of related variables to assess extent of transfer), would help greatly in understanding the nature of any effects that microcomputers produce in young children and in determining the effects' longevity.

Microcomputers are an exciting and promising new technology, with many interesting possible uses for preschool-age children. Although some researchers have begun to answer pertinent questions about microcomputer use by preschoolers, much empirical work still needs to be done. It is hoped that research-based answers to some of the critical questions concerning if, when, and how microcomputers can best be used by this age group will begin to emerge in the near future.

REFERENCES

Atkinson, R. C., & Fletcher, J. D. (1972). Teaching children to read with a computer. *The Reading Teacher, 25*, 319–327.

Barnes, B. J., & Hill, S. (1983). Should young children work with microcomputers: LOGO before Lego? *The Computing Teacher, 10*(9), 11–14.

Bitter, G. (1982). It's never too early to learn: Getting K–3 students involved with computers. *Educational Computer Magazine, 2*(3), 12.

Bork, A. (1984). Computer futures for education. *Creative Computing, 10*, 178–180.

Bowman, R. P., & Rotter, J. C. (1983). Computer games: Friend or foe? *Elementary School Guidance and Counseling Journal, 18*, 25–33.

Brady, E. H., & Hill, S. (1984). Young children and microcomputers: Research issues and directions. *Young Children, 39*(3), 49–61.

Burg, K. (1984). The microcomputer in the kindergarten. *Young Children, 39*(3), 28–33.

Campbell, S. (1985). Early childhood: Preschoolers meet a high tech turtle. *Science and Children, 22*(7), 37–40.

Campbell, T., & Stanley, J. C. (1971). *Experimental and quasi-experimental designs for research.* Chicago: Rand McNally.

Casey, J. C. (1984, March). *Beginning reading in-*

struction: Using the LEA approach with and without microcomputer intervention. Paper presented at the annual meeting of the Western Regional Conference of the International Reading Association, Reno. (ERIC Document Reproduction Service No. ED 245 192)

Chatman, S., Love-Clark, P., & Ash, M. (1984, April). Microcomputers in early childhood psychological research. Paper presented at the annual meeting of the American Educational Research Association, New Orleans.

Chin, K. (1984a). In the school room 'A' is for access. InfoWorld, 6(8), 26–27.

Chin, K. (1984b). Personal computing: Too much, too soon? InfoWorld, 6(8), 24–26.

Clark, R. E. (1984, April). Learning from computers: Theoretical problems. Paper presented at the annual meeting of the American Educational Research Association, New Orleans.

Clements, D. H., & Gullo, D. F. (1984). Effects of computer programming on young children's cognition. Journal of Educational Psychology, 76, 1051–1058.

Cuffaro, H. K. (1984). Microcomputers in education: Why is earlier better? Teachers College Record, 85, 559–568.

Cuneo, D. O. (1985, April). Young children and turtle graphics programming: Understanding turtle commands. Paper presented at the biennial meeting of the Society for Research in Child Development, Toronto. (ERIC Document Reproduction Service No. ED 260 800)

Damarin, S. K. (1982). The impact of computer technology on children. Paper presented at the symposium on the Impact of Computer Technology on Children, American Society of Information Scientists, Columbus, OH.

Dickerson, L., & Pritchard, W. H. (1981). Microcomputers and education: Planning for the coming revolution in the classroom. Educational Technology, 21(1), 7–12.

Emihovich, C., Miller, G. E., & Clare, V. (1985, March–April). Learning LOGO: The social context of cognition. Paper presented at the annual meeting of the American Educational Research Association, Chicago. (ERIC Document Reproduction Service No. ED 261 662)

Favaro, P. (1983). My five year old knows BASIC. Creative Computing, 9, 158–166.

Fletcher, J. D., & Atkinson, R. C. (1972). Evaluation of the Stanford CAI program in initial reading. Journal of Educational Psychology, 63, 597–602.

Feldman, D. H., & Sears, P. S. (1970). Effects of computer assisted instruction on children's behavior. Educational Technology, 20(3), 11–14.

Gallini, J. K. (1983). What computer-assisted instruction can offer toward the encouragement of creative thinking. Educational Technology, 23(4), 7–11.

Getman, G. N. (1983). Computers in the classroom, Bane or boon? Academic Therapy, 18, 517–524.

Goodwin, L. D., Goodwin, W. L., Nansel, A., & Helm, C. (in press). Cognitive and affective effects of various types of microcomputer use by preschoolers. American Educational Research Journal.

Hines, S. N. (1983). Computer programming abilities of 5-year-old children. Educational Computer Magazine, 3(4), 10–12.

Hirschberg, P. (1981). Compu-tots and other joys of museum life. Instructional Innovator, 26(6), 28–31.

Hoot, J. L. (1984). Computers and very young children: Educational promise and problems. (ERIC Document Reproduction Service No. ED 235 897)

Hungate, H. (1982). Computers in the kindergarten. The Computing Teacher, 9(5), 15–18.

Hungate, H., & Heller, J. I. (1984, April). Preschool children and microcomputers. Paper presented at the annual meeting of the American Educational Research Association, New Orleans.

Johnson, J. E. (1985). Characteristics of preschoolers interested in microcomputers. Journal of Educational Research, 78, 299–305.

Jones, R. (1980). Microcomputers: Their uses in primary schools. Cambridge Journal of Education, 10, 144–153.

Keller, J., & Shanahan, D. (1983). Robots in the kindergarten. The Computing Teacher, 10(9), 66–67.

Kimmel, S. (1981). Programs for preschoolers: Starting out young. Creative Computing, 7(10), 44–53.

Klinzing, D. G. (1985, March–April). A study of the behavior of children in a preschool equipped with computers. Paper presented at the annual meeting of the American Educational Research Association, Chicago.

Lawler, R. W. (1980). One child's learning: Introducing writing with a computer. (ERIC Document Reproduction Service No. ED 208 415)

Lee, M. W. (1984, November). An electric preschool: Pros and cons. Paper presented at the annual meeting of the National Association for the Education of Young Children, Los Angeles. (ERIC Document Reproduction Service No. ED 257 551)

Lipinski, J. M., Nida, R. E., Shade, D. D., & Watson, J. A. (1984). Competence, gender, and preschoolers' free play choices when a microcomputer is present in the classroom. (ERIC Document Reproduction Service No. ED 243 609)

Lucas, J. P. (1980). Programs for small children. Creative Computing, 6(3), 136–137.

Magarrell, J. (1982). Notes on computers. The Chronicle of Higher Education, 25(8), 3.

Mandell, A. (1983). Mind their Ps and Qs. *Classroom Computer News, 3*(3), 66.

Martin, K. (1981). The learning machines. *Arithmetic Teacher, 29*(3), 41–43.

McCrory, J. C. (1984, March). *So you have one computer? What now?* Paper presented at the annual meeting of the Southern Association for Children Under Six, Lexington, KY. (ERIC Document Reproduction Service No. ED 251 190)

Monahan, B., & Monahan, T. A. (1982). *Compute first, read and write later.* (ERIC Document Reproduction Service No. ED 226 357)

Muller, A. A., & Perlmutter, M. (1984). *Preschool children's problem-solving interactions at computers and jigsaw puzzles.* (ERIC Document Reproduction Service No. ED 248 013)

Muller, J. (1983). The million dollar smile. *The Computing Teacher, 10*(6), 20–22.

Nida, R. E., Lipinski, J. M., Shade, D. D., & Watson, J. A. (1984). *Introducing a microcomputer to a preschool classroom: The effects on children's social interacting.* (ERIC Document Reproduction Service No. ED 243 607)

Ohanian, S. (1983). Beware the rosy view! *Classroom Computer Learning 4*(3), 22–27.

Olds, H. F. (1982). Logic at play in moptown. *Classroom Computer News, 3*(2), 54–59.

O'Malley, C. (1985). Boosting your child's creativity. *Personal Computing, 9*(3), 100–107.

Papert, S. (1980). *Mindstorms: Children, computers, and powerful ideas.* New York: Basic.

Paris, C. L., & Morris, S. K. (1985, March). *The computer in the early childhood classroom: Peer helping and peer teaching.* Paper presented at the Microworld for Young Children Conference, College Park, MD. (ERIC Document Reproduction Service No. ED 257 555)

Partridge, S. (1984). *Using computers with little children: A discussion.* (ERIC Document Reproduction Service No. ED 253 349)

Petitto, A. L., & Newman, D. (1984, April). *Forming new goals in microcomputer interactions.* Paper presented at the annual meeting of the American Educational Research Association, New Orleans.

Piaget, J., & Inhelder, B. (1969). *The psychology of the child.* New York: Basic.

Piestrup, A. M. (1981). *Preschool children use Apple II to test reading skills programs.* (ERIC Document Reproduction Service No. ED 202 476)

Piestrup, A. M. (1982). *Young children use computer graphics.* (ERIC Document Reproduction Service No. ED 224 564)

Preschoolers learn using microcomputers (1982). *Classroom Computer News, 2*(5), 13–14.

Prinz, P. M., Nelson, K. E., & Stedt, J. D. (1982). Early reading in young deaf children using microcomputer technology. *American Annals of the Deaf, 127,* 528–535.

Ross, S. M., & Campbell, L. (1983). Computer-based education in the Montessori classroom: A compatible mixture? *Technologic Horizons in Education, 10*(6), 105–109.

Rotenberg, L. (1984). Two nationwide programs that use computers to teach reading. *Teaching and Computers, 1*(8), 16–19.

School uses of microcomputers: Reports from a national survey (Issue No. 1). (1983). Baltimore: Johns-Hopkins University, Center for Social Organization of Schools.

Shade, D. D., Daniel, G. E., Nida, R. E., Lipinski, J. M., & Watson, J. A. (1983). *Microcomputers: A close look at what happens when preschool children interact with age-appropriate software.* (ERIC Document Reproduction Service No. ED 243 608)

Shade, D. D., & Watson, J. A. (1985, April). *In mother's lap: The effect of microcomputers on mother teaching behavior and young children's classification skills.* Paper presented at the biennial meeting of the Society for Research in Child Development, Toronto. (ERIC Document Reproduction Service No. ED 257 581)

Shaw, D. G., Swigger, K. M., & Herndon, J. (1984, April). *Children's questions: A study of questions children ask while learning to use a computer.* Paper presented at the annual meeting of the American Educational Research Association, New Orleans.

Sherman, J., Divine, K. P., & Johnson, B. (1985). An analysis of computer software preferences of preschool children. *Educational Technology, 25*(5), 39–41.

Silvern, S. G. (1983). Opening the door to the microworld. *Childhood Education, 59,* 219–221.

Simon, T. (1985). Play and learning with computers. *Early Child Development and Care, 19,* 69–78.

Smithy-Willis, D., Riley, M. T., & Smith, D. (1982). Visual discrimination and preschoolers. *Educational Computer Magazine, 2*(6), 19, 45.

Snyder, T. D. (1985). Trends in education. *Principal, 65*(1), 57–61.

Spencer, M., & Baskin, L. (1983). *Microcomputers in early childhood education.* (ERIC Document Reproduction Service No. ED 227 967)

Staples, B. (1981). A visit to Sesame Place. *Creative Computing 7*(1), 56–60.

Staples, B. (1984). Growing up literate. *Creative Computing, 10*(4), 64–76.

Steffin, S. A. (1982). A challenge to Seymour Papert. *Educational Computer Magazine, 2*(4), 34, 36.

Streibel, M. J. (1984, April). *An analysis of the theoretical foundations for the use of microcomputers in early childhood education.* Paper presented at the annual meeting of the American Educational Research Association, New Orleans. (ERIC Document Reproduction Service No. ED 248 971)

Strein, W., & Kachman, W. (1984). Effects of computer games on young children's cooperative behavior: An exploratory study. *Journal of Research and Development in Education, 18*(1), 40–43.

Swigger, K. M. (1983a). Do you know a four-year-old child who can program? *Educational Computer Magazine, 3*(5), 70, 88.

Swigger, K. M. (1983b). More programs for kids. *Educational Computer Magazine, 3*(3), 24–25.

Swigger, K. M., Campbell, J., & Swigger, B. K. (1983). Preschool children's preferences of different types of CAI programs. *Educational Computer Magazine, 3*(1), 38–40.

Swigger, K. M., & Swigger, B. K. (1984). Social patterns and computer use among preschool children. *AEDS Journal, 17*(3), 35–41.

Tan, L. E. (1985). Computers in pre-school education. *Early Child Development and Care, 19,* 319–336.

Tursman, C. (1982). Powerful ideas. *Educational Leadership, 40*(2), 68–70.

Vaidya, S. R. (1984). Making LOGO accessible to preschool children. *Educational Technology, 24*(7), 30–31.

Vartuli, S., Hill, S., Loncar, K., & Caccamo, N. (1984a). *Research on using computers with preschool-age children.* (ERIC Document Reproduction Service No. ED 256 516)

Vartuli, S., Hill, S., Loncar, K., & Caccamo, N. (1984b). *Selecting and evaluating software for use in a preschool classroom: From the young child's and researcher's perspective.* (ERIC Document Reproduction Service No. ED 259 838)

Vockell, E. L. (1983). *Educational research.* New York: Macmillan.

Walker, D. F. (1983). Reflections on the educational potential and limitations of microcomputers. *Phi Delta Kappan, 65*(2), 103–107.

Warash, B. G. (1984, April). *Computer language experience approach.* Paper presented at the annual meeting of the National Council of Teachers of English Spring Conference, Columbus, OH. (ERIC Document Reproduction Service No. ED 244 264)

Watkins, M. W., & Abram, S. (1985). Reading CAI with first grade students. *The Computing Teacher, 12*(7), 43–45.

Watt, D. (1982). LOGO in the schools. *BYTE, 7*(8), 116–134.

Weir, S., Russell, S. J., & Valente, J. A. (1982). LOGO: An approach to educating disabled children. *BYTE, 7*(9), 342–360.

Worden, P. E., Kee, D. W., & Ingle, M. J. (1985, April). *Preschoolers' alphabet learning activities with their parents: Picture-book vs. personal computer software.* Paper presented at the biennial meeting of the Society for Research in Child Development, Toronto. (ERIC Document Reproduction Service No. ED 258 710)

Ziajka, A. (1983). Microcomputers in early childhood education? A first look. *Young Children, 38*(5), 61–67.

ASK YOURSELF:
Identifying Issues for Debate and Advocacy

1. Gersten and White (1986) contend that equating child-initiated activities with active learning and teacher-directed activities with passive learning misrepresents various preschool curriculum models and preschoolers' actual experiences. They believe that early childhood education needs to move away from emotional phrases such as *high quality* and *whole child* and carefully examine what is happening in preschool settings. Do you agree or disagree with these arguments? Explain. For example, is a quality learning experience one where a child moves to a sandbox, builds a sand castle, and then hears a teacher say that she or he did a nice job of castle building?

2. Does a preschool child have any use for reading, or is play the preschool child's work?

3. If children learn to read early, will they be more likely to experience success in elementary school?

4. What is an appropriate context for the literacy development of young children?

5. Why are workbooks inappropriate instructional materials for young children? (Also see Kamii, 1985.)

6. Is use of a microcomputer by preschool children a significant educational experience in an early childhood program? Why or why not? (Also see Bredekamp, 1987).

7. What kinds of information should a teacher have before instituting a new curriculum or new technology? What are the sources of such information? Why should learning processes as well as learning outcomes be considered in the evaluation of educational materials and technology?

8. Every day at Cross Roads Day Care Center, the children gather at 9:15 for the calendar routine. For example, on the 24th of March, they counted the numbers on the calendar up to 24. Then they counted using first, second, third, and so on. Next, the preschoolers were asked what day it was, the weather outside, the name of the month, the name of the season, and the year. After this routine, the children moved into a circle for circle time and sang songs that they requested. Evaluate this routine in terms of the young child's early concept development.

9. Why are many parents interested in developing "superbabies"? Is this a syndrome of today's parents? (Also see Langway, Jackson, Zabarsky, Shirley, & Whitmore, 1983, and Sigel, 1987). Are these practices harmful or beneficial to young children?

10. How might an early childhood program undermine children's confidence in their own thinking (Katz, 1987)? How might assessment methods undermine young children's confidence in their own thinking? What would be alternatives to such programs or assessment methods?

11. If development were viewed in terms of long-term effects, transformational changes, and cumulative effects rather than in terms of developmental norms (Katz, 1987), what would be appropriate curriculum activities? What should preschoolers be doing now in terms of desirable long-term effects?

12. Are published guidelines for developmentally appropriate practices useful? Or are they too vague and too open to diverse interpretations? Explain. (How might such guidelines be misused? What precautions, if any, should be taken to guard against possible misuses?)

APPLICATION/ADVOCACY EXERCISES

1. Imagine that Cindy, the young mother in the vignette at the beginning of this chapter, comes to you with concerns about the kit and wants advice about responding to Grandma Kramer. In a small group with your classmates, prepare strategies and arguments to convince Grandma Kramer that this kit is an inappropriate activity. Consider what young children can do and what young children should do. Incorporate ideas from your readings.

2. Visit a kindergarten or nursery school classroom. Observe how much time is devoted to play or child-initiated activities. When are reading or literacy activities introduced? What types of literacy activities, if any, are occurring in the program? What types of teacher-led activities occur in the program? If computers are present, how are they used?

3. Using the information you have gathered from reading these selections and from class presentations, develop media materials (newspaper article, newsletter article, slide show, or videotape presentation) related to what are and are not developmentally appropriate practices in early education programs. Direct your remarks to parents or to the general public, and include visuals as well as oral or written messages that advocate developmentally appropriate programs for young children. Include examples of classroom methods, interaction styles, and materials. An alternative format would be a graphic, public information/advocacy display.

REFERENCES & SUGGESTED READINGS

Beardsley, L. V., & Marecek-Zeman, M. (1987). Making connections: Facilitating literacy in young children. *Childhood Education, 63,* 159–166.

Bredekamp, S. (Ed.). (1987). *Developmentally appropriate practice in early childhood programs serving children from birth through age 8.* Washington, DC: National Association for the Education of Young Children. (Major portions of this publication can be found in the September 1986 and January 1988 issues of *Young Children.*)

Cataldo, C. Z. (1984, January). Infant-toddler education: Blending the best approaches. *Young Children, 39,* 25–32.

Colangelo, N., & Fleuridas, C. (1986). The abdication of childhood. *Journal of Counseling and Development, 64,* 561–563.

Cuffaro, H. (1984). Microcomputers in the classroom: Why is earlier better? *Teachers College Record, 85,* 559–568.

Gersten, R., & White, W. A. T. (1986, November). Castles in the sand:

Response to Schweinhart and Weikart. *Educational Leadership, 19–20.*

Hitz, R., & Wright, D. (1988, May). Kindergarten issues: A practitioners' survey. *Principal, 28–30.*

Kamii, C. (1985, September). Leading primary education toward excellence: Beyond worksheets and drill. *Young Children, 40,* 3–9.

Karnowski, L. (1986, September). How young writers communicate. *Educational Leadership, 58–60.*

Katz, L. G. (1987, April). Discussion. In L. S. Scott (Chair), *Curricular demands appropriate for the urban kindergarten.* Symposium conducted at the meeting of the American Educational Research Association, Washington, DC.

Katz, L. G. (1987, October). Lilian Katz: Let's not underestimate young children's intellects. *Instructor, 16–19.*

Kitano, M. K. (1985). Ethnography of a preschool for the gifted: What gifted young children actually do. *Gifted Child Quarterly, 29,* 67–71.

Langway, L., Jackson, T., Zabarsky, M., Shirley, D., & Whitmore, J. (1983, March 28). Bringing up superbaby. *Newsweek, 62–68.*

Moyer, J., Egertson, H., & Isenberg, J. (1987). The child-centered kindergarten. *Childhood Education, 63,* 235–242.

On kindergarten graduations. (1988). *Childhood Education, 64,* 283.

Sigel, I. (1987). Does hothousing rob children of their childhood? *Early Childhood Research Quarterly, 2,* 211–225.

CHAPTER 10

Educating/Mainstreaming Handicapped and High-Risk Children

The Ins and Outs of Mainstreaming

"The last item on our policy board agenda concerns a letter from the Department of Social Services. I presume all of you have had time to read the copy that was mailed to you. The issue, of course, is whether our nursery school is able to accommodate an emotionally disturbed child."

"Just a minute, madam chairperson," interrupted Janice. "I've been doing an informal canvas of our car pool, and most mothers are very reluctant to admit a child who is so disruptive! We're all sympathetic with the plight of this particular family and want to help. But we wonder first of all whether it's our problem, and second, whether our children will suffer because of the extra care and attention that will be needed for this child. Many of us feel that we are paying good money for a high-quality educational experience for our children, and we think admitting this child will mess up a good thing."

Questions

1. Imagine that the chairperson of the policy board turns to you, a teacher at the nursery school, and asks for your opinion on the feasibility of enrolling this child. Would you agree or disagree with Janice? What would you say to advocate for or against inclusion of this child? Consider what conditions in classroom setting, teacher behavior, and parent relations would have to exist or be established for this child to be successfully enrolled.

2. If a teacher modifies the classroom structure to accommodate a handicapped child, is this change "fair" to the non-handicapped children? Why or why not?

PREVIEW

How would you feel if three special needs children were enrolled in your team-teaching classroom? What feelings of emotional stress might you experience? Do you think you might hear yourself say: "No problem really. Just cut back on the sugar in her diet and she'll be all right." "This poor, deaf child will never know the beauty of music." "I'm afraid I won't know what to do." "He can't go on the field trip to the wildlife preserve; he might get too tired." "Nothing I do will make much difference with this child" (White & Phair, 1986).

Successful education and integration of special needs children depends heavily upon the attitude of teachers. Anne H. Widerstrom and Curtis Dudley-Marling open this chapter with a discussion of the myths commonly associated with handicapped children. Next, Barbara J. Smith and Phillip S. Strain discuss issues associated with program quality and implementation of the 1986 federal legislation for early childhood special education. Samuel J. Meisels and Seymour J. Friedland propose that regular early childhood programs are uniquely suited to mainstreaming under certain conditions. Finally, Robert J. Trotter profiles the research of Tiffany Field on effective intervention with high-risk infants.

Living with a Handicapped Child: Myth and Reality

Anne H. Widerstrom and Curtis Dudley-Marling

During the past decade there has been much emphasis in the educational community on providing services to handicapped children. As services for these children and their families have multiplied, so has the interest of researchers in the dynamics involved in having a handicapped child in the family.

Early studies reported devastating effects of handicapping conditions on families, ranging from higher divorce rates for parents of handicapped children (Farber, 1959; Peck and Stephens, 1960) to higher incidence of emotional disturbance in siblings (Farber and Ryckman, 1965). These results led to certain myths concerning handicapped children and their families which may adversely affect the way teachers, psychologists and other professionals interact with these families in the delivery of services. These myths may especially affect expectations professionals have regarding the families' behavior and performance.

While it is obviously more difficult in some ways to have a handicapped child in the family, recent research suggests that for many families the effect is not so devastating as the myths might lead us to believe. In the following sections we will examine the research regarding several of these myths.

MYTH: Families with a handicapped child have more difficulty coping with daily living than families with nonhandicapped children.

It is often thought that living with a handicapped child must be a highly stressful experience, causing economic hardship, interfering with social and recreational activities, and resulting in poorly adjusted family members. This scenario may be representative of some families who have a handicapped member, but it also probably describes many families without a handicapped child. Although a few studies have reported a reduced quality of life for families of handicapped children, the research literature does not, for the most part, confirm such a stereotype. The studies that identify differences between families with handicapped children and other families tend to predate the passage of Public Law 94-142, the Education for All Handicapped Children Act, in 1975.

Waisbren (1980) compared the life of families with handicapped children in the United States with similar families in Denmark. The study included nonhandicapped control families in both countries. Families with a handicapped child were strikingly similar to families with a nonhandicapped child on dimensions of circumstances of the child's birth, mental health of the family, influence of the baby on the marriage, the parents' relationship with the child's siblings, support networks and future plans.

Both groups reported increased stress as a result of having a new baby. Suelzle and Keenan (1981) confirm that the birth of an infant almost always requires major adjustments of the parents as well as new role definitions. Waisbren (1980) reports that on the dimension of professional support—i.e., contact with medical professions—both American and Danish families with a handicapped

Source: Anne H. Widerstrom & Curtis Dudley-Marling (1986). Living with a handicapped child: Myth and reality. *Childhood Education, 62,* 359, 362, 364–367. Reprinted by permission of Anne H. Widerstrom, Curtis Dudley-Marling, and The Association for Childhood Education International, 11141 Georgia Avenue, Suite 200, Wheaton, MD. Copyright © 1986 by the Association.

child reported more involvement than those with a nonhandicapped child and found the professional services to be adequate and helpful to family adjustment. Like several other authors, Waisbren (1980) pointed out that all families experience stress at certain times; families with a handicapped child are no exception. In some ways these families experience more stress, but the families generally cope successfully.

Dunlap, in a comprehensive study of 400 families with developmentally disabled children in rural Alabama (Dunlap, 1976; Dunlap and Hollingsworth, 1977) found that the large majority of these families felt that their handicapped child did not create additional stress in their daily life. More specifically, these family members did not believe that the disabled child affected the choices or decisions made by the family, its closeness, or the employment of family members. The majority reported no effect on family recreation (64 percent) or outings (71 percent), on the father's job (85 percent) or whether the mother worked outside the home (72 percent) or on where the family lived (91 percent). Many other respondents who felt the handicapped child did have an effect on the family's life believed it to be a positive one. Most parents in this study perceived their disabled child to be well adjusted to family members, including siblings and grandparents, as well as to neighbors. Dunlap and Hollingsworth (1977) also reported that the degree of family adjustment depends to some extent on the child's handicapping condition, with more serious disorders like cerebral palsy and epilepsy being more stressful.

Several other studies have examined the negative effects on families with severely impaired children. Holroyd and McArthur (1976) examined the problems reported by mothers of autistic as compared to mothers of Down syndrome children and children who were undergoing evaluation in a neuropsychiatric clinic, and found more serious effects reported by mothers of the autistic children. These effects included worry about their child's impact on the rest of the family and more difficulties related to daily coping with the autistic child: physical care, keeping the child occupied and dealing with behavior problems. These mothers perceived their families as being less well integrated as a result of the child's presence. It should be noted that at the time of the study they were not reported to be receiving any pro-

fessional services (beyond diagnosis of the child's condition). Holroyd and McArthur (1976) found that the mothers of Down syndrome children and the mothers of the outpatient group believed their families to be well adjusted. It would appear that stress is, in this case, related to the severity of the child's handicap. This conclusion supports an early literature review by Farber and Ryckman (1965).

While certain characteristics of severely handicapped children may add to the family's stress (e.g., difficult behaviors, social obtrusiveness or low self-help abilities), Bristol and Schopler (1984) found that the family's adaptation to the child was more closely related to the perceived adequacy of both professional services and informal social support than to the severity of the handicap. In regard to services, Bristol and Schopler's (1984) longitudinal study of families of autistic children found that an important factor differentiating high-stress from low-stress families was the amount of training and support services the parents received. Availability of day care was seen as critical by Bristol and Schopler (1984) and Bronfenbrenner, Avgar and Henderson (1977). Wikler, Wasow and Hatfield (1981) determined through interviews conducted with a group of parents of mentally retarded children that they required a continuum of services over their entire life span. The parents in this study reported that their "chronic sorrow" was periodic, not continuous, and they needed professional services primarily during those stressful periods. They stated that availability of effective professional services during those periods was an important factor in their successful daily coping.

In regard to social support, Bristol and Schopler (1984) found the parents' belief system, especially the mother's, predictive of family adjustment and therefore of good family integration and cohesiveness. Better-adjusted families had a strong emphasis on moral or religious beliefs and on absence of guilt feelings or self-blame for the child's handicap. This is confirmed by Bradshaw and Lawton (1978). A third predictive factor was active involvement in recreation by the family as a group. Healthy families tended to be more involved in recreational activities.

In a naturalistic study of 12 families, 6 with a mentally retarded child and 6 with an orthopedically handicapped child, Turnbull, Summers and Brotherson (1983) found that while having a mentally retarded child is a stressful experience for a family at every stage of the life cycle, certain factors contribute to the family's adjustment and acceptance of the handicapped member. These factors include an effective system of communication among family members, a stable husband/wife relationship, adequate family income and adequate social support. Turnbull et al. (1983) gave several examples of the positive effect a handicapped child may have on the family's daily life, including helping elderly parents fight loneliness, helping siblings to learn to value differences in people and drawing the family closer together as a unit.

Several studies have suggested that single-parent families and families with nonworking mothers experience higher stress levels. Beckman-Bell (1980) and Holroyd (1974), for example, reported mothers in single-parent families to be under more stress than those in two-parent families. Tavormina, Boll, Dunn, Luncomb and Taylor (1975) found mothers employed outside the home to exhibit less stress in coping with family routine than nonworking mothers. Bristol and Schopler (1984), however, found few differences in the daily lives of the families they interviewed, whether they were single-parent or two-parent families, with or without mothers employed outside the home. The large majority of the families interviewed by Bristol and Schopler (1984) reported acceptance of their child, well-adjusted siblings and an average daily life.

In examining the daily life of a family, social interactions are an important variable. Two studies appear to present somewhat conflicting conclusions. An early study (McAllister, Butler and Lei, 1972) found that families with a retarded child participated in fewer informal neighborhood activities than families without a retarded child. Gath (1977), in a study of Down syndrome families, reported that parents of Down infants went out socially, including visits to grandparents, as often as parents of nonhandicapped infants did. Gath's (1977) findings are consistent with those of Dunlap and Hollingsworth (1977) reported above.

In summary, most of the recent literature related to families with a handicapped child does not lend support to the myth of increased stress in family daily life. While there is no denying that having a handicapped child is a stressful experience, to label such families as unable to cope is to seriously underestimate them.

MYTH: Parents of a handicapped child have a higher divorce rate and greater marital disharmony.

It is commonly assumed that handicapped children, by their very presence, will have a negative effect on their parents' marriage. Indeed, a number of reports published before 1980 support this conclusion. In these studies parents of handicapped children have been found to have more frequent marital conflict (Boles, 1959; Gath, 1977; Tavormina and Kralj, 1975), more feelings of dissatisfaction with their marriages (Cummings, 1976; Gath, 1978), increased sexual difficulties (Cummings, 1976) and higher rates of divorce (Gath, 1978; Tew, Payne and Laurence, 1974) compared to parents of nonhandicapped children. These effects were reported for a wide range of handicapping conditions including mental retardation (e.g., Farber, 1959; Gath, 1978; McAllister et al., 1973) and behavior disorders (e.g., Marcus, 1977). It also was reported that these negative effects may increase as the handicapped child gets older (Farber, 1959; Schipper, 1959). Some studies indicated that mothers of handicapped children withdraw from their husbands and become more involved with their handicapped children (Farber, 1964, 1972; Illingworth, 1967). Consistent with this view, Doernberg (1978) noted that mothers of the handicapped must often function as therapists, teachers, trainers and transporters; she speculated that this may make it harder to provide for other relationships including marriage.

Studies that report negative marital consequences suggest that, although the presence of a handicapped child may negatively affect some marriages, not all or even most marriages are affected. For example, Tew et al. (1974) interviewed 59 families of children with spina bifida and 59 parents on nonhandicapped children. Seventy percent of both groups reported having happy marriages when their children were born. Forty-six percent of the parents of the spina bifida children and 79 percent of the comparison parents reported having satisfactory marriages when their children were 9 years of age. While the parents of the handicapped children were less likely to report satisfactory marriages when their children were older, nearly half did report satisfactory marriages despite the fact that spina bifida is a fairly severe handicap with many demands on parents. Similarly, Gath (1977) interviewed parents of Down syndrome children six times over a period of two years and found that, compared to parents of non-handicapped children, the Down parents were just as likely to have happy marriages. McAndrew (1976) reported similar findings for parents of physically handicapped children. Bristol and Schopler (1984) found divorce rates for parents of autistic children to be no higher than those for the general population.

A number of other authors have not found significant differences in marital integration of parents of handicapped and nonhandicapped children (Bernard, 1974; Dunlap and Hollingsworth, 1977; Freeston, 1971; Korn, Chess and Fernandez, 1978; Waisbren, 1980). In general, while parents of handicapped children may be at greater risk for marital disharmony compared to parents of non-handicapped children, this effect will not obtain for all parents of the handicapped. In fact, several of the authors mentioned above stated that the deciding factor was the degree of stability of the marriage before the handicapped child's birth.

MYTH: Fathers of a handicapped child have greater difficulty accepting the child.

There appears to be general agreement among early authors that fathers of handicapped children have difficulty accepting their children (Chigier, 1972; Farber and Ryckman, 1965; Grossman, 1972; Gumz and Gubrium, 1972; Reed and Reed, 1965). Carver and Carver (1972) reported that fathers may react more negatively to their handicapped child if mothers are told first by professionals that the child is handicapped. Acceptance of handicapped children was reported to be influenced by the sex of the child (Chigier, 1972; Farber, 1962; Farber and Ryckman, 1965; Grossman, 1972), with fathers reacting in the extreme of total involvement or total withdrawal if the child is a boy (Chiegier, 1972) and more accepting if the child is a girl (Grossman, 1972). Sibling position (Farber, 1962), level of occupational stress (Korn et al., 1978) and the nature of the handicap (Farber and Ryckman, 1965) may also be factors in fathers' reactions. Fathers seem best able to cope with handicaps other than retardation, and they are more effective with their retarded sons than with retarded daughters.

Also, fathers exhibited greater stress with the birth of retarded sons, while mothers exhibited greater stress with retarded daughters (Farber and Ryckman, 1965).

Recent studies have identified factors that result in acceptance by fathers. These include being involved in the handicapped child's daily care (Price-Bonham and Addison, 1978); acceptance of the child by the father's own parents (Waisbren, 1980); and informal support from friends and family (Moran, 1982; Waisbren, 1980).

Conclusion

In reviewing research on handicapped children and their parents, the striking differences between effects reported in earlier and more recent studies are of interest. If teachers and other service providers of young handicapped children base their interactions with families on old stereotypes that predict failure and disintegration, the resulting lowered expectations may interfere with the families' progress in dealing with their children. If, on the other hand, families are generally seen as capable of dealing effectively with the stress of having a handicapped child, it is more likely that the prophecy will self-fulfill and good adjustment will result.

It is of interest to speculate about the reasons for the more positive effects families have reported recently. Two factors appear relevant to this review, although several others probably exist. First, we have witnessed some rather far-reaching changes in attitude during the past decade in American society, toward handicapped persons and toward sex-roles. Attitudes toward the handicapped have become more accepting, especially since the passage of P.L. 94-142, so that it is possible parents do not feel as much stigma surrounding their handicapped child. Additionally, progress has been made in perceiving the positive impact that a handicapped child can have on family life (Turnbull et al., 1983). As social attitudes toward sex roles have changed, the burden of caring for a handicapped child becomes more evenly shared between fathers and mothers, brothers and sisters.

A second factor of interest is the great improvement in services to families with handicapped members since the passage of P.L. 94-142 in 1975. This is due in part to an increase in the number of related service personnel trained to work with young handicapped children and their families, and to higher standards of training required, especially among teachers of preschool children who are increasingly required to hold public school certification (Widerstrom, Domyslawski and McNulty, 1986). This trend is likely to continue as services become mandated for more handicapped children from birth, resulting in families receiving more effective support earlier in raising their child.

REFERENCES

Beckman-Bell, P. "Characteristics of Handicapped Infants: A Study of the Relationship Between Child Characteristics and Stress as Reported by Mothers." Unpublished doctoral dissertation, University of North Carolina—Chapel Hill, 1980.

Bernard, A. W. "A Comparative Study of Marital Integration and Sibling Role Tension Differences Between Families Who Have a Severely Mentally Retarded Child and Families of Nonhandicapped." *Dissertation Abstract International* 35A, 5 (1974): 2800–01.

Boles, G. "Personality Factors in Mothers of Cerebral Palsied Children." *Genetic Psychological Monographs* (1959): 159–218.

Bradshaw, J., and D. Lawton. "Tracing the Causes of Stress in Families with Handicapped Children." *British Journal of Social Work* 8, 2 (1978): 181–92.

Bristol, M., and E. Schopler. "A Developmental Perspective on Stress and Coping in Families of Autistic Children." In J. Blacher, ed., *Severely Handicapped Young Children and Their Families: Research in Review*. New York: Academic Press, 1984, pp. 91–142.

Bronfenbrenner, U.; A. Avgar and C. Henderson. "An Analysis of Family Stresses and Supports." Unpublished manuscript, 1977.

Carver, N., and J. Carver. *"The Family of the Retarded Child."* Syracuse, NY: Syracuse University Press, 1972.

Chigier, E. *Down's Syndrome*. Lexington, MA: Heath, 1972.

Cummings, S. T. "The Impact of the Child's Deficiency on the Father: A Study of Fathers of Mentally Retarded and of Chronically Ill Children." *American Journal of Orthopsychiatry* 46 (1976): 246–55.

Doernberg, N. "Some Negative Effects on Family Integration of Health and Educational Services for Young Handicapped Children." *Rehabilitation Literature* 39, 4 (1978): 107–10.

Dunlap, W. R. "Services for Families of the Developmentally Disabled." *Social Work* 21 (1976): 220–23.

Dunlap, W. R., and J. S. Hollingsworth. "How Does a Handicapped Child Affect the Family? Implications for Practitioners." *The Family Coordinator* 26 (1977): 286–93.

Farber, B. "Effects of a Severely Mentally Retarded Child on Family Integration." *Monographs of the Society for Research in Child Development* 24, 2 (1959).

———. "Effects of a Severely Mentally Retarded Child on Family." In E. P. Trapp, ed., *Reading on the Exceptional Child*. New York: Appleton-Century, 1962.

———. *Family Organization and Interaction*. San Francisco: Chandler, 1964.

Farber, B., and D. B. Ryckman. "Effects of Severely Retarded Children on Family Relationships." *Mental Retardation Abstracts* 2 (1965): 1–17.

Freeston, B. M. "An Enquiry into the Effect of a Spina Bifida Child Upon the Family." *Developmental Medicine and Child Neurology* 13 (1971): 456–61.

Gath, A. "The Impact of an Abnormal Child Upon the Parents." *British Journal of Psychiatry* 130 (1977): 405–10.

———. *Down's Syndrome and the Family*. London: Academic Press, 1978.

Grossman, F. K. *Brothers and Sisters of Retarded Children*. Syracuse, NY: Syracuse University Press, 1972.

Gumz, E. J., and G. F. Gubrium. "Comparative Parental Perceptions of a Mentally Retarded Child." *American Journal of Mental Deficiency* 77 (1972): 175–80.

Holroyd, J. "The Questionnaire on Resources and Stress: An Instrument to Measure Family Response to a Handicapped Family Member." *Journal of Community Psychology* 2 (1974): 92–94.

Holroyd, J., and D. McArthur. "Mental Retardation and Stress on the Parents: A Contrast between Down's Syndrome and Childhood Autism." *American Journal of Mental Deficiency* 80 (1976): 431–36.

Illingworth, R. S. "Counseling the Parents of the Mentally Retarded Child." *Clinical Pediatrics* 6 (1967): 340–48.

Korn, S.; S. Chess and P. Fernandez. "The Impact of Children's Handicaps on Marital and Family Interaction." In R. M. Lerner and B. B. Spanier, eds., *Child Influences on Marital and Family Interaction—A Life-Span Perspective*. New York: Academic Press, 1978.

McAllister, R.; E. Butler and T. Lei. "Patterns of Social Interaction Among Families of Behaviorally Retarded Children." *Journal of Marriage and the Family* 35 (1972): 93–99.

McAndrew, I. "Children with a Handicap and Their Families." *Child Care, Health and Development* 2, 4 (1976): 213–30.

Marcus, L. M. "Patterns of Coping in Families of Psychotic Children." *American Journal of Orthopsychiatry* 47 (1977): 388–98.

Moran, M. "Living with a Handicapped Child: Findings on Families and Early Intervention." Paper presented at the 60th Annual International Convention of the Council for Exceptional Children, Houston, Texas, April 1982.

Peck, J. R., and W. B. Stephens. "A Study of the Relationship of Parents and That of Their Mentally Defective Child." *American Journal of Mental Deficiency* 64 (1960): 839–44.

Price-Bonham, S., and S. Addison. "Families and Mentally Retarded Children: Emphasis on the Father." *The Family Coordinator* 27, 3 (1978): 221–30.

Reed, E. W., and S. C. Reed. *Mental Retardation: A Family Study.* Philadelphia: Saunders, 1965.

Schipper, M. T. "The Child with Mongolism in the Home." *Pediatrics* 24 (1959): 132–44.

Suelzle, M., and V. Keenan. "Changes in Family Support Networks on the Life Cycle of Mentally Retarded Persons." *American Journal of Mental Deficiency* 86, 3 (1981): 267–74.

Tavormina, J. B., and M. M. Kralj. "Facilitating Family Dynamics: Family System Issues in the Overall Management of the Handicapped Infant." Paper presented at the Exceptional Infant Symposium, Charlottesville, Virginia, 1975.

Tavormina, J. B.; P. J. Boll; N. J. Dunn; R. Luncomb and J. Taylor. "Psychological Effects of Raising a Physically Handicapped Child on Parents." Paper presented at the meeting of the American Psychological Association, Chicago, 1975.

Tew, B.; H. Payne and K. Laurence. "Must a Family with a Handicapped Child be a Handicapped Family?" *Developmental Medicine and Child Neurology* 16 (1974): 32–35.

Turnbull, A. P.; J. A. Summers and M. J. Brotherson. "The Impact of Young Handicapped Children on Families: Future Research Directions." Kansas Research and Training Center on Independent Living. University of Kansas—Lawrence, 1983.

Waisbren, S. E. "Parents' Reactions After the Birth of a Developmentally Disabled Child." *American Journal of Mental Deficiency* 84 (1980): 345–51.

Widerstrom, A. H.; D. Domyslawski and B. McNulty. "Rural Outreach Training in Early Childhood Special Education: A Cooperative Model." *Journal of the Division for Early Childhood* 10, 1 (1986): 84–92.

Wikler, L.; M. Wasow and E. Hatfield. "Chronic Sorrow Revisited: Parent vs. Professional Depiction of Adjustment of Parents of Mentally Retarded Children." *American Journal of Orthopsychiatry* 51, 1 (1981): 63–70.

Anne H. Widerstrom, Associate Professor, School of Education, The University of Colorado at Denver, and Curtis Dudley-Marling, Assistant Professor of Special Education, York University, Toronto, Ontario.

Early Childhood Special Education in the Next Decade: Implementing and Expanding P.L. 99-457

Barbara J. Smith and Phillip S. Strain

In this article, the authors propose several future challenges for the early childhood special education (ECSE) field. In the next decade, ECSE public policy developments will be related both to implementing current policy (e.g., P.L. 99-457), and to expanding policy in order to assure that quality services are available to all children and families who need early intervention and preschool services. In addition to discussing future policy issues, the article also describes possible roles and responsibilities of professionals and other advocates in shaping future policy.

In the next decade, it is likely that significant early childhood special education (ECSE) developments will be achieved only partially through legislation. Laws like P.L. 99-457, The Education of the Handicapped Act Amendments of 1986, may play a role in future ECSE developments, but that role may contribute less to changes in the field than laws have in the previous decade. With P.L. 99-457 and related state policy developments, ECSE can achieve the fundamental programmatic framework from which to operate. The challenges ahead for ECSE will be the full and effective implementation of the provisions and intent of P.L. 99-457 at state and local levels as well as the expansion of the existing knowledge base to ensure that all children and families benefit from what has been learned about factors that enhance development.

Four critical areas of implementation and expansion are the focus of this article: funding and resource utilization, eligible populations, integrated services, and program quality. These areas not only have direct implications

for public policy but also will challenge our abilities as professionals to help shape the future of the field.

Funding and Resource Utilization

While funding for early childhood special education services has increased dramatically over the last 20 years, it is still insufficient. The Congress has not yet repaired the discrepancy between its promise of funding and its reality of appropriations. Consequently, many programs continue to struggle to survive. Site visits often reveal overstretched resources and administrators faced with the reality of moving resources from one program to another, children on waiting lists, or the need to prioritize children and families based on the severity of their needs. In this context, it is troubling that professionals, legislators, and the public demand that early intervention demonstrate its cost-effectiveness. As we move into the next decade, with likely pressures to increase funding for exceptional in-

Source: Barbara J. Smith & Phillip S. Strain (1988). Early childhood special education in the next decade: Implementing and expanding P.L. 99-457. *Topics in Early Childhood Special Education*, 8, 37–47. Reprinted by the permission of the publisher.

fants and preschoolers, the demands for cost-effectiveness data will probably increase as well.

If funding for ECSE is to increase, we need to build a certain and secure *moral consensus* that appropriate funding for early intervention is the right thing to do. Some may argue that the building of a moral consensus is a step backward from the scientific progress that has been made in the area of cost-effectiveness analysis. That, in our opinion, would be an error in judgment. Cost-effectiveness analysis is potentially quite useful, but it should be applied in a purely technological sense to better enable us to choose *between* program options, not between some intervention and none, or between early intervention and some other social/humanitarian need.

A significant increase in funding at the federal as well as the state level is a requirement for the next decade of ECSE progress. We will achieve increased resources only if we are able to continue to raise the consciousness of the public and policy makers about the needs of young children and convince them that funding these services is indeed a moral obligation of society.

In addition to new funds, in an effort to require states to make the best use of existing resources, P.L. 99-457 requires that funds from other sources (e.g., Medicaid, Maternal and Child Health, etc.) be utilized to provide early intervention services. Particularly Part H, the Infant/Toddler Program, amplifies the need to coordinate and utilize existing resources—programs and funds—rather than create overlapping services. Indeed, House Report 99-860 states:

> It is the Congress' intent that other funding sources continue; that there be greater coordination among agencies regarding the payment of costs; and that funds made available under Part H be used only for direct services . . . that are not otherwise provided from other public or private sources. (U.S. House of Representatives, 1986, p. 15)

This "payor of last resort" provision of P.L. 99-457 requires that states use the menagerie of existing federal, state, local, and private resources more efficiently and cooperatively. Implementing the "shared resources" provisions of the Act presents the profession with one of the most significant challenges for the coming decade. If this provision is to work effectively, communication and cooperation among affected federal, state, local, and private agencies, programs, and individuals will be necessary. More specifically, rigorous preservice and inservice training will be required among professionals in various programs and agencies regarding the needs of young handicapped children and their families, what each program has to offer, and how expertise and resources may be shared. Revisions and amendments to federal and state laws governing relevant programs may be required to mandate participation and to abolish counterproductive policies prohibiting sharing of funds, personnel, and services. In order to assess and analyze the adequacy of these various resources, states and localities will need to conduct interagency assessments of all available funding strands (local, state, and federal) as well as to provide recommendations to the funding sources regarding legislative or administrative revisions necessary to facilitate sharing and cooperative planning.

The goals of such cooperative activities should be improved services to children and families, unduplicated and efficient service systems, and less red tape and counterproductive regulations. Interagency efforts could result in cooperative planning and written cooperative agreements that delineate the nature and extent of the cooperation. For example, interagency agreements might establish cooperative efforts related to: (a) fiscal responsibilities for particular services, (b) personnel resources, (c) monitoring and evaluation procedures, and (d) paperwork and data collection requirements (Smith, 1986). These cooperative efforts should not be restricted to state-level agencies and councils, but should be made on a local and/or regional basis as well.

In addition to increasing funding and coordinating existing resources, a third strategy for resource utilization is the development of a continuum of services. A full continuum of services should be available in all communities to meet the individual needs of children and families, as well as to provide the most cost-effective program of early intervention. All children and families do not have the same needs or require same services or intensity of services. In early intervention one size does *not* fit all. Therefore, a range of service options from the least intensive to the most intensive is necessary. An example of such a range or continuum is shown in Figure 1. Some families will need and want only periodic developmental monitoring. Others will need and want intensive residential or hospital-based programs. Children and families should be referred to services (options) based on their individual needs as outlined in their Individualized Family Service Plan (IFSP) or Individualized Education Program (IEP).

The services constituting the continuum should utilize existing resources and, of course, all services should meet state standards. New or additional programs should be created only when that particular service does not exist. Individual placement decisions should be made by a multidisciplinary team and coordinated by a case manager.

Eligible Populations

Any discussion about which children should have access to early intervention, whether the debate occurs in Congress, state legislatures, professional meetings, or college classrooms, eventually reaches the perplexing and morally difficult question of which children should *not* receive early intervention. Currently, professionals are required to engage in the unpleasant and questionable strategy of determining eligibility on the basis of some rules that restrict eligibility. In order to provide services to a fortunate few, a determination must be made of which children are the most handicapped, poor, sick, neglected, or abused. It is an exercise that far surpasses our technical skill and sensitivity of existing instruments.

Currently, states facing the challenge of implementing P.L. 99-457 are spending many hours on the development of eligibility criteria. In the case of 3- through 5-year-olds, state

and local officials must determine which disability identification procedures to use and then decide whether to identify children by disability labels or noncategorically; that is, by generic terms such as "developmentally delayed," or "preschool special needs."

Under P.L. 99-457, the determination of eligibility for birth- to 2-year-olds is confounded by the addition of the at-risk population. The Act allows, but does not require, states to extend services to children who are at risk for developing developmental delay, either because of medical or environmental factors. Hence, many state policy makers are facing the difficult task of trying to determine which factors render which children at risk.

One challenge before us is the need to extend early intervention services to at-risk children from *birth to 5 years*. Under current federal policy, if a state included at-risk children as eligible for Part H services, at the age of 3 years these at-risk children are no longer eligible for such services. It is certainly not documented that the need for services disappears at 36 months. If the intent of Congress under P.L. 99-457 is to provide support to those children and families who need early intervention, then Congress should amend the law to fully serve all at-risk children. Congress should extend that right to services past the arbitrary age of 2 years and 11 months and to require, rather than allow, the states to serve at-risk children.

As early childhood professionals, we must also turn our attention and our political will toward ensuring that ESCE services are available to any child or family that may benefit from them. The technologies and methods of ESCE have been proven to be effective in enhancing the development of handicapped as well as nonhandicapped children (Smith & Strain, 1984). Is there a child or family that

FIGURE 1 *Early Intervention Continuum of Services*

Prevention services	Tracking and monitoring	Parent intervention and training	Day care with support services	Home-based program	Center-based program that includes nonhandicapped children (integrated)	Center-based program and extensive family support services	Residential program

273

cannot benefit from carefully applied, individually based, educational, and other developmental services? The United States faces a crisis in the need for more, and better, child care and preschool opportunities. The number of young children living in poverty is rising—and yet programs such as Head Start are currently capable of serving fewer than 30% of the eligible children; teen pregnancy is increasing, while related publicly supported programs are being cut back; and over 50% of mothers with children under the age of 6 are working (Schweinhart, Koshel & Bridgman, 1987). Providing voluntary early childhood programs to all young children based upon their individual needs would be more humane; would provide large-scale, long-term, positive effects related to preventing school failure; and would, in one broad sweep, reduce administrative costs and bureaucratic red tape tenfold by eliminating our elaborate systems of determining who gets in and who doesn't.

ECSE professionals need to join ranks with other child care advocacy groups in an effort to obtain federal and state legislation that would make available high quality early childhood programming for all children. These universal services would be individually determined, developmentally integrated, and offer a wide variety of specialized services where needed.

Integrated Services

Probably no other concept in the history of special education has been more abused, misused, and confused than providing services in the least restrictive environment (LRE). At various times and in various circumstances, it has been an organizational battle cry, the plague to be avoided at all cost, a logistical nightmare, and a crowning achievement. It is strange that attempts to provide handicapped individuals with access to nonhandicapped or less handicapped persons would be so mercurial for a profession and society dedicated to the development of children.

The concept of least restrictive alternative is a legal doctrine that historically was applied to non-education-related civil rights cases. The doctrine, simply put, requires that when government attempts to restrict an individual's fundamental liberty, it can do so only with full due process of law. Applied to special education, through litigation and many state statutes, as well as P.L. 94-142, The Education for All Handicapped Children Act, this doctrine has been translated as the least restrictive alternative educational setting or the least restrictive environment (LRE). Johnson (1976) explained the least restrictive alternative doctrine and its relationship to special education as follows:

Placement in special environments for educational purposes can, without appropriate safeguards, become a restriction of fundamental liberties.

It is required, then, that substantive efforts be made by educators to maintain handicapped children with their peers in a regular education setting, and that the state *(as represented by individual school districts)* bear the burden of proof when making placements or when applying treatments which involve partial or complete removal of handicapped children from their normal peers. (p. 60)

It is important to note that the term LRE, as used historically in education, had its basis in the notion of *removal from* the regular class environment. Thus, the relationship of the term LRE and services for children from birth through 5 years of age, for whom there is no regular class, is complex. While the *legal* relationship of LRE and preschool services has yet to be clarified, it is important for professionals and other advocates not to lose sight of the *scientific* basis for integrating young handicapped children with their nonhandicapped peers (Strain, Guralnick, & Walker, 1986; Strain & Odom, 1986). The burden of proof is on the system to demonstrate when integrated services are not appropriate for an individual child. Thus, our concern may be more appropriately focused on the need for integrated services, and not on the LRE per se.

However, given the predictable struggles that integration will bring, is it worth the effort? Is it worth alienating some parents, confronting otherwise supportive administrators, or expending disproportionate time and professional resources? This is doubtful, given the way in which integration is currently practiced in many locales. Integration defined as "sharing the same program administrators," "occupying a room in one wing of an elementary school," "eating lunch together," "sharing a playground," and the like, is at best only cos-

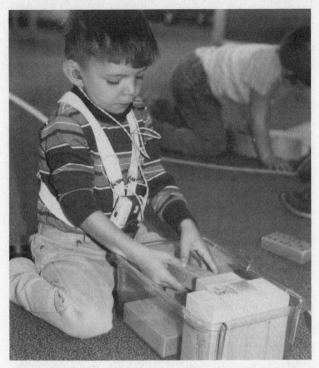

Consistent, sustained, and well-conceived interactions between nonhandicapped and handicapped young children can improve both the social and communicative performance of handicapped children.

metic. We know of no evidence that such episodic flirtations between nonhandicapped and handicapped children do more than draw down dollars with LRE tags attached.

On the other hand, it is quite clear that consistent, sustained, and well-conceived interactions between nonhandicapped and handicapped young children can improve both the social and communicative performance of handicapped children (see Strain et al., 1986, for extensive reviews). Moreover, there is evidence that inconsistent, unsustained, and ill-conceived interchanges between nonhandicapped and handicapped children are developmentally insignificant (Strain & Odom, 1986).

There are numerous administrative arrangements that can lead to developmentally significant integrated services. A brief list would include (a) enrollment of handicapped children in appropriate family- or center-based day care or preschool; (b) enrollment of handicapped children in Head Start; (c) enrollment of nonhandicapped children in specialized programs; and (d) enrollment of handicapped children in school-sponsored preschools and kindergartens. Of course, none of these setting arrangements by themselves lead directly to developmentally significant programming. That can be achieved only when children share an instructional and social environment and when teachers and children are specifically trained to facilitate interaction (Strain & Cordisco, 1983).

Not only is integration a central issue for early childhood service models, but it is just as relevant to the future placement of the program graduates. We must not forget that the regular classrooms that will accept ECSE graduates can also be the settings that yield illiterate junior high students; that provide minimal academic instruction; that promote stereotyping and scapegoating; and that achieve de facto segregation. If placement in nonsegregated settings is to have meaning beyond the early intervention years, ECSE professionals must be involved in retraining regular education personnel. In the next decade, we must be willing to share knowledge, techniques, and methodology that have proven to be effective with administrators, teachers, and related personnel in regular education. The logistical and fiscal enormity of such an enterprise must not be underestimated. However, if we as early childhood special educators wish to "move" children and families to regular class options, we had better be sure those options are worthwhile!

Program Quality

Early childhood professionals must avoid "winning the battle but losing the war" by obtaining legislation and funding for programs while failing to ensure the quality of those programs. There are several generic quality assurance ingredients that appear to be particularly critical in the delivery of early intervention and preschool services. Consider the following recent events.

In addition to program improvements like P.L. 99-457 for handicapped young children, some states are initiating early childhood programs for portions of the population under 5 years old. Such policies are evidence that policy makers are becoming convinced of the positive effects of early intervention and prevention services. In 1986, 22 states appropriated $330 million for early childhood programs to serve poor children, as compared to $160 million spent by only eight states in

1984 (Schweinhart, Koshel, & Bridgman, 1987). This movement adds to the ECSE program increases, provides more potential for integrated settings, and is a step toward universal early childhood services.

However, ECSE professionals need to ensure that these efforts are directed by individuals that are knowledgeable of the needs of very young children. Practices that are modeled after those for older children, teachers that are trained to work with school-aged populations rather than young children, and administrators that make decisions regarding philosophy or curriculum on the basis of their experience with older children are examples of situations that need to be avoided.

Early childhood professionals need to extend the leadership role we have played in the legislative arena to leadership roles in the implementation arena. We must now ensure that the programs and services that we have helped to create reflect the best that our knowledge and science has to offer. We must also work to be included in state and local decision making regarding early childhood program development.

What are the quality indicators that need to be monitored by professionals? The National Association for the Education of Young Children (NAEYC), among others, reports several critical factors affecting the quality and appropriateness of programs for very young children. These factors include the following:

• Group Size and Child Ratios: Young children require smaller ratios of adults to children and smaller groupings than do children of school age. Recommended minimum ratios that have been associated with desirable classroom performance of nonhandicapped children are 1:3 or 1:4 for infants or toddlers and 1:7 to 1:10 for 3- through 5-year-olds. Group sizes should be limited to groups of eight for infants and 15 to 20 for 2- through 5-year-olds (Moore, 1984; NAEYC, 1983).

• Facilities: Facilities should provide the space that young children need to accommodate a variety of developmentally appropriate activities. There should be at least 35 square feet of indoor space and 75 square feet of outdoor space per child. Facilities should contain equipment and materials designed for the age group and developmental level of the children served (NAEYC, 1983).

• Personnel Skills: One of the key factors shown to be related to program effectiveness is the skill level of the staff. Early childhood personnel should be specially trained and experienced in the developmental needs of young children with whom they work. On-going, job-related staff training has been shown to be a significant predictor of the quality and effectiveness of early childhood programs (Moore, 1984; Schweinhart et al., 1987).

• Specialized Services Indicators: In addition to those generic effectiveness indicators for all early childhood programs, programs for children with handicaps have been found to be more effective if they include (a) individualized programming, (b) involvement of parents, and (c) structured curricula that include frequent assessment and monitoring of the child's progress (Smith & Strain, 1984).

Conclusions

Legislative reforms, such as P.L. 99-457, may not be the primary avenue of change in the next decade. Rather, ensuring the quality and expansion of programs provided under current legislative authority may be the recipe for positive change over the next 10 years. These changes will necessitate that we as professionals monitor the implementation of P.L. 99-457 and related state policies to ensure that not only the intent of the law is met, but that best practices are incorporated and that children and families receive the highest quality of services. We can begin to meet this challenge by (a) becoming active in the quality assurance or program monitoring mechanisms in our states and localities; (b) serving on state and local decision-making boards and commissions that will drive the development of early childhood programs; (c) encouraging professional and parent organizations to become effective political forces in not only the legislative arenas but in the shaping of political platforms and in the support of candidates for public office; and, finally, (d) taking individual action such as voting, professional development, and advocating the highest professional standards and ethics among colleagues.

Authors' Note

Preparation of this paper was supported by Contract No. 300-82-0368 (Early Childhood Research Institute) from the Department of Education to the University of Pittsburgh. However, the opinions expressed herein do not necessarily reflect the position of or policy of the U.S. Department of Education, and no official endorsement by the Department should be inferred.

REFERENCES

Johnson, R. A. (1976). Renewal of school placement systems for the handicapped. In F. Weintraub, A. Abeson, J. Ballard, & M. LaVor (Eds.), *Public policy and the education of exceptional children* (pp. 47–61). Reston, VA: The Council for Exceptional Children.

Moore, S. (1984, November). Keynote address, Policy Conference on Young Children. Anchorage, AK.

National Association for the Education of Young Children (NAEYC). (1983). *How to choose a good early childhood program.* Washington, DC: Author.

Schweinhart, L., Koshel, J., & Bridgman, A. (1987, March). Policy options for preschool programs. *Phi Delta Kappan,* pp. 524–529.

Smith, B. J. (1986). *A comparative analysis of selected federal programs serving young children.* Chapel Hill, NC: START Publications.

Smith, B. J., & Strain, P. S. (1984). The argument for early intervention (Factsheet) *ERIC Digest.* Reston, VA: The Council for Exceptional Children.

Strain, P. S., & Cordisco, L. K. (1983). Child characteristics and outcomes related to mainstreaming. In J. Anderson & T. Black (Eds.), *Issues in preschool mainstreaming* (pp. 47–64). Chapel Hill, NC: TADS Publications.

Strain, P. S., Guralnick, M. J., & Walker, H. M. (Eds.). (1986). *Children's social behavior: Assessment, development, and modification.* New York: Academic Press.

Strain, P. S., & Odom, S. L. (1986). Peer social initiations: An effective intervention for social skills deficits of exceptional children. *Exceptional Children, 52,* 543–551.

U.S. House of Representatives (1986). House Report 99-860. Washington, DC: Government Printing Office.

Mainstreaming Young Emotionally Disturbed Children: Rationale and Restraints

Samuel J. Meisels and Seymour J. Friedland

Abstract.   Young emotionally disturbed children have only recently been intentionally integrated into regular classrooms. In this paper, reasons are presented concerning why young behaviorally disordered children have not previously been identified or assisted in participating in mainstreamed classrooms. It is argued that in order for these children to profit from the experience of the regular classroom, two general conditions must be met. First, the regular classroom structure, typical teacher behaviors and established patterns of relationships with parents must be modified. Second, the potential of a modified regular classroom to meet all of the therapeutic needs of young disturbed children should be carefully assessed. The addition of a specialized clinical milieu may be a necessary concomitant of mainstreaming for many children with behavioral disorders.

Introduction

The integration of handicapped children into regular classrooms has taken place without sufficient attention being devoted to individual differences in the populations of handicapped children. Early emphasis was placed on integrating retarded children in elementary schools (Birch, 1974; Dunn, 1968; Hammons, 1974) and models developed for this specific age group and handicapping conditions were then assumed to be applicable to all age groups and disabilities (Reger, 1974; Wynne, Dakof and Ulfeder, 1975). However, preschool and kindergarten children pose very different problems and issues from those posed by elementary-aged children. Similarly, emotionally disturbed children present issues and challenges that are different from those of mentally retarded or physically handicapped children. This paper examines some of the

unique issues of integrating or mainsteaming preschool and kindergarten emotionally disturbed children.

Issues Unique to the Young Emotionally Disturbed Child

Until the 1960's school-aged emotionally disturbed children received very little attention or support in public schools. Trippe (1963) reports that behaviorally disordered children were all but completely ignored in public school classrooms if their behavior was compliant. Non-compliant, emotionally disturbed children generally were not permitted to enroll in public school programs. Paul (1977) notes that these children were frequently "left in psychiatric hopsitals . . . because there was no appropriate educational program in the schools, misplaced in classes for the retarded,

Source: Samuel J. Meisels & Seymour J. Friedland (1978). Mainstreaming young emotionally disturbed children: Rationale and restraints. Behavioral Disorders, 3, 178–185. Reprinted by permission of the Council for Children with Behavioral Disorders.

or excluded from school altogether because of behavior problems and the school's inability to cope with or respond to their needs" (pp. 8–9).

Even fewer educational options were available for preschool and kindergarten-aged children with behavior disorders. In general, the development of early intervention programs for young emotionally disturbed children was not considered urgent. Some of the factors that contributed to this neglect can be identified. First, the early dominance of maturational psychologists such as Gesell (1940) led to a view of young children as inexorably governed by physical timeclocks that could not be tampered with significantly, either for purposes of acceleration or remediation. This view of the immutable progression of nature negated the importance or need for programs designed to identify and remediate deficits at an early age.

A second reason young emotionally disturbed children were not identified or assisted in their development originates with one of the most significant characteristics of this age group. Development is rapid during this period. Changes in cognitive, physical and emotional skills occur during very short periods of time. This factor promotes the notion that it is sensible to wait and see if a deficit will disappear or be "outgrown," rather than deciding to label and intervene early. Third, much of the behavior seen in preschool children is generally considered reactive; that is, it is explained as a product of the immediate situation (Group for the Advancement of Psychiatry, 1966). This view leads to the assumption that behavioral deficits appearing early in development do not represent enduring traits, but responses to immediate environmental events. Such a view suggests that most disturbances in young children may be transient, thus minimizing the importance of early intervention. Finally, there has been a tendency in clinical diagnosis to assume that if a child displays apparently permanent, non-reactive difficulties, then these difficulties must be generated by physical factors. Hence, the emotional disorder is interpreted as an organic deficit. An excellent example of this phenomenon is the diagnosis of Minimal Brain Dysfunction so widely applied to preschool children who display antisocial behavior.

Thus, a dichotomous approach to providing educational services for children has evolved. On the one hand, because of the extreme nature of their disorders, preschool children with psychotic tendencies or autistic characteristics are usually placed in segregated programs. In contrast, children who show less severe signs of disturbance are frequently not clearly identified or provided with specialized services. Since their condition is seen as temporary, due to maturational or environmental factors, or is mistakenly identified as organic, these children are placed in regular preschool and kindergarten programs, not because of the value of integration, but because of the difficulty of making an early diagnosis of emotional disturbance. In examining "integrated" programs for young emotionally disturbed children, one is thus frequently discussing programming for a population that may not be clearly defined and whose deficit may not really be acknowledged as a disability.

It is the contention of this paper that the purposeful and conscious integration or mainstreaming of mildly and moderately disturbed children into the regular classroom can be valuable. In the following section the rationale for mainstreaming young emotionally disturbed children is given. The next section identifies some modifications of the mainstream that may promote a more successful experience for behaviorally disordered children. The final section identifies some constraints of the regular classroom that should be considered when mainstreaming young emotionally disturbed children.

Rationale: Beneficial Features of Regular Classrooms for Emotionally Disturbed Children

In a paper that explores the implications for teacher training entailed by mainstreaming emotionally disturbed children, Fink (1977) notes that there are several advantages of special class placement which should not be abandoned in the movement toward mainstreaming. In Fink's view, behaviorally disordered children who participate in special education programs benefit from "The Three R's of Special Education": 1) respite, 2) repair, and 3) renewal.

In Fink's terms, the emotionally disturbed child enrolled in a special class can obtain *respite* from the network of tension, stress and discomfort in which he finds himself. Such experience also makes possible the *repair* and development of skills, and ultimately provides an experience of *renewal* of the whole person.

These features of the special class can also play a significant role in an integrated preschool or kindergarten classroom. Respite takes several forms for young behaviorally disordered children in mainstreamed classrooms. If the child is a member of an unstable or inconsistent family group, the regularity, stability and potentially nurturant qualities of an organized preschool or kindergarten program staffed by able and dependable teachers may be extremely beneficial. Similarly, if the chid is treated "like other children," and is systematically exposed to a set of relatively common expectations and limits, he may experience some relief or respite from his own inability to govern his impulses and manage his behavior.

The quality of respite in the mainstreamed classroom overlaps with that of repair. In the integrated classroom an emotionally disturbed child may have opportunities to be exposed to corrective emotional experiences. The provocative child may discover that not all adults react with rejection and anger to his or her behavior. The child with little basic trust may find adults who are responsive and who can be involved in reciprocal relationships. The depressed child may be stimulated by the affective investment of non-disabled children. These experiences offer an opportunity for emotional repair to young disturbed children.

Finally, the integrated early childhood program offers numerous opportunities for renewal of the whole person. A competent early childhood program is designed to help children obtain a strong sense of selfhood and ego. As Fink (1977) notes, renewal draws upon respite from stress and repair of significant intellectual and interpersonal skills. Regular early childhood programs provide numerous opportunities for children to experience success, as well as reinforcement of positive behaviors and exposure to pleasurable interpersonal experiences. Taken together, these experiences have the potential of improving a disturbed child's sense of self and the role he can play in the world.

These features of regular early childhood programs are paralleled by three other characteristics of integrated programs: 1) maturation, 2) mastery and 3) modelling. Maturation refers to the wide range of normality represented in most preschool and kindergarten programs. Children under the age of six mature at dramatically different rates, hence justifying a range of behavior that is not typically expected in classrooms for older elementary-aged children. This range of normality permits the integration of disturbed children to take place without these children's behaviors being isolated or highlighted as exceptionally bizarre or atypical.

Another aspect of early childhood programs that is beneficial for mainstreaming is the orientation of these programs toward mastery experiences. Many early childhood programs are formally or informally criterion-referenced, in the sense that a child's performance or behavior is referenced to a specific task or content area, rather than to the child's relative position to other children in some undifferentiated normative grouping (Meisels, 1976). The typical early childhood and kindergarten program is not deficit-oriented; rather, it is oriented toward encouraging children to attain a degree of knowledge or level of performance that is individually appropriate. Children who display various levels of mastery can still be reinforced and respected for the abilities that they demonstrate. The wide range of activities that may be considered mastery experiences in early childhood programs could contribute to a disturbed child's potential experience of effectance, autonomy and competence (see White, 1959).

Finally, the integrated classroom offers emotionally disturbed children opportunities to interact with positive role models as well as occasions to serve as positive models for other children. Bandura (1973) has shown that under certain circumstances, negative behavior is modelled more readily and more frequently than positive behavior. This is one reason classrooms composed entirely of behaviorally disordered children may frequently have a negative impact on the children enrolled in these programs. Several researchers, including Csapo (1972), Hartup (1970), Guralnick (1976) and Solomon and Wahler (1973) have shown that with systematic planning, exposure of special needs children to positive non-handicapped role models will result in a marked increase in socially positive behaviors on the part of special needs children. The integrated classroom, with its focus on normality and on "typical" behavior, is thus capable of providing emotionally disturbed children with experience with positive peer models.

Integrated classrooms also provide opportunities for emotionally disturbed children to serve as positive role models for their nondisturbed peers. Given the ability of the majority of the children in an integrated classroom to respond favorably to positive, competent and purposeful activity, when disturbed children display mastery and effectance, they are likely to be reinforced for these actions by their peers. This reinforcement may take the form of other children directly imitating their actions, desiring to spend time with them, or including them in their spontaneous play groups.

Thus, there is a place for emotionally disturbed children in mainstreamed early childhood programs. However, not all of a disturbed child's needs can be met in the regular classroom unless that program is modified in certain significant respects.

Modifying the Mainstream

Behaviorally disordered children present a number of distinct characteristics that distinguish them from other children. These characteristics differ in quality and intensity from one child to another. In order to create an educational setting that is appropriate for these children, a number of modifications in the regular classroom may have to be made by the teacher. Several examples of classroom adaptations follow.

1. *Classroom schedule:* In order for an emotionally disturbed child to be successfully integrated, teachers may have to adjust their classroom routines to create a sense of greater stability and predictability. A definite classroom schedule may have to be formulated—at least for the children with special needs—and then followed with regularity. Abrupt or unusual transitions may prove particularly difficult for children who have serious problems paying attention and trusting others (Swap, 1974). Such children should receive special preparation and attention at transitional points (e.g., at clean-up, snack time, end of the day or end of an activity), and may profit from a ritual such as an early warning, a timer, or a special place or cushion in the classroom.

2. *Classroom objectives:* In general, goals and outcome objectives formulated for use with emotionally disturbed children are process-oriented rather than product-oriented. Although skill development is crucial in order for

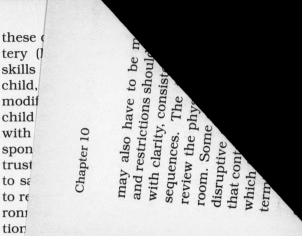

these
tery (
skills
child,
modif
child
with
spon
trust
to sa
to re
ron
tion
effectively
mate" of a classroom, rather than
uniform progression of activities.

3. *Unusual behaviors:* Children with behavioral disorders frequently display a disproportionate amount of disruptive behavior (Pastor and Swap, in press). Teachers who integrate emotionally disturbed children into their classes must be willing to accept more disruptive behavior in their classrooms than would typically be expected. These teachers must also learn how to help children who are acting out, who are disruptive or who are prone to tantrums. Some techniques which are useful include knowing how to hold and restrain these children, how to implement selective segregation or "time out" from the classroom, and how to help these children acquire inner controls and the ability to verbalize.

Children who display profound isolation and withdrawal can also prove disruptive in the classroom. Teachers must learn how to intervene in the behavior of these children by interrupting their withdrawn behavior and insisting on classroom participation that is consistent with their capabilities.

4. *New teaching skills:* The previous sections identify a number of skills of individualization that may have to be learned for the first time by a regular classroom teacher. Although individualized programming is a fairly common concomitant of early childhood programs, behavior modification techniques are not typically used in regular classrooms for young children. Since many emotionally disturbed children require consistent and dependable rewards for modifying their behavior, it would be helpful for teachers who integrate disturbed children into their classrooms to have an awareness of the effects of interpersonal and environmental reinforcement on young children.

The teacher's approach to limit-setting

281

odified. Limits, rules
be devised and applied
ency and attention to con-
teacher may also have to
ical arrangement of the class-
hildren who are impulsive and
respond favorably to a classroom
ains a number of small, safe places in
unctions are clear and boundaries de-
ned.

Finally, teachers who are working with
emotionally disturbed children may have to
learn to cope with primitive issues with which
they might be uncomfortable. Issues such as
death, aggression, sexuality or elimination
may arise at any time. Teachers have to be familiar with their feelings concerning these issues and must be prepared to help children
cope with and begin to govern their own potentially powerful feelings.

It is important to note that non-disturbed
children may also engage in unusual or disruptive behavior some of the time. Thus, the
techniques developed or refined specifically
for mainstreamed emotionally disturbed children will probably have general usefulness for
teachers in their work with all the children in
their classrooms.

5. *Peer relationships in the classroom:*
Young children are frequently frightened by
children who act differently from them, particularly if they are exposed to angry, disruptive,
acting-out behavior. Teachers in integrated
settings will have to learn techniques of explaining and interpreting children's actions in
behaviorally observable terms so that non-disturbed children will be able to mediate and understand some of this behavior. Other useful
techniques for maximizing positive interactions between special needs children and
other children include: arranging with parents
for children to play together outside of school;
establishing respect for individuals as a prime
classroom value; creating a safe, protected environment so that children can risk forming
relationships; explaining individual differences to chidren in a neutral, value-free manner; and designing and guiding positive
interactions between children based on a common interest or curricular experience (see
Meisels, 1977).

6. *Parent relationships:* Teachers also have to
learn to work effectively with the parents of
emotionally disturbed children. Their children
are frequently a source of stress for them, and
they—as is the case with most parents of special needs children—should be given advice
about how to manage their child at home and
how to support their child's growth and development.

Frequently, if the child is receiving therapy,
the parents are also involved in some form of
counseling or therapy. This type of arrangement is usually considered optimal, because it
enables the parents to become closely involved with the child's therapeutic program.
However, it may have effects on the teacher-
parent relationship. For example, the participation of a clinical "authority" may dilute the
teacher's authority. When conflicting messages come from the teacher and the therapist, the credibility of the teacher may decline.
Moreover, since the focus of therapy is typically on the maladaptive aspects of relationships between the child and family, the more
generally adaptive experiences in the classroom may not be valued as highly by the parents. In order to avoid some of these
misunderstandings, teachers, parents and
therapists should stay in close communication
with one another and should make a significant effort to support and respect each's contribution to the child's well-being.

Restraints: Therapeutic Needs That Cannot Be Met in the Integrated Classroom

Due to its structure and intrinsic nature, the
regular classroom usually cannot meet a number of therapeutic needs of young emotionally
disturbed children. Failure to recognize the
limitations of the regular classroom may
result in the inappropriate attempt to incorporate techniques developed for the clinical situation into the regular classroom. What follows
is a discussion of those therapeutic needs of
the preschool child that usually cannot be met
in the regular classroom.

The disturbing behavior of many emotionally disturbed children often takes the form of
acting and functioning at developmental levels well below chronological age. For example,
the excessive clinging and crying that is most
often found in the toddler may be a prominent
characteristic of the emotionally disturbed
three- or four-year-old. For many disturbed
children there may be therapeutic value in
functioning at this regressed level. The opportunity to act in such a regressed manner in a
safe environment may provide the child with
the experience of satisfying specific needs and

impulses within a context that is low in anxiety. Children who engage in a great deal of clinging and crying may discover that attachment and attention can result from such behaviors and that they need not perpetually experience frustration in the face of basic dependency needs. Such experiences may then allow the child to progress to more mature ways of relating to others. The overly-socialized child with a harsh superego may benefit from being regressed from rule games into symbolic and practice play (Friedland and Shilkret, 1977). Children who are having difficulty in the later stages of identification may need to experiment with developmentally earlier tasks concerning the expression and inhibition of feelings. Permission for regressed behavior and the fostering of regression are common techniques of the clinical situation. Because of the physical organization of the therapeutic setting and because of the clinician's ability to monitor the child, therapists can tolerate a level of regression in clinical situations that is unacceptable in the classroom. No matter how permissive a classroom, highly regressed behavior will be disruptive and can frequently be destructive, leading to the danger of affective contagion, of harm to other children and of heightened guilt and fear in the child. For many emotionally disturbed children, there may be a need to provide other therapeutic situations, such as play therapy, that can allow for therapeutic regression.

Another example of disturbed behavior that is inappropriate for the classroom focuses on the expression of particularly threatening play themes. By means of proper equipment, spatial design and teacher intervention, most well-designed preschool or kindergarten classrooms facilitate play representing a number of critical developmental issues. Identity issues, fears and controls are confronted as an everyday occurrence in the dress-up corner. Yet, there may be some themes of importance to the emotionally disturbed child that may be disturbing or traumatic to other children because of their content and manner of portrayal. The explicit confrontation of issues concerning death, separation, elimination, annihilation, and anger may be overwhelming to the observing or participating non-disturbed child. However, such working-through in play may be essential for a disturbed child. This represents another circumstance in which the individual therapy situation may be a necessary concomitant of the integrated program.

Many young emotionally disturbed children require a suspension of the ongoing process of life in order to establish controls, get distance from anxiety-provoking stimuli, and experiment with new coping devices. These therapeutic experiences usually require a place and time that is set apart distinctly from everyday life. Often, the artificiality of the treatment room and situation provides such a vehicle. By delimiting the therapeutic situation in time, housing it in a building that the child attends only for a single purpose, and restricting the nature of available materials, a separation from and suspension of the common and the familiar is suggested to the child. In contrast, the classroom is usually designed as a microcosm of the familiar and common world of the child. Its adult staffing, grouping of children, and carefully selected furnishings frequently are attempts to promote the notion of a miniature representation of the society at large. Many emotionally disturbed children may, for therapeutic reasons, require a temporary release from this type of experience. The sole use of the integrated classroom as a treatment setting would impede the progress of such children.

Finally, the integrated program may not be able to meet some of the therapeutic needs presented by the parents of the disturbed child. Frequently, the treatment of the child may require changes in patterns of parenting, and an acceptance by the parents of some of the negative feelings and behaviors presented by their child. The traditional perception of the educational institution and classroom as child-focused mitigates against establishing contracts with parents that would be of therapeutic value to the child. The clinical situation can more typically make such demands. The parents of the disturbed child have explicitly brought their child to a change-agent who may then openly expect parental involvement. In contrast, the integrated classroom may be so quickly assimilated to the parent's concept of the typical classroom, that expectations of change may not be appropriate. For such changes to take place, a partnership between teachers, parents and therapists is usually a prerequisite.

Conclusion

The integrated classroom is an effective setting for many young mildly or moderately emotionally disturbed children. There are a number of reasons for integrating disturbed children in early childhood programs. The success of this integration, however, rests generally on two conditions. First, the main-streamed classroom must be modified for the emotionally disturbed child in terms of structure, teacher behavior and expectations and parent-teacher relationships. Second, since the regular classroom program may be unable to meet all of the behaviorally disordered child's needs, the addition of a clinical or therapeutic milieu should be carefully considered.

REFERENCES

Bandura, A. *Aggression: A social learning analysis.* Englewood Cliffs, New Jersey: Prentice-Hall, 1973.

Birch, J. W. *Mainstreaming educable mentally retarded children in regular classes.* Reston, Va.: Council for Exceptional Children, 1974.

Csapo, M. Peer models reverse the "One bad apple spoils the barrel" theory. *Teaching Exceptional Children*, 1972, *5* (1), 20–24.

Dunn, L. M. Special education for the mildly retarded—is much of it justifiable? *Exceptional Children*, 1968, *35* (1), 5–22.

Fink, A. H. Implications for teacher preparation. In A. J. Pappanikou, and J. L. Paul, (Eds.), *Mainstreaming emotionally disturbed children.* Syracuse, New York: Syracuse University Press, 1977.

Friedland, S. J. and Shilkret, R. B. *The concept of functional regression: Its value for Piagetian theory and its clinical application.* Paper presented at the seventh annual UAP-USC conference on Piaget and the Helping Professions. Los Angeles. 1977.

Gesell, A. et al. *The first five years of life.* New York: Harper, 1940.

Group for the Advancement of Psychiatry, *Psychopathological disorders in childhood: Theoretical consideration and a proposed classification.* New York: Group for the Advancement of Psychiatry, 1966.

Guralnick, M. J. The value of integrating handicapped and nonhandicapped preschool children. *American Journal of Orthopsychiatry*, 1976, *46* (2), 236–245.

Hammons, G. N. Educating the mildly retarded: a review. *Exceptional Children*, 1972, *38* (7), 565–570.

Hartup, W. Peer interaction and social organization. In P. Mussen. (Ed.) *Carmichael's Manual of Child Psychology*, Vol. 2. New York: John Wiley, 1970.

Hewett, F. *The emotionally disturbed child in the classroom.* Boston: Allyn & Bacon, 1968.

Meisels, S. J. A personal-social theory for the cognitive-developmental classroom. *Viewpoints*, (Bulletin of the School of Education, Indiana University), *52* (4), 1976, 15–24.

Meisels, S. J. First steps in mainstreaming, *Young Children*, 1977, *33* (1), 4–13.

Pastor, D. L. and Swap, S. M. An ecological study of emotionally disturbed preschoolers in special and regular classes. *Exceptional Children* (in press).

Paul, J. L. Mainstreaming emotionally disturbed children. In A. J. Pappanikou, and J. L. Paul, (Eds.), *Mainstreaming emotionally disturbed children.* Syracuse, New York: Syracuse University Press, 1977.

Reger, R. What does "mainstreaming" mean? *Journal of Learning Disabilities*, 1974, *7* (8), 57–59.

Solomon, R. and Wahler, R. Peer reinforcement control of classroom problem behavior. *Journal of Applied Behavior Analysis*, 1973, *6* (1), 49–56.

Swap, S. M. Disturbing classroom behaviors: An ecological and developmental view. *Exceptional Children*, 1974, *41*, 163–172.

Trippe, M. Conceptual problems in research on educational provisions for disturbed children. *Exceptional Children*, 1963, *29*, 400–406.

White, R. W. Motivation reconsidered: The concept of competence. *Psychological Review*, 1959, *66*, (5), 297–333.

Wood, M. M. *The Rutland Center model for treating emotionally disturbed children.* Athens, Georgia: Rutland Center Technical Assistance Office, 1972.

Wood, M. M. A developmental curriculum for social and emotional growth. In D. L. Lillie, (Ed.) *Early childhood education.* Chicago: Science Research Associates, 1975.

Wynne, S., Ulfeder, L. S. & Dakof, G. *Mainstreaming and early childhood education for handicapped children: Review and implications of research*, Final Report, Bureau of Education for the Handicapped, OEC-74-9056, 1975.

Samuel J. Meisels, Associate Professor, Child Study Department, Tufts University, Medford, Massachusetts.

Seymour Friedland, Framingham Child Guidance Clinic, Framingham, Massachusetts.

The Play's the Thing
Profile Tiffany Field

Robert J. Trotter

Tiffany Field loves babies. You can tell she loves babies by the way her eyes light up and her voice becomes positively animated whenever the topic turns to infants—and it usually does. For the past 10 years, Field has devoted most of her research time and efforts to the study of infants, toddlers and preschool children. Specifically, she has focused on the various ways newborns make contact with their parents and the world.

These first interactions, Field says, set the stage for social, emotional and cognitive development. It has been shown, for instance, that children who experienced disturbed interaction patterns during infancy still have similar problems or are having language development and behavioral problems at 2 years of age. "If you don't develop relatively harmonious interaction patterns early in life," Field explains, "you are going to have difficulty with peer relations and in social situations. We know that kids who have disturbed peer interactions are the ones most likely to end up being delinquent or psychologically disturbed."

Field reached this conclusion after several years as a psychotherapist. In the mid 1960s, when group therapy was coming into vogue, Field and a group of Washington, D.C., therapists founded the Psychiatric Institutes of America. She did a lot of art, play and dance therapy with disturbed children. "It was fun," she says, "but then I went on a sailing trip halfway around the world on a 31-foot sloop and did a lot of soul-searching. I realized that we really didn't know what we were doing, that we didn't know why psychotherapy was working or not working. I decided I should get some research skills, so I went for a Ph.D."

While studying developmental psychology at the University of Massachusetts at Amherst, Field became very interested in the kind of social and emotional disturbances she had seen in many of the children she had worked with as a therapist. "They were emotionally flat. There was very little variation in their vocal patterns," she says. "But the disturbed interaction pattern I really got interested in, because I had seen a lot of it in these kids, was gaze aversion. You'd be talking to a kid, or one kid would be talking to another and there would be very little eye contact. That ended up in frustration on the part of the speaker—no interaction got generated."

This pattern can begin in infancy, Field says. While still in graduate school, she got a grant to study high-risk infants—those born early, late or suffering from various congenital or hereditary problems. She found these infants a good group to study because they often have difficult interactions with their mothers. Many of them are hard to feed, unresponsive, fussy and cranky. The mothers may feel guilty, anxious or depressed and disappointed in the infant's unresponsiveness and lack of cuddliness, feelings that detract from normal mother-infant interactions. Field documented this in her first research paper, which compared the developmental and interaction patterns of 40 postmature infants with those of 40 normal infants.

Postmaturity occurs when a fetus stays in the womb too long. The placenta usually begins to calcify after about 38 weeks, the normal gestation period, and no longer functions as efficiently as it should, depriving the fetus of nutrients and oxygen. Infants born after 40 weeks often have peeling, parchmentlike skin, a long, thin body, and a wizened look. Subtle long-term effects may include learning difficulties, hyperactivity and problems with peer relationships. Although postmature infants appear physically normal by about 4 months of age, they do not do as well as full-term infants on behavioral and social measures. They tend to be fussy rather than cuddly and have trouble maintaining eye contact while being fed or played with by their mothers.

"Face-to-face interactions between infants and their mothers provide a foundation for the development of the infant's communication skills," Field explains. "How to take turns, how to engage in eye contact, how to go up and down with the flow of conversation—we can see babies doing all of those things at a very early age." The disturbed interaction pattern seen in postmaturely born infants, along with their physical problems, she suggests, could be related to the social and learning difficulties they have later.

After one year of postdoctoral research in Massachusetts, Field took a job at the Mailman Center for Child Development, the perfect place to continue her work with high-risk infants. The center, a research and training facility located in the heart of Miami, is affiliated with the University of Miami as well as with its medical school and hospital. Every year about 10 percent of the more than 10,000 infants born at the hospital are treated in the intensive-care unit, either because they are premature or because they have some other problem. These children are then seen in follow-up clinics until they are 8 years old. This never-ending supply of high-risk infants provides Field and her colleagues with a wide variety of problems to tackle.

Having been a therapist for many years, Field is still clinically oriented—perhaps too much so, she says. "What tends to happen, particularly in a setting like this where clinical problems are emerging all over the place, is you tend to jump around. You are trying to finish one study and you find another group of kids that have another problem you have to look at."

Aptly described as a bundle of energy by her colleagues, Field has managed to tackle many of these problems, almost always with an emphasis on early interaction patterns. One study even suggests that it may be a good idea for a mother to start getting to know her child before it is born. Previous research has indicated that high levels of maternal anxiety during pregnancy can have negative effects on the fetus and may contribute to hyperactivity and irritability in the newborn infant. Field and her colleagues reasoned that reducing the expectant mother's anxiety might produce a better newborn, one who's less irritable, more responsive.

Because a lot of anxiety results from worries about the developing fetus, the researchers used routine ultrasound examinations to show a group of pregnant women that their fetuses were in good condition and were developing normally. While the women were watching the fetus on the video monitor, the researcher talked them through the examination, saying things like "Look, there's the fingers, there's the toes. See, your kid can already smile."

They compared the women who received this visual and verbal feedback with a similar group who were given only a summary of the results of the ultrasound examination. According to Field, the feedback reduced pregnancy anxiety, resulted in fewer birth complications and produced healthier, less irritable babies. "It would appear," Field concludes, "that ultrasound feedback is a cost-effective way to reduce pregnancy anxiety and produce better babies."

Reductions in such anxiety may have other benefits as well. According to Field, pregnancy anxiety has been linked with cranio-facial anomalies, such as cleft palate and harelip. These problems can be hereditary, she explains, but experiments have shown that rats exposed to stress during pregnancy more likely give birth to pups with cranio-facial anomalies.

This facial disfigurement may also lead to some social discrimination. Disfigured infants may be more difficult to interact with, says Field, both because they are less attractive and because their deformity makes their facial expressions more difficult to read.

Field and her colleagues monitored the face-to-face interactions between 12 such infants and their mothers and found important differences compared with normal mother-infant pairs. Although mothers look at these infants as much as mothers of normal infants look at theirs, they are not as smiling and lively as the other mothers. There is less eye contact, smiling, vocalization, imitation and reactivity. "These less-than-optimal interactions may contribute to later social problems," Field says. Follow-up studies will determine whether these infants continue to be less attentive and reactive and whether corrective surgery leads to more social responsivity.

During one such follow-up exam, Field's playfulness and love of children serendipitously led to several ground-breaking findings regarding the remarkable abilities of very young infants. "Often, during these follow-ups," she explains, "we have trouble keeping the babies alert. So I started clowning around, making monkeyshine faces, singing funny songs and so on, and we noticed that the newborns appeared to be mimicking us. Facial imitation had never been documented in infants this young, so we designed an imitation study."

Newborns, approximately 3 days old, were held in a face-to-face position by an examiner who made a happy, sad or surprised-looking face. The examiner sustained the expression until the infant looked away; then, after a couple of deep knee-bends and tongue clicks, made another face (or repeated the same expression) until the infant looked away again. An observer who could see only the infant's face would then guess, based on the infant's expression, which expression was being modeled. The chance of guessing correctly would be only 33 percent, but the observers did much better. Expressions of surprise were guessed correctly 76 percent of the time; happy, 58 percent; and sad, 59 percent. Field and her colleagues concluded that the infants' facial movements were an attempt at imitation, an attempt so obvious that it could be recognized.

The 3-day-olds also displayed some unexpected basic learning ability, apparently learning to recognize and discriminate among the expressions. This was indicated by the amount of time they looked at each one. When an expression is modeled for the first time, for example, an infant will stare at it with interest. If the same expression is presented several times in a row, the infant will look at it less each time. This is called habituation, a basic sign of learning. If a different expression is displayed, the infant stares at it longer. This dishabituation indicates that even very young infants can discriminate among basic facial expressions.

Not all of the newborns tested were imitative at such an early age, but Field believes that "the more imitative kids and those who have more developed recognition skills are going to be better interaction partners, primarily because they are more expressive. And if they have more sophisticated recognition skills, they can recognize the signals of the mother and will develop a smoother interaction pattern."

While doing the imitation studies, Field and her colleagues decided that it would be fun to show the mothers what their kids could do. "A lot of mothers still think that the normal newborn cannot see or hear," explains Field, "so they are always very surprised, and it's fun watching them be surprised. We wanted to show them as much as we could about their newborns, hoping we could turn them on to doing more. But when we started working with the mothers, we were the ones who were surprised. We realized that the newborns were acting differently with the mothers than they had been with us. They were visually discriminating the mothers from us."

Previous studies had shown that newborns could discriminate their mother's voice, but not her face, from that of a stranger. It is possible that infants can learn features of their mother's voice, but certainly not her face, while still in the womb.

The researchers designed another study. This time, infants approximately 4 days old were placed in an infant seat in front of a trap door that opened to reveal either the face of the mother or of a stranger. During four trials, each infant saw each twice while observers recorded the number of seconds the infant looked at each face. According to Field, the newborns showed a clear preference for the mother's face. This is remarkable, she says, especially since these babies had spent a total of only about four hours with their mothers during feedings. It appears that newborns can learn some distinctive features of the mother's face during the first hours of life.

The infants also showed an ability to discriminate between the mother and a stranger. This may serve an adaptive function, Field explains. Newborns who can discriminate their mother's face may elicit more nurturing behavior from her.

The imitation and recognition studies gained Field and the Mailman Center a lot of publicity because people are always fascinated by sensational findings about the abilities of newborns. But there is also a practical side to this research. "It's a sensitizing phenomenon," Field explains. "The more parents know about the abilities of their babies, the more likely they are to take advantage of that knowledge for developing healthy interaction patterns with their babies." And the more researchers and clinicians know about such patterns, the more they can do to correct disturbed patterns.

Premature infants, for example, have serious difficulties interacting with their mothers

Games Parents Play

"Pat-a-cake" and "peek-a-boo" are more than just fun and games, says Field. These and other games introduce infants to the rules of social behavior. Being highly repetitive with simple roles for both parent and infant, these games help infants learn such things as the rules of give-and-take during conversations. Even when infants are too young to play an active role, Field explains, the structure of the repetitive games may help them grasp the turn-taking nature of social interaction.

In one study, Field documented the most often-played parent-infant games. In addition to "pat-a-cake" and "peek-a-boo," they included:

• "Tell-me-a-story," in which the parent asks the baby to tell a story, the baby coos or makes some other sound and the parent then supplies the words for both the story and the reactions to the story. This helps teach the infant that his or her responses will elicit a response from the parent.

• "I'm gonna get you," in which a wide-eyed parent repeatedly looms toward the infant saying such things as "Ah, boom!" or "I'm gonna get you." This repetitious behavior usually makes the infant smile or laugh, and the parent continues the game until the infant no longer responds.

• "Walking fingers" or "creepie crawlies," in which the parent's fingers crawl spider-like up the body of the baby, usually make the baby laugh.

• "So big," a game in which the parent extends the infant's arms upwards and says, "So big," providing the infant with a combination of visual, auditory and tactile stimulation.

Unfortunately, according to Field, high-risk infants may miss out on some of the important social learning experiences this game playing provides. Twenty normal 4-month-old infants, 20 premature and 20 postmature infants and their parents were videotaped during a play situation. The parents of the normal babies played games with their infants almost 40 percent of the time. Parents of both groups of high-risk infants played games less than 30 percent of the time.

Field says these parents probably play less because high-risk infants usually are more difficult to deal with than normal babies. Premature infants, for instance, tend to be floppy, underactive, unresponsive and have a weak cry. Postmature infants are overactive, fussy and have a cry like a donkey's bray. These difficulties limit the playfulness of the parents, which further limits the responsiveness of the infants. Parents, especially the parents of high-risk infants, Field suggests, should be more aware of the importance games play in the social development of their children.

because of their weakened and undeveloped condition. They make less eye contact, in part, because they are too weak to hold their heads up. In addition, preemies have a limited attention span and usually need more stimulation than normal infants before they will respond.

"A mother walks a very fine line with a preemie," says Field. "She may not provide enough stimulation to get the child to respond, or she may be too stimulating. She's got to be really sensitive to the baby's signals."

Field and her colleagues use coaching sessions to teach mothers of premature and other high-risk infants more effective ways of interacting with their children. If a mother tends to be too active, for example, they tell her to try imitating the baby's behavior. This gets the mother to slow down and limit her behavior. It also makes her very sensitive to her baby's signals and generally turns into an imitation game, with the mother and the baby imitating each other. It is also very effective in getting a baby to stop crying. Just imitate the baby's crying, Field says, and often the baby will stop and pay attention to your crying. It's almost as if the infant were thinking, "What's going on here? I was the one that was crying, not you."

Finally, overstimulating mothers are taught to stop talking or interacting when the baby looks away. "This is the kid's signal that it's time for a break," Field says. "We tell the mothers not to start talking again until the baby turns back and looks at you again. That's pretty effective."

Getting mothers to slow down is usually easy, Field says. Getting mothers who are depressed, passive and noninteractive to liven up is a lot more difficult. One thing Field and her colleagues have tried is a bug-in-the ear device through which they coach the mothers.

"The animation in our voices sometimes carries over to their behavior. Or we'll teach them a nursery rhyme and have them sing it. They may feel ridiculous, but when they see the kid's reaction they start laughing. That sometimes works, but it's a lot harder to liven them up than to slow them down."

Assessing Amazing Abilities

Field has found that teaching mothers to rate the behavior of their infants the way a pediatrician would sensitizes them to the amazing abilities of their newborns and can enhance mother-child interactions. The following questions are among those included in the Mother's Assessment of the Behavior of Her Infant.

When you play with your baby he or she is often
1. *sleepy*
2. *alert*
3. *upset*

How much do you have to stimulate your baby to get him or her to look at you?
1. *not very much*
2. *a fair amount*
3. *a lot*

When your baby is upset what does he or she do to quiet himself or herself?
1. *bring hand to mouth*
2. *sucks with nothing in his or her mouth*
3. *looks at you*

Try talking to your baby holding your face about one foot away from his or her face and then slowly move your face to one side and then to the other as you continue talking. When you do this your baby
1. *doesn't look at you*
2. *becomes quiet and looks at you*
3. *follows your face to each side with his or her head and eyes*
4. *follows your face with his or her head and eyes, up and down and to each side*

Now try the same thing, only move your face without talking. When you do this your baby
1. *doesn't look at you*
2. *becomes quiet*

3. *follows your face with head and eyes*
4. *follows your face with his or her head and eyes, up and down and to each side*

Try talking to your baby from one side of his or her head and then from the other. When you do this he or she
1. *has no reaction or blinks*
2. *becomes quiet*
3. *turns eyes and head to your voice once or twice*
4. *turns eyes and head to your voice more than two times*

Now try holding a colorful toy or some shiny object in front of your baby's face and then move it slowly to each side of his or her head and then up and down. When you do this he or she
1. *doesn't look at the toy*
2. *becomes quiet and looks at toy*
3. *follows the toy you are moving with head and eyes*
4. *follows the toy you are moving with head and eyes, up and down and to each side*

Try shaking a rattle on one side of your baby's head and then on the other side. When you do this he or she
1. *has no reaction or blinks*
2. *becomes quiet*
3. *turns eyes and head to the rattle once or twice*
4. *turns eyes and head to the rattle more than two times*

When you did the above things with your baby he or she usually
1. *paid little attention to you or the toy*
2. *had short periods of watching you or the toy*
3. *watched for a fairly long time*
4. *paid attention most of the time*

(cont.)

How does your baby feel when you handle or hold him or her?
1. *limp like a rag doll*
2. *limp some of time*
3. *relaxed but firm*
4. *very tense*

When your baby moves his or her arms the movements are
1. *jerky most of the time*
2. *jerky some of the time*
3. *smooth some of the time*
4. *smooth most of the time*

When you pick up your baby and hold him or her in a rocking position he or she
1. *often swings his or her arms and kicks his or her legs and squirms a lot*
2. *is like a sack of meal in your arms*
3. *relaxes and nestles his or her head in the crook of your arms*
4. *moves his or her face toward you and reaches out to grab your clothing*

When your baby is crying very hard
1. *nothing seems to quiet him or her*
2. *only a pacifier will quiet him or her*
3. *holding and rocking will quiet him or her*
4. *talking and holding your hand on his or her stomach quiets him or her*

Please circle those activities that upset your baby
1. *changing his or her diaper*
2. *undressing or dressing him or her*
3. *putting him or her back in the bassinet*
4. *lying him or her on his or her stomach*

How often does your baby tremble when he or she is warmly dressed?
1. *not very often*
2. *occasionally*
3. *fairly often*
4. *very often*

When your baby is crying, how successful is he or she at quieting himself or herself?
1. *cannot quiet himself or herself*
2. *makes several attempts to quiet himself or herself but is usually unsuccessful*
3. *has many brief sessions at quieting himself or herself*
4. *often quiets himself or herself for long periods of time.*

How would you describe your baby's hand-to-mouth activity?
1. *makes no attempt to bring his or her hands to his or her mouth*
2. *often brings a hand next to his or her mouth*
3. *sometimes puts his or her fist or fingers in his or her mouth*
4. *sometimes sucks on fist or fingers for as long as 15 seconds at a time*

How many times has your baby looked like he or she was smiling at you?

Baby Massage

One of the reasons I got very involved with premature infants," says Field, "was that my 10-year-old daughter was a preemie." Ever since then, the problems of premature infants have been a special concern for Field. Some of her most recent research shows that massaging premature infants can help them catch up developmentally with full-term infants.

Field and her colleagues studied 40 preemies who had just been released from the intensive-care unit and placed in the transitional, or "grower," nursery. Twenty of these babies received special tactile and kinesthetic stimulation for three 15-minute periods at the beginning of three consecutive hours every morning for 10 weekdays. For the tactile stimulation, the infant was placed on its stomach and gently stroked. Beginning with the head and neck, the massage would proceed downward to the feet and from the shoulders to the hands. The infant was then rolled over for the kinesthetic stimulation, which involved flexing and extending each arm and leg and then both legs together. Then the tactile stimulation was repeated.

The massaged babies gained 47 percent more weight than the others, even though both groups had the same number of feedings per day and averaged the same intake of formula. The massaged infants were more active, more alert and performed better on the Brazelton scale. Finally, their hospital stay was about six days shorter than that of the nonmassaged infants. This saved approximately $3,000 per infant, Field says, making massage a cost-effective way to help premature infants.

The increased activity of the massaged infants would seem to work against weight gain, but similar findings have been made with rat pups. And Field has found that even the activity of sucking on a pacifier can lead to increased weight gain in premature infants. Infants allowed to suck on a pacifier while being fed intravenously gained more weight than those who were simply given tube feeding. Field thinks that in both cases the increased activity may result in increased gastrointestinal and metabolic effi-

ciency. "We're going to have to do all kinds of tests to document that," she says, "but I think that's the bottom line. And we do know that putting malnourished children on an exercise regimen helps them gain weight."

The massaged infants were also more socially interactive than the others. "This," Field suggests, "may be because infant massage, like adult massage, gets some kind of intimacy going and produces a better baby. And if you have a better baby, you have a happier parent who is going to interact better and be more responsive. It's like a criss-cross effect. After a while you don't know who did what to whom. But it's the end result that counts—better babies."

Unfortunately, if the mothers don't liven up, their depression can carry over to their infants. Field's research suggests that infants as young as 3 months of age appear to be affected by living with a depressed mother. They talk less and smile less than infants do with normal mothers. The infants may simply be imitating their mothers or they may be depressed because of the minimal stimulation provided by their mothers. The question now, says Field, is whether this depressed behavior generalizes to other adults. "Have these infants already developed a depressed style of interacting," she asks, "or are they just flat and deadpan when they are with their mothers?" A study to answer these questions is getting under way.

Another form of intervention that Field and colleagues have found very effective involves teaching mothers to administer a modified form of the Brazelton Neonatal Assessment Scale (a test used by child specialists and pediatricians to measure various aspects of infant development—see "Assessing Amazing Abilities," this article). Using this test to teach mothers the amazing skills of their newborns, Field suggests, may facilitate early interactions which, in turn, may contribute to early cognitive development.

She bases this conclusion on a study of teenage mothers and their premature infants, who are likely to suffer interaction disturbances and cognitive delays because of their prematurity and parenting by teenagers. The

mothers were asked to administer the Brazelton scale to their infants at birth and at one-week-intervals during the first month. These mothers and their infants were then compared at 1, 4 and 12 months with a similar group who had not been taught the Brazelton. At each testing, the mothers who had used the Brazelton talked more to their infants and had more face-to-face contact than did the other mothers. At the 12-month assessment their infants also scored higher on a test of mental development.

It appears that sensitizing mothers to their infant's unique abilities through the Brazelton scale can make early interactions more effective, Field says. The mothers become more interested in observing their child's development and more active in providing stimulation and interaction that fosters development. And previous studies have found that more effective early mother-infant interactions foster later cognitive development.

"So it all comes down to those first interactions," says Field. "I think that the early interactions the baby has with the world are critical for setting a foundation for later interactions. The important thing is to make parents aware of the amazing skills of the newborn, make them aware that they have a very active, lively, interactive creature from the very start. Once this is established, the parents just need to make contact and interact so the baby can get practice in those skills."

Robert J. Trotter is a senior editor at Psychology Today.

ASK YOURSELF:
Identifying Issues for Debate and Advocacy

1. Is mainstreaming a passing fad?

2. What are the rights of parents of a handicapped child? What are the rights of children (handicapped and non-handicapped)? What are the rights of teachers?

3. Do physically handicapped children create unnecessary fears in their normal preschool peers? Why or why not?

4. What are the effects on the mainstreamed child when he or she is socially isolated by peers? Are mainstreamed children often social isolates in regular classrooms?

5. What knowledges and skills do teachers need to have to be able to work with handicapped children?

6. What measures should be taken to ensure appropriate educational placements for handicapped or high-risk children?

7. Sue, a legally blind child, is enrolled in Sandbox Nursery School. As part of the special education aid provided for Sue, a special education teacher from the Board of Cooperative Education Services (BOCES) comes three times a week to work with Sue. This teacher works with her during a time of the session when Sue will not miss out on specially planned activities. The special education teacher also incorporates activities that involve the entire class. The directors contacted an organization called Lighthouse to help them get Sue's parents to accept her disability. Sue has come a long way. When she was first enrolled, she could not participate in snack because she could not feed herself and refused to hold a cup. The changed attitudes of her parents also have fostered quicker progress at home. Examine and discuss this situation in light of suggestions made by Meisels and Freidland for mainstreaming.

8. Mrs. Bates, a center director, says that their program cannot mainsteam handicapped children because their building is not equipped to meet the needs of handicapped children. What assumptions about mainstreaming and handicapped children is Mrs. Bates making?

9. Is infant education and stimulation beneficial for high-risk infants? Why or why not? In your response, consider the work of Tiffany Field and the following conversation:
   CATHY: OK, Donna, let's go over our list of purchases for the baby room.
   1. Lullaby records?
   DONNA: Check.

CATHY: 2. Four mobiles?

DONNA: Check.

CATHY: 3. Four crib protectors, two with ducky designs and two with piglets?

DONNA: Check.

CATHY: Looks good! Now, did you decide on the colors for the headboards?

DONNA: Two orange and two yellow.

CATHY: Great! With all the stimulation stuff we've ordered for the infant intervention program, I'm hoping we'll get approval as a university research and training site, so we can get some extra help. I'm sure that when the university's infant program supervisor comes to visit our program, she will see the artist's murals on the wall as an added visual plus.

10. Under what circumstances is enrollment of an infant in some type of intervention program justified?

11. How should education for handicapped or high-risk children (ages birth to five years) be funded (public, corporate, private, state, federal, or local)? Why?

APPLICATION/ADVOCACY EXERCISES

1. In order to better understand diverse perceptions and responses to special needs learners, interview a nursery school teacher, a day care teacher, and a kindergarten teacher. Request an interview with each teacher and state your purpose (i.e., to gather information about identification of and curricular adaptations for developmentally delayed and handicapped learners). Based on information gathered from this and the previous chapter, compose four to six interview questions that you wish to ask each person. (Avoid questions that can be answered with a yes-no only response.) Take notes during the interview in order to obtain a record of the interviewee's responses. After the interviews, write a synopsis of the interviews, including the questions asked, each interviewee's responses, and your interpretation of responses in relation to readings in this chapter. Then compare interview findings with guidelines for developmentally appropriate curriculum practices (Bredekamp, 1987; Nebraska State Board of Education, 1984). Share your information in class in a panel discussion.

2. On October 8, 1986, PL 99-457 was signed into law. These amendments to PL 94-142 provide federal assistance to states for intervention services and preschool programs

293

for handicapped children (birth to five years) and for intervention services aimed at high-risk infants and toddlers. All states have decided to apply for these funds. Contact an early childhood special education representative in your state (e.g., in the State Education Department or in the State Mental Health Department). Find out how your state plans to implement the provisions of this amendment. What "lead agency" is (will be) designated to oversee and monitor implementation of these provisions? What types of agencies or institutions are (will be) the major providers of services (e.g., public versus private)? How are (will) handicapped or at-risk children (be) identified? What proportion of the children served in the state have language delays or speech impairments? What proportion of the children served in the state have each of various handicapping or at-risk conditions? What provisions (will) exist to train staff for these programs?

REFERENCES & SUGGESTED READINGS

Bredekamp, S. (Ed.). (1987). *Developmentally appropriate practice in early childhood programs serving children from birth through age 8*. Washington, DC: National Association for the Education of Young Children. (Major portions of this publication can be found in the September 1986 and January 1988 issues of *Young Children*.)

Demerest, E. (1983, January–February). Perspectives on mainstreaming: A parent's view. *Children Today*, 26, 37.

Guralnick, M. J. (1982). Mainstreaming young handicapped children: A public policy and ecological systems analysis. In B. Spodek (Ed.), *Handbook of research in early childhood education* (pp. 456–500). New York: The Free Press, Macmillan.

Nebraska State Board of Education. (1984, October). *What's best for 5-year-olds?* Position statement on kindergarten. Lincoln, NE: Author. (Included in Chapter 9.)

O'Connell, J. C. (1983). Education of handicapped preschoolers: A national survey of services and personnel requirements. *Exceptional Children*, 49, 538–540.

Vuola, S. (1983, January–February). Perspectives on mainstreaming: A teacher's view. *Children Today*, 27.

Wang, M. C., Reynolds, M. C., & Walberg, H. J. (1986, September). Rethinking special education. *Educational Leadership*, 26–31.

White, B. P., & Phair, M. A. (1986, January). "It'll be a challenge!" Managing emotional stress in teaching disabled children. *Young Children*, 41, 44–48.

Widerstrom, A. H. (1986, December). Educating young handicapped children: What can early childhood education contribute? *Childhood Education*, 63, 78–83.

CHAPTER 11

Multicultural and Bilingual Education

Thanksgiving: Time for a Unit on Indians? *

Mrs. Jones teaches kindergarten in a middle-sized city in the Northeast. She's really concerned about all of her children who have black, Hispanic, and a number of different European ethnic backgrounds. Through the grapevine, Mrs. Jones learns that there are three children in her class who are said to be Indians:

> *Ramona and her family have just moved to the city from a southwestern reservation, where she attended a government-sponsored Head Start program for Indian children. She is bilingual in her native language and English.*
>
> *Mary has heard that she has an Indian great-grandmother on her father's side of the family. The family doesn't know where this great-grandmother was born and doesn't know any Indian people who might help them trace their ancestry.*
>
> *Tom's parents have lived in the city for 15 years, but the family keeps in touch with relatives living in an Indian community 100 miles away. Tom's mother belongs to the city's Native American Cultural Center and occasionally attends dinners and social dances there, but Tom's father hasn't attended for some years; the dinners conflict with his bowling league. Tom doesn't speak an Indian language.*

---

*Adapted from Z. Chevalier and S. Roark-Calnek (1982, November). Meeting the challenge of cultural pluralism. Workshop presented at the National Conference of the National Association for the Education of Young Children, Washington, DC.

Mrs. Jones decides to teach a unit on traditional Indian culture "because that's part of our history, our past." This is the only unit using ethnic or cultural content that she will teach this year; she wants to "make the Indian children feel special." The unit will be taught at Thanksgiving time. She sets up a Plains-style tipi in her room and plans a series of learning activities on a buffalo-hunting theme.

On the day that she introduces the unit, Mrs. Jones announces to her class, "We have three real Indians in this room and they're going to help us learn about themselves." She encourages other children to direct questions to Tom, Mary, and Ramona.

As Mrs. Jones begins her lesson, Ramona goes to the bathroom and hangs around the sink, washing her hands. She pulls out paper towels one by one and carefully drops them in the wastebasket. When Mrs. Jones calls on her to answer a question, she looks away, answers "dunno," and sits down in the back of the story circle, behind another child.

Mary has moved up to sit next to Mrs. Jones, who is reading a story and showing its illustrations to the children. She reaches over and pats Mrs. Jones on the leg, smiling at her. When Mrs. Jones addresses questions to Mary, she answers readily at first but soon begins to fidget. Mrs. Jones asks her why the Indian boy in the story is wearing a feather in his hair, and Mary hesitates before stammering out an answer. She's interrupted by several other children: "Dummy! You made that up. When I saw that on TV. . . ." Mary bursts into tears.

The three Indian children are given notes to take home to their parents and told, "I'm asking your mommies and daddies to come in and tell us about how Indians live. Maybe they can bring in something your grandmas and grandpas used a long time ago."

Tom slouches down when he hears this and mumbles, "I bet I'm going to lose that note!" He remains stonily silent during the course of the day. At the end of the day, he rips the note from his jacket and stuffs it down behind a cushion. Mrs. Jones is distressed.

Questions

1. Why do you think Ramona, Mary, and Tom are reacting in these ways?

2. What is Mrs. Jones trying to accomplish? What should she know about these children? How could we help her to know? How else might she accomplish her goals?

PREVIEW

Different views on multicultural education often stem from values attributed to a melting-pot culture versus a pluralistic culture. Those who espouse the first position believe that so-

ciety's needs will best be served when everyone works toward reaching consensus on norms and values. Those who favor the latter view believe that acknowledging differences in ethnic and cultural traditions as well as diverse ways of communicating contribute to the freshness, richness, and openness of a society. Which of these positions best meets the needs of all children and their families? Should we assume that all people wish to retain their distinctive cultural identities? Do some wish to blend in more readily with the dominant culture? Or is it possible or even beneficial to have "the best of both worlds"?

In the first selection of this chapter, Allan C. Ornstein and Daniel U. Levine examine the history and recent trends in multicultural education and then discuss potential pitfalls for today's multicultural programs. Next, Patricia G. Ramsey points out some of the common misconceptions about multicultural education in early childhood. Luis M. Laosa stresses the importance of designing programs for children that provide continuity with the sociocultural environment of the home and argues that bilingual programs are not detrimental to the child's academic success. Frances Smardo Dowd and Velma Schmidt review research on the development of attitudes about ethnic and racial differences and recommend use of materials that better children's understanding of various cultural lifestyles and customs. Finally, Alice J. Kawakami and Kathryn Hu-pei Au describe a kindergarten program designed to reflect the cultural language interaction styles of Hawaiian children.

Multicultural Education: Trends and Issues

Allan C. Ornstein and Daniel U. Levine

Concern with multicultural education in the United States grew through the 1970s and promises to increase in the 1980s. This concern reflects problems involving intergroup contact and individual and group opportunity encountered by a nation of many ethnic groups and subcultures. It also reflects the prevailing notion that the melting pot theme has not worked for some non-white ethnic groups.

Recognizing and responding to social trends emphasizing the desirability of multicultural education, educators examined and developed ways to achieve a constructive pluralism in the U.S. educational system. School officials at every level of this system developed specific approaches for translating the goals of multicultural education into classroom practice. In particular, state departments of education, national professional organizations, local school district curriculum developers and supervisors, and colleges of teacher education introduced guidelines for providing constructive multicultural education for all students.

Multicultural Instruction

Differential instructional approaches appropriate for teaching students with differing ethnic and racial backgrounds are a key to developing effective approaches for multicultural education. Important and frequently discussed approaches include student learning styles, dialect differences among ethnic and racial groups and bilingual education.

Student Learning Styles

A serious attempt to explore differentiating instruction according to learning styles associated with students' backgrounds is the "bicognitive" approach advocated by Manuel Ramirez and Alfredo Castaneda (1974). After conducting preliminary research with Hispanic students, Ramirez and Castaneda concluded that these children tend to be more "field sensitive" than non-minority children. Field-sensitive children are described as being more influenced by personal relationships and by praise or disapproval from authority figures than are "field-independent" students.

Ramirez and Castaneda reviewed the implications of these findings for instruction and concluded that a "field-sensitive curriculum" should be "humanized through use of narration, humor, drama, and fantasy" and should emphasize "description of wholes and generalities" and be "structured in such a way that children work cooperatively with peers or with the teacher in a variety of activities."

Although "bicognitive" instruction and similar approaches may potentially improve instruction for many minority students in the future, little current research documents the proven value of such methods. The learning styles of field-sensitive minority students, moreover, may be associated as much or more with low socioeconomic status as with ethnicity or race per se.

Another example of an effort to identify instructional approaches uniquely suited to students' ethnic or racial backgrounds has been provided by Vera John-Steiner and Larry Smith (1978), who have worked with Pueblo Indian children in the Southwest. They concluded that schooling for these children would be more successful if it took better account of their "primary learning" patterns (learning outside the school) and organized classroom instruction in a manner more compatible with

Source: Allan C. Ornstein & Daniel U. Levine (1982). Multicultural education: Trends and issues. *Childhood Education, 58,* 241–245. Reprinted by permission of Allan C. Ornstein and Daniel U. Levine and the Association for Childhood Education International, 11141 Georgia Avenue, Suite 200, Wheaton, MD. Copyright © 1982 by the Association.

these patterns. These investigators point out that primary learning tends to take place in personal communication with emotionally significant individuals, in tutorial situations (face-to-face) in which learning is pervasive (not limited to a single setting) and highly adaptive (closely linked to the concerns and needs of the community).

In the case of Pueblo children, the researchers found that primary learning also emphasized verbal instruction, exploratory play, and monitoring of the complex activity of elders, and that children's observations centered on individuals—such as a favorite uncle—who were particularly important to a child. Researchers concluded that teachers should do more to match their techniques with the previous learning of the child, especially in the middle and upper grades. The value of this approach, however, is not well documented, and its specific implications for classroom instruction have not been worked out in much detail.

Recognition of Dialect Differences

Many educators are concerned with the problems of teaching students who speak nonstandard dialects that may hamper their progress in the traditional classroom. Historically, U.S. public schools have attempted to teach "proper" or standard English to students who speak nonstandard dialects, but simplistic insistence on proper English sometimes has caused students either to reject their own cultural background or to view such efforts by teachers as demeaning and hostile.

In recent years educators have been particularly concerned with learning problems encountered by students who speak Black English. A number of scholars studied the Black English dialect and succeeded in identifying its underlying grammatical forms and differences from standard English (Dillard, 1972). Because Black English seems to be the basic form of speech of many low-income black students who are not succeeding academically, some educators propose the school teach such students in Black English until they learn to read. Other proposals and experiments have advocated teaching English as a foreign language to students who speak Black English or other nonstandard dialects, emphasizing students' personal experiences in teaching language and other transitional techniques.

Research on teaching in Black English or other dialects has not indicated that students will gain academically if initially taught in their own dialect. Thus one review of the research stated "there is, as yet, no conclusive empirical evidence in the literature supporting the belief that using any of the methods which purport to minimize the interference of Black English or reading performance . . . is more successful than the traditional standard instructional materials" (Harber and Bryan, 1976). In addition, members of dialect communities usually disagree about the way schools should teach English. In working-class black communities, for example, many parents believe their children should be taught only in "proper" English in order to acquire language skills required for success in the larger society.

Despite lack of research indicating the superiority of any particular method for teaching students with nonstandard dialects, educators still should seek constructive ways to overcome the learning problems many of these students encounter in standard English classrooms. This task became particularly important when a federal judge ruled in 1979 that the Ann Arbor, Michigan, school district must recognize that students who speak Black English may need special help in learning standard English (Schools . . . 1979). The court ordered the school district to submit a plan defining the steps it would take to identify children who speak Black English and then to take their dialect into consideration in teaching them to read. Although the decision is being appealed and is not binding on anyone outside the Ann Arbor schools, it may have an important future influence in many school districts struggling to provide effective multicultural education for students who speak nonstandard dialects.

Bilingual / Bicultural Education

Bilingual education, which provides instruction for non-English speaking students in their native language, has been an expanding activity in U.S. public schools. In 1968 Congress passed the Bilingual Education Act and in 1974 the Supreme Court ruled in Lau v. Nichols that schools must take steps to help students who "are certain to find their classroom experiences wholly incomprehensible" because they do not understand English. Congressional appropriations for bilingual education increased from $7.5 million to 1969 to $158.6 million in 1979. Although the federal and state governments fund bilingual projects for more than 60 language groups speaking various Asian, Indo-European and Native American languages, the large majority (70 percent) of children in these projects are Hispanic.

Bilingual education has been expanding partly because the federal Office of Civil Rights (OCR) insists that educational opportunities be improved for limited-English speaking (LES) and non-English speaking (NES) students. The Supreme Court's unanimous decision in the Lau case involving Chinese children in San Francisco did not focus on bilingual education as the only remedy for teaching non-English speaking students. Instead, the Court said, "Teaching English to the students of Chinese ancestry is one choice. Giving instruction to this group in Chinese is another. There may be others." In practice, however, federal regulations for implementing the Lau decision have tended to focus on bilingual education as the most common solution for helping LES and NES students, generally suggesting that school districts initiate bilingual programs if they enroll more than twenty students of a given language group at a particular grade level. Bilingual programs have proliferated accordingly, but considerable disagreement exists concerning the kinds of programs that can or should be offered.

Controversies over bilingual education have become somewhat embittered as federal and state actions have led to the establishment of additional programs. As in the case of teaching through dialect, there are arguments between those who would "immerse" children in an English-language environment and those who believe initial instruction will be more effective in the native language. Divided on this issue, residents in some ethnic neighborhoods have engaged in bitter internal struggles over the establishment of bilingual programs in the public schools.

Educators and laypeople concerned with LES and NES students also argue over whether emphasis should be placed on teaching in the native language over a long period (maintenance) or proceeding to teach in English as soon as possible (transitional). On the one side, those who favor maintenance feel that this will help build or maintain a constructive sense of identity among ethnic or racial minorities. On the other side are those

who believe that cultural maintenance programs are harmful because they separate groups from one another or discourage students from mastering English well enough to function successfully in the larger society.

Adherents and opponents of bilingual education also differ on the related issues of whether bilingual programs sometimes or frequently are designed to provide teaching jobs for native language speakers and whether individuals who fill these jobs are competent in English. Observers who favor bilingual/bicultural maintenance tend to believe that the schools need many adults who can teach LES or NES students in their own language, while many observers who favor transitional programs feel that relatively few staff are required for a legitimate program.

Another major controversy involving bilingual education concerns whether this approach is effective in improving the performance of low-achieving students. Most scholars who have examined the research agree that bilingual education has effected little if any improvement in the performance of participating students. Other scholars partially disagree and argue that programs implemented well can result in significant achievement gains. There is considerable agreement, however, that much more than bilingual/bicultural education is needed to improve the performance of economically disadvantaged LES and NES students. In this regard, Joshua Fishman (1977) has summarized the research literature by stating that, "on the whole," bilingual education is "too frail a device in and of itself, to significantly alter the learning experiences of the minority-mother-tongue in general or their majority-language-learning success in particular . . . precisely because there are so many other pervasive reasons why such children achieve poorly . . . removing the extra burden . . . does not usually do the trick."

Dangers in Multicultural Education

Multicultural education can be indispensable in helping to achieve constructive cultural pluralism in a nation composed of diverse ethnic groups. At the same time, however, multicultural education can be potentially harmful or damaging. In general, the potential dangers of multicultural education are the same as those associated with the larger concept of cultural pluralism. Major dangers are that:

1. Multicultural education can emphasize separatism in a way that is divisive and disunifying. If too much emphasis in multicultural education is placed on differences and separation, educators may neglect unifying themes and similarities that are desirable in a society in which groups are interdependent. Emphasis on differences may lead to neglect of the need to develop citizens who understand and act on national and universal responsibilities of citizenship.

In addition, educational arrangements for some aspects of multicultural education such as bilingualism may conflict with constitutional requirements for ethnic and racial desegregation. For example, bringing students from particular ethnic groups together in a bilingual program may increase their segregation within a school district or school.

2. Multicultural education may be used to justify second-rate education for economically disadvantaged students or minority students. Encouraging the separation of disadvantaged students in "remedial" education programs or of minority students in "ethnic studies" programs under the guise of cultural pluralism can result in the establishment or maintenance of programs that are widely viewed as second rate. Unless great efforts are made to maintain the quality and reputation of such programs, students who participate in them may find that the diplomas or degrees they receive are viewed as worthless or second class.

3. Multicultural education may lead to fragmentation of the school curriculum. For example, to the extent that attempts are made to broaden the curriculum to achieve all the possible goals of cultural pluralism, attention may be diverted from other equally or more important topics. Ethnic identity by itself, a language, cuisine, folk customs and quaint stories about middle-class models or super heroes do not necessarily qualify for subject matter beyond the elementary curriculum in publicly supported schools. Attempts to incorporate much material on ethnic diversity may trivialize rather than enrich the curriculum.

Summary

Historically, school boards have resisted a differential curriculum for different ethnic or racial groups. In the early 1970s indications appeared of a reversal from the "melting pot" theme to the concept of cultural pluralism. The latter idea embraces the ideals of mutual appreciation and understanding of various cultures in society; cooperation of diverse groups; coexistence of different languages, religious beliefs and life styles; and autonomy for each group to work out its own social purposes and future without interfering with the rights of other groups. Some of the pitfalls of cultural pluralism are linked with increased tribalism, isolation and hostility among ethnic groups, and fear that the curriculum will be watered down.

REFERENCES

Dillard, Joey L. *Black English.* New York: Random House, 1972.

Fishman, Joshua A. "Bilingual Education—A Perspective," *IRCD Bulletin* (Spring 1977): 5.

Harber, J. R. and D. N. Bryan. "Black English and the Teaching of Reading." *Review of Educational Research* (Summer 1976): 397–98.

John-Steiner, Vera, and Larry Smith. "The Educational Promise of Cultural Pluralism." Paper prepared for National Conference on Urban Education, St. Louis, MO, 1978.

Ramirez, Manuel, and Alfredo Castaneda. *Cultural Democracy, Bicognitive Development, and Education.* New York: Academic Press, 1974. P. 142. See also James A. Vasquez, "Bilingual Education's Needed Third Dimension," *Educational Leadership* (Nov. 1979): 166–69.

"Schools Must Help Break Down the 'Black English' Barrier." *Phi Delta Kappan* (October 1979): 144.

Allan C. Ornstein is Professor of Education, School of Education, Loyola University of Chicago.

Daniel U. Levine is Professor of Education, School of Education, University of Missouri–Kansas City.

Multicultural Education in Early Childhood

Patricia G. Ramsey

"How can we teach children about other cultures when they don't even know what their own ethnic heritages are?" "I have real problems finding materials that don't stereotype cultural or ethnic groups." Questions and comments such as these are frequently voiced by early childhood teachers in response to advocates of multicultural education. Theoreticians and practitioners can point to ample evidence that young children cannot grasp the concept of different countries nor the relationships and correspondences among different cultural groups within a country. In his study of children's views of their homeland, Piaget (1951) found that children before the age of six could not relate the concept of town, state, and country. Many teachers have reported that their children enjoyed the variety of activities involved in United Nations Week programs but were unable to understand the categories of different countries and cultures. Finding information about ethnic groups in this country that is simple enough for children to understand and yet not superficial and stereotypical is another challenge to teachers who integrate multicultural education into the curriculum for young children.

At the same time, there is evidence that children's attitudes toward their own race and toward other racial groups start to form in the preschool years (Goodman 1964; Porter 1971). Infants recognize differences in social objects (Thurman and Lewis 1979) and negative stereotypes appear to be readily absorbed by young children. We once had an Algonquin woman visit our school. Several three-year-olds began to cry and shriek with fright as soon as the visitor mentioned that she was an Indian. Similar accounts of children's stereotyped misconceptions are frequently described by teachers (Califf 1977; Ramsey

1979). During the early years, children are forming their initial social patterns and preferences and their basic approaches to learning about the physical and social worlds. Thus, the difficulties of designing effective multicultural education for young children appear to be considerable; however, there is compelling evidence that in order to influence children's basic racial and cultural attitudes, we must start with the very young.

Challenging Some Misconceptions

How can we resolve this apparent contradiction? First, there are several prevalent misconceptions about the nature of multicultural education and the rationale for it that need to be challenged. One prevailing idea is that multicultural education should focus on information about other countries and cultures. Plans for implementing multicultural education are often reminiscent of the geography or history lessons that we learned as children. There is an emphasis on names of countries, their capitals, flags, exports, typical artifacts, and famous people. Efforts to have International Week or to cover a country a week often fall into the trap of teaching children facts for which they have no context. We frequently stress information that is meaningful to adults but not necessarily to children. Moreover, the emphasis on exotic differences often accentuates the "we" and "they" polarity. Thus, in many respects, this type of curriculum may actually work against the goal of understanding the shared experiences of all people.

A second misconception is the notion that multicultural education is only relevant in classrooms with students who are members of the cultural and racial groups to be studied. When I suggested the topic of multicultural education for a workshop I was to give, the teachers quickly said that because they did not have any Blacks or members of other minority groups in their classrooms, such a workshop would be irrelevant. These responses reflected a limited view of the effects and responsibilities of intergroup relationships. The fact that teachers and children in this country feel disassociated from issues related to race and culture underscores the importance of multicultural education for children of all cultural groups.

From an early age children who grow up in culturally mixed settings or as members of minority groups are exposed to the idea that our society is comprised of many groups. Through television, books, and school they have been exposed to the life styles and expectations of the Anglo-American middle class. From their own experiences they may also be aware of the existence and effects of discrimination. Many American children however, can grow to adulthood unaware of and insensitive to the experiences of other cultural groups. The extent of this isolation is illustrated by the following incident. Recently, in Boston, a Black, high school football player was shot during a game in a White community. In a subsequent discussion in a class of student teachers, the people working in the inner city talked about the questions and reactions expressed by their young students. In contrast, the students teaching in the suburbs a few miles away reported that neither the teachers nor the children mentioned the incident.

In order to increase the potential for positive relationships among groups of people, all children need to expand their realm of awareness and concern beyond their immediate experience. Since education in this country traditionally has been dominated by the Anglo-American point of view, one important task of multicultural education is to try to balance this lopsided learning by helping children look into and beyond their relatively insulated environments.

A third misconception, that there should be a unified set of goals and curriculum for multicultural education, contradicts the underlying purpose of multicultural education to provide relevant and meaningful education to children from all cultural backgrounds. Many books and activity kits designed for multicultural education describe curriculum with no mention of the cultural backgrounds and attitudes of the children in the class. In order to design effective multicultural education, teachers need to learn about the racial, cultural, and socioeconomic background of children in their care, what experiences they have had with people from other groups, and their attitudes toward their own and other groups. In order to respond to these variations, the goals and the curriculum will differ considerably from classroom to classroom.

For instance, in a classroom of children from diverse backgrounds, the primary goal might be to help the children understand the extent of their similarities and the nature of some of their differences. Learning how to communicate if there is not a shared language might also be a major focus of the classroom. However, for a group of White middle-class children who have grown up in a relatively monocultural environment, the emphasis would be in seeing the diversity that exists among the group members and grasping the idea that there are many other cultures and ways of life. For children from low-status groups, one initial goal would be to foster their respect and appreciation for their own culture. Children of high-status groups often need to become more realistic about the relative value of their own culture. The social and political climate of the school and community should also be taken into account. The state of intergroup relationships and the prevalence of negative or positive perceptions of the groups influence the children's attitudes. While published multicultural materials can be used as resources for information and, in some cases, activities, each education program should be designed to fit the backgrounds, awareness levels, and attitudes of the particular group of children in each class.

Finally, the misconception that multicultural education is a set of activities added on to the existing curriculum needs to be reexamined. Multicultural education embodies a perspective rather than a curriculum. Just as teachers constantly assess and address children's social skills, emotional states, and cognitive abilities, so should teachers consider children's cultural identities and attitudes. This type of learning can occur every minute of the day. Effective teachers are ingenious at incorporating language skills, problem-solving abilities, and social experience into all activities. Likewise, teachers can seize opportunities to foster the children's awareness of their immediate and broader social world. A child's comment about a picture of an unfamiliarly clothed person, the arrival of a child who does not speak English, a conflict between two children, the advent of a holiday season, and a visiting grandparent are a few of the many moments that can become opportunities to introduce and reinforce the idea that people share many of the same feelings and needs yet express them in many different ways. In addition to incidental teaching moments, all aspects of the planned curriculum can incorporate a multicultural perspective. Decisions about materials, program structure, the role of parents, and the selection of curriculum topics all reflect attitudes toward cultures.

The Role of the Teacher

The design and implementation of multicultural education rests, in large part, with the attitudes, skills, and knowledge of the teacher. One initial step is for teachers to become aware of their own cultural backgrounds, their relationships with the larger society, and their attitudes toward other people. This process requires a great deal of honesty and is often painful. However, it is important that we all recognize our biases and ignorance. It is tempting to deny our prejudices and to claim that we find all children equally appealing. Many teachers, in their efforts to minimize differences, maintain that children are all alike. While such comments emerge from genuine intentions to be fair and impartial in their perceptions and their relationships with children, they also reflect a naiveté about the power and effects of social attitudes and conditions. As teachers we need to accept the fact that we, like our young charges, have inevitably been influenced by the stereotypes and the one-sided view of society that prevail in the schools and the media.

I spent several weeks observing in an elementary school noted for its humanistic, child-centered approach to learning. The teachers had met the challenges of mainstreaming special needs children with commitment, sensitivity, and imagination. However, in our conversations, there were frequent disparaging allusions to the "foreign student element." Clearly frustrated by the extra work that these recent immigrants required, the teachers tended to dwell on the things that the children "didn't even know."

Differences in life style and language were interpreted as ignorance. Neither the school nor the individual teachers attempted to learn about the diverse cultures of the children or to incorporate that richness into the classrooms. These kinds of attitudes obscure our own biases and restrict our realm of knowledge. Thus, it is important that we dispel the illusion that we are totally without prejudice and recognize that there are many valid ways of life beyond our immediate experience. Humility and a genuine desire to know more about other people are absolute prerequisites for designing and implementing multicultural education. From this perspective, we can genuinely learn about the children's cultural backgrounds and attitudes and start to form effective and reciprocal collaborations with parents and people in the community. This knowledge can then provide the base to design ways of promoting cultural identity and positive attitudes toward various cultural and ethnic groups. Once a multicultural perspective has been incorporated into our view of children and educational goals, many ways of implementing it in our classrooms become obvious.

Conclusion

Multicultural education can be incorporated effectively into every aspect of early childhood programs. While multicultural education may seem to be most immediately relevant to classes with minority children, it is even more important that all children in this country understand the culturally pluralistic nature of our society. Teachers need to be conscious of their own views and the limits of their knowledge in order to learn about the backgrounds and attitudes of the children in their classes. Using this information, they can design appropriate goals and curricula.

The concept of shared human experience and cultural diversity can be woven into all aspects of the curriculum. The emphasis on social and emotional development can be expanded to incorporate the enhancement of children's cultural identity and their awareness, concern, and respect for other people. Through a variety of materials and activities, young children can become accustomed to the idea that there are many ways of doing things. For primary school children, there should be a continued emphasis on the development of self-concepts, cultural identities, and social skills. As these children start to express curiosity about the world and gain skills to seek information, they should have access to materials that will foster their awareness of the diversity of human experience as well as its common themes.

Despite the complexity of its issues and content, multicultural education is far from incompatible with early childhood education. In fact, by incorporating one with the other, we can enrich and expand the lives of the children with whom we work.

REFERENCES

Califf, J. "What One Teacher Has Done." In *Unlearning "Indian" Stereotypes.* New York: Council on Interracial Books for Children, 1977.

Goodman, M. E. *Race Awareness in Young Children.* New York: Collier, 1964.

Piaget, J. "The Development in Children of the Idea of the Homeland and of Relations with Other Countries." *International Social Science Journal* (Autumn 1951): 561–578.

Porter, J. D. R. *Black Child, White Child: The Development of Racial Attitudes.* Cambridge, Mass.: Harvard University Press, 1971.

Ramsey, P. G. "Beyond Turkeys and 'Ten Little Indians': Alternative Approaches to Thanksgiving." *Young Children* 34, no. 6 (September 1979): 28–32, 49–52.

Thurman, S. K., and Lewis, M. "Children's Responses to Differences: Some Possible Implications for Mainstreaming." *Exceptional Children* 45, no. 6 (March 1979): 468–470.

Patricia G. Ramsey, Ed.D., is Assistant Professor, Early Childhood Education, Wheelock College, Boston.

Socialization, Education, and Continuity:

The Importance of the Sociocultural Context

Luis M. Laosa

What are some of the factors which affect the transition children must make between the family's sociocultural context and the often quite different sociocultural context of the school?

Children from families of certain minority groups in the United States—groups that typically bear a disproportionately high representation in the lower socioeconomic status (SES) categories—tend to do poorly academically. For example, the U.S. Commission on Civil Rights published a large-scale study (1971) which showed that 40 percent of the Mexican-American[1] and 33 percent of the Black-American children in the five southwestern states of the United States who enter first grade never complete high school; in contrast, only 14 percent of the Anglo-American[2] students in the region fail to graduate. Statistics regarding several other ethnic minority groups are just as depressing. I am not aware of any evidence pointing to a significant improvement in this situation during the past six years.

The early attempts in the 1960s to remedy this depressing state of affairs were principally based on the premise that there was some *deficiency* in these minority children and their respective cultures that had to be corrected. More recently, however, on the basis of new empirical and theoretical evidence, there is an increasing acceptance of another view of the existing problems. This view posits that there are *differences* between minority and nonminority children and also differences among and within the various subcultural communities. Since public schooling is generally oriented toward the middle SES nonminority child, the minority child often is less able to profit from school experiences, gradually tun-

ing out and eventually turning off school completely (Cárdenas and Cárdenas 1973; Cole and Bruner 1971; Kleinfeld 1973; Laosa 1974a, 1974b; Tulkin 1972). Educational practices must be modified and corrected to accommodate and capitalize on the characteristics of each child.

There is wide variability within any one ethnic or cultural group (LeCorgne and Laosa 1976) and one may find individual instances of deficiencies in any group. However, one should not mistakenly equate cultural characteristics with deficiencies or mistakenly define as a deficiency a characteristic that may actually represent a cultural difference. Research such as that reported by Lesser, Fifer, and Clark (1965) tends to show that children from different ethnic groups may possess different patterns of ability, learning styles, and ways of approaching problem solving. Probably the most important finding of their study was that, while SES affects the *level* of performance across various mental abilities, each ethnic group evidences a unique *pattern* of mental abilities. That is, each ethnic group has its own areas of strength, but regardless of ethnic group, lower SES children perform less well than middle SES children.

Only a few of these educationally relevant characteristics associated with ethnic group membership have been identified, since research in this area is just beginning. The findings which are emerging lend support to the hypothesis that serious discontinuities exist between the early environments of minority children and the environments they encounter in school—discontinuities which appear to explain early academic failure. But there is much we still do not know about *specific* learning styles, motivational characteristics, interpersonal styles, and problem-solving strategies which children, particularly those from ethnic minority backgrounds, develop early in life. We also know very little about factors affecting the transition children must make between the family's sociocultural context and the often quite different sociocultural context of the school. The studies reported here offer insights in two areas where discontinuities between the family and school are often found.

Maternal Teaching Strategies

These observational studies were designed to investigate whether there are ethnic group differences in the way young children are taught by their own mothers—whether there are ethnic group differences in young children's first experiences with activities involving teaching and learning in relation to adults. In addition, I was interested in determining the extent to

Children from different ethnic groups may possess different learning styles, motivational characteristics, interpersonal styles, and problem-solving strategies.

which the variability in maternal teaching behaviors within ethnic groups is related to SES.

Forty mothers and their five-year-old children, all from intact families, were selected for this study. Twenty of the mother-child dyads were Mexican-American and twenty were Anglo-American. The Mexican-American and the Anglo-American mothers were closely matched by pairs based on the husband's occupation. In addition, when examining the statistical significance of the ethnic group differences in maternal teaching behaviors, both the husbands' and wives' schooling attainment levels were controlled for the analyses. The husbands' occupations included semi-skilled, technical, and professional workers. These families were individually visited in their own homes by trained observers who were bilingual Mexican-Americans. During these visits, the mothers were asked to teach their own children how to solve problems involving perceptual-cognitive and motor abilities. Each mother's behaviors while teaching her child were coded by the observers.

What have the results shown? Comparisons of the Mexican-American and Anglo-American mothers revealed that there were no ethnic group differences in the *total number* of teaching behaviors directed to the children. Both the Mexican-American and Anglo-American mothers directed approximately the same number of teaching behaviors to their children. Examination of the ratio of verbal to nonverbal behaviors for each ethnic group, however, indicates that the interactions which the Mexican-American children received from their mothers were more frequently of a *nonverbal* nature. On the other hand, the Anglo-American children received more *verbal* types of interactions from their mothers. When these interactions were analyzed by the specific types of verbal and nonverbal behaviors they involved, additional ethnic group differences in maternal instructional strategies emerged. The Anglo-American mothers asked the children more *questions* while teaching them than the Mexican-American mothers.

These findings provide clear evidence, then, that Mexican-American and Anglo-American children from similar SES backgrounds are exposed to different adult-child interaction styles and instructional strategies in the home. From these findings we are able to understand better the dynamics underlying a child's behavior in the typical testing situation: Modes or "rules" for interacting with adults which a young child has learned in the home will determine the child's expectations and behaviors toward adults (such as an examiner in a test situation) and this, of course, will influence how the child performs. Often, *performance* (what the child does or fails to do) in a situation is taken as a measure of *competence* (what the child is able to do under circumstances that maximally elicit the required performance). Performance and competence, however, are not synonymous, since performance in any given situation is determined by a number of factors, including the "rules of interaction" (Getzels 1974) which young children have learned in the sociocultural context of their homes. Thus, the typical test situation in which an adult examiner asks the child questions will be a more familiar and culturally appropriate situation for an Anglo-American than for a Mexican-American child.

I also examined maternal teaching styles within ethnic groups in relation to SES of the families. The findings indicate that SES differences in maternal teaching behaviors *within* any one ethnic group may be much greater than the differences between ethnic groups. For example, results involving a sample of 43 Mexican-American families revealed that mothers with relatively more years of schooling (about a twelfth grade education) employed a teaching strategy characterized by more frequent questions (rather than commands) and a greater tendency to let the child perform the task on his or her own than mothers who had fewer years of schooling. Mexican-American mothers with fewer years of schooling (about a sixth grade education) used significantly fewer questions and more commands, and were much more likely to perform the task for the child than the mothers who had completed more years in school.

Another important finding of this study is that the pattern of correlations between specific maternal behaviors and the children's cognitive development varied by ethnic group. Maternal behavior which has one kind of influence on child development for one ethnic group does not necessarily have the same effect or "meaning" for another ethnic group (Laosa 1976).

By better understanding specific aspects of children's home environments, we are better able to design educational programs which capitalize on the problem-solving, relational,

and instructional styles and other characteristics and "rules of interaction" that are unique to each group, thus providing an articulated continuity between the home and other institutions. There is an urgent need to look very closely at the experiences that children from various ethnic minorities encounter in school and at the transitions they are forced to make between the sociocultural contexts of home and school, in order to identify the specific areas in which schools could be made more responsive to the unique needs and characteristics of all children and their families.

Language Patterns in Home and School

Linguistic characteristics represent one of the most visible areas of child functioning in which there may be discontinuity between the home and other settings. When different cultural or linguistic groups come into contact with one another, varying degrees of bilingualism usually ensue. Bilingual situations may range from instances in which speakers seldom use anything but their native language to speakers who use a second language in varying degrees to the rarely encountered ambilinguals who achieve complete mastery of both languages (Halliday 1968). In situations where languages come in contact, languages or language variants *sometimes* replace each other among *some* speakers in *certain* domains of language behavior. One way of determining a particular community's sociolinguistic characteristics is to identify social domains (Fishman 1968) in a group (i.e., major spheres of activity in a culture such as family, education, etc.) and obtain information about the languages used in the various domains.

I recently conducted an empirical study (Laosa 1975a) examining the use of language patterns in specific social contexts among children and adults in their families from three different Hispanic urban groups in the United States: Central Texas Mexican-Americans, New York Puerto Ricans, and Miami Cuban-Americans. A total of 295 children in the first, second, and third grades and their families participated in the study. The general pattern of socioeconomic and educational status of the families in the three ethnic samples was similar to the U.S. national averages for each group. The mother and teacher of each child were individually interviewed by trained persons who were indigenous to the ethnic, linguistic, and geographical group of each interviewee. Information was obtained regarding the language pattern used most often in the home by the child and the adults. In addition, information was obtained regarding which language was used as the principal medium of instruction in the child's classroom.

Results showed that in the overwhelming majority of both the New York Puerto Rican and the Miami Cuban-American families, the adults living with the children used Spanish as the most frequent means of verbal communication in the home. Among the Central Texas Mexican-American families, Spanish-English "mixture" was the single most frequently used language by adults in 40 percent of the homes, Spanish in approximately one-fourth of the families, and English in approximately the remaining one-fourth. Previous research evidence on the linguistic nature of language "mixing" (Cornejo 1973) suggests that the mixture of English and Spanish among Mexican-Americans follows a very systematic pattern. There is a high degree of "grammaticalness" in the structural and lexical blending and mixture present in the language of Mexican-American children.

These findings indicate that there are differences in the language environments to which Hispanic-American children are exposed in their homes, depending on the particular ethnic and geographical group to which they belong. Even *within* a single community there may be significant differences, so we must question the frequent assumption in research and educational policy involving persons from non-English-speaking backgrounds that such groups are homogeneous.

In both the New York Puerto Rican and Cuban-American groups, the majority of the children used Spanish as the most frequent means of verbal communication in the home. Only about 10 percent of the children in the Cuban-American and the Puerto Rican families used English, and almost none used a "mixture," as the single most frequent familial language. Among the Central Texas Mexican-American children, 30 percent used a "mixture" in the familial context, 23 percent used both English and Spanish with equal frequency without mixing, and 45 percent used English.

The relatively greater use of English among the Mexican-American than among the Puerto Rican or Cuban-American families can be explained by two principal factors. Mexican-Americans in the southwestern United States have experienced contact with the English language more intensely and for a much longer period than either of the other two groups. Moreover, Mexican-Americans have experienced great pressures to give up their native language for English; the Southwest has a long history of prohibiting the speaking of Spanish in schools (Carter 1970) and of using various forms of punishment to enforce the "no Spanish rule." Only recently has this situation begun to change with the large-scale implementation of bilingual education programs. Caution should therefore be exercised when generalizing the language use findings of this study to different geographical regions.

What about the language used in these children's classrooms as the medium of instruction for content subjects? With over 90 percent of the Mexican-American children, over 40 percent of the Cuban-American children, and 26 percent of the Puerto Rican children, English was the language primarily used as the medium of instruction. For 21 percent of the Puerto Rican children, English and Spanish were used with approximately equal frequency, and for 52 percent of the Puerto Rican children, Spanish was the primary language of instruction.

Thus we see that, except for some Puerto Rican children, there were abrupt discontinuities for many of the children between the linguistic environment experienced at home and school. I should point out that the Puerto Rican children in the sample were in a rather unique school situation. The school principal was Puerto Rican and fully committed to bilingual-bicultural education and to providing an educational context in school compatible with the children's home environment. This situation seems to have had a positive impact on the children's intellectual development, since their performance on a test of general nonverbal intelligence (Raven Coloured Progressive Matrices) was much higher than that of the other groups, even though the Puerto Rican children came from homes with the lowest average SES.

It should be noted that classroom instruction through a second language is probably not the only or perhaps even the principal reason so many children from non-English- or limited-English-speaking families perform poorly academically. In fact, Anglo-American English-monolingual children who have been immersed in a Spanish-only program (Cohen and Laosa 1976) in which teachers pretended not to know English and used only Spanish from the beginning of kindergarten, have been found to do as well academically by the end of the third grade as children who go through a regular English program. But for the Anglo-American children in the Spanish immersion program, language was the only factor which differed significantly and abruptly from the sociocultural context of their homes. It appears that the abrupt discontinuity in the *total sociocultural context*, compounded by issues related to attitudes and behaviors from individuals representing the two sociocultural contexts, may be at the root of the problems affecting minority children's academic development.

Conclusions

My intent in this article has been to stress the importance of the sociocultural contexts which represent the total life space or "ecology" (Bronfenbrenner 1974) in which each child's development takes place. The research evidence I have presented reveals that children's environments show quite unique characteristics depending on their membership in particular sociocultural groups—and that even *within* particular subcultural communities sometimes one may find considerable variability. At times, the same observed behavior, such as a particular teaching strategy, may have quite a different "meaning" in terms of its influence on children's development depending on the sociocultural context in which it occurs. These findings raise serious questions concerning whether environments which we impose on children are designed to provide sufficient *articulated continuity with the early and ongoing sociocultural environment of the home*. There is still much we do not know about the total ecologies of children in the various cultural groups in our pluralistic society. We are just beginning to catch a glimpse of the rich and complex variability in our changing nation as it begins its third century.

ENDNOTES

1. The term *Mexican-American* refers to persons who were born in Mexico and now hold United States citizenship or otherwise live in the United States, or whose parents or more remote ancestors immigrated to the United States from Mexico. It also refers to persons who trace their lineage to Hispanic or Indo-Hispanic forebears who resided within Spanish or Mexican territory that is now part of the southwestern United States.
2. The term *Anglo-American* refers to White, native United States, English-speaking persons who are not Mexican-American or members of other Hispanic or Indo-Hispanic groups.

REFERENCES

Bronfenbrenner, U. "Developmental Research, Public Policy, and the Ecology of Childhood." *Child Development* 45 (1974): 1–5.

Cárdenas, B., and Cárdenas, J. A. "Chicano—Bright Eyed, Bilingual, Brown, and Beautiful." *Today's Education* 62 (1973): 49–51.

Carter, T. P. *Mexican Americans in Schools: A History of Educational Neglect.* New York: College Entrance Examination Board, 1970.

Cohen, A. D., and Laosa, L. M. "Second Language Instruction: Some Research Considerations." *Journal of Curriculum Studies*, 8 (1976): 149–165.

Cole, M., and Bruner, J. S. "Cultural Differences and Inferences about Psychological Processes." *American Psychologist* 26 (1971): 867–876.

Cornejo, R. J. "The Acquisition of Lexicon in the Speech of Bilingual Children." In *Bilingualism in the Southwest*, edited by P. T. Turner, pp. 67–93. Tucson, Ariz.: University of Arizona Press, 1973.

Fishman, J. A. "Sociolinguistic Perspective on the Study of Bilingualism." *Linguistics 39* (1968): 21–49.

Getzels, F. W. "Socialization and Education: A Note on Discontinuities." *Teachers College Record* 76 (1974): 218–225.

Halliday, M. A. K. "The Users and Uses of Language." In *Readings in the Sociology of Language*, edited by J. A. Fishman, pp. 139–169. The Hague, Netherlands: Mouton, 1968.

Kleinfeld, J. S. "Intellectual Strengths in Culturally Different Groups: An Eskimo Illustration." *Review of Educational Research* 43 (1973): 341–359.

Laosa, L. M. "Bilingualism in Three United States Hispanic Groups: Contextual Use of Language by Children and Adults in Their Families." *Journal of Educational Psychology* 67 (1975a): 617–627.

Laosa, L. M. "Child Care and the Culturally Different Child." *Child Care Quarterly* 3 (1974a): 214–224.

Laosa, L. M. "Teaching Problem-Solving to Their Young Children: Strategies Used by Mexican-

American and Anglo-American Mothers. Preliminary Analysis." Paper presented at the SVI Interamerican Congress of Psychology, December 1976, Miami Beach, Florida.

Laosa, L. M. "Toward a Research Model of Multicultural Competency-Based Teacher Education." In *Multicultural Education Through Competency-Based Teacher Education*, edited by W. A. Hunter, pp. 135–145. Washington, D.C.: American Association of Colleges for Teacher Education, 1974b.

Laosa, L. M. "What Languages Do Bilingual Children Speak with Whom? Research Evidence and Implications for Education." Paper presented at the Annual Convention of Teachers of English to Speakers of Other Languages (TESOL), March 1975b, Los Angeles.

LeCorgne, L. L., and Laosa, L. M. "Father Absence in Low-Income Mexican-American Families: Children's Social Adjustment and Conceptual Differentiation of Sex Role Attributes." *Developmental Psychology* 12 (1976): 470–471.

Lesser, G. S.; Fifer, G.; and Clark, D. H. "Mental Abilities of Children from Different Social Class and Cultural Groups." *Monographs of the Society for Research in Child Development* 30, no. 4 (1965).

Tulkin, S. R. "An Analysis of the Concept of Cultural Deprivation." *Developmental Psychology* 6 (1972): 326–339.

U.S. Bureau of the Census. "Persons of Spanish Origin in the U.S.: March, 1973." *Current Population Reports.* 1974, Series P-20, no. 264. Washington, D.C.: U.S. Government Printing Office.

U.S. Commission on Civil Rights. *The Unfinished Education. Report II of the Mexican American Educational Series.* Washington, D.C.: U.S. Government Printing Office, 1971.

Luis M. Laosa, Ph.D., is a research psychologist at the Educational Testing Service in Princeton, New Jersey. Formerly he was on the early childhood development faculty of the Graduate School of Education, University of California, Los Angeles. His research focuses on child development and cross-cultural issues in psychology and education.

Developing Multicultural Awareness

Frances Smardo Dowd and Velma Schmidt

"I don't need children's books with black or Mexican-American characters in them, because at our child care center we have only white children."

"Would you believe that Seong Wan brought me a note today from his mother asking me not to allow him to write with his left hand! Yet she's a neurological nurse and admits that Seong shows a definite preference for left-handedness!"

"Tommy Lightfoot never looks me straight in the eye when I talk to him although I always tell him to. It infuriates me. He's so defiant. He just stares down at the floor."

"Today at school Shafonda asked me how the class will celebrate Juneteenth. What is she talking about?"

"Guillermo is the name of the only Mexican-American child in my class. Since I can't pronounce his name, I told him we were all going to call him 'Bill.' I thought he'd like the nickname, but instead he seems despondent!"

"I expected the Jewish children in my class to be absent on Yom Kippur. But I just can't understand why Jewish parents and children did not attend the open house at our center the evening before."

Comments and questions like these, which concern religious, ethnic and racial groups, are often made by teachers. All six of the remarks quoted reveal one common need—a better understanding of the various cultural lifestyles and customs practiced in our country.

The first teacher failed to recognize that her need for multicultural materials was even greater simply *because* all of the children in her classroom were white. Seong Wan's teacher did not know that to some Asian Americans it is considered a disgrace and very *bad manners* to be left-handed. Tommy Lightfoot's teacher did not realize that traditionally Native American Indian children are taught that it is a sign of *respect* to look down when an older person who is in a role of authority speaks to them.

Shafonda's teacher had not been exposed to the fact that on June 19 black Americans in Texas, and in many Southern states, celebrate an important historical event. They commemorate the fact that two years after the Emancipation Proclamation was issued the order to free the slaves was finally given to Texan troops.

Guillermo's teacher was insensitive to the child's rightful sense of pride in his ethnic heritage and in his own distinctive Spanish name. The last teacher referred to was unaware that Yom Kippur, like other Jewish holidays, is observed from sundown of one day to sundown of the next.

Source: Frances Smardo Dowd & Velma Schmidt (1983, May–June). Developing multicultural awareness. *Children Today*, pp. 23–25. Reprinted by permission of Frances Smardo Dowd.

If these teachers had had a better awareness of, and sensitivity to, ethnic and religious traditions, their own attitudes toward diverse groups would improve and their effectiveness as educators might increase. Moreover, if teachers display an accepting and sensitive attitude toward cultural diversity in their classrooms, their students may well develop a deeper understanding of the basic likeness of all peoples, as well as of the distinctiveness of cultural lifestyles, which adds a richness to our society as a whole.

Children's Perceptions

Early research findings indicated that the preschool years are crucial in forming attitudes toward oneself and others[1] and that ethnic awareness emerges in children between the ages of three and five.[2] More recent studies support those results. For instance, one researcher reported that most children have the capacity to distinguish clues associated with race by age five.[3]

A considerable body of research demonstrates that children in the United States are aware, at a *very* early age, of physical and cultural differences among people and that they learn the prevailing social attitudes toward these differences, whether or not they are in direct contact with people different from themselves.[4]

One study, in which preschool, day care and elementary school teachers recorded children's comments about racial identity, revealed the following:

• Children three to five years of age indicated most interest in physical characteristics of themselves and others. A second but lesser area of interest was that of such readily observable cultural characteristics as dress and language.
• Children five to eight years of age indicated a greater interest in cultural characteristics. They also worked at integrating biological and cultural factors which defined racial and national identity, as well as the interrelationships between group and country membership. Their major tasks at that age seemed to be developing an extensive repertoire of accurate information, deepening pride in their identity and learning authentic information about others.
• Children nine to 12 years of age indicated

that they were beginning to understand historical and geographical aspects of racial identity as well as the concepts of "ancestry."[5]

In reviewing studies on prejudice, one researcher found that prejudice could be reduced among people when the following conditions remain constant: knowing each other as individuals, having equal status and sharing common interests, as well as a favorable climate established by an authority figure.[6] This researcher also concluded that an individual who has a high degree of self-acceptance will be more likely to have a low degree of prejudice.

Based upon her own research and a review of the findings of other studies, another researcher offered the following three suggestions on helping children develop positive racial attitudes:

• Initiate activities and discussion to build a positive racial/cultural self-identity. This might include admiring the physical characteristics of other children in the same racial group or offering books that depict racial groups in a positive manner.
• Offer activities and lead discussions to develop positive attitudes toward racial/cultural groups different from the child's heritage. These activities might involve such concrete experiences as celebrating multi-ethnic holidays, cooking ethnic foods or inviting persons from various cultural groups to visit the class or center.
• Help children recognize stereotypes in books, television, greeting cards, movies and other materials.[7]

Multicultural Materials

All children need accurate information about ethnic groups. The material should be presented through a multicultural program that is integrated into the curriculum. This approach to cultural diversity will assist children in developing an appreciation of and respect for diverse racial, religious and ethnic groups.

Research on children's responses to literature and the use of multicultural materials indicate that these resources *do* affect children's attitudes, achievements and concepts.[8] Literature can contribute to children's development of values, if adults select quality literary materials and then lead children in active discussion. Teachers can help children take the point

313

of view of a character so that students can better understand motive and actions. In addition, teachers can help children find elements in a story which are relevant to their own life experiences. This comparison may mean looking for universal themes, such as pride in one's heritage or embarrassment at being labeled "different."[9]

Evaluating Multicultural Materials

Many instructional materials available for young children are, unfortunately, culturally inappropriate. The Council on Interracial Books For Children (CIBC) publishes materials which can assist one in critically evaluating resources and identifying any bias and stereotypes present. The CIBC has also published a "recommended" list of multicultural books (CIBC, 1981).[10]

The criteria which the CIBC uses to analyze materials involve these factors: authenticity, stereotypes, perspectives and negative or positive portrayal of the culture. Material is authentic, for example, if the culture and the people are depicted realistically for the historical period of the story. An author or illustrator often stereotypes a character by oversimplification or a generalization that presents a negative message. The perspective of the author and illustrator should reflect the point of view of the culture depicted, rather than the viewpoint of the writer, should he or she be of a different culture. Negative portrayal of a culture can involve unfavorable cultural myths, demeaning statements and loaded words.

Perhaps there is an even more important point to remember in evaluating multicultural materials. It is that commonalities basic to all peoples should be emphasized, while considering the distinctiveness of particular cultural, racial or ethnic groups. For example, as Peter Spier notes in *People* (Doubleday, 1980), all of us communicate, eat, play, work and need shelter and clothing! However, languages and alphabets differ, menus vary, games and occupations are distinctive, and there are many types of homes and dress. It would certainly be a dull and drab world if this were not so.

ENDNOTES

1. K. B. Clark, "Skin Color as a Factor in Racial Identification of Negro Preschool Children," *Journal of Social Psychology*, Vol. 11, February 1940.
2. R. Goodman, *Race Awareness In Young Children*, Cambridge, Mass., Addison-Wesley, 1952.
3. P. Katz, "Perception of Racial Cues In Preschool Children: A New Look," *Developmental Psychology*, Vol. 8, March 1973.
4. See, for example, K. B. Clark, *Prejudice and Your Child*, Boston, Beacon Press, 1963; L. Derman-Sparks, C. Higa and B. Sparks, "Children, Race and Racism: How Race Awareness Develops," *Interracial Books for Children Bulletin*, Vol. 11, Nos. 3 and 4, 1980; D. Milner, *Children and Race*, New York, Penguin Books, 1975; and H. Trager and M. Radke-Yarrow, *They Learn What They Live*, New York, Harper and Row, 1952.
5. Derman-Sparks, Higa and Sparks, op. cit.
6. G. Pate, "Research on Prejudice Reduction," *Educational Leadership*, Vol. 38, January 1981.
7. L. Derman-Sparks, "Suggestions for Developing Positive Racial Attitudes," *Interracial Books for Children Bulletin*, Vol. 22, Nos. 3 and 4, 1980.
8. See, for example, E. M. Aoki, "Are You Chinese? Are You Japanese? Or Are You Just A Mixed-Up Kid? Using Asian American Children's Literature," *Reading Teacher*, Vol. 34, No. 4, January 1981; P. Campbell and J. Wirtenberg, "How Books Influence Children: What The Research Shows," *Interracial Books for Children Bulletin*, Vol. 11, No. 6, 1980; Council on Interracial Books for Children, "Positive Books: The Ideal Gift," *Interracial Books for Children Bulletin*, Vol. 12, No. 6, 1981; and D. Milner, "Are Multicultural Classroom Materials Effective?," *Interracial Books For Children Bulletin*, Vol. 12, No. 1, 1981.
9. Aoki, op. cit.
10. See Council on Interracial Books for Children, op. cit. The Council also has published "Guidelines for Selecting Bias-Free Textbooks and Story Books, 1980." For these and other materials, including booklets, lesson plans, filmstrips and checklists to evaluate books for racism, sexism, "handicapism" and other biases, write to the Council at 1841 Broadway, New York, N.Y. 10023.

Dr. Frances Smardo Dowd is Assistant Professor, School of Library and Information Studies, Texas Woman's University, Denton, TX 76204.

Velma Schmidt is Professor of Early Childhood Education, North Texas State University, Denton.

Encouraging Reading and Language Development in Cultural Minority Children

Alice J. Kawakami and Kathryn Hu-pei Au

The Kamehameha Elementary Education Program (KEEP) in Honolulu, Hawaii, was established as a research and development unit to create programs to increase the reading achievement of educationally at-risk students of Polynesian-Hawaiian ancestry. Efforts have centered on students in kindergarten through third grade who, in the past, had consistently scored at about the 30th percentile or lower on standardized tests of reading achievement. These students have scored near national norms when in the KEEP reading program (for further information on program evaluation, see Tharp, 1982). The evaluation data speak for the effectiveness of the program as a whole. The relative contributions of individual elements of the program, such as small-group comprehension instruction, have not been studied.

The present study was conducted in classrooms in the KEEP laboratory school. In developing the KEEP reading program, a model of least change was adopted. In taking this approach, the staff at KEEP sought to redesign familiar instructional events in critical ways to make them more effective for the target population. This strategy may be a more productive method of improving children's learning than strategies that require radically changing whole classrooms by introducing new materials, personnel, or management systems.

The first language of KEEP's Hawaiian students is the local English dialect or Hawaiian Creole English. The children have varying degrees of knowledge of standard English, but all are bidialectal to some extent. That is, they are all able to comprehend and use some features of standard English. In this regard, the children are similar to those in other cultural-minority, dialect-speaking populations in the U.S. mainland (Alexander, 1979).

The work to be described did not concentrate on remediating deficiencies in standard English, but instead followed a strategy of adjusting lessons to build on the children's strengths. Two areas of strength were targeted. The first was the children's familiarity with home and community speech events using a "talk story" interactional style. The second was the children's knowledge of real-world events. The redesigned lessons may thus be said to have two general properties: they are conducted in a culturally compatible interactional style, and they are oriented toward helping children draw relationships between text information and their own background experiences and knowledge.

Interactional Style

In working to improve the reading and language learning of cultural-minority students, it is important to understand that their home preparation for literacy, and the interactional styles they bring to school, may differ substantially from those of mainstream students. Children from the dominant culture, and middle-class children in particular, often experience dyadic interactions with parents from their infancy (Taylor, 1982). Hawaiian children, and lower-income Hawaiian children in particular, do not frequently participate in one-to-one conversations with adults. Interaction in Hawaiian households tends to occur in group rather than dyadic form. It involves many adults and children and is based on norms that are consistent with the dynamics

Source: Reprinted from *Topics in Language Disorders*, Vol. 6, No. 2, pp. 71–80, with permission of A. J. Kawakami and Aspen Publishers, Inc., © March 1986.

of groups (D'Amato, personal communication, April 1984).

Group interactions among Hawaiian children were studied by Watson (1975) and Watson-Gegeo and Boggs (1977). They examined a speech event called "talk story." Watson (1975) defines talk story as "a rambling personal experience narrative mixed with folk materials" (p. 54). In talk story, the children cooperate in producing narratives. That is, the first child begins a story, for example, about a camping trip. A second child will join in, adding another event or detail to the narrative. Other children may also join in the conversation. The children will then continue the narrative by speaking alternately with one another. Watson-Gegeo and Boggs (1977) discovered that Hawaiian children participating in talk story valued performance in collaboration with others over individual performance. This talk story pattern of speaking and interacting is seen in home events involving both children and adults, as well as in events involving only children.

As these studies of talk story show, the home experiences of cultural-minority children often differ from the experiences of their counterparts in the dominant culture. For example, children from the dominant culture, specifically middle-class children, experience bedtime story reading with a parent from a very young age. These experiences with books seem to play an important part in preparing children to learn reading and language skills (Clay, 1979; Teale, 1981). In the homes of educationally at-risk Hawaiian children, such dyadic, book-centered interactions between parent and child often do not occur. However, group talk story sessions about television programs (with conarration, overlapping speech, and highly animated talk) are often observed (D'Amato, personal communication, April 1984).

This body of information suggests how school events may be structured to capitalize on students' knowledge about effective communication gained in the home culture. Previous KEEP research conducted by Au (1980), involving the close analysis of videotapes, shows that effective reading lessons can be carried out in the talk story style already familiar to young Hawaiian children. About half of the discussion time in these lessons occurs in *open turns*. In this type of turn, the teacher does not call on any one child to answer. Rather, any student who knows all or part of the answer may speak in response to the teacher's question. Often, two, three, or even four children will appear to be speaking at the same time.

To those unfamiliar with the interactional style of Hawaiian children, so much overlapping speech may convey the impression of chaos. However, experienced teachers in the KEEP program have no trouble channeling all of this talk to further the group's understanding of the story being read. The teachers accomplish this by repeating or paraphrasing the best responses given by the children. After one question has been answered, the teacher goes on to ask another and again listens for and elicits the best responses. In another study, Au and Mason (1981) found that more academically engaged time occurred in lessons conducted in the talk story manner than in lessons in which dyadic or single-turn speaking was the rule.

Transcripts of sample lessons reveal that the children work cooperatively much of the time to answer the teacher's questions, with each child contributing one part of the answer. Several benefits for learning reading and speaking in standard English are made possible through the use of the talk-story style. First, the teacher always speaks in standard English, though permitting the children to speak in the dialect. Often the teacher repeats in standard English what the child has just said in the dialect. This procedure provides the children with models of standard English expression. Gradually, and in a completely natural way, they incorporate more and more standard English forms in their own speech.

Second, because the children are permitted to speak following already familiar rules for interaction, they feel comfortable participating in lessons and are almost always actively involved. Since the talk-story style allows more than one child to speak at a time, more responses can be given than would be possible in a conventional reading lesson. It can be argued, then, that in lessons conducted in the talk-story style, the children probably have more opportunity to discuss text ideas and to use standard English than would otherwise be the case.

Background Knowledge

Background knowledge, or what the reader already knows, plays an extremely important role in reading for understanding, as many studies have demonstrated (for a review, see Langer, 1982). In fact, what the reader brings to the text seems to be as important in the process of constructing meaning as the wording of the text itself. For example, given the exact same text, black students may comprehend a passage as a description of "sounding," a ritual exchange of verbal insults, while white students assume it to be about a physical rather than verbal confrontation (Reynolds, Taylor, Steffenson, Shirey, & Anderson, 1982).

The instructional implications growing from these studies is that students need to be alerted to the importance of applying background knowledge when reading, because meaning resides as much in the mind of the reader as on the printed page. Thus, particularly when working with young children who have not had many home experiences with books, teachers should help them learn to recall pieces of background knowledge that are pertinent to the understanding of a particular text.

At KEEP, the experience-text-relationship (ETR) method was developed to give teachers an instructional framework for helping students learn about the importance of background knowledge to reading with understanding (Au, 1979). ETR lessons consist of three phases. In the *experience phase*, the teacher asks the children questions about background experiences relevant to an understanding of the story.

Following this introductory discussion, the lesson moves into the *text phase*, during which the teacher sets a purpose for reading, generally based on the children's predictions about what might happen in the story. The story might be read aloud to the children, or they may read it silently to themselves. Generally, only a small part of the story is read at a time. After each interval of reading, the teacher helps the children validate or reject the predictions they made about story events, and generate new predictions. Other interesting or important story information is also discussed.

Text phases generally alternate with *relationship phases*, during which the teacher helps the children draw relationships between story ideas and experiences in their own lives. In this way, the teacher is able to communicate the idea that reading can be interesting and have a bearing on a child's life outside of school. Thus background knowledge and experiences come into play during both relation-

ship and experience phases. Cultural-minority students, at risk educationally, will not necessarily learn to value reading unless teachers encourage them to explore these relationships, as they do during relationship phases.

Whole-Class Story Reading Lessons

Thus, school experiences can profitably allow minority children to capitalize on their interactional skills and background knowledge and so learn to read and use standard English. Story-reading activities during the first years of school may be structured so that these students can participate confidently in discussions of text ideas.

A series of discourse analyses of videotaped story-reading lessons is currently in progress at KEEP. These analyses indicate that story-reading lessons provide young Hawaiian children with a solid foundation for literacy and language development (Kawakami, 1984). Redesigned story-reading lessons include the two important general principles: familiar interactional patterns and the knowledge that children bring with them from home.

The goal of these story-reading lessons in kindergarten classes is to encourage language and reading development. The primary objective of story reading is to make obvious the relationship between children's real-life knowledge and specific ideas in the text by allowing them to participate in culturally compatible interactions with a teacher and other children.

The following excerpt was taken from a transcript of a videotaped lesson of *Birthday Surprise* (Sabin, 1981). This sequence illustrates a typical experience phase during a story-reading lesson. In this KEEP kindergarten class, the children were seated on the floor in front of the teacher. (Brackets indicate overlapping speech. The participants are the teacher, Kehau, Alan, and Moki; X = an unidentified student speaker, and _____ = undecipherable speech.)

T:	And when it's your birthday, people usually do some kind of special thing for you, right?
K:	Right
X:	⎡ Right
M:	⎢ They buy some things.
T:	⎣ What are some of the things that people do for you?

X: ⌈ They give you something!
A: ⌊ They might give you a present.
X: ⌈ A fish
K: ⌊ They buy something.
A: Bring you presents
T: They might bring you presents.

In this sequence, the children were asked to share their ideas about birthdays before the story was read. In asking what the children knew about birthdays, the teacher began the lesson by tapping the children's prior knowledge of concepts that were an integral part of the text. The lesson was carried out in the talk-story style of interaction. Children spoke individually, with one or two other speakers, or in chorus with multiple speakers, as indicated by utterances in brackets. By using open turns rather than nominating individual children to answer, the teacher allowed discussion points to be constructed jointly as the story reading activity proceeded.

In the text phase of the lesson, the text rather than background knowledge became the focus of discussion. At this point in the lesson, the teacher had already read a few pages to the class, and the students were looking at a page showing the main character, Sammy the skunk. (Words printed in the book are bold-faced. Brackets indicate overlapping speech. The participants are the teacher, Cheri, Liko, Bobbie, Violet, and Nona.)

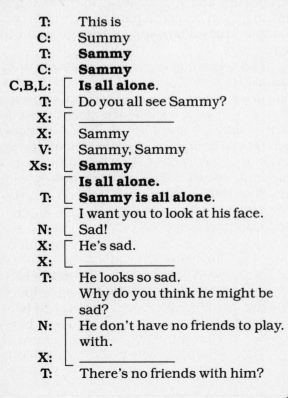

T: This is
C: Summy
T: **Sammy**
C: **Sammy**
C,B,L: ⌈ **Is all alone**.
T: ⌊ Do you all see Sammy?
X: ⌈ _____
X: Sammy
V: Sammy, Sammy
Xs: ⌊ **Sammy**
    ⌈ **Is all alone**.
T: ⌊ **Sammy is all alone**.
    ⌈ I want you to look at his face.
N: ⌊ Sad!
X: ⌈ He's sad.
X: ⌊ _____
T: He looks so sad.
    Why do you think he might be sad?
N: ⌈ He don't have no friends to play with.
X: ⌊ _____
T: There's no friends with him?

In this excerpt, the discussion was again carried out in the talk-story style, with ideas being presented both by single speakers and by the teacher and students speaking simultaneously. In this phase, the children commented on and speculated about text events. Interactions were not limited to talk about text ideas but also included "reading along" with the teacher. This "reading along" allows children to become familiar with the language of books or patterns of written language that they do not normally encounter in their daily conversations.

In lessons such as these, children are guided by the teacher through the experience and text phases of the ETR approach. To increase students' knowledge of written texts, stories are selected from a wide variety of genres. These redesigned story-reading events promote language development as well as reading comprehension skills, because discussion about relevant background knowledge and text ideas allows students to practice organizing and talking about their thoughts.

Story-reading activities that build on the children's strengths offer cultural-minority children a bridge to literacy. Opportunities for interaction with texts allow them to move into more demanding instructional settings in which their skills in reading comprehension and language can be developed further.

Small-Group Reading Comprehension Lessons

The principles of using a culturally compatible style of interaction and building on students' background knowledge apply in small-group reading lessons as well as in large-group story-reading lessons. Small-group reading lessons are at the heart of the KEEP reading program for students from the first grade on. Children in KEEP classes are homogeneously grouped for reading instruction on the basis of criterion-referenced tests that are part of the Kamehameha Reading Objective System (Crowell, 1981). Most classrooms have from 25 to 30 students and either four or five reading groups with approximately five students in each reading group. Each group meets daily with the teacher for a 20-minute to 25-minute reading lesson. In the meantime, the rest of the class works at learning centers on a variety of reading and writing activities.

The small-group reading lessons are also conducted following the ETR approach. Although trade books, magazine articles, and other materials may be used from time to time, most lessons center on selections from basal readers. In general, because the stories are read a few pages at a time, the reading of an entire story may take three to four days.

In a sample lesson, the teacher began by asking the children to read the title of the story, "A Surprise for Pat." She then pointed out that Pat was a nickname and asked if they knew anyone who might have that nickname. There happened to be a boy in the class named Patrick, and the children easily made the connection. Continuing on with the experience phase of the lesson, the teacher asked what kind of surprise Pat might have. The children guessed that it might be Pat's birthday and that he might receive a present.

After exploring the topic of surprises further, the teacher showed the children the illustration on the first two pages of the story. It showed, among other things, a leafless tree and snow on the ground. The teacher then drew upon the chidren's background knowledge by asking if they thought Pat lived in Hawaii. The discussion was conducted in the talk-story style, with much overlapping speech. Only on one occasion did the teacher call on a particular child to answer. (Brackets indicate overlapping speech. The participants are the teacher, Jeffery, Mickey, Cindy, and Brenda.)

T: Do you think Pat lives in Hawaii?
J: Maybe he might have
M: Uh-uh.
T: Why not?
M: In the Mainland.
T: How do you know he's
J: Because he's in the winter.
T: in the Mainland?
It doesn't say.
J: Because got snow.
T: Cindy?
B: Get snow.
C: Because then it's snow.
T: And what does it mean if it's snowing?
M: Cause we don't have snow on our island.
T: Yeah, we don't, do we, Mickey?
C: Only have sun.

This lesson exemplifies several of the ways in which teachers giving ETR lessons help children learn to read by building on existing background knowledge. The children are taught to read with the same texts as those used with children from majority-culture backgrounds. But to make the texts meaningful to the children, the teacher attempts to make explicit the connections between the text and what the children already know. In the case of the nickname Pat and the concept of surprises, the teacher simply helped the children tap existing background knowledge. But in the case of the setting of the story, in a locale cold enough to have snow, the teacher had to ask the children to contrast the place in which Pat lived with Hawaii.

Summary and Implications

The research described in this paper examined two types of events commonly found in elementary school classrooms: large-group story-reading lessons and small-group reading lessons. In both cases, by beginning the lessons with a prereading discussion of a topic that is already likely to be familiar to the children, teachers are able to involve them actively in lessons. This approach also allows the teachers to show the children the importance of background knowledge in constructing meaning from text. By conducting the lessons in a talk-story style of interaction, with open turns and overlapping speech, the teacher creates a comfortable environment for learning. Because the students are already proficient with this style of interaction, they are able to focus on learning to read rather than on figuring out how to participate appropriately in the discussion.

Teachers and language specialists should determine what their students already know and redesign reading and language lessons to capitalize on these strengths. Familiar patterns of interaction and prior knowledge are two aspects of students' culture-specific learning that were built on the redesigned lessons at KEEP, a strategy that can be adopted to other settings. Teachers of other cultural minorities might begin to gather similar information about children in their classes.

It has been argued here that teachers' use of the talk-story style of interaction helps educationally at-risk Hawaiian students to benefit from classroom reading lessons. For other minority groups, adopting styles of interaction that are consistent with the values of the students' homes might also have a positive effect on school learning. For example, Erickson and Mohatt (1982) found that Odawa Indian students were more responsive to teachers who made requests in an indirect manner, without putting the "teacher spotlight" on individual students. Another aspect of this interactional style was teachers' use of private conversations with students as opposed to a more public form of interaction, such as calling out to students from across the room. In studying a classroom of Mexican-American students, Cazden, Carrasco, Maldonado-Guzman, and Erickson (1980) discovered that much of teachers' effectiveness seemed to be related to their use of an interactional style that communicated a sense of caring. They asked questions reflecting their knowledge of the students' families and a concern for their well-being.

These studies bring out aspects of interactional style that may be important to students from particular cultural-minority backgrounds. Teachers should be aware of the importance of considering cultural differences in interactional style when attempting to redesign reading and language lessons (see Cazden, John, & Hymes, 1972; Chu-Chang, 1983; Trueba, Guthrie, & Au, 1981).

In addition to interactional style, the background knowledge that minority students bring to school should be considered. Generally, considerable information about students' background knowledge is available, but teachers and language specialists may not be making full use of this information for such purposes as planning prereading discussions. In the early grades, for example, "sharing" is a common and popular activity. During this time, children tell the rest of the class about things that are important in their lives outside of school. When students speak about visits from relatives, prized possessions, red-letter days, athletic achievements, and similar topics, the teacher can gain insights about their interests and abilities. Another source of information is students' writing. Dialogue journals (Staton, 1980) and writing following a process approach (Graves, 1983), with the children choosing their own topics, give teachers opportunities to become acquainted with students. Writing for children as young as kindergartners (Crowell, Kawakami, & Wong, 1984) can provide an outlet for concerns that a student may not want to share verbally with the whole class. If teachers are observant,

daily interactions with students can also be a rich source of information.

To work effectively with cultural-minority children, the first question should be: "What strengths can I build upon?" By approaching instructional issues in this way, teachers are led to look at ways of changing school environments, as in the redesigning of reading lessons. Equally important, they are not led to look at the children's background as a problem. Many teachers and language specialists today work in classrooms or clinical settings in which the children are from a number of different cultural backgrounds. When they use students' strengths as a starting point for instruction, they can view cultural diversity as a resource rather than as a deficiency.

REFERENCES

Alexander, C. F. (1979). Black English dialect and the classroom teacher. *The Reading Teacher*, *33*(5), 571–577.

Au, K. H. (1979). Using the experience-text-relationship method with minority children. *The Reading Teacher*, *32*(6), 677–679.

Au, K. H. (1980). Participation structures in a reading lesson with Hawaiian children: Analysis of a culturally appropriate instructional event. *Anthropology and Education Quarterly 11* (2), 91–115.

Au, K. H., & Mason, J. M. (1981). Social organizational factors in learning to read: The balance of rights hypothesis. *Reading Research Quarterly*, *17*(1), 115–152.

Cazden, C. B., Carrasco, R., Maldonado-Guzman, A. A., & Erickson, F. (1980). The contribution of ethnographic research to bicultural bilingual education. In J. Alatis (Ed.), *Current issues in bilingual education* (pp. 64–80). Washington, DC: Georgetown University Press.

Cazden, C. B., John, V., & Hymes, D. (Eds.). (1972). *Functions of language in the classroom.* New York: Teachers College Press.

Chu-Chang, M. (Ed.) (1983). *Comparative research in bilingual education: Asian-Pacific-American perspectives.* New York: Teachers College Press.

Clay, M. M. (1979). *Reading: The patterning of complex behavior.* Auckland, New Zealand: Heinemann Educational Books.

Crowell, D. (1981). *Kamehameha reading objective system.* Honolulu, HI: Kamehameha Schools, Kamehameha Early Education Program.

Crowell, D., Kawakami, A. J., & Wong, J. L. (1984). *Emerging literacy: Observations in a kinder-*

garten classroom. Honolulu, HI: Kamehameha Schools, Kamehameha Elementary Education Program.

Erickson, F., & Mohatt, G. (1982). Cultural organization of participation structures in two classrooms of Indian students. In G. D. Spindler (Ed.), Doing the ethnography of schooling: Educational anthropology in action (pp. 132–174). New York: Holt-Rinehart and Winston.

Graves, D. H. (1983). Writing: Teachers and children at work. Exeter, NH: Heinemann Educational Books.

Kawakami, A. J. (1984, December). Promoting active involvement with text through story reading. Paper presented at the National Reading Conference, St. Petersburg, Florida.

Langer, J. A. (1982). The reading process. In A. Berger & H. A. Robinson (Eds.), Secondary school reading: What research reveals for classroom practice (pp. 39–57). Urbana, IL: National Conference on Research in English and ERIC Clearinghouse on Reading and Communicating Skills.

Reynolds, R. E., Taylor, M. A., Steffenson, M. S., Shirey, L. L., & Anderson, R. C. (1982). Cultural schemata and reading comprehension. Reading Research Quarterly, 17, 353–366.

Sabin, L. (1981). Birthday surprise. Mahwah, NJ: Troll Associates.

Staton, J. (1980). Writing and counseling: Using a dialogue journal. Language Arts, 57(5), 514–518.

Taylor, D. (1982). Family literacy: Young children learning to read and write. Exeter, NH: Heinemann Educational Books.

Teale, W. H. (1981). Parents reading to their children: what we know and what we need to know. Language Arts, 58, 902–912.

Tharp, R. G. (1982). The effective instruction of comprehension: Results and description of the Kamehameha Early Education Program. Reading Research Quarterly, 17(4), 503–527.

Trueba, H. T., Guthrie, G. P., & Au, K. H. (1981). Culture and the bilingual classroom: Studies in classroom ethnography. Rowley, MA: Newbury House.

Watson, K. A. (1975). Transferable communicative routines: Strategies and group identity in two speech events. Language in Society, 4, 53–72.

Watson-Gegeo, K. A., & Boggs, S. T. (1977). From verbal play to talk story: The role routine in speech events among Hawaiian children. In S. Ervin-Tripp & C. Mitchell-Kernan (Eds.), Child discourse (pp. 67–70). New York: Academic Press.

ASK YOURSELF:
Identifying Issues for Debate and Advocacy

1. Is bilingualism detrimental to school achievement and the development of social competence? Why or why not? Should children from immigrant families be taught in their dominant or native language for no more than two years upon immigrating to the United States? Why or why not?

2. Is preserving customs of immigrants detrimental to their child's adaptation to school? Why or why not? Should schools strive for cultural continuity between home and school? Why or why not?

3. Are laws and programs for bilingual/multicultural education effective? Why or why not?

4. Honeysuckle Day Care and Nursery School is located in an upper middle-class community. Most children come from two-parent, working families. Noting the community in which this program is located, the director explains

321

that there has never been a need for bilingual or multi-cultural education. She is uncertain how the staff would "handle such a situation if it were to arise." She guesses that probably the center would not accept the child because the child most likely would be considered a child with special needs, and the center does not accept special needs children. Analyze the assumptions and value positions held in this situation in terms of views expressed by Ramsey and other authors of your readings.

5. Is there a paradox that exists between recognition for ethnic differences and encouragement of American patriotism? Why or why not?

6. Some persons espouse the position that cultural traditions should be taught only by members of that society. They argue that outsiders are cultural "foreigners," unable to grasp the subtleties of another person's culture. Moreover, our thoughts and feelings are sifted through our own cultural lenses. Thus, attempts to teach native children about cultures different from one's own are seen as paternalistic and patronizing. What implications does this view have for the early childhood teacher? Does this preclude finding out about other cultures and societies? Why or why not?

7. If parents of your private, cooperative nursery school object to sliding scale fees because low-income, minority children "who use street language" might enroll, how would you as a nursery school director respond?

APPLICATION/ADVOCACY EXERCISES

1. If possible, arrange for a visit to a bilingual, early childhood classroom. Compare and contrast what you observe with viewpoints expressed in the readings of this chapter and Chapter 9.

2. Carefully read the following letters and then consider what ways of coping with ethnicity each of these letters exemplifies. In your response to each letter, concentrate on the child's perspective and what the four- or five-year-old child is learning. Should the school ignore these requests? Why or why not?

Dear Teacher,
    I would appreciate it if you did not call attention to Shenoa's Indian background during Thanksgiving. My new husband is American and has adopted Shenoa. He wants her to be a real Yankee like himself, and so do I.
Thank you,
Mrs. Sally Porter

Dear Teacher,

I didn't get much of a chance to talk to you at open house last Thursday night because there were so many people standing around. However, I want you to know that even though Rhonda's skin is as fair as yours and mine, she is Black. And I want her to be proud of her African heritage. So please, when you begin to talk about Black History on Martin Luther King's birthday, be sure to ask Rhonda to tell the class about the many struggles of our people for equal rights. For a five-year-old, she is extremely well informed. She has been attending the Title IV program and knows a lot about her ancestry.
Thank you,
Mrs. Janice Bethany

Dear Teacher,

I won't be coming to International Night at the school, and I would rather not send in my recipe for churros. When my husband, Jose, and I emigrated from Puerto Rico and came here, we decided on two things:

1. We would practice our old ways only at home with our friends and family.
2. With strangers and on our jobs, we would try to blend in with other people.

We want our children to do the same things that we do. They know who they are, but they know that it's a competitive world out there, and that they will have to be like everyone else in order to get ahead.
Thank you,
Mrs. Rorita Rodriguez

3. View the filmstrip "Unlearning Indian Stereotypes" (Council on Interracial Books for Children, Inc.). In small groups, develop a list of dos and don'ts to guide decisions on classroom interactions and curriculum when teaching about Native Americans. Incorporate ideas from readings as well as from the filmstrip.

4. Describe a classroom pattern of organization and two multicultural activities that are consistent with principles espoused in the readings and that could be implemented with the kindergarten class described in the vignette at the beginning of this chapter.

REFERENCES & SUGGESTED READINGS

Arenas, S. (1980, May–June). Innovations in bilingual/multicultural curriculum development. *Children Today*, 17–21.
Carrasco, R. L. (1981). Expanded awareness of student performance: A case study in applied ethnographic monitoring in a bilingual

classroom. In H. L. Treuba, G. P. Guthrie, & K. H. P. Au (Eds.), *Culture and the bilingual classroom: Studies in classroom ethnography* (pp. 153–177). Rowley, MA: Newbury House.

Dixon, G. T., & Fraser, S. (1986, March/April). Teaching preschoolers in a multilingual classroom. *Childhood Education, 62,* 272–275.

Juarez and Associates. (1982). *An evaluation of the Head Start bilingual bicultural curriculum models* (DHSS Publication, Final Report). Washington, DC: U.S. Government Printing Office.

Katz, P. A. (1982). Development of children's racial awareness and intergroup attitudes. In L. G. Katz (Ed.), *Current topics in early childhood education* (Vol. 4) (pp. 17–54). Norwood, NJ: Ablex.

Rashid, H. M. (1984, July). Promoting biculturalism in young African-American children. *Young Children, 39,* 13–23.

Rodriguez, R. (1980/81, Winter). Aria: A memoir of a bilingual child. *American Scholar, 50,* 25–54.

CHAPTER 12

The Family: Parent Involvement, Parent Education, and Parent Rights

A License to Help?

Mrs. Yancey, a kindergarten teacher, watches the departing father of five-year-old Pete with tears in her eyes. "Where did I go wrong? I was only trying to help. I even offered to help Pete get some exercise by taking him ice skating after school. I know that Mr. Freeman works long hours and has his hands full as a single parent. I sure had a tough time getting him in here, and now he's left in a huff! I only casually mentioned that I thought Pete's grandmother shouldn't send four peanut butter and jellies, two Hostess Twinkies, a banana, and a can of pop for lunch when the child is 25 pounds overweight. I just suggested that Pete's compulsive eating habits would be relieved if Mr. Freeman spent more time with his son."

Questions

1. Suppose you were Mr. Freeman. How would you describe the conference with Mrs. Yancey?

2. What is the difference between giving advice and offering suggestions?

3. In what ways can a teacher's overidentification with a child interfere with home/school relationships?

4. What steps should a teacher take when she believes a child is nutritionally at risk?

PREVIEW

For the past 20 years, families have been changing from the traditional model where the man is the breadwinner and the woman stays home. And today, many children, at some point, will experience living in a single-parent family. If early childhood programs play a role in supporting the family, how can they best help to strengthen today's family? At the very least, teachers need to be sensitive to family circumstances, routines, and values. Also, parent involvement in school programs can strengthen the connections between home and school and can enhance the meaningfulness of the curriculum for the child. As part of parent involvement, parents should be informed about their child's developmental progress, but parents should also be encouraged to communicate to the teacher their knowledge of the child and their expectations as well as their concerns for the child. Teachers should be sensitive to the need for communication to occur in both directions.

In the first selection of this chapter, George Levinger examines the issue of family stability in our society. Next, Ira J. Gordon reviews the history of parent education and parent involvement, and then addresses the assumptions underlying current models of parent education and parent involvement. In an interview, Penny Hauser-Cram, a veteran day care director and teacher, shares her insights into helping roles teachers should avoid when dealing with parents. Finally, Michael K. Meyerhoff and Burton L. White describe the development and evaluation of their New Parents as Teachers project—a parent education program that seeks to alleviate the stresses of new parents and to reach children in their first three years of life.

Where Is the Family Going?

George Levinger

Imagine, for a moment, two contrasting models of society. In Society X, all marriages last for a lifetime. In Society Y, no marriages are allowed to continue beyond the partners' fourth wedding anniversary. In the first society, the barrier against family breakup is very strong; in the second, there is no barrier.

Society X assumes a stability which has not been uncommon in the history of the Western family; even today, it remains the ideal in much of America and in many regions of the world. The marital vow is here considered sacred; it represents a contract not only on earth, but also in heaven. The vow creates a bond between man and wife; it also ties together irrevocably two families and their communities. In Society X, one's marriage is as important as one's birth and death. The spouse becomes, in all likelihood, the mother or father of all one's children; only in widowhood does one continue living without the partner.

Family relationships in Society X are remarkable stable. Once allied through the nuptial bond, kinship lines are unbroken unless death comes before there are children; the couple is part of a larger clan—of parents and grandparents, aunts and uncles, cousins and nephews. The adventurous may find such social stability excessively static; they may feel oppressed by the pressures of family and community.

Now consider a society where family relations are founded on instability. Society Y emphasizes the individual's mobility and readiness to cut ties of intimacy, and the exploration of many successive personal relationships. In Society Y, all marriages by law are temporary; if and when they attain the statutory four-year limit, their warranty expires and they become officially null. One's marriage is like a four-year college course or a stint in the army.

The recurrent dissolution of intimate relationships in Society Y makes its citizens more dependent on larger institutions—government, corporations, unions. It encourages job changes and geographical shifts. The care of children, their financial support, and their assimiliation into adult society become to a large extent the responsibility of the state. So do the care and comfort of aging parents or ex-spouses. Neighborhood and family ties fade.

While citizens of Society Y believe that this system enables them to "maximize self-growth" and "fulfill personal happiness," the total society is also affected. Adults are so busy with the formation, maintenance, and termination of personal relationships that they pay little heed to the workings of the larger community; left in charge is a managerial elite.

While Societies X and Y present almost polar opposites, they do share one common property. Both illustrate the effect of the rigid application of rules that may fit reality under some conditions but become sources of strain or even social pathology under other conditions.

A flat ban on divorce may make sense in a tightly knit society where there is little geographic movement, great homogeneity among eligible partners, and little change in people's tastes or opportunities over the course of their lives. But if the same injunction remains intact in a culture of instability and impersonality—such as modern Western urban culture—the prohibition itself may become a source of marital strain. Despite formal adherence to the marriage contract, the frequency of informal violations—infidelity, desertion, separation—goes up. For example, in Catholic

Italy, before divorce was legalized, some observers estimated that 40,000 de facto divorces occurred annually in the 1950s.

Similarly, Society Y's prescription of regular breakup—which some contemporary writers appear almost to advocate—is also likely to be intolerable. It may fit a kind of Brave New World where all adults move to new locations every four years, where childbirth is highly restricted and child-rearing is an impersonal function. But where such conditions do not prevail, a ban on permanent marriage would be oppressive.

In short, marriage and family—which involve our most personal relationships—are inseparable from the nature of the society in which they exist. High divorce rates in the America of the 1970s reflect far more than the aggregate of individual choices and actions or fluctuations in social mores. They also reflect broad changes in economic conditions, social mobility, and technology.

But the interplay of these forces is extremely difficult to disentangle. We have demographic and economic data; we have polls showing changes in attitudes toward marriage; we have statistics on church attendance, divorce decrees, welfare rolls; we have studies of divorcées in Boston; we have national studies of "happiness" by researchers in Michigan and analyses underway elsewhere of the effects of new "no-fault" divorce laws. But such studies vary greatly in their scope, method, and conclusions.

We don't have answers to some basic questions. Are the increases in divorce rates due mostly to (1) a lowering of barriers around the marital relationship, (2) a lowering of the attractiveness of staying married, or (3) a rise in the attractiveness of alternatives outside of marriage?[1]

The Eroding Barriers

We know that American divorce laws have been liberalized over the past half-century and that attitudes toward marriage have changed. According to a 1974 Roper Survey, some 60 per cent of all Americans believe in divorce as "a way out of a marriage that isn't working." No good media research studies seem to be available, but analyses of trends in news coverage, popular fiction, and television dramas would probably show a large increase in sympathetic or neutral portrayals of divorce over

the last three decades. We also know that divorced American politicians are no longer disqualified in the eyes of voters from seeking election or reelection.

It is likely that, today, spouses' feelings of obligation toward marriage are lower than those of previous generations. For some people, this decline may be related to their own experience of divorce. Others' attitudes may be shaped by a history of divorce in their parents' marriage. Indeed, an increasing proportion of American children whose parents have been separated are growing up—children who are therefore less likely to expect a permanent marriage in their own future. In a 1976 analysis of national survey data, two Iowa sociologists, Hallowell Pope and Charles W. Mueller, found that children from homes broken by divorce were slightly more likely to go through divorce in their own marriages than were those who grew up in intact homes or in homes broken by a parent's death. This "intergenerational transmission effect" of divorce rates is not yet well understood; obviously, if this effect were found to be stronger, the impact over time on American society could be considerable.

The Ties That Bind

Another past "barrier" to family breakup has been the spouses' religious beliefs. Practicing Catholics, Jews, and conservative Protestants have tended to have far lower divorce rates than non-church attenders, according to reputable data. As religious orthodoxy weakens, so does the churches' overall influence in holding marriages together.

If barriers to divorce have grown weaker, have marriages also become less attractive? Who knows? There are few good data to answer that question. The more extreme representatives of the women's liberation movement, as well as certain popular male writers, argue variously that conventional marriage is repressive for women and inhibiting for men. Nevertheless, judging by the polls, the average American views "getting married" as less important to a successful life than was the case decades or centuries ago. Almost all young people today still aspire to get married *eventually,* and most divorced people try to get remarried (although more men than women succeed). Most Americans—men and women alike—expect their spouses to continue being in love, to remain sexually compatible, to enjoy similar interests and activities, and to resolve all conflicts through honest communication. However, research on "happiness" suggests that the early peak experiences are eventually followed by a slide toward a more prosaic routine which does not match earlier expectations.

If Americans in the 1970s tend to demand more of a "good" marriage, they may also be quicker to rate a marriage as "bad." In the 1974 Roper Survey, for example, about half of all respondents said that a *sufficient reason* for considering divorce is "no longer being in love"; agreeing with that statement were 59 per cent among 18–29-year-olds, and 45 per cent among 50–59-year-olds. While younger people revealed somewhat higher expectations than older people, all segments of our society placed high demands on marriage, demands that are often hard to meet in the real world of jobs, children, and installment payments.

On a more concrete level, census and other survey data show clear evidence that a husband's low income and low employment stability are associated with marital instability. For example, Phillips Cutright, in a 1971 analysis of 1960 U.S. census data, found that a husband's income was a far clearer clue to intact marriage than either his occupation or his education. In a more recent analysis, sociologist Andrew Cherlin found a husband's job stability to be even more important than his income. So did Heather Ross and Isabel Sawhill in their 1975 analysis of data from the University of Michigan's *Panel Study of Income Dynamics.* They concluded that layoffs, discrimination, and marginal employment help explain high marital breakup rates among low-income blacks.

What Makes the Grass Greener?

Even if a marriage seems unattractive and the costs of terminating it are low, it will not be broken unless some alternative becomes more attractive, unless the grass looks greener elsewhere. What, then, are the social forces that have enhanced alternative attractions?

Oddly enough, researchers have only recently recognized that the husband's income and employment are only one part of the divorce picture. As women's own income-earning opportunities have risen, as their aspi-

rations to independence have climbed, they have become able to consider divorces that earlier seemed financially impossible.[2] Other research indicated that a wife's independent income at all economic levels is correlated with a propensity toward divorce; my own research at a divorce court in Cleveland, Ohio, indicated that female divorce applicants who earned wages were significantly less likely to dismiss their divorce suits than were those who did not. Hence, the rising participation of married women in the labor force, especially in the professions, seems likely to have future impact on family stability. Again, no one knows what offsetting effects might also occur.

Because state or federal programs of aid to dependent children subsidize low-income, one-parent families, but not low-income, two-parent families, another potential economic incentive is provided for marital breakup. But Oliver C. Moles's analysis of 1960–1970 welfare programs suggests that any link between divorce and the level of welfare payments is tenuous at best. Others, notably Ross and Sawhill, have suggested that rather than promoting marital breakups, such payments may tend to deter already-separated welfare mothers from seeking remarriage to the available men whose low incomes may not match government support to single mothers.

At all income levels, the divorced or separated woman no longer suffers the social stigma of two decades ago. If we believe evidence that divorce rates rise with the social acceptability of divorcées, then this shift signals another important weakening to barriers to divorce.

The ethic of "self-actualization" is important, too. Not only in the literature of the women's movement, but in Western cultures generally, we have witnessed a rising desire to pursue individual happiness, variously defined. The achievement of "self-growth" in career or in romance often seems to conflict with continued obligations to those others who are near and dear. Like Hollywood stars, American middle-class spouses may seek out external opportunities or pursue the paradox of an "open marriage," and thereby fatally neglect their existing obligations.

Curbing Breakups

Let us now look at the other side of the issue. What social policies act to keep down the rate of marital breakup? While easier divorce and separation may provide American society with necessary escape valves, their benefits may eventually become lower than their costs—costs to children, to family and friends, to the social fabric, and especially to the ex-partners themselves. And these costs, variously perceived, have already elicited public declarations from politicians, church leaders, and academics in favor of "preserving the family."

If increasing legal permissiveness (such as "no-fault" divorce) over the past decade has tended to erode the barriers against divorce, a reversal would tend to raise them. In some totalitarian societies—such as the Soviet Union or the People's Republic of China—reversals of policy have indeed occurred. After an early post-revolutionary period of official permissiveness, government policy changed to make divorce difficult and unlikely.[3]

American social policy lacks coherence; it is, instead, a contradictory patchwork attempting to satisfy competing interests. If divorce is tolerated, or even tacitly encouraged, by local social custom in Beverly Hills, on Park Avenue, or in Watts, there are many communities where more traditional views prevail. Few Americans, it may be assumed, are in favor of going all the way back to something like Society X. But if divorce trends continue, some reaction in social and legal policy may indeed occur during the next decade, if only to ward off the spectre of something like Society Y.

Perhaps the most palatable device for increasing the seriousness of marital commitments would be to make it more difficult for people to get married in the first place. Increasing the obstacles to "quickie" marriage may merit some social experimentation—raising the legal age for marriage or requiring lengthy engagements, for example. Making it harder to marry might force men and women to consider marriage more carefully and enable them to predict better what their marriage would be like.

An obvious major contributor to disruption of American families is economic instability, as we have seen. Subsidies that would support two-parent families (as distinguished from one-parent families headed by the mother) might help increase the attractiveness of remaining married for low-income people with children. Such a policy might be part of a federal program of reducing extreme financial distress in general—notably by increasing low incomes. We do not know if money alone would lessen the high breakup rate in poor families; we only know that the poor divorce more than the non-poor.

A Hazy Picture

Finally, a "psychological" note. The current hazy picture of personal and social dissatisfaction suggests that many Americans' "interpersonal expectations" have risen faster than the ability to meet them. Is it possible to foresee political leadership that will, among other goals, seek to encourage American men and women to become more realistic in their expectations, and hence lower the risk of disillusionment?

One doubts it. The United States is still a country heavily committed to optimism, personal enhancement, and change for the better. Moreover, the constant thrust of political rhetoric and consumer advertising, of themes in women's magazines and television drama, is to stir great expectations, to create confidence in quick remedies ("fast, fast, *fast* relief"), and to evoke visions of a richer life for all. Such visions, indeed, are implicit in much of the "advocacy" research dealing with marriage, divorce, and the changing socioeconomic role of men and women. We may be in for continuing tumult.

Already, conflicting views of the family and its future are reflected (and often distorted) in the current debates over abortion laws, the Equal Rights Amendment, "no-fault" divorce legislation, day-care programs, and welfare reform. But as I have indicated in this essay, serious gaps still exist in scholarly knowledge of the social causes and effects of family disruption. We know some important statistics. We know America is somewhere between Society X and Society Y; but exactly where we are headed, and why, remains largely conjectural. In any case, when a national debate on family policy begins, as it surely will if present divorce trends persist, none of us should overestimate the efficacy of policy-makers in hastening or reversing changes in the role and structure of the American family.

ENDNOTES

1. My own social-psychological approach to divorce and separation assumes that people stay in marriages because (a) they are attracted to

them and/or (b) they are barred from leaving them by law, custom, or economic penalities. Furthermore, I assume that, consciously or not, men and women compare a current relationship with alternative ones. If the internal attractions and the barriers surrounding the present relationship become distinctly weaker than those of a promising alternative, the result is apt to be breakup. This theoretical perspective translates the effects of cultural trends, social pressures, or economic shocks into psychological forces experienced by individuals or couples.

2. According to survey data analyzed by Cherlin in 1976 and other data reported by Ross and Sawhill in 1975.
3. Soviet policy shifted again; the Russians now have a "Western" divorce rate.

AUTHOR'S NOTE: Listed below are specialized studies cited in this essay or otherwise worthy of note:

"Hedonic Relativism and Planning the Good Society" by Philip Brickman and Donald T. Campbell, in *Adaptation-Level Theory*, M. H. Appley, ed. (Academic Press, 1971).

"Differentials in Marital Instability: 1970" by L. L. Bumpass and J. A. Sweet, in *American Sociological Review* (no. 37, 1972).

"Social and Economic Determinants of Marital Separation" by Andrew Cherlin, unpublished doctoral dissertation, University of California, Los Angeles (1976).

"Income and Family Events: Marital Stability" by P. Cutright, in *Journal of Marriage and the Family* (no. 33, 1971).

"Marital Satisfaction and Instability: A Cross-Cultural Analysis of Divorce Rates" by W. J. Goode, in *International Social Science Journal* (no. 14, 1962).

"Boys in Fatherless Families" by E. Herzog and C. E. Sudia, U. S. Department of Health, Education, and Welfare, Children's Bureau (U.S. Government Printing Office: no. 72–33, 1971).

"The Aftermath of Divorce" by Mavis Hetherington, paper presented at the 1976 meeting of the American Psychological Association.

"The Intergenerational Transmission of Marital Instability: Comparisons by Race and Sex" by Hallowell Pope and Charles W. Mueller, in *Journal of Social Issues* (vol. 32, no. 1, 1976).

"Marital Instability by Race and Income, Based on 1960 Census Data" by J. R. Udry, in *American Journal of Sociology* (no. 6, 1967).

"Effects of Parental Divorce: Experiences of the Child in Early Latency" by J. Wallerstein and J. Kelly, paper presented at the 1975 meeting of the American Orthopsychiatric Association.

George Levinger, 49, is a professor of social psychology at the University of Massachusetts at Amherst. Born in Berlin, he grew up in Germany, Britain, and the United States, and served in the U.S. Army. He graduated from Columbia (1946), obtained his Ph.D. in social psychology from Michigan (1955), and taught at Bryn Mawr and Western Reserve before coming to the University of Massachusetts in 1965. He was co-editor with Oliver C. Moles of a special omnibus issue of the Journal of Social Issues *(Winter 1976) devoted to "Divorce and Separation."*

Parent Education and Parent Involvement:
Retrospect and Prospect

Ira J. Gordon

Retrospect

Parent education probably began with the first grandmother in the cave telling her daughter how to rear a newly arrived infant. Of the many biblical references we can quote, my favorite is the injunction in Leviticus instructing the Hebrews "Thou shalt teach . . . diligently unto thy children."

Skipping several thousand years, we might place the beginning of the modern era of parent education at 1801, when Pestalozzi (1801) wrote *How Gertrude Teaches Her Children.* He states in a letter to a friend:

> *From the moment that a mother takes a child upon her lap she teaches him. She brings nearer to his senses what nature has scattered afar over large areas and in confusion, and makes the action of receiving sense-impressions and the knowledge derived from them, easy, pleasant, and delightful to him (cited in Kessen 1965, p. 102).*

During the next few decades, emerging concern for the early years of life and the role of the parent can be found in the beginnings of the kindergarten movement and (in the early 1840s) in Froebel's book, *Mother's Songs, Games, and Stories.* One of those illustrated games is "patche-kuchen," which you will recognize as "Pattycake"!

Before the turn of the twentieth century, the United States began to feel the effects of Pestalozzi and Froebel. Parent education and parent involvement in the U.S.A. have followed two main directions.

1. The first, stemming from the European influence, essentially involved middle-class and well-educated people. It was linked intimately in the 1920s with the Progressive Education movement and Deweyian thought. Examples can be found in the child study movement and in the development of the PTA, mental health associations, and parent cooperative nursery schools, as they emerged in the 1930s. These efforts often used group approaches to both parent education and parent involvement. Parents generated activities which, in cooperation with professionals, led to lay organizational programs. The aims were not simply to learn about rearing one's own children but also, in keeping with Deweyian doctrine, to influence and shape the broader society. Schlossman (1976) has reviewed this direction in his study of the history of parent education from 1897 to 1928.

2. Paralleling this approach was one that in today's jargon we might call *mainstreaming.* This called for utilizing parent education and home visitations to integrate the flow of immigrants into the mainstream. The schools were obviously involved in stirring the mix in the melting pot. But some efforts transcended schools—examples were the visiting nurse programs, home visitors to people such as my grandparents on New York's lower side, the social work movement in the settlement houses, and the emergence of the adult education movement. In rural America these two approaches were linked through the work of the agricultural extension service and the home demonstration agent.

Establishment of the Children's Bureau in 1913 was originally designed to strike a blow at child labor. But the Bureau very soon found itself developing pamphlets and other materials on childrearing practices for parents. These pamphlets were disseminated through the home-demonstration system and also through hospitals and other means, including Congress, to the parents of newborn children. Because understanding the language of the pamphlets required a high degree of literacy, however, they did not really have an impact on the mainstreaming effort.

Most materials developed during this period reflected the middle-class pattern. The content stressed either descriptive norms of development or parent behavior to rear socially acceptable and academically successful children. Examples of such publications are the National Society for the Study of Education 1929 yearbook, *Preschool and Parental Education*; books by John B. Watson and Arnold Gesell; and the series of Iowa child welfare pamphlets of the 1930s and early '40s, including one by Ralph Ojemann (1941) on reading.

A lull occurred during or immediately after World War II, especially in the "mainstreaming" side of the picture. Massive immigration had long since ceased, and our energies were diverted to other things.

In the 1960s the two diverse approaches reemerged with some strength. The middle-class parent education approach changed from the progressive education type of emphasis to one more psychotherapeutic in nature, especially therapy as represented by the ideas of Carl Rogers and his associates (Baruch 1949; T. Gordon 1970; Ginott 1965). In the 1970s suggestions for parenting begin to reemerge from the conditioning orientation, this time not from the classical one of Watson but from the operant conditioning movement (Becker 1974).

Counterparts to the earlier organizational efforts are those of various groups of parents with special problems, the organizations stressing natural childbirth or breast feeding, and the informal groups of parents of infants and toddlers and the like. Of course, the PTA, the mental health associations, and parent cooperatives have continued since their founding.

Mainstreaming shifted from a concern for the integration of the immigrants from Europe to an awareness of groups in the American population *outside* the mainstream: our own indigent poor, the immigrant waves from the farm to the city represented by the movement of southern blacks, the immigration of Puerto Ricans to New York and other urban centers, the Chicano in the Southwestern United States, and the Appalachian poor in thirteen states on the Eastern Seaboard. The best single representation of all that effort, beginning about 1965, was the "War on Poverty." Of all of the influences in the American society since the turn of the century, this was the first large-scale federal government effort since the initial establishment of the Children's Bureau in 1913. Basic to the effort were longitudinal early intervention research projects (Weikart 1970; Gray 1970; Levenstein 1970; and Gordon 1967, 1969). Government programs are represented by Head Start, Parent and Child Centers, Home Start, Parent Child Development Centers, Title I, and Follow Through.

While these developments were going on here, similar developments occurred abroad. A parent education movement in the middle-class tradition, founded at the turn of the century in France, led by 1964 to the formation of the International Federation for Parent Education. This federation developed general policy statements that resembled those supporting government efforts and the variety of private efforts and publications in the United States.

Central themes common to these parallel lines of middle class and mainstreaming, in Europe and the United States, can be summed up in three statements: (1) the home is important and basic for human development; (2) parents need help in creating the most effective home environment for that development; and (3) the early years of life are important for lifelong development.

Today

Several reviews give us an updated picture of the state of the art of parent education, especially in the mainstreaming dimension: Gordon 1970; Goodson and Hess 1975; Gordon et al. 1975; and Honig 1975. It is no coincidence that the last three reviews have a 1975 date. Two ACEI pamphlets grew out of papers presented at the 1975 Texas Conference on Infancy directed by Joe Frost: *Understanding and Nurturing Infant Development* (1976) and *Developing Programs for Infants and Toddlers* (1977).

U.S. Secretary of Health, Education, and Welfare (HEW) Joseph Califano has indicated that strengthening the family rather than strengthening institutions to deal with the family will be a major thrust of his department in the days ahead. The Office of Child Development (OCD)—now called the Administration for Children, Youth and Families—continues, fortunately, to support Parent Child Development Centers, Child and Family Resource programs, Home Start efforts within Head Start, and Head Start itself. Unfortunately, however, most of these local programs are small-scale and non-longitudinal. The Office of Education (OE) through its regulations for Title I, Follow Through and PL94-142 requires parent involvement as distinct from parent education.

Prospect

Let us look at where we are in 1977. Are we climbing aboard a new educational bandwagon? Do we see parenting education and parent involvement as a new kind of panacea? We have to address certain critical questions:

1. What are the philosophical assumptions underlying programs? Do they still perpetuate the separate mainstreaming and middle-class movements?
2. What is the place of parent education outside of parent involvement in the school?
3. What is the role of the school (or agency) in parent education vis-a-vis the role of the family in parent involvement in the school? If there are parent-directed emergent group efforts, as we have seen in the middle-class tradition, and government-required parent involvement in the decision process in the mainstreaming, how do these roles of parents relate to those of parents as receivers of child development or educational information?
4. What are the evidences that various programs have been successful and what is meant by success?

Assuming answers can be found to the above, newcomers to the parent-movement typically face another set of questions:

How do you select and train and supervise home visitors, if that is the model you plan to use?

What should be the level of training of personnel who work with parents?

What are the comparative advantages of home visitor or center or mixed type of programs?

How should television and other media be used?

How do you design multi-discipline approaches?

How do you get parents to participate?

How do you sustain their level of involvement?

How do you build flexibility into a program?

Crassly, where do you get the money? How do you convince legislators and educational bureaucrats that educational dollars should be spent outside the classroom?

How do you improve the pre- and inservice training of teachers and other professionals in reference to working with parents?

Some answers are found scattered in the literature. But generally the answers are not available in any comprehensive, organized fashion. This may not be possible. What, then, can one say?

For a long time I have been concerned about the American tendency to seek the short-term, easy, package-solution to problems and, within that context, to view the school as the remedial agent for society's ills. This single shot, "offer a course" approach often ignores the social context, assumes a power for formal education it most likely does not possess, and overlooks the fact that schools are but one subsystem within the society.

A useful analytic approach is the systems viewpoint. By placing the issue of parent involvement and parent education in a systems context (Brim 1975; Bronfenbrenner 1976), we can examine assumptions that underlie current programs and deal with our first question.

Three Models
• *Family Impact.* At the heart of the mainstream tradition is the Family Impact Model, whereby parent education from local agency or school is designed to have an impact on the family so that the child will "fit" the school and the system's goals—to get those who are out of the system into it.

Underlying such efforts is a set of assumptions. Applied to parent education, these are: that specific answers exist; that the family wants to be "in" but doesn't know how; that changing the parent, in some way, without changing anything else, will enable entry; that knowledge and attitudes of parents are keys to entry. In the middle-class tradition, the assumptions are also that "the" right way to rear a child can be learned from books, peers or experts, and that the parents, using these, can be successful childrearers. To state these assumptions is not to deny their power or validity. This model is the basic one for all formal education. The larger core assumptions are that there is a body of information necessary for life and for a career, that a teacher knows and teaches it, and that individuals learn and apply it. This view, which holds sway from "basic skills" to postgraduate refresher courses in medicine or education, is a legitimate and respectable approach.

This model is the major thrust of most school-based efforts and of many state-supported child mental health and Appalachian Regional Commission projects.

With some justification, some people feel that this strategy treats symptoms (parent-child behaviors, family transactional patterns) without attacking root causes, without clearly understanding subcultural strengths, and/or without recognizing the varieties of positive ways of childrearing. Nevertheless, if we attend to these programs' goals, the data seem reasonably clear from both the longitudinal early intervention studies as summarized in Palmer (1977) and Goodson and Hess (1975), that lasting effects are evident on the intellectual and academic performance of children. The research efforts have been generally small-scale, with heavy university involvement.

For example, our Florida families—whose parents we home-visited beginning when the children were three months old and who were involved for at least two continuous years before they were three years old—have a significantly lower percentage of their children assigned to special education in third grade (six years later) and significantly higher percentage of their children who performed better on the MAT than did children who had been randomly assigned to the control population. That is a long-term positive effect.

With emerging concern for cross-generational efforts and parenting education programs for high school youth, the parent-oriented early education programs offer possible models for the involvement of youth in efforts that not only are socially useful in the community but also provide them with understanding of families and of child development in ways that should impact upon their own roles as parents. It would be rather easy to incorporate the home-visit program, with suitable supervision, into a variety of high school efforts in which high school youth are trained as home visitors. Further, in the many places in which infant centers are located on school grounds, the activities developed in programs lend themselves to use in infant and early childhood centers.

Adult-education and family-life education people are also drawing implications from the two strands of parent education work. In a recent position paper, they state such goals as:

a. *Developing educational potentials of parents for the social, mental, emotional and physical growth of children.*
b. *Improving parent-child communication throughout the life cycle.*
c. *Clarifying parental responsibilities and competencies in developing emotional stability of all family members young and old. . . .*
d. *Expanding and upgrading community resources supporting parents, including child care facilities (Cromwell and Bartz 1976, pp. 18–19).*

Although the Family Impact Model is time-honored and seemingly successful, we still need to raise some issues concerning its prospects.

Both parent-education traditions use forms of the family-impact model. The middle-class tradition is voluntary, self-selective, often informal and group self-managed, and the content based upon the parents' perceptions of need. The "mainstreaming" tradition is usually programmatic, funded or connected to a government agency, run by professionals, and based upon "expert" perception of parents' needs.

Today we need ways to synthesize the strengths of both traditions. For example, new parents, regardless of social class, may need more specific help than in the past in the physical health and cognitive as well as the affective domains.

To accomplish this synthesis, if we see the school system as the major social agency, we need to answer such questions as:

1. Where do the schools acquire the wisdom to know what parents need? (Our evaluation of programs—Gordon et al. 1975—showed the nonexistence of need assessment.)
2. Do such programs run the risk of seeing parents as clients and lowering parent self-esteem and sense of potency vis-a-vis the system?
3. Where do school personnel get the training and develop the attitudes and skills necessary for working with parents from diverse backgrounds?
4. Is this a new version of the melting pot—like the home visitors of the 1890s who dealt with my grandparents? Is that necessarily bad? As a corollary,
5. Are there universal parent-child behaviors we wish to foster? What is the evidence?

I cannot answer the first four questions, but we have data on the fifth. If a common system goal is still "making it" in schools as they are, the data are clear.

We find many indications, across culture, of common family variables that influence scholastic achievement. The data from American studies (Coleman 1966; Mayeske 1975; Gordon 1969, 1977; Hess 1969), from the international educational achievement studies (Coleman, 1975; Keeves 1972, 1975; Purves 1973; Thorndike 1973), and from British longitudinal studies (Pringle, Butler and Davie 1966; Davie, Butler and Goldstein 1972; Wedge and Prosser 1973) all show that the variables are not magical. They have to do with, among others, whether: (1) parents see themselves as teachers of their children; (2) they talk with them, not at them; (3) they take them to the libraries or the museums or the parks; (4) they sit around the dinner table and share and plan; (5) they listen; (6) they display a child's work on the refrigerator or the wall; (7) they themselves read and talk about what they read.

Further to be noted are such variables as communication processes, values, sense of family and family pride, self-concept and sense of potency of the family members, which also influence the child's development. Some of these may be functions of class and caste. The American intervention studies show, however, *within* social class and caste, that these variables are important (Gordon 1976; Carew 1977; and Elardo, Bradley and Caldwell 1975).

• *School Impact Model.* Here the issues are the same as those Moynihan (1969) raised when he analyzed four views of community intervention in decision-making:

> *The essential problem with community action was that one term concealed at least four quite distinct meanings. Organizing the power structure, as in the Ford Foundation Programs . . . expanding the power structure, as in the delinquency program . . . confronting the power structure as in the Industrial Areas Foundation program . . . and finally, assisting the power structure as in the Peace Corps (Moynihan 1969, p. 168).*

Another type of maximum feasible misunderstanding arises out of the fact that many programs incorporate both the Family Impact and the School Impact models in the same project. Head Start, Home Start and to some degree Follow Through and Title I are examples. What is the maximum feasible misunderstanding?

Try this logic tree: Your young child is not doing well in school. (1) This is because you need help—you are out of the system. (2) This is because you lack knowledge/skills in childrearing (or dominant culture childrearing). (3) Therefore, we will help you learn. (4) But, since this is your child, you should have something to say. (5) Therefore, even though you are either deficient or different, we will put you on the policy council to tell us what to do! But, as Moynihan said, "The exercise of power in an effective manner is an ability acquired through apprenticeship and seasoning" (p. 137). Parent involvement for this model requires a form of parent education different from learning to improve one's own home—such as education in budgeting, parliamentary procedure, knowledge of local agency and federal regulations, skill in communication with the power structure, group decision-making processes and the like.

In practice, despite a certain sense to this model, it can lead to conflict *unless* both parents and program people recognize their *mutual* needs to learn *from each other*. Parent involvement for this model also requires a new form of teacher education! Teachers and school administrators, or any other professional involved in working with this model, need to learn new attitudes toward parents, new skills in communication and group processes and sharing. Both groups need help in relating to each other when the task is common decision-making.

If we are serious about the second model, it may intrude very heavily on the first. Parents may not see any need for the parent education that school people design, or they may see needs to change *teacher* behavior, rather than their own.

Implementing this model calls forth another set of concerns:

1. How do we reconcile conflicting views about what is good for children?
2. How do we solve the possible struggle for power over programs?
3. How do we resolve the maximum feasible misunderstanding, in which school systems may want (or permit) parent involvement in decision-making if it enhances the school system *as is* (the Peace Corps meaning), and parents may want to make major modifications in the school system (the Industrial Areas Foundation meaning)?

Some say that *both* models are merely topical treatments—that what is needed to help the family is to change the larger systems in which it is embedded. For example, within our American framework, changes might be required in the systems of welfare, health care, work (flextime, mobility for promotion), media, etc.

• *Community Impact Model.* As applied to parent education and parent intervention, this third model is usually represented by a so-called "comprehensive service" component. But, here again, we face the strategy issues of the previous two models. Many parent involvement/parent education programs adopt the strategy of helping parents learn about available services or find ways to get them *to* services—both within the Family Impact Model. Others try, through parent councils and parent advisory committees or child advisory committees, to give parents something to say about who should deliver services and where and how these should be delivered (School Impact Model).

Although both strategies are useful, they place the blame for obviously needed change upon one of the weaker agencies in the system—the family. The family has no lobby, local or national; the American Medical Association does. If the families in programs, as they usually were from mid-1960s to now, were the "outside the system" ones, this places perhaps an unattainable expectation on them. We, the "powerful"—the educators and social service and health bureaucracies—are *telling* them to change us!

If the families are middle class, they are usually primarily interested in getting the system to be more responsive to their individual needs and are not interested in fundamental change.

The community impact model may seem the weakest or most futile, requiring us to step back and view our society and its efforts as a whole. It may make us feel overwhelmed, like Sisyphus, rolling the rock up the hill. It may imply that the other models should be abandoned. Such an analysis may seem unduly cynical or pessimistic, giving aid and comfort to the enemy; but that is not my intent. Much that is good and useful can be found in the variety of Parent Education/Parent Involvement efforts in which many of us have engaged. Results *do* show that the Family Impact Model works. The School Impact Model, too, has led to changes in the way parents and professionals see each other and, in some situations, to legislation and local district change. The Community Impact Model, as used in Head Start, clearly improved the health of many children, at least for the time they were in the program, and brought many formerly powerless people into the political mainstream.

Indeed, a National Survey of the Impacts of Head Start Centers on Community Institutions reported that

> *there does seem to be a relationship between the degree of parental participation in Head Start centers and the extent of centers' involvement in the institutional change process. . . . It would seem that Head Start involved the poor (the parents) in its organizational structure, this structure in turn had a tendency to become a vehicle through which Head Start contributed to the background for change (Kirschner, 1970).*

We sometimes forget that Head Start was funded under the community action agency legislation and, in this area, made a significant impact.

Efforts in all three models need to continue and to be enlarged. Today our prospects are so improved that we can develop and use a Community Impact Model as well as continue and strengthen the other two more micro models. Much will be required of us to move to this level. We will make errors, be faced with fragmentation of effort, and suffer territorial agency wars. The odds are high, but so are the stakes. My overriding concern is that our efforts not continue to be piecemeal, unsynthesized, small-scale and sporadic, but that they be placed in the broader social system context. We need to tie, where possible, parent education efforts to work, family income, and housing and zoning programs, medicare and medicaid, teacher education, professional education of social workers, psychologists, etc.

The American family, school and many elements of the system at all levels are in a state of flux. Change is not pleasant, and planned change is not always either possible or the outcome predictable. Further, change takes time. We need to ask ourselves not only the tactical questions, which relate to the state of the art and to what we have learned about the "how-to's," the retrospective questions; but also the strategic issues—why are we doing this? How does it fit into the larger social scheme? What do we hope to accomplish within the narrow confines of a specific program? What else ought to be done? What are our basic assumptions about people—what they need and want, how they learn and grow, what we desire for them? These prospective questions face us and the administration.

As you have seen, the issues and approaches have been with us for a long time. Although many of us *are* trying diligently to teach our chidren, the content has changed. Sharing Pestalozzi's dream, we must apply it to men and women, fathers as well as mothers. Many of us *are* working for change within the larger system, and our hopes are still high.

REFERENCES

Baruch, D. *New Ways in Discipline*. New York: Appleton-Century-Crofts, 1949.

Becker, W., & J. Becker. *Successful Parenthood*. Champaign, IL: Research Press Co., 1974.

Brim, O. G. *Education for Child Rearing*. New York: The Free Press, 1965.

———. "Macro-Structural Influences on Child Development and the Need for Childhood Social Indicators." *American Journal of Orthopsychiatry* 45, 4 (1975): 516–24.

Bronfenbrenner, U. "The Experimental Ecology of Education." *Educational Researcher* 5 (1976): 5–15.

Carew, J. V. "Effective Home Learning Environments in the Preschool Years." In *Update: The First Ten Years of Life*. Gainesville, FL: Division of Continuing Education, University of Florida, 1977.

Coleman, J. *Equality of Education Opportunity*. Washington, DC: United States Government Printing Office, 1966.

Cromwell, R., & K. Bartz. *The American Family: Its Impact on the Quality of Life*. Paper presented at Bicentennial Congress on Adult Continuing Education, New York, Nov. 19, 1976. Reprinted by permission of National Association for Public Continuing and Adult Education, Washington, DC.

Davie, R.; N. Butler; & H. Goldstein. *From Birth to Seven*. London: Longman, 1972.

Douglas, J. W. B.; J. M. Ross; & H. R. Simpson. *All Our Future*. London: Panther Books Ltd., 1971.

Elardo, R.; R. Bradley; & B. Caldwell. "The Relation of Infants' Home Environments to Mental Test Performance from Six to Thirty-six Months: A Longitudinal Analysis." *Child Development* 46, 11 (1975): 71–76. Reprinted by permission of The Society for Research in Child Development, Chicago.

Froebel, F. *Mother's Songs, Games and Stories*. Translated by Frances and Emily Ford. London: William Rice, 1907.

Frost, J., et al. *Understanding and Nurturing Infant Development*. Washington, DC: Association for Childhood Education International, 1976.

———. *Developing Programs for Infants and Toddlers*. Washington, DC: Association for Childhood Education International, 1977.

Ginott, H. *Between Parent and Child*. New York: Macmillan, 1965.

Goodson, B., & R. Hess. *Parents as Teachers of Young Children: An Evaluative Review of Some Contemporary Concepts and Programs*. Stanford, CA: Stanford University Press, 1975.

Gordon, I. J. *A Parent Education Approach to Provision of Early Stimulation for the Culturally Disadvantaged*. Final Report to Ford Foundation. Gainesville, FL: Institute for Development of Human Resources, 1967.

———. *Early Child Stimulation Through Parent Education*. Final report to Children's Bureau, Department of Health, Education, and Welfare, Grant No. PHS-R-306. Gainesville, FL: Institute for Development of Human Resources, 1969.

———. *Parent Involvement in Compensatory Education*. Urbana, IL: University of Illinois Press, 1970.

———. *An Investigation into the Social Roots of Competence*. Final report to NIMH, Project No. 1 RO1 MH 22724. Gainesville, FL: Institute for Development of Human Resources, Oct., 1974.

———. *The Infant Experience*. Columbus, OH: Charles G. Merrill, 1975.

———. "Intervention in Infant Education." In *Understanding and Nurturing Infant Development*, Joe Frost et al. Washington, DC: Association for Childhood Education International, 1976. Pp. 3–19.

———. "Parenting Teaching and Child Development." *Young Children* 16, 3 (1976): 173–83.

———. "What Are Effective Home Learning Environments for School Age Children?" In *Update: The First Ten Years of Life*. Gainesville, FL: Division of Continuing Education, University of Florida, 1977.

Gordon, I. J., & W. Breivogel, eds. *Building Effective Home-School Relationships*. Boston: Allyn & Bacon, 1976.

Gordon, I. J.; M. Hanes; L. Lamme; P. Schlenker; & H. Barnett. *Parent-oriented Home-based Early Childhood Education Programs*. Research report to United States Office of Education, contract from Region IV, P.L. 90-35, Title V, Part D, COP Grant. Gainesville, FL: Institute for Development of Human Resources, May 1975.

Gordon, I. J., & R. E. Jester. *Instructional Strategies in Infant Stimulation*. JSAS Selected Documents 3 (1972): 122.

Gordon, T. *Parent Effectiveness Training*. New York: Wyden Press, 1970.

Gray, S., & R. Klaus. The Early Training Project: A Seventh Year Report. *Child Development* 42 (1970), 909–924.

Guinagh, B., & I. J. Gordon. *School Performance as a Function of Early Stimulation*. Final report to Office of Child Development on Grant #NIH-HEW-OCD-09-C-638. Gainesville, FL: Institute for Development of Human Resources, Dec. 1976.

Honig, A. *Parent Involvement in Early Childhood Education*. Washington, DC: National Association for the Education of Young Children, 1975.

International Federation for Parent Education. Brochure. Paris, France, 1973.

Keeves, J. P. *Educational Environment and Student Achievement*. Stockholm: Almqvist & Wiksell, 1972.

———. "The Home, the School, and Achievement in Mathematics and Science." *Science Education* 59, 4 (1975): 439–60.

Kessen, W. ed. *The Child*. New York: John Wiley & Sons, 1965. Reprinted by permission.

Kirschner Associates, Inc., ed. *A National Survey of the Impacts of Head Start Centers on Community Institutions*. Washington, DC: Kirschner Associates, Inc. May 1970. Pp. 119, 121, 125. Reprinted by permission.

Levenstein, P. "Cognitive Growth in Preschoolers Through Verbal Interaction with Mothers." *American Journal of Orthopsychiatry* (April 1970): 426–32.

Mayeske, G. W., & A. E. Beaton. *Special Studies of Our Nation's Students*. Washington, DC: U.S. Department of Health, Education, and Welfare, 1975.

Miller, G. W. *Educational Opportunity and the Home*. London: Longman, 1971.

Moynihan, D. P. *Maximum Feasible Misunderstanding*. New York: Macmillan Publishing Co., 1969. Reprinted by permission.

National Society for the Study of Education. *The Relationship Between Persistence in School and Home Conditions*. Fifteenth Yearbook, Part II. Charles E. Hollye, Chairperson. Bloomington, IL: Public School Publishing Co., 1916.

———. *Preschool and Parental Education*. Twenty-eighth Yearbook. Lois Meek, Chairperson. Bloomington, IL: Public School Publishing Co., 1929.

———. *Early Childhood Education*. Seventy-first Yearbook, Part II. Ira J. Gordon, Chairperson. Chicago: University of Chicago Press, 1972.

Ojemann, R. *The Child and His Reading*. Child Welfare Pamphlet #16. Iowa City, IA: University of Iowa Press, 1941.

Palmer, F. H. "Has Compensatory Education Failed?" In *Update: The First Ten Years of Life*. Gainesville, FL: Division of Continuing Education, University of Florida, 1977.

Pestalozzi, J. H. *How Gertrude Teaches Her Children*. Translated by Lucy E. Holland & F. C. Turner. Syracuse, NY: Bardeen, 1894. First published in German, 1801. Letters IX and X reprinted in *The Child*, edited by W. Kessen. New York: John Wiley & Sons, 1965.

Pringle, M. L. Kellmer; N. R. Butler; & R. Davie. *11,000 Seven-Year-Olds*. London: Longman, 1966.

Purves, A. C. "Literature Education in Ten Countries." *International Studies in Evaluation*. Vol. 2. Stockholm: Almqvist & Wiksell, 1973.

Purves, A., & D. Levine. *Educational Policy and International Assessment*. Berkeley, CA: McCutchan Publishing Corp., 1975.

Schlossman, S. "Before Home Start: Notes Toward a History of Parent Education in America, 1987–1928." *Harvard Education Review* 46, 3 (1976): 436–67.

Southern Association of Colleges and Schools. *Together Is Best, Families and Schools, Findings of the Parent Education Demonstration Project in Region IV*. August 1976.

Thorndike, R. L. "Reading Comprehension Education in Fifteen Countries." *International Studies in Evaluation.* Vol. 3. Stockholm: Almqvist & Wiksell, 1973.

Van Leer, Bernard, Foundation, *Parent Involvement in Early Childhood Education—Selected Titles.* The Hague, Netherlands, Bernard Van Leer Foundation, 1976.

Wedge, P., & H. Prosser. *Born to Fail?* London: Arrow Books, 1973.

Weikart, D. P., et al. *Longitudinal Results of Ypsilanti Perry Preschool Project.* Ypsilanti, MI: High/Scope Educational Research Foundation, 1970.

Ira J. Gordon was Dean, College of Education, University of North Carolina at Chapel Hill.

Backing Away Helpfully: Some Roles Teachers Shouldn't Fill

Based on an Interview with Penny Hauser-Cram

I suspect that if you asked for a definition of a good teacher most families would describe a cross between a chameleon and Wonderwoman—someone who is part developmental scholar, pediatrician, artist, and therapist, with a little bit of toy designer, janitor, and athlete mixed in. But based on my years as a teacher and a director, I have come to believe that there are at least some roles that teachers can't and shouldn't fill. Two roles that I have seen cause tension and hard feelings come immediately to mind: the role of family therapist and the role of parenting expert.

Parents need and want other adults in each of these roles. Since teachers and parents share an intimate, ongoing relationship centered on children they both care about, it is tempting for all sides to move from educational and developmental issues to personal, and even therapeutic, ones. A big challenge for teachers is to help parents find the help they need, without adopting those helping roles themselves.

Sharing Children's Development

Parents and teachers really do share children. Together they are involved in seeing one, and sometimes several, children through some of the largest developmental events of the early years: the transition from the home to school or a center, the process of making friends, the joys and struggles of learning to talk or even to begin reading. Because of daily involvement with a child, a teacher is often the first outsider to know the in's and out's of a family's workings: whether they ignore or attend to a child's illness, when they have had periods of disorganization, how they handle the stresses of being late, bathroom accidents, or a missing favorite book or toy. A teacher also learns a great deal of very revealing information about individual children: how late or early a baby sits up, walks, says a first word; how shy or aggressive a three year old is; how challenging or cooperative a four year old may be. Unlike friends or neighbors, who may have similar insights, teachers are in a position to evaluate—they can compare a family or a child to many others they know.

Together parents and teachers are involved in seeing children through some of the major developmental events of the early years.

Source: Backing away helpfully: Some roles teachers shouldn't fill (1986, Spring). *Beginnings,* pp. 18–20. Reprinted with permission from Exchange Press, Inc., P.O. Box 2890, Redmond, WA 98073.

A Charged Situation

Since parents are often deeply invested in how their children are developing, their discussions with teachers are often charged with emotion. Some parents resent or distrust teachers, particularly in cases where teachers and family members see the child or the purposes of early education differently. For example, imagine what happens when a father sees a boy as *active* and a teacher sees that child as *aggressive* or when a mother wants her three year old to practice number facts and a teacher insists blocks and beads provide the *right* kinds of early mathematical experiences.

Other parents react to a teacher's knowledge by thinking: "Here is someone who already knows and cares about us. At last, here is someone I can really talk to." Then, when a teacher asks a question in a conference related to a child's life at home, the parent may see it as an invitation to go far beyond issues of the child's behavior or schooling. Suddenly, the teacher is catapulted into the role of a therapist or expert.

Spotting Difficult Situations

Sometimes teachers can anticipate that parents may desire additional advice, especially when a child's behavior has undergone a dramatic change. Discussing that change with parents is an important part of a teacher's responsibility, but such discussions can sometimes lead to areas beyond the scope and expertise of the teacher.

Imagine that during a conference a teacher says: "I have been wondering about Michael. The last two weeks he hasn't been playing with friends. He seems listless and tired. Has he been sleeping well?" The parent comes back with: "You're right. I'm glad you mentioned it. Things have been tough . . . there have been a lot of fights at night. We're thinking of separating, and I'm worried about Michael. What shall I do?" Without meaning to, the teacher touched a nerve. The parent responded with a flood of intimate information and a request for help. Within a few moments, the teacher has become a parent's counselor.

A different type of difficult situation sometimes occurs when a mother and father come to a conference with different points of view. Before the teacher can say much, it is clear that they see their child quite differently. One

insists: "Shelly is a cry-baby." The other interrupts: "She is not. She is just more sensitive than other children." Both turn to the teacher for confirmation. Suddenly, the teacher is playing the part of an arbitrator in a family dispute.

It is early Wednesday morning. Lucia, rubbing her eyes, comes into the classroom dragging behind her father. A teacher greets her and then comments to Lucia's father that she looks a bit tired. Sighing, he replies: "She's so difficult at home. We can't get her to eat her dinner or go to sleep at a reasonable hour. And she's always starting fights with her brother. We're exhausted. What can we do?" All at once, the teacher has gone from making an observation to being the dispenser of advice.

Each of these is a delicate situation—parents are genuinely seeking help. But they are also asking their children's teachers to go beyond what teachers can reasonably do. The requests are tempting—they complement teachers' knowledge, and often they seem like only a small extension of teachers' concern for children's development.

Backing Away Helpfully

Far from being trapped, teachers can take steps to help parents understand the difference between the roles of teachers, therapists, and experts—steps that clarify without abandoning or ignoring the distress or confusion that parents may feel.

1. **Acknowledge what has been said.** When parents open up their private lives, they make themselves vulnerable. If a teacher tries to change the topic or gloss over the issues raised, the parent may be hurt or angry. Teachers must recognize what's been revealed: "That helps me to understand why Michael has been tired. It sounds difficult for all of you."

2. **Categorize the kind of problem.** Once a parent has talked about a problem, a teacher must decide: Is this a classroom problem, a mild developmental issue, or an acute issue in children's or parents' lives deserving professional help? Deciding is not always easy, but here are some examples which may help:

   • **Classroom problems:** Learning to concentrate on a task; being able to take turns or share with other children; conflicts between parents and teachers over how early to start toilet training; a child's reluctance to come to school in the morning.

- **Mild family issues:** A child being unwilling to play at other children's homes; a child being afraid of monsters and refusing to go to sleep at night; parent-child conflicts over eating habits, thumb sucking, getting dressed in the morning.
- **Acute problems:** Marked delay in the child's development; extreme aggression, fears, or apathy in children; marital conflict; family abuse; severe mental or physical illness or death in the family.

It is important to categorize because teachers have the skills and information to work on classroom issues. Venturing into family issues or acute problems saddles teachers with responsibilities and demands too great to handle.

3. **Make a plan for classroom issues.** It is vital that parents know teachers are willing and able to work on problems of learning, behavior, and development in the classroom. Go right to work: find out what is bothering the parent, describe your view of the issue, work out joint strategies, and arrange a time to talk over progress in the near future.

4. **For other kinds of problems, inform parents of other resources.** If a parent brings up something other than a classroom issue, she should not be left alone with her problem neglected. Teachers can help responsibly by alerting parents to other, more appropriate resources.

- **Resources for mild developmental issues:** I have seen two kinds of center-based parent resources work very well. At Eliot-Pearson, we have a parents' group led by a social worker (trained in child development), not a teacher. The group meets at the school, with no teachers or director attending. Since the group mixes parents of children of different ages and from different classrooms, the discussion doesn't turn to teachers or curriculum. Also, because of that mix, parents of younger children can learn from the mothers and fathers of older children. Parents of older children can look back and appreciate all the distance they have come.

At the Brookline Early Education Pro-ject, there were specific *call-in hours* each week—just as some pediatricians have. Trained social workers and child development specialists took calls from parents concerned about issues such as sleep difficulties, sibling relationships, or changes in behavior.

- **Resources for acute issues:** Always have a list of community resources on hand: When parents announce their needs, they are feeling them acutely. That is not the time to say: "Hmmm, I once had a friend who used a good family counselor. Let me see if I can find out who that was." Instead, it is the time to offer a well thought-out list of resources. The list should include a variety of services in a range of areas: developmental screening clinics, therapists who work with children, family therapists, marriage counselors. The list should contain services in a number of different locations and at varying levels of expense. Every resource listed must have been carefully checked.

5. **Agree to collaborate.** By limiting their roles, teachers aren't signing off. They can agree to work with families and outside resources to solve issues. They can work closely with parents to help children develop better eating habits or self-control. They can share information about what works in the classroom or offer observations when parents come to pick up children. They can offer to talk to a professional who will be testing the child, make it possible for that person to observe in the classroom, and meet with parents to go over any final reports.

Conclusion

The way in which teachers are pulled into acting as therapists or experts is part of a much larger situation. Families often have nowhere else to turn. Many, maybe even most, parents live apart from their own families of origin. Few pediatricians or nurses are trained to discuss and solve developmental issues. For over a century, parents have been *trained* to turn to outside experts—like Gesell or Spock—for answers. For many people, it is a large, bewildering, and expensive step to start hunting for professional help. Not surprisingly, it is teachers who inherit the flock of questions, concerns, and worries parents have.

The other side of the coin is that teachers are trained to notice and respond to the needs of other human beings. For many of them, saying "No" to a request for help feels wrong, like shutting off some very basic perception.

But I am not suggesting that teachers turn a cold shoulder on family's needs. Instead, teachers should think about where they can be most helpful and where being helpful lies in pointing the way to more appropriate resources.

New Parents as Teachers

Michael K. Meyerhoff and Burton L. White

In 1981, the Missouri State Department of Education hired us to design a model parent education program and to help implement it at four different sites. The success of the New Parents as Teachers program has been so remarkable that the Missouri legislature has made the availability of parent education mandatory in the state. As the word spreads, we expect to see other states doing the same.

How did this come about? A fair amount of credit goes to some very dedicated people in Missouri, including the state's director of early childhood education, the commissioner of education, a representative from the Danforth Foundation, and the then incumbent governor (who became a first-time father in his early forties). Credit also is due to the very talented parent educators who staffed the initial programs. The rest of the credit can go to our research of the last 20 years on the early learning process and how parents can help their children get the best possible start in life.

The Lessons of Project Head Start

Prior to 1965, very few people thought that any significant learning took place before a child entered school at age five or six. However, largely in the context of the civil rights movement that blossomed during the early 1960s, an increasing number of parents and professionals came to the realization that many children—particularly those from low-income, minority communities—were already educationally disadvantaged at kindergarten age and were destined to perform poorly in the classroom. In 1965, the federal government initiated Project Head Start, a nationwide network of center-based programs for three- to six-year-old children, designed to ensure that they would not miss out on important preschool educational experiences evidently available to their more fortunate peers.

Unfortunately, from an educational standpoint, Project Head Start and its various spin-off programs, such as Home Start and Follow Through, have failed to accomplish this goal. A handful of well-funded, carefully designed programs staffed by highly trained personnel (such as David Weikart's Perry Preschool Project in Ypsilanti, Michigan) have demonstrated that under special conditions such programs can achieve modest success. However, while the children apparently were somewhat better off than they would have been had they not participated in these programs they still were not exhibiting even average, much less superior, levels of achievement during the school-age years.

Project Head Start did succeed in demonstrating two points very clearly. First, most of the children headed for scholastic difficulty at age six and beyond are by age three already significantly behind their peers in terms of intellectual and linguistic skills. Rather than giving children a "head start," these programs are more likely helping them "catch up." Second, such remedial work is extraordinarily expensive, difficult to do, and, even under the best of circumstances, not likely to completely reverse early losses.

The Harvard Preschool Project

Our research with the Harvard Preschool Project also began in 1965. However, unlike Head Start programs, our interest went beyond children from poor families heading for problems in school to helping all children achieve the best possible start in life. We were also interested in social, as well as academic, aspects of development.

In the early stages of our research, we focused on preschool children who, by anyone's definition and in everyone's opinion, were "most likely to succeed." These children came from a wide range of socioeconomic and cultural backgrounds, but they all shared intellectual, linguistic, and social skills that clearly set them apart from their average and below-average peers. We soon realized that these children were exhibiting an impressive pattern of abilities by the time they were three years old.

We then went to their parents to find out which ones had another child coming along. When the new siblings were between one and three, we went into their homes every other week and recorded all we could about their experiences and the childrearing practices of their parents.

Later we took what we had learned from these "successes of nature," combined it with the research of others like Piaget, Hunt, and Ainsworth, and then translated it into information and support programs for new parents. In addition to our early, university-based efforts, we joined with a local school district in conducting a special parent education program known as the Brookline Early Education Program. Through these experiences, we gained additional knowledge about early development, as well as expertise in working with diverse young families.

The Center for Parent Education

We published the results of our basic research on early development[1] and our guidelines for parents[2] between 1973 and 1979. We reached three central conclusions.

- The educational consequences of the experiences of the first three years of life contribute heavily to lifelong development.
- The practice of offering little or no preparation or assistance to the child's parents often leads to more stress, reduced pleasure, and educational losses for all involved.
- Although much research remained to be done, it was possible to implement effective programs, as much reliable and useful information existed that parents and professionals simply weren't getting.

With this motivation, in 1978 we established the Center for Parent Education, an independent, nonprofit organization based in Newton, Massachusetts. We had two primary goals: to increase public awareness of these issues and to provide resource, consulting, and training services to professionals concerned with the education of children during the first three years of life, especially those interested in working with parents in their role as their children's first and most important teachers.

Subsequently, we had contact with thousands of grassroots parent education programs that were springing up throughout the United States and Canada. Unfortunately, most government agencies did not respond with the same enthusiasm. At the federal level, Project Head Start continued to receive nearly all the money and personnel allocated for early education. While its educational track record remained weak, the fact that it was focusing attention on a long-neglected segment of the population and channeling much-needed funds into their communities made it politically popular and powerful. At the state level, the inertial effects of doing things as they had always been done were strong, and key decision makers still felt that there was insufficient evidence for changing the traditional approach to education.

The Missouri Initiative

In the late 1960s two Missouri women became determined that their state would lead the country into a new educational era. From the end of that decade and throughout the 1970s, Mildred Winter, the state's director of early childhood education, and Jane Paine, a representative of the Danforth Foundation, conducted an extensive and exhaustive political and public relations campaign aimed at getting Missouri to commit some of its educational resources to the kind of programs we were advocating. Eventually, they were joined by Arthur Mallory, the state commissioner of education, and Governor Christopher Bond. By 1981, the stage was set for Missouri's New Parents as Teachers project.

We selected four school districts (urban, suburban, small town, and rural) to host the initial programs, which were to be based on our model of an ideal parent preparation and support program. Together, the families they served approximated a fair representation of the total population of Missouri, covering a wide socioeconomic spectrum and a variety of cultural backgrounds. The program was open to all first-time parents, and a thorough outreach effort was conducted to ensure that all segments of the population were included and to avoid "self-selected" samples.

Using mostly federal funds, over which the state department of education had discretionary power, and contributions from local school districts, we hired two full-time parent educators to serve between 60 and 100 families in each district. Also, employing mostly unused elementary school classroom space, we established a resource and operations center at each site. Through a grant from the Danforth Foundation, we were contracted to provide the parent educators with specialized training, help equip the resource centers, prepare the sites for operations, and supply guidance and supervision for the entire effort. By January 1982, services to families were begun, which continued for three years.

The Structure of the Program

Services offered to the families featured group get-togethers at the resource center, where 10 to 12 parents would meet with a parent educator, and private home visits, in which a parent educator would meet one-to-one with parents. Services began during the third trimester of pregnancy and continued until the child's third birthday, with increasing emphasis on private visits after the child was five or six months of age. The average amount of contact with families was once a month for an hour to an hour-and-a-half.

Comprehensive educational screening services were provided to monitor each child's intellectual, linguistic, and social progress, and an extensive referral system was instituted to promptly provide parents with any special assistance they might require. In other words, the parents were virtually guaranteed that their children could not develop an educational problem without their knowing about it immediately and receiving appropriate information about where and how to get help. Since the staff maintained a strict identity as educational specialists only, this referral system also helped the parents with monetary, marital, medical, or other noneducational problems.

Furthermore, the parents had access to the resource centers, where they could examine an extensive collection of books, magazines, toys, and other materials relating to early development and parenting, and obtain guidance from the staff regarding the evaluation and selection of potentially useful items. They also could meet with other new parents and even take advantage of cooperative babysit-ting arrangements, which would enable them to have regular (and often requisite) time off from their childrearing responsibilities.

The Content of the Program

Through the group and private sessions, the parents were given basic information about what children are like at different stages of development and what sorts of things help or hinder their progress. They were shown videotapes demonstrating typical behaviors of infants and toddlers,[3] and they received curriculum materials that outlined the interests and abilities of children at each stage of development, suggested appropriate activities, and alerted them to new developments to expect in the upcoming stages.[4]

The information and advice conveyed through these mechanisms were neither highly elaborate nor overly extensive. Since we were interested in promoting well-balanced, all-around development, we did not advocate high-pressure procedures designed to produce precocities in specific areas. Unlike the many "infant stimulation" or "super-baby" programs that have sprung up in recent years, we focused on a comfortable style of parenting that would make the early educational process enjoyable, as well as effective. We felt that a highly intensive, structured set of specific activities might dampen the children's intrinsic interest in learning and take a lot of the fun out of the daily interactions between parents and children. The following are examples of information that we shared with the parents.

Language learning. All too often, attention to early linguistic development focuses on children's speech. We knew from our research that, although many well-developing children do not say very much until they are almost two years old, their capacity to understand simple words and instructions usually begins to develop between six and eight months of age. Since most sane people tend not to talk to things that don't talk back—such as chairs, fire hydrants, and babies—many parents miss out on several months' worth of opportunities for teaching language. In homes where children were developing impressive linguistic abilities, we noticed that parents had talked to them a lot from birth.

Moreover, once the children began exhibiting signs of language awareness, the parents

347

did not engage them in vocabulary exercises using flashcards, labeling books, or other such devices. They simply waited for the many daily instances when their children approached them for comfort, assistance, or to share their excitement over some new discovery. At these times, they would respond to their children, using simple language to expand upon what the children were focusing on.

Intellectual development. "Doing what comes naturally" can be counterproductive at times. For instance, when children reach the second half of the first year, they start crawling and climbing. They enter a period when accidental falls, poisonings, and other serious mishaps are apt to occur and when they may wreak havoc with plants, china, and other valuable items they encounter. Many well-meaning parents react by restricting their children to a small but safe area, such as a playpen. They provide "educational" toys to keep the children occupied and occasionally let them loose for carefully supervised "learning" sessions.

However, in homes where children were developing impressive intellectual abilities, we noticed that their parents took a different tack. Rather than restricting their children, they simply redesigned their homes, making most of the living area safe for (and from) newly mobile babies. In this way, the children were given access to a large and interesting learning environment. They could explore, investigate, and experiment with a world of exciting and enriching objects and experiences virtually at will.

Those parents were good observers of their children and were usually available to act as personal consultants, providing assistance when necessary and sharing excitement when appropriate. They also were ready and willing to provide new learning opportunities, not through expensive toys or specific games, but rather by letting the children help bake cookies or accompany them on a trip to the supermarket. Instead of setting aside specific and structured time to "teach" their children, they simply and spontaneously set up interesting environments, allowed their children to indulge their natural curiosity, and then followed whatever leads the children provided.

Social skills. We discovered that bright three-year-olds were relatively common as compared to nice three-year-olds. Many parents, especially first-timers, mistakenly assume that children come already civilized, or at least acquire common courtesies on their own. Even when presented with increasing evidence to the contrary, many parents have trouble cracking down on their children's unacceptable behaviors, understandably but misguidedly fearing they might lose the love of these precious and wonderful additions to lives. As a result, the "terrible two's" and the unpleasant temper tantrums of the third year of life are all too common.

Temper tantrums during the third year are not inevitable. In homes where children were developing into people who were both bright and a pleasure to live with, we noticed that the parents were not afraid to set realistic but firm boundaries on their children's behavior, and they started doing so before the first birthday. During the first months of life, these parents lavished love and attention upon the children and responded almost unconditionally to their every demand. However, starting at about eight months of age, when the children's demands were no longer a result of need but often reflected the exploration and testing of what they could and could not get away with (especially during the normal period of "negativism" between 15 and 24 months), these parents let the children know in no uncertain terms that infringements on the rights of others would not be tolerated.

We also learned that consistency in setting such limits often was overrated as compared to persistency. Sooner or later, all parents would admonish their children for certain undesirable activities, but the effective parents always followed through. If the admonishments were ignored or the undesirable activities later resumed, they acted swiftly and firmly. Moreover, their disciplinary strategies were appropriate to their children's level of understanding. For instance, rather than saying something like, "If you don't stop pulling on the drapes, we won't take you to Nana's house next Christmas," to an 18-month-old, they quickly removed the child from the scene and physically restrained the child from engaging in the offending behavior.

These few examples represent the sorts of points we stressed and the style of childrearing we encouraged the parents to adopt. Since program participation was voluntary, we could not require them to follow our prescriptions. However, we have found that first-time parents are eager for information and quite willing to accept guidance from people who demonstrate genuine expertise in these areas.

The Results

As the children of the participating families approached their third birthdays, we contracted with Research and Training Associates of Overland Park, Kansas, an independent organization with no prior involvement in the project, to evaluate the program's effectiveness. Their report was published in September 1985,[5] and the results were even better than we had expected.

First, the participating parents highly valued the program. Of the 300+ families, close to 90 percent remained in the program to its conclusion, and only one or two of the dropouts did so for reasons other than the fact that they had moved out of a participating district. Moreover, 99 percent of the families reported satisfaction with the program, and many of their comments to the evaluators were highly complimentary.

More important, a comparison of 75 randomly selected project children with a carefully matched sample of children from nonparticipating school districts whose parents had not received services revealed that we had made a substantial difference on a variety of dimensions. Unfortunately, while the data collected strongly suggested outstanding social development in the project children, since the science of measuring social skills in very young children remains rather crude, solid evidence for improvements in this aspect of development could not be firmly established. However, sophisticated measures of intellectual and linguistic development—the Kaufman Assessment Battery for Children and the Zimmerman Preschool Language Scales—left little doubt of our success in enhancing the educational prospects of the project children.

All children tested, both project and comparison, were first-born children. With respect to intellectual development, the Kaufman measure has four subscales. The comparison children scored 113, 107, 107, and 110 on these subscales—substantially above national averages, which is to be expected in the case of first-born children. The project children scored 117, 117, 117, and 123, respectively.

The significance of the differences on the second, third, and fourth subscales was .003, .001, and greater than .001, respectively. With regard to linguistic development, the Zimmerman measure has three subscales. Once again, the comparison children scored well above national averages—127, 117, and 123, and the project children scored significantly better—140, 130, and 138, respectively. In all cases, significance was beyond the .001 level.

Implications of the Study

In cases where children were suffering from severe pathology, such as Down's Syndrome or deafness, or where the parents had overwhelming problems, such as alcoholism or abject poverty, that overshadowed educational issues, we did not exclude the families from receiving services, but we made it clear that our program could not deal with their extraordinary circumstances. To that extent, we cannot say that this type of program will have a comparable impact on every family with young children.

On the other hand, these evaluation results are probably applicable to the approximately 85 percent of the population without such special needs. We had success with families in which both parents had Ph.D.'s, and with those in which both parents failed to finish high school. Some families had an annual income in excess of $40,000, and others were living below the poverty line. There were black families and white families. Some parents were in their late thirties, others were teenagers, and a number of them were single parents.

We have demonstrated some basic principles that we feel could—and should—revolutionize the traditional approach to education. First, in order to make a significant difference in the academic prospects of young children, you should reach them during the first three years of life, when the foundations for key aspects of development are being laid. Second, if you want to do so inexpensively and efficiently, work through the people who have the greatest influence on their lives during this period—their parents. Finally, most parents, regardless of socioeconomic status, educational level, or cultural background, are eager to receive the information and support they need to be effective in the role as their children's first and most important teachers.

ENDNOTES

1. The results of the Harvard Preschool Project research have been published in B. L. White et al., *Experience and Environment: Major Influences on the Development of the Young Child, Vol. 1 and Vol. 2* (Englewood Cliffs, N.J.: Prentice-Hall, 1973, 1978); B. L. White et al., *The Origins of Human Competence: The Final Report of the Harvard Preschool Project* (Lexington, Mass.: Lexington Books, 1979).

2. Specific recommendations for parents based on our research have been published in B. L. White, *The First Three Years of Life* (Englewood Cliffs, N.J.: Prentice-Hall, 1975, rev. ed., 1985).

3. The videotape series used in the New Parents as Teachers project is *The First Three Years*, produced by the Westinghouse Broadcasting Company in 1977, and available through the Center for Parent Education, 55 Chapel St., Newton, MA 02160.

4. The curriculum materials used in the New Parents as Teachers project are produced by the Missouri State Department of Education. They are available through New Parents as Teachers, Attention: Debbie Murphey, Director, Missouri Department of Education, P.O. Box 480, Jefferson City, MO 65102.

5. The final evaluation of the New Parents as Teachers project was prepared by Research and Training Associates of Overland Park, Kansas. Copies are available from the Missouri State Department of Education at the address above.

Michael K. Meyerhoff is Associate Director and Burton L. White is Director, Center of Parent Education, 55 Chapel St., Newton, MA 02160.

ASK YOURSELF:
Identifying Issues for Debate and Advocacy

1. If parents were educated to create more effective home environments, would there be fewer problems in the school? Why or why not?

2. Will parent involvement in school programs and in policy decisions minimize the influence of the professional? Why or why not?

3. Is formal parent education helpful to becoming an effective parent? Do home environments (family income, culture, and functioning) influence the effectiveness of parent education programs? Do the personality orientations and childrearing beliefs of parents influence the effectiveness of parent education programs? (What types of parent education do parents want and need?) Explain. (Also see Powell, 1986.)

4. When is parent involvement in school programs preferable to home visits by school personnel? When is the reverse true?

5. Should parents' expectations for their child in an early education program (as revealed by talking with them) influence a teacher's curriculum decisions? Why or why not?

6. What adjustments, if any, should a teacher make when working with single parents? Explain.

7. In relationships with parents, how can teachers help without doing harm? (See the article "Backing Away Helpfully" in this chapter.)

APPLICATION/ADVOCACY EXERCISES

1. Uncertainties or differences about role responsibilities and limitations often curtail collaboration and communication between teachers and parents of young children. This four-part activity will help you to better understand some of the perceptions and underlying issues that can create distrust between teachers and parents.

   a. *Carefully* read the following propositions:

     Proposition 1: The family operates as the primary socializing agent for stimulating and supporting educational, developmental, and cultural influences in the lives of young children (Hanson, 1980).

     Proposition 2: The "mothering" and the informal education provided in the family can be described as different from the teaching and "formal" education provided in the school (Katz, 1980).

     Proposition 3: To develop the full potential of the child, the "education" provided by the family and by the school should have distinctive aims/goals (Hanson, 1980).

     Proposition 4: The goal of home/school relations in school should be one of parent empowerment, where supportive emphasis is placed on parents' self-efficacy (versus helplessness) and on their abilities to solve their own problems (versus reliance on "experts").

   b. In two columns, identify some distinctive aims or goals for education in the family versus education in preschool or kindergarten programs.

   c. Differentiate between *parent education* for this informal education in the family setting and *parent involvement* in the school setting. In what important ways do they differ? (Incorporate ideas from Gordon in your response.)

   d. Given the difficulties with communication and role definition that Mrs. Yancey (the kindergarten teacher in the vignette at the beginning of this chapter) had in her conference with Mr. Freeman, how would you manage the conference differently? (In your response, keep in mind: that (1) the parent-teacher conference is a form of parent involvement, and (2) parent empowerment is important in home/school relations.)

2. This modification of a jigsaw activity (Moskowitz, Malvin, Schaeffer, & Schaps, 1983; Slavin, 1980) uses an assortment of articles (see list below) about stress factors that

351

contribute to parent burnout in today's family. The steps of this jigsaw activity are:

a. Separate into five to seven home teams and assign one of the articles listed below to each team member. Each person reads his or her article.

Caplan, P. J. (1986, October). Take the blame off mother. *Psychology Today*, 70–71.

Gagnon, J. (1981, January). Baby Sam needs you. *Working Mother*, 103, 153–155.

Kontos, S., & Wells, W. (1986). Attitudes of caregivers and the day care experiences of families. *Early Childhood Research Quarterly*, *1*, 47–67.

Reder, N. (1986, July). Women & work: Where does it leave us? *The National Voter*, 6–9.

Shapiro, J. L. (1987, January). The expectant father. *Psychology Today*, 36–39, 42.

Shreve, A. (1982, November 21). Careers and the lure of motherhood. *The New York Times Magazine*, 38–43, 46, 48, 50, 52, 56.

Weissbourd, B., & Grimm, C. (1981, March–April). Family Focus: Supporting families in the community. *Children Today*, 6–11.

b. Next, the students, who have the same article, meet in expert teams: (1) to identify the factors contributing to parental stress, (2) to analyze the author's point of view and arguments, and (3) to help each other prepare to teach the ideas and issues presented in their article when they return to their home teams.

c. Upon return to their home teams, each "expert," in turn, presents an article and shares insights and conclusions.

d. Finally, home team members discuss one or more of the following questions:
- How do schools contribute to parent burnout?
- Are there ways that schools can help to alleviate parent burnout?
- How can the school and the home work together to alleviate parent burnout? (Also see the article "Backing Away Helpfully.")
- What social policies would help to alleviate parental stress? (Also see the article "New Parents as Teachers.")

3. To better understand the importance of parent expectations for education, interview a preschool and kindergarten parent. Request an interview and state your purpose (i.e., to learn more about what they expect for their child in terms of a preschool or kindergarten experience). Compose four to six questions that you wish to ask each parent about school expectations each has for his or her child. (Write open-ended questions; avoid suggesting spe-

cific responses and avoid questions that can be answered with a yes-no only response. Include some questions related to issues discussed in this book.) Take notes during the interviews in order to obtain a record of responses. After the interviews, write a summary, including the interview questions and followup probe questions, the responses of each interviewee, and your interpretation and analysis of responses in terms of how this information might be helpful to a teacher. Compare and contrast responses of the preschool and kindergarten parent. Incorporate ideas from readings in your interpretations.

4. Develop a pamphlet for parents describing various ways in which to become more involved in child care programs (both inside and outside the classroom) and in improving the quality of their child's learning experiences in the school program. Incorporate meaningful visuals as well as printed information. Include references or sources for further information.

REFERENCES & SUGGESTED READINGS

Bronfenbrenner, U. (1985, May). The three worlds of childhood. *Principal*, 7–11.

Hanson, B. A. (1980, October). Personal communication.

Katz, L. G. (1980). Mothering and teaching—Some significant distinctions. In L. G. Katz (Ed.), *Current topics in early childhood education* (Vol. 3) (pp. 47–63). Norwood, NJ: Ablex.

Kristensen, N., & Billman, J. (1987). Supporting parents and young children: Minnesota Early Childhood Family Education Program. *Childhood Education, 63,* 276–282.

Moskowitz, J. M., Malvin, J. H., Schaeffer, G. A., & Schaps, E. (1983). Evaluation of a cooperative learning strategy. *American Educational Research Journal, 20,* 687–696.

Powell, D. R. (1986, March). Parent education and support programs. *Young Children, 41,* 47–53.

Slavin, R. E. (1980). Cooperative learning. *Review of Educational Research, 50,* 315–342.

CHAPTER 13

Advocacy: Influencing Policy and Regulations

Pie Slicing?

"Thank you so much for taking time out of your busy schedule to see me, Assemblyman Toplure. I'll get right to the point. I'm here to discuss the impact of the changes in national policy on the children in our state, specifically, cuts in day care funds. You're aware, I'm certain, that the reduction of monies in the Social Services Block Grant has meant a $60 million loss this fiscal year. And, in spite of the fact that the need for child care services has increased with escalating numbers of single and divorced parents, day care is being reduced all over the state. Moreover, I'm sure you recognize that cuts in funding of licensing agencies for Social Services has meant that more and more of our children are being cared for in illegal, substandard settings."

"Well now, Mrs. Knight, I am well acquainted with the figures as well as the problems. And I think I can safely speak for the rest of my colleagues, Democrat and Republican. We are aware of the issues and their importance, but our problem is that we can't deal with issues piecemeal. We must take a look at the whole social picture. And with economic circumstances the way they are today, it's difficult to know how to allocate the meager resources available to us. For example, what about AIDS and the problems of the homeless? . . . Oh, oh! The buzzer is sounding for roll call vote. Sorry, I must go now. But I do thank you for stopping in. It's always nice to meet one of my constituents."

Questions

1. Suppose you received a polite brush-off similar to the one just described. What would be your next step?
2. Given today's budget deficits, how can child care be made a priority for public spending?

PREVIEW

How do cultural assumptions about child care outside the home affect child care policy (Klass, 1986)? When both parents hold jobs, who should provide care for preschool children and how should such care be regulated by the government? How can adequate care be insured with the continuing increase in the number of day care centers, day care homes, and other group-care programs and the present number of state licensing staff? How can program evaluation best support quality child care services and advocacy efforts for child care funding?

In the first selection of this chapter, Alice Sterling Honig describes child care programs in three different countries: East Germany, China, and France. Elizabeth Sestini then examines the national policies for preschool programs found in three African countries. Although the United States has a wide array of programs for young children, it has no national policy on child care. Edward E. Gotts argues for policies that support quality child care for young children in terms of the needs of the contemporary family. Next, Gwen G. Morgan explains how both regulatory and nonregulatory approaches can help to achieve the goals of quality child care. Amy Wilkins and Helen Blank then discuss how to improve child care funding and standards through orchestrated advocacy efforts. The final selection is a set of guidelines from Child Care, Inc., to use when visiting public officials to advocate for child care issues.

Comparison of Child Care in Different Countries

Alice Sterling Honig

Child care needs are met in different ways in different countries. Some nations have given more attention, some much less, to the needs of children and their families for safe and intellectually and emotionally nourishing environments in which to grow. These needs may be particularly acute if parents are working or are immigrants in a country.

From my travels as a visitor to child care facilities in many lands, I should like to present some examples of child care facilities found in different societies that have dealt with the problem of child care in different ways. Governments and citizens have shown different degrees of awareness of the developmental needs of young children, and different degrees of commitment to help organize quality child care facilities.

In East Germany, working women have the right to day care facilities for their children for ten hours per day. The Clara Zetkin Day Care Center in Jena, for example, houses programs for infants, toddlers, and preschoolers. Health care standards are very strict. The Director is required to have three years of special child care education and staff is expected to have two years of training. An impressively thick child care manual spells out clearly the tasks and responsibilities of staff. Infants were cuddled and talked to while being diapered; gentle relaxed toilet training procedures were used. Teachers sang with toddlers and proudly showed off, using a pitch pipe to help the little one begin, how well their toddlers could sing songs as "Teddy, teddy, tanze!" The staff was professional and loving; they promoted educational as well as practical living goals with very young children. Outdoors in the large play yard, an artificially created stream allowed water play for more than the usual four children that can be accommodated at a rectangular water play table.

To child care facilities visited in The People's Republic of China, day care equipment varied greatly, depending on the economic resources available in each community. But even in an agricultural commune, where few frills or toys existed for children, the caregivers obviously were courteous, concerned, warm, attentive and proud of the little ones in their care. Many physical games were used to help build skills and agility and give pleasure in body movement as well as promote sharing and cooperation. Paper mache brightly colored props, obviously hand made, were used to permit sociodramatic play such as riding a choo-choo train, or pretending to plant and harvest giant vegetables from a garden. Despite the lack of Western material resources and toys in many urban and rural centers visited, there was a strong emphasis on aesthetics in Chinese child care centers (Honig, 1978a, 1978b). Facial make-up and homemade costumes or crepe paper streamers and flowers often served to enhance children's play and performance. Songs were an integral part of the curriculum. Adults and children obviously had spent a great deal of time together singing and learning songs and little dances. Even during a chance meeting of day care teachers and their preschoolers on a path on a tea plantation commune, we were able to enjoy brief songs and accompanying actions as the children and adults carried out singing play games. Another important aspect of Chinese child care during two separate visits to such facilities (both during and four years after the Cultural Revolution) was the strong emphasis given to teaching and encouraging prosocial and caring interpersonal actions

Source: Alice Sterling Honig (1984). Comparison of child care in different countries. *Child Resource World Review*, 1(1), pp. 1–2. Reprinted by permission of the author and Kenneth Jaffe, Executive Director, International Child Resource Institute.

357

among children. Just as teaching colors or shapes might be important for a preschool teacher in the West, teaching moral concern for the rights and needs of others was built into informal games, formal lessons and into even the type of playground equipment used. Some of the games and swings worked best if children cooperated in moving and swinging legs together. Despite lack of formal training in Piaget or Erikson, more integration of developmental principles with very young children was observed than in many child care settings in the West, where child development theorists are far better known. The children's responses to a visitor's gifts, such as balloons or soap bubble jars or slinkies, showed how well the prosocial curricula have worked. There was intense interest and desire for new toys but also very little shoving or pushing to get something before another child did.

In Paris, France, where large numbers of North African immigrants work in the automobile factories and at other jobs, child care is available for infants in creches and in the public school Ecole Maternelle for children from $2^{1}/_{2}$ years of age. Social workers make every effort to help families enroll small children in the Ecole Maternelle as this is considered the most rapid way for a child to learn to speak French and to learn basic cognitive and social skills that will be required on entrance to early school grades. The quality of the care differs very much in different communities. Some of the Ecole Maternelles I visited were filled with equipment, toys, art materials and construction materials in a profusion of shapes and colors. Sometimes caregivers seemed to have less knowledge about the *process* of luring and motivating and arousing the curiosity and love of learning in young children. How important *individual* teachers seemed! Rather than fancy toys as a panacea, what comes clear after visiting a variety of such educational settings, is how important are adult qualities of: insight, sensitivity, caring, sense of humor, and genuine interest and pleasure in each child's *unique* way of developing and learning.

Where custodial or routinized child care situations exist in different places, whether in Western or in developing nations, then young children are being shortchanged, even though their working parents may feel relief that child care of any kind is available. Visits to child care facilities in a variety of cultural settings confirms the important fact that when governments really believe that small children are priceless resources, then they will help to establish child care settings not only as aids to working parents, but as places where young chidren can learn how to become intellectually ready for school tasks as well as socially concerned for each other and for adults. Quality child care, even with limited material resources, can create good playmates, good learners, and caring human beings as well as serve the needs of working parents.

REFERENCES

Honig, A. S. (1978a). Aesthetics in Asian child care environments. *Childhood Education*, 54, 251–255.

Honig, A. S. (1978b). Comparison of child-rearing practices in Japan and in the People's Republic of China: A personal view. *International Journal of Group Tensions*, 8(2), 6–32.

Pre-School Policies and Programmes in Low-Income Countries

Elizabeth Sestini

Summary. *Many countries in Africa have responded to a widespread demand for pre-school provision and have established expensive college based initial teacher training courses to professionalize staff and upgrade the standards of pre-school education. Government policies generally emphasize community responsibility for pre-school education and recognize the potential of pre-schools for community development as well as promoting children's physical, social, emotional and cognitive development. Yet pressure from parents in both rural and urban communities is for early entry into education for their children and despite broadly based curriculum guidelines, the emphasis in most pre-schools is on an academic curriculum geared to preparing children for primary school. Pre-schools are generally characterized by lack of liaison with other services, by professional barriers to the involvement of parents, parental opposition to para-professionals and to a community based curriculum, and sometimes barriers also to the use of children's mother tongues.*

Have recent U.S. research findings on the positive long term effects of "high quality" pre-school education any relevance for countries experiencing financial constraints, food shortages, and rapid population expansion? Most developing countries have urgent needs for health, nutrition and child care. Yet there is a lack of coordination of services for the under 5s. Can expenditure on pre-school education with professional teachers be justified in low-income countries where the achievement of U.P.E. (Universal Primary Education) or continuity of U.P.E. is under threat?

Would these countries benefit more from alternative approaches to pre-school provision which involve "para-professional" training and community based curricula?

Characteristics of pre-school provision for early childhood education in Malawi are compared with pre-school provision and training for pre-school teachers in Kenya and Zambia.

Initially it would seem difficult to substantiate pre-school education as a national priority in countries experiencing economic difficulties and where the achievement of U.P.E. is under threat because of population expansion. What factors then have influenced policy making and have affected the structure of training programmes?

I have selected aspects of developments in Kenya, Zambia and Malawi for consideration

Source: Elizabeth Sestini (1985). Pre-School Policies and Programmes in Low-Income Countries. *The International Journal of Early Childhood, 17,* 23–28. Reprinted by permission of the publisher.

because part of my own role, as tutor for the DAES-B. Phil. Course in the *Development and Education of Young Children* at the University of Newcastle upon Tyne, is to work with teachers from these countries who are seconded (on sabbatical) for one year and who return to their respective countries as trainers of pre-school teachers, inspectors, or as trainers of pre-school play group leaders.

In both Kenya and Zambia there is government commitment to the professionalization of pre-school education and through institutions appointed to develop and implement policy, national objectives have been drawn up and training programmes established to upgrade teachers.

Government involvement in pre-school education is partly a reflection of the increased need for child care provision, due to the changing economic and social structure. In Kenya, "the introduction of a new land tenure system in favor of private landholding has brought with it a concomitant breakdown of the extended family and a reduction in the size of livestock herds, both of which had definite custodial and educative functions for children." Under U.P.E. programmes, older children entered school and were no longer able to care for younger ones.

Government involvement was also a response to the widespread demand after independence, from all communities for access to education for their children. Parents view pre-school education as "an investment in their children's educational futures, a way of ensuring success in future schooling." In this they are encouraged by the general belief in the economic value of education. Government statements have also reinforced this belief by declaring education to be the foundation for national economic progress. In Kenya, the Ministry of Education referred to the rapid expansion of pre-school provision as the reflection of "the demand and concern for the education of young children to ensure national development and advancement" (H. J. Kanina, Director of Education, 1978). Both Kenyan and Zambian Government policies recognize the role of pre-school education in forging a national identity and the achievement of national ideological goals. In Zambia pre-school objectives include:

1.4 promote the child's
  1.4.1 social attitudes
  1.4.2 correct values
  1.4.3 patriotism and culture

and pre-school education was planned to meet "the social, economic and cultural needs of the country."

Another major factor in Government involvement was the availability of funding from a sponsoring agency. In Kenya funding came from the Bernard Van Leer Foundation, an international foundation specifically concerned with projects to assist the development of young children in disadvantaged communities. This foundation brought its own philosophy to bear on the aims of the pre-school training programme and on the role of the teacher. The Van Leer Foundation advocated the principle that parents are legitimate educators in their own right and have a voice in the kind of education provided. They were concerned to facilitate a partnership between home and school and viewed pre-school training as helping the teacher in Kenya "to relate to the local community councils as a professional person, to get their authority as teacher accepted, and to organize the community in a support rather than directive role so as to get a constructive pedagogy in the school."

The pre-school training programme was also a response by the government to grass roots initiatives which established community pre-schools throughout the country. It was seen as a way of raising the standard of pre-school education, in Kenya necessary when already by 1976, 17.6% of the population of 3–6 year olds were attending pre-schools. In Kenya there are approximately 6,000 nursery schools with over 7,500 teachers, over half of whom have not yet been trained and who have generally only attained the primary education certificate (CPE).

Untrained teachers were recognized to be using inappropriate formal rote-learning teaching methods. The Kenya Pre-school Education Report noted that teachers "felt that children learn largely by reciting" and that "children only learn when a teacher is in front of them teaching something." There was therefore an evident need to introduce approaches that reflected more understanding of child development, and of the kinds of learning experiences appropriate for young children.

The objectives of the Kenya pre-school training programme include the concept of community participation, and curriculum guidelines emphasize the need for community relevance and the use of local resources. Programmes focus on the outreach function of the school and the need for parents to work as "para-professional" teacher aides. The state objectives of the training programme include "to develop abilities in trainees to explore ways and means whereby nursery schools can contribute to development in the community and the community can contribute to the activities of the nursery schools," and to "guide the professional growth of the trainees by helping them change their attitudes to teaching, their teaching styles and their expectations of the children they teach." Yet in practice these objectives are not easily realized.

In Zambia, the development of pre-schools owes much to the Zambia Pre-School Association which, supported by the Ministry of Education, carried out national and local training programmes in pre-school education. In 1975 the Ministry of Education initiated a national pre-school policy, to coordinate pre-school activities on a national level. They recommended that "curricula should be controlled by the Ministry of Education" but that the "organization, administration and running of the community pre-schools should be left in the hands of the communities concerned . . . and that parents should be encouraged to have an interest in their children's education." Currently, in Zambia, government policy and the objectives of the Zambia Pre-School Association include: "to sensitize the Zambian public, and especially parents, to the educational needs of younger children" and "to Zambianize pre-school education materials and approaches to teaching" (Play with a Purpose, 1982). The use of local materials, teaching approaches and the use of Zambian languages are emphasized as "positive steps in the growth of children."

In both countries, therefore, training programmes recognize the need for "professionals" who are skilled in developing curricula which reflect local conditions and resources and in adapting to the realities of their teaching situations. Yet there are major obstacles in each country to the implementation of the teaching roles and kinds of curricula advocated by government policy. These obstacles stem from the institutions that employ pre-school teachers, values inherent in educa-

tional systems, parental expectations and from the "professional" roles teachers assume in practice.

A first major obstacle to curriculum development in pre-schools is the range of pre-school institutions that employ teachers and the functions that they are seen to serve. In both Kenya and Zambia the employment of pre-school teachers is in the hands of a variety of agencies—private, churches, companies, city and community councils—and teachers are accountable to their employers.

Private nursery schools in both Kenya and Zambia provide the models that parents seek for the education of their children. These schools were originally established by expatriates for their own children but continue to flourish in educational systems which despite broadly based government policies reflect elitist academic values.

In Zambia (1978) government policy recommended that although "private people should be allowed to continue running pre-schools, fees charged should be scrutinized with a view to controlling them." In practice private nursery schools generally charge high fees and provide an academic curriculum which introduces children to English and the 3Rs and enables them to gain entry into favoured primary schools.

In Kenya, similarly, the Pre-school Project Evaluation Team noted that the educational system is frequently criticized as being irrelevant, tending to alienate pupils from their communities, and their report suggested that this "may be as a result of the elitist curriculum development approaches which have emphasized theory and professionalism at the expense of wider participation." The objective of training programmes may be community focused but difficulties arise in practice because many pre-schools in rural areas in Kenya are supervised by the local primary school headteacher and are very much influenced by the primary school curriculum. In urban areas also there is a close tie with primary schools, and pre-schools have become extensions of primary education. In Kenya pre-school teachers are frequently accountable to both primary school headteachers and to standard one primary teachers. A survey of the expectations of primary heads indicated that 73% viewed pre-school as preparing children for school by teaching basic skills—oral, reading, writing and number, and 27% as training children to be social and use school facilities. Standard one teachers had similar expectations of pre-schools, i.e. academic preparation 72%, and social skills 28%.

Despite the participatory aims of training programmes, both parents and teachers viewed the main role of parents as paying school fees. In a small survey of parental perceptions of pre-school 44% emphasized academic preparation, 35% personality development and 21% custodial functions. A related survey of teachers' perceptions of the parental role included: paying school fees 28%, and providing finance 25%, labour 21% and materials 12%.

Parents feel that their fees should be used to pay for a "professional" teacher and there is pressure on pre-schools to sponsor training for their teachers. Training is dependent upon the institution's resources and in Kenya the training programmes had to be flexible. Two types were developed, a two year programme for pre-school teachers in Nairobi, and a six month, part-time in-service programme for rural teachers conducted by district trainers.

The training programmes in both Kenya and Zambia are influenced by "expatriate expertise" both directly and indirectly. Trainers are sent to the UK (United Kingdom) and other universities on advanced study courses, where their thinking is influenced by the study of current UK research, theory and educational practice. Trainers themselves study in English and they tend to implement training programmes in their own countries through the medium of English. This decision is mainly a consequence of the multi-lingual nature of their own societies, but it is another obstacle to the training aim of "community participation." In Kenya the training programmes are conducted through English "because all the instructional materials were in English" and some of the concepts were difficult to translate into mother tongue. Most pre-school teachers lack a working knowledge of English so not surprisingly the evaluation team noted that the "child development course was found to be difficult by a large number of teachers" as English was "a language that the majority of teachers had not mastered well due to their low academic standard."

If training programmes are committed to the concept of cultural diversity and community participation, it would seem more appropriate for district trainers to collaborate with parents in each community to produce written materials in mother tongue and to develop a curriculum based on community resources, needs and local traditions. Use of mother tongue is now recognized in multi-cultural Europe as intrinsic to children's personal and social identity. It provides access to the culture of the family and community, and its maintenance in school is essential if parents and teachers are to collaborate as partners and if education is not to set some groups at educational disadvantage. Yet pre-school teachers who share these values are in conflict with parents, primary teachers and their Pre-school Committees who regard pre-school education through English as a desirable aid to entry into primary school. Despite their own lack of fluency most pre-school teachers introduce English to young children, and in Nairobi some pre-schools use only English.

A more serious obstacle to the implementation of a pre-school curriculum which meets community needs is the inequality in community resources. While most of the pre-schools in the southern highlands of Kenya have feeding programmes, in other areas there is inadequate food within the communities to support such a programme. The Kenya pre-school evaluation report noted that "the valley experiences chronic and severe famines" and that "pre-school children were therefore poorly fed and consequently tended to drop out of school." Health and medical facilities are sparse and in some areas parents have to rely on traditional medicines. Pre-school provision is also inadequate in the poorest areas because parents are unable to pay the minimum fees to support a pre-school.

Children's basic health and nutritional needs are of paramount importance and in very socially disadvantaged areas support from local or central government is essential to establish pre-school centres where health and feeding programmes are integrated with care and educational functions. In view of rapid population expansion and the frequent uncertainty of local food supplies such support is essential. Pre-school teachers can fulfill a vital role in ensuring that food aid reaches the most needy children, and in monitoring children's health and physical development. Meeting health and nutritional needs is a pre-requisite for education, but despite official recognition of the importance of coordinating services for the under fives, coordination is frequently inhibited by professional boundaries and negative attitudes towards collaboration with other agencies and professional bodies.

Although attempts were made in Kenya at the interministerial level for coordination of services for the under 5s, at the local level they encountered "professional" barriers. For example, plans for model pre-schools in poor areas were not implemented because the Health Department who ran some of the nurseries, "viewed the use of the schools in a negative way." Placing "trained" teachers in these nurseries was seen as an attempt to take over the nurseries by the Department of Education.

In practice, trained pre-school teachers are cast into a role mainly determined by the expectations of others and which is defined for them. They also find it necessary to emphasize their specialist training and "educational" role in order to improve their physical working conditions, salaries and conditions of service. It is education that carries status, not responsibility for children's physical welfare or community participation. It is as "qualified specialists" that teachers can claim salaries commensurate with their expertise!

A fundamental question is whether expenditure on enabling teachers to gain "the advanced knowledge" of child development and early learning processes can be justified in many low income countries. Is pre-school education as distinct from pre-school child-care provision necessary when in most European countries young children are cared for by nursery assistants not teachers?

In most low income countries professional criteria may be impossible to achieve. It is impossible to achieve "professional standards" in teaching situations where one teacher may have up to 60 children in a class, and lack basic physical facilities and reading and writing materials.

What evidence is there that early childhood education as distinct from care is beneficial for children? In the 1960s and 70s in the UK and the U.S.A. pre-school education was viewed primarily as a means of compensating for social disadvantage. It reflected the assumption that national economic development is dependent on a highly educated population and that the failure rate of working class children could be reduced by early education which would compensate for social disadvantage. Disillusionment grew with initial reports of "head start" programmes in the U.S.A. which indi-

cated little lasting effect on children's later performance in school. In 1974 Tizard wrote "in so far then as the expansion of early schooling is seen as a way of avoiding later school failure or of closing the social gap in achievement, we already know it to be doomed to failure."

Yet recent evidence from later follow up studies of experimental pre-school programmes in the U.S.A. indicates that high quality pre-school education has significant long term outcomes, not only for the child but also for the community. Weikart's findings revealed that as young adults, children who attended the programme made greater gains in education, employment and social responsibility than similar young adults who did not attend pre-school. He concluded that "high quality" early childhood education also "reduces major social and economic problems within a community" and that "preventing life long problems in high risk children is a better community investment than attempting to correct them." Of relevance for training policies in low income countries is that Weikart's evidence indicated that it is not the training or qualifications of teachers but the quality of the programmes and the systematic approach to their implementation that is critical for "high quality."

The Commission of the European Communities in their report on *Pre-School Education in the European Community* (1980), identified two opposing trends, "one demanding more advanced training for teaching staff in pre-school establishments, at least equal to teacher training of primary schools, and one which would like pre-school education to be 'deprofessionalized'." They suggest that the demand for "more professionalism" comes from countries where teacher training is not very advanced, and where professionalism is not yet established, and opposition from those who see "specialists assuming sole charge of education to the detriment of other members of the community, especially parents who, convinced of their own incompetence, end up by relinquishing their educational roles."

The Commission expressed its own views on the European context where specialism was seen to be increasing. "Excessively narrow specialist training and school attendance at an ever younger age for an ever longer period risk leading inevitably to parental dispossession." They warned that if there is also too big a gap between the educational values of the nursery school and the community's socio-cultural character, the latter might deteriorate and the children become torn between two conflicting worlds."

The Commission Report referred to countries where teacher training was not very advanced and suggested that as the introduction of large scale teacher training programmes for pre-schools is very costly, "pre-school education might conceivably be better in every respect in the hands of parents organizing play groups with possibly some support from the authorities."

In Malawi, this is the model that the government has endorsed nationally. Play groups are run by an elected committee of parents and are staffed by volunteer "para-professionals." "The education plan in Malawi reflects the Government's concern to ensure that education is developed along lines which are not wasteful of resources and are in the national interest." Like Kenya and Zambia, nurseries were originally established by the European population for their own children, and after independence in 1966 there was a strong demand for similar pre-school provision. A Pre-school Play Group Association was formed in 1970 and play groups now coexist with private nurseries. Two week basic courses are conducted for play group leaders, and a full time national organizer is employed to organize these and refresher courses for the leaders. Prospective pre-school play group leaders work on a voluntary basis and each leader has the responsibility for looking after 20 children. By 1982, play group centres had been established on a self help basis, 247 play group leaders had been trained, and over 4,500 children were attending play groups. Pressures towards professionalization were experienced and in Malawi problems arose over the use of the title "play group leader" because of "its implication of a status inferior to that of a teacher." Volunteers were used initially because of the acute shortage of teachers in both elementary and secondary schools but as the movement developed, they became seen by the trainers as the most appropriate way of meeting young children's needs, and national needs. "We must continually discover new approaches in promoting the standard of pre-school education, with joint efforts the gap must be closed for the young child's involvement in rural and national development." Parental cooperation is emphasized in training courses which includes the aim to "make leaders aware of the importance of working with parents and the community, and how to enlist their cooperation."

In many respects the objectives and strategies for developing a curriculum in Malawi are very similar to guidelines developed in Kenya and Zambia. There is a concern for "educational standards" but recognition that "professionalization" and teacher "status" can lead to discontinuity in children's learning experiences and barriers to liaison with parents and parental involvement. Should pre-school play groups focus on "educational" goals and standards? Para-professionals can also find that they face demands to assume "professional" teaching roles for which they are unqualified, and demands for standards that are unattainable.

Blank (1981) distinguishes between "academic pre-schools" and "shared rearing pre-schools." The "advantages" in the professional teacher model are insights that stem from theoretical knowledge and research, skills developed through lengthy initial training programmes in curriculum planning, in teaching and evaluation of children's learning. The "advantages" of the alternative "shared rearing" approach lie in the values to both child and the community of supporting and enhancing family and community experience. Blank suggests that the main goal of such programmes should be "to offer a service that will help parents and the entire family to function in a more effective and enjoyable manner," and that they should not "take on educational purposes which they were never intended to serve and which they may well not be suited to fulfill."

There is no easy solution to the problems facing low income countries where despite government policies to facilitate community based pre-school curricula, communities demand academic pre-schools. The paradox is that although there may be little justification for professional teachers in pre-schools, if pre-schools are to become community based and fulfill a much wider range of needs, a great deal of "professional" skill will be necessary. Parents need to be persuaded that the kinds of experiences which would be the best investment for their children's future are not "academic" but are ones appropriate to developmental needs, reflecting their social and cultural environments and which enable children to develop greater awareness and appreciation of their own circumstances and to develop relationships based on mutual respect and consideration for others.

The aims of the training programmes in Kenya, Zambia and in Malawi include enabling trainees to develop a curriculum which draws on children's everyday experiences, reflects community values and involves parents. The assumption is that by drawing parents into the educational process, parents will come to recognize the need for social relevance, recognize their own importance as "educators" and reappraise their belief in the value of academic pre-school education. Unfortunately, though educationists and trainers may advocate wider participation and community focused pre-schools, changes in parental attitudes and beliefs do not come easily and pressure from all communities is still strongly for an extension of the existing school system with professional teachers despite accumulating evidence of its failure to fulfill expectations.

REFERENCES

Berrueta-Clement, J. R., Schweinhart, L. J., Barnett, W. C., Epstein, A. S. and Weikart, D. P. *Changed Lives: The Effect of the Perry Pre-school Program on Youth through Age 19.* High Scope Ed. Research Foundation, Ypsilanti, U.S.A. 1984.

Blank, M. "Pre-school and/or education: A comment" in *Child Development 0–5,* (ed.) M. Roberts and J. Tamburrini. Holmes McDougall, 1981.

Commission of the European Communities, *Pre-school Education in the European Community,* ECSC Brussels—Luxembourg, 1980.

Everest, I. C. "School and Community: The potentials and constraints of the private foundation as a promoter of innovation and change" in *School and Community in Developing Countries.* Proceedings of 22nd Conference ATOE Newcastle upon Tyne, 1983.

Kenya Institute of Education with B. Van Leer Foundation. *The Evaluation of the Pre-school Education Project.* 1982.

Ministry of Education Kenya with B. Van Leer Foundation. *A Report on the Pre-school Education Project.* Kenya, 1978.

Ministry of Education, Zambia. "National goals for pre-school education" in *New Policy Directions.* 1975.

Padambo, M. "Malawi" in *Watoto wa Africa,* Vol. 5, 1982.

Padambo, M. Para-professional training in early childhood education in Malawi, *PPA,* Malawi (no date).

Tizard, B. *Early Childhood Education.* NFER, 1974.

Zambia Pre-School Association, *Play with a Purpose,* 1982.

Elizabeth Sestini is a tutor for the Development and Education of Young Children course at the University of Newcastle upon Tyne, School of Education.

The Right to Quality Child Care

Edward E. Gotts

At the time of the last White House Conference on Children (1970), the Association for Childhood Education International published a position paper on *The Child's Right to Quality Day Care* (Butler, 1970). In this statement the late Annie Butler clearly identified trends and facts that called for priority action:

1. Mothers were entering the workforce in rapidly increasing numbers.
2. The U.S. Department of Labor had publicized the widespread need for child care.
3. Quality care was expensive and lay beyond the financial means of many families.
4. Standards for care needed to encompass the comprehensive range of services.
5. Insufficient and poor-quality care meant lost developmental and educational opportunities for children.

Yet a decade later, the White House Conference on Families (1980) declared that the need for affordable quality care still loomed large in America. At present, child care access has become a concern of not only parents, childhood educators and other professional groups, but also the business community (Committee for Economic Development, 1987).

ACEI Position Statement

ACEI affirms that the first duty of family and society is to protect, guide and give care to the young. Therefore, we declare that the child's right to quality care is fundamental.

Families the world over are passing through times that bewilder; many of the old solutions no longer work. Parents are now stretched beyond resiliency to both survive and give care. The media all too faithfully portray these forces and their consequences for children. We must as a society of caring people answer the cry, "Who will care for the children—indeed, who if not ourselves?" Business, governmental agencies, religious organizations, foundations, service groups, school systems, professionals and private citizens can all share in solving the child care dilemma. We welcome all constructive efforts.

ACEI believes that:

• Children must receive care while parents are unavailable due to work or other causes. The care must be affordable, reliable and accessible. Custodial care will not do; the needs of children require quality care. If we correctly align our priorities, we will not fail.

• In center-based programs, care must be: 1) developmentally focused and culturally salient; 2) offered by qualified adults who are wise and caring; 3) provided in environments designed and equipped for learning, arranged for safety and privacy as well as activity and interaction; 4) professionally directed and managed; 5) assisted by community service providers. Moreover, such programs must attend to health, nutrition and social concerns and encourage lively parent involvement. They must be educational in the broadest sense.

• In family-based care, providers must receive ongoing training and professional support of their performance as natural extensions of the child's own family.

• In all settings, children's health must be maintained through prevention, sanitation and other recognized means of infection control.

ACEI recognizes that, whatever the setting, the quality of adult-child interactions is

Source: E. E. Gotts (1988). The right to quality child care. *Childhood Education, 64*(5), 268–275. Reprinted by permission of Edward E. Gotts and the Association for Childhood International, 11141 Georgia Avenue, Suite 200, Wheaton, MD. Copyright © 1988 by the Association.

the most vital ingredient. Staff morale and turnover, thereover, become critical concerns in providing quality care. Caregivers themselves must receive care, in the form of improved compensation and benefits, reasonable workload, continuing education, creative supervision and an interpersonally supportive work environment.

ACEI affirms the benefits of quality child care and cautions against low-quality care, which involves risks. Nevertheless, we recognize that our knowledge is limited. Hence, we commit ourselves to devising ways and means for parents and caregivers to evaluate the care that children experience.

ACEI believes that parents should have freedom of choice in child care arrangements. In support of their informed choice, we pledge ourselves to assist in developing and providing current child care information and referral services. Such services shall present information that assists parents to consider child care from the standpoint of compatibility with family characteristics and style. We further recognize that, because of ambivalence and confusion about chid care, some parents may require guidance and counseling as they make their choices.

When necessary, we shall work together through the various levels of government to improve the standards for personnel and provider licensing.

Reasons and Evidence for Child Care

ACEI's position, as stated above, is supported by the following observations and evidence:

Care: A Fundamental Right

A sleeping infant stirs and begins to stretch. Soon he is fully awake, reaching out to be lifted and held. A toddler points to something beyond reach and expresses a nearly intelligible request to have it. A preschool child appears intently inquisitive about the workings of a mechanical device, asking, "Why did it do that?" An elementary age child arrives home from school, admits herself to the house, and then locks the door to make sure an intruder does not disturb or harm her. A young adolescent works on a project assigned by his teacher—works, that is, until he reaches an impasse and cannot decide how to proceed. These happenings are so ordinary, so unre-

markable, they are to be expected as daily events in the lives of children. Needing help is as natural as reaching or pointing or asking, as fundamental as feeling lonely and frightened or trying hard but getting lost along the way.

Thus, it is natural and fundamental that children need care. This is, of course, what families are for: to give children care. Erikson (1950) suggests that in giving care to the young, adults express, develop and actualize in themselves an essential human quality he calls *generativity.* As adults practice their generativity, or nurturance, children are helped to practice trust, autonomy, initiative and industry and to develop identity. And so they progress from infancy through the adolescent years. If these nurturing interactions did not occur between children and adults, then children would not thrive or develop in the five essential human outcomes of childhood described by Erikson (1950).

Families today cannot always be with their children when they need help. Yet it is easy to lose sight of the fact that families throughout history have experienced times when they needed others to help with their children (Aries, 1962). After all, what is schooling if not an arrangement by which adults from outside the family help children with important aspects of their development. Schooling in this sense has become an extension of the family's child-rearing activities in both developed and developing countries. As such, schooling has become a recognized right, just as belonging to a family is a right (United Nations, 1959).

Child care is also an arrangement by which adults from outside the family help children with important aspects of their development— aspects that are natural, fundamental and necessary. Similarly, the United Nations (1959) declares that children are entitled to special protection, support and facilities. Child care, then, should be regarded as a right. The United States stands almost alone among the more developed nations in failing to recognize child care as a right and in having no national policy on child care (Martinez, 1986).

Care: An Urgent Priority

In recent discussion, many have advanced the case for universal preschool education and expansion of kindergarten to a full-day program. Many parents may be seeking to meet their own needs for quality child care rather than wanting early academics, according to the former first Director of the Office of Child Development (Zigler, 1987). The supply of affordable child care services continues to lag far behind the demand (Gunzenhauser & Caldwell, 1986). Because schooling is viewed as a right and a solution to social ills, it is being advanced also as a cure for the problem of insufficient public child care. As Zigler (1987) argues, citing Head Start and other early childhood research, it is the wrong solution for the wrong problem. Yet that is what develops when people see no other way out.

Galinsky (1986) notes in her review of current child care patterns that by 1985, 62% of all mothers of school-age children were part of the workforce. This rate is expected to continue rising gradually through the 1990s. By 1982 only 31% of children of working mothers were cared for in their own homes (O'Connell & Rogers, 1983). Preschool enrollment had jumped by 1983 to almost 53% of this age group (cited in Galinsky, 1986), probably in response to child care needs. But considering children of all ages who have full-time employed parents, 46% have no identifiable child care arrangements (Children's Defense Fund, 1982). This means that many of the 46% are likely looking after themselves. Galinsky (1986) further reveals from another study that a large majority of parents surveyed stated that they find it difficult to locate child care services. Parents are forced to cope with conflicting responsibilities of work and child care, resulting in higher rates of absenteeism from work. Competent child care, to the contrary, is known to increase worker satisfaction and productivity (Committee for Economic Development, 1987).

Affordability is also a central issue. In 1982 one out of five women workers were the main support of their family (U.S. Department of Labor, 1983). The average annual (median) wage for full-time women workers in 1981 was $12,001, only 59% of the comparable figure for men (U.S. Department of Labor, 1983), leaving 23% of female-maintained households below the official poverty level. In the face of these limited resources, the annual cost of caring for one child at that time was around $3,000 (Rothman, 1986), or 25% of the typical gross income. For the typical family, the cost of child care is now estimated to consume 10–20% of its income. This comes in the face of reductions in state funds for subsidized child care in 28 states since 1981 (Wilson, 1988).

In many areas of the United States, children go home to an empty dwelling at the end of the school day. Forced to care for themselves, they are undeniably exposed to considerable risk to their safety. By one estimate, latchkey children numbered 7 million in 1983 (Strother, 1984). Child care programs for school-age children were in fact uncommon before 1980 (Seligson, 1986). Self-care by latchkey children has been found to cause greater academic and social problems and to result in loneliness, fear and boredom. Latchkey children are believed to be involved more often in sexual experimentation (Strother, 1984). It would be an obvious overstatement to imply that self-care has a uniformly detrimental effect. Under certain circumstances, self-care may be an enhancing experience. The point is that school-age children should not be left on their own simply because child care is unavailable.

Indeed, the scope of need for child care is great, including children of infancy through school age. Most investigators in this area of study consider that after age 14, most children are capable of self-care and thus lie outside the range of those needing services. The need for care is universal. The forces of social change extend beyond national boundaries and racial-ethnic concerns as, everywhere, growing numbers of single parents and employed women cope with the often conflicting responsibilities of work and child care. The care of children is an urgent priority.

Care: The Need for Quality

Historically, child care outside the family developed in America as a two-tier or two-track system: one track for the children of the more affluent and one for the poor. Care was provided primarily for children in the post-toddler through preschool years; infants, most toddlers, and school-age children were outside the system. Middle and upper class parents shopped for quality care based on the reputation of programs. Even when necessity dictated child care for them, these parents actively sought to secure beneficial experiences. The poor took their children to designated child care providers, who were approved for reimbursement or subsidized payment. Social caseworkers helped link them up with qualified resources. Children of more affluent families received early childhood education, under whatever name offered, while children of the poor got custodial day care.

With the further passage of time, the meaning boundaries of quality were stretched to include infants, toddlers and school-age children. The distinction between day care and early education began to blur as children of the poor received Head Start and as, increasingly, employed middle class mothers needed day care as well as preschool education for their offspring. Social changes had thus given families a common problem that signaled an end to the old two-track system of child care. As the system expanded in scope and complexity, so too the standards of quality were strained to accommodate an emerging reality far more complicated than early childhood education. Consequently, much effort has been invested since the mid-1960s in defining the expanded meaning of quality child care (American Academy of Pediatrics, 1985; American Home Economics Association, 1975; Gunzenhauser & Caldwell, 1986; National Association for the Education of Young Children, 1984; U.S. Department of Health and Human Services, 1985; Zigler & Gordon, 1982).

Education. An educational emphasis in child care is important (Butler, 1970; Gunzenhauser & Caldwell, 1986), but this must not become a blindly applied goal that attempts to make the entire day resemble the operation of an elementary classroom (Zigler, 1987). Yet a whole mythology of what should be done is leading some adults to push children as rapidly as possible through childhood (Salholz, Wingert, Burgower, Michael & Joseph, 1987). This quickening pace has led some thoughtful observers to fear that childhood may be missed altogether. They urge that these years be preserved for the important developmental issues that are also at risk of being bypassed (Elkind, 1981; Zigler, 1987). Quality demands that education occur, while time is left for the issues of childhood. Child care and education must be integrated into a single childrearing extension and supplement to the family. An early childhood rather than elementary school model is more likely to meet the currently unmet needs of children throughout the broad range of the childhood years (Butler, Gotts & Quisenberry, 1978, chap. 9).

Staffing. Staff characteristics are essential ingredients in a quality program; the most crucial one is combined training in early childhood education and child development (Smith, 1986). A differentiated staffing pattern should be followed, with supervising teachers, paraprofessional teachers or child development associates (CDAs), and classroom aides assigned in a cost-effective manner. Staff must be fond of children and experienced in their care, conscientious, tolerant of others' views, well-supervised (Kagan, Kearsley & Zelazo, 1978), and culturally and ethically sensitive.

State standards for child-to-staff ratios vary widely (Martinez, 1986). They are the *minimum* standards recommended by each state. Research suggests, nevertheless, that quality is more likely to be present when staffing ratios are based on the intensity of care required by the children involved. For infants and toddlers up to 24 months, the desirable ratio is about 3:1 (Children's Bureau, 1975; Kagan et al., 1978), while state standards most typically set this ratio between 4:1 and 6:1 (Wolverton & Kinard, 1971). From 24 to 36 months, state standards most typically call for 8:1; from 36 months to school age, 10:1, although ratios of 12:1 and 15:1 are also common. School-age children up to the mid-teens typically have one of these three ratios: 10:1, 20:1, 25:1 (Wolverton & Kinard, 1971). These ratios are moderated, however, by the frequent requirement that two staff be present in each group of children or that a staff member not be left in the center without back-up help. Several states do not regulate school-age child care by licensing. Although federal requirements set smaller ratios for all ages, they have never been enforced and essentially have now been set aside (Martinez, 1986).

Yet smaller group size and a ratio of 10:1 have been associated with both improved child behavior and cognitive performance (Committee for Economic Development, 1987). Larger ratios may result in a more group-focused program, excessive emphasis on conformity and a custodial atmosphere, and increased risk of injury. The presence of handicapped children in any group signals the need to adjust the ratio downward (Butler, 1970; Gunzenhauser & Caldwell, 1986). In any event, an adult providing child care should have someone available to assist in case of emergency, even if the recommended ratios are otherwise being met. Inevitably, of

369

course, smaller ratios translate into higher per-child program cost. Family care child-adult ratios are another matter, since state laws commonly limit the number of children in these settings either to 5:1 or 6:1 and further reduce them if infants or toddlers are present.

Environment. Because of their social interaction, preschool children may do well with 50 square feet per child indoors plus 100 square feet of enclosed outdoor space per child (Butler, 1970). Considering children of all ages, state standards for indoor space per child range from 20 to 50 square feet, with most states calling for 35 square feet (Wolverton & Kinard, 1971). The comparable range for enclosed outdoor space per child is from 40–200 square feet, with a median of 75 square feet.

A quality environment further refers to the materials and equipment that should be available as developmentally appropriate for children of differing age levels. Butler, Gotts and Quisenberry (1978, Appendix C) compiled lists of equipment and materials recommended for building and construction activities, dramatic play, physical activity, creative arts, music, mathematics, science, perceptual-motor and language arts. Moreover, they rated and recommended materials as either essential, desirable or supplemental for each of three age groupings (nursery, kindergarten and early elementary). Unfortunately, there have been no systematic studies of materials that would more definitively establish developmentally oriented standards of quality, although state licensing standards typically offer some guidance.

In addition, it is necessary to evaluate a center's equipment and materials and their physical layout or arrangement in terms of safety for the ages of the children served (Aronson, 1986). Finally, adequate lighting and regulated noise and temperature are essential to environmental quality.

Services. Child care centers must provide for comprehensive services, among them:
- Nutrition
- Integration of the handicapped
- Parent involvement
- Preventive and other health care
- Monitoring of child development
- Planned and organized activities
- Continuing staff growth and development
- Space for resting
- Provision for the child who is ill or out of sorts
- Consultation with outside specialists about individual child and family needs
- Infection control
- Advocacy
- Insurance coverage for relevant contingencies
- Referral to outside resources.

Obviously, not all of these services are needed on a daily basis. Their scope, nevertheless, indicates the varied service needs for which the program or center director must make provision.

The Cost of Caring

Staff members in child care settings are typically paid low wages (Wilson, 1988), without essential benefits such as health care and retirement plans. In fact, it is estimated that 58% of center-based and 90% of family care workers are paid wages below the poverty level (Trotter, 1987). Often they are under-appreciated in other ways, suffer from low status image and encounter stressful interactions with some parents. In the face of these working conditions, they often experience low morale (Gunzenhauser & Caldwell, 1986). When recent headlines portrayed child care workers as sexually exploitative and otherwise abusive of children, the low morale problem was compounded. For these reasons, directors must constantly seek ways to improve the lot of their staff. Job security, supportive co-workers, quality inservice, appreciative supervision and similar measures work to improve staff morale and self-esteem.

The health risks of group care must be considered (Centers for Disease Control, 1984). Excessive fatigue may result from a full-day program; resting times and space must be provided. Proper immunization and clean environments will prevent many of the usual childhood diseases. Upper respiratory and middle ear infections may flare up seasonally. Attention to handwashing and isolation of infected children are necessary procedures of risk control. Parasite control is also essential, from ringworm to intestinal infestations with pinworm. There is a potential in group settings for the spread of heptatitis and CMV or cytomegalovirus (Pass, Hutto, Ricks & Cloud, 1986). These pose a risk not only to children and staff but also to unsuspecting family members. The risk of maternal exposure to any virus during pregnancy must be weighed carefully in the decision to place children in a care program, especially during the first trimester of a pregnancy. Recent reports have highlighted AIDS exposure of infants born to intravenous drug users. These children are showing up with increased frequency in some major urban centers such as New York City. Such youngsters have been described as chronically ill. Standards will need to be developed for their proper care and management. Since many states require that even mildly ill children be isolated in child care centers, they may eventually be cared for in special sick child centers modeled after those appearing in many urban centers (Topolnicki, 1987). For further guidance on child health in care settings, see American Academy of Pediatrics (1985), Aronson (1986) and Centers for Disease Control (1984).

Despite the foregoing concerns, it can be affirmed that research evidence supports the view that quality child care in a center generally is not harmful or measurably less effective than remaining at home (Belsky & Steinberg, 1978; Kagan et al., 1978). Family child care may produce less positive results, perhaps due to limited materials and an emphasis on conformity (Clarke-Stewart, 1982). Quality care programs may in fact favorably affect the development of children from low income backgrounds (Zigler, 1987). They result in more positive interactions with adults and more focused and interactive play (Schindler, Moely & Frank, 1987; Vandell & Powers, 1983), as well as richer mother-child verbal interaction and greater compliance (Peterson & Peterson, 1986). Nevertheless, a new generation of research on infant and toddler participation in child care has again raised the question of whether parent-child attachment may thereby be weakened (Meredith, 1986), especially in boys (Belsky & Rovine, 1988). The long-term consequences of these findings have not yet been studied, so it is premature to view them as more than cause for caution and further study.

For the school-age child, several potential benefits may be realized from participation in after-school care, including an increased sense of personal safety and improved supervision of leisure time. Advice and suggested resources on school-age child care are accessible in Ap-

palachia Educational Laboratory (no date), Seligson (1986) and Strother (1984). Levine (1978) has studied and discussed different models of public school involvement in child care, and should be consulted on this subject. Zigler (1987) has approached public school child care from a programmatic perspective for children of all ages.

Practicing Care: Conclusions

We need neither a custodial nor a narrowly educational approach to child care. *Developmental child care* suggests the protective and child-maintaining sense of *custodial*, plus the stimulating sense of *educational*. It suggests a program for the developing individual who at each level of maturity has special needs, interests and possibilities. Developmental care further suggests a comprehensive approach that includes issues of health, family, nutrition and social well-being. It requires enabling child care environments, personnel and organizational arrangements.

In developmental child care, play is a primary modality of learning. Further, it is an expression and vehicle for the broader issues of human development (Erikson, 1950). We have advocated that programs for preschool and primary age children should view developmental play as both a framework for program planning and an instructional tool (Butler et al., 1978; Isenberg & Quisenberry, 1988). Careful study of the research literature on play convinces us of its potential to contribute comprehensively to nearly all aspects of development (Butler et al., 1978). Closely rereading Erikson (1950) will further expand the potential for using chid care to promote trust, autonomy and other fundamental outcomes of childhood. This is the care to which children, their families and society have a right. Let us then give care.

REFERENCES

American Academy of Pediatrics. (1985). *Recommendations for day care centers for infants and children.* Evanston, IL: American Academy of Pediatrics.

American Home Economics Association. (1975). *Child care handbook.* Washington, DC: American Home Economics Association.

Appalachia Educational Laboratory. (no date). *Policy issues. Latchkey children and school-age child care.* Charleston, WV: AEL, Inc.

Aries, P. (1962). *Centuries of childhood: A social history of family life.* New York: Vintage Books, Random House.

Aronson, S. S. (1986). Maintaining health in child care settings. In N. Gunzenhauser & B. M. Caldwell (Eds.), *Group care for young children.* Skillman, NJ: Johnson & Johnson.

Belsky, J., & Steinberg, L. D. (1978). The effects of day care: A critical review. *Child Development, 49,* 929–949.

Belsky, J., & Rovine, M. J. (1988). Nonmaternal care in the first year of life and the security of infant-parent attachment. *Child Development, 59,* 157–167.

Butler, A. L. (1970). The child's right to quality day care. *Childhood Education, 47* (2), 58–65.

Butler, A. L., Gotts, E. E., & Quisenberry, N. L. (1978). *Play as development.* Columbus, OH: Charles E. Merrill.

Centers for Disease Control. (1984). *Stop disease in child day care centers.* Washington, DC: U.S. Government Printing Office.

Children's Bureau. (1975). *Using Title XX to serve children and youth.* Washington, DC: U.S. Government Printing Office.

Children's Defense Fund. (1982). *Employed parents and their children: A data book.* Washington, DC: Children's Defense Fund.

Clarke-Stewart, A. (1982). *Day care.* Cambridge, MA: Harvard University Press.

Committee for Economic Development. (1987). *Children in need. Investment strategies for the educationally disadvantaged.* New York: Committee for Economic Development.

Elkind, D. (1981). *The hurrried child.* Boston, MA: Addison-Wesley.

Erikson, E. (1950). *Childhood and society.* New York: Norton.

Galinsky, E. (1986). Contemporary patterns of child care. In N. Gunzenhauser & B. M. Caldwell (Eds.), *Group care for young children* (pp. 13–24). Skillman, NJ: Johnson & Johnson.

Gunzenhauser, N., & Caldwell, B. M. (Eds.). (1986). *Group care for young children.* Skillman, NJ: Johnson & Johnson.

Isenberg, J., & Quisenberry, N. L. (1988). Play: A necessity for all children. *Childhood Education, 64* (3), 138–145.

Kagan, J., Kearsley, R. B., & Zelazo, P. R. (1978). *Infancy: Its place in human development.* Cambridge, MA: Harvard University Press.

Levine, J. A. (1978). *Day care and the public schools. Profiles of five communities.* Newton, MA: Educational Development Center.

Martinez, S. (1986). Child care and public policy. In N. Gunzenhauser & B. M. Caldwell (Eds.), *Group care for young children* (pp. 71–81). Skillman, NJ: Johnson & Johnson.

Meredith, D. (1986). Day-care. The nine-to-five dilemma. *Psychology Today, 20* (2), 36–44.

National Association for the Education of Young Children. (1984). *Position statements on child care licensing and family day care regulation.* Washington, DC: National Association for the Education of Young Children.

O'Connell, M., & Rogers, C. C. (1983). Child care arrangements of working mothers: June 1982. *Current population reports,* special studies, series P-23, No. 129. Washington, DC: U.S. Department of Commerce, Bureau of the Census.

Pass, R. F., Hutto, C., Ricks, R., & Cloud, G. A. (1986). Increased rate of cytomegalovirus infection among parents of children attending day-care centers. *The New England Journal of Medicine, 314,* 1414–1418.

Peterson, C., & Peterson, R. (1986). Parent-child interaction and daycare: Does quality of daycare matter? *Journal of Applied Developmental Psychology, 7,* 1–15.

Rothman, R. (1986, January 11). Democrats in Congress open new push for child care aid. *Congressional Quarterly Weekly Report, 44* (2), 63–67.

Salholz, E., Wingert, P., Burgower, B., Michael, R., & Joseph, N. (1987, January 2). Kids need time to be kids. *Newsweek, 109* (5), 56–58.

Schindler, P. J., Moely, B. E., & Frank, A. L. (1987). Time in day care and social participation of young children. *Developmental Psychology, 23,* 255–261.

Seligson, M. (1986). Child care for the school age child. *Phi Delta Kappan, 67,* 637–640.

Smith, M. M. (1986). Promoting quality in child care personnel. In M. Gunzenhauser & B. M. Caldwell (Eds.), *Group care for young children.* Skillman, NJ: Johnson & Johnson.

Strother, D. B. (1984). Latchkey children: The fastest-growing special interest group in the schools. *Phi Delta Kappan, 66,* 290–293.

Topolnicki, D. M. (1987, November). Daycare for sick children. *Good Housekeeping, 205* (5), 245.

Trotter, R. J. (1987). Project day-care. *Psychology Today, 21* (12), 32–38.

United Nations. (1959, November 20). *Declaration of the rights of the child.* Resolution 1386 (XIV). New York: United Nations.

U.S. Department of Health and Human Services. (1985). *Model child care standards act: Guidance to states to prevent child abuse in day care facilities.* Washington, DC: U.S. Government Printing Office.

U.S. Department of Labor. Women's Bureau. (1983). *Time of change: 1983 handbook of women workers.* Washington, DC: U.S. Government Printing Office.

Vandell, D. L., & Powers, C. P. (1983). Day care quality and children's free play activities. *American Journal of Orthopsychiatry, 53,* 493–500.

White House Conference on Children. (1970). *Re-*

port to the President. Washington, DC: U.S. Government Printing Office.

White House Conference on Families. (1980). *Listening to America's families, action for the 80s. The report to the President, Congress and families of the nation.* Washington, DC: U.S. Government Printing Office.

Wilson, V. (1988, February 15). A crisis in child care. *Newsweek, 111* (7), 57.

Wolverton, E. D. L., & Kinard, C. (1971). *Abstracts of state day care licensing requirements. Part 2: Day care centers.* Washington, DC: U.S. Government Printing Office.

Zigler, E. F. (1987). Formal schooling for four-year-olds? No. *American Psychologist, 42,* 254–260.

Zigler, E. F., & Gordon, E. W. (Eds.). (1982). *Daycare: Scientific and social policy issues.* Boston, MA: Auburn House.

Edward E. Gotts is Director of Psychology, Madison State Hospital, Madison, Indiana, and serves as Principal Investigator for AEL, Inc., Charleston, West Virginia.

Regulation: One Approach to Quality Child Care

Gwen G. Morgan

Licensing and other forms of regulation affecting the quality of preschool and day care programs for children is a major policy arena. This article will examine some common assumptions about licensing, identify the major regulatory and nonregulatory policies affecting child care programs, and relate these policies to the issue of quality care for children.

Common Assumptions

Strong support is needed from early childhood educators if regulation is to be helpful and effective. Sometimes we have been ineffective in our support of sound regulatory policy because of our lack of expertise in law and regulatory administration. We early childhood professionals have often supported high standards for licensing, but we have been fickle in our support of the enforcement of those standards. Our idealism and our ambivalence toward the use of authority has sometimes led to conflict between us and those trying to implement regulatory policy. As one licensor put it, "With friends like these, who needs enemies?"

I would not suggest blind loyalty and support of regulators, because I believe that one of the greatest dangers to the future of regulatory effectiveness is poor regulatory practice. However, in the field of child development and early childhood education, there are some unexamined assumptions about the goals and nature of regulation that get in the way of our understanding of effective regulatory administration.

Some of these assumptions may be incorrect notions, and all are worthy of thinking through more carefully than we have done. Here are some examples:

Assumption: The goal of licensing is to achieve high quality day care. Many early childhood specialists have concluded that licensing is a failure if it does not achieve high quality care. Under the law, licensing is the base line of quality below which a program may not legally operate. It is doubtful that even early childhood educators, much less the general public, would support closing down programs and putting program operators in jail for failure to achieve ideals. Further, this assumption fails to take into account the many roads to quality, of which licensing is just one, and it fails to distinguish levels of quality.

Assumption: Licensing only covers the health and safety of children, therefore, it fails to achieve quality, which has to do with program. There are several ideas intertwined in this common assumption. The first, that licensing does not address program, is simply incorrect for most states. There are explicit sections of the licensing requirements in many states addressed to the requirements for program activities, requirements for the training and experience of staff, and the type and quantity of materials.

People who make this assumption may well be confused about differences between licensing and the two other major regulatory systems outside licensing that also affect early childhood programs—building safety regulation and health regulation. But the major question to raise about this assumption is: Just how much control of program do we want

Source: Gwen G. Morgan (1979, September). Regulation: One approach to quality child care. *Young Children*, pp. 22–27. Copyright © 1979 by the Association for the Education of Young Children. Reprinted by permission of the publisher.

the state to impose and how much control do we want the classroom staff to retain? It is difficult, but not impossible, to write explicit requirements that would stand up in a court of law, spelling out the particulars of a program. I suspect, however, that we would be appalled at the results of state regulatory control of programming. Our support might better be directed toward regulation requiring some general evidence that there is an appropriate, well thought out program carried out by competent and qualified people.

Assumption: *Quality equals college trained staff.* As a college teacher, I certainly value higher education, and I welcome the recent evidence from the Abt Center Study and other studies that training in a specialized field relating to children has a positive measurable effect on children. However, no study has found that only college training can produce this effect. The assumption could blind us to children's needs for role models in their own community, role models who may have less access to college than middle class people from outside the community. It may cause us to downgrade the competencies some staff gain through training on the job.

Assumption: *The use of police power is bad.* Licensing is the use of state police powers. Those opposed to using policing power must seek nonregulatory ways of achieving their aims. Those of us who support licensing believe that children and their families have a right not to experience harmful conditions in early childhood programs, and the right to expect that children's developmental needs will be met. A "cop for kids" is not necessarily a bad thing. What is bad is the misuse of power.

Assumption: *Licensing standards, and the licensors who enforce them, should be flexible.* Enforcement of the law cannot be arbitrary. It cannot be applied forcefully to some and gently to others. Licensing requirements are laws, and the law must be fairly and uniformly applied to all. This means they have to be written in a way that makes uniform interpretation possible, not with vague words like *adequate* and *appropriate*.

Of course, there are times when the harsh application of a requirement would cause terrible hardship. In such cases, the first question to ask is whether the requirement was justified in the first place. Was it really so important to have this requirement, if it is now so

important not to apply it? If the requirement is important, then there need to be articulated alternative ways of meeting it, including the structured use of waivers to cover unforeseen ways of meeting the intent of the requirement. This is flexible policy.

Assumption: *We know what "quality" is, and we can guarantee it through licensing.* Those of us who have had a lot of experience with early childhood programs do know quality when we see it. We feel welcome as we enter the door of a good program. Quality is evident in the way children respond to us, to each other, and to the staff. There are many clues. But of these, how many can be regulated?

Any of us could make a list of the virtues caregivers should have. But by the time we get to "sense of humor" and "stamina," we may be uncomfortable about regulation as a way of ensuring that staff have these virtues. We can document the needs of children through research findings, but some of these needs, such as continuity, do not lend themselves to regulation.

Licensing is only one of many forms of regulation aimed at children's services. There are also a number of nonregulatory activities that are just as important for the achievement of quality. It is a mistake in our zeal to put all our eggs of quality into the licensing basket. We need to sort out the different levels of quality that can be achieved through different means, and the different avenues for reaching quality.

If we want to be effective in bringing our knowledge to bear on policy, the appropriate question is not "What should the licensing standards be?" but the prior and broader question, "What is the most feasible and desirable mix of regulatory and nonregulatory actions that can eliminate harmful programs and stimulate high quality programs?"

In order to answer that question, we need to be familiar with all the different forms of regulation and other ways of achieving quality.

Forms of Regulation

Licensing is permission by the state to operate legally, and is given after basic requirements are met. Licensing represents a state-established base line of quality below which no program may lawfully fall, and operation below this line is punishable. These requirements are a floor of quality protecting all children. This floor can be as high or as low as a state wishes, but wherever it is set, it is the least tolerable or "minimum" by definition. Also at the base line are two other major regulatory activities of two other major bureaucracies under two other statutory authorities: safety regulation and health regulation.

Safety regulation and health regulation. These two sets of regulations mandate state permission to occupy a building and carry on a service there (permission is given on the basis of meeting building and fire safety requirements, designed to prevent loss of life and property in unsafe buildings; and sanitation requirements, designed to prevent the spread of epidemic disease and eliminate environmental health hazards). Inspections are usually done by two local officials with different professional expertise, a building safety inspector and a sanitarian who report to their own government agencies. The trend is for these two codes to be uniform statewide codes, but there are places where additional local requirements also apply. These three different regulatory systems are seldom integrated systematically to cut down on the time spent in regulation and to offer more coordinated help to the would-be licensee—a major problem for programs.

Zoning is the regulation of land use by local planning officials under state enabling law. Zoning ordinances are developed through dividing a locality into zones and spelling out what may take place in each zone. These ordinances often either exclude early childhood programs by not listing them among specific permitted uses, or force them to conform to an inappropriate classification by applying the next closest category listed. Zoning is used for the protection of property values and the preservation of space and has sometimes been misused as a tool to keep needed services out of a community. Some state laws have been amended to prohibit communities from misusing their zoning powers.

Fiscal regulation is specification of the level of quality for which a public agency will spend its purchasing dollar. A good example of this type of regulation is the Federal Interagency Day Care Requirements (FIDCR) that have been under review this summer. Logically, the standards for purchase can be set at a higher level than the base line of quality required of anyone wanting to care for children without public funds. The other side of the coin of fiscal regulation is *rate-setting*, the method used by the government to establish what it will pay on a per-child basis for child care meeting government specifications. If the public dollars, or the rate of reimbursement, are not adequate to cover the costs spent in meeting the fiscal requirements, the system is hypocritical.

Credentialing, another form of regulation, is a method of certifying that credentialed staff have competencies for work with children that noncredentialed staff would not necessarily have. Therefore jobs in the field can be exclusively reserved for staff with the credential, and licensing or purchase requirements can include a requirement of credentialed staff. A credential may also be developed without this exclusivity merely to give the holder of the credential an edge in the open job market.

If we can develop foolproof ways of measuring competence, this may be one of the most important ways to achieve quality. One example of a credential is the Child Development Associate; others are some state requirements for academic work or taking particular courses. Credentialing regulates staff while licensing and fiscal regulation regulate the entire facility, which includes building, staff, administration, and program.

Accreditation is a broad general term that means identification of certain model programs as those meeting high standards agreed on by some group (public agency, private peer group, or consumer group). Accreditation can be either voluntary or required, but either way if offers the possibility of a tier above the licensing and fiscal regulatory standards, identifying a third, and higher, level of quality (Fig. 1). No program is required to be accredited, although a state might decide to fund only accredited programs, thereby collapsing the top two tiers into one. Generally accreditation has been voluntary. Programs wishing to be known as high quality programs apply for the accreditation and receive consultation and help from the accrediting group, as well as some kind of "seal of approval." Were there such a method widely in place, those who were only licensed might be less likely to wave their licenses on high as banners of quality since **a license is merely permission to operate.**

Above all these levels of regulatory and nonregulatory means for achieving quality (Fig. 2) are the goals or ideals recognized by

FIGURE 1 *Three Possible Tiers of Quality*

Type of Regulation	To Whom Applied	By Whom Implemented
Accreditation	All who voluntarily seek it	Peer group, local 4-C, state agency, consumer group
Fiscal regulation/rate-setting	All programs funded by the agency that regulates the program	Funding agency or its agent
Approval	All publicly operated programs	Public operating or approving agency
Licensing	All private programs as defined in statue	State or local licensing agency

FIGURE 2 *Methods for Achieving Quality Child Care*

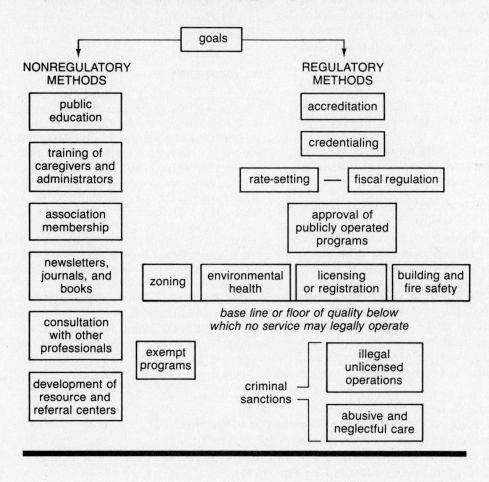

the field, always changing as we learn more about children's programs.

Nonregulatory Approaches to Achieve Quality

There are a number of other important activities that support quality children's programs. Sometimes these actions are taken by the same agency responsible for licensing or sometimes by other organizations. A few of these approaches are:

Educate the public. Parent and community expectations for child care must be raised, so that all efforts to achieve quality or to regulate programs will have public support, and so that parents will make use of regulation as a consumer protection.

Train caregivers and administrators. There are many models for training staff, including the traditional academic model of preservice training; the consultative model of ongoing personal development; and the materials model with a place where books, filmstrips, and other learning materials are available.

Associations. When centers or family day care providers form associations, the opportunity to share knowledge often results in increased status, more information about ways to improve quality, and better communication with funding sources and the public.

Newsletters. Associations, state licensing agencies, state and national organizations, and private individuals have developed newsletters and other publications that offer information to improve services to children.

Consultation. Consultation is a relationship voluntarily entered into by two parties and freely ended by either party at any time. Many consultants are available in early childhood education. Consultation related to licensing requirements continues to be a part of regula-

tion; other kinds of consultation are sometimes also offered by licensing staff, or the licensing staff may provide names of other consultants. When the regulator provides consultation, it is very important that both regulator and program staff be clear on the difference between requirements and advice.

Resource and referral centers have sprung up spontaneously out of the need for parents to have one place to go to find out about their child care options, and the need of the child care field for information, technical assistance, advocacy, and support.

Both the nonregulatory roads to quality and the various levels of regulation should be considered when the early childhood professional examines ways to achieve quality child care. We must avoid putting undue expectations on any one method and allow each to operate optimally in context of the overall system. When we do this, we can effectively support licensing as one piece of child care regulatory policy.

BIBLIOGRAPHY

Class, N. E. *Licensing of Child Care Facilities by State Welfare Departments.* Washington, D.C.: Department of Health, Education, and Welfare, 1968. Children's Bureau Publication #462.

Davis, K. C. *Administrative Law.* St. Paul, Minn.: West Publishing, 1951.

DHEW. *Report on the Appropriateness of Federal Interagency Day Care Requirements.* Washington, D.C.: Department of Health, Education, and Welfare, August 1978.

Morgan, G. G. "Federal Day Care Standards and the Law." Washington, D.C.: Department of Health, Education, and Welfare, October 15, 1976.

Morgan, G. G. "Regulation of Early Childhood Programs." Washington, D.C.: Day Care and Child Development Council of America, 1971.

Paulsen, M. G. "The Licensing of Child Care Facilities—A Look at the Law." *Alabama Law Review* 21, no. 1 (Fall 1968): 1–24.

Gwen G. Morgan, M.A., is Instructor and Coordinator of Summer Day Care Seminars, Wheelock College, Boston; Child Care Specialist, American Institutes for Research; and an independent consultant. She is also Advisor, Association for Regulatory Administration; member, NAEYC Commission on Licensing and Regulation; and Vice President, Day Care and Child Development Council of America.

Child Care: Strategies to Move the Issue Forward

Amy Wilkins and Helen Blank

Child care advocates have recently won a number of improvements in their states' level of funding and standards for child care. These victories are the result of well-planned and carefully executed legislative campaigns. The strategies used in the campaigns vary according to resources available to advocates and the political and economic climate of their states. This article examines four key elements of successful advocacy present in several state efforts:

- Select and focus the issue.
- Develop a core constituency.
- Work with the media.
- Build legislative support.

Select and Focus the Issue

Advocates campaigning to improve child care in their state face many choices because no single effort can address all of the gaps and problems in child care. Successful advocates must first determine the priority issues and then relate them to the political climate. For example, Ohio and North Carolina advocates targeted the 1985–86 legislative session to improve their state child care licensing standards, knowing negative media attention to child abuse in child care settings had created a climate to work toward much needed licensing improvements. Similarly, Virginia advocates capitalized on their state's rapid economic expansion and new employment opportunities to win funding for child care assistance targeted at low-income working families. Public support for an issue depends not only on its merits, but also on how proponents focus their message. Great care is essential to develop the words and concepts used to describe the problem and its legislative solution.

While most advocates understand that each child care issue involves a number of complex concepts, the general public, including the media and legislators, seldom have such sophistication. Longtime child care advocates and providers, like members of other professions, also tend to use professional jargon. Such jargon is often incomprehensible to people outside the field, and may alienate and confuse potential supporters. A set of simple, clear, and consistent themes must be developed and used throughout the campaign.

How an issue is focused also depends upon the current political and economic climate of the state. One test of how effectively an initiative has been portrayed is whether or not it is able to win bipartisan support. Successful advocates describe an initiative in a way that allows groups and individuals with a wide variety of political views to embrace their plan.

A good example of an effective issue campaign is Minnesota's effort to expand the state sliding fee scale program. The slogan—"Child Care Works"—linked child care to employment, a major issue in Minnesota. This link made child care a priority issue. Virginia child care advocates chose a similar theme in their campaign to increase funds and raise income eligibility limits for child care assistance. Their report to the legislature, *Child Care: An Investment in Virginia's Future*, stressed the importance of providing assistance for child care costs in order to help low-income families gain economic self-sufficiency and thus strengthen the state's economy.

A different tactic, and one that is particu-

Source: Amy Wilkins and Helen Blank (1986, November). Childcare: Strategies to move the issue forward. *Young Children, 42,* pp. 68–72. Reprinted by permission of the authors.

379

larly effective if the climate is ripe for highlighting several issues, is to develop a comprehensive child care improvement package. Such a comprehensive theme marked the Ohio and Massachusetts campaigns. The Ohio package included licensing improvements, a new state child care tax credit, and a $5 million increase in financial aid for low-income families. Linking quality and affordability issues helped to protect against charges that improved licensing standards would increase the cost of child care beyond the reach of working families, because advocates could assure skeptics that their package included a tax credit and an increase in financial aid to address affordability.

Ohio advocates also paid particular attention to how they presented the issues involved in improving state licensing standards. Their bill was vulnerable not only to charges that it would raise the cost of care, but also to accusations that improved state standards for child care facilities promoted too much government involvement in the family. The bill was such an ambitious attempt to improve licensing standards that it had to involve many details including staff-child ratios, square footage requirements, structural and fire safety standards, and teacher qualifications. Such a complex bill can overwhelm the public and legislators. Ohio advocates responded by developing one overarching and simple theme of the state's obligation to protect children in care. Given the basic theme of protection, they constructed secondary themes to highlight their five top priorities. Simplifying the complex legislation allowed the Ohio group to summarize the 64-page bill on a 1-page fact sheet.

Massachusetts advocates also stressed the comprehensive nature of their initiative. Their child care agenda was very broad and included provisions to increase provider reimbursement rates, increase the number of subsidized child care slots, fund resource and referral programs, and create a corporate child care unit within the Executive Office of Economic Affairs. Calling the legislation a comprehensive agenda unified what otherwise might seem diverse and unrelated issues.

Build a Constituency

Successful legislative campaigns depend heavily on the active support of a large and diverse constituency. The ideal constituency represents the largest possible group of individuals and organizations with the broadest spectrum of interests. It is equally important that there be a high degree of organizational unity and discipline within the core group of supporters. Internal conflict can be even more harmful than outside opposition in a legislative effort.

While two groups, the Ohio Association for the Education of Young Children (AEYC) and the Children's Defense Fund-Ohio (CDF-Ohio) formed the core of support for the Ohio child care initiative, more than 150 organizations endorsed the bills, testified at hearings, and lobbied for the legislation. Development of the coalition began long before the bills were actually drafted. CDF-Ohio coalition members laid the groundwork by giving speeches on child care to groups they believed would be helpful to their campaign, such as Kiwanis and Rotary Clubs and Chambers of Commerce. The speeches not only educated the audiences about the importance of child care and the need to improve Ohio's system, but also developed contacts who could later be called upon to support the legislation.

In discussing the Ohio coalition's development, Mark Real, director of the CDF-Ohio office, commented, "We only asked other groups and individuals to buy into the pieces that they could buy into—we didn't push them to endorse more than they could." Pushing potential allies to go too far beyond the limits of their own agendas and resources may eliminate potential supporters. While the for-profit centers objected to three aspects of the licensing improvement bill, they have long agreed with the nonprofits on the need for increased state funding for child care. Therefore, compromises in the licensing bill could be made and the $5 million increase in financial aid passed. This strategy of not pushing allies beyond their limits led to the endorsement of the tax credit component by 174 Ohio organizations. Real also stressed the importance of unity within the coalition, "Everyone in the coalition agreed that passage of the tax credit was important and no one attempted to bring in other issues."

Pennsylvania advocates used a somewhat different coalition model to win an increase in the number of subsidized child care slots and in the rate at which the state reimbursed those providing subsidized care. The Women's

Agenda, a group of individuals and organizations focused on issues affecting women and children, identified increasing the number of the state's subsidized child care slots as a legislative priority for 1985. The Pennsylvania Child Care Association (PACCA) was planning a legislative effort to increase provider reimbursement rates. Rather than developing separate campaigns that would compete against each other for the finite dollars in the state's budget surplus, the groups combined the two proposals into a single child care improvement package.

An even larger coalition model was used by Minnesota child care advocates. The success of "Child Care Works" depended on a coalition of 141 organizations and individuals. Unlike previous child care advocacy efforts, that drew most of their support from the Minneapolis-St. Paul area, the "Child Care Works" campaign developed statewide support for their agenda. The group was assisted in their efforts to build a geographically diverse coalition with funding from a private foundation that allowed them to hire a paid organizer.

While developing outside support for a legislative agenda is crucial, successful advocacy efforts also require building support for the legislation in the related department in state government. Basic rules for developing and maintaining this support are

• a clear understanding of the department with responsibility for the implementation and administration of the program;
• early and continued communication between advocates and the department throughout the course of the campaign; and
• informing the department about the release of reports, press conferences, and testimony about the issue. Failure to do this may result in alienating key department staff.

The rewards for gaining administrative support are clear. Minnesota's lieutenant governor agreed to serve as the honorary co-chair of the "Child Care Works" coalition. In Virginia, advocates were able to participate in writing the regulations for the use of newly won funds and have established a continuing relationship to improve child care in their state.

Support from local officials for legislative initiatives can also be helpful. In Indiana, advocates for successful school-age child care legislation sought and won the support of local fire officials and county prosecutors, arguing that unsupervised children are more likely to hurt themselves and others than children in supervised programs.

Reports and Fact Sheets

One of the most useful tools, not only in developing a broad constituency for an issue, but also in working with the media and legislators, are well-prepared, accurate documents. Such documents help publicize campaign issues and provide supporting data. Documents may range from brief brochures, such as that published by Minnesota's campaign to extensive reports like that published in Ohio.

No matter what the length, a document about the issue has several benefits:

• It acts as a focal point for the campaign.
• It provides a standard set of facts, helping to ensure your message is consistent.
• It helps to establish your group as experts on the issue.

Advocates in Minnesota and Ohio used data from a number of state and private sources to document the child care problems their legislative initiatives were designed to address. In both states, the advocacy reports were the sole source of such consolidated data.

In Virginia, the state legislature had mandated an annual "Child Care Plan" to be prepared by the state's Office for Children. The first plan included three child care priorities for the state. Child care advocates helped ensure that child care assistance for low-income working families was the top item in this plan. The state's top priority became the point of departure for the legislative campaign and the focus of the advocates' report, which supplied data on the need for financial child care assistance, information not found in the state plan. In Massachusetts, advocates used a report prepared by the Governor's (Child Care) Partnership Project as the basis of their campaign, highlighting key issues and recommendations with independent fact sheets. In each of these states, the documents lent weight, credibility, and focus to the campaign.

Work with the Media

Once a core constituency is built and themes describing the bill are developed, the next step

381

is to present the issue to the public. The best ways to use the media to promote public attention must be determined by a careful analysis of the political climate in the state. Media coverage is not always necessary or even desirable. CDF's Virginia campaign, for example, received no media coverage until *after* the bill's passage.

Advocates who decide media coverage will help their campaign must aggressively attract its attention. Timing is also very important. Poorly timed coverage can waste organizational resources, while well-timed coverage can be a real shot in the arm.

In some cases, advocates have sought general coverage of child care before launching their campaign. Minnesota advocates worked with a business reporter who developed a series of articles on various aspects of child care prior to the release of their legislative agenda. The series was published in the "Business" section. This strategy not only presented the issue to an important new audience, it also helped set the stage for presenting child care as an employment and jobs issue.

Ohio child care advocates used the press extensively. They began by releasing a report on the state of child care in Ohio. In addition, they tailored press releases to provide reporters throughout the state with detailed information about their local child care situation. Providing the media with local angles generally increases coverage. Coverage was also enhanced because advocates personally met with news editors around the state.

Lobbying

The ultimate goal of any campaign is to influence the legislature to vote favorably on the initiative. All of the steps described in this piece move toward that goal. While lobbying may sound intimidating, it is nothing more than getting the right information to the right people at the right time. Child care advocates around the country have developed a number of creative lobbying techniques.

Before beginning a lobby effort, you must understand how your state legislature works. This information can be obtained from your secretary of state's office. The legislative clerk's office will also be able to supply lists of the legislators, their districts, and their committees. Other necessary information includes the committees the initiative has to pass

through, and if the initiative calls for funds, the nature of the state's budget process.

In addition to this formal information, informal information can also be very helpful. Does the representative have children? Any in child care? What about grandchildren? Do any members of the legislator's family work in child care? All of this information, in conjunction with an understanding of the political climate, helps fashion an effective lobby campaign.

As in working with the media, the level of a campaign's visibility depends upon the state's political climate. Successful tactics in one state may backfire in another. High visibility campaigns are generally more exciting and allow more individuals and organizations to be involved. However, low visibility campaigns, as in the case of CDF's Virginia project, can be equally successful. For example, Ohio and North Carolina used very different legislative strategies. Ohio's campaign was highly visible and included buttons, a great deal of media coverage, and committee hearings in which large numbers of supporters turned out. North Carolina advocates kept a low profile in the statehouse and did *not* turn out in mass at hearings on licensing improvements, but the opposition did. North Carolina legislators found this mass turnout intimidating and voted in favor of improved standards.

Regular communication with legislators is crucial to any lobbying effort:

- meetings with the legislators, both in the capital and in their home districts;
- letter-writing campaigns; and
- telephone calls.

Personal meetings are most effective. Each legislator should generally be visited at least once during the session, while members of the leadership should be visited more frequently.

There are any number of ways to keep in touch with your legislators. New York advocates sponsor annual Child Care Lobby Days. Child care providers and parents from across the state go to the state capital on the same day to meet with their legislators and discuss pending child care legislation. They also sponsor a series of brown bag lunches for legislators over the course of the session to discuss child care issues. Iowa child care programs adopt key legislators for the length of the session, invite them to lunch at the center from time to time, send them pictures and paint-

Face-to-face communication with legislators is crucial to any lobbying effort.

ings the children have made, and take children to visit the legislator's offices.

Other approaches can help to keep an issue alive in the minds of legislators. For example, the Pennsylvania Women's Agenda developed a postcard series depicting a range of child care issues. The postcards were distributed to parents, child care providers, and other supportive individuals along with a list of names and addresses of legislators. Individuals need to write their own messages to legislators because mass produced cards are likely to end up in the trash unread.

California advocates, who had seen their school-age child care bill vetoed twice, sent thousands of old keys to the governor and the lieutenant governor to show the popular support for the bill. While gimmicks like these can help attract media attention, they cannot substitute for the political savvy and face-to-face meetings required for effective lobbying.

The same basic rules that apply to building constituencies among the public also hold within the legislature. Efforts should be made to gain support from every legislator who is not diametrically opposed to your bill. For example, the Ohio licensing bill had 30 cosponsors. Cosponsors included the chairpersons of the committees that heard the bill; the princi-

pal House sponsor was a Democrat, while the principal Senate sponsor was a Republican.

One Last Step

A key phase in any legislative campaign, whether the initiative is successful or not, is after the legislators have voted on the issue. It is critical to thank the legislators who supported the effort. If possible or politically feasible, you may want to make known the lack of support or opposition received from those voting against the bill. Depending on the political climate and available resources, expressing your appreciation may be very public—as in California, where advocates hold an annual awards dinner to recognize legislators supportive of child care issues—or as low-key as the thank you cards sent to key legislators in Virginia. But one way or another, you must thank those who have supported you, because you will want to work with them in the future on new issues.

Finally, after the dust has settled, be sure to evaluate the campaign. What was done well, what could have been done better? Without such evaluation, it is all but impossible to profit from the experience of your efforts.

Amy Wilkins, B.A., is a Program Associate with the Child Care Division of the Children's Defense Fund.

Helen Blank, M.A., is the Director of that division.

Visiting Public Officials

Child Care, Inc., New York City

Talking directly to public officials about issues that concern you can be a very effective form of advocacy. It lets us present more material to them than a letter can, and counters their arguments immediately with our own arguments. In some cases, a visit may help to persuade ignorant public officials that we do in fact exist, live in their districts, vote, and do not have fangs and horns.

Step #1: In this as in all activities, our first step must be to get clear information on what the problem is, what our position is, who is responsible for the problem, and how, when and where we should get to them.

Step #2: Select one person to call on behalf of the group to make the appointment. The representative should tell the official's staff who we are, how many of us wish to see him/her, what we wish to see him/her about, and should give some kind of time frame. It often is a good idea to write a confirming letter to follow up on this. We should also decide whether we will accept a meeting with one of the official's assistants, or whether we want to meet with the official herself or himself. This is not an issue of principle—it is a practical question of who we think we need to get to at this time on this issue. Be persistent, since it may take several phone calls and a letter before we are able to pin down any kind of meeting.

Step #3: Assemble the delegation to visit the official. It's a good idea to mix the delegation as much as possible, to show the range of interest in the issue. For instance, we want to include both workers and management, professionals and parents, ministers and business persons, day care and non-day care people, to show that our concern is a universal human concern, rather than a narrow "special interest."

Step #4: Always caucus before meeting with the official to plan details of the meeting. Often we can simply meet an hour earlier, in a coffee shop or meeting room near the official's office. We need to agree on exactly who will say what, and in what order. This planning helps to overcome the tendency for one or two people to do all the talking, and helps people to overcome their shyness and their reluctance to be forceful with a public official. This planning also keeps us from wasting the official's time (or our own) in repetitions, and gives the official a vivid sense of our unity.

Step #5: Be succinct and polite in the meeting, but don't give up the point. Avoid rhetoric as much as possible (there's little use these days in talking about how much we love children), and avoid begging or weeping. State the case and stick to it.

Step #6: Caucus again immediately after the meeting, to evaluate it, and to agree on the follow-up steps. Again, this is something we can do in a coffee shop, a meeting room, or simply in the lobby after the meeting.

Step #7: Write a thank-you letter on behalf of everyone who visited the official, and in the letter summarize clearly the points we made, and any agreements or disagreements, that we reached with the official.

Step #8: In this, as in all activities, give the larger group that you represent feedback on what happened, through informal reports, meetings, memoranda, newsletters, or whatever.

Source: Visiting public officials. (n.d.). New York: Child Care, Inc. Reprinted by permission of Child Care, Inc., New York City.

ASK YOURSELF:
Identifying Issues for Debate and Advocacy

1. What are the differences between policies, laws, and regulations?

2. How can we make the American public aware of the need for licensing child care facilities?

3. Consider your home community. What information sources are available that would help you determine the need for child care?

4. If the state government funded preschool education, would accompanying regulations lead to pressure for academically oriented programs for young children? Why or why not?

APPLICATION / ADVOCACY EXERCISES

1. View Bronfenbrenner's film "Three Worlds of Childhood" (A-V Resource Center, Cornell University). Then discuss the ideas and views expressed in the film in terms of the following sociopolitical dimensions (Robinson & Robinson, 1972), which strongly influence the kinds of programs for early education and care undertaken in a society:

   a. Economic Status

Mass poverty	High standard of living

Wide discrepancies in income and aspirations	Large, middle-income group

   b. Economic Organization

Free enterprise (consumer control)	Socialist (agency control)

   c. Welfare Orientation

Emergency-induced welfare programming	Future-oriented welfare programming

   d. Planning

Lack of overall planning	Mechanisms for establishing national priorities

e. Centralization

⟵─────────────────────────────────⟶

Local control and influence	Central government control

f. Coordination Among Programs

⟵─────────────────────────────────⟶

Lack of continuity across services and age levels	Continuity across services and age levels

g. Cultural Heterogeneity

⟵─────────────────────────────────⟶

Hetergeneous population with need to be sensitive to local conditions and culture	Homogeneous population with a common framework of socialization goals

h. Role of Women

⟵─────────────────────────────────⟶

Society approves of working mothers	Society disapproves of working mothers

i. Neighborhoods and the World of Work

⟵─────────────────────────────────⟶

Homogeneous environments where field trips become necessary	Varied environments mixing industry (or agriculture) and residences

j. Mass Media

⟵─────────────────────────────────⟶

Low media impact on socialization	High media impact on socialization

k. Family/Society Compact

⟵─────────────────────────────────⟶

Child care and socialization are the exclusive responsibility of parents; concepts of "charity" and "privilege" affect services	Society is an active partner in child care and socialization; services aimed at all children

l. Conceptions about the Nature of Early Childhood

⟵─────────────────────────────────⟶

Weak belief in the importance of this period	Strong belief in the importance of this period

Goals for early childhood are individualistic and less clearly stated	Goals for early childhood are differentiated, especially socialization goals.

2. As a small group, choose one of the countries described by Honig or Sestini or another nation with a child care policy. Investigate further the child care programs and policies of this country. Then compare and contrast your findings with what you know about child care programs in the United States in terms of the sociopolitical dimensions listed in exercise 1. (For this analysis, you may need to read the Robinson and Robinson (1972) article.)

3. Invite a licensing agent from social services to class to discuss state day care regulations and how they are implemented or monitored. Ask the licensing agent to estimate the impact of licensing on the quality of child care being provided in your state.

4. Invite an early childhood program director or a validator, who has participated in the Center Accreditation Program of the National Association for the Education of Young Children, to share his or her experiences with the class.

5. Using ideas for influencing policy decisions presented in this chapter and the guidelines for visiting a public official, organize a small group to visit a legislator. Discuss a current child advocacy issue that he or she will be addressing in upcoming sessions, or discuss the rights of children and families in our society to quality child care. If you are unable to organize a group, write an advocacy letter to one of your governmental officials or to a governmental commission on child care and share your thoughts on an issue of concern. Use the letter-writing guidelines listed in Chapter 2 as you compose your letter.

REFERENCES & SUGGESTED READINGS

Bredekamp, S., & Apple, P. L. (1986, November). How early childhood programs get accredited: An analysis of accreditation decisions. *Young Children, 41*, 34–37.

Bredekamp, S., & Berby, J. (1987, November). Maintaining quality: Accredited programs one year later. *Young Children, 42*, 13–15.

Collins, R. C. (1983, July). Child care and the states: The comparative licensing study. *Young Children, 38*, 3–11.

Klass, C. S. (1986). *The autonomous child.* New York: The Falmer Press.

Kontos, S., & Stevens, R. (1985, January). High quality child care: Does your center measure up? *Young Children, 40*, 9–13.

National Academy of Early Childhood Programs. (1984). *Accreditation criteria & procedures.* Washington, DC: National Association for the Education of Young Children.

Robinson, N., & Robinson, H. (1972). A cross-cultural view of early education. In I. J. Gordon (Ed.), *The seventy-first yearbook of the National Society for the Study of Education: Part 2. Early childhood education* (pp. 291–315). Chicago: The University of Chicago Press.

Weiser, M. G. (1982). Public policy: For or against children and families? An international perspective. *Childhood Education, 58,* 227–234.

INDEX